THE ROUTLEDGE COMPANION TO TWENTY-FIRST CENTURY LITERARY FICTION

The study of contemporary fiction is a fascinating yet challenging one. Contemporary fiction has immediate relevance to popular culture, the news, scholarly organizations and education – where it is found on the syllabus in schools and universities – but it also offers challenges. What is 'contemporary'? How do we track cultural shifts and changes? *The Routledge Companion to Twenty-First Century Literary Fiction* takes on this challenge, mapping key literary trends from the year 2000 onwards, as the landscape of our century continues to take shape around us. A significant and central intervention into contemporary literature, this *Companion* offers essential coverage of writers who have risen to prominence since then, such as Hari Kunzru, Jennifer Egan, David Mitchell, Jonathan Lethem, Ali Smith, A. L. Kennedy, Hilary Mantel, Marilynne Robinson, and Colson Whitehead.

Thirty-eight essays by leading and emerging international scholars cover topics such as:

* Identity, including race, sexuality, class, and religion in the twenty-first century;
* The impact of technology, terrorism, activism, and the global economy on the modern world and modern literature;
* The form and format of twenty-first century literary fiction, including analysis of established genres such as the pastoral, graphic novels, and comedic writing, and how these have been adapted in recent years.

Accessible to experts, students, and general readers, *The Routledge Companion to Twenty-First Century Literary Fiction* provides a map of the critical issues central to the discipline, as well as uncovering new perspectives and new directions for the development of the field. It is essential reading for anyone interested in the past, present, and future of contemporary literature.

Daniel O'Gorman is Lecturer in Twentieth and Twenty-First Century Literature at Oxford Brookes University, UK. He works on contemporary literature and terror.

Robert Eaglestone is Professor of Contemporary Literature and Thought at Royal Holloway, University of London, UK and works on contemporary literature and literary theory, contemporary philosophy and on Holocaust and Genocide studies.

ROUTLEDGE COMPANIONS TO LITERATURE SERIES

Also available in this series

The Routledge Companion to Twenty-First Century Literature
Edited by Daniel O'Gormon and Robert Eaglestone

The Routledge Companion to Literature and Economics
Edited by Michelle Chihara and Matt Seybold

The Routledge Companion to Pakistani Anglophone Writing
Edited by Aroosa Kanwal and Saiyma Aslam

The Routledge Companion to World Literature and World History
Edited by May Hawas

The Routledge Companion to Picturebooks
Edited by Bettina Kümmerling-Meibauer

The Routledge Companion to International Children's Literature
Edited by John Stephens, with Celia Abicalil Belmiro, Alice Curry, Li Lifang and Yasmine S. Motawy

The Routledge Companion to the Environmental Humanities
Edited by Ursula K. Heise, Jon Christensen and Michelle Niemann

The Routledge Companion to Inter-American Studies
Edited by Wilfried Raussert

The Routledge Companion to Literature and Religion
Edited by Mark Knight

The Routledge Companion to Travel Writing
Edited by Carl Thompson

The Routledge Companion to Native American Literature
Edited by Deborah L. Madsen

For more information on this series, please visit: www.routledge.com/literature/series/RC4444

THE ROUTLEDGE COMPANION TO TWENTY-FIRST CENTURY LITERARY FICTION

Edited by Daniel O'Gorman and Robert Eaglestone

Routledge
Taylor & Francis Group

LONDON AND NEW YORK

First published 2019
by Routledge
2 Park Square, Milton Park, Abingdon, Oxon OX14 4RN

and by Routledge
52 Vanderbilt Avenue, New York, NY 10017

Routledge is an imprint of the Taylor & Francis Group, an informa business

British Library Cataloguing-in-Publication Data
A catalogue record for this book is available from the British Library

Library of Congress Cataloging-in-Publication Data
Names: Eaglestone, Robert, 1968- editor. | O'Gormon, Daniel, editor.
Title: The Routledge companion to twenty-first century literary fiction /
edited by Robert Eaglestone and Daniel O'Gormon.
Description: Abingdon, Oxon ; New York, NY : Routledge, 2019. | Series:
Routledge companions to literature series | Includes bibliographical references.
Identifiers: LCCN 2018033561 | ISBN 9780415716048 (hardback : alk. paper) |
ISBN 9781315880235 (ebk) | ISBN 9781134743773 (epub) | ISBN 9781134743704
(pdf) | ISBN 9781134743841 (mobikindle)
Subjects: LCSH: English fiction—21st century—History and criticism. |
American fiction—21st century—History and criticism.
Classification: LCC PR889 .R68 2019 | DDC 823/.9209—dc23
LC record available at https://lccn.loc.gov/2018033561

ISBN: 978-0-415-71604-8 (hbk)
ISBN: 978-1-315-88023-5 (ebk)

Typeset in Bembo
by Apex CoVantage, LLC

Printed and bound by CPI Group (UK) Ltd, Croydon, CR0 4YY

CONTENTS

Contents

Contents

Contents

ACKNOWLEDGEMENTS

Editing a volume like this is a learning experience, and we have both discovered new ideas, texts, theories and trends while working with these fascinating chapters. The project has been long in the making, and in the time between its inception and its publication, the literary landscape has transformed in exciting new ways. Our contributors have worked hard to keep alert to these changes, adapting and honing their arguments as the field has expanded around them, and for this we would like to extend our immense gratitude: their talent and collegiality has made the process a joy. In addition, we would like to thank Zoe Meyer, Stacey Carter and Polly Dodson at Routledge for their patient overseeing of the project, as well as our project manager, Sheri Sipka, for her meticulous attention to detail in the final stages.

Daniel O'Gorman: I would like to thank Alexandra Parsons for her endless support and generous feedback on ideas for the Introduction; Alex Trott for her friendship and encouragement, and for organising a thought-provoking discussion about metamodernism at Oxford Brookes in March 2018; Adam Alston, Will Philps and Carl-Henrik Bjerström for keeping me on my toes about contemporary culture beyond the literary; Sam Solnick for lunchtime chats about contemporary writing; Thomas Hilder for his friendship and perspective; and my students and colleagues at Oxford Brookes over the past two years, for their inspiring ideas about contemporary literature and the literary, especially on the module 'Contemporary Literature'. Thanks also to Amila Lokuge, Veena Naganathar, Asil Tahir, Luke Deller, Joey Bania, Miranda Prag and Viyaasan Mahalingasivam, as well as to Stefan, Eija and Christopher O'Gorman, for their continuing friendship and support, especially during my occasional spells in academic hermitage. And thanks, finally, to Bob Eaglestone for being a fantastic co-editor on this project.

Robert Eaglestone: I'd like to thank my wife, Poppy Eaglestone, and my children, Alex and Bella, for their support, as well as my wider family and friends. My students, on 'Ideas in Contemporary Fiction' have been a constant source of inspiration. And in addition to thanking our contributors above, I'd also like to dedicate the book to them too. Contemporary fiction is a growing field, and it seems to me to be characterized by scholars and writers full of energy, intellectual curiosity, enthusiasm and collegiality: the contributors are prime exemplars of these. And so are the many members of the *British Association for Contemporary Literary Studies* which came into existence during the gestation of this volume: in that respect, we also all owe special thanks to Caroline Edwards, one of the BACLS co-founders, for her commitment and foresight. Finally, perhaps

unusually, I'd like to dedicate this book to the other co-editor: he's astute, well-informed, inde-
fatigable and thoughtful. Thank you, Dan!

Chapter 1, 'The Networked Novel', contains revised material from *Utopia and the Contemporary
British Novel* (Cambridge University Press: 2019). Forthcoming.

Chapter 3, 'Sincerity', contains revised material from *Literature Against Criticism: University English
and Contemporary Fiction in Conflict* (Cambridge: Open Book Publishers, 2016).

Chapter 8, 'Pastoral', contains revised material from *The New Pastoral in Contemporary British Writing* (Routledge: 2019). Forthcoming.

Chapter 19, '(The) Digital', is adapted from 'Being Social in a Postdigital World in *Catfish* and
How Should a Person Be?', originally published in *The Digital Banal: New Media and American
Literature and Culture*, by Zara Dinnen. Copyright © 2018 Columbia University Press. Used
by permission of Columbia University Press.

Chapter 21, 'Displacement' by Emily Hogg, was written with financial support from the Danish
National Research Foundation (grant number DNRF127).

Chapter 25, 'War on Terror', contains revised material from 'Ambivalent Alterities: Pakistani post-
9/11 Fiction in English', originally published in *Fictions of the War on Terror: Difference and
the Transnational 9/11 Novel*, by Daniel O'Gorman. Copyright © 2015 Palgrave Macmillan.

CONTRIBUTORS

Timothy C. Baker is Senior Lecturer in English at the University of Aberdeen. His recent publications include *Contemporary Scottish Gothic: Mourning, Authenticity, and Tradition* (2014).

Jenny Bavidge is Academic Director and University Senior Lecturer in English Literature, Institute of Continuing Education, University of Cambridge, and has published widely on contemporary literature and the environment.

Arthur Bradley is Professor of Comparative Literature at Lancaster University. His recent publications include *Originary Technicity: The Theory of Technology from Marx to Derrida* (2011) and, co-edited with Andrew Tate, *The New Atheist Novel: Fiction, Philosophy and Polemic after 9/11* (2010).

Joseph Brooker is Reader in Modern Literature at Birkbeck, University of London. The author of *Joyce's Critics* (2004), *Flann O'Brien* (2005), *Literature of the 1980s* (2010) and *Jonathan Lethem and the Galaxy of Writing* (2019), he has also edited special issues of the *Journal of Law & Society, New Formations, Textual Practice* and *Critical Quarterly*.

Stephen J. Burn is Reader in English Literature at the University of Glasgow. His publications include *Jonathan Franzen at the End of Postmodernism* (2008) and, as editor, *American literature in transition* (2017).

Dorothy Butchard is Lecturer in Contemporary Literature & Digital Cultures at the University of Birmingham and has published widely in the field.

Paul Crosthwaite is Senior Lecturer in English at the University of Edinburgh. His publications include *Trauma, Postmodernism, and the Aftermath of World War II* (2009) and, as editor, and *Show Me the Money: The Image of Finance, 1700 to the Present* (2014).

E. Dawson Varughese is a writer, critic and performer who works in global cultural studies specialising in post-millennial Indian literary and visual cultures. Recent academic publications include *Genre Fiction of New India* (2016) and *Visuality and Identity in Post-millennial Indian Graphic Narratives* (2017).

Sarah Dillon is University Lecturer in Literature and Film at the University of Cambridge and a broadcaster. Her recent publications include *Deconstruction, Feminism, Film* (2018) and, co-editor *Maggie Gee: Critical Essays* (2015).

Zara Dinnen is Lecturer in Twentieth and Twenty-First Century Literature at Queen Mary, University of London. Her recent publications include *The Digital Banal: New Media and American Literature and Culture* (2018), and as co-editor *The Edinburgh Companion to Contemporary Narrative Theories* (2018).

Robert Eaglestone is Professor of Contemporary Literature and Thought at Royal Holloway, University of London. His recent publications include *The Broken Voice: reading post-Holocaust literature* (2017), *Literature: why it matters* (2018) and, as editor *Brexit and Literature: Critical and Cultural Responses* (2018) and, with Gail Marshall, *English: Shared Futures*.

Harriet E.H. Earle is Lecturer in English and Creative Writing at Sheffield Hallam University. Her recent publications include *Comics, Trauma and the New Art of War* (2017).

Caroline Edwards is Senior Lecturer in Modern & Contemporary Literature at Birkbeck, University of London. Her recent publications include *Utopia and the Contemporary British Novel* (2019) and, as co-editor, *China Miéville: Critical Essays* (2015) and *Maggie Gee: Critical Essays* (2015). She is co-founder of the Open Library of the Humanities.

Martin Paul Eve is Professor of Literature, Technology and Publishing at Birkbeck, University of London. His most recent books include *Password* (2016) and *Literature Against Criticism: University English & Contemporary Fiction in Conflict* (2016). He is co-founder of the Open Library of the Humanities.

Anna Hartnell is Senior Lecturer in English at Birkbeck, University of London. Her recent publications include *After Katrina: Race, Neoliberalism, and the End of the American Century* (2017).

Jennifer Hodgson is a writer, critic and broadcaster. Her recent publications include *The Unmapped Country* (2018), a collection of the 'lost' short stories and fragments by Ann Quin.

Emily J. Hogg is Assistant Professor in the Department for the Study of Culture at the University of Southern Denmark. She has published on human rights and feminism.

Emily Horton is Lecturer in English Literature at Brunel University. Her recent publications include *Contemporary Crisis Fictions: Affect and Ethics in the Modern British Novel* (2014) and co-edited volumes on *1980s: A Decade in Contemporary Fiction* and on *Ali Smith* (2014).

Carole Jones is Lecturer in English at the University of Edinburgh, and has published widely on Scottish Literature.

Leila Kamali is Lecturer in American and English Literature at King's College London. Her recent publications include *The Cultural Memory of Africa in African American and Black British Fiction, 1970–2000* (2016).

Arin Keeble is Lecturer in Contemporary Literature and Culture at Edinburgh Napier University. His recent publications include *Narratives of Katrina: Literature, Film and Television* (2018) and *The 9/11 Novel: Trauma, Politics and Identity* (2014).

Daniel Lea is Professor of Contemporary Literature at Oxford Brookes University. His recent publications include *Twenty-First Century Fiction: Contemporary British Voices* (2016).

Deborah Lilley is a writer and editor based in San Francisco, and has published widely on the relationship between the environment and literature. Her *New Pastoral in Contemporary British Writing* is forthcoming.

Christopher Lloyd is Lecturer in English Literature at the University of Hertfordshire. His recent publications include *Rooting Memory, Rooting Place: Regionalism in the Twenty-First-Century American South* (2015).

Lucienne Loh is Senior Lecturer in English Literature at the University of Liverpool. Her most recent books include *The Postcolonial Country in Contemporary Literature* (2013) and, co-edited with Malcolm Sen, *Postcolonial Literature and Challenges for the New Millennium* (2016).

Caroline Magennis is Lecturer in Twentieth and Twenty-First Century Literature at the University of Salford. Her publications include *Sons of Ulster: Masculinities in the Contemporary Northern Irish Novel* (2010) and many articles in the field.

Xavier Marcó del Pont has published widely on contemporary American fiction, with a focus on postmodernism, narrative theory and the novels of Thomas Pynchon.

Huw Marsh is Lecturer in Modernist and Contemporary Literature at Queen Mary, University of London. His recent publications include *Beryl Bainbridge* (2014).

Daniel O'Gorman is Lecturer in Twentieth and Twenty-First Century Literature at Oxford Brookes University, and author of *Fictions of the War on Terror: Difference and the Transnational 9/11 Novel*.

Alexandra Parsons teaches at UCL and Queen Mary, University of London, and recently completed a period as Visiting Assistant in Research in English Literature and LGBT Studies at Yale University.

Danielle Sands is Lecturer in Comparative Literature and Culture at Royal Holloway, University of London. Her recent publications include *Animals, Plants, Things: Nonhuman Storytelling Between Philosophy and Literature* (2019).

Katy Shaw is Professor of Contemporary Writings at Northumbria University. Her most recent publications include *Hauntology* (2018), *Crunch Lit: Twenty-First Century Genre Fiction* (2015) and, as editor, *Jim Crace* (2018).

Kristian Shaw is Senior Lecturer in English Literature at the University of Lincoln. His recent publications include *Cosmopolitanism in Twenty-First Century Fiction* (2017).

Sam Solnick is Lecturer in English Literature at the University of Liverpool. His recent publications include *Poetry and the Anthropocene: Ecology, Biology and Technology in Contemporary British and Irish Poetry* (2016).

Rachel Sykes is Lecturer in Contemporary American Literature at the University of Birmingham. Her recent publications include *The Quiet Contemporary American Novel* (2017) and *Marilynne Robinson: Essays* (2019).

Andrew Tate is Reader in Literature, Religion and Aesthetics at Lancaster University. His recent publications include *Apocalyptic Fiction* (2017), with Arthur Bradley, *The New Atheist Novel: Fiction, Philosophy and Polemic after 9/11* (2010), and, as co-editor, *Literature and the Bible: A Reader* (2014).

Sara Upstone is Associate Professor in English at Kingston University. Her recent publications include *Literary Theory: A Complete Introduction* (2017) and, as co-editor *Postmodern Literature and Race* (2015).

Sophie Vlacos is Lecturer in English Literature post-1900 at the University of Glasgow. Her recent publications include *Ricoeur, Literature and Imagination* (2014).

Agnes Woolley is Lecturer in Transnational Literature and Migration Cultures at Birkbeck, University of London. Her recent publications include *Contemporary Asylum Narratives: Representing Refugees in the Twenty-First Century* (2014) and, as co-editor, *Refugee Writing: Contemporary Research Across the Humanities* (2019).

INTRODUCTION

Daniel O'Gorman and Robert Eaglestone

Landscapes of the now

This book is an experiment in critical cartography: its contributors have taken up the difficult challenge of mapping key literary trends as the landscape and perhaps even the underlying geology of our century continue to take shape around us. This is an intellectually precarious undertaking. Both the territory and its charting will change rapidly over the next eighty years: some of the fictional trends identified in this volume will solidify as others erode, and critical directions and interests will shift. If literature is still studied by the century's end, perhaps only some of the authors, texts, and themes covered in these 38 chapters will orient future generations of scholars: others, possibly all, may have vanished into the obscurity of paths not taken.

Of course, there is nothing new about changing literary and critical trends and the ensuing re-evaluation of periods: but what this book offers is an invitation for readers to engage with the mapping of our present *as it is taking place*, contributing in an active way to our current self-understanding. This is why we do not think that, despite covering work from only a fifth of the 'Twenty-First Century' to which we refer in the title, this book is premature. Indeed, this book instantiates a growing critical and theoretical interest in and study of our present moment, usually employing the definite article: '*the* contemporary'. Over the past twenty years there has been a period of intense self-periodization: 'Contemporary Literature' is a rapidly growing field of academic study in its own right, especially in American and British universities.

This field begs questions. For example, when, after all, does the contemporary begin? Often in academic texts and university modules, and in our case here, the year 2000, the 'Common Era' millennium, is chosen, but this is an open issue. Should 'mere chronology' define a period? Or do significant political events (an election, a war) inaugurate it? Or, perhaps more appropriately in this context, should a major literary event begin a literary period? And, perhaps more saliently for this volume, when do contemporary texts *stop* being contemporary? Or, most of all: can the contemporary even be characterized?

In an influential essay published a decade ago, Giorgio Agamben asked, 'What is the Contemporary?' He focused on the term's relativity: that which is contemporary to one person or group of people is not necessarily contemporary to another. 'Contemporariness', he writes, 'is, then, a singular relationship with one's own time, which adheres to it and, at the same time, keeps a distance from it' (2011: 11). To be contemporary is to experience a closeness with one's time, but not a complete absorption by it: there remains a degree of distance, or reflection. More, being the contemporary of another is to recognize some shared experience or identity with that other, while also acknowledging the other's distinctness or difference: we can be contemporary with each other in some ways, while not in others. The experience of contemporaneity, then, is always, inevitably, relative: one can only be contemporary in relation to someone or something else. Consider, for instance, the case of John Williams' 1965 novel *Stoner*, largely ignored upon its original publication and obscure for decades, only to be brought to wild popularity and commercial success through its translation and championing by French author Anna Gavalda in 2013 (Barnes 2013). As reviewer Sarah Hampson put it at the time, 'Perhaps it is simply a matter of a book finding its perfect moment. We live in an era in which happiness and success are pursued ruthlessly, selfishly. . . . This is a novel that serves as an antidote to that expectation' (Hampson 2013). Additionally, there is certainly much to be said for the role played in *Stoner*'s recent success by the widespread contemporary appetite for autofictional sincerity, especially in the work of Ben Lerner, Sheila Heti and Maggie Nelson, which has made the market ripe for a deeply emotive novel only faintly masking its author's real life experiences.

A novel like William Gibson's *Pattern Recognition* (2003), on the other hand, strives hard for contemporaneity. Yet its frequent references to early 2000s popular culture and technology mean that, a decade-and-a-half on, it reads as a document of that very specific moment in time: a world of Hotmail, Netscape, and iBook, rather than WhatsApp, Uber, and Deliveroo. This is not to say that it hasn't remained contemporary in other ways: its depiction of corporate data harvesting has, if anything, become more powerful in the wake of the recent Cambridge Analytica scandals. What becomes apparent, when reading the novel in 2019, is quite simply the inevitable relativity of the contemporary as a periodizing category: in contrast to other 'periods' in literary history, the contemporary eludes – and sometimes actively resists – the fixity and definition which periodization necessarily aims to entrench. The contemporary can be untimely. Indeed, as this volume demonstrates throughout, to be a critic of the contemporary moment is to identify its trends while simultaneously foregrounding its position within a constellation of other contemporary moments, in different parts of the world, or at different points in time. Gibson's widely cited axiom, that the 'future is already here – it's just not evenly distributed' is even more complexly and powerfully true of the contemporary.

Critical constellations

Literary critics and theorists, as well as critics of contemporary arts and culture more broadly, have in recent years been clambering for a definitive term for the new era many feel we are entering in the early twenty-first century. A consensus has emerged around the idea that postmodernism, the critical paradigm of late twentieth century arts and culture, has begun to fizzle out gradually, replaced by works that maintain postmodernism's self-reflexive playfulness while also adhering to an underlying sense of emotional truthfulness, whether in the form of sincerity (Wallace 1993; Kelly 2010), reconstruction (Funk 2015), solace (James 2019), or a 'Turn to the Human' (Timmer 2010: 51). This trend, sometimes referred to using the unfortunate catch-all and clumsy term 'post-postmodernism', has been prompted in part by a response to shifts in the way that we experience the world in the twenty-first century. The irony and occasional cynicism that is often seen to characterize postmodern writing has, for some, come to feel self-indulgent in an era in which, for instance, it has become indisputable that humanity will face mass displacement and famine in the absence of urgent and committed collective action against climate change. From another perspective, digital culture has ushered in an age in which it is virtually impossible to be disconnected from others: whether friends, work colleagues or distant relatives in faraway parts of the world, anyone with a smartphone – including, notoriously, the President of the United States – can be contacted instantly at the touch of a button, no matter their physical distance. As Alison Gibbons has put it, 'Whether one takes the critical position that postmodernism is past/passed or passing, the recent fervor for ethical, political, social, and environmental commitments is telling in that it appears to indicate, at the very least, an epistemological shift away from the superficiality of postmodern irony and, at its greatest, the onset of a more substantial post-postmodern turn' (Gibbons 2015: 29–30).

A far from exhaustive list of the many terms proposed for this new period includes, for instance: altermodernism, hypermodernism, supermodernism, hysterical realism, digimodernism, The New Sincerity and metamodernism. Of these, the last two have held most sway in literary studies, though by no means uncontroversially so. The New Sincerity, proposed by Adam Kelly, draws on a provocation made by David Foster Wallace in his 1993 essay, 'E Unibus, Plurum', and argues that a trend has emerged amongst (mostly) American writers such as Dave Eggers, as well as Wallace himself, whereby '[f]ormer divisions between self and other morph into conflicts within the self, and a recursive and paranoid cycle of endless anticipation begins, putting in doubt the very referents of terms like "self" and "other", "inner" and "outer"' (Kelly 2010: 136). To borrow from David Shields' influential *Reality Hunger* (2010), we can see this kind of self-conscious sincerity at play very clearly in Eggers' breakthrough memoir *A Heartbreaking Work of Staggering Genius* (1999), a book that is 'full of the same self-conscious apparatus that had bored everyone silly until it got tethered to what felt like someone's "real life" (even if the author constantly reminded us how fictionalized that life was)' (Shields 2010: 5).

Metamodernism, meanwhile, likewise identifies at the heart of contemporary culture a persistent fluctuation between irony and sincerity, emphasizing a dissolution in the boundary between the two. The term was theorized in 2010 by Timotheus Vermeulen and Robin van der Akker, who posit it as a discourse 'oscillating between a modern enthusiasm and a postmodern irony' (2010: 5–6). Arguably broader in scope than the text-focused New Sincerity, metamodernism does not describe an artistic trend so much as a wider cultural condition. In Vermeulen and van der Akker's words, it 'should be understood as a spacetime that is both-neither ordered and disordered. Metamodernism displaces the parameters of the present with those of a future presence that is futureless; and it displaces the boundaries of our place with those of a surreal place that is placeless' (2010: 12). Or, putting it another way, the artist Luke Turner – known for his high profile work with fellow self-proclaimed metamodernists Shia LaBeouf and Nastja Säde Rönkkö – has argued that metamodernism

> describe[s] the climate in which a yearning for utopias, despite their futile nature, has come to the fore. The metamodernism discourse is thus descriptive rather than prescriptive; an inclusive means of articulating the ongoing developments associated with a structure of feeling for which the vocabulary of postmodern critique is no longer sufficient, but whose future paths have yet to be constructed.
>
> (Turner 2015)

Turner's intervention in this critical debate is indicative of a trend that is apparent throughout the chapters of this book: namely, that it is not only critics, but also *authors* themselves who have been striving to give definition to the era we currently occupy. Writers like Jonathan Lethem, Ali Smith, and Jennifer Egan (who have chapters dedicated to them in this collection), or Ben Lerner, George Saunders, Mohsin Hamid and Zadie Smith (who appear repeatedly in chapters throughout), have made it part of their project to sketch out the contours of our time. As the narrator of Lerner's autofictional *10:04* self-reflexively puts it right at the start of that novel, consciously evoking recent academic debates about postmodernism's seeming decline, 'I'll work my way from irony to sincerity in the sinking city, a would-be Whitman of the vulnerable grid' (Lerner 2014: 4). Or, from a different perspective, we can see an echo of Agamben's disjunctive relationship with the contemporary in Ali Smith's 2017 Goldsmiths Prize lecture, when she argued that, among many other reasons, 'the novel matters because the contemporary state of the novel is always related to the state of whatever's new to us in the contemporary' (Smith 2017).

Technically, of course, everything published in the contemporary period is contemporary. However, on 'Contemporary Literature' modules at universities, and in books like this one, we tend to focus on texts that somehow tap into or encapsulate contemporaneity in some way, revealing to us an essence of something that we literary critics identify as being inherently characteristic of the early twenty-first century. This revelation can emerge through either a text's thematic content or its form. Novels like Smith's *Autumn* (2016) or *Winter* (2017), for instance, strive for contemporaneity by responding to events that have taken place barely 12 months before their publication (here, the 2016 British EU referendum and ensuing chaos). Meanwhile, playful narrative forms such as Sheila Heti's *How Should a Person Be?* (2010), Adam Thirlwell's *Kapow!* (2012), or Nicola Barker's *H(A)PPY* (2017), attempt to capture something of the contemporary in the very mechanics of their storytelling, incorporating elements of digital or material culture in a way that lends their work a sense of twenty-first century authenticity.

However, as Judith Butler has argued influentially, any critical consideration of the contemporary must also start 'with a question of how temporality is organized along spatial lines' (2009: 101). By this, she means that the contemporary moment, like all temporal categories, is geographically bounded: the contemporary in one place, within one culture, will not be the same contemporary experienced in another place, by another culture. While of course there will always be overlaps and intersections, for instance in what Teju Cole calls the 'continuity' that exists between the diversities of big global cities, it is important to hold back from the assumption that the contemporary is a universal category (2017: 200). In Cole's words, 'What is interesting is to find . . . the less obvious differences of texture: the signs, the markings, the assemblages, the things hiding in plain sight in each cityscape or landscape' (2017: 200). Meanwhile, Butler explains that 'the problem is that certain notions of relevant geopolitical space – including the spatial boundedness of minority communities – are circumscribed by [the] story of a progressive modernity; certain notions of what 'this time' can and must be are similarly construed on the basis of circumscribing the 'where' of its happening' (2009: 103). While all contemporary fiction is – at least for the moment – also twenty-first century fiction, twenty-first century fiction is not all, necessarily, contemporary. This is a crucial point to acknowledge at the beginning of a volume such as the present one: while we have aimed for as diverse a spread of topics and authors as possible, our perspectives on twenty-first century literary fiction, as a collection of mainly Western literary critics, are necessarily both spatially and culturally bounded. Nonetheless, one thing that the chapters in this book share is an understanding that the contemporary experience of time is simultaneously situated and unfixed: to borrow from literary critic Lionel Ruffel, '[it] feels more like a concordance of temporalities than a single time, a concordance that is also more subjective than collective: it's not postulating that a single unique, unified present is shared by the community but rather that what the community shares is a subjectivized polychronicity' (2018: 178).

'Reality is a question of perspective', Salman Rushdie wrote in his 1981 novel, *Midnight's Children*: 'the further you get from the past, the more concrete and plausible it seems – but as you approach the present, it inevitably seems more and more incredible' (2008: 229). Using the example of a cinemagoer who slowly moves up towards the screen, his narrator goes on to explain that 'Gradually the stars' faces dissolve into dancing grain; tiny details assume grotesque proportions; the illusion dissolves – or rather, it becomes clear that the illusion itself is reality' (229). The contributors to this volume are each like one of Rushdie's cinemagoers, their faces inexorably pressed up against the screen's dancing grain. Each offers a unique, spatially bounded perspective on twenty-first century literary fiction. Collectively, however, these 38 perspectives trace a more panoramic view: one that helps us, slowly, to begin mapping a twenty-first century literary constellation.

The question of the literary

Despite its focus on the contemporary, the title of this volume contains a word with long, tangled roots: *Literary*. In English in the fourteenth century, it meant roughly 'knowing about books' and only added the meaning which refers to a certain sort of writing (say: 'literature with a capital L') in the eighteenth century. 'Literary' is a term that is by turns complex, multifaceted, historically rich, and problematic. It's far from clear what literature even is: what do Sappho and Orwell, Morrison and Dante, Beckett and Spenser, have in common? We might usefully adapt Wittgenstein's metaphor of a rope: made of threads turned one upon another, a rope does not have a single strand that runs from end to end. Instead, its strength relies on the interweaving of the many threads together. Similarly, literature is not made up of one thread: there is no single 'literary' filament, and it's vain to search for one (and partisan to champion one over another). However, in this volume we are concerned with a more focused but no less problematic and controversial sense of the literary: literary fiction. Our choice in this requires explanation.

To sketch a rough literary history: from the 1930s to the 1970s, the academy, and the high-culture associated with it, divided contemporary fiction – if it even concerned itself with contemporary fiction – into 'literary' and 'genre'. The arguments made in Q. D. Leavis' *Fiction and the Reading Public* (1932) cast a long shadow. Literary fiction was considered serious, cultivated, the inheritor of the canonical greats and – crucially – of literary value. In contrast, genre fiction – including science fiction, fantasy, the romance novel, the crime novel, young adult and children's fiction – was seen as formulaic, popular, and populist, shallow, entertainment, and relegated to, at best, sociological study (with notable exceptions, of course). In the face of this division, writers, critics, and readers of these genres fought to establish the creation, production, and study of 'genre' as worthy of serious attention. Rightly, they won these arguments, revealing the depth of thought, significance, seriousness, and value of genre fiction. More, in reframing debates over literary value and the canon – over what literature is or might be, in fact – this played a part in uncovering and calling to account hitherto unquestioned forms of sexism, racism, classism, and other forms of prejudice in intellectual life: questions of the canon and of literary value are a place where aesthetic and political matters are impossible to disentangle.

To stay with this crude chronology, from the 1980s and 90s, the academic study of genre fiction became instituted in multifaceted and thought-provoking ways: there were major advances in the study of romance (for example, Janice Radway, *Reading the Romance*), travel writing (another example, Mary Louis Pratt, *Imperial Eyes*) and young adult or children's literature (say, Jacqueline Rose, *The Case of Peter Pan*). These changes took longer, perhaps, to disseminate through to wider cultures, but only very rarely does one now hear 'genre fiction' disparaged just because it is 'genre'. Indeed, for example, the role of science fiction as a literature of ideas is praised; the strong narrative drive of young adult fiction is admired; and the crime novel is lauded. More, just as once literary fiction made a claim to be rooted powerful in literary traditions, so genre fiction has acquired this sense too. A series of novels about the colonization of Mars, like Kim Stanley Robinson's, is rooted in and responds to all the previous stories of Mars. Again, just as literary fiction was seen to respond to events in literary and contemporary culture, so too, now is genre fiction. *Harry Potter* is as much a response to its time as *1984* was to 1948

But now, in the wider cultural and literary world, genre now utterly dominates the mainstream, even more than it did in 1932. For example, in response to a journalist's question suggesting that science fiction was 'ghettoised', the leading UK science fiction writer, theorist, and critic Adam Roberts wondered if 'the ghetto doesn't figure the opposite way to how it's often invoked. It's not that SFF [science fiction and fantasy] is a ghetto inside the glorious city of "Literary Fiction", but the reverse. "Literary" novels sell abominably badly, by and large; popular culture in the main belongs to SF and Fantasy, eighteen of the top twenty highest grossing movies of all time are SFF; everybody recognises SFF icons and memes' (Shenoy 2018). Indeed, other genre forms are thriving too: the thriller, the crime story and the romance also dominate both popular fiction and the small screen; the fantasy adventure, science fiction – or classic or modern Western – are the major modes for the computer game. Even given the access to the world provided by the web and the creativity it fosters, this is a competitive environment for what was once called the literary novel, and even more so for experimental fiction.

One response to this environment is the idea that literary fiction is simply one genre amongst others. And, in terms of the external branding of consumer choice that shapes the category of genre (and literature in general), this is clearly so: as Sarah Brouillette reminds us, 'the literary field's tendencies and capacities are tied to the fate of the real economy' (2017: 281). However, as the editors of this collection, we want to argue, tentatively, a different view: one with which we by no means expect all of our readers, nor even, perhaps, all of the contributors to this volume to agree. We suggest that there is something else internal to literary fiction: that, in contrast to genre writing, the literary remains in a deep way free and unbound. To clarify: any work of genre fiction to some degree accepts, develops or challenges (and so reinforces) generic conventions of content, plot, style, form, and so on, consensually understood by its readers, writers, and publishers. The conventions mark the 'brand' of a genre: a consensually predetermind set of signifiers to which literary fiction need not subscribe.

This idea, that genre is ruled by its conventions, underlies David Shields' purposely provocative dictum that genre 'is a minimum-security prison' (Shields 2010: 210). In contrast, what makes literary fiction 'literary' is not simply a different set of rules ('the maverick detective who doesn't do it by the book' in a crime novel against the more demanding literary character in literary fiction; the pacey prose of a thriller against a more challenging 'literary' style). Instead, literary fiction is characterized by potential absence of these rules altogether. As Derrida puts it, the literary is a 'strange institution': the 'institution of fiction . . . gives in principle the power to say everything, to break free of the rules' (Derrida 1992: 37). A literary fiction can choose its forebears (and one part of critical work is to draw out the significance of these choices); its subject, its form, its own questions. It is unbound, intrinsically, and internally unbranded. It may even, as Margaret Atwood famously does in her speculative fiction, draw on genre tropes: Indeed, two chapters in this book focus on authors who do something similar – Jonathan Lethem and Colson Whitehead. This unboundedness does not mean that a work of literary fiction never lapses into cliché (the 'adultery-in-Hampstead' novel or the tiresome middle-aged man 'revivified' by a stereotyped 'manic pixie dream girl', for example). Rather, it means that a work of literary fiction, potentially and its best, holds open a virtually infinite range of possibilities for the expression of what it means to be.

A consequence of this is that the literary is defined by being impossible to define: a contradiction, an aporia. But through this impossibility of definition, the literary can open up radically new spaces for understanding the world and one's place within it. In a rapidly digitalizing world – in which, as Wendy Hui Kyong Chun has memorably suggested, even the newest of New Media 'races simultaneously towards the future and the past, towards what we might call the bleeding edge of obsolescence' (2008: 148) – the literary continues to offer an alternative experience, a territory different from neoliberal teleology or instrumentalizing reason: a landscape neither utopian nor dystopian, but radically *open*. It is for this reason that we draw attention to and focus on literary fiction, an old and contested term but one whose full range of potential continues to make itself known in new and exciting ways. The diversity of contributions to this volume, we hope, demonstrates this, and the continuing relevance and value of the literary.

Orientation

The book is divided into four sections: 'Forms', 'Identities', 'Ruptures' and 'Case Studies'. Part 1, 'Forms', sketches out some of the most salient formal trends in literary fiction of the early twenty-first century. It opens with Caroline Edwards' theorization of 'The Networked Novel': a highly contemporary form which 'knit[s] together a disparate set of temporal (and frequently disjunct spatial) locations that are interconnected at the level of narrative structure, as well as being thematically interlaced' (p. 15). The networked novel is, as Edwards shows, reflective of a twenty-first century that is networked in multiple ways: through globaliza-tion, the internet, multinational financial capital, migration, and increasing awareness about humanity's collective experience of climate change. Next, Kristian Shaw takes the idea of networked fiction further by zooming in on a particular strand of contemporary fiction deal-ing with globalization: the major subgenre of twenty-first century writing that has come to be known as 'global fiction'.

Following Shaw, Part 1 moves on to two interrelated chapters that engage with the post-postmodern impulse, outlined earlier in this Introduction, towards writing that draws on post-modern tropes and techniques while adhering to an essence of emotional fidelity or truth: Martin Paul Eve's 'Sincerity' and Timothy Baker's 'Autobiografiction'. Jennifer Hodgson then continues to trace a pattern of sincerity underlying contemporary experimental fiction, while Huw Marsh's chapter on comedy goes on to identity a 'funny turn' (Marsh: p. 67) in twenty-first century fiction, focusing in particular on the American experimental author George Saunders (another writer often associated with the contemporary impulse for sincerity). Subsequently, Part 1 moves on to three chapters that focus on contemporary reimaginings of established forms: Xavier Marcó del Pont's 'Metafiction', Deborah Lilley's 'Pastoral', and Sophie Vlacos' 'Realisms'. These chapters demonstrate some of the many ways in which contemporary literary fiction is rooted in the past via complex and overlapping strands of history, while also speaking, again, to the multiple ways in which twenty-first century writers have sought to reimagine our sense of past and present by rendering familiar forms in exciting new ways. Finally, Part 1 closes with Harriet E.H. Earle's chapter exploring the surge in literary comics and graphic novels in a century that 'has seen comics come into its own, with an ever-increasing corpus of notable texts and creators'.

Part 2, 'Identities', shifts the books primary focus to the various ways in which contemporary debates about identity have been explored in twenty-first century fiction. Sara Upstone's chap-ter, 'Black British Fiction', opens the section with a reflection on developments in this diverse field over the past two decades. Placing Black British fiction into context via discussion of the controversial 2014 'Exhibit B' exhibition in London, the Grenfell Tower disaster in 2017, and the structual racism leading up to the recent Windrush scandal, Upstone argues that it frequently presents readers with 'a heteroglossic discourse': one that 'at points indicates both departure from and resonance with not only earlier British born voices of the 1980s and 1990s, but also that incredibly crucial black presence of the post-Windrush migrant generation' (p. 126). Next,

Alexandra Parsons' chapter, 'Queer', goes on to map the complex and diverse directions that LQBTQ+ fiction has taken in the past two decades, including a discussion of its intersections with ethnicity, race, and gender in the family. Stephen J. Burn's chapter on 'Family' follows, arguing that contemporary fiction's 'renewed interest in the family is multifaceted, moving from the surface obsessions of recent works . . . to deeper, axial questions that engage with the contemporary novel's clock, and its signature forms' (p. 148). Family is, again, a touch-point for Arthur Bradley and Andrew Tate in their chapter, 'Religion'. Via an exploration of contemporary fiction's fascination with religious experience – from re-writings of gospel narratives to representations of Islam and Islamism – Bradley and Tate suggest that twenty-first century writing on such topics frequently 'reveals all the other deep fiduciary investments in Big Others that circulate unnoticed within the contemporary novel: family, work and, most destructively, capital' (p. 160).

Part 2 then shifts its focus back to ethnic and national identity, with Leila Kamali's writing on 'Diaspora', E. Dawson Varughese on 'Indian Fiction in English', and Caroline Magennis on 'Northern Irish Fiction'. Again, in these three chapters, trends identified in Part 1 are brought to the fore: global networks in Kamali's and Dawson Varughese's chapters, and sincerity in Magennis' chapters, via its focus on intimacy. Finally, Part 2 closes with a discussion of posthumanism in Danielle Sand's chapter on 'Animals'. With a particular focus on insects, Sands argues that 'these tiny creatures offer the potential for a transformation of our understanding of empathy, attentiveness and kinship' (p. 199).

Part 3, 'Ruptures', examines literary fiction's responses to some of the early twenty-first century's most paradigm-shifting events. Via an analysis of Heti's *How Should A Person Be*, Zara Dinnen's '(The) Digital' argues that in our hyper-connected era of Web 2.0, social media and the Cloud, 'understanding literary fiction as part of an ecology of cultural practices, instructions, and sites is a way to encounter the normative action of digital media as we are co-constituted as subjects with it' (p. 215). Next, in 'Anthropocene', Sam Solnick turns the volume's attention to what scientists have described as a nascent ecological epoch defined by humans' impact on the Earth, tracing how contemporary literary fiction has explored the ways in which humanity writes itself into the fabric of the planet. It has been predicted that climate change will lead to an increase in the mass displacement that we are already witnessing in the context of the current refugee crisis, a global emergency that Part 3's next two chapters engage with from different angles. In 'Displacement', Emily Hogg explores a particular definition of the term that arises from four contemporary literary texts, showing that 'To speak of displacement is inevitably to speak of what it means to be at home' (p. 239). Agnes Woolley's chapter, 'Asylum', then analyses the next stage in displacement: refuge. Woolley shows that in contrast with escalation of anti-immigration policy and rhetoric in Europe, Australia, and North America (not least in the hateful narratives of Donald Trump and Brexit), 'fictional representations of contemporary asylum and displacement eschew simplified legal and media forms' (p. 250).

Paul Crosthwaite then shifts Part 3's focus to another of the century's key crises: the financial collapse of 2008. In his chapter, 'Finance', Crosthwaite argues that writers engaging with money and markets in the twenty-first century 'are united by their foregrounding of the profound ways in which human emotion and imagination are implicated in the abstract processes of financial exchange' (p. 262). Arin Keeble and Daniel O'Gorman follow with two interrelated chapters: 'The 9/11 Novel' and 'War on Terror'. Keeble sketches the development of the '9/11 novel', which has become a subgenre in its own right in contemporary literary fiction, while O'Gorman explores the ways in which the event's reverberations have been felt globally, with a particular focus on Anglophone writing from Pakistan. Both chapters show that literary writers have strived to challenge the reductive narratives about terrorism and counterterrorism that have dominated media and political discourse over the past two decades by placing 9/11 in a complex historical context.

Anna Hartnell's chapter, 'From Civil Rights to #BLM', continues this historical emphasis by tracing the roots of the Black Lives Matter movement in acts of twentieth century anti-racist resistance in the United States, with a particular focus on the novels of Toni Morrison and Jesmyn Ward.

Part 3's focus on history in the twenty-first century then comes to a head with Robert Eaglestone's chapter, 'The Past', which looks at the ways in which many contemporary novels – from fables and science fiction to Neo-Victorian works – are haunted by history. Finally, Emily Horton closes the section with an analysis of two contemporary authors who have attempted to offer active participation in challenging some of the twenty-first century 'Ruptures' that Part 3 has focused on. Looking in particular at the work of Ben Lerner and Ali Smith, Horton argues that both of these authors '[negotiate] modernist techniques as a means to reconceiving novelistic sentiment, rejecting irony and cynicism in favour of candour and hope' (p. 321). In doing so, she once again underlines the volume's repeated emphasis on sincerity running through twenty-first century literature.

Finally, Part 4, 'Case Studies' collects ten chapters that zoom in on particular authors, who have been chosen for the ways in which they put into play many of the topics discussed throughout the volume. By no means an exhaustive list of the century's most significant authors, this section is, as it's heading suggests, a selection that exemplifies some of the twenty-first century's most salient literary and cultural trends. It begins with Katy Shaw's chapter, '*Granta*'s Best of Young British Novelists', which analyses the significance of cities in the work of those selected in the most recent round of the influential literary magazine's prominent, once-per-decade prize. Shaw argues that this focus on cities '[reframes] our relationship with the environment in the new millennium' (p. 336). Globalization, digital culture and the networked novel are represented in the next three chapters: Lucienne Loh on Hari Kunzru, Dorothy Butchard on Jennifer Egan, and Sarah Dillon on David Mitchell.

Defining the contemporary comes to the fore in the next two chapters: Joseph Brooker on Jonathan Lethem and Daniel Lea on Ali Smith. Two very different authors from different backgrounds, Lethem and Smith are both shown to oscillate between irony and sincerity in a way that exemplifies this overarching metamodernist trend in contemporary writing more broadly. According to Brooker, Lethem does this through a subversion of the border between literary and genre fiction, while Lea shows how Smith does it by pushing the boundaries of social realism in innovative new ways. Following on this theme, Carole Jones argues that A.L. Kennedy likewise reworks realism for the twenty-first century, by drawing on postmodern metafiction 'to counter the most radical effects of postmodernist discourse, particularly its moral relativism and textualizing of reality' (p. 406).

Part 4's final three chapters turn once again to contemporary fiction's haunting by the past. In her chapter on Hilary Mantel, Jenny Bavidge explores the author's curious contradictions: Mantel, she writes, is 'a Dame of the British Empire who writes short stories imagining the assassination of the Prime Minister, and a historical novelist fond of pointing out the limitations of our historical knowledge' (p. 415). Next, Rachel Sykes argues for the urgent, disjunctive contemporaneity of the writing of Marilynne Robinson, outlining Robinson's outspoken opposition to postmodernism while also critiquing 'the willingness of critics and reviewers to assign the style and concerns of her writing to the past' (p. 424). Finally, the collection closes with Christopher Lloyd's chapter on Colson Whitehead, one of the most significant writers of literary fiction to have emerged in the United States this century. As Lloyd shows, Whitehead's uncategorizable writing – like that of Mitchell, Lethem or Smith – pushes at the boundary between literary and genre fiction, realism, and fantasy, in order to delve deep into the history of race in America, showing that 'African American history and memory suffuse every corner of US identity' (p. 434).

Throughout the volume, we have encouraged contributors to favor argument and ideas over exhaustive coverage. This has resulted in productive and creative intersections, revealing networks of knowledge about the contemporary, rather like those identified by Edwards in the novels that she analyses in Chapter 1. As we mentioned above, many authors who do not have dedicated chapters reappear: Mohsin Hamid, Kazuo Ishiguro, David Foster Wallace, Ben Lerner and Zadie Smith, to name a few. Similarly, the length of this volume has allowed for a more nuanced exploration of themes, giving contributors the opportunity to explore similar topics from a multitude of varying angles, perspectives, and contexts. As we stated at the outset, this book is an experiment in cartography, with the aim of beginning to map the already diverse, expansive and shifting regions of literary fiction in the twenty-first century. Each chapter traces a different path through this still-growing, still-evolving contemporary environment.

Works cited

Agamben, G. (2011) 'What Is the Contemporary?' *Nudities*, trans. D. Kishik and S. Pedatella. Stanford: Stanford University Press. 10–20.

Barnes, J. (2013) 'Stoner: The Must-Read Novel of 2013.' *Guardian*. 13 Dec. www.theguardian.com/books/2013/dec/13/stoner-john-williams-julian-barnes

Brouillette, S. (2017) 'Neoliberalism and the Demise of the Literary.' *Neoliberalism and Contemporary Literary Culture*, ed. Mitchum Huehls and Rachel Greenwald Smith. 277–290.

Butler, J. (2009) *Frames of War: When Is Life Grievable?* New York and London: Verso.

Chun, W.H.K. (2008) "The Enduring Ephemeral, or the Future Is a Memory." *Critical Inquiry* 35:Autumn. 148–171.

Cole, T. (2017) *Blind Spot*. New York: Penguin Random House.

Derrida, J. (1992) 'This Strange Institution Called Literature.' *Acts of Literature*, ed. D. Attridge. London: Routledge.

Funk, W. (2015) *The Literature of Reconstruction: Authentic Fiction in the New Millennium*. London: Bloomsbury.

Gibbons, A. (2015) '"Take That You Intellectuals!" and "kaPOW!": Adam Thirlwell and the Metamodernist Future of Style.' *Studia Neophilologica* 87:1. 29–43.

Hampson, S. (2013) 'Stoner: How the Story of a Failure Became an All-Out Publishing Success.' 11 May. https://www.theglobeandmail.com/arts/books-and-media/stoner-how-the-story-of-a-failure-became-an-all-out-publishing-success/article15803253/

James, D. (2019) *Discrepant Solace: Contemporary Writing and the Work of Consolation*. Oxford: Oxford University Press.

Kelly, A. (2010) 'David Foster Wallace and the New Sincerity in American Fiction.' *Consider David Foster Wallace*, ed. D. Hering. Los Angeles and Austin: Sideshow Media Group Press. 131–146.

Lerner, B. (2014) *10:04*. London: Granta.

Ruffel, L. (2018) *Brouhaha: Worlds of the Contemporary*. Minnesota: University of Minnesota Press.

Rushdie, S. (2008) *Midnight's Children*. London: Vintage.

Shenoy, G. (2018) '"We're Winning the War": A Q&A with SF Writer, Critic and Historian, Adam Roberts.' *Factor Daily*. https://factordaily.com/adam-roberts-interview/

Shields, D. (2010) *Reality Hunger: A Manifesto*. London: Hamish Hamilton.

Smith, A. (2017) 'Ali Smith's Goldsmiths Prize lecture: The novel in the age of Trump.' *New Statesman*. 15 October. https://www.newstatesman.com/culture/books/2017/10/ali-smith-s-goldsmiths-prize-lecture-novel-age-trump

Timmer, N. (2010) *Do You Feel It Too? The Post-Postmodern Syndrome in American Fiction at the Turn of the Millennium*. Amsterdam: Rodopi.

Turner, L. (2015) 'Metamodernism: A Brief Introduction.' *Queen Mob's Teahouse*. 5 Jan. http://queenmobs.com/2015/01/metamodernism-brief-introduction/

Vermeulen, R., and T. van der Akker (2010) 'Notes on Metamodernism.' *Journal of Aesthetics & Culture* 2. 1–14.

Wallace D.F. (1993) 'E Unibus Plurum: Television and U.S. Fiction.' *Review of Contemporary Fiction* 13:2. 151–194.

PART I

Forms

1

THE NETWORKED NOVEL

Caroline Edwards

Contemporary literature, as the term suggests, is defined by its relationship to the condition of being contemporary, or contemporaneity. We can debate the parameters by which we choose to periodise the contemporary: does it, for instance, begin in 1945 with the beginning of the postwar period and its welfarism, immigration and economic stability? Or should we consider the neoliberal recalibration of economic policy with Thatcher and Reagan as building the bedrock for our financial, political and economic situation today? Perhaps we wish to take a more millennial approach and suggest that contemporary literature can be periodised from 2000 onwards, with the terrorist attacks of 9/11 marking the beginning of a new century with its increasingly globalised geopolitics, the rise of stateless networked terrorist organisations and the transnational pressures upon individual nation-states provoked by international financial transactions and the ethical, legal and market frontiers of the digital realm.

Beyond periodising claims, however, lies the paradox of contemporaneity itself. As Giorgio Agamben (2009) notes in his essay 'What is the Contemporary?,' our time is yoked with another time or, rather, many other times, and the relationship between them signifies their *contemporary* nature. Since *to be contemporary* suggests being with other times, our perception of contemporaneity is then held up for scrutiny in terms of its distance – or proximity – to the present 'now.' The study of contemporary literature is thus rooted within a complex philosophical discussion concerning the nature of temporal experience as it mediates between historical time and lived, subjective time. Moreover, the literary form of the novel (with which I shall be concerned in this chapter) is uniquely positioned to convey the qualitatively different kinds of subjective and 'clock' times that organise our lives, as well as the possibilities afforded by narrative organisation to represent such lived times. As Paul Ricoeur enthusiastically observes in *Time and Narrative*, *Vol. 2*: 'What resources fiction has for following the subtle variations between the time of consciousness and chronological time!' (Ricoeur 1985: 107). Examining this relationship between consciousness and narrative time, there has been much written about the times of the modernist novel, as well as the postmodernist novel. Modernist narrative innovators such as Virginia Woolf, James Joyce, Dorothy Richardson and Katherine Mansfield were acutely aware of the temporal distinctions to be made between the chronometric regularity of standardised time, and the private times of subjective experience that stretch out the smallest, most mundane moments into extended reveries: throwing up memories into the melee of a chaotic present and secreting distant utopian yearnings. What Henri Bergson referred to as the intuitive, fluid encounters with *durée* – in which the essence of a singular moment may be felt as an interruption into the spatial-ised time of the clock's steady ticking of seconds, minutes and hours (*l'étendu*) (Bergson 1911) – can be charted in Woolf's 'moments of being' or Joyce's stream of consciousness, which unfolds the fluxional process of temporal experience (for influential readings of time in the modernist novel, see Schleifer 2000; Kern 2003; Randall 2007; Barrows 2011; Murphy 2011). Meanwhile, readings of time in the postmodern novel have clustered around the central questions of prolif-erating forks and temporal branchings – those texts which foreground impossible times, simul-taneous times, multiple alternate possible trajectories, and loops of chance containing moments whose temporal plasticity offers narrative analogies to Salvador Dalí's soft clocks (Heise 1997: 51; Gomel 2010). Here, we find writers such as Christine Brooke-Rose, Alain Robbe-Grillet, Thomas Pynchon and Julio Cortázar: chosen for their complex and contradictory timeframes, their experimentation with non-linear narrative form, and their articulation of the increasingly splenetic, globalised times of media production, spectacle-laden simulation and paranoid con-sumption from the mid- to late-twentieth century.

More recently, however, the dominant paradigm of literary postmodernism has waned and the twenty-first century novel finds itself in an interesting position with respect to the question of time. Over the past two decades a resurgence of interest has sprung up around questions of temporal experience, both within theoretical discussions as well as in the contemporary novel. Recent developments in queer theory, for example, have given fresh impetus to studies of the phi-losophy of time. Bringing queer phenomenology into contact with studies of temporality, critics have emphasised the way in which a queer experience of time is qualitatively distinct to that of heteronormative subjects and produces a challenge to so-called 'chrononormativity' through alternative times of being (Halberstam 2005; Ahmed 2006; Edelman 2004; Freeman 2010). The relationship between queer subjectivity and queer times can similarly be traced in a number of recent novels that examine questions of historical time and linear progress, the anachronism of contemporaneity's relationship with the past, as well as the possibilities for queer futurity. Jeanette Winterson's *The PowerBook* (2000) embeds the idea of disembodied Internet chatroom anonym-ity into a fluid consideration of gender and identity that stretches across various historical times as the central characters morph between selves. Meanwhile, Alison Bechdel's graphic memoir *Fun Home: A Family Tragicomic* (2006) uses the non-linear possibilities of graphic storytelling to great effect in an examination of queer identity that blurs past and present. Lynn Breedlove's 2002 novel *Godspeed* (2002) also constructs an alternative temporality that Judith Halberstam describes as ludic, using drugs to create a 'junk time' inspired by William Burroughs and animating a les-bian picaresque narrative with the speed of accelerated narcotic times and possible alternate his-tories (Halberstam 2005: 5). Similarly, what has been called the post-AIDS 'anti-historical novel' of Jeremy Reed's *The Grid* (2008) uses queer identity to reconsider the relationship between past and future in an erotically charged temporal register that pits sexual desire against an apocalyptic backdrop (Stanivukovic 2014: 227).

In addition to the temporal possibilities of queer fiction, a recent spate of novels featuring dead narrators similarly challenge linear narratives of temporal progress in the seamless blending of the living present with the afterlives of deceased characters given narrative voice in a number of striking ways. As Alice Bennett (2012) has argued, such 'narrative afterlives' use experimental forms to offer complex combinations of narrative temporal order and causality, employing pro-lepsis and analepsis to construct supernatural, 'un-lifelike types of temporality' that challenge the predominance of mimetic representation in contemporary literary realism (Bennett 73). Novels such as Ali Smith's *Hotel World* (2001); Alice Sebold's *The Lovely Bones* (2002); John Burnside's *Glister* (2008) and Jon McGregor's *Even the Dogs* (2010) feature dead narrators whose temporal location in a narrative position 'outside' or 'beyond' the time of the narrative present affords them an otherworldly and distinctly post-secular perspective on events that unfold within the storyworld. Meanwhile, texts such as Glenn Duncan's *I, Lucifer* (2003) and Margaret Atwood's *The Penelopiad* (2005) employ an afterlife perspective to deconstruct the hierarchical privileging of present time over past and future; whilst Kate Atkinson's *Life After Life* (2013) sees its central protagonist Ursula living out her life again and again, each time in a different historical period. These temporal structures seem apposite to the transtemporal, transmedial and transnational patterns of connection experienced in the twenty-first-century, in which time and space are felt as increasingly compressed, accelerated and abstracted. The digital network of global communications that charts our progressively computerised lifeworlds stands as the figure for our times and casts its shadow over the contemporary novel in interesting ways. The challenge of wrenching the historical form of the novel into a networked aesthetic appropriate to our digital encounters thus provides fresh opportunities for a plethora of distinctly new temporal engagements that move us beyond modernist and postmodernist timeframes.

This preoccupation with many different kinds of time in the contemporary novel is thus reimagining mimetic representation through a number of innovations in narrative voice, structure and temporality. Such texts might productively be considered as what Ricoeur called 'tales about time,' in which 'it is the very experience of time that is at stake' (Ricoeur 1985: 101). One of the most striking examples of such innovation can be identified in what I am calling the 'networked novel.' Networked novels knit together a disparate set of temporal (and frequently disjunct spatial) locations that are interconnected at the level of narrative structure, as well as being thematically interlaced. Such novels stretch the boundaries between the novel and the short story collection, pulling into contiguity characters that are dotted throughout historical time to present a story that takes as its primary figural terrain the image of the network. In so doing, many contemporary networked novels engage with the idea of transmigration, in which disembodied spirit characters move between host bodies or characters appear to be reincarnated across different time periods (Virginia Woolf's fictional 1928 biography *Orlando* can be identified here as the contemporary networked novel's ur-text, which offers a plasticity of subjective identity and temporal experience as Orlando lives more than 300 years and changes biological sex). Douglas Coupland has touched upon this aspect of what I am calling the networked novel, arguing that texts such as Hari Kunzru's *Gods Without Men* (2011); David Mitchell's *Cloud Atlas* (2004a); and Michael Cunningham's *The Hours* (1998) exemplify what he calls 'translit novels,' which 'cross history without being historical; [and] span geography without changing psychic place' (Coupland 2012). Similarly, the relationship between such temporal networking and the notion of a global narrative form has been considered by Caren Irr in *Toward the Geopolitical Novel: U.S. Fiction in the Twenty-First Century* (2014). Over the last three decades, the increasingly visible use of multiple novelistic settings, global peregrinations, and networked connections between divergent locales reveals the ambitions of a 'certain kind of contemporary writer' to construct what Irr terms the 'world novel':

> Maxine Hong Kingston, Kazuo Ishiguro, and others have imagined a new 'epic' that spans many locations, documents the simultaneous and multidirectional movements of the world's populations, and registers without being swamped by the new communication technologies. They hope that such works will address the major issues of our era, including peace, ecological crisis, and nuclear threats.
>
> (Irr 2014: 175)

To Irr and Coupland's mini-oeuvre, we might also add Haruki Murakami's epic three-volumed *1Q84* (2009–2011), Bernardine Evaristo's poetic autobiography *Lara* (2009); Nick Harkaway's multi-genre-spanning *Angelmaker* (2012); and Ali Smith's *How to be Both* (2014), which connects the fifteenth-century painter Francesco del Cossa with a teenager in contemporary England.

In contextualising the twenty-first-century networked novel we might consider scholarship that has developed the idea of networked narratives in contemporary cinema. As Wendy Everett has argued, the concept of the network has impacted upon the narrative structure of contemporary films: 'echoing the random growth of the network, there is little or no linear development, and stories and events instead form complex web-like structures' (Everett 167). Films such as Paul Thomas Anderson's *Magnolia* (1999); Paul Haggis' *Crash* (2004); Alejandro González Iñárritu's *21 Grams* (2003) and *Babel* (2006), and Gaspar Noé's *Irréversible* (2002) thus suggest cyberspace through the way in which their multiple narratives are networked together across space and time. Also sometimes referred to as 'database' (Kinder 2002) or 'modular' narratives (Cameron 2008), the anachronic and episodic temporal structures that these films construct recast temporal anxieties for the digital age. The film critic Roger Ebert defines this kind of cinema with reference to the digitised metaphor of the hyperlink: 'a hyperlink movie shows apparently unrelated stories and characters that have a gradually revealed, hidden connection' and cites Robert Altman's acclaimed musical drama *Nashville* (1975), which features 24 main characters ranged across numerous storylines (Ebert 2007).

Rita Barnard connects such globalised cinematic storytelling with the contemporary novel, arguing that the British writer David Mitchell's 1999 novel *Ghostwritten* intersperses a series of short stories set in disjunct locales and time periods via the idea of a 'highlighted hyperlink,' which she calls 'Mitchell's deliberate effort to imagine some sort of global narrative form' (Barnard 2009: 211). Mitchell has become the literary exemplar of this new kind of globalised narrative, whose networking structure has been described by critics as evidencing a twenty-first-century reimagination of the novel as a transnational literary form, modified to express a contemporary mode of cosmopolitan identity (Schoene 2009; O'Donnell 2015: 5–6; Barnard 2009: 211). Since *Ghostwritten* in 1999, Mitchell has been praised for the ambitious scope and energy of his novels, his acute ear for distinct narrative styles and the ability to move from genre to genre with apparent ease. With each new novel, what critics have termed 'the Mitchellverse' (Berry 2015) has expanded as characters reappear across his texts and increasingly complex backstories become slowly unfolded. As Patrick O'Donnell describes, the architecture of Mitchell's narrative structures is 'neither carpenter's gothic nor that of the sedimented multinovel, but a capacious assemblage of narratives connected to each other in differential patterns' (O'Donnell 2015: 1). But perhaps most distinctively, Mitchell has been committed to exploring the narrative function of transmigratory characters since a wandering soul known as Arupadhatu transmigrated into the body of a young Danish backpacker travelling through Ulan Bator in the 'Mongolia' section of *Ghostwritten*. These two seemingly disjunct figures – the backpacker and the transmigratory soul – offer Mitchell an illustration of the rootlessness of contemporary globalised life. As Arupadhatu muses, backpackers and wandering souls have much in common:

> We live nowhere, and we are strangers everywhere. We drift, often on a whim, searching for something to search for. We are both parasites: I live in my hosts' minds, and drift through his or her memories to understand the world. Caspar's breed live in a host country that is never their own, and use its culture and landscape to learn, or stave off boredom. To the world at large we are both immaterial and invisible.
>
> (G 160)

Mitchell returned to this theme in his 2004 bestseller *Cloud Atlas*, in which nearly all of the novel's characters are reincarnations of the same soul and share a comet-shaped birthmark. In his 2010 historical fiction *The Thousand Autumns of Jacob de Zoet*, Mitchell further probed the narrative possibilities of transmigration through the mysterious character of Lord Enomoto, who claims to have cheated death by harvesting and distilling souls for over 600 years. The theme of soul-harvesting ('animicide') is given a fuller account in *The Bone Clocks*, where the character of Marinus – who, in a former incarnation, appeared as a Dutch physician working at Dejima, Nagasaki in *The Thousand Autumns* – is revealed to be a transmigratory spirit who has lived for over 1400 years in 39 different host bodies.

As I have argued elsewhere (Edwards 2011), Mitchell's use of the figure of transmigration in *Ghostwritten* and *Cloud Atlas* allows him to network together a disjunct set of characters stretched across various historical times and locales into a forceful critique of colonial power. The theme of violent colonisation and the rise and fall of empires has preoccupied Mitchell throughout his texts, and is given structural impetus in the nested *matrioshka* Russian doll presentation of embedded narratives in *Cloud Atlas* in which, as Mitchell himself has said, '[e]ach block of narrative is subsumed by the next, like a row of ever-bigger fish eating the one in front' (Mitchell 2004b). The themes of European colonisation, genocide, slavery and the destruction of indigenous cultures are revisited in *The Bone Clocks*. The narrative is divided into six chapters, each narrated by a different character in a different time, stretching from 1984 to an apocalyptic near-future, when the West Coast of Ireland slides into anarchy after a series of global calamities in 2043. Neatly sidestepping the linear time of modernity that equated progress with an expanding world system of capitalist and colonial predations, *The Bone Clocks* offers an alternative historical register. As the character of Esther Little reveals to Lucas Marinus, transmigration has marked her ancient soul with numerous cultural inheritances that originated with the Aboriginal Noongar and has experienced more than 25 centuries, 'predat[ing] Rome, Troy, Egypt, Peking, Nineveh and Ur' (*BC* 415).

The theme of transmigration similarly offers a networked narrative structure to the British novelist Marina Warner's *The Leto Bundle* (2001), in which the destitute Titan goddess Leto (raped by Zeus and subsequently banished from Olympus by Hera) raises her twins Apollo and Artemis in a number of different historical periods. Similarly, the Jamaican-Canadian writer Nalo Hopkinson reworks diasporic consciousness within a transnational and transhistorical community in *The Salt Roads* (2003). The novel weaves together four female first-person narrative voices: Mer is a slave and a healer working on a sugar plantation in colonial Saint-Domingue in the 1750s, shortly before the Haitian Revolution (1791–1804); the beautiful mixed-race Haitian-French dancer Jeanne Duval, Charles Baudelaire's lover, struggles against discrimination, penury and ill health between 1842 and 1862; and in 345 CE a young Nubian–Egyptian slave and prostitute Thaïs (whose Egyptian name is Meritet, shortened to Meri) journeys from her master in Alexandria to the Roman garrison of Aelia Capitolina in Jerusalem where she suffers a miscarriage inside the Church of the Sepulchre and becomes deified as Saint Mary of Egypt (indicating a linguistic slippage between Meri/Mary). Interlacing these three women's stories is the fourth narrative voice of Ezili, a newborn Caribbean deity who is delivered as Mer buries a stillborn child in a river. Ezili floats through time, transmigrating into the host bodies of Mer, Jeanne and Thaïs, as well as drifting into a detemporalised spirit world of the Ginen: the sacred homeland of the Haitian slaves, whose religious culture blends West African Yoruba spirituality with Haitian and Christian elements. Ezili thus figuratively connects diasporic African identities through her travels in the 'aether world,' with its metaleptic layers of salt and its '[m]any flows, combining, separating, all stories of African people' (*TSR* 193). The fluid imagery of water and salt – extending from the brackish seawater and briny stench of the Middle Passage, to the amniotic fluid holding unborn children, to jism, sweat, cooking and the ritual uses of salt in religious ceremonies – form interconnecting 'joined tributaries' and 'watery webs' (*TSR* 213) between the novel's central characters.

This fluidity connects each historical time in *The Salt Roads* at the level of a shared set of motifs which are clustered around water and salt (each woman struggles against male oppression, rape, working in prostitution, and expressing a positive female sexuality outside of these parameters). Ezili thus mediates between 'human time' or 'the mortal world of time' and 'the flowing world of stories' (*TSR* 293, 326). Read via a Ricoeurian analysis, we can therefore identify her temporal networking of the other characters, and the Ginen as a whole, as reconciling individual time with cosmic time:

> We are all here, all the powers of the Ginen lives for all the centuries that they have been in existence, and we all fight. We change when change is needed. We are a little different in each place that the Ginen have come to rest, and any one of [us] is already many powers. No cancer can fell us all, no blight cover us completely.
>
> (TSR 387)

Like Warner's deified figure of Leto in *The Leto Bundle*, Ezili functions to network together various syncretic historical times and spaces into a hybridised mode of what we might call *hypertemporal* being. Ezili's narrative exteriority to the mortal time of humanity is nonetheless suffused with temporal resonances, experienced as a vast ocean of diasporic suffering, dreams and ambitions. 'Time has no past or future for me, just an eternal now' (*TSR* 322) Ezili states, asserting her non-linear experience of spiritual time: 'Time does not flow for me. Not for me the progression in a straight line from earliest to latest. Time eddies. I am now then, now there, sometimes simultaneously' (*TSR* 42). This temporal eddying not only connects the characters of *The Salt Roads* across different centuries and continents, but also works real historical figures into a fictional reimagining of the past: Hopkinson's narrative features François Mackandal, the voodoo priest and Haitian fugitive leader of the runaway Maroon slaves; Baudelaire's lover Jeanne Duval who inspired his 'Black Venus' poems; Queen Nzingha of Matramba; Rosa Parks; and the trans activist and 'street queen' Marsha P. Johnson (whose occlusion from conventional accounts of the Stonewall Riots in 1969 is mirrored in the novel's interrogation of historical record and its blindness to lower-class women's agency). Hopkinson's employment of transmigration to network together her mixed-race set of characters owes a debt to Caryl Phillips' 1993 novel, *Crossing the River*, which similarly reimagines the African diaspora across historical time: stretching over a period of 250 years from the transatlantic slave trade, to the late 1830s and the beginning of WWII. Hopkinson's non-linear fragmented narrative structure in *The Salt Roads* thus builds upon Phillips' earlier experiment with a polyphonic transmigration between characters whose interconnected stories arc across continents and centuries. Both novels reject an exclusionary model of historical time, which posits a pre-historical anteriority of non-European experience against which modern colonial powers define themselves, and the historical narrative of civilised European modernity with its normative temporalities of calendric number and the productive units of clock-time (West-Pavlov 2013: 163). Moreover, Hopkinson's exploration of lesbian and bisexual relationships in *The Salt Roads* explicitly positions a different quality of what Julia Kristeva has called 'women's time' by privileging the extrasubjective times of *jouissance* and pleasure in contradistinction to the 'cursive time' (as Nietzsche called it) of capitalist production and colonial mastery, which reveals the temporal structure of slavery within its master-slave dialectic (Kristeva 1981: 16, 14).

A similarly delinearised chronology is employed in Hari Kunzru's 2011 novel *Gods Without Men*. Building on his earlier novelistic interest in networked patterns of connection (as explored in his 2004 novel *Transmission*, which brings together globalised circuits of production with diasporic characters travelling around the world), *Gods Without Men* embeds interconnecting narratives within a transhistorical story that actuates what Kunzru has called 'a networked art form' (Kunzru in Hodgkinson 2012). The novel's non-linear structure sutures a variety of different historical times – 1947, 2008, 1958, 1969, 1920, 1778, 1871, 1970 and 2009 – all set in the Californian Mojave desert. This networked mode of storytelling earned the novel some rather mixed reviews. As one critic complained: 'It feels as if [Kunzru] has shackled his enterprise to a conceptual apparatus that . . . has run amok,' asking: 'Why laboriously split and splice narratives instead of pursuing a central theme or story?' (Linklater 2011). Whilst critics recognise the relevance of Kunzru's aesthetic project of networking the different times of *Gods Without Men* to our contemporary digitised lifeworld of multiple, simultaneous overlapping timescales, their dislike of narrative discontinuity has led to accusations of Kunzru's residual postmodernist style. I would contend, however, that the novel's structural fragmentation is adequately matched to its thematic networking. Kunzru's networked novel thus matches form with content: a narrative concerned with the way in which a single location (the Mojave desert) constructs a model of present time that is suffused with historical resonances, is narrated in a narrative structure in which each different timescale is connected. It is the central figure of the missing child – Lisa and Jaz's son Raj, who disappears in 2008 at the Trona Pinnacles in the Western Mojave desert – that brings together the novel's different historical times. In a world in which, as Jaz thinks, '[e]verything seemed to be linked to everything else' (*GWM* 141), the globally interconnected, algorithmic temporalities of computational exchange – whether the short-selling of stocks and shares by the Walter software, or the Asian gameworlds whose simulated universes have spawned their own markets for trading virtual commodities – become subordinated to the image of futurity contained within the figure of the child. Raj transmigrates across the novel's different narrative timescales, seen by characters in different time periods, from the 1920s to 2008. In his association with the mythical Coyote figure who moves between the living and the dead, Raj becomes a redemptive figure explicitly connected to the narrative's otherworldliness after his miraculous return: the other 'paths and flows' (*GWM* 357) of Coyote's polytemporal wanderings having marked Raj as different, with his inexplicable knowledge and uncanny abilities.

This use of a networked narrative structure to explore a particular setting (as opposed to bringing together multiple geographically dispersed settings) can also be discerned in Michael Cunningham's fourth novel *Specimen Days* (2005). Cunningham borrows from the title of Walt Whitman's 1882 autobiography to transcribe the lives of three main characters reincarnated in different historical periods, through the iterated stories of Simon, his fiancée Catherine, and his younger brother Lucas/Luke. The first timescale is set in 1867, featuring Catherine and Lucas shortly after Simon's abrupt death in a factory accident. When Lucas replaces his brother's place on the factory floor the workshop's deafening, insatiable machines sound to him like the incantatory rhythms of Whitman's *Leaves of Grass* (extensive sections of which he can quote from memory), and Lucas starts to hear his dead brother's voice issuing from the machinery, lulling him into 'a continuum: machines, then grass and trees, then horses and dogs, then human beings' (*SD* 19). The novel's second timescale is set in the early 2000s and is narrated in the style of a police procedural, in which Cat is a forensic psychologist tracking juvenile terrorists, including Luke, who are sacrificing themselves as suicide bombers for an apocalyptic religious sect whose sacred text is Whitman's *Leaves of Grass*. Finally, the novel's third timescale shifts into a dystopian New York in the mid-twenty-second century. In this post-catastrophe future, Simon has literally become a machine: a cyborg who earns his living by playing a mugger in Manhattan in a theme park for wealthy Asian tourists; meanwhile, Catereen is an alien refugee with lizard features, and Luke has morphed into a messianic child worshipped by a Christian sect. The three narratives of Cunningham's novel are connected through the unified location of New York as well as references to Walt Whitman's poetry and his transcendentalist notions of cyclical existence. The theme of

Buddhist rebirth reverberates across each narrative timescale; as Jacqueline Rose has suggested, in *Specimen Days* '[n]one of the dead disappears. Everyone comes round more than once (the formal repetition, or rhyming structure, of his novels is his way of saying this)' (Rose 2005). Cunningham's Ricoeurian 'tale about time' thus not only enacts what Aris Mousoutzanis has called the *Unheimlich* Freudian repetition of 'the trauma of industrialization' (Mousoutzanis 2009: 130) across each of its narrative times but, moreover, offers a compelling reimagination of the Whitmanesque eternal present in which, as W. J. Johnson suggests, Whitman's poetic vision of the rhythmic flow of all organic and inorganic life presents a model of time in which the '*Hic et nun* ("here and now") becomes part of the *illud tempus* ("that time"), and in this still center, this timeless present, there is no death' (Johnson 1982: 185).

Whilst Whitman's poetic influence shapes Cunningham's consideration of networked times in *Specimen Days*, it is Marcel Proust whose influence can be discerned in another significant example of the networked novel in recent years: Jennifer Egan's fourth novel, *A Visit from the Goon Squad* (2010). Egan has said in interview that the novel's non-linear structure was inspired by Quentin Tarantino's *Pulp Fiction* (1994) (she even named the character Jules after the film), widely considered the acme of postmodern cinematic intertextuality and pastiche. The novel is organised into 13 chapters which jump around in time, stretching from the 1970s to the near-future of the 2020s, encompassing Los Angeles, San Francisco, New York, a Kenyan safari park, and the barricaded compound of a genocidal dictator (location unspecified). Across these times and spaces we encounter a loose cluster of central characters, as well as numerous peripheral figures, grouped around two nodal characters: Sasha Grady (third-person point of view narrative in the mid-2000s), a kleptomaniac in her early 30s working in the music industry, whose adolescence was marked by her absconding father, several suicide attempts and years of therapy; and her boss Bennie Salazar (third-person point of view narrative in the same time period), a Chicano music producer originally from San Francisco whose fortunes rise and fall over the course of the story.

Networking the delinearised narrative progression of these loosely interconnected groups of characters is a shared pattern of eddying leitmotifs: there are numerous references to the trauma of 9/11 and the shocking absence of the Twin Towers at Ground Zero ('he followed her eyes to the empty space where the Twin Towers had been. "There should be something, you know?" she said, not looking at Bennie. "Like an echo. Or an outline"' [*VGS* 38]); several characters reflect upon their own fractured subjectivities and the congruence of multiple identities and selves; and the theme of shame reverberates from chapter to chapter as characters address their flaws and transgressions (from Sasha's kleptomania to Bennie's childhood humiliations, infidelities and corporate transactions, as well as his wife Stephanie's minor victory at being inaugurated into the country club set). But it is Egan's iterated recourse to a Proustian *mémoire involontaire* that forms the pivotal structuring device of the novel. Proust differentiated between the controlled, deliberate recollection of the past (*mémoire volontaire*) and those piercing lances of memory which punctuate our experience as unbidden visceral flashbacks, particularly associated with unconscious sensory recollection (*mémoire involontaire*) (Carter 2004: 176). Citing Proust in the novel's epigraph, Egan proceeds to stud her narrative with a catalogue of *mémoire involontaire*: 'the memory overcame Bennie (had the word 'sisters' brought it on?)' (*VGS* 21); 'He idled now in front of Christopher's school, waiting for the memory spasm to pass' (*VGS* 25); 'he concentrated on Sasha, just to his right, hew sweet-bitter smell, and found himself remembering a girl he'd chased at a party when he first came to New York and was selling vinyl on the Lower East Side a hundred years ago' (*VGS* 33); 'Stephanie had a flash of how they'd been as kids, an almost-physical sense of Jules as her protector . . . That feeling had been buried under Jules' chaotic intervening years, but now it pushed back up, warm and vital, sending tears into Stephanie's eyes' (*VGS* 138). It is the felt physicality of these unbidden memories that marks Egan's aesthetic preoccupation with the relationship between past and present, specifically in terms of her characters' awareness of what it is they have lost.

In its networking together of disjunct narrative times ranged across a cast of characters and in a host of different settings, Egan's Ricoeurian 'tale about time' thus matches form with content. As Sarah Churchwell has observed, *A Visit from the Goon Squad* is 'neither a novel nor a collection of short stories, but something in between: a series of chapters featuring interlocking characters at different points in their lives, whose individual voices combine to a create a symphonic work that uses its interconnected form to explore ideas about human interconnectedness' (Churchwell 2011). Whilst the novel proceeds non-chronologically – although, we should note, digital readers are afforded the opportunity to shuffle the chapters into any order of their preference, approaching the 'card shuffle' or 'model kit' novel-in-a-box experimentation of Marc Saporta's *Composition No. 1* (1961) or B. S. Johnson's *The Unfortunates* (1969) (Egan in Gallagher n. dat.) – its delinearised mode of storytelling is apposite to Egan's investigation of the workings of memory, the Proustian examination of 'lost time' and the unbidden reflexes of *mémoire involontaire*. The novel progresses via narrative loops and thematic eddies, gradually building an expanding network of characters through a lengthening chain of connection that has nodal points as well as indirect vertices. Through this recursive networked aesthetic, lost time gradually coalesces into a central novelistic concern as Egan's cast of characters explore the theme of loss. Jocelyn's mother, for instance, reflects upon the 'lost time' of her drug-addled twenties (*VGS* 90). Meanwhile, as Sasha tells Rob, 'there were kids who were just lost. You knew they were never going to get back to what they'd been, or have a normal life' (*VGS* 206). Later, Sasha's uncle Ted, an Art History lecture, experiences an intense aesthetic response to a painting of Orpheus and Eurydice, which 'mashed some delicate glassware in his chest' as he contemplates their 'unspeakable knowledge that everything is lost' (*VGS* 222).

In addition to 'lost time,' the reader is also shown a number of other temporal modes in the novel. The elasticity of subjective temporal experience, established in contradistinction to the relentless progress of regularised 'clock-time,' is conveyed at various points ('Stephanie hunched in the dirt for a long time, or what felt like a long time – maybe it was only a minute' [*VGS* 143], 'his week of solitude, a week that felt like both a month and a minute' [*VGS* 217]). Then there is the alternative temporality of an architectural, inanimate time posed in contradistinction to the brevity of human time: '[Ted] imagined he was an element of the palace itself, a sensate molding or step whose fate it was to witness the ebb and flow of generations, to feel the place relax its medieval bulk more deeply into the earth. Another year, another fifty' (*VGS* 239). In terms of narrative organisation, Egan's periodic arrest of story-time to allow the omniscient heterodiegetic narrator to comment on characters and events through the use of knowing asides effects a series of temporal interruptions apposite to the novel's non-linear form ('But we're getting off the subject' [*VGS* 85], 'He thinks, I'll remember this night for the rest of my life. And he's right' [*VGS* 66]); as well as the cyclical time of narrative loops (Jocelyn observes that 'We're back to the beginning' [*VGS* 95], 'Bennie was caught in a loop from twenty years ago' [*VGS* 22]), which are embedded within the text's narrative structure: the closing chapter from Alex's point of view is enfolded back within the first chapter which details Sasha's disastrous date with Alex. Moreover, the decrepit musician Boscoe's observation that 'Time's a goon, right? Isn't that the expression?' (*VGS* 134) offers a metafictional reflection upon Egan's own goonish experiments with narrative time. There is a character named Chronos (*VGS* 69), the obligatory references to quantum mechanics required of any time text (as Jules discusses 'entangled particles' in a footnote of his article [*VGS* 177]), and a curious incorporation of proleptic futurity within Charlene and Rolph's safari trip narrated in Chapter 4. In an interesting twist on Proustian *mémoire involontaire*, Egan presents us here with what we might call *l'avenir involontaire* (or involuntary futurity), as Charlene experiences the physical pang of a future self, looking back at the present with the foreknowledge of an omniscient narrator:

> and each time the experience of music pouring directly against her eardrums – hers alone – is a shock that makes her eyes well up; the privacy of it, the way it transforms her surroundings into a golden montage, as if she were looking back on this lark in Africa with Lou from some distant future.
>
> (VGS 68)

Charlene experiences this shock iteratively, 'each time' the music is played. Music is similarly important in Proust's *In Search of Lost Time*: the narrator falls in love with Odette in *Swann in Love* (Proust 2002) whilst listening to a violin sonata at Madame Verdurin's salon, and subsequently insists on hearing the same snatch of this unknown musical composition again and again in an attempt to recapture his initial feeling of elation.

Egan's networked novel can thus be considered within a larger, and growing, corpus of twenty-first-century texts that are centrally preoccupied with the workings of time. As we have seen, such networked novels offer a broad range of temporal registers that complicate notions of historical time, narratives of progress, the old modernist distinction between public and private time, as well as reworking postmodernist tropes of simultaneity, chaos, contingency and chance. These texts demand new strategies of reading sensitive to their complex engagements with time, which can modulate between a content-based analysis of the philosophical questions temporal experience raises, as well as consider the structural and formal possibilities that narrative time can actuate within the literary form of the novel.

Works cited

Agamben, G. (2009) 'What Is the Contemporary?' In *What Is an Apparatus? And Other Essays*, trans. David Kishik and Stefan Pedatella. Stanford, CA: University of California Press, 39–54.

Ahmed, S. (2006) *Queer Phenomenology: Orientations, Objects, Others*. Durham, NC: Duke University Press.

Altman, R. (Dir.) (1975) *Nashville*. Paramount Pictures.

Anderson, P. T. (Dir.) (1999) *Magnolia*. New Line Cinema.

Atkinson, K. (2013) *Life after Life*. London: Doubleday.

Atwood, M. (2005) *The Penelopiad*. New York: Alfred A. Knopf.

Barnard, R. (2009) 'Fictions of the Global.' *Novel: A Fiction on Forum* 42(2): 207–215.

Barrows, A. (2011) *The Cosmic Time of Empire: Modern Britain and World Literature*. Berkeley, CA, Los Angeles: University of California Press.

Bechdel, A. (2006) *Fun Home: A Family Tragicomic*. London: Jonathan Cape.

Bennett, A. (2012) *Afterlife and Narrative in Contemporary Fiction*. Basingstoke: Palgrave Macmillan.

Bergson, H. (1911) *Creative Evolution*, trans. Arthur Mitchell. Lanham, MD: University Press of America.

Berry, M. (2015) "Review: *Slade House* by David Mitchell." *San Francisco Chronicle*, 22 October (accessed 30 March 2018): www.sfchronicle.com/books/article/Slade-House-by-David-Mitchell-6584756.php

Breedlove, L. (2002) *Godspeed*. New York: St. Martin's Press.

Burnside, J. (2008) *Glister*. London: Jonathan Cape.

Cameron, A. (2008) *Modular Narratives in Contemporary Cinema*. Basingstoke: Palgrave Macmillan.

Carter, W. C. (2004) 'The Vast Structure of Recollection: From Life to Literature.' In Harold Bloom (ed.) *Marcel Proust*. Broomall, PA: Chelsea House Publishers, 165–184.

Churchwell, S. (2011) 'Review of *A Visit from the Goon Squad* by *Jennifer Egan*.' *The Observer*, 13 March (accessed 11 February 2015): www.theguardian.com/books/2011/mar/13/jennifer-egan-visit-goon-squad

Coupland, D. (2012) 'Convergences: Review of *Gods without Men* by Hari Kunzru.' *New York Times*, 8 March (accessed 15 August 2012): www.nytimes.com/2012/03/11/books/review/gods-without-men-by-hari-kunzru.html?pagewanted=all

Cunningham, M. (1998) *The Hours*. New York: Farrar, Strauss and Giroux.
—— (2005) *Specimen Days*. London: Harper Perennial.
Duncan, G. (2003) *I, Lucifer*. London: Scribner.
Ebert, R. (2007) 'Think beyond the Top Layer.' *RoberEbert.com*, 6 September (accessed 18 February 2012): www.rogerebert.com/answer-man/think-beyond-the-top-layer
Edelman, L. (2004) *No Future: Queer Theory and the Death Drive*. Durham, NC: Duke University Press.
Edwards, C. (2011) '"Strange Transactions": Utopia, Transmigration and Time in *Ghostwritten* and *Cloud Atlas*.' In Sarah Dillon (ed.) *David Mitchell: Critical Essays*. Canterbury: Gylphi, 177–200.
Egan, J. (2010) *A Visit from the Goon Squad*. London: Corsair.
Evaristo, B. (2009) *Lara: The Family is Like Water*. Eastburn: Bloodaxe Books.
Freeman, E. (2010) *Time Binds: Queer Temporalities, Queer Histories*. Durham, NC: Duke University Press.
Gallagher, P. (n. date) 'Interview: Jennifer Egan on *A Visit from the Goon Squad*.' *Scottish Book Trust*, n. date (accessed 12 February 2015): www.scottishbooktrust.com/booktalk/jennifer-egan-goon-squad-interview
Gomel, E. (2010) *Postmodern Science Fiction and Temporal Imagination*. London: Continuum.
Haggis, P. (Dir.) (2004) *Crash*. Lionsgate Films.
Halberstam, J. (2005) *In a Queer Time and Place: Transgender Bodies, Subcultural Lives*. New York: New York University Press.
Harkaway, N. (2012) *Angelmaker*. London: Random House.
Heise, U. K. (1997) *Chronoschisms: Time, Narrative, and Postmodernism*. Cambridge: Cambridge University Press.
Hodgkinson, T. (2012) 'Interview with Hari Kunzru.' *Granta*, 10 March (accessed 30 March 2018): https://granta.com/interview-hari-kunzru/
Hopkinson, N. (2003) *The Salt Roads*. New York: Warner Books.
Iñárritu, A. G. (Dir.) (2003) *21 Grams*. Focus Features.
Iñárritu, A. G. (Dir.) (2006) *Babel*. Paramount Vintage.
Irr, C. (2014) *Toward the Geopolitical Novel: U.S. Fiction in the Twenty-First Century*. New York: Columbia University Press.
Johnson, W. R. (1982) *The Idea of Lyric: Lyric Modes in Ancient and Modern Poetry*. Berkeley, CA: University of California Press.
Kern, S. (2003) *The Culture of Time and Space, 1880–1918: With a New Preface*. Cambridge, MA: Harvard University Press.
Kinder, M. (2002) 'Hot Spots, Avatars and Narrative Fields Forever: Buñuel's Legacy for New Digital Media and Interactive Database Narrative.' *Film Quarterly*: 2–15.
Kristeva, J. (1981) 'Women's Time.' Trans. Alice Jardine and Harry Blake. *Signs* 7(1): 13–35.
Kunzru, H. (2004) *Transmission*. London: Quality Paperbacks Direct.
—— (2011) *Gods without Men*. London: Penguin.
Linklater, A. (2011) '*Gods without Men*: Review.' *The Observer*, 31 July (accessed 3 July 2012): www.guardian.co.uk/books/2011/jul/31/gods-without-men-hari-kunzru
McGregor, J. (2010) *Even the Dogs*. London: Bloomsbury.
Mitchell, D. (1999) *Ghostwritten*. London: Sceptre.
—— (2001) *Number9Dream*. London: Sceptre.
—— (2004a) *Cloud Atlas*. London: Sceptre.
—— (2004b) 'Q&A: Book World Talks with David Mitchell.' *The Washington Post*, 22 August (accessed 18 February 2015): www.washingtonpost.com/wp-dyn/articles/A17231-2004Aug19.html
—— (2010) *The Thousand Autumns of Jacob de Zoet*. London: Sceptre.
—— (2014) *The Bone Clocks*. London: Sceptre.
Mousoutzanis, A. (2009) 'Uncanny Repetition: Trauma, and Displacement in Michael Cunningham's *Specimen Days*.' *Critical Survey* 21(2): 129–141.
Murakami, H. (2012) *IQ84: The Complete Trilogy*. London: Vintage.
Murphy, P. (2001) *Time is of the Essence: Temporality, Gender, and the New Woman*. New York: State University of New York Press.
Noé, G. (Dir.) (2002) *Irréversible*. Mars Distribution.
O'Donnell, P. (2015) *A Temporary Future: The Fiction of David Mitchell*. New York: Bloomsbury Academic.
Proust, M. (2002) *In Search of Lost Time, Vol. 1: The Way by Swann's*, trans. Lydia Davis. London: Penguin.
Randall, B. (2007) *Modernism, Daily Time and Everyday Life*. Cambridge: Cambridge University Press.
Reed, J. (2008) *The Grid*. London: Peter Owen.
Ricoeur, P. (1985) *Time and Narrative*, Vol. 2, trans. Kathleen McLaughlin and David Pellauer. Chicago: The University of Chicago Press.

Rose, J. (2005) 'Entryism: Review of *Specimen Days* by Michael Cunningham.' *London Review of Books* 27(18), 22 September (accessed 9 February 2015): www.lrb.co.uk/v27/n18/jacqueline-rose/entryism

Schleifer, R. (2000) *Modernism and Time: The Logic of Abundance in Literature, Science, and Culture 1880–1930.* Cambridge: Cambridge University Press.

Schoene, B. (2009) *The Cosmopolitan Novel.* Edinburgh: Edinburgh University Press.

Sebold, A. (2002) *The Lovely Bones.* London: Picador.

Smith, A. (2001) *Hotel World.* London: Penguin.

—— (2014) *How to Be Both.* London: Hamish Hamilton.

Stanivukovic, G. (2014) 'Queer Early Modern Temporalities and the Sexual Dystopia of Biography and Patronage in Jeremy Reed's *The Grid.*' In Ana María Sánchez-Arce (ed.) *Identity and Form in Contemporary Literature.* New York: Routledge, 227–245.

Tarantino, T. (Dir.) (1994). *Pulp Fiction.* Miramax.

Warner, M. (2001) *The Leto Bundle.* London: Vintage.

West-Pavlov, R. (2013) *Temporalities.* New York: Routledge.

Winterson, J. (2000) *The PowerBook.* London: Vintage.

2

GLOBALIZATION

Kristian Shaw

In an opening address to nongovernmental organisations before the United Nations Millennium Summit on 6th September 2000, former UN Secretary-General Kofi Annan declared: 'arguing against globalization is like arguing against the laws of gravity' (Crossette 2000). The subsequent three-day summit meeting brought together over a hundred of the world's leaders in order to discuss the economic, political and cultural consequences of globalization, which Annan asserted should be 'an engine that lifts people out of hardship and misery, not a force that holds them down' (Crossette 2000). The summit's intense focus on this process, topping the agenda for their first meeting in the new millennium, attests to the critical importance of globalization and its far-reaching impact on our contemporary moment.

We should begin by asking the most obvious question: what is globalization? After all, the term defies simple explanation and as a result is in danger of becoming a portmanteau for various cultural processes shaping the post-millennium. As Michael Hardt and Antonio Negri emphasise, globalization 'is not one thing, and the multiple processes that we recognize as globalization are not unified or univocal' (2000: xv). Globalization's potency derives both from its ubiquitous deployment as well as the insufficiency (and even unavailability) of existing terminology to accurately describe recent transformations in twenty-first century fiction and culture more widely. This chapter will unpack prevailing definitions of this term, outlining the socio-cultural and economic systems of integration associated with its usage. But more importantly, it will be suggested that such processes find traction and representation within literary studies, illustrating how the novel form provides pragmatic and meaningful responses attuned to the complex heterogeneity of twenty-first century life.

According to David Held et al. globalization refers 'to the widening, deepening and speeding up of global interconnection' engendering 'a transformation in the organization of human affairs' (1999: 14). The intensification in transnational forms of mobility and extensive technological change, as well as the accelerated movement of capital, services and products, contribute to the proposed transformation. For this reason, however, globalization is often employed as a synonym for universalism, implying a level of homogenization that neglects the inherent heterogeneity of world culture. As Mike Featherstone notes, perceiving the world as 'a single place' neglects the asymmetrical power relations governing contemporary life and creates 'a sense of false concreteness and unity' (1996: 70). Globalization is thus best understood as a socio-cultural and economic phenomenon which deepens existing forms of exclusion and inequalities of access as much as it activates new patterns of connectivity. The reconfiguration of cultural attachments and economic relations creates what Ulrich Beck heralds as 'a new historical reality [. . .] in which people view themselves simultaneously as part of a threatened world and as part of their local situations and histories', resulting in connectivity between cultures being tempered by a raised awareness of global risks (2006: 48). It is therefore important to consider how individuals and communities respond to the emergent cosmopolitical problems that global interconnectedness brings.

Processes of globalization are evident in twenty-first century fiction's engagement with digital communicative technology and labour markets, commercialization and commodity fetishism, terrorism and the spread of Western media, transnational mobilities and migration, and the environmentally detrimental practices of multinational corporations and global tourism. Recent works of literature have also attempted to register individual experiences of globalization, illustrating a sense of distanciation felt by many communities due to a compression of cultural space. The selected British, American and Indian fictions examined in this chapter share a willingness to forge a future-oriented dialogue between local experiences and global flows, and imagine new modes of belonging sensitive to the cross-cultural interdependencies of world society. A central characteristic of globalization studies has been this focus on the diminishing relevance or sovereignty of nation-states, as these new configurations of connectivity override national borders and concerns. The final section of this chapter will therefore look towards a shift in this dynamic, pointing to recent political developments in Western Europe and North America that necessitate a re-evaluation of globalization as a seemingly unstoppable force and acknowledge an incipient resistance to its cultural effects. The chapter will conclude by considering how literature responds to this shift, demonstrating the novel's capacity to engage with emergent political realities.

Arjun Appadurai asserts that globalization has induced a 'complex, overlapping, disjunctive order that cannot any longer be understood in terms of existing center-periphery models' (1996: 32). Discourses of globalization have therefore led to a reshaping of late-twentieth century literary paradigms such as postmodernism and postcolonialism, resulting in a vast array of literary terms and theories that extend these paradigms in new and innovative directions. As Michel Bérubé writes, 'postmodernism aligns with postcolonialism not because they're both post-something [. . .] but because they are epiphenomena of globalization itself' (2002: 7). With this in mind, globalization should not be perceived as simply a continuation of colonial ideologies, but rather responsible for the intrinsic restructuring of existing hierarchies and systems, engendering an unprecedented change in planetary interconnectedness

In discussions of contemporary literature, globalization is often employed as periodizing term, rather than positioned as a geopolitical project, involving a range of socio-economic transformations that reshaped cultural relations from the late 1980s onwards. James Annesley's *Fictions of Globalization* (2006), for example, details how the contemporary American novel engages with the malign and detrimental effects of consumer culture as a by-product of widespread neoliberalism, evident in the work of Jonathan Franzen, Bret Easton Ellis and Don DeLillo. This concentration on American fiction is understandable as globalization is often considered 'an extension of the economic and political domination of the United States, which thrusts its hegemonic cultural productions to all parts of the world and effectively erases local forms of expression' (Childs and Green 2013: 17). Indeed, the term itself functions as a synonym for Westernization in the social sciences and retains a hegemonic rhetoric. However, there is no denying that the discipline of English Literature – through the spread of Western influence – undoubtedly contributes to this cultural phenomenon. English is a global language and mirrors globalization via its imposition of a unitary code which is then adapted to meet the demands of specific cultures.

Annesley identifies that contemporary literature should 'refine ways of knowing globalization's discourses' and respond to developing processes of consumer capitalism (2006: 6). Dave Eggers' *A Hologram for the King* (2013) answers this charge, providing a snapshot of the (post-financial crisis) global economy by moving beyond outdated centre-periphery paradigms in order to critique the decline of American manufacturing in the post-millennium. The novel follows Alan Clay, a middle-aged, divorced salesman from Boston, as he attempts to win a lucrative IT contract for his employer Reliant. Unfit to compete in the accelerated global marketplace, and unable to pay his daughter's tuition fees, Clay wastes several weeks of his life waiting for the King of Saudi Arabia to materialise so he can present his marketing pitch. Clay's failure to win the contract or forge a meaningful relationship with his potential clients indicates that an intensification in cultural interdependencies fails to engender a corresponding development in mutual relationality or cosmopolitan openness. Rather than capturing the planetary interconnectedness of the globalized era, the novel merely expresses a narrow nostalgia for the heyday of American hegemony before the widespread outsourcing of labour. Clay's nostalgic vision of his own past, when he was more than simply 'tangential to the making of things' and intimately involved in the production process of Schwinn bicycles, is an idealised fiction that both neglects the role immigrants played in this construction of this 'American' product and his own complicity with the practice of outsourcing: 'Alan knew, and the retailer knew [. . .] that that bike had been made by hand a few hundred miles north, by a dizzying array of workers, most of them immigrants – Germans, Italians, Swedes, Irish, plenty of Japanese and of course a slew of Poles' (2013: 12–13, 49–50). Although fictions of globalization predominantly focus on white, middle-class males from privileged nation-states, as evident in *A Hologram for the King*, this chapter will also examine novels which provide non-Western perspectives and experiences of heightened connectivity from marginalized positions, providing a more negative stance to cultural engagement and globalized life than found in Annesley's analysis of American fiction. In so doing, it will be argued that the globalized world is not 'a seamless whole without boundaries. Rather, it is a space of structured circulations, of mobility and immobility. It is a space of dense interconnections and black holes' (Inda and Rosaldo 2008: 35).

As the introduction proposed, the novel requires a unique form of narrative representation in order to capture the transformational effects of globalization on contemporary society. David Mitchell's debut novel *Ghostwritten: A Novel in Nine Parts* (1999), published at the turn of the millennium, anticipates several concerns that come to define the twenty-first century novel from rampant consumerism and Western neoliberalism, to ecological degradation and religious fundamentalism, to global tourism and the maintenance of racial imperialism. Mitchell's later novel, *Cloud Atlas* (2004), retains this concentration on cultural homogenization, but positions globalization as a continuation of historical process, merely adapting many nocuous practices at work under imperial rule (thus weakening claims that globalization should be perceived merely as a periodizing term only applicable to post-millennial life). By incorporating anxieties regarding globalizing processes into the architectural fabric of his fiction, Mitchell indicates how convergence culture results in an unprecedented level of planetary relatedness. In Mitchell's own words, 'the world is a web' where 'links become more apparent [. . .] A button can be pushed in Hong Kong and a factory gets closed in Sydney' (Mitchell 2011). Rita Barnard identifies Mitchell's text as a key early example of emergent 'global fictions', which involve a focus on 'human interconnection, causality, temporality, social space' and thus 'provide the conceptual preconditions for a cosmopolitan society' (2009: 208). Crucially, however, Mitchell avoids a depiction of millennial society as a unified scene of harmonious cosmopolitanization, concentrating on the conflict and discord globalization engenders as impersonal forces begin to dismantle cultural identities and infringe upon territorial belonging.

Ghostwritten contains nine interconnected narratives and a brief coda, beginning in Okinawa before traversing various locations in a sweeping geographical movement from East to West, concluding in Ireland and New York. Mitchell, who spent many years residing in Japan and later Ireland, details how globalized society is characterised by 'overlapping communities of fate', which Held argues bind individuals together in a complex constellation of cultural interdependence: 'developments at the local level [. . .] can acquire almost instantaneous global consequences' creating 'an extraordinary potential space for human development as well as for disruption and destruction by individuals, groups or states' (2010: 295; 296). The interlinked narratives betray an evident critique of Westernization and its role in eroding cultural diversity, indicating how globalization itself emerges 'from the centers of the West, pushing other alternatives out of existence' (Hannerz 1996: 24). The novel's opening chapter, Okinawa, inspired by the terrorist attacks of the Aum Shinrikyo cult in 1995, follows the actions of Quasar, a young cult member charged with the responsibility of detonating Sarin nerve gas on the Tokyo subway. Quasar directs his anger and resentment at his fellow countrymen, who have permitted Western homogenization to irreversibly transform the architectural face of his beloved city: '[t]he same shops are anywhere else . . . Burger King, Benetton, Nike . . . High streets are becoming the same all over the world' (Mitchell 1999: 12).

The novel's title is reflective of this cultural infringement as disempowered actors become progressively disembedded in specific localities that are irrevocably reshaped by anonymous forces beyond their purview: '[w]e all think we're in control of our own lives, but really they're pre-ghostwritten by forces around us' (1999: 296). The fourth chapter, Holy Mountain, charts the solitary life of a nameless tea shack owner on Mount Emei in China. The mountain – an isolated site existing on the periphery of globalized culture – suffers progressive acts of deteritorialization as it becomes a space of cultural contestation for late feudalism, Eastern communism, economic reform under Deng Xiaopong, and finally global tourism: 'somebody called Russia, somebody else called Europe [. . .] What world had these men come from?' (1999: 115). The purposely nameless old woman, functioning as an immobile and impotent actor subject to the accelerating force of cultural mobilities, epitomizes John Tomlinson's assertion that 'the paradigmatic experience of global modernity for most people [. . .] is that of staying in one place but experiencing the "displacement" that global modernity brings to them' (1999: 9). And yet, Mitchell avoids signalling the advent of the borderless world or the end of the nation-state as a political system, instead fashioning 'glocal' spatialities in which global and local forces operate in dynamic interplay, complicating and reconfiguring local landscapes and cultural identities.

As Peter Boxall states, Mitchell's fiction 'exhibit[s] at once a tendency [. . .] towards an expanded form in which we might see the world whole, and an opposite tendency towards fragmentation, towards a kind of broken failure of collective sight' (2013: 191). The novel's coda, 'Underground', provides a cyclical return to the opening chapter, concluding the terrorist activities of disenfranchised Quasar within a Tokyo subway carriage, yet provides a more damning indictment of the detrimental effects of globalization in exploiting indigenous customs and landscapes for the sake of corporate profit. The coda reduces the characters of the previous eight chapters to mere global advertising lining the carriage, raising the separate narratives to the same ontological level. The carriage – a terrifying commodified vision of world society – encapsulates the McDonaldization of Tokyo, as commodity fetishism and rampant consumerism inexorably eviscerate and engulf the cultural heterogeneity constructed over the previous chapters, altering the structural formal organization of the novel itself. The coda's final image of the subway carriage 'accelerating into the darkness' represents the intensifying immediacy and compression of globalized life, with transnational citizens enclosed in a risk society from which there is no immediate escape (Mitchell 1999: 436).

An examination of the intensification of transnational mobilities – of which immigration is an integral element – is especially relevant to any discussion of globalized fiction as these processes contribute to Edward Said's 'revision [. . .] of the idea that literature exists in a national framework' (2001: 64). Contemporary works including *Girl in Translation* (2010) by Jean Kwok, *The Lowland* (2013) by Jhumpa Lahiri, *We Need New Names* (2013) by NoViolet Bulawayo, *Americanah* (2013) by Chimamanda Ngozi Adichie, and *Behold the Dreamers* (2016) by Imbolo Mbue, traverse and exceed national space in their portrayals of intense cross-cultural engagement. In Britain, the late-twentieth century had already witnessed a generation of authors attempting, as Ian Baucom so provocatively puts it, 'to stew England in the migrant's gastric juices, and to return England to itself as markedly, perhaps aromatically, different' (1999: 208). The recent transformation of post-millennial British society has brought further reconfiguration of the literary landscape, as authors from diverse cultural backgrounds revitalize the novel form.

Patrick Parrinder went so far as to declare that 'the novel of immigration [is] now recognised as the most vital form of English fiction at the beginning of the twenty-first century' (2006: 380). Monica Ali's *Brick Lane* (2003), Xiaolu Guo's *A Concise Chinese-English Dictionary for Lovers* (2008), and Zia Rahman's *In the Light of What We Know* (2014) are key examples of novels which chronicle the lives of migrants striving for a sense of belonging in British society, exploring the historical legacies of diaspora and trauma in post-millennial life. This cosmopolitanization of British literature was reflected in the 2013 Granta list – celebrating the twenty most promising authors under the age of 40. Whereas late-twentieth century Granta lists were dominated by white, male postmodernists such as Will Self or Julian Barnes, the 2013 list included authors of Pakistani, Chinese, Ghanaian and Indian heritage, revealing a renewed effort by publishers to introduce more culturally diverse voices to the literary marketplace.

Such pervasive ethnic heterogeneity as a corollary of globalization becomes a dominant feature in the localized landscapes of black British and British Asian fiction. The multicultural optimism of Zadie Smith's *White Teeth* (2000), published at the turn of the millennium, looks beyond the 'past tense' of British imperial history to an almost utopian 'future perfect' where 'roots won't matter anymore' (2000: 527). Smith's debut novel, winner of countless awards including the James Tait Black Memorial Prize for fiction in 2000, became the quintessential model for later 'London fictions' actively interrogating multicultural relations within the capital. Smith herself was lauded as the felicitous new voice of the British literary scene. While *White Teeth*'s Magid, an Asian youth, becomes a 'pukka Englishman' despite his father's attempts to force Bangladeshi culture upon him, Gautam Malkani's *Londonstani* (2006) reverses this pattern, disrupting reader's expectations by revealing the seemingly Hindu protagonist to be a white youth whose speech is a distinct fusion of cockney slang, Hindi argot and AAVE gleaned from hip-hop music videos (2000: 407). Such fictions evince a heightened global consciousness in British fiction, sensitive to the syncretic tensions and cultural incongruities reshaping the nation.

Concerns surrounding globalization's destabilizing effects also find fertile ground in contemporary Indian fictions, in which local settings are often employed as microcosmic analogies for transformations affecting the wider world. Kiran Desai's *The Inheritance of Loss*, winner of the 2006 Man Booker Prize, examines the sense of dislocation and alienation experienced by economic migrants, linking cultural globalization to a wider history of colonization and imperialism, thus revealing how individuals inherit a sense of personal loss from the previous generation. Set in Kalimpong, an east Indian town in the Himalayan foothills, the novel charts the fates of Sai, 'a westernized Indian brought up by English nuns, an estranged Indian living in India', and Biju, the son of a cook who secures a tourist visa to search for employment in New York (2006: 210). The isolated locale of Kalimpong becomes a complex glocal site of cultural contestation, torn apart by the seductive influence of cultural Westernization and a neo-nationalist Gorkhaland movement.

Sai's exposure to a Westernized education teaches her that 'cake was better than laddoos, fork spoon knife better than hands [. . .] English was better than Hindi', epitomising globalization's penetration of Kalimpong, creating tension and anxiety as communities are reshaped by their response to cultural interdependence (2006: 30). Sai's homestead – the decaying mansion Cho Oyu – was built by a Scotsman, thus mirroring the fractured, hybrid cultural identities of its inhabitants, caught between the urge to embrace Western influence and the desire to maintain deep-rooted traditions specific to east Indian life. Over the course of the novel her family become passive victims in the socio-political cosmopolitanization of their hometown, demonstrating how globalization can lead to the socio-cultural and psychological dislocation of individuals who do not even leave their locality.

Biju's corresponding narrative strand details his sense of stasis and immobility as he works a series of menial restaurants jobs in basements and cellars across New York. The design of his employer's restaurant, Le Colonial, overtly gestures towards the maintenance of hierarchical racial structures within the Western World, delivering: 'the authentic colonial experience. On top, rich colonial, and down below, poor native. Colombian, Tunisian, Ecuadorian, Gambian' (2006: 21). Dismissed as 'a brown curry-smelling reptile' by white American citizens, Biju fails to assimilate into his new environment, remaining in a liminal state before ultimately returning to Kalimpong in defeat and humiliation: a disposable component in the global economic system. In channelling an anti-globalist critique aimed at the creeping insidiousness of Westernization and the lingering legacy of imperial rule, Desai avoids pointing towards new configurations of cultural connectivity or cosmopolitan forms of belonging, instead indicating the staggering adversity migrants face in breaking away from their cultural inheritance.

Aravind Adiga's debut novel *The White Tiger* (2008), winner of the Man Booker Prize two years later, echoes Desai's focus on class and caste by providing a related critique of neoliberal globalization and the injurious effects of technological change on contemporary India. Balram Halwai, an unprivileged village boy, provides a retrospective assessment of his personal rise from the son of a rickshaw puller to a successful entrepreneur with his own taxi firm in Bangalore. Balram reports his account in a series of letters addressed to Mr Jiabao, the Chinese premier. Rather than 'writing back' to the dominant West, a narrative technique associated with late-twentieth century postcolonial literature, Balram directs his attention eastwards to a burgeoning Chinese superpower, echoing Adiga's own claim that in an age of globalization China 'is likely to inherit the world from the west' (Jeffries 2008).

The narrative reveals the stark ethnic and cultural divisions in the country between those in the 'Darkness', containing the majority of the Indian underclass, and the lucky minority in the 'Light', populated by those with the affluence to enjoy transnational forms of mobility. Access to capital, rather than the existing caste system, becomes the decisive factor in determining the social hierarchy as citizens abandon familial or communal ties in favour of individual financial gain. The shopping mall in the novel – the symbol of capitalist wealth and consumerism – excludes those without footwear and the very word itself becomes a signifier of social status in the appropriation of the English language: 'I kept saying "maal", and they kept asking me to repeat it, and then giggled hysterically each time I did so' (2008: 147). Before his own personal progression, Balram accuses his employer, Mr Ashok, of such indifference to his fellow countryman: 'Here you are, sitting in glass buildings and talking on the phone night after night to Americans who are thousands of miles away, but you don't even have the faintest idea what's happening to the man who's driving your car!' (2008: 257).

By equating success with the appropriation and adoption of a selfish individualistic outlook, Balram deteriorates into a megalomaniacal entrepreneur worshipping at the altar of neoliberalism, perceiving himself to be a 'white tiger' emblematic of the ambitious ascendancy of East Asian culture. His systematic acts of corruption, theft, bribery of government officials, and the eventual murder of his employer, represent a broader deterioration of ethical values in Bangalore – the world's fastest growing city. Although globalization can be responsible for eliminating cultural heterogeneity, Adiga's novel demonstrates how it also operates as a polarizing force, exacerbating rather than ameliorating systems of segregation and exclusion, and compelling individuals to abandon a sense of cosmopolitan empathy for their fellow citizens: 'These days there are just two castes: Men with Big Bellies, and Men with Small Bellies. And only two destinies: eat – or get eaten up' (2008: 64).

Hari Kunzru's *Transmission* (2004) continues this concentration on Indian economic migrants in an age of globalization. Kunzru, born to a Kashmiri father and an English mother, acknowledged in a personal interview that his fiction echoes Mitchell's *Ghostwritten* in articulating the 'networked nature of contemporary life', but accentuated that 'what I do with interconnectedness is not quite what David Mitchell does with it', being 'messier and less resolved' than his counterpart in highlighting the cultural discrepancies that globalization produces (Kunzru 2014). While both works offer chilling millennial visions of the recent intensification in socio-cultural interdependence, *Transmission* imparts a more direct critique of digital connectivity and exposes the exploitative underbelly of capitalist discourses. This rapid acceleration of digital communicative technologies is a distinguishing feature of contemporary globalization. Novels such as *JPod* (2006) by Douglas Coupland, *Super Sad True Love Story* (2010) by Gary Shteyngart, *The Circle* (2013) by Dave Eggers, *Bleeding Edge* (2013) by Thomas Pynchon, and *The Book of Numbers* (2015) by Joshua Cohen respond to the immediacy with which digital technology now connects disparate peoples, creating new virtual communities that overcome territorial divides and destabilize notions of proximity and distance. *Transmission*, however, goes further than these works in positioning digital connectivity to be an emergent form of cultural imperialism, responsible for enhancing rather than alleviating socio-economic inequalities.

The novel follows the actions of Arjun Mehta, an Indian computer engineer, as he attempts to gain employment in the Western digital sector. Although Arjun subsequently relocates to the United States to work for a company named Databodies, he soon experiences a sense of stasis and stagnation in this world of flows, revealing the marginalization of migrants by the dominant power-structures of transnational corporations. The corporation's name betrays their odious work practice of employing migrants on 'slave visas', paying 'a fraction of what it would cost [. . .] to hire an American engineer', and essentially stripping them of their cultural idiosyncrasies until they are little more than 'databodies' serving and satisfying the wired world (2004: 65). Rather than ameliorating forms of discrimination, empowering localities and individuals within an interconnected web, the novel exposes Kunzru's own incredulity that a networked society can function as a cultural leveller. Instead, as evident in *The Inheritance of Loss*, migrants are simply uprooted from their localities and suffer a form of dislocation as they struggle to navigate the sinuous flows of globalization. By perpetuating this exploitation of disposable labour, Databodies remains blind to the suffering of its migrant workers, resulting in further homogenization of cultural values and transferring racial asymmetry into the digital domain.

Transmission also tackles the related issues of sovereignty and national citizenship, anticipating the racial discourses that were to emerge in Western, anti-globalist, populist movements a decade later. Kunzru's satirical depiction of the European Union, reimagined as a 'Pan European Border Authority' (PEBA), calls into question existing immigration policies and the preservation of racial hierarchies (2004: 130). In attempting to develop a common border policy based on biometric data for the purposes of securitization, PEBA merely improves relations between Western member states while reinforcing Europe's perimeters from perceived 'Eastern' cultural contagion, forging spurious connections between immigration and acts of terrorism. The organization seeks the advice of Guy Swift, an English CEO of a global advertising firm, to rebrand Europe as an elite cultural space, harmonising 'the immigration and customs regimes of all the member states' (2004: 130). While Guy enjoys the 'sublime mobility of those who travel without ever touching the ground', Arjun's contrapuntal narrative reveals 'what lies below, the other mobility, the forced motion' experienced by digital migrants (2004: 47). Guy's design for a Fortress Europe with a gated community and an imperial outlook – an elitist space that operates on systems of inclusion and exclusion – exposes how non-white immigrants still exist on the periphery of globalized life and how their very presence provokes a surge in belligerent nationalism.

The concluding stages of the narrative provide a form of poetic justice. In a desperate attempt to remain in the United States and avoid forthcoming redundancies, the novel's dislocated protagonist, Arjun, unwittingly unleashes a digital virus that destabilizes global operating systems: 'the revenge of the uncontrollable world' (2004: 159). The digital virus disrupts global information systems and PEBA's own centralised databases – deleting immigration records – and results in Guy being mistaken for an asylum seeker. The rapid dissemination of the virus, a hyperbolic manifestation of 'what is lurking outside our perimeter', operates as a highly mobile and mutable form of digital terrorism across fixed territorial boundaries (2004: 271). Forced to suffer the indignity of deportation, the narrative places Guy in the role of marginalized 'other'. He is forced to experience the physical corporeality of nation-state borders in a (supposedly) borderless world: the very perimeter he aimed to manipulate and police to enforce forms of racial exclusion.

Although the virus – a destructive force of radical multiplicity condemned as 'an informational disaster, a holocaust of bits' – is ultimately a failed and desperate attempt by Arjun to alter the unequal world and reposition himself within the Western narrative, its transmission certainly harbours subversive potential (2004: 272). The articulation of new forms of alterity within its innumerable strains is representative of the multitude exploited by corporate control, conveying how migrants may prevent digital communicative technology remaining an insidious tool of privileged elites, and begin to reroute Western systems of control to their own ends. By offering an outsider perspective of globalization, Kunzru provides a potent critique of nation-states in exploiting fears surrounding immigration and the failure of Western nations to acknowledge the ways by which non-elite migrant workers are integral to the globalized system. These contemporary novels suggest that a revival of territorial borders is not a form of progress or reclamation of national sovereignty, but rather a direct challenge to the emergent risks of the twenty-first century life and a retreat from globalized culture.

As many social scientists and economists argue, the fall of the Berlin Wall marked the advent of contemporary globalization, intensifying the free movement of people, products, services and capital across territorial borders, resulting in new forms of socio-cultural connectivity and the subsequent weakening of the nation-state system. If we are to accept this historical moment as a cultural and economic marker, then Britain's recent rejection of the European Union and the surge in populist movements across North America and Western Europe undoubtedly signal an emergent backlash against the processes of globalization, the notion of open borders, and the act of migration. Peter Boxall points towards Dave Eggers' *What is the What* (2006) and Chimamanda Ngozi Adichie's *Half of a Yellow Sun* (2006) as diverse examples of a contemporary impetus to acknowledge 'a shared understanding both of the persistence of national categories in the global imagination, and of the difficult necessity of thinking beyond them, of imagining communal modes of being that are not made available by the current global networks for the distribution of wealth and cultural power' (2013: 178). However, whereas Boxall argues that the more general condition of contemporary globalization might allow 'new postnational identities to emerge', the current spread of nationalist political ideology in Western nation-states suggests a staunch resistance to the erasure of national paradigms and local forms of cultural identification (2013: 179).

Ashcroft polling during the EU referendum campaign found that 78% of Remain voters considered globalization to be a good thing, compared with only 49% of Leave voters, affirming Craig Calhoun's assertion that while globalization may have destabilized forms of national belonging, it 'has not put an end to nationalism [. . .] nor the role of nationalist categories in organizing ordinary people's sense of belonging in the world' (2007: 171). Although Theresa May, unveiling her blueprints for a 'Global Britain', asserted that Britain's act of political isolationism presents the opportunity for greater economic interdependence without suffering further foreign influence, her political rhetoric betrayed an intrinsic opposition to discourses of globalization and cosmopolitan belonging: 'If you believe you're a citizen of the world, you're a citizen of nowhere' (May 2016). In order to provide an updated analysis of fictions of globalization, we must examine to what extent literature responds, and becomes a vehicle of resistance, to this purposeful retreat from a world community *sans frontières*.

At the heart of the EU referendum debate was the question of national borders. Are permeable borders an inevitable necessity in an age of globalization, or does a nation have a responsibility to strengthen its borders in order to defend citizens from the transnational risks of undocumented immigration and Jihadi terrorism? The Syrian refugee crisis, fictionalized in Mohsin Hamid's *Exit West* (2017), was partly responsible for the xenophobic responses to immigration in the media, with Angela Merkel recognizing that the crisis constituted 'our rendezvous with globalization' (Merkel 2016). *Exit West* follows the movements of a young Muslim couple as they flee an unnamed Middle Eastern country on the brink of civil war, engaging with the broader ethno-political issues that influenced the referendum campaign. Hamid − a Pakistan author whose earlier works include *The Reluctant Fundamentalist* (2007), a timely novel that responds to Western anxieties surrounding Islamic fundamentalism in the wake of 9/11 − positions contemporary asylum to be yet another inevitable consequence of globalization's capacity for deterritorialization. However, the sudden appearance of magical black doors in the novel, allowing free access across territorial borders, allows *Exit West* to retain a hopeful sentiment that new forms of cosmopolitan connectivity in the twenty-first century will overcome the current securitization and surveillance measures of Western nation-states: 'they had grasped that the doors could not be closed, and new doors would continue to open' (2017: 164).

Anthony Cartwright's *The Cut* (2016) provides an internalized response to the Brexit debate, dramatizing events within Britain before and after the fateful result, building on the class-based concerns that characterised his earlier works, *Heartland* (2009) and *Iron Towns* (2016). The novel's title, alluding to the abandoned canals of a disfigured, post-industrial Black Country landscape (open scars of a forgotten community), encapsulates the fractious social divide at the core of the nation. The novel's formal organization mimics this fissure as dual narrative strands represent opposing factions of the British public. Grace Trevithick, a film maker from London completing a documentary on the EU referendum, begins a tense relationship with Cairo Jukes, an ex-boxer now supporting himself as a labourer on zero-hour contracts. Grace initially dismisses Cairo's anxieties regarding the decline of the industrial sector in Dudley, perceiving his self-destructive nostalgia to be little more than narrow-minded bigotry, failing to note how nationalist rhetoric emerges as a psychological defiance to immigration and the destabilizing effects of the global economy.

As the analysis of contemporary Indian fictions suggested earlier, there will always be those who benefit less from globalizing processes. Cairo's decision to contribute to Grace's documentary, presenting an opportunity 'to say something, about the sense of his world being made invisible, mute', symbolises how the Brexit vote became a desperate means of voicing the impotent rage felt by white working-class voters: 'retribution on some grand, futile scale' (2017: 30; 24). By acknowledging the geographic inequality and economic disparity of individuals and communities left behind by globalization in the 'edgelands' of the North and the Midlands – 'here were the ruins, and here were the ghost people among them, lost tribes' – *The Cut* suggests that the EU referendum merely revealed a wider discontent with globalized culture that had been bubbling under the surface of British society for decades (2016: 100). Crucially, the exploration of local and national concerns in the novel avoids satirising cultural prejudices or chastising working-class communities resistant to globalizing forces, instead proposing the need for a more nuanced dialogue that transcends the liberal echo chamber and heals the inherent divisions of our fractured nation.

This culture clash between an outward-facing globalism and an inward-looking parochialism also defined the 2016 US Presidential election. Running on a platform of aggressive nationalist ideology and xenophobic rage, the divisive figure of Donald Trump inspired the emergence of satirical works such as Howard Jacobson's *Pussy* (2017). Globalization can serve as a positive force in the spread of cosmopolitan ideals, yet it remains to be seen how these emergent 'post-truth' novels respond to the populist desire to retreat from more integrated systems of democratic governance and the development of institutional community-building. Sunjeev Sahota, author of *The Year of the Runaways* (2015), shortlisted for the 2015 Man Booker Prize and winner of the European Union Prize for Literature in 2017, predicts that Britain's less splendid isolation will be a catalyst for the proliferation of literary texts that gesture towards the novel's unique capacity for empathy, cultural relationality and imaginative world-creation: 'I think writers will continue to write globally and won't be hemmed in by these boundaries that politicians try to impose on our minds. I think writers will write truth to power' (Sahota 2017). The first two instalments of Ali Smith's planned seasonal quartet, *Autumn* (2016) and *Winter* (2017), evince such a literary retaliation to these divisive cosmopolitical events. Developing a form of narrative hospitality sensitive to the tensions of globalized life, Smith forges an empathetic response to cultural otherness in an age of renewed nationalistic fervour: 'always try to welcome people into the home of your story' (2016: 119).

The novel form, then, plays an integral role in responding to the globalized contemporaneity of twenty-first century life. As Martha Nussbaum emphasises: '[n]arratives, especially novels [. . .] speak to the reader as a human being, not simply as a member of some local culture; and works of literature frequently cross cultural boundaries far more easily than works of religion and philosophy' (1990: 391). Fiction possesses the power to make narrative concerns universal, compelling individuals to identify with different cultures and recognize shared concerns. The selected fictions in this chapter demonstrate how globalizing discourses impact upon localized communities and landscapes, linking disparate individuals in a networked society of mutual dependence, and expressing an increased awareness of planetary co-presence. Although homogenization and deterritorialization emerge as key characteristics of globalization (weakening calls for more productive forms of interconnectedness), a subsequent engagement with, or purposeful resistance to, these practices will undoubtedly define future societal developments. If, as Held theorizes, globalization naturally engenders 'communities of fate', then the value of the novel lies in its ability to reveal radical inequalities of access, actively interrogate transformational changes profoundly reshaping our contemporary moment, and imagine new approaches for sharing a convergent, but not unified, world (2010: 295).

Works cited

Adiga, A. (2008). *The White Tiger*. London: Atlantic Books.
Annesley, J. (2006). *Fictions of Globalization: Consumption, the Market and the Contemporary American Novel*. London: Continuum.

Appadurai, A. (1996). *Modernity at Large: Cultural Dimensions of Globalization.* Minneapolis, MN: University of Minnesota Press.

Barnard, R. (2009). Fictions of the Global. *Novel: A Forum on Fiction*, 42(2), 207–215.

Baucom, I. (1999). *Out of Place: Englishness, Empire, and the Locations of Identity.* Princeton, NJ: Princeton University Press.

Beck, U. (2006). *Cosmopolitan Vision.* Trans. C. Cronin. Cambridge: Polity.

Bérubé, M. (2002). Introduction: Worldly English. *Modern Fiction Studies*, 48(1), 1–17.

Boxall, P. (2013). *Twenty-First-Century Fiction: A Critical Introduction.* New York: Cambridge University Press.

Calhoun, C. (2007). *Nations Matter: Culture, History and the Cosmopolitan Dream.* London: Routledge.

Cartwright, A. (2016). *The Cut.* London: Peirene Press.

Childs, P. and Green, J. (2013). *Aesthetics and Ethics in Twenty-First Century British Novels: Zadie Smith, Nadeem Aslam, Hari Kunzru and David Mitchell.* London: Bloomsbury.

Crossette, B. (2000). Globalization Tops 3-Day UN Agenda for World Leaders. *New York Times.* [Online]. 3 September. [Accessed 29 December 2017]. Available from: www.nytimes.com/2000/09/03/world/globalization-tops-3-day-un-agenda-for-world-leaders.html

Desai, K. (2006). *The Inheritance of Loss.* London: Penguin.

Eggers, D. (2013). *A Hologram for the King.* London: Penguin.

Featherstone, M. (1996). Localism, Globalism, and Cultural Identity. In: R. Wilson and W. Dissanayake, eds. *Global/Local: Cultural Production and the Transnational Imaginary.* Durham, NC: Duke University Press, 46–77.

Hamid, M. (2017). *Exit West.* London: Hamish Hamilton.

Hannerz, U. (1996). *Transnational Connections: Culture, People, Places.* London and New York: Routledge.

Hardt, M. and Negri, A. (2000). *Empire.* Cambridge, MA: Harvard University Press.

Held, D. (2010). Reframing Global Governance: Apocalypse Soon or Reform! In: G. W. Brown and D. Held, eds. *The Cosmopolitanism Reader.* Cambridge: Polity, 293–311.

Held, D. et al. (1999). *Global Transformations: Politics, Economics and Culture.* Cambridge: Polity.

Inda, J. X. and Rosaldo, R. (2008). Tracking Global Flows. In: J. X. Inda and R. Rosaldo, eds. *The Anthropology of Globalization: A Reader.* 2nd ed. Oxford: Blackwell, 3–46.

Jeffries, S. (2008). Roars of Anger. *The Guardian.* [Online]. 16 October. [Accessed 3 January 2018]. Available from: www.theguardian.com/books/2008/oct/16/booker-prize

Kunzru, H. (2004). *Transmission.* London: Penguin.

—— (2014). Transmission: A Conversation with Hari Kunzru. Interview with K. Shaw, 29 June.

May, T. (2016). Keynote Address. Conservative Party Conference, The ICC Birmingham. 5 October.

Merkel, A. (2016). Merkel: Germany Should Play Bigger Role on World Stage. *DW.* [Online]. 2 March. [Accessed 4 January 2018]. Available from: www.dw.com/en/merkel-germany-should-play-bigger-role-on-world-stage/a-19088542

Mitchell, D. (1999). *Ghostwritten: A Novel in Nine Parts.* London: Sceptre.

—— (2004). *Cloud Atlas.* London: Sceptre.

—— (2011). The Thousand Styles of David Mitchell. Interview with G. Williamson for Sydney Writers' Festival, 20 May.

Nussbaum, M. C. (1990). *Love's Knowledge: Essays on Philosophy and Literature.* Oxford: Oxford University Press.

Parrinder, P. (2006). *Nation and Novel: The English Novel from Its Origins to the Present Day.* Oxford: Oxford University Press.

Sahota, S. (2017). Living by the Pen: In Conversation with Sunjeev Sahota. Interview with K. Shaw, 1 June.

Said, E. (2001). Globalizing Literary Study. *PMLA* 116(1), 64–68.

Smith, A. (2016). *Autumn.* London: Hamish Hamilton.

Smith, Z. (2000). *White Teeth.* London: Hamish Hamilton.

Tomlinson, J. (1999). *Globalization and Culture.* Cambridge: Polity.

3

SINCERITY

Martin Paul Eve

Relatively close to the beginning of David Foster Wallace's 2001 short story, 'Good Old Neon', the narrator's psychoanalyst, Dr. Gustafson, outlines the basic problem of 'sincerity' faced by the piece's protagonist:

> 'If I understand you right', he says, 'you're saying that you're basically a calculating, manipulating person who always says what you think will get somebody to approve of you or form some impression of you you think you want'.
>
> (Wallace 2005: 145)

While Neal, the story's narrator, notes that this is an overly simplistic representation of his mental state, he confirms its basic accuracy in the story and goes on to give his theory of a 'fraudulence paradox':

> The fraudulence paradox was that the more time and effort you put into trying to appear impressive or attractive to other people, the less impressive or attractive you felt inside – you were a fraud. And the more of a fraud you felt like, the harder you tried to convey an impressive or likable image of yourself so that other people wouldn't find out what a hollow, fraudulent person you really were.
>
> (Wallace 2005: 147)

In this chapter, following the cue of Adam Kelly, I will argue that the problem of 'sincerity' raised here sits at the thematic heart of a body of post-boomer authors, including David Foster Wallace, Dave Eggers, Jennifer Egan, George Saunders, Rachel Kushner and Jonathan Franzen (Kelly 2010, 2011, 2012a, 2012b, 2016, 2017a, 2017b). As I will show, this is no accident but, instead, a calculated, reactionary response against a perceived fraudulence paradox within a specific style of mid-to-late twentieth-century writing: ironic postmodern metafiction, to which I will turn later. Finally, however, I will also complicate the straight narrative of a turn to 'sincerity' as overly simplistic; it is never just a case of sincerity or irony and the two can co-exist.

To explore these claims and the historical lineage within which they sit, this chapter will consist of three sections. The first section will set out the traits and definitions of 'sincerity', 'authenticity' and the 'postmodern metafiction' against which the (New) Sincerity movement must be framed. The second section will turn to the manifesto documents of the 'group', a significant portion of which will examine specific statements of David Foster Wallace, the acknowledged progenitor of this 'movement'. The final section will detail the ways in which these statements manifest themselves within several contemporary works, while also bringing attention to a range of authors who continue to consciously rebel against this turn. Ultimately, while providing a broad narrative of the historical emergence of this trend, I also want to re-think some of the assertions made about secrecy and performance that have surrounded its description to-date.

Sincerity, authenticity and postmodern irony

The brief excerpts above from 'Good Old Neon' illustrate one of the core problems of writing about sincerity: the term is clearly closely linked to, but separate from, 'authenticity'. So what is the difference? Is there a difference? Elizabeth Markovits and others deny that such a divide exists, or at least claim that it is of little use for many discussions (Markovits 2008: 21). However, in a distinction first taken seriously in the contemporary era by Lionel Trilling, authenticity is usually thought of as an exact correlation between one's hidden inner 'self' and one's outer assertion and behaviour; a mode in which 'there is no within and without' (Trilling 1972: 93). Unfortunately, if authenticity is about the erasure of a divide between an individual's inner essence and its outer expression, a number of difficulties emerge. For one, this authenticity can only be seen as true if one knows one's own inner essence. However, does this 'inner essence' even exist and what is it? Such questions show that authenticity is actually embroiled in the difficulties of knowing oneself that are inherent in any age after psychoanalysis, although these queries also reach back to the slogan of the Delphic oracle. After all, how can you be true to your 'inner self' or 'essence' if you don't wholly know yourself? That said, most people have a belief that they do know how they feel and also possess an internal representation of themselves – a self-image – that could be said to constitute their authentic self.

Sincerity, on the other hand, is seen in antiquity as a 'moral excellence' deriving from Book Four of Aristotle's *Nicomachean Ethics* wherein a person is deemed sincere if he or she is 'truthful in both speech and conduct when no considerations of honesty come in' (Aristotle 2009: 102–103).[1] Sincerity is, in the interpretation that I will advance here, a type of honesty that is not merely concerned with an accuracy in one's *statements* to others but is rather based on checking future actions against previous speech and behaviour.[2] Although this differs somewhat from Trilling's definition of sincerity as 'a congruence between avowal and actual feeling' (Trilling 1972: 2), this is unavoidable: the only way in which 'actual feeling' can be seen is through action that is verified in a social situation. If you say you will do something, do you make every effort to follow through on it truthfully? If you state a belief, do you truly mean it and can this be publicly seen in your subsequent actions?

Of course, it is possible and frequently necessary to *believe* someone else is speaking sincerely before one has seen the public proof that he or she will follow through on his or her words – it would be a grim world were it otherwise. We have all developed strategies for dealing with this unknowable future and lack of proof, using, for example, a person's past record for truthfulness and the persuasiveness of his or her avowal as signifiers; '"I love you", s/he said'. However, any future betrayal of this sincerity will mean that such a belief was misplaced. Sincerity is, therefore, a social phenomenon pertaining to trust that unfolds between a faith in the present performance of avowal (a belief in a person's words and intentions) and the empirical verification of future action (the proof that they have made good on their words). Sincerity is an ongoing negotiation between trust, public performance and proof, between the rhetoric of the present and the action of the future.[3]

As ideas of sincerity and authenticity are not unchanging but differ from culture to culture, a few examples will serve to demonstrate the differentiation between sincerity and authenticity as they currently exist before we return to literature. Firstly, assuming that authenticity really exists, it is possible to behave authentically, but insincerely. If your authentic self is a liar and you make a promise on which you subsequently renege, you were insincere but authentic. Secondly, in an example that I owe to Orlando Patterson, one can be sincere but inauthentic. Patterson notes that people may be authentically prejudiced but that this does not prohibit them from behaving according to negotiated standards of society, decency and self-consistency (sincerity):

> I couldn't care less whether my neighbors and co-workers are authentically sexist, racist or ageist. What matters is that they behave with civility and tolerance, obey the rules of social interaction and are sincere about it. The criteria of sincerity are unambiguous: Will they keep their promises? Will they honor the meanings and understandings we tacitly negotiate? Are their gestures of cordiality offered in conscious good faith?
>
> (Patterson 2006)

This is an instance of sincere inauthenticity. The other permutations (insincere inauthenticity and authentic sincerity) are also possible but I will refrain from laying these out in detail here (for a full analysis of these, see Eve 2016: 123). The take-away point, however, is that the terms 'authenticity' and 'sincerity' are linked as they both focus on a truth to oneself, but they are also fundamentally distinct in the interpretation I am advancing here: only an individual can tell whether they are being authentic (if they even can) but sincerity is a societal, public virtue that can be verified and judged by others.

As a final note, Trilling's thesis is that, when he was writing in the 1970s, contemporary society had become fixated on notions of authenticity at the expense of sincerity. Since that time, however, there seems to have been another reversal back to sincerity (although critics might question whether these shifts are true movements or simply different priorities of classification). This shift back to sincerity from the late-1980s, as Markovits reads it, finds its clearest articulation in Jürgen Habermas's project of communicative action. Under such a theory, sincerity forms a new cornerstone in the field of so-called discourse ethics. In other words, as I intimated earlier, 'mutual trust', fostered through sincerity, is a crucial prerequisite to any kind of societal cooperation, in Habermas's formulation (Habermas 1990: 136; Markovits 2008: 20).

This shift back towards a focus on sincerity can also be seen in various art-forms. Consider, for example, the 1993 film *Groundhog Day*, in which Bill Murray is doomed to repeat the same twenty-four hours over and over until he comes to a more ethical existence. In the film, Murray at first behaves insincerely in his attempts to win over Andie MacDowell's character; he tries to learn her desires and to feign a set of false coincidences in their interests so that she will sleep with him. As the film progresses and it becomes clear that this will not work – and also that Murray's character cannot die – he decides to spend his energies ensuring that, for one day, he does nothing but help other people, thereby improving himself. As a result of this, his authentic self is changed and MacDowell's character falls in love with Murray's. Once more, this demonstrates Trilling's thesis that authenticity is privileged. However, Murray's character is also no longer insincere; he avows, feels and acts without irony. His inner self has been changed so that he has no desire to be insincere any longer. He is a straight-talking, sincere (and now loveable) character. In this way, he becomes authentically sincere and the two are once more linked. What this means for contemporary fiction, however, requires some unpacking.

★★★

To understand the literary turn towards sincerity in the last twenty-five years, it is crucial to trawl back through the history of a certain mode of literary fiction that came to prominence circa 1960s America: postmodern metafiction. As we will see shortly, when I turn to David Foster Wallace's 'manifesto' documents, the primary targets against which the sincerity group act – at least in the sphere of literary fiction, rather than poetry – are a series of, for the most part white, male writers whose writings were the subject of intense academic critical scrutiny from the 1970s onwards, namely: John Barth, Thomas Pynchon, Jorge Luis Borges, Don DeLillo, E. L. Doctorow, Robert Coover, Donald Bartheme, William H. Gass, William Gaddis, Kurt Vonnegut, Richard Powers; and, on the other side of the Pond: Umberto Eco and John Fowles. While the stylistic traits that these writers share can also be seen in, for instance, the novels of Toni Morrison or Ishmael Reed, the status of these latter authors as 'African American writers' has led to a privileging of the sociological and historical aspects of their work over its aesthetic qualities and thus the similarities between these writers and their white postmodern counterparts has received less attention (Jablon 1997: 21).

For the discussion at hand, the predominant stylistic and thematic characteristics of this subset of postmodern literature can easily be summarised as: irony; reflexivity and metafiction (fiction about fiction or the act of writing itself); reworkings of history; a playful mode that teases the reader; paranoia; and non-linearity (both of narrative and of the chronologies represented). These authors embrace and extend the project of high modernist experiment with often-lengthy and fragmented works that seek new modes of representation to counter the perceived failings of literary realism, namely that the supposedly objective and linear aspects of the nineteenth-century realist novel are not commensurate with lived experience. The undoing of the linear chronology and categorical moral certitude of the nineteenth-century realist novel finds its climax in the representations of a fragmented, complex and overlapping body of literature that the postmodernists claim more accurately represents life.

To understand sincerity in literature, as we shall see shortly with a return to David Foster Wallace, one of the core components that needs to be analysed is the supposition that the irony of postmodern literature 'is parasitic on sincerity', a claim that Markovits complicates (Markovits 2008: 36). Indeed, those contemporary authors seeking new ways of engaging with sincerity in their fiction are not rejecting all aspects of postmodern literature; the complexity, fragmentation and even the historical subject matter often remains (see, for instance Letzler 2017: 87). Instead, the core facet that these authors of the (New) Sincerity reject in their aesthetic is postmodern irony while in their philosophy they retain a postmodern incredulity at the idea of an authentic self. Interestingly, this complicates any narrative of a swing from authenticity to sincerity but is rather focused on the way in which irony, framed as an incongruity, is antithetical to a sincere public ethic (Gordon 1996: 134; Markovits 2008: 90). While I will deal with the 'why?' aspect of this in the next section, it is worth taking a few moments to consider how this might appear in a literary sense; after all, from my above examples, it seems clear what it could mean for a person to behave with differing degrees of sincerity, but it is less obvious what the literary equivalent of this might be. In order to understand this transcription of a behavioural description to the literary realm, it is important to think about two different spheres of 'action', both within narrative and without: authorship and intra-textual voice.

To begin with the author's position with regard to sincerity, I can think of no better example than the one already furnished by Kelly who notes of Wallace's short-story 'Octet' that it is extremely difficult – or even impossible – for a work of fiction to truly (or sincerely) interrogate the truth of its own performance (Kelly 2010: 143). This is because for an author of fiction to be sincere, they should communicate in some way within a text that they are aware of the falsehood inherent to literary representation; fiction should be, at least to some extent, self-aware metafiction. However, as Mark Currie sees it, this is not truly possible: '[i]t is not enough that metafiction knows that it is fiction; it must also know that it is metafiction if its self-knowledge is adequate', thus prompting an infinite regress (Currie 1995: 1). This leads Kelly to conclude that 'in Wallace's fiction the guarantee of the writer's sincere intentions cannot finally lie in representation – sincerity is rather the kind of secret that must always break with representation' (Kelly 2010: 143). The first half of this statement – that fiction cannot represent the writer's sincere intentions – seems uncontentious and forms the basis of the many reading methods that disregard authorial intent, such as those of Roland Barthes that have their roots in the New Critical movement. The second half, though, is more difficult. In the definition of sincerity that I outlined above, sincerity is always *only* about a trade-off between belief and representation and its future self-consistency; whether or not the hidden inner state of an 'authentic' self is truly represented in that consistency can be seen, as does Patterson, as irrelevant. Like Wittgenstein's 'private object', it 'drops out of consideration' (Wittgenstein 2001, sec. 293).

These limitations of fictional representation are well laid out by David Shields who, in *Reality Hunger: A Manifesto*, appears sceptical of the novel's future (and instead seems to champion a type of literary journalism, a form to which Wallace was much accustomed). Instead, Shields signals the interlinked problems of authenticity and sincerity that the novel will never wholly master (and that literary journalism should instead honestly face): 'What does it mean to set another person before the camera, trying to extract something of his or her soul? [. . .] Do you promise to tell the truth, the whole truth, and nothing but the truth?' (Shields 2011: 79–80). The novel never can.

In this sense, then, a sincere author can never be represented within the text and this is not the point of the New Sincerity. As Kelly puts it, 'It is difficult to imagine why one would write fiction if convincing the reader of one's own sincerity was the prime motivation' (Kelly 2017a: 21). This does not mean, however, that nothing can be done because, in at least my reading, the consistency of a text's 'truth to itself' can stand in for this function. This is distinctly *not* to mean that a text cannot contradict itself; to contain Walt Whitman's famous multitudes is the prerog- ative of literature. It is instead to say that fiction must drop any claim to the representation of an author's inner truth: literature is always an outward performance, a representation. Instead, to be sincere, in my reading (and departing from Kelly's) literature must make good on its function to represent well (to engender *belief* in the reason for its avowals – even when metaphorical and implausible) and to represent in a manner consistent with its subject (which stands in for future verification of the avowal, even when contested through varying interpretation). Literature that persuades the reader of the necessity of its aesthetic composition is analogous to the individual who convincingly says: 'I promise'. Whether the promise is borne out is deferred, perhaps indef- initely, into the future.

There are many instances in literary history that do not hold up to this standard of sincerity or occasions where the understanding of a text's sincerity has changed. Consider, for instance, the failure of *Jane Eyre* through the disjunct between Brontë's statement that 'conventionality is not morality' and the subsequent need for the death of Bertha Mason in the novel that allows Jane to marry, as is made clear in the many postcolonial readings of this text. Likewise, in a very different epoch of the novel, the sincerity of Kurt Vonnegut's *Slaughterhouse-Five* is cast into doubt when his deeply sardonic text can only write its counter-narrative of the Dresden bombing through denigration of the Holocaust and the use of the research work of a Holocaust-denier, David Irving (see Watts 1994). Of course, there are problems here of interpretation, ambiguity, reader reception, authorial intention (or otherwise). That said, sincerity in literature, decoupled from authenticity, is – at least in part – about appropriateness and consistency of representation.

The sincerity manifesto

As I have previously outlined in an article on 'metamodernism' (Eve 2012), David Foster Wallace's 1995 novel, *Infinite Jest*, was, in part, an attempt to evade the problems of postmodern irony, problems that he had previously described in an interview as 'sarcasm, cynicism, a manic ennui, suspicion of all authority, [and a] suspicion of all constraints on conduct' (McCaffery 1993: 147). It is, however, in DFW's 1993 article 'E Unibus Pluram' (an inversion of the usual motto of the United States that in this case reads: 'from one, many') that he most clearly outlines the problems that he saw emerging from postmodern fiction and from the attempts that were already under steam to resolve them. It is this document, above all others, that could be called 'the sincerity manifesto'.

Given this claim – that this is a manifesto for *fiction* – you might find it strange to learn that 'E Unibus Pluram' is an essay primarily concerned with television. More specifically, it is an essay that details the ways in which various televisual tropes of irony directly informed specific writers' approaches. To comprehend this, it is first of all important to understand the specific definition of irony with which Wallace's essay is playing. In his view, the reason that 'television was practically *made* for irony' is that 'TV is a bisensuous medium' (Wallace 1993: 161). In this setup it becomes possible for the visual to undermine the aural, for the presentation of 'sights that undercut what's said' (Wallace 1993: 161). Although Wallace doesn't make the explicit connection, despite not being 'bisensuous', writing is also capable of (at least) two simultaneously different presentations: form and content. While this distinction is somewhat false – after all, form is a type of content – it is possible to signal one set of values in writing through what is represented and to undermine them through the way in which it is represented. For the most trivial visual instance, a poem that described a circle while being laid out in a square would achieve this. More frequently in fiction, however, this ironic conflict is played out in sarcastic humour being used to describe events that are beyond laughter; Thomas Pynchon's ironic quip in *V.* that '[t]his is only 1 per cent of six million, but still pretty good' deploys black humour in its representation of both the Herero genocide in the German Südwest and the later systematic extermination of the Jewish people, homosexuals, Roma, Slavs, the disabled, communists, socialists and others in the Holocaust (Pynchon 1995: 245).

The area where Wallace does signal two conflicting modes in postmodern fiction is in its frequent combination of 'high' (difficult) and 'low' (popular) cultural components. Just two of the examples that Wallace gives of this are Pynchon's character Slothrop in *Gravity's Rainbow* meeting Mickey Rooney while on a secret drugs run known as the 'Potsdam Pickup' and DeLillo's characters' discussion of Elvis Presley in *White Noise* in obscenely analytical/academic terms (Wallace 1993: 166). Of this phenomenon, as well as noting that DeLillo and Pynchon were ahead of their time (not necessarily in a good way), Wallace diagnoses the reason why this can work: 'Americans seemed no longer united so much by common feelings as by common images: what binds us became what we stood witness to. No one did or does see this as a good change' (Wallace 1993: 166). Furthermore, in contrast to Modernism's similar techniques, the way in which these 'low' cultural images are used in contemporary literary fiction, for Wallace, are: '(1) to help create a mood of irony and irreverence, (2) to make us uneasy and so 'comment' on the vapidity of U.S. culture, and (3) most important, these days, to be just plain realistic' (Wallace 1993: 167).

Before moving on from Wallace, who must by rights occupy a prominent place in any discussion of a turn towards sincerity, it is worth closing the second part of this chapter by examining the state of affairs as they stood in 1993 and also by framing Wallace's prescription remedy for such problems. Mid-way through 'E Unibus Pluram', Wallace sets out his core statements that set sincerity in motion:

I want to convince you that irony, poker-faced silence, and fear of ridicule are distinctive of those features of contemporary U.S. culture (of which cutting-edge fiction is a part) that enjoy any significant relation to the television whose weird pretty hand has my generation by the throat.

[. . .]

My two big premises are that a certain subgenre of pop-conscious postmodern fiction, written mostly by young Americans, has lately arisen and made a real attempt to transfigure a world of and for appearance, mass appeal, and television; and that, on the other hand, televisual culture has somehow evolved to a point where it seems invulnerable to any such transfiguring assault.

(Wallace 1993: 171)

From Wallace's essay – which I would recommend that readers consult in its entirety – we see a lineage traced that points the way to a clear future trajectory. From the founding fathers of postmodernism, we move to 'image-fiction', which is the next stage (the 'subgenre of pop-conscious postmodern fiction' to which Wallace refers). Examples of image fiction are found in Coover's *The Public Burning*, Max Apple, William T. Vollman's *You Bright and Risen Angels* and *The Rainbow Stories*, Mark Leyner's *My Cousin, My Gastroenterologist* and the later fictions of both Pynchon and, especially, Don DeLillo. But image fiction is not the be-all and end-all. Namely, for Wallace, it shares too much in common with postmodern fiction's tendency to represent pop-cultural phenomena with a vaguely condescending tone of irony and self-consciousness, rather than truly breaking down the distinction between high and low culture. 'And make no mistake', Wallace writes, 'irony tyrannizes us' (Wallace 1993: 183). If we must always refer to our cultural landscape in a tone that undercuts belief, it becomes impossible be sincere. Wallace, the physician, attempts to heal himself in his later works *Infinite Jest* and *The Pale King* (with some success) but for the rest of this chapter, in which I will look at the authors influenced by this statement, he prescribes two potential routes: 1.) the fiction writer can become reactionary and turn to conservatism, as I will argue is sometimes the case for Jonathan Franzen; or, 2.) the fiction writer can risk being deemed 'sentimental' – they can risk affect, or feeling, in their work (Wallace 1993: 193).

Contemporary writers exploring sincerity

Since Wallace wrote, the literary field has changed considerably; after all, this is only to be expected when gazing more than a decade into the future. In the remainder of this chapter I will attempt to give a 'map' of some current American writers who have followed in Wallace's wake specifically in terms of their relationship to this school of sincerity – Jonathan Franzen, Jennifer Egan and Rachel Kushner – and I will also present the dissenters, framed through the continuing outputs in the twenty-first century of Thomas Pynchon and Ishmael Reed.

Of the writers who sit in a lineage from David Foster Wallace, Jonathan Franzen has a particular claim to the inheritance. An early pen-pal of Wallace (who was somewhat inexplicably in awe of Franzen's muddy novel *The Twenty-Seventh City* (1988)) they remained friends until the end of Wallace's life. This was a complex friendship, both marred by a rivalry in which Wallace wrote of being 'so jealous, so sickly searingly envious of you' (Max 2012) and subsequently contaminated by the understandable expression of pain that Franzen felt in the wake of his grief at Wallace's suicide, a grief that led him to condemn the popular beatification of Wallace and even to write that 'I will pass over the question of diagnosis (it's possible he was not simply depressive) and the question of how such a beautiful human being had come by such vividly intimate knowledge of the thoughts of hideous men' (Franzen 2011).

While, of course, as here and below, more comprehensive guides to these writers can be found elsewhere in this volume, Franzen's relationship to a new-found school of sincerity is most clearly played out in the movement from *The Corrections* (2006) to *Freedom* (2010). Eschewing the density of his previous works (*The Twenty-Seventh City* and *Strong Motion* (1992)), *The Corrections* is a nonetheless lengthy novel that demonstrates a 'continued affinit[y] to postmodernism', as Stephen J. Burn puts it (Burn 2008: 128). This is most clearly demonstrated in Franzen's choice both to feature an academic as a protagonist (Chip Lambert) and in his reconfiguration of a single phrase ('the corrections') to hold multiple meanings at different points in the text (as seen in Pynchon's *V.* (1963)). This latter aspect carries with it a sense of irony. This is because, with any new encounter of the term 'the corrections', the reader disregards his or her old understanding of the term as naïve and incongruous; an insufficiently experienced reading. So, for example, Chip's 'major, quick set of corrections' (Franzen 2006: 34) to his script gives way to an italicised discussion of the world's first modern prison, '*still the basic model for corrections in the United States today*' (Franzen 2006: 239), which then yields to Alfred's belief that 'a last child was a last opportunity to learn from one's mistakes and make corrections' (Franzen 2006: 323) until we encounter the final meaning of the term with regard to the technological boom: '[t]he correction, when it finally came, was not an overnight bursting of a bubble but a much more gentle letdown, a year-long leakage of value from key financial markets, a contraction too gradual to generate headlines and too predictable to seriously hurt anybody but fools and the working poor' (Franzen 2006: 647). If the text's purported core ethic pertains to self-reflection and change (making corrections to oneself), then *The Corrections* represents that phenomenon, but does so through cynicism and ironic awareness of one's past self.

Franzen's later novel, *Freedom* (2010), takes a very different tack. While this text represents a return to the ecological themes that had first surfaced in *Strong Motion*, the narrative is chronologically linear (except at one key point which I will discuss shortly), uncomplicated and departmentalised. The text contains far fewer nods to its postmodern forebears but seems to want to show the problems of moral action. Indeed, every single character in *Freedom* is compromised in one way or another: from Joey, the young Republican who nonetheless enters into a business deal that endangers the lives of American soldiers, through to Walter, the all-round nice-guy and environmentalist who is willing to sell out to a mining company so long as they protect just one single species of (not even currently endangered) bird. In some senses, then, *Freedom* represents its subject well, in the ethical sense. In at least one reading, however, Franzen blows it. While open, ambiguous endings are the hallmark of postmodern fiction, in Franzen's choice to close *Freedom* with the definitive reunion of Walter and Patty, the novel retreats into the conservatism of which Wallace warned. This is because the reunion is only made possible through the death of Lalitha, a character who seems little more than a plot device and who is consistently sexualised and referred to as 'dark-skinned', an awful stereotyping that finds its locus in her need 'to do the Downward Dog and be whammed from behind' (Franzen 2010: 466).

Despite this potential problem in Franzen's later output, there is a portion of the text (and the way in which it specifically narrates Lalitha's death) that is worth quoting:

> The woman he loved loved him. He knew this for certain, but it was all he knew for certain, then or ever; the other vital facts remained unknown. Whether she did, in fact, drive carefully. [. . .] Whether a coal truck had come flying around one of the curves and done what a coal truck did somewhere in West Virginia every week. Or whether

somebody in a high-clearance 4x4 [. . .] veered into her lane or tailgated her or passed her too narrowly or even deliberately forced her off the shoulderless road.

(Franzen 2010: 500)

This moment of intense emotional anguish for Walter and the reader is framed through a temporal anomaly in which, suddenly, everything is once more speculative and unknown. While, as I have noted, this death of a woman of Indian descent is problematically 'used' in *Freedom* to allow the white American reunion at the end, it does signal a particular affective (i.e. 'emotional') strategy in contemporary fiction. For, by abruptly jutting between time periods within the narrative it becomes possible for the novelist to achieve the poignancy of the knowledge of future hindsight; a type of anticipated retrospection. At the same time, this is coupled with a naivety in the moment; a presentness that doesn't resort to any kind of disdainful dramatic irony. In other words, this narrative is not authentic because the authorial perspective at this point *does not know* the authentic truth. In doing so, it brings sincerity to the fore.

A superb example of this technique is also found in Jennifer Egan's acclaimed novel, *A Visit from the Goon Squad* (2010). In a gut-wrenching moment in this text, two young teenagers – a brother and sister – are dancing with one another. At this point, the action suddenly jumps forward, within a single sentence, to reveal that this moment, the two children dancing, will be a memory that Charlie 'will return to again and again, for the rest of her life, long after Rolph has shot himself in the head in their father's house at twenty-eight' (Egan 2011: 87). This type of time-distortion is common in both postmodern and 'post-postmodern' fiction. Indeed, one can think also of Frobischer in David Mitchell's *Cloud Atlas*, who writes in his own diary of how he 'Shot [himself] through the roof of [his] mouth at [the upcoming] 5 a.m.' (Mitchell 2008: 487). While Mitchell's use is cynical and ironic, and while both of these examples focus on death, the way in which Egan deploys this technique is in the service of pathos. As I have already noted, this pathos is the function of two different moments of knowledge, at three different locations. The two types of knowledge, and their three places are: 1.) Charlie's naivety (or lack of knowledge) at the current moment in the text; 2.) Charlie's knowledge in the future of her brother's death and the memory of the moment when he was alive and they were dancing; and 3.) the reader's knowledge, outside the text, of both of these aspects. While, strictly speaking, characters in a book do not have 'knowledge' in the same way as a reader, the depiction of these human situations in fiction allows us to think of them as though they are real because we can empathise with the position. This conjunction of pathos, empathy and naivety fused with knowledge is not used, in Egan's worlds, to cynically deplore the naivety of the present, but to value it more highly and to create affect. Wallace accurately noted the danger of this mode for the writer: it can cross over into being branded as 'sentimental'. Whether or not this is the case will depend, of course, upon how cynical you yourself are as a reader. Egan's framework, though, is ethically consistent in its vision to present a world where there is irony and cynicism, but to do so without cynicism.

Finally, this acceptance, but progression, from tropes of irony is also well-reflected in Rachel Kushner's strange text, *The Flamethrowers* (2013). Clearly a historical novel, to at least some degree, the text explores a genealogy of Italian art, from the Futurists through to the motorcycle/photographic landscape art of the narrative's 1970's protagonist. One of the core aspects of this novel is the linkage of the various depictions of misogyny, violence, sexuality and aggression to the art-forms of speed, which are historically backed by fascism. However, the generic placement of this text is far from straightforward. The novel contains so many metatextual elements, historical ironies and aspects of time-distortion (via the trope of 'speed') that it would be easy to situate it within a postmodern framework. That it does so, however, in a mode that seems not only unsentimental but also, as noted in many reviews, 'hyper-masculine', brings us back to thinking about sincerity and 'straight-talking' once more.

To give just a few instances in this novel that examine this trope, one could think of the fact that Ronnie's art, in the novel, is deemed 'too flatly ironic' (Kushner 2013: 144) or the metatextual moment wherein the story of the core motorcycle accident that Sandro relates is framed as 'far-fetched, outlandish' (Kushner 2013: 179), evoking the mode of the texts that James Wood has dubbed 'hysterical realism'. Aspects of sincerity are also seen, however, in the way in which the novel makes knowledge/naivety subjective and time-rooted. So, for example, in the discussion of whether it is now passé to attempt to shock through transparent dresses, Gloria is cynical, noting that the phenomenon dates back to 1971. The narrator, however, outside of Gloria's cynical, critical and insincere speech, simply states: 'But it's new *to her*, I should have said but didn't. She's on *her* timeline, Gloria, not yours or anyone else's' (Kushner 2013: 306).

However, and to conclude, it is in Kushner's novel that we find, to date, one of the strongest expressions of what it means to write about sincerity in contemporary literature. It is not, as has been proposed, a simple matter of transcribing statements about sincerity into the mouths of characters and/or narrators, as seen above. It seems, rather, to be about exploring the histories of irony's dominance and the need for sincerity within fiction and reality. It is, therefore, apt that, when Reno confronts Ronnie about his brother, he retorts:

> Let me introduce you to a concept. Two concepts, actually. Important tools for surviving the human condition. One is called irony. Say it with me. *Eye-ron-ee*. Now, the next is harder to pronounce, but let's try. *Diss-sim-you-lay-shon*. Giving the false appearance that you are not some thing.
>
> (Kushner 2013: 315)

As Ronnie ('I, Ronnie'/'*Eye-ron-ee*'/irony) sees it, irony is not the truth but it is an important rhetorical tool for surviving one's own timeline; it is a mode of self-preservation, an aspect overlooked by those who seek only pure conformity to the ideals of sincere speech. What is clear from all of the above is that a delicate balance is always maintained in fiction between the use of irony and the desire to speak the truth about reality – and to speak it plainly. Much contemporary fiction, particularly American, has taken this as one of its preoccupations in a reaction against the privileging of authenticity but also in a move against postmodern irony.

As a final remark, it is worth noting that several writers of the postmodern school evidently frame the assault on irony and swing towards sincerity as an over-reaction. Thomas Pynchon's 2013 novel, *Bleeding Edge*, for instance, swipes at Wallace's counter-ironic stance, scathingly noting of Heidi's article in that text that it 'argues that irony, assumed to be a key element of urban gay humor and popular through the nineties, has now become another collateral casualty of 11 September because somehow it did not keep the tragedy from happening' (Pynchon 2013: 335; Eve 2014: 27).

Likewise, in 2011, after an 18 year hiatus from writing novels, Ishmael Reed published *Juice!* with the Dalkey Archive Press. The novel is narrated from the perspective of Paul ('Bear') Blessings, a cartoonist who is obsessed with the OJ Simpson trials and who rigorously protests the innocence of the former NFL star and actor. Indeed, at every instance possible, Bear reads OJ's troubles as enhanced, or more frequently entirely produced, by structural racism; after all, 'The men who run the networks prefer blondes' (Reed 2011: 75). Were this simply a tool of communication, though, a polemic rant on the continued deplorable state of US race-relations, *Juice!* could hardly be said to merit its sub-title, '*a novel*'. Instead, often through an ironic parody of academic discourse, Reed seeks to complicate his protagonist's distorted narrator in order to extend the traditional postmodernist deconstruction of binaries (Reed 2011: 193). Indeed, Bear alternates between poles of paranoia and viable critique, the one continually undercutting the plausibility of the latter in order to show, at one remove, how it is that cultural reading practices of paranoia and truth degrade the efficacy of radical critique. Such an act of extreme ironic complication in recent contemporary fiction shows that, regardless of how much we would like to impose taxonomies, the battles of the sincerity wars are far from over.

Notes

1 Note, though, that Plato's concept of *parrhesia*, later explored extensively by Michel Foucault, could also be seen as intimately related to notions of 'sincerity' (see Markovits 2008).
2 One also has to be careful that this appraisal of consistency is local and specific, though; a type of appraisal that Markovits calls 'trustworthiness' (204).
3 The latter portions of this definition evolved from a conversation with Ruth Charnock, to whom I am extremely grateful.

Works cited

Aristotle (2009) *The Nicomachean Ethics*. Translated by D. Ross. Oxford: Oxford University Press.

Burn, S. J. (2008) *Jonathan Franzen at the End of Postmodernism*. London: Continuum.

Currie, M. (1995) 'Introduction', in Currie, M. (ed.) *Metafiction*. London: Longman.

Egan, J. (2011) *A Visit from the Goon Squad*. London: Corsair.

Eve, M. P. (2012) 'Thomas Pynchon, David Foster Wallace and the Problems of "Metamodernism": Post-Millennial Post-Postmodernism?', *C21 Literature: Journal of 21st-Century Writings*, 1(1), 7–25.

—— (2014) *Pynchon and Philosophy: Wittgenstein, Foucault and Adorno*. London: Palgrave Macmillan.

—— (2016) *Literature against Criticism: University English and Contemporary Fiction in Conflict*. Cambridge: Open Book Publishers.

Franzen, J. (2006) *The Corrections*. London: Harper Perennial.

—— (2010) *Freedom*. London: Fourth Estate.

—— (2011) 'Farther Away', *The New Yorker*, 18 April. Available at: www.newyorker.com/reporting/2011/04/18/110418fa_fact_franzen?currentPage=all (Accessed: 10 January 2014).

Gordon, J. (1996) 'Against Vlastos on Complex Irony', *The Classical Quarterly*, 46(1), 131–137.

Habermas, J. (1990) *Moral Consciousness and Communicative Action*. Cambridge, MA: MIT Press.

Jablon, M. (1997) *Black Metafiction: Self-Consciousness in African American Literature*. Iowa City: University of Iowa Press.

Kelly, A. (2010) 'David Foster Wallace and the New Sincerity in American Fiction', in Hering, D. (ed.) *Consider David Foster Wallace*. Amazon Kindle edition. Los Angeles and Austin: SSMG Press, 131–146.

—— (2011) 'Beginning with Postmodernism', *Twentieth Century Literature*, 57(3/4), 391–422.

—— (2012a) 'Development through Dialogue: David Foster Wallace and the Novel of Ideas', *Studies in the Novel*, 44(3), 267–283.

—— (2012b) '"Who Is Responsible?": Revisiting the Radical Years in Dana Spiotta's Eat the Document', in Coleman, P. and Matterson, S. (eds.) *'Forever Young?' The Changing Images of America*. Heidelberg: Universitatsverlag Winter, 219–230.

—— (2016) 'The New Sincerity', in Gladstone, J., Hoberek, A., and Worden, D. (eds.) *Postmodern/Postwar and After: Rethinking American Literature*. Iowa City: University of Iowa Press, 197–208.

—— (2017a) 'David Foster Wallace and New Sincerity Aesthetics: A Reply to Edward Jackson and Joel Nicholson-Roberts', *Orbit: A Journal of American Literature*, 5(2). doi: 10.16995/orbit.224.

—— (2017b) 'Language between Lyricism and Corporatism: George Saunders's New Sincerity', in Coleman, P. and Ellerhoff, S. G. (eds.) *George Saunders: Critical Essays*. Basingstoke: Palgrave, 41–58.

Kushner, R. (2013) *The Flamethrowers*. New York: Scribner.

Letzler, D. (2017) *The Cruft of Fiction: Mega-Novels and the Science of Paying Attention*. Lincoln: University of Nebraska Press (Frontiers of narrative).

Markovits, E. (2008) *The Politics of Sincerity: Plato, Frank Speech, and Democratic Judgment*. University Park: Pennsylvania State University Press.

Max, D. T. (2012) 'David Foster Wallace on the Brink of "Infinite Jest"', *Newsweek*. Available at: www.newsweek.com/david-foster-wallace-brink-infinite-jest-64425 (Accessed: 10 January 2014).

McCaffery, L. (1993) 'Interview with David Foster Wallace', *Review of Contemporary Fiction*, 13(2), 127–150.

Mitchell, D. (2008) *Cloud Atlas*. London: Sceptre.

Patterson, O. (2006) 'Our Overrated Inner Self', *The New York Times*, 26 December. Available at: www.nytimes.com/2006/12/26/opinion/26patterson.html (Accessed: 4 January 2014).

Pynchon, T. (1995) *V*. London: Vintage.

—— (2013) *Bleeding Edge*. London: Jonathan Cape.

Reed, I. (2011) *Juice!: A Novel*. Champaign: Dalkey Archive Press.

Shields, D. (2011) *Reality Hunger: A Manifesto*. London: Hamish Hamilton.

Trilling, L. (1972) *Sincerity and Authenticity*. Cambridge, MA: Harvard University Press.

Wallace, D. F. (1993) 'E Unibus Pluram: Television and U.S. Fiction', *Review of Contemporary Fiction*, 13(2), 151–198.

—— (2005) 'Good Old Neon', in *Oblivion: Stories*. London: Abacus, 141–181.

Watts, P. (1994) 'Rewriting History: Céline and Kurt Vonnegut', *The South Atlantic Quarterly*, 93, 265–278.

Wittgenstein, L. (2001) *Philosophical Investigations: The German Text, with a Revised English Translation*. Oxford: Blackwell.

4

AUTOBIOGRAFICTION

Timothy C. Baker

In 2010, David Shields released his aesthetic manifesto *Reality Hunger* to sustained media attention. Consisting of 618 numbered sections arranged by alphabetical themes, the book combines hundreds of unacknowledged quotations with Shields's own musings on the nature of art in the twenty-first century, collapsing the division between primary and secondary texts, and arguably redefining the role of the author as a single, stable locus of meaning and intent. In the 'overture', Shields reflects on Dave Eggers's popular memoir *A Heartbreaking Work of Staggering Genius* (2000), finding that it 'was full of the same self-conscious apparatus that had bored everyone silly until it got tethered to what felt like someone's "real life"'; even a book that explicitly reminds its readers of its artifice, Shields finds, can still provide a moment of 'authenticity' (Shields 2010: 5). Works such as Eggers's, he argues, serve as examples of a new artistic movement founded on elements such as 'deliberate unartiness', 'reader/viewer participation', 'criticism as autobiography', 'self-reflexivity', and finally 'a blurring (to the point of invisibility) of any distinction between fiction and nonfiction: the lure and blur of the real' (5). As James Wood comments in a review of Sheila Heti's *How Should a Person Be?* (2012) Shields's title is particularly apposite: '[r]ealism is perpetually hungry [. . .] because no bound manuscript can ever be "real" enough' (Wood 2012). In a variety of forms, ranging from *romans à clef* and fictionalised autobiographies to fiction presented in the form of autobiographies, diaries, and memoirs, as well as texts that problematise all categorical distinctions, contemporary writers constantly renegotiate the value of the 'real'.

The blurring of divisions between fiction and nonfiction is certainly not new; it has been commented on by critics of autobiography since the early nineteenth century, while Northrop Frye influentially argued in the mid-twentieth century that rather than designating 'falsehood or unreality', 'the word fiction [. . .] could be applied in criticism to any work of literary art in a radically continuous form', including autobiography (1971: 303). The widely publicised controversy surrounding James Frey's *A Million Little Pieces* in 2006 – a text initially marketed as a memoir and later revealed to incorporate fictional elements, to the dismay of many of its readers – reveals, however, the persistent idea that there is not only an 'identity of name' between author, narrator, and protagonist, as established by Philippe Lejeune's 'autobiographical pact' (1989: 14), but further what could be called an 'identity of experience'. For many readers, 'the strength of memoir is precisely its claim of literal truth' (Mills 2004: 116). An autobiographical novel may exaggerate or condense events, while a text labelled as memoir is presumed to offer a true record of experience. This generic horizon of expectation is confounded to different extents in each of the texts discussed below; each author uses the blurring of fiction and nonfiction as a way to question the larger relation between self and text.

One of the clearest examples of authorial and generic reinvention can be found in J.M. Coetzee's work over the past two decades. As opposed to the impersonal style of his earlier novels, his recent texts highlight the relation between autobiography and what he elsewhere calls '*autrebiography*' (1992: 394). This shift in focus can be dated to the delivery of the Tanner Lectures at Princeton University in 1997–8, later published as *The Lives of Animals* (1999) and incorporated into the subsequent novel *Elizabeth Costello* (2003). The lectures consist of two short stories in which Costello, an Australian novelist, herself presents two lectures on animal ethics. These texts immediately confound the reader's expectations of what might be the proper work of fiction: they are dramatically unbalanced in favour of philosophical and ethical discourse, and while there are significant differences between Coetzee and Costello as personae, it is frequently implied that Costello's views may be Coetzee's own, even as Costello questions her own thinking. *The Lives of Animals* contains four responses from prominent critics, each of whom responds to the moral arguments put forward in the lectures, rather than elements of narrative or characterisation. *Elizabeth Costello* adds another six 'lessons' to these first two, beginning with a discussion of realism:

> Realism has never been comfortable with ideas. It could not be otherwise: realism is premised on the idea that ideas have no autonomous existence, can only exist in things. So when it needs to debate ideas, as here, realism is driven to invent situations – walks in the countryside, conversations – in which characters give voice to contending ideas and thereby in a certain sense embody them. The notion of *embodying* turns out to be pivotal.
>
> (Coetzee 2004: 9)

Costello certainly can be seen to embody ideas, however uncomfortably. Whether in scenes that draw on realist conventions or more surreal sequences derived from Kafka, the reader approaches the novel as a work of both narrative and criticism. The tension between the reader's awareness that Costello is a fictional construct and their equal awareness that the ideas she embodies are neither attributable to her nor Coetzee in any straightforward way, however, never resolves. The fictional frame does not provide access to the 'real', but instead destabilises it. Realism, Coetzee implies, can only be achieved through a denial of realistic techniques. Costello is neither simply a spokesperson for abstract or philosophical ideas, nor a fully developed character in her own right; rather, by occupying the space between these poles she is used to challenge the reader's pre-established ideas of how fiction might be used as a vehicle for ethical argument.

This destabilisation is further complicated in *Slow Man* (2005), a sequel of sorts. While the novel begins as an account of the protagonist Paul Raymond's recovery from a dehabilitating accident, its apparent conventional realism is called into question when Costello appears midway through, claiming that Raymond is only a character in her writing. Furthermore, she attests that she is 'not in command of what comes to me' (2006: 81), but instead occupies Raymond's house, waiting to see what happens next. Neither Costello nor Coetzee can be positioned as the source of the ideas and stories the reader encounters; in their absence the reader becomes the arbiter of meaning and ethical consideration. As Coetzee writes in the persona of Señor C, an elderly writer in Sydney, in *Diary of a Bad Year* (2007): 'Authority must be earned; on the novelist author lies the onus to build up, out of nothing, such authority' (2008: 149). In each of these three texts the assumed author abdicates responsibility. Indeed, the pages of *Diary* are divided into three distinct parts, comprising Señor C's essays on various topics (which in turn echo Costello's lectures), his diary entries concerning his typist, Anya, and her often contradictory account of their relation. No single text is true, or authoritative: rather, in each of these novels, the 'real' lies in the interplay of various narratives and ideas, progressively divorced from their apparent source. Especially in *Diary*, the reader must devise their own reading strategies, choosing whether to read a page in the order presented or follow each of the narratives separately. By empowering the reader in this way, Coetzee suggests that no text can point to a fixed, predetermined reality; rather, the 'real' is co-created in the relation between author and reader.

This authorial abdication is also the theme of Coetzee's concurrent experiments in memoir. *Boyhood* (1997) and *Youth* (2002) present a selective, third person account of Coetzee's childhood. While the names provided were fictionalised at the request of his American publishers, the significant absence of names is altogether more striking. The earlier volume begins simply '[t]hey live on a housing estate outside the town of Worcester' (Coetzee 1998: 1), with no indication of who this 'they' might be. In both novels there is no attempt to introduce the various characters; rather, the reader is assumed already to know who they are. The protagonist, referred to as 'he' throughout, is finally named as 'John' in a letter late in the text, while his statement that '[h]is grandfather is the only Coetzee' at the family farm strongly implies the perpetuation of the family name (97). Given that the text is labelled as fiction, however, there is no necessary reason for the reader to believe that the events depicted in the text are particularly true. Neither, however, is there any reason to doubt them. In *Youth* the narrator considers Flaubert's *Madame Bovary*, arguing that she 'was not created out of nothing: she had her origin in the flesh and blood experiences of her author, experiences that were then subjected to the transfiguring fire of art' (Coetzee 2003: 25). In these texts, however, the extent of such a transfiguration remains unclear. In this way, Coetzee reverses the traditional horizon of expectation: if the reader of an autobiography assumes the truth of the text but looks for fiction, here they assume fiction but look for truth. This reversal is compounded in *Summertime* (2009). Here, Coetzee is named; the novel is presented as a series of interviews his academic biographer conducts with people who may have known him, following his death sometime after writing *Youth*. If Coetzee is present but unnamed in the previous texts, here he is an absent centre around whom the story revolves. Yet many of the interviewees position Coetzee as a 'minor character' in their own narratives (Coetzee 2010: 44), and are keen to emphasise his inadequacies. The text presents a rare instance of a memoir in which the primary subject appears to have no right of reply. As a former colleague argues, Coetzee 'believed our life-stories are ours to construct as we wish, within or even against the constraints imposed by the real world' (227). In each of these volumes Coetzee constructs a life story for himself, but also foregrounds not merely the unreliability that is inevitable to any reconstructed autobiographical project, but also the insufficiency of every such attempt.

Coetzee's twenty-first century novels represent the difficulties faced by any texts that attempt to blur the lines between fiction and autobiography. As the autobiography theorist Paul John Eakin writes, throughout nineteenth- and twentieth-century memoirs 'the fictive nature of self-hood [. . .] is held to be a biographical fact' (1985: 182). Like Lejeune, Eakin argues that the primary separation between autobiography and fiction is one of identity: the autobiographical text can be recognised by the writer choosing to appear, often under his or her own name, as autobiographer. Coetzee's presentation as Elizabeth Costello, Señor C, He, and John Coetzee, however, all complicate this notion: in each instance the reader is finally unable to ascribe a single perspective or truth to the author. Coetzee's work is thus far more destabilised than a memoir such as Salman Rushdie's *Joseph Anton* (2012) which, although presented in the third person and under an assumed name, is still readable as a guide to Rushdie's life. As such, Coetzee's works can be seen as what is alternatively termed 'autofiction', 'autobiografiction', 'auto/biografiction', and even, for the cartoonist Lynda Barry, 'autobifictionalography' (Miller 2007: 539). Although each of these terms has their adherents, 'autobiografiction' is especially useful since, as Max Saunders argues, it foregrounds not the relation between fiction and the self, as 'autofiction' might, but between fiction and the self's autobiography (2012: 7). This is certainly true of each of Coetzee's texts, which construct an uneasy relationship between self, author, reader, and text: in each, the reader must learn to deconstruct the fictive nature of selfhood and accept the ambiguity of the text's apparent references to lived experience. As the texts raise questions of authorial control, the reader is forced to confront the ethical implications of their own reading, as they simultaneously must interpret a text as fiction and as a record of a particular reality.

Although often assumed to be a recent coinage, the term 'autobiografiction' first appears in Stephen Reynolds's 1906 article of that name; while he laments that the word itself is 'rather dreadful', he defines it most simply as 'a record of real spiritual experiences strung on a credible but more or less fictitious autobiographical narrative' (1906: 28). For Reynolds autobiografiction is differentiated from autobiographical fiction by a focus on subjective and internal, rather than external, experience. This focus is evident in the influence of a number of works from the 1990s, most notably Seamus Deane's *Reading in the Dark* (1996) and the novels of W.G. Sebald, as well as Chris Kraus's hybrid text *I Love Dick* (1997), that combine fiction and autobiography in various ways. Perhaps the clearest example of a recent autobiografictional text in relation to Reynolds's definition is Heti's *How Should a Person Be?*, which begins with an investigation of the title question. The protagonist, Sheila, asks the question of everyone she meets, writing: 'I know that personality is just an invention of the media. I know that character exists from the outside alone. [. . .] So how do you build your soul?' (2013: 2). The majority of the novel consists of Sheila's conversations with her friend Margaux, presented alternately as theatrical playscript and prose narrative. Many of these scenes are drawn from e-mails and recorded conversations, so as to present what appears to be a true record of events. Sheila reveals her ambition to be emotionally naked, to write a play that will change the world, and to have a life 'no less ugly than the rest' (272). The solution to Sheila's existential and creative unhappiness, Margaux tells her, is to write honestly, and answer the title question so as not to think about it again. As Sheila begins to write, she comments that

> I'd never before wanted to uncover all the molecules of shit that were such a part of my deepest being which, once released, would smell forever of the shit that I was, and which nothing – not exile, not fame – could ever disappear. But I threw the shit and the trash and the sand, and for years and years I just threw it. And I began to light up my soul with scenes.
> I made what I could with what I had. And I finally became a real girl.

> (277)

If Heti's novel ultimately resembles many other accounts of growth into artistic maturity, it remains remarkable for the appearance of honesty. While Coetzee's self-abnegation begins when he is already recognised as one of the most important living writers, Heti's self-presentation is arguably riskier. Indeed, as Laura Marcus argues, 'definitions of the autobiographical genre and theories of autobiography in general, derived almost entirely from texts by male authors, and a very selective group of male authors at that, acquired an intrinsic androcentric bias' (1994: 230). Autobiography, Marcus argues, is inevitably seen as a male genre. This is perhaps especially true of artistic autobiography and autobiografiction. While the Norwegian novelist Karl Ove Knausgaard's six-volume autobiografiction *My Struggle*, which similarly presents often mundane experience in great detail, has become a worldwide phenomenon, critical reaction to Heti's perceived narcissism has been much more strident. Heti's work has been criticised for its perceived formlessness and lack of polish; by presenting her creative process as inherently unfinished, the novel refuses many of fiction's traditional consolations.

Heti's novel can be placed in a recent tradition of what might be called 'theoretical fictions' (Hawkins 2006: 263), inaugurated by Chris Kraus and Michelle Tea, where writing the story of a woman's intellectual life is positioned as a challenge to normative and masculine ideas of autobiography. Recent examples include Eileen Myles's *Inferno (A Poet's Novel)* (2010) and Lynn Crosbie's *Life is about Losing Everything* (2012). Both authors are better known for their poetry and, in Crosbie's case, journalism, as well as more academic writings. If Myles's text never explicitly answers the questions suggested by its subtitle – the definition of a 'poet's novel' and how might it be different than a memoir or a novelist's novel – the text highlights its own construction. At the beginning of the second of three parts, she provides an abstract in which she argues that she is 'following both Dante and Freud's models for "existence"'; the conjunction is necessary because women 'might actually be a little more medieval than men. We don't start off being "human". I mean that's been my experience' (Myles 2010: 95). Like Heti's novel, Myles's alternates between immediate experience – in both cases most often located in conversations with named individuals – and larger inquiries into the role of the artist. As Myles reflects, here specifically on Knut Hamsun:

> Nobody ever told me how to live, they told me what not to do. In all these books about the lives of artists that I read I mean they weren't guidebooks but they took the simple beliefs in art and freedom and carried them to outrageous lengths. I could do that.
>
> (75)

The 'outrageous lengths' in Myles's text include retaining struck-through fragments of text; at one point she asks '~~Who's asking these questions anyhow~~' (141). At the same time that Myles charts her own creative journey, she also points to the failure of earlier texts or external voices to provide direction. While Heti substantially revised her novel between its original Canadian publication in 2010 and its British publication in 2013, producing a shorter, more focused text, Myles's novel at times reads like an unfinished draft. Both authors use the experimental techniques of autobiografiction to challenge any anxiety of influence: lacking autobiographical precedents, they showcase both their lives and novels as involved in a process of constant change.

The experimental account of a writer's journey is rendered still more outrageous in Crosbie's *Life is About Losing Everything*. The text opens with a list of 'fabrications [. . .] for the reader to consider': the 'names of actual people in this book have been changed, as have the actual people', while the book's 'chronology is impossible to follow' (Crosbie 2012: n.p.). Crosbie immediately positions herself as an unreliable narrator of her own life: scenes of drug and alcohol abuse are rendered absurd by comparison to George Herbert's religious writing, while the apparent veracity of the story is challenged when she includes surreal scenes of, for instance, a relationship with an inch-high man. The entire text is a rebuttal to her professor's claim that 'No one gives a damn what you feel or remember' (134). Unlike Heti's and Myles's texts, where historical details and even the existence of other characters can be verified by the reader, Crosbie's text posits her feelings and memories as the only locus of the 'real'. Her novel is one of the best examples of E.H. Jones's claim that autofiction, or autobiografiction, 'is a genre in which the uniqueness of the author is foregrounded not only in the form but also in the very content of the work' (2010: 181). Such texts, she argues, do not transcend genre, but instead approach pre-existing literary genres as sources of innovation and self-expression. Even more than her contemporaries, Crosbie challenges pre-conceived expectations of 'memoir' and 'novel', and between the real and the invented, creating a kaleidoscopic text that moves easily between both modes. Like Heti and Myles, however, she also highlights the extent to which any self is necessarily fictive: presenting a 'true' picture of the self's development necessitates overturning the conventions of life writing.

The more surreal elements of Crosbie's narrative are echoed in recent work by Will Self and Bret Easton Ellis. In *Walking to Hollywood* (2010) and *Lunar Park* (2005) respectively, the authors present caricatured portraits of themselves in order to undermine their own reliability and status as public figures. *Lunar Park* opens with an account of the writing of Ellis's previous novels, lamenting that *Less Than Zero*, his first novel, 'was mistaken for autobiography' (2005: 7). Here, the Ellis persona suggests, he will set the record straight. The opening contains publicity material and accounts of public events that are easily verifiable; indeed, it constitutes one of the better accounts of Ellis's work. Yet Ellis also discusses his marriage to the actress Jayne Dennis, who does not exist: material that is readily 'true' is juxtaposed with material that is clearly fictional without any explanation. As the novel progresses and Ellis not only encounters characters from his previous novels but malevolent spirits, it becomes evident that 'Ellis' the protagonist may only bare a superficial resemblance to Ellis the author. Like earlier novels by Paul Auster and Philip Roth featuring protagonists bearing the authors' names, *Lunar Park* foregrounds to extent to which the idea of the author is already a construct, not necessarily anchored to the real world. As Ellis summarises his own career: 'I was adept at erasing reality. As a writer, it was easy for me to dream up the more viable scenario than the one that had actually played itself out' (147). That the 'more viable scenario' in this case devolves into familiar horror tropes only highlights the extent to which any writing self is not only fictive, but unknowable. At the same time, however, the final pages of the novel reveal it to have been a grief work in which Ellis attempts to come to terms with the death of his father. The correspondence of the Ellis persona with the actual author is by this point irrelevant; rather, it is the confusion between the two that permits emotional recovery. The passages that appear most honest in all of Ellis's writings only appear when the very idea of honesty has already been undermined.

Walking to Hollywood initially appears more stable than Ellis's novel. The first of the novel's three sections depicts a psychogeographical expedition, copiously illustrated, that is much indebted to Sebald's work. Like Crosbie, however, Self opens the text with a claim that while the names of real persons are used, 'these characters appear in fictionalized settings that are manifestly a product of the narrator's delusions' (2010: n.p.). Self soon encounters the psychiatrist Zack Busner, 'the fixed point of a turning world' (119); as the reader recognises, but the novel elides, Busner is the most common recurring character in Self's fiction. This confusion of fact and fiction is embellished when Self journeys to Hollywood, where he believes that everyone he meets is played by a famous actor: he himself is played by David Thewlis, while Bret Easton Ellis, with whom he has dinner, is played by mid-period Orson Welles. He congratulates Ellis on *Lunar Park*, saying he 'love[s] the way you play with your own identity' (236). Although, like Ellis's novel, Self's becomes gradually more surreal as it continues, losing all anchoring to any recognisable reality, a brief afterword suddenly reverses this apparent pastiche. Coming shortly a fight with Death himself, Self opens the afterword with a real time and place, 17 July 2008 in Stockwell, South London, where he is witness to events surrounding the death of Frederick Moody Boateng, 'the twenty-first teenage fatality from a stabbing in London that year' (429). The text suddenly reasserts itself as a place to memorialise a now nearly forgotten crime. In both Ellis's and Self's novels, the confusion between memoir and novel initially appears to be a way of heightening the comic aspects of the work. As both novels assume familiarity not only with the authors' previous texts, but also with their public personae, the outrageousness of events can be seen as mocking the constructed selves that appear in wider media. Yet in both texts something of the 'real' intrudes in the final pages. The self-cancelling memoir becomes a way to speak of something that would otherwise be forgotten or ignored.

The use of autobiografiction to comment on the confusion between public and private lives is also found in the work of a younger generation of American experimental writers. Marie Calloway's *What Purpose Did I Serve in Your Life* (2013) juxtaposes semi-fictional stories with screenshots of presumably real social media conversations, while Tao Lin's *Richard Yates* (2010) tells an autobiographical love story where the protagonists' names have been replaced by those of the actors Dakota Fanning and Haley Joel Osment. Both writers work in a contemporary idiom that gives the appearance of artlessness, as if their material was drawn unfiltered from life. Perhaps because of this perception, both writers have been the subject of significant controversy surrounding their treatment of other people. While in Heti's and Myles's texts the appearance of other people is often a matter of public record, and in Crosbie's, Self's, and Ellis's the degree of caricature is generally clear, in Lin's and Calloway's work, as in Kraus's, their contemporaries are described in thinly fictionalised ways but are still recognisable. While such work may not be libellous, it nevertheless raises the possibility of misrepresentation. This dilemma is most clearly expressed in the work of Rachel Cusk. The author of a number of novels and memoirs, her autobiographical text *Aftermath* (2012) outlines the 'new reality' of her divorce; her husband's belief that she 'had treated him monstrously' is dismissed with the claim that '[i]t was his story, and lately I have come to hate stories' (2012: 2). Nevertheless, Cusk's memoir was held to be overly partial; the British press especially presented arguments that it was unethical to present an account such as this when young children were involved.

Cusk's response, the novel *Outline* (2014) – the first of a trilogy including *Transit* (2014) and *Kudos* (2018) – may be the most ambitious and innovative work of autobiografiction produced in recent years. The novel consists of a series of episodes concerning a woman teaching a writing course in Athens. The protagonist, who is only referred to by name once in each volume and closely resembles Cusk, states that she is 'no longer interested in literature as a form of snobbery or even self-definition. [. . .] What I knew personally to be true had come to seem unrelated to the process of persuading others' (2014: 19). All that the reader learns about the protagonist in the text that follows comes from a series of conversations; despite the first-person narration, the writer is only defined in opposition to other, more fully developed characters. Cusk both completes the process of authorial abdication and self-effacement found in Coetzee and at the same time reasserts the power and control of the writing self. The protagonist chooses to live 'a life as unmarked by self-will as possible', on the grounds that all desire leads to an artificial vision (170). At the same time, however, by voicing these concerns, the protagonist, or Cusk, comes to find a new way of considering the relation between self and others. As she describes watching a family of strangers on a boat:

> I was beginning to see my own fears and desires manifested outside myself, was beginning to see in other people's lives a commentary on my own. [. . .] Those people were living in their moment, and though I could see it I could no more return to that moment than I could walk across the water that separated us. And of those two ways of living – living in the moment and living outside it – which was the more real?
>
> (75)

The 'real', Cusk implies, is not necessarily located in experience, nor is it dependent on the desires of an individual self. Instead the real is located somewhere else, a place that may be approached in the intersection of text and self, but which can never be reached. This radical turn from realist conventions allows Cusk to present a text in which the relation between author and protagonist is not only opaque, but ultimately irrelevant. As much as the text appears to be autobiographical, the reader's impulse to connect events with real world experience is rendered futile. Instead, Cusk constructs a genuinely hybrid form of memoir and novel that foregrounds Shields's desired 'blur of the real'.

Each of the texts discussed above wrestles not only with the question of how best to relate the reality of individual experience, but also with the impossibility of creating something original within generic conventions. As Lars Iyer bemoans at the beginning of his trilogy of comic, philosophical autobiografictions, when faced with 'literature itself', '[w]hat could we do, simple apes, but exhaust ourselves in imitation' (2011: 19). Each of these authors uses the constraints and expectations of both the memoir and novel as a catalyst for creating a new form and ultimately, perhaps, a new sense of realism. Similar experiments can be found in a variety of other works; Lydia Davis's autobiografictional short stories, for instance, challenge the reader's preconceptions of the amount of context and setting required for narrative. Such experimentation is not limited to the Anglophone world: as well as the tremendous success of Knausgaard's texts, similar approaches can be found in the work of the French novelist Frédéric Beigbeder and the continued popularity of the Japanese 'I-novel'. Generic distinctions are also been blurred between memoir and criticism in Kate Zambreno's *Heroines* (2012) and between fiction and criticism in Ali Smith's *Artful* (2012)The growth of the graphic novel has further collapsed distinctions, most particularly in Alison Bechdel's *Are You My Mother?* (2012), which combines elements of memoir, literary criticism, and psychoanalytic theory all in graphic form. Each of these authors displays a dissatisfaction with received ideas of realism and genre. Each highlights the extent to which any idea of realism is insufficient, and to which every individual text must create its own strategy for combining the autobiographical and the fictional.

As Saunders concludes his study of autobiografictional texts, such work challenges the basis of a separation between fiction and nonfiction: autobiografiction is not only the recognition that autobiography and fiction each incorporate aspects of the other, 'but is also the recognition that they are inseparable; and that they have been since the beginning' (2012: 526). Such work highlights contemporary anxieties concerning the nature of the 'real', but also can function as a panacea. Each of these texts suggests an individual locus of the real, but also makes the question of the real into a shared experience between the author, text, and reader. As Knausgaard summarises the autobiografictional dilemma at the close of *A Man in Love*:

> Language is shared, we grow into it, and the forms we use it in are also shared, so irrespective of how idiosyncratic you and your notions are, in literature you can never free yourself from others. It is the other way round, it is literature which draws us closer together. Through its language, which none of us owns and which indeed we can hardly have any influence on, and through its form, which no one can break free of alone, and if anyone should do so, it is only meaningful if it is immediately followed by others. Form draws you out of yourself, distances you from yourself, and it is this distance which is the prerequisite for closeness to others.
>
> (2013: 496)

The creation of a new genre, or a new language for realism, necessarily refers back to earlier models which have themselves often proved insufficient. Yet in demonstrating the extent to which every text is free to negotiate these boundaries, autobiografictional work requires a personal response from the reader that takes account of both aesthetic and ethical ambiguities. These suggest that there is no meaning, and perhaps no reality, other than that which is shared: whatever 'realism' might mean in the twenty-first century, it can only be reached through the active collaboration of text, author, and reader.

Works cited

Coetzee, J. M. (1992) *Doubling the Point: J.M. Coetzee, Essays and Interviews*, ed. D. Attwell, Cambridge, MA: Harvard University Press.

—— (1998) *Boyhood: Scenes from Provincial Life*, London: Vintage.

—— (1999) *The Lives of Animals*, ed. Amy Gutmann, Princeton: Princeton University Press.

—— (2003) *Youth*, London: Vintage.

—— (2004) *Elizabeth Costello*, London: Vintage.

—— (2006) *Slow Man*, London: Vintage.

—— (2008) *Diary of a Bad Year*, London: Vintage.

—— (2010) *Summertime: Scenes from Provincial Life*, London: Vintage.

Crosbie, L. (2012) *Life Is about Losing Everything*, Toronto: House of Anansi.

Cusk, R. (2012) *Aftermath: On Marriage and Separation*, London: Faber.

—— (2014) *Outline*, London: Faber.

Eakin, P. J. (1985) *Fictions in Autobiography: Studies in the Art of Self-Invention*, Princeton: Princeton University Press.

Ellis, B. E. (2005) *Lunar Park*, London: Picador.

Frye, N. (1971) *Anatomy of Criticism: Four Essays*, Princeton: Princeton University Press.

Hawkins, J. (2006) 'Afterword: Theoretical Fictions', in C. Kraus, *I Love Dick*, Los Angeles: Semiotext(e), 263–277.

Heti, S. (2013) *How Should a Person Be?*, London: Harvill Secker.

Iyer, L. (2011) *Spurious*, New York: Melville House.

Jones, E. H. (2010) 'Autofiction: A Brief History of a Neologism', in R. Bradford (ed.), *Life Writing: Essays on Autobiography, Biography and Literature*, Basingstoke: Palgrave Macmillan, 174–184.

Knausgaard, K. O. (2013) *A Man in Love: My Struggle: 2*, trans. D. Bartlett, London: Vintage.

Lejeune, P. (1989) *On Autobiography*, ed. P. J. Eakin, trans. K. Leary, Minneapolis: University of Minnesota Press.

Marcus, L. (1994) *Auto/Biographical Discourses: Theory, Criticism, Practice*, Manchester: Manchester University Press.

Miller, N. K. (2007) 'The Entangled Self: Genre Bondage in the Age of the Memoir', *PMLA* 122.2: 539–548.

Mills, C. (2004) 'Friendship, Fiction, and Memoir: Trust and Betrayal in Writing from One's Own Life', in P. J. Eakin (ed.), *The Ethics of Life Writing*, Ithaca and London: Cornell University Press, 101–120.

Myles, E. (2010) *Inferno (A Poet's Novel)*, New York: OR Books.

Reynolds, S. (1906) 'Autobiografiction', *The Speaker: The Liberal Review* 15.366: 28–30.

Saunders, M. (2012) *Self Impression: Life-Writing, Autobiografiction, and the Forms of Modern Literature*, Oxford: Oxford University Press.

Self, W. (2010) *Walking to Hollywood: Memories of before the Fall*, London: Bloomsbury.

Shields, D. (2010) *Reality Hunger: A Manifesto*, London: Hamish Hamilton.

Wood, J. (2012) 'True Lives', *The New Yorker* (25 June), www.newyorker.com/magazine/2012/06/25/true-lives-2, accessed 24 December, 2014.

5

EXPERIMENT

Jennifer Hodgson

'Are we ready for a new generation of experimental fiction?' asked literary critic and novelist Lee Rourke in 2008 (Rourke 2008). During the rash of *fin-de-siècle* literary stock-taking that appeared during the first decade of the new millennium, the answer seemed to be, resoundingly: no. The symbolic potency of the turn of a new century, along with the transformative events of its early years – 9/11 (which came to signal the belated and catastrophic point of entry into the new era), the subsequent War on Terror, the 2008 financial crash and its aftermath – all seemed to call for new representational strategies capable of articulating a new and radically different kind of real. The increasing awareness that the rise of digital cultures may well signal a new and distinct phase of late modernity and a growing recognition of the waning of the postmodern project also seemed to demand novelistic innovations that might attest to the continuing relevance of an ancient and venerable tradition. But as the forms and functions of twenty-first-century fiction and the role of the writer were speculated upon, the outlook for experiment amongst what was only then beginning to be periodised as 'post-millennial fiction' was not good.

During the first decade of the new millennium, there was an abiding sense amongst literary intellectuals that the halcyon days of fictional innovation were long past. A picture emerged of an archetypal Anglophone – but more specifically British – novel: complacent, innocuous and socially impotent, it was perceived as being dominated by the realist forms of the past, still shackled to an outdated liberal humanist worldview. In 2012, the novelist Colm Tóibín described Britain's literary output as monopolised by novels that were 'well made, low on ambition and filled with restraint, taking [their] bearings from a world that Philip Larkin made in his own image' (Tóibín 2012). The same year, China Miéville argued that the 'culturally dominant strain of the English novel has for years been . . . the remorseless prioritisation of recognition over estrangement' (Miéville 2012). The troubled category of 'literary fiction' was judged to have fossilised into near self-parody. It had become dominated by, as Will Self writes in 2008, 'jolly good reads' that double as ethical heuristics, and which depict the trials and tribulations of a 'morally vacillating protagonist' before culminating neatly with their 'almost mandatory redemption' (Self 2012).

Whilst some literary intellectuals lamented the non-appearance of new forms to give shape to the lived present and respond to newly emergent political possibilities, others raised more fundamental doubts. Many were sceptical about the capacity for the novel, a literary form long privileged with making sense of our lives and our selves, to reflect the way we live now in a post-industrial, neo-corporate, globally connected world – still less to fulfil its traditional role (as Raymond Williams had argued) of court of human appeal. David Shields' epoch-defining manifesto *Reality Hunger* (2010) argues that a deep and abiding need for the real is ill-served by mainstream fiction's 'pretense [*sic*] of actuality' (Shields 2010: 30). He instead proposes a multitude of alternatives, including literary modes such as life writing and the lyric essay that are, he argues, capable of containing raw and unmediated 'chunks of "reality"' (ibid.: 1). Other critics called into question the appropriateness of those logics of disruption and subversion frequently associated with experimental writing, given the perceived failure of the artistic and cultural interventions made by postmodernism. They tentatively identified a move away from postmodern modes of scepticism, deconstruction and self-reflexive irony, towards new fictional registers of sincerity and authenticity. The new was framed as a return to realism, be it hysterical, hyper-, specula-tive, contested, problematised, paranoid, critical or dirty.[1] In a now-infamous 2002 polemic, the American novelist Jonathan Franzen inveighed against literary experiment's traditional role as a form of political opposition. Making a plea for the pleasures of 'self-expression', 'communication' and 'connectedness' as the bases of the novel's continuing relevance, he argues that 'as the decades pass . . . the notion of formal experimentation as an act of resistance . . . begins to seem seriously misconceived' (Franzen 2002).

However, as we have settled into the new millennium, it seems that literary experiment has, to a certain extent, been welcomed in from the cold. Eimear McBride's scarcely recuperable novel of phenomenological, semi-expressionist rendition, *A Girl Is a Half-Formed Thing* (2013), with its private language and broken syntax, became the multi-award-winning, rapturously received toast of British book culture – advertised on the sides of buses, no less. Relatedly, the advent of a twenty-first-century modernism, called for by Gabriel Josipovici's *What Ever Happened to Modernism?* (2010) and manifested in the work of Tom McCarthy, recent novels by Will Self, and McBride, is being debated within the books pages of the broadsheets. And beyond the timely re-emergence – or arguably the new recognition of the continuity – of older forms, commentators are also beginning to point to new lines in fictional narrative. A significant tendency can be identified in the innovative writing of emerging Anglo-American authors including Ned Beauman, Adam Thirlwell, Rachel Kushner, Teju Cole, Ben Lerner, Evie Wyld, Lee Rourke and Lars Iyer, amongst others. These writers are variously affiliated through their antipathy toward 'the literary' and novelistic convention. Amongst their works we see the abandonment of novelistic irony in favour of a predominant mode of sincerity, undercut by affective flattening and (as prophesised by Shields) a tendency to blur the lines between the fictional, the essayistic and the autobiographical.

Elsewhere, book culture is beginning to grasp the nettle of digital media. One of the most prominent (and most controversial) outcrops of new experimental writing, particularly in the United States, is that associated with 'Alt Lit'. This hazily defined community of born-digital writers, small presses and lit blogs includes amongst its most prominent figures Tao Lin, Sheila Heti and Noah Cicero.[2] The broader impact of digital media upon the novel is noticeable too; mainstream book culture has been challenged and shows signs of being transformed by a lively literary counterculture that has in part flourished online. New and emerging indie publish-ers such as And Other Stories, Melville House, Galley Beggars Press and Fitzcarraldo Editions, together with offshoot imprints, such as Faber Finds, have seized the opportunities provided by digital technology for new methods of distribution, funding and publicity, crowd-sourcing the editorial process, and funding books via subscription models. The success, for example, of *Swimming Home* (And Other Stories), Deborah Levy's mesmeric 2011 novel about the brittle-ness of domestic life, or of McBride's *A Girl Is A Half-Formed Thing* (Galley Beggars) (which famously spent nine years in mainstream publishers' slush piles) is testament to readers' appetite for innovation. As McBride herself has commented, their ability to meet the challenge posed by so-called 'difficult' novels (and their willingness to do so) has been consistently underestimated (Cochrane 2014).

This sense of a revitalised literary scene that is open to and curious about the new is evident in other areas too. Not insubstantial audiences have coalesced around lit blogs and magazines like *n+1*, *The White Review*, *Triple Canopy* and *The New Inquiry*. Increasingly, literary innovation is also being nurtured and recognised by new literary awards, such as the Goldsmiths and Folio prizes. Moreover, demand for fiction in translation, which has long been an embarrassing blind spot in monolingual Anglophone literary cultures, is now booming (thanks in part to 'Nordic Noir'). This has drawn new attention to an older generation of writers such as the South Americans Roberto Bolaño and Clarice Lispector and the Italian Elena Ferrente, as well as younger authors, like the Norwegian Karl Ove Knausgaard, and the South Korean Han Kang. Similarly, the short story, which has tended to be, at times, derided as the novel's inferior relation, has undergone a renaissance. Veteran writers like Lydia Davis and George Saunders have recently enjoyed late-coming commercial success and critical recognition.

The impetus to look back as well as forwards for innovative and ambitious writing is also evident in the new attention that has been brought to bear on forgotten corners of literary history. The significance of neglected British experimental writers of the sixties for example, such as B.S. Johnson, Ann Quin, Christine Brooke-Rose and Brigid Brophy, has been reassessed in recent years. Clearly, then, as Miéville comments in characteristic style, 'it is not quite qliphothic [meaning emptied out, or husk-like] business as usual' (ibid.). Does all of this signal, then, a genuine renaissance of experiment amongst the emergent forms of twenty-first-century fiction?

★★★

Contingent, slippery and often troubled, the term 'experiment' remains a contested one. It is loose to the point of unwieldy, describing neither a periodisable aesthetic movement, nor a recognisable aggregate of aesthetic practises. Instead it designates a more complex and apparently paradoxical (in Harold Rosenberg's words) 'tradition of the new' (Rosenberg 1971). In use, its meaning hovers uncertainly between a sense of vitalising replenishment implied by one of its synonyms, *innovation* and a more challenging affront to the mainstream indicated by another, *avant-garde*. Whilst recognising what may turn out to be a modest renaissance for experiment in fiction, it is crucial to note that although the experimental novel's stock seems to have risen of late, it never really went away. Mainstream accounts, tempered by their obligations to categorisation, periodisation and positioning, almost always rehearse a version of literary history that is far less richly variegated than the realities of literary production.[3] But still, today, to speak of an 'experimental novel' seems like a quaint anachronism, given that the non-linearity, chronological displacement, fragmentary selves, metafictional self-consciousness, multi-modality and trans-mediality that were the markers of twentieth-century experiment are seen up and down fiction best-seller lists (in the work, for example, of Ali Smith, David Mitchell, Jon McGregor amongst others). If the innovations of previous eras have now been assimilated into the mainstream, can there be anything left for experiment to overturn, problematise or otherwise have its wicked way with?

Despite its manifest associations with aesthetic newness, vitality, originality and innovation, the term 'experiment' has often tended to be more frequently employed to identify a backwards-looking quality within innovative writing: the emulative gesture, the homage to long-neglected forms or the retreat into aesthetic introversion. In the recent resurgence of debates about the forms and functions of fiction, literary experiment has tended to be situated as an adjunct to concerns about the appropriateness of realistic writing for giving literary form to contemporary experience. Zadie Smith's timely and influential essay on the future of fiction in English laments that '[t]hese aren't particularly healthy times' (Smith 2008). She goes on to argue that a 'breed of lyrical Realism' that amounts to a 'perfectly done' but inauthentic image 'of what we have been taught to value in fiction' has 'had the freedom of the highway for some time now with most other exits blocked' (ibid.). Other recent accounts have, like Smith's, tended to set up an opposition between a detached, obscure and aloof experimentalism, overshadowed by the towering legacies of modernism – 'a heroic bivouac on the edge of a civilisation in denial' (Parks 2013) as Tim Parks recently put it – and an ailing but liberal and humane tradition of realist fiction.[4]

In the terms and the tenor of these current debates we can identify a return to anxieties artic-ulated, perhaps most prominently but by no means for the first time, in the 'death of the novel' controversies of the 1960s and 1970s. During the period, novelists were perceived to confront a markedly similar dilemma to the one described by present-day commentators – the 'crossroads' famously imagined by David Lodge, for example, between the central thoroughfare of realistic writing and the side alleys of experiment has been almost directly reprised by Smith (Lodge 1978). The precedent is an important, and yet often overlooked, one.[5] For the innovative novel-ists of that era, the perceived moribundity of the novel signalled not the exhaustion of the form itself, but of a dominant mode of realistic narrative, and provided the impetus for an extraordi-nary flowering of experimental energies – which is evident in the work of sixties authors whose significance (as I note above) is only now being recognised. And similarly, the writing of the twenty-first-century is beginning to demonstrate that this latest iteration of concerns about the novel's demise should by no means be a cause for despair – and may well signal a kind of rebirth.

Nevertheless, such attitudes beg important questions: how do writers go about making the 'new of old' new again, what might be the rationale for such a project? And relatedly: is the fic-tion of the twenty-first-century capable of moving beyond the gestures of literary homage that Tom McCarthy has criticised as the 'nineteenth-century novel with a few Joycean knobs on' (James 2012: 40)? Can such writing truly rehabilitate and revivify the experimental forms and stylistic gambits of the past? In part, what follows will explore some of the ways in which inno-vative writers of the twenty-first-century are navigating the legacies of successive incursions of literary experimentation and will consider the ways in which the innovative strategies of previous generations are being fruitfully deployed within new climates and to new ends. But in equal measure, it will look to how contemporary writers are finding new ways to challenge the novel's history. And how, in doing so, they are moving beyond both the reinvention and inward-looking interrogation of older forms, to tentatively re-envision new possibilities for the novel.

Perhaps the most notable instance of the re-emergence of past innovations in present-day lit-erary fiction has been the growth of interest in literary modernism amongst novelists and critics alike. Whilst critics such as Mikhail Epstein, Laura Marcus and others have identified a return to modernist forms,[6] others such as Josipovici, McCarthy and Neil Levi have drawn upon Alain Badiou's designation of the 'event' as a sudden rupture in normal circumstances that opens up a space of political and aesthetic possibility to argue for the ongoing relevance of modernism as an unfinished project. To ignore the modernist avant-garde, claims McCarthy, 'is the equivalent of ignoring Darwin' (Purdon 2010). Levi proposes, following Badiou, that twenty-first-century modernism is 'modernist differently' (Levi 2009: 120), that it does 'not anachronistically . . . imitate modernist models but . . . see[s] modernist works as events whose implications demand continued investigation' (ibid.). McBride's *A Girl is a Half-formed Thing* is one example of the 'differently modern' – a contemporary novel which engages with and extends modernist modes in order to reinvent and reinvigorate them. The narrative, a bildungsroman parody, plumbs the subterranean depths of a teenage girl's psychic collapse. In the novel, to be born a girl is to be exiled in girlhood, slung out into a 'vinegar world' as a disembodied, disassociated and fragile kernel of a self (McBride 2013: 5). It is from here that the strange, self-abnegating voice of the narrative emanates, registering in her own private language a barrage of sense-perceptions from an ever-encroaching external world. The novel's story of abuse, trauma and religious fanaticism in Catholic Ireland, in the recent but distant-seeming past, is rendered via allusive fragments, condensed syntax, mingled voices and compound words – readers have to work to parse its horror.

Critics have been quick to locate modernist precedents for McBride's novel: primarily Joyce, but also Faulkner and Beckett.[7] But *Girl* . . . is not simply a virtuosic rehearsal of the familiar modernist means of capturing the mind and fixing it on the page. Accounts of the novel have been slower to situate it within a rich tradition of women's experimental writing from the modernist period and beyond. There are very direct echoes here with the literary impressionism of Gertrude Stein and her sensitivity to what Ellen G. Friedman and Miriam Fuchs call the '"wordness" of words' (Friedman and Fuchs 2014: 15). There are further resonances with Virginia Woolf's phenomenological renderings of the perceptual imagination and with Julia Kristeva's ideas about the archaic origins of the self and of language. Perhaps most of all, the novel recalls the struggle, seen in the work of Ann Quin, to recover the presence of a radically different mode of experience within the parameters of a communal language. The surprise success of *Girl* . . . is perhaps because it so audaciously captures the mood of the moment, connecting this literary tradition with the recent emergence of a fourth-wave feminism. McBride draws upon and transforms a modernist inheritance in order to respond to timely questions, such as: how can we speak about the unspeakable aspects of female experience? And how can we create a new language with which to do so? On the one hand, there is now scepticism about the romantic valorisation of the feminine as a politically necessary position of radical marginality that has been offered by previous incursions of feminist thought (French feminism, second-wave feminism). On the other, post-feminism's erasure of difference and strategic embrace of the illusion of equality, has also been called into question – not least in recent discourse surrounding privilege and intersectionality. In such a climate, how can we develop a kind of feminine demotic which is capable of capturing, preserving and, crucially, communicating the contents of those experiences? As such, the novel goes some way to answering Jacqueline Rose's recent call for a 'bold, scandalous feminism' (Rose 2014). This feminism, Rose argues powerfully, will entail the creation of a 'new language' that at once 'allows women to claim their place in the world' but also 'burrows beneath its surface to confront the subterranean aspects of history and the human mind, which our dominant political vocabularies most often cannot bear to face' (ibid.). Many other new, innovative fictions by women, including Levy's *Swimming Home*, Claire Louise Bennett's *Pond* (2015); Sheila Heti's *How Should a Person Be?* (2013); Zoe Pilger's *Eat My Heart Out* (2014) and Rachel Kushner's *The Flamethrowers* (2013), also inhabit this space of productive tension. Like *Girl* . . ., these works are driven to present the female subject as a coherent and powerful agent in the world, whilst at once emphasising the provisionality of such a position and simultaneously using this position to voice experiences of oppression and disempowerment.[8]

In such ways, authors like McBride engage with a modernist inheritance as a rich, generative point of departure for present-day literary innovation. Elsewhere, however, the attempt to reach past previous experimental strategies and the problematic legacies of twentieth-century thought is evident; these have seemingly hardened into new orthodoxies to be resisted, subverted and somehow moved beyond. The restless apathete narrator of Adam Thirlwell's *Kapow!* (2012), for example, admits his preference for the 'irony of counter-revolution' over the fruitless negation of political engagement (Thirlwell 2012: 11), which merely amounts to lurching between 'one thing, then the opposite, then the opposite of the opposite' (5). Postmodern claims about the fictiveness of all truths, he reflects, have become a 'convention' that is 'too convenient': 'The real! The real could never be described. I knew all about the scepticism. I'd grown up with it' (16). Residually distrustful of narratives, but nonetheless seeking a framework with which to corral a proliferation of 'content', the narrator commits an act of wilful cultural appropriation by embarking upon the Borgesian task of writing his own Arabic novel about the Arab Spring. 'I didn't see why you couldn't become international', he comments, 'the era was world-historical, so why not, then, dip into what Salman Rushdie refers to as the "sea of stories", pick one at will and tell it as your own?' (17). Indeed, the novel's exploded format, with its concertinaed pages and embedded marginalia flowing in multiple directions, is a kind of formal pastiche of the epic, nation-building ambition that characterises extended narratives like Rushdie's. This novel's scale and multiplicity mimics ironically the attempt by such totalising fictions to find new ways to panoramically capture the broad sweep of life. *Kapow!* is a kind of psychomachia reflecting the globalised consciousness' hyper-connected estrangement and hyper-informed ignorance. Thirlwell's myriad digressions, his self-conscious refusal of the authorial functions of selection and organisation, reflect the dizzying complexity and inscrutability of his ostensible subject:

> You never know which facts turn out to be real. That's why you need to keep on thinking as much detail as possible. There's no point adding in lianas and tendrils of your own to this jungle and outback. You have to try to keep looking – as everything splits into its infinite directions.
>
> (52–53)

'It would really take a great epic poet to describe the events that we were witnessing', notes cab-driver Faryaq, whose story about his friends in Egypt provides the basis for – but quickly becomes entirely secondary to – a fabulation of the narrator's own invention, '[i]t would take a very great writer indeed'. (12) Thirlwell, of course, is not that writer, and this is – gleefully, carousingly – not that book. But neither is it the meditation in fiction upon whether such a book is possible that we have come to expect from previous strains of the self-scrutinising novel. Instead, *Kapow!* functions as a kind of *reductio ad absurdum* of storytelling, in a 'post-truth' era so unimpeachably incredulous that it is sceptical even of its own scepticism.

Ben Lerner's *Leaving the Atocha Station* is another recent novel that takes as one of its themes the reassessment of how literature can perform ethical and political work. In the opening passages of the novel protagonist Adam (another ill-made malcontent) encounters a man 'los[ing] his shit' in front of the artworks at Madrid's Prado Gallery (Lerner 2011: 9). Adam wonders incredulously whether the man is 'having a *profound experience of art*' (8, italics his). He finds this impossible to believe; the 'closest [he'd] come to having a profound experience of art' was a 'profound experience of the absence of profundity' (9). At length, Adam decides the man must be a 'great artist' and the whole episode a spectacle designed to enact a critique of artistic institutions (10). He too is undertaking such a performance. Adam is in Madrid on a prestigious fellowship, focusing upon the representation of the civil war in Spanish poetry, and yet he knows very little about either. He draws upon a mish-mash of part-digested late-twentieth-century avant-garde theorisations of writerly engagement and commitment in order to justify this quandary as a valid and productive artistic gesture. The renunciation and evasion of his position as a writer, he argues, is a performance that enacts the absurdity of such a position:

> If I was a poet, I had become one because poetry, more intensely than any other practice, could not evade its own anachronism and marginality, and so constituted a kind of acknowledgment of my own preposterousness, admitting my bad faith in good faith, so to speak. I could lie about my interest in the literary response to war because by making a mockery of the notion that literature could be commensurate with mass murder I was not defaming victims of the latter, but the dilettantes of the former, rejecting the

political claims repeatedly made by the so-called left for a poetry radical only in its unpopularity.

(101)

However, the paucity and crudity of this response is underlined a few pages later. Following the terrorist attack upon Madrid's Atocha train station, Adam suggests to his gallerist friend Arturo that he should cover the gallery's exhibits 'with a black cloth as a memorial, a visual moment of silence' (121) that would appropriately acknowledge the incommensurability of art and atrocity. At the exhibition opening, as attendees look 'long and thoughtfully' at the covered paintings 'as if they weren't covered', both Adam and his not-quite lover, Teresa, ponder simultaneously whether 'any of them will sell' (124). The strategies of negation and silence, which were elevated during the sixties and seventies as the ultimate avant-gardist gesture, have become co-opted and commodified as a kind of ghoulish commercial cache.

Lerner's novel, like Thirlwell's, then, asserts the necessity of a fresh departure in fictional writing that moves beyond what they perceive as the jaundiced, atrophied and corrupted interrogation of the conditions of its own possibilities of meaning. In one essayistic digression, Adam reflects upon the poems of John Ashbery, noting that they are 'written [as if] on the other side of a mirrored surface, and you saw only the reflection of your reading', and 'this keeps the virtual possibilities of poetry intact because the true poem remains beyond you, inscribed on the far side of the mirror' (91). However, there is the sense throughout this novel that what Adam relishes initially as the 'ability to dwell among possible referents, to let them interfere and separate like waves, to abandon the law of excluded middle' (14) is, at least for fiction, no longer sufficient.

★★★

In their recent study, *The Good of the Novel* (2011), Liam McIlvanney and Ray Ryan attempt to identify the novel's special claim to knowledge, arguing that '[n]ovelistic truth . . . has to do with character' and 'the novel's key strength is the disclosure of interiority' (McIlvanney and Ryan 2011: xii). But when the narrator of *Kapow!* admits that he is 'doubting this thing called I very much' (Thirlwell 2012: 12), or the protagonist of *Leaving the Atocha Station* asks '[w]ho wasn't squatting in one of the handful of prefabricated subject positions . . . [and] lying every time she said "I"' (Lerner 2011: 101), they express a vision of the self evinced throughout some of the most interesting twenty-first-century writing. The notion of a deep interior – and the subsequent nostalgia for this idea of the self – that can be said to have characterised twentieth-century fiction, has given way to a concept of the self which is no longer even minimal. It is far less substantial than that: ephemeral, devoid of essence, presence or unity. The Indian writer Pankaj Mishra has commented upon the ways in which 'global citizenship' – and with it the 'loss of the knowable small world' – has engendered a new 'crisis of the subject' in which that which was previously felt as an 'abstract philosophical problem' has become an 'urgently existential' one (Shamsie and Mishra 2014).

These are fictions which describe a world where the real has already been thoroughly managed and mediated. Here characters confront the challenge of situating themselves in relation to a world made strange by unanthropomorphisable hypercapitalist and technocratic forces. Both Adam in *Leaving the Atocha Station* and the narrator of *Kapow!* self-medicate with cocktails of uppers and downers – hash, caffeine, various pharmaceuticals – in an attempt to mitigate the experience of an increasingly phantasmagoric reality. It becomes clear over the course of Lerner's novel that the subject of Adam's research is in fact himself, and the aim of his project is to artificially synthesise a sense of self-presence or what Sartre calls 'ipseity': a sense of selfhood, that is, of fundamental self-givenness. Although eager to 'create the impression that I was . . . busy accumulating experience' (19) for friends back home, Adam's experience is almost always confined to the experience of experience itself. He lives in a state of the subjunctive: '[i]n retrospect, I would find this beautiful' (123) he notes at one point. His own witnessing of the aftermath of the Atocha bombing is interposed by the 'newspaper accounts modifying and replacing [his] memory of what [he'd] seen' (119). But, given the correct combination of white and yellow pills and the right slant of afternoon sun, Adam is able to access the sense of 'equilibrium' he could not grasp at the Prado: 'a small wave of euphoria would break over me . . . I would begin to feel a rush of what I considered love' (15).

There are similar stakes in Tom McCarthy's *Remainder*, which, like Lerner's novel, is in part a disquisition upon the place of art in a commodified world. The novel's narrator, having suffered an unspecified accident, finds himself having to relearn the life functions that used to be second nature and in the process, all that was previously a given is suddenly made strange. He recalls:

> I closed my fingers around the carrot. It felt – well, it *felt*; that was enough to start short-circuiting the operation. It had texture; it had mass. The whole week I'd been gearing up to lift it, I'd thought of my hands, my fingers, my rerouted brain as active agents, and the carrot as a nothing – a hollow, a carved space for me to grasp and move. This carrot though was more active than me: the way it bumped and wrinkled; how it crawled with grit.
>
> (McCarthy 2011: 20)

If repetition is the means by which walking, lighting a cigarette – or holding a carrot – become intuitive, he deduces, then perhaps it is also the means by which he can re-attune himself to the world. Perhaps, at length, he would be able to remove what he calls 'the detour': the self-reflexive awareness that now precedes his experience. Using his accident compensation, he hires a phalanx of networked agents, facilitators, project managers and special effects workers to painstakingly reconstruct scenes half-remembered from his past. He cannot help but fail to recover their presence, but in the process he apprehends the presence of something else. The real takes on a new cast; things have an 'almost toxic level of significance' and there is 'something excessive about [their] sheer presence, something overwhelming' (13).

McCarthy's novel is about narrative form as a kind of consolation – its capacity to make sense of a world that is now beyond our ken – that undoes itself as it reveals the losses and holes in the real. A similar presence is also glimpsed in Lerner's novel. In one of the many self-conscious non-sequiturs of *Leaving the Atocha Station*, Adam reflects that '[t]hese periods of rain or periods in between rains in which I was smoking and reading Tolstoy would be . . . impossible to narrate' (63). But it is precisely those in-between times to which the novel turns its attention and where, for Lerner, the texture of the real is found. Intermittently throughout the novel, but especially in its closing passages, the narrative voice suddenly takes a lyrical, hyper-referential, occasionally marxisant, quasi-cut-up turn. He returns repeatedly to a description of '*that other thing* . . . life's white machine, shadows massing in the distance . . . the texture of et cetera itself'. (16) Here too in the failure of the narrative function – the absence of a sense of meaningful time and significant events – is found the real that eludes conventional narrative. Similarly, the staged formal breakdown of Thirlwell's novel reveals a story that is smaller but more profound in scope. 'All this is, after all', the narrator admits, 'is a small exploded story, just a place, like one of Rauschenberg's combines, where some things happen' (80).

Teju Cole, in a recent profile in the *New York Times*, comments that '"the novel" is overrated . . . the writers I find most interesting find ways to escape it' (Cole 2014). However, it seems that many of the emerging innovative writers of the twenty-first-century are not quite so ready to abscond. For these writers the idea that the novel, in its traditional form, is no longer fit for purpose is now a given. But their works seek to demonstrate that the failure and malfunctioning of its narrative principles and conventions can still perform important work. This is metafiction – but not as we know it. Twenty-first-century literary experiment continues to draw upon the self-metaphorising capacities of the novel to propose that if contemporary life is already beyond belief, if the truth is already stranger than fiction, then perhaps (at last) it is to fiction that we should turn, in order to experience the feeling of the real.

Notes

1 Such coinages emerged in essays including James Wood's 'Human, All Too Inhuman' (Wood 2000) and Peter Ackroyd's 'The English Novel Now' (Ackroyd 2001).
2 Although, as with most critical attempts to christen and therefore concretise emergent literary tendencies, the accuracy and the usefulness of this term is debatable – and has generally been promptly disputed by the diverse coterie of writers to whom it has been applied. See, for example, Allie Jones, 'Alt Lit is Dead and Its Women Writers Are Creating Their Own Scene' (Jones 2014) – amongst many others.
3 Elsewhere, Patricia Waugh and I have traced the 'hidden' continuities of an ongoing tradition of experiment in fictional narrative that far exceeds pre-existing accounts of the so-called inward turn of modernism, or the turning inside out of fictional convention in the postmodern, or the double perspectivism of the post-colonial (Waugh and Hodgson 2013).
4 See also, for example, the novelist Lars Iyer's essay 'Nude in Your Hot Tub Facing the Abyss (A literary manifesto after the end of Literature and Manifestos)' (Iyer 2011).
5 It has also been noted by David James in an essay exploring the contemporary relevance of Iris Murdoch's conceptualisation of the 'crystalline novel' (James 2012).
6 Contemporary writers, Marcus argues, are increasingly appealing to modernist forms as 'spaces in and through which questions of art, life and value can be reposed and reconfigured' (Marcus 2007: 82). Mikhail Epstein has theorised a return to the concepts of modernity with the prefix *trans-* (Epstein 1995).
7 See, amongst many others, James Wood, 'Useless Prayers' (Wood 2014). McBride too has acknowledged her debt to Joyce: 'reading *Ulysses* really set [her] world on its end' (McBride 2014).
8 Levy, in a recent extended essay *Things I Don't Want to Know* (Levy 2013: 26) encapsulates the predicament of the twenty-first-century woman writer thus:

> When a female writer walks a female character into the centre of her literary enquiry (or a forest) and this character starts to project shadow and light all over the place, she will have to find a language that is in part to do with learning how to become a subject rather than a delusion, and in part to do with unknotting the ways in which she has been put together by the Societal System in the first place. She will have to be canny about doing this because she will have many delusions of her own. In fact it would be best if she was uncanny when she sets about doing this. It's exhausting to learn how to become a subject, it's hard enough learning how to become a writer.

Works cited

Ackroyd, P. 'The English Novel Now.' In *The Collection*, 321–327. London: Chatto and Windus, 2001.
Cochrane, K. 'Eimear McBride: "There Are Serious Readers Who Want to Be Challenged".' *Guardian*, June 5, 2014. Accessed August 22, 2014. www.theguardian.com/books/2014/jun/05/eimear-mcbride-serious-readers-challenged-baileys-womens-prize
Cole, T. 'Teju Cole: By the Book.' *New York Times Sunday Book Review*, March 6, 2014. Accessed March 30, 2014. www.nytimes.com/2014/03/09/books/review/teju-cole-by-the-book.html.
Epstein, M. *After the Future: The Paradoxes of Postmodernism and Contemporary Russian Culture.* Amherst, MA: University of Massachusetts Press, 1995.
Franzen, J. 'Mr Difficult: William Gaddis and the Problem of Hard-to-Read Books.' *New Yorker*, September 30, 2002. Accessed July 3, 2011. www.newyorker.com/magazine/2002/09/30/mr-difficult
Friedman, E. G. and M. Fuchs, eds. 'Context and Continuities.' In *Breaking the Sequence: Women's Experimental Fiction.* Princeton, NJ: Princeton University Press, 2014.

Heti, S. *How Should a Person Be?* New York: Random House, 2013.

Iyer, L. 'Nude in Your Hot Tub Facing the Abyss (A Literary Manifesto after the End of Literature and Manifestos).' *The White Review*, November 2011. Accessed March 7, 2012. www.thewhitereview.org/features/nude-in-your-hot-tub-facing-the-abyss-a-literary-manifesto-after-the-end-of-literature-and-manifestos/

James, D. *Modernist Futures: Innovation and Inheritance in the Contemporary Novel.* Cambridge: Cambridge University Press, 2012.

——— 'A Renaissance for the Crystalline Novel?' *Contemporary Literature*, Volume 53, Number 4, Winter 2012, 845–874.

Jones, A. 'Alt Lit is Dead and Its Women Writers Are Creating Their Own Scene,' *Gawker*, October 3, 2014. Accessed October 20, 2014. http://gawker.com/alt-lit-is-dead-and-its-women-writers-are-creating-thei-1642110662

Josipovici, G. *What Ever Happened to Modernism?* London: Yale University Press, 2010.

Lerner, B. *Leaving the Atocha Station.* London: Granta, 2011.

Levi, N. 'Alt Lit is Dead and Its Women Writers Are Creating Their Own Scene,' In *Modernism and Theory: A Critical Debate*, edited by Stephen Ross, 117–126. London: Routledge, 2009.

Levy, D. *Swimming Home.* London: And Other Stories, 2011.

——— *Things I Don't Want to Know.* London: Penguin, 2013.

Lodge, D. 'The Novelist at the Crossroads.' In *The Novel Today*, edited by Malcolm Bradbury. London: Fontana, 1978.

Marcus, L. 'The Legacies of Modernism.' In *The Cambridge Companion to the Modernist Novel*, edited by Morag Shiach, 82–98. Cambridge, Cambridge University Press, 2007.

McBride, E. *A Girl Is a Half-Formed Thing.* Norwich: Gallery Beggars, 2013.

——— 'My Hero: Eimear McBride on James Joyce.' *Guardian*, June 9, 2014. Accessed June 10, 2014. www.theguardian.com/books/2014/jun/06/my-hero-eimear-mcbride-james-joyce

McCarthy, T. *Remainder.* London: Alma Books, 2011.

McIlvanney, L. and R. Ryan, eds. *The Good of the Novel.* London: Faber & Faber 2011.

Miéville, C. 'The Future of the Novel.' *Guardian*, August 21, 2012. Accessed August 22, 2012. www.theguardian.com/books/2012/aug/21/china-mieville-the-future-of-the-novel

Parks, T. 'Trapped Inside the Novel.' *New York Review of Books Blog*, October 28, 2013. Accessed November 3, 2013. www.nybooks.com/blogs/nyrblog/2013/oct/28/novel-trap/

Pilger, Z. *Eat My Heart Out.* London: Serpent's Tail, 2014.

Purdon, J. 'Tom McCarthy: "To Ignore the Avant Garde Is Akin to Ignoring Darwin".' *Observer*, August 1, 2010. Accessed February 14, 2011. www.theguardian.com/books/2010/aug/01/tom-mccarthy-c-james-purdon

Rose, J. 'We Need a Bold, Scandalous Feminism.' *Guardian*, October 17, 2014. Accessed October 20, 2014. www.theguardian.com/books/2014/oct/17/we-need-bold-scandalous-feminism-malala-yousafzai

Rosenberg, H. *The Tradition of the New.* New York: Books for Libraries Press, 1971.

Rourke, L. 'The Return of British Avant Garde Fiction.' *Guardian*, July 14, 2008. Accessed July 27, 2014. www.theguardian.com/books/booksblog/2008/jul/14/post27

Self, W. 'Will Self: Modernism and Me.' *Guardian*, August 3, 2012. Accessed August 22, 2012. www.theguardian.com/books/2012/aug/03/will-self-modernism-and-me

Shamsie, K. and P. Mishra. 'Where's the Rage?' *Guernica*, February 3, 2014. Accessed October 10, 2014. www.guernicamag.com/interviews/wheres-the-rage/

Shields, D. *Reality Hunger: A Manifesto.* London: Hamish Hamilton, 2010.

Smith, Z. 'Two Paths for the Novel.' *New York Review of Books*, November 20, 2008. Accessed July 3, 2011. www.nybooks.com/articles/archives/2008/nov/20/two-paths-for-the-novel/.

Thirwell, A. *Kapow!* London: Visual Editions, 2012.

Tóibín, C. 'Going beyond the Limits.' *New York Review of Books*, May 10, 2012. Accessed June 25, 2012. www.nybooks.com/articles/archives/2012/may/10/julian-barnes-going-beyond-limits.

Waugh, P. and J. Hodgson. 'On the Exaggerated Reports of a Decline in British Fiction.' *The White Review*, Spring 2013.

Wood, J. 'Human, All Too Inhuman.' *New Republic*, July 24, 2000. Accessed March 15 2015. www.newrepublic.com/article/61361/human-all-too-inhuman

——— 'Useless Prayers.' *New Yorker*, September 29, 2014. Accessed October 3, 2014. www.newyorker.com/magazine/2014/09/29/useless-prayers

6

COMEDY

Huw Marsh

Introduction: a funny turn?

This chapter makes a claim for the significance of comedy in contemporary fiction, arguing that it has taken an identifiable funny turn. By funny turn I mean not only that much of the most interesting contemporary writing is funny and that there is a comic tendency in contemporary Anglophone fiction, but also that this humour, this comic license, allows writers of contemporary fiction to do peculiar and interesting things – things that are funny in the sense of odd or strange and which may in turn inspire a funny turn in readers. To have a funny turn is to feel peculiar or light-headed, to feel that something is awry, and at its best and most powerful, comic writing can inspire just such peculiar feelings. In the short stories of George Saunders, for example, humour mingles with horror and pity at the increasingly desperate circumstances of his protagonists. Or in the twisted picaresques of Nicola Barker, comic laughter can move between shock and repulsion, through uneasy recognition to eventual understanding or even identification. And while some may argue over the relative preponderance and merits of US versus UK humour in fiction,[1] it is certainly true to say that much of the most innovative and interesting fiction on both sides of the Atlantic is comic. Any list, and indeed any entry on a subject, is necessarily limiting, but a discussion of the topic could, in addition to the writers already mentioned, include Michael Chabon, Paul Beatty, Magnus Mills, Jennifer Egan, Jonathan Coe, Junot Diaz, Ali Smith, Will Self, Gary Shteyngart and many more besides, along with an even larger body of writers whose work includes comic moments or interludes. Fictional comedy is hard to categorise or codify in the same way as theatrical comedy – this may be one reason why the topic has received comparatively little scholarly attention – but as a working definition I define the comic as that which is designed to be humorous. This necessarily introduces an element of intentionality, but it is important to separate that which is funny because it is intended to be funny from that which is accidentally humorous. There is a significant difference between *I, Partridge* (2011), the 'autobiography' of the fictional radio DJ Alan Partridge, a comic character played by Steve Coogan, and *Poptastic!* (2007), the often unintentionally hilarious autobiography of real-life radio DJ Tony Blackburn: both may inspire laughter, but there is a significant difference in intent.[2]

Despite the preponderance of contemporary fiction which treats serious topics in a comic manner, the funny turn in fiction has received relatively little academic scrutiny, although a number of scholars have made important contributions, including Robin Mookerjee (2013) on the 'new satirists' such as Irvine Welsh, Bret Easton Ellis and Martin Amis (Gregson: 2006), on caricature in contemporary fiction; Michael Ross (2006) on comedy and ethnicity; and Margaret D. Stetz on women's comic fiction (2001). Important earlier contributions include James F. English's *Comic Transactions* (1994) and Gail Finney's collection *Look Who's Laughing: Gender and Comedy* (1994). More often, when it is remarked upon at all the fact that a novel or story is humorous is taken for granted, and yet humour is predicated on an affective response, is identifiable by a particular style or aesthetic, and often speaks to questions of identity and community, inclusion and exclusion, all of which are live debates in the discipline.

The paucity of scholarship in this area is due in part to a series of historical concerns both within the academy and without. In *The Art of Fiction* (1992), for example, David Lodge describes the comic novel as 'a very English, or at least British and Irish, kind of fiction, that does not always travel well'. He goes on to quote John Updike's review of Kingsley Amis's novel *Jake's Thing* (1978), and Updike's dismissive conclusion that Amis suffers from being 'in thrall to the "comic novel"', that 'There is no need to write "funny novels" when life's actual juxtapositions, set down attentively, are comedy enough' (1992: 110). Lodge, a writer of comic novels himself, and understandably somewhat defensive, goes on to list the strength of the comic tradition in both overtly comic fiction (Fielding, Sterne, Smollett, Austen, Dickens, Waugh) and in fiction that contains comic episodes within a structure whose prevailing tone is not necessarily comic (Eliot, Hardy, Forster). These brief comments by Lodge and Updike highlight some of the difficulties inherent in any discussion of comedy and fiction, or in comic fiction more narrowly defined. In Lodge's remarks we see the suggestion of particularity and regionality, even parochialism, followed by a list of precursors that both reinforces this sense of parochialism by naming only British and Irish authors and then stretches the definition of comic novel almost to breaking point. And in Updike's scornful review we can see a suspicion of, even snobbery against, writers who work in a comic tradition; comic fiction is not, it seems, sufficiently literary: rather than being a structure imposed upon fiction, comedy should inhere in the representation of everyday life.

More recently, Howard Jacobson – who, as a writer of comic novels, has his own agenda – again reminded readers of comedy's centrality to the history of the novel. He is similarly dismissive of the term 'comic novelist', finding it 'as redundant and off-putting as the term "literary novelist"', but he makes a strong claim both for the importance of the comic tradition and for its gradual denigration in the literary marketplace and intellectual life more broadly: 'we have created a false division between laughter and thought', he argues, 'between comedy and seriousness, between the exhilaration that the great novels offer when they are at their funniest, and whatever else it is we now think we want from literature' (2010). This 'false division' between comedy and seriousness is perhaps not as pronounced as Jacobson suggests,[3] but his comments, as well as his work in the 1997 book and television series *Seriously Funny*, do gesture towards some further questions faced by both writers *of* comic fiction and those who write *on* comic fiction. For example, how can we treat seriously that which is apparently unserious? And does the distinction between 'comic fiction' and 'literary fiction' impose limits on the text? In the argument which follows I outline some of the ways in which we can address the first of these questions and begin to think about comedy *as comedy* rather than as a light-hearted adjunct to the serious work of literature. My answer to the second question broadly follows those of Updike, Lodge and Jacobson in dismissing the unhelpful term 'comic fiction' or the 'comic novel'. Like many genre classifications, such categories suggest a series of tendencies or rules that fall apart under scrutiny: Henry Fielding, Jane Austen, Charles Dickens, Mark Twain, P.G. Wodehouse, Evelyn Waugh, Thomas Pynchon, Martin Amis, Lydia Davis, David Foster Wallace, all of this disparate list of writers at times write in a comic mode, but it would be hard to identify a series of features that tie them to a particular genre or style. As Andrew Stott suggests, 'comedy is as much a tonal quality as a structural one' (2005: 2) and these authors do not conform to unifying genre tropes. They write what Robert Eaglestone calls 'open' fiction, 'able to cover anything, in any form' (2013: 1098), though they often do so in ways that inspire laughter. Rather than codifying such texts within a set of common traits or structures, it is more profitable to ask what comedy does in these texts and what an understanding of the role of comedy can add to our understanding of fiction. This chapter aims to address these questions and to suggest some of the defining tendencies in contemporary US and UK comedy.

The discussion which follows focuses on three different approaches or frameworks for thinking about three seemingly quite different authors. It aims to suggest not only why these texts are funny but also how they are funny and what the significance of this humour might be. Firstly, it examines the short stories of George Saunders and the ways in which Saunders represents the postmodern workplace as an affective or, in the terminology of Sianne Ngai, 'zany' space. Secondly, it looks at the stylistics of comedy and the ways in which style and humour are bound up with questions of class in the recent fiction of Martin Amis. And thirdly, it looks at the relationship between comedy and community in the fiction of Zadie Smith. These approaches draw from current debates in literary studies (affect studies, the resurgent interest in literary form, and debates about irony and the 'new sincerity' respectively), but are applied to the question of how comedy operates and what an understanding of comedy can add to our understanding of fiction.

Thinking Positive/Saying Positive: the zany workplaces of George Saunders

In his essay 'Mr Vonnegut in Sumatra', George Saunders offers a theory of humour that is in keeping with a writer who specialises in the short story form. 'Humor', he says, 'is what happens when we're told the truth quicker and more directly than we're used to. The comic is the truth stripped of the habitual, the cushioning, the easy consolation' (2009: 80). Comedy does not, on this view, soften or diminish serious topics but rather provides 'rapid-truthing', unencumbered by the niceties and circumlocutions of other modes. Saunders's putative subject is his first encounter, aged twenty three, with Kurt Vonnegut's *Slaughterhouse Five* (1969), and in this section of the essay he focuses on the enlightening effect of following Vonnegut's 'unusual vector' through the topic of war, in which jokes and a sense of the absurd replace the 'usual conceptual packaging we associate with "war" and "soldiers" and "prisoners of war"' (2009: 80). Similarly enlightening was Vonnegut's use of science fiction and the fantastic, a subversion of mimesis that allowed Saunders to see how his own experiences could inform fiction that wasn't strictly realist but which nevertheless contained truths of its own; indeed, *Slaughterhouse-Five* seemed to suggest that 'our most profound experiences may *require* this artistic uncoupling from the actual' (2009: 79). In Saunders's writing this uncoupling from the actual and the rapid-truthing of the comic mode combine in stories that are at once based on a recognisable reality and full of exaggerations and absurdist conceits, at once riotously funny and deadly serious. In particular, they are acutely observant of the contemporary workplace and the language and demands of a late-capitalist economy in which clocking on and completing a day's work is no longer enough.[4]

Sianne Ngai's *Our Aesthetic Categories* (2012) offers a way to think about Saunders's fiction in the context of broader socio-economic and aesthetic shifts that have taken place in the late-twentieth and early twenty-first centuries. Ngai identifies three under-examined and marginal aesthetic categories which are nevertheless 'the ones in our current repertoire best suited to grasping how aesthetic experience has been transformed by the hypercommodified, information-saturated, performance-driven conditions of late capitalism' (2012: 1). The zany, the cute and the interesting relate to categories of production, circulation and consumption respectively, and as such represent an aesthetic suited to our times. There is much to be said about Ngai's rich and rewarding text, but the topic of most interest here is her discussion of the zany, an aesthetic linked to the move towards a post-Fordist service economy in which the affective requirements of the workplace begin to trouble the distinction between work and play: 'Zaniness is the only aesthetic category in our contemporary repertoire explicitly about this politically ambiguous intersection between cultural and occupational performance, acting and service, playing and labouring' (2012: 182). Zaniness, as represented by the obsessive role-playing of the eponymous character in Jim Carrey's *The Cable Guy* (1996), for example, represents how workers are no longer required merely to work, but also to *perform* (2012: 201–202). It is this performative aspect of the postmodern workplace that forms one of the central subjects of Saunders's comic vision of the world, in which compression ('rapid-truthing') combines with absurd or exaggerated versions of working life – most commonly represented by the theme park worker – that are nevertheless recognisable versions of the challenges and dilemmas facing workers in a service economy.

Saunders's first collection of stories, *CivilWarLand in Bad Decline* (1996) includes stories set in a water park ('The Wavemaker Falters'); a museum of curiosities and cod-historical interactive exhibits ('Downtrodden Mary's Failed Campaign of Terror'); a nightmarish resort for the rich citizens of a dystopian version of the United States ('Bounty'); a company named Humane Raccoon Alternatives, which is a purportedly 'humane' trap-and-release operation that in reality dispatches racoons with a tyre iron before burying them in a pit ('The 400-Pound CEO'); and a crumbling Civil War theme park besieged by marauding gangs (the titular 'CivilWarLand in Bad Decline'). Subsequent collections have continued this interest in comically exaggerated versions of American workplaces, and Saunders has suggested that, when writing the earliest of his published stories 'The Wavemaker Falters', it was the theme park setting that liberated him from 'faux-Hemingway element' of his earlier work: 'Placing a story in a theme park became a way of ensuring that the story would lurch over into the realm of the comic, which meant I would be able to finish it, and it would not collapse under the conceptual/thematic weight I tended to put on a so-called realist story' (Saunders, 2013b). More than this, it allowed Saunders to develop a comic voice and a vision of the world that encapsulates through exaggeration many of the problems and paradoxes of the late-capitalist economy. This continues in stories such as 'Escape from Spiderhead', 'Exhortation' and 'My Chivalric Fiasco' from his most recent collection *Tenth of December* (2013a), but here I will focus on the title story from his second collection *Pastoralia* (2000), a tragicomic treatment of the American service economy.

The narrator of 'Pastoralia' lives and works in a theme park and is an actor in a living diorama of the imagined lives of prehistoric cave dwellers. During the park's opening hours he and his co-worker Janet must perform as cave people for the ever-dwindling number of visitors to the park. There is a viewing hole through which visitors can watch them going about their daily business, but the story is punctuated by the refrain 'No one pokes their head in', and it is clear that visitor numbers are in decline. The narrator and Janet must roast goat carcasses over an open fire, communicate with each other in faux-primitive grunts, and give the illusion that they are living without modern conveniences. But increasingly Janet disobeys orders and ignores the park's dictum that employees should be 'Thinking Positive/Saying Positive' at all times. 'Thinking Positive/Saying Positive' is an example of the empty corporate speak that Saunders is so adept at parodying and is suggestive of the way in which, as Ngai outlines, in the post-1970s economy 'human competences once viewed as outside capital – affect, subjectivity, and sociability – are systematically put to work for the extraction of surplus value' (2012: 202): it is not enough simply to do one's job, one must act, even think, in the prescribed way. Performance is essential to the work at the theme park; it is vital that the narrator and Janet not only work, but also perform at all times: their work *is* performance, and that that performance is monitored via a Daily Partner

Performance Evaluation Form (DPPEF). The dutiful narrator, determined to stay in character and conform to the park's rules, remains loyal to Janet even when personal pressures, the prospect of redundancy and an increasingly erratic food supply lead her to break character with increasing frequency, including in the presence of visitors. The narrator's DPPEF repeats the same lines each day, with little variation: 'Do I note any attitudinal difficulties? I do not. How do I rate my Partner overall? Very good. Are there any situations which require Mediation? There are not' (5). Yet still the pressure builds, particularly when Janet's problems with her errant son, Bradley, start to affect her ability to work and to maintain her performance. The park manager, Nordstrom, realises that the narrator is lying in his DPPEFs and forces him to tell the truth. When the narrator warns Janet that in future he will have to be honest, Nordstrom writes a furious note: '*Do you really think I care about how she is? I KNOW how she is. She is BAD. But what I need is for you to SAY IT. For reasons of documentation. Do you have any idea how hard it is to fire a gal, not to mention an old gal, not to mention and old gal with so many years of withered service under her ancient withered belt? There is so much you don't know about the Remixing, about our plans!*' (27, italics in original). The language of performance evaluation and personal development is here laid bare as less about improving Janet's service as an employee and more about constructing a case for her dismissal. It becomes a meta-performance, in which employees – actors – are given the illusion of autonomy whilst having to follow a continually changing script rendered in an inarticulate and increasingly aggressive form of management speak. Terms such as 'Remixing', like its cousin 'downsizing', become a method of coding and hiding a pernicious subtext.

Much of the humour in Saunders's fiction comes precisely from his ability to evoke exaggerated but pitch-perfect forms of vernacular speech and writing, and in 'Pastoralia' the contorted arguments and language of Nordstrom's memos force his employees to contort themselves in turn. First, there is the question of the 'Disposal Debit', colloquially known as the 'Shit Fee', which is deducted from all employees' wages to pay for waste disposal ('*It is as if you expect us to provide [. . .] Cokes for free, just because you thirst. Do Cokes grow on trees? Well, the other thing that does not grow on trees is a poop truck*'. (47, italics in original)), and then there is the question of the goat carcass the narrator and Janet receive daily, the roasting of which signals the authenticity of the caveperson lifestyle: '*In terms of austerity [. . .]. No goat today. In terms of verisimilitude, mount this fake goat and tend as if real*' (49, italics in original). The narrator and Janet continue to mime the catching and eating of insects and to grunt in the required manner, but Janet finally breaks character when she answers back to an obnoxious visiting family. The father's feedback form, or Client Vignette Evaluation, is damning: 'Under *Learning Value* he's written *Disastrous. We learned that some cave ladies had potty mouths. I certainly felt like I was in the actual Neanderthal days. Not!*' (57, italics in original). The narrator faxes in a truthful DPPEF and Nordstrom has the evidence he needs to fire Janet. As the Remixing continues and the park steadily winds down, Janet is replaced by Linda, whose rigour at performing as a caveperson surpasses even the narrator's own. At the conclusion there is a comic reversal in which the narrator seeks to bond and share a joke with Linda as he once had with Janet. His advances are met with stony indifference and '*strict verisimilitude*' (64, italics in original):

All afternoon we pretend to catch and eat small bugs. We pretend to catch and eat more pretend bugs than could ever actually live in one cave. The number of pretend bugs we pretend to catch and eat would in reality fill a cave the size of our cave. It feels like we're racing. At one point, she gives me a look, like: Slow down, going so fast is inauthentic. I slow down. I slow down, monitoring my rate so that I am pretending to catch and eat small bugs at the same rate at which she is pretending to catch and eat small bugs, which seems to me prudent, I mean, there is no way she could have a problem with the

way I'm pretending to catch and eat small bugs if I'm doing it exactly the same way
she's doing it.

No one pokes their head in.

(66)

The narrator continues Thinking Positive/Saying Positive and performs even when there is no
audience there to witness it, whirling around after imaginary bugs to give the impression of
greater conviction and more authenticity, in short to *perform* more effectively. Saunders's theme
park vision of the American workplace is less an absurdist conceit than an exaggerated version
of wider tendencies within late-capitalist society, and the zany aesthetic is closely related to the
movement of affect into the workplace, particularly in the service industries. As Ngai argues,
comedy is the genre or 'representational practice' that incorporates the zany, and Saunders's comedy may be zany but it is not light; it is representative of the fact that 'the zany is not just funny
but angry' (Ngai 2012: 3, 218).

A grave disquisition: style and class in Martin Amis's *Lionel Asbo* (2012)

Also angry, but in a very different way, is Martin Amis's Lionel Asbo, the central character in
the 2012 novel *Lionel Asbo: State of England*. As the subtitle suggests, this is a novel which seeks
to say something about contemporary Britain, and as the title suggests, this is also a comedy.
ASBO is an acronym for Anti-Social Behaviour Order, a notorious measure introduced into
British law in 1998, designed 'to protect the public from behaviour that causes or is likely to
cause harassment, alarm or distress' and containing 'conditions prohibiting an individual from
carrying out specific anti-social acts or (for example) from entering defined areas' (Crown
Prosecution Service 2014). Amis's Lionel views his series of ASBOs as a source of pride to the
extent that at age eighteen he changes his surname from Peppardine to Asbo because it '*has a
nice ring to it*' (27, italics in original). Lionel is a petty criminal who finds fame when he wins
£139,999,999.50 on the National Lottery, and whose rise and eventual downfall is contrasted
with his studious nephew Des Peppardine, who pursues education, family life and stability. This
is a novel which is self-consciously about contemporary Britain, and particularly its class politics
and the roles of money and celebrity. It is not hard to see parallels between the character Lionel
Asbo and the real-life Michael Carroll, the self-styled 'King of Chavs'[5] who in 2002 became
notorious after winning nearly ten million pounds on the UK National Lottery. The tabloid
press made much of Carroll's criminal past and branded him the 'Lotto Lout' (the title of part
two of *Lionel Asbo*) when he spent his money publicly and ostentatiously. The same press then
delighted in the subsequent loss of his fortune and return to working life in a biscuit factory.
Moreover, in a further parallel with tabloid news stories of the preceding decade, Amis's novel
also features a love interest known as 'Threnody', a glamour model with poetic ambitions who
is rival to Danube, a character surely based on Jordan – now known by her birth name Katie
Price – a former glamour model turned entrepreneur who also published a series of bestselling
autobiographies, novels and children's books. Price was for many years both courted and reviled
by the tabloid press, her every movement the subject of intense speculation.

By the time *Lionel Asbo* was published these knowing references to tabloid celebrities already
looked dated, but they are emblematic of the comically exaggerated version of contemporary
Britain found in Amis's novel. Lionel and Threnody are grotesques, but as in all satire they are
grotesques anchored in a recognisable world. Moreover, they are grotesques who are invoked via
Amis's customarily stylish prose, and it is this style, and specifically Amis's negotiation of different stylistic registers, which is the source of much of the novel's humour. Take, for example, this

passage from early in the book, in which Lionel educates his nephew, Des, on the finer points of English criminal law:

> There followed a grave debate, or a grave disquisition, on the difference between ABH and GBH – between Actual Bodily Harm and its sterner older brother, Griev-ous. Like many career delinquents, Lionel was up to PhD level on questions of criminal law. Criminal law, after all, was the third element in his vocational trinity, the other two being villainy and prison. When Lionel talked about the law (reaching for a kind of high style), Des always paid close attention. Criminal law was in any case much on his mind.
>
> In a nutshell, Des, in a nutshell, it's the difference between the first-aid kit and the casualty ward.
>
> (17)

While the narrator holds forth with customary eloquence, preparing us for a 'grave disquisition' and suggesting that Lionel is 'reaching for a kind of high style' – note the modifying 'reaching for' and 'kind of' – what we get is a bathetic cliché followed by an analogy that can't compete with the preceding 'sterner older brother' metaphor. This mixture of the demotic voice and the high style is what Jeremy Scott refers to in relation to the earlier Amis novels *Money* (1984) and *London Fields* (1989), as Amis's 'double-voicedness', or the complex 'intersection between the demotic and the hieratic' (2009: 159). For Scott it is this linguistic play, this *style* which shapes character in Amis's fiction; indeed it '*is* style which is the substance of the fiction' (2009: 170, italics in original); to this I would add that it is this stylistic interplay which generates much of the humour in Amis's fiction. Amis has more than once suggested that 'style *is* morality' (2001: 121n, italics in original, 2002: 467),[6] and if this is the case then it begs the question, what does this reliance on the bathetic juxtaposition of registers suggest about the relationship between the narrator, the characters, and ultimately the reader?

One answer to the question can, I believe, be found in David Herman's work on style shift-ing in Edith Wharton's *The House of Mirth* (1905). In *Story Logic*, Herman suggests that style shifting 'occurs when a speaker shifts, for example, from casual to formal speech or vice versa', and furthermore that '*a reported utterance is evaluated more negatively the more it differs from the degree of formality, type of speech variety, and mode of situational appropriateness of the style in which the report is couched*' (2002: 197, 201, italics in original). In *The House of Mirth*, Herman argues, these stylistic shifts index class relations and serve to align the reader with the upper-class Lily Barth and against the working-class Mrs Haffen. Such alignments also occur in Amis's fiction and raise questions about who is laughing and at whose expense the joke is being told. To take a further example from the dialogue between Lionel and Des quoted from above, one can see this style shifting at work when Des further questions Lionel about an unprovoked assault in the Hobgoblin pub:

> 'And this Ross Knowles, Uncle Li. How long's he been in Diston General?' asked Des (referring to the worst hospital in England).
>
> Oy. Objection. That's prejudicial.
>
> [. . .]
>
> Why Prejudicial?
>
> 'Hypothesis'. *Hypoffesis*. 'I give Ross Knowles a little tap in a fair fight, he comes out of the Hobgoblin – and walks under a truck'. Truck: pronounced truc-kuh (with a glottal stop on the terminal plosive). 'See? Prejudicial.'

Des nodded. It was in fact strongly rumoured that Ross came out of the Hobgoblin on a stretcher.

(17)

The 'strongly rumoured' is the heavily ironic punchline to this dialogue, which in the space of a few short lines shifts between multiple registers and styles. In addition to Des's and Lionel's spoken words there are the interjections of a more distant, correcting narrator[7] and, in the final sentences a moment of third-person counterpoint inflected with Des's point of view. Lionel is not dismissed as a complete fool – however misguided, he does have some grasp of legal niceties – but his distance from the voice in which the speech is couched is associated, both inherently and explicitly, with language and with questions of class. It would be hard to reclaim or redeem Lionel's attitudes, but what is problematic is the way in which his status as the object of satire is so closely aligned to demotic speech and how much of the novel's humour is aimed at this linguistic variation. Rather than rendering Lionel's speech in an approximation of phonetic spelling,[8] Amis's narrator actually interjects like a judgemental grammarian to indicate just how far Lionel diverges from Received Pronunciation. And these jokes are not only at Lionel's expense. In the opening pages the autodidact Des is implicitly mocked for his inconsistent spelling, grammar and punctuation via excerpts from a letter he is drafting to a tabloid agony aunt. It is only later in the novel, when he has the benefit of a university education, that Des escapes this judgement and his voice begins to align with that of the narrator. In the concluding pages Amis strikes a more elegiac tone and we get passages such as this: 'The air seemed to ripple with infant voices . . . Des assumed that this feeling would one day subside, this riven feeling, with its equal parts of panic and rapture' (273). These moments, focalised through Des, suggest a moral equivalence between the articulateness brought about by education and Des's ability to tell his story without interruption: there is no ironic, external narrator to comment on or correct his perceptions.

The ending of Amis's novel, in which Des finds love and stability with his partner Dawn and their new-born daughter Cilla, does suggest some form of hope or redemption – Cilla sings in imitation of 'the birds you could still sometimes hear, up on the thirty-third floor, so high above Diston Town' (275) – but throughout there is an evident discomfort and distaste for working-class speech and culture, as indexed through style shifting and commentary on the lexicon and dialect of working-class characters: the debasement of British culture, which is a running theme, is seen to go hand in hand with the debasement of language. As Lawrence Driscoll has suggested of Amis's earlier fiction, 'the real target of Amis's satire is his working-class characters, and it is them we are laughing at, while siding with the very stable positions that the novel provides' (2009: 102). This is not to suggest that the character Lionel Asbo should be seen as wholly emblematic of working-class people or culture – he is after all a violent criminal – but it is to suggest that the novel finds humour in the juxtaposition of Amis's famously 'high' style and forms of demotic speech, and that this juxtaposition is problematic because of the forms of hierarchy and judgement it introduces. As Herman suggests, 'Style is content' and 'Content is style' and 'styles invite reflection on how discourse is an instrument that can either work against or reinforce patterns of conflict' (2002: 194, 207), a series of suggestions not dissimilar to Amis's own assertion that 'style *is* morality'. But when applied to Amis's own *Lionel Asbo* we find a clear indication not only of which style of language is grammatically correct but also of which style of language is *morally* correct. The suggestion is that the only way to remedy the moral failing of inarticulate and inelegant speech is through standardisation via the conventional route of a university education: to express oneself otherwise is to be, well, laughable.

Talking about things we don't want to talk about: comedy and community in Zadie Smith's *NW*

Published in the same year as *Lionel Asbo*, but suggesting a very different picture of class and community, Zadie Smith's *NW* (2012) was frequently referred to by reviewers as a funny novel. Perhaps most notable among these was Philip Hensher, who suggested that *NW* 'is intensely funny in its disillusioned way, both laughing with its characters, and, sometimes in angry judgment, at them' (Hensher, 2012). This question of laughing 'with' and 'at' has been important to the preceding discussions of *Lionel Asbo* and Saunders's 'Pastoralia' and it is the question that most clearly delineates the politics of joke work. As Hensher suggests, in Smith's novel we are not given certainties or fixed positions but rather a more mutable sense of the comic tendencies and absurdities of people individually and collectively. In *Comic Transactions* (1994), James English describes a form of postcolonial joke work which 'attempts to work *through* the crisis point toward a new laughter of community which would not celebrate a common identity, and a new politics of community which would not strive either to realize a common essence or to perform a common work'. He further suggests that it is the nature of such texts that they challenge such models of community as soon as they are set-up, instead preferring what Georges Bataille describes as an evolving 'community of those who have no community' (1994: 236–237). Whilst being careful to distinguish Smith's novel of multicultural contemporary London from the specifically post-colonial context in which English discusses Salman Rushdie's *The Satanic Verses* (1988), it seems to me that *NW* shares a similar concern with the laughter of community, not only in the simple sense of bringing individuals together through shared joking, but as a way of recognising difference not as something to laugh *at* but as something to laugh *through*.

NW principally centres on four characters living in the environs of the fictional Caldwell council estate in the real-life area of Willesden, north-west London: Leah Hanwell, treading water in an undemanding job allocating funding to charities; Natalie (formerly Keisha) Blake, Leah's childhood friend now a barrister apparently living the ideal bourgeois lifestyle; Nathan Bogle, a childhood crush of Natalie's who has fallen on difficult times; and Felix Cooper, a mechanic keen to put the problems of his past behind him. These characters' lives intersect to varying degrees and build a necessarily fragmentary picture of life in this corner of London. As with *Lionel Asbo*, social class is an implicit concern in this novel, but it is seen as a fluid thing, bound up with questions of ethnicity, education, experience, language and geography. As Lynn Wells argues, 'Smith challenges us to look beyond social narratives – whether racial, socioeconomic or gendered – to seek the hidden, complex lives of those around us, stories they long to tell and have told' (2013: 110–111). Wells's essay focuses on the power of secrets, and more importantly on the power of revealing the truth, and it seems to me that there is a similar power at work in the novel's humour – in the telling of jokes as well as the telling of secrets.

In the 2008 essay 'Dead Man Laughing', Smith remembers her father and their shared love of comedy. She recalls how the British comedian Tony Hancock and his comic progeny 'served as a constant source of conversation between my father and me, a vital link between us when, classwise, and in every other wise, each year placed us further and further apart'; it is shared laughter and a shared sense of humour which neutralises, at least temporarily, class and other divides. For Smith, 'it was a way of talking about things we didn't want to talk about' (2009: 239). In *NW* we see how this shared laughter works in both a partially negative sense – Leah's mother and Leah's partner Michel are sworn enemies except in the delight they take in laughing at Leah's mistakes and foibles (2012: 18) – and as a way of talking about and talking through hidden or difficult topics. At one point Felix goes to visit his father and afterwards falls into conversation with his father's neighbour Phil Barnes ('Barnesy'), and it is the lightness, the back-and-forth humour of their conversation that allows Phil to ask after Felix's brother Devon, who is serving time in prison for armed robbery. 'Phil was the only person on the estate who asked after Devon' (114), we are told, and after a moment of reflection the two friends, one white and one black, one middle-aged and one in his early thirties, are soon joking again: 'Laughter again, bent with laughter, hands on knees' (115). Here laughter does not dissipate the serious topic of their conversation, as is sometimes argued of humour, but has rather *allowed* the conversation to take place. A shared sense of humour allows stories to be shared and allows conversations across boundaries of age and ethnicity.

This and other episodes are at once comic (though not in the sense of conventional set-up and punchline jokes) and *about* the relationship between comedy and community, its capacity both to bring people together and push them apart. Later, Felix travels to central London to buy a second-hand car and meets Tom Mercer, who is selling the car on behalf of his wealthy father. The two come from very different parts of London and they engage in often awkward conversation as they negotiate on price. At one point Felix, always seemingly in control of the situation, tells Tom 'No one's gonna pay six hundred for this. This one you won't be able to sell to no one but a mechanic, I promise you':

> Tom looked up, squinting.
> Good thing you're a mechanic then, isn't it?
> There was something funny about the way he said it. Both men laughed: Felix in his big gulping way, Tom into his hand like a child.
>
> (124)

Laughter and, to use the British vernacular, the ability for both sides to take the piss out of one another, allows a degree of connection to develop, though it is only later that Tom recognises this connection. When Felix offers Tom some heartfelt but admittedly clichéd self-help advice, Tom oversteps the tacit boundaries of their relationship and takes the joking too far:

> He nodded at Felix deeply, satirically, samurai-style. 'Thank you, Felix', he said. 'I'll remember that. Best you that you can be. Personal equals eternal. You seem like a bloke who's got it all figured out'. He lifted his empty glass to clink against Felix's, but Felix was not impervious to irony and left his own glass where it was.
>
> (131)

On reflection, Tom realises he has enjoyed Felix's over-familiarity and that his misjudgement has soured their joking relationship. Indeed, following this recognition we get a passage, focalised through Tom, in which he takes stock of his life and the problems caused by his ironic detachment from events and other people. The comedy of the exchanges between Felix and Tom is one primarily of awkwardness and misreadings, but in moments such as their shared joking and Tom's misjudged quip at Felix's expense, Smith's novel explores the importance and power of humour as a social force that has the potential for both cohesion and division.

What distinguishes *NW* from Amis's *Lionel Asbo*, for example, is this interplay between laughing *with* and laughing *at*, and it is this which is perhaps the difference between humour and satire.[9] More than this, it is also linked to the way in which Smith negotiates registers, voices and points and view,[10] a technique which makes it hard to isolate a particular object or victim of her humour: just as we are about to write Tom off as an arrogant and spoilt rich boy, there is a moment of interiority and introspection that reveals a coming awareness of his privileged position and, perhaps, a need to change. Passages such as these are closer to what James Wood, who was so sceptical about Smith's first novel *White Teeth*,[11] would call the comedy of forgiveness, 'a way of laughing with' (2004: 4) than to the more corrective and judgemental tone prevalent in *Lionel Asbo*. This process is not a perfect one and Smith's novel does not suggest that humour and joking are solutions to problems of community, but it does suggest that, to return to the James English comments which opened this section, we can work 'toward a new laughter of community' not through collapsing difference into sameness but rather by recognising and discussing difference through joke work.

Concluding remarks

What these three readings have sought to explore are some of the many and various ways in which comedy functions in contemporary literary fiction. The zany aesthetic of George Saunders's stories engages with and satirises the affective and performative aspects of the post-industrial workspace; Martin Amis's style shifting in *Lionel Asbo* indexes class hierarchies through the juxtaposition of the demotic and the self-consciously 'high' or literary; and Zadie Smith's *NW* explores the relationship between comedy and community, the ways in which humour offers a way of talking through unspoken or difficult topics, acting as a powerful (though not always conciliatory) force in shaping interpersonal relations. These readings seek to open up comedy as a topic for further investigation and to demonstrate its centrality to much of the most interesting and complex contemporary fiction. Such is the prominence of the comic voice in contemporary fiction that this identifiable 'funny turn' demands further work in order to explore not only what is funny, but how and why it is funny, and what an understanding of these aspects of comedy can add to our understanding of literature.

Notes

1 See, for example, the 2014 debate between Philip Hensher and Harry Mount, published in the *Guardian*.
2 Blackburn's autobiography was one of the sources of inspiration for *I, Partridge* (de Semlyen, 2013), and is full of lines that could easily be spoken by Partridge, Coogan's un-self-aware and often pompous comic masterpiece. In a further turn of the intertextual screw, award-winning stand-up comedian and commercial indie digital DJ John Robins has written his own autobiography, *A Robins Amongst the Pigeons*, a pitch-perfect homage to both Partridge and Blackburn.
3 Fuelled by Jacobson's own comments on the marginalisation of comic literature, many commentators suggested Jacobson's *The Finkler Question* was the first comic novel to win the Man Booker Prize. See, for example, Singh (2010) and Aspden (2010). That this discounts previous winners such as J.G. Farrell's *The Siege of Krishnapur* (1973) and Kingsley Amis's *The Old Devils* (1986) suggests something about both the marketing and publicity surrounding such awards and the difficulty of deciding how to classify a text as out-and-out comic fiction. See Jordison (2010) for a rebuttal of the claims made for Jacobson's novel and English, 2005, 197–210 for a discussion of some of the complexities of the Booker Prize and its publicity machine.
4 For a persuasive reading of George Saunders's 'Sea Oak' from the perspective of postmodern categories of class, as well as alternative take on the politics of the workplace, see Rando (2012). Rando argues that 'the "actual" in Saunders is often the moment of comic shock that uncouples his text from the conventions of narrative realism and satire' (451).
5 As Owen Jones (2012) notes, the term 'Chav' originates from the Romany work 'chavi', meaning child, but has spread into wider usage as a derogatory term for working-class youths.
6 See James (2012) for a discussion of the relationship between aesthetics and ethics in Amis's *Money*.
7 There are parallels here with what James Wood describes as the 'comedy of correction' in which we laugh *at* rather than *with*. (See Wood, 2004: 1–16).
8 As Geoffrey Leech and Michael Short remind us in *Style in Fiction*, such writing is an example of 'EYE-DIALECT, where the impression of rendering non-standard speech by non-standard spelling is pure illusion'. Moreover, 'non-standard speech is typically associated with objects of comedy and satire: characters whom we see from the outside only' (Leech and Short 2007, 136–137).

9   The nature and effects of satire continue to be debated, but it is worth noting that modern satire, like its Roman forbears, tends to have a target, which it exposes, challenges or critiques. As Andrew Stott notes: 'Satire aims to denounce folly and vice and urge ethical and political reform through the subjection of ideas to humorous analysis' (2005: 109).

10 As many commentators on the novel have noted, *NW* owes much to modernist modes of narration in its experiments with voice and typography. See, for example, Knepper (2013); Lorentzen (2012) and, more sceptically, Mars-Jones (2012).

11 In a 2000 *New Republic* review, Wood famously described *White Teeth* as an example of Dickensian 'hysterical realism' and expressed his frustration at the novel whilst still finding much to admire (2004: 167–183). *NW* was less equivocally praised in his 2012 *New Yorker* books of the year list (Wood, 2012).

Works cited

Amis, M. [2000] 2001. *Experience*. London: Vintage.
—— [2001] 2002. *The War against Cliché: Essays and Reviews 1971–2000*. London: Vintage.
—— 2012. *Lionel Asbo: State of England*. London: Jonathan Cape.
Aspden, P. 2010. Comic Novel Wins Booker Prize. *Financial Times* [online] 10 October. Available at: www.ft.com/cms/s/0/dc508888-d632-11df-81f0-00144feabdc0.html#axzz3SZ38XBCX [Accessed 21 September 2017].
Blackburn, T. 2007. *Poptastic!: My Life in Radio*. London: Cassell.
Crown Prosecution Service, 2014. *Anti-Social Behaviour Orders on Conviction (ASBOs)*. Available at: www.cps.gov.uk/legal/a_to_c/anti_social_behaviour_guidance/ [Accessed 21 September 2017].
de Semlyen, N. 2013. Steve Coogan Talks Alan Partridge. *Empire* [online]. Available at: www.empireonline.com/interviews/interview.asp?IID=1757 [Accessed 23 February 2015].
Driscoll, L. 2009. *Evading Class in Contemporary British Literature*. New York: Palgrave Macmillan.
Eaglestone, R. 2013. Contemporary Fiction in the Academy: Towards a Manifesto. *Textual Practice*, 27(7), 1089–1101.
English, J. F. 1994. *Comic Transactions: Literature, Humor and the Politics of Community in Twentieth-Century Britain*. Ithaca, NY: Cornell University Press.
—— 2005. *The Economy of Prestige: Prizes, Awards, and the Circulation of Cultural Value*. Cambridge, MA: Harvard University Press.
Finney, G. ed., 1994. *Look Who's Laughing: Gender and Comedy*. Langhorne, PA: Gordon and Breach.
Gibbons, R., Gibbons, N., Ianucci, A. and Coogan, S. 2011. *I, Partridge: We Need to Talk about Alan*. London: HarperCollins.
Gregson, I. 2006. *Character and Satire in Contemporary Fiction*. London: Continuum.
Hensher, P. 2012. *NW* by Zadie Smith. *Telegraph* [online] 3 September. Available at: www.telegraph.co.uk/culture/books/9508844/NW-by-Zadie-Smith-review.html [Accessed 21 September 2017].
Hensher, P. and Mount, Harry, 2014. Is Alan Bennett Right to Prefer US Literature? *Guardian* [online] 10 May. Available at: www.theguardian.com/commentisfree/2014/may/10/alan-bennett-american-literature-debate-mount-hensher [Accessed 21 September 2017].
Herman, D. 2002. *Story Logic: Problems and Possibilities of Narrative*. Lincoln, NE: University of Nebraska Press.
Jacobson, H. 1997. *Seriously Funny: From the Ridiculous to the Sublime*. London: Viking.
—— 2010. Howard Jacobson on Taking Comic Novels Seriously. *Guardian* [online] 9 October. Available at: www.theguardian.com/books/2010/oct/09/howard-jacobson-comic-novels [Accessed 21 September 2017].
James, D. 2012. 'Style Is Morality'? Aesthetics and Politics in the Amis Era. *Textual Practice*, 26(1), 11–25.
Jones, O. 2012. *Chavs: The Demonization of the Working Class*. 2nd ed. London: Verso.
Jordison, S. 2010. Booker prize disdains comedy? What a joke. *Guardian* [online] 14 October. Available at: https://www.theguardian.com/books/booksblog/2010/oct/14/booker-prize-disdains-comedy-joke [Accessed 7 September 2018].
Knepper, W. 2013. Revisionary Modernism and Postmillenial Experimentation in Zadie Smith's *NW*. In: P. Tew, ed. *Reading Zadie Smith: The First Decade and Beyond*. London: Bloomsbury Academic. 111–126.
Leech, G. and Short, M. 2007. *Style in Fiction: A Linguistic Introduction to English Fictional Prose*. 2nd ed. Harlow: Pearson.
Lodge, D. 1992. *The Art of Fiction*. London: Penguin.
Lorentzen, C. 2012. Why Am I so Fucked Up? *London Review of Books*, 8 November, 21–22.

Mars-Jones, A. 2012. NW by Zadie Smith: Review. *Guardian* [online] 31 August. Available at: www.theguardian.com/books/2012/aug/31/nw-zadie-smith-review [Accessed 21 September 2017].

Mookerjee, R. 2013. *Transgressive Fiction: The New Satiric Tradition.* Basingstoke: Palgrave Macmillan.

Ngai, S. 2012. *Our Aesthetic Categories: Zany, Cute, Interesting.* Cambridge, MA: Harvard University Press.

Rando, D. P. 2012. George Saunders and the Postmodern Working Class. *Contemporary Literature*, 23(3), 437–460.

Robins, J. 2015. *A Robins amongst the Pigeons.* Available at: https://arobinsamongstthepigeons.tumblr.com/ [Accessed 21 September 2017].

Ross, M. L. 2006. *Race Riots: Comedy and Ethnicity in Modern British Fiction.* Montreal and Kingston: McGill-Queen's University Press.

Saunders, G. [1996] 1997. *CivilWarLand in Bad Decline.* London: Vintage.

—— [2000] 2001. *Pastoralia.* London: Bloomsbury.

—— [2008] 2009. *The Brain-Dead Megaphone.* London: Bloomsbury.

—— 2013a. *Tenth of December.* London: Bloomsbury.

—— 2013b. CivilWarLand in Bad Decline: Preface. Repr. in *Paris Review* [online]. Available at: www.theparisreview.org/blog/2013/01/07/civilwarland-in-bad-decline-preface/ [Accessed 21 September 2017].

Scott, J. 2009. *The Demotic Voice in Contemporary British Fiction.* Basingstoke: Palgrave Macmillan.

Singh, A. 2010. Man Booker Prize: Howard Jacobson Is Surprise Winner. *Telegraph* [online] 12 October. Available at: www.telegraph.co.uk/culture/books/booker-prize/8060132/Man-Booker-Prize-Howard-Jacobson-is-surprise-winner.html [Accessed 23 February 2015].

Smith Z. 2009. *Changing My Mind: Occasional Essays.* London: Penguin.

—— [2012] 2013. *NW.* London: Penguin.

Stetz, M. D. 2001. *British Women's Comic Fiction, 1890–1990.* Aldershot: Ashgate.

Stott, A. 2005. *Comedy.* New York: Routledge.

Wells, L. 2013. The Right to a Secret: Zadie Smith's *NW*. In: P. Tew, ed. *Reading Zadie Smith: The First Decade and Beyond.* London: Bloomsbury Academic. 97–110.

Wood, J. 2004. *The Irresponsible Self: On Laughter and the Novel.* London: Jonathan Cape.

—— 2012. Books of the Year. *New Yorker* [online] 17 December. Available at: www.newyorker.com/books/page-turner/books-of-the-year [Accessed 23 February 2015].

7

METAFICTION

Xavier Marcó del Pont

Definition and context

Simplifying to the extreme, I define metafiction as a text's incredulity towards both itself and the presupposed truth-building power of narrative and the written word. It is usually discussed in terms of the text's self-consciousness or self-awareness, and often results in a revelation of the writing process: as this moves to the fore, the stitching itself not only becomes visible, but comes to be essential to the very pattern of the narrative's texture. The coinage of the term metafiction is attributed to William Gass. In his 1970 essay 'Philosophy and the Form of Fiction,' Gass put forth the term as a counterpart to the 'lingos to converse about lingos' that many disciplines possess, such as meta-ethics in ethics or metatheorems in logic and mathematics (Gass 1970: 24). He drew a line, however, rejecting 'those drearily predictable pieces about writers who are writing about what they are writing'; under the category of metafiction, Gass included those works 'in which the forms of fiction serve as the material upon which further forms can be imposed,' drawing a distinction between metafiction and the anti-novel (Gass 1970: 24–25). It would be erroneous to describe metafiction as either a literary form or a genre, as it may take different formal con-figurations and be classified under a number of stylistic categorizations; it is a mode. It also bears mentioning that some narratives fully embrace the metafictional mode throughout – as is the case with Salvador Plascencia's *The People of Paper* (2005) – whilst others merely dip their figurative toes in its waters – like Ian McEwan's *Atonement* (2001) – though the effect remains within a spectrum that includes narrative destabilisation and purposeful readerly alienation.

Scholars have signalled towards several possible definitional problems with metafiction. As Mark Currie argues, ascribing self-consciousness to a text is not only problematic in and of itself, but there is also the matter of the infinite regression, as if in a hall of mirrors, that this situation would bring about: to be truly self-conscious, the text would have to be conscious of its self-consciousness, and conscious of this, and so on (Currie 2013: 1). However, since we do not nec-essarily see this endless regression as an obstacle to describing humankind as self-conscious, and given that the term is a widely understood shorthand, there is no actual problem with describing metafiction as self-conscious fiction, though we may use the term self-reflexive instead. In any case, we can think of the self-consciousness of metafiction as that which the reader experiences when confronted with a text constructed in a way that highlights its own artificiality. Or, for that matter, the fact that characters in metafiction are sometimes rendered as either being or becoming self-aware of their own fictional nature. The real problem that often emerges when discussing metafiction is the matter of the personification of the text, an example of which may be taken from the very first sentence of this chapter, where I referred to metafictional texts as displaying incredulity. Furthermore, there are plenty of pre-twentieth century texts that would fit most scholars' definition of the term: metafiction *avant la lettre*, so to speak (Currie 2013: 1–5). Pointing out that metafiction predates postmodernism has become commonplace amongst critics, with each subsequent scholar attempting to outdo the next by identifying an earlier precursor. None-theless, one of the most frequently mentioned examples is Cervantes' *Don Quixote* (1605–1615), particularly the second volume, which, besides its many remarks on the materiality of the text, contains mocking references to a second apocryphal volume that appeared in the decade between the publication of the two parts of *Don Quixote*. Whilst there are certainly complexities inherent to the concept of metafiction, we can nonetheless agree that it is a useful taxonomical term for a narrative mode and aesthetic that grew enormously in popularity during the twentieth century and with which writers of literary fiction have since been grappling in the twenty-first. One of its most quoted, if not most vocal, recent detractors was David Foster Wallace, who decried what he saw as the ironic detachment of postmodernism and metafiction yet, ultimately, did not himself break away from the metafictional mode.

This chapter will explore twenty-first century literary metafiction, its wide range of tech-niques and approaches, as well as its implications for the very act of reading. First, it will delineate the concept of metafiction, before exploring the different ways in which the textual self-awareness of metafiction makes itself manifest in twenty-first century literature; second, it will examine the concept of historiographic metafiction, problematizing it and attempting to formulate a few notes for a revised taxonomy of twenty-first century metafictions, exploring and questioning the connections between metafiction and postmodernism by way of the metafictional challenge to grand narratives. Finally, it will consider the privileged position from which metafiction can help us navigate the contemporary world. After all, metafictional narratives were one of the most important weapons in the armoury of twentieth century postmodern literature, and contempo-rary authors have been hard at work attempting to reinvent metafiction in a shape that will better suit our still adolescent century or, at the very least, discover what metafiction can contribute to our interpretations and interactions with our times.

Metafiction is a form of narrative *trompe l'œil* as it, simultaneously, blurs the distinction between the fictional and the non-fictional, whilst drawing attention to its own artifice. The metafictional novel often presents us with a plurality of refracted perspectives and, in general, metafiction is more interested in posing questions than providing definitive answers. Patricia Waugh claims that all fiction stands on some point of the metafictional spectrum (Waugh 1984: 18–19), therefore positing the notion of a gradation of metafictions. One of the most useful ways of understanding the concept of metafiction is Currie's idea of metafiction as being of a liminal nature, a discourse at the borderline between fiction and criticism, yet also between reality and representation. As Robert Scholes asserts, '[m]etafiction assimilates all the perspectives of criticism into the fictional process itself' (Scholes 1970: 106). Due to this liminal nature, metafiction has been able to defend itself from attacks in the past by simply doing so, being comfortable in its own textual skin. A classic example can be drawn from B.S. Johnson, who pre-empts criticism of *Albert Angelo* in the novel's very text, '[t]o dismiss such techniques as gimmicks, or to refuse to take them seriously, is crassly to miss the point' (Johnson 1964: 176). Contemporary metafiction's liminality is the result of crosspollination between the literary and academic worlds. Since the 1960s many lit-erary authors have had to supplement their income by producing criticism and, this century, by becoming embedded in the ever-growing creative writing industry at universities, which in the twenty-first century has even produced metafictions about the creative writing industry, such as

Nicholas Royle's *First Novel* (2013). Likewise, academics have also often tried their hand at writing fiction with great success, as is the case with Umberto Eco and Laurent Binet, whose works this chapter will discuss later on, and many others, this cross-fertilization in turn expanding the horizons of the metafictional mode.

Self-aware fiction

Self-conscious fiction takes many forms, a characteristic example of which is what Amy J. Elias refers to as the 'work as text machine' (Elias 2011: 18). These works draw attention to their own fictionality through a number of narrative techniques. Creating a comprehensive list of the devices employed by writers of metafiction would be reductive, as any such catalogue would be provisional and subject to revision, since metafiction itself remains an evolving mode. However, amongst them we may count authorial self-insertion, extended narratorial reflections on the processes involved in either writing or reading, narrative devices or textual idiosyncrasies that highlight the materiality of the text, conspicuous narrative architectonics, for example *mise-en-abyme*, crossing narrative frames, book-within-a-book embedded narratives, and extensive use of intertextual references. Illustrative examples of self-insertion, prominent narrative shape, and a marked emphasis on writing/reading procedures may be taken from US author Bret Easton Ellis' 2005 novel *Lunar Park*. *Lunar Park* is structured metafictionally, the text initially presenting itself as a straightforward memoir. However, the narrative eventually diverges noticeably from the author's actual biography, as if allowing Ellis to take a different, imagined path in life, poaching elements of the horror genre along the way. Yet, already the very beginning of the novel is unequivocally metafictional, since the text's first line is a quotation from 'the first line of *Lunar Park*,' as the narrator – a fictional construct claiming to be more than a mere character – indicates (Ellis 2005: 3). In the initial chapter, the narrator then proceeds to quote the first sentences of Ellis' four previously published novels. Yet the metafictional conundrum has already been presented to us in the first two sentences of the novel. After all, the first line of a novel cannot be a quotation of its own first line, since – for something to be a quotation – it must be a reiteration and, therefore, must first appear elsewhere. Yet the sentence reappears as the first line in the second chapter, therefore making *Lunar Park* simultaneously the book the reader holds in their hands and a book within that book. Structurally, this is how *Lunar Park* announces from the outset its metafictional, even ouroboric, nature; moreover, the first sentence itself also constitutes a textual confession of the entire metafictional thematic of the novel, as the narrator either lets slip or confides his imitative nature to the reader: 'You do an awfully good impression of yourself' (Ellis 2005: 3). Like a finger pointing at itself, *Lunar Park*'s apparent parthenogenesis has an effect of disorientation on the uninitiated reader, forcing them to do a double-take. As such, the narrative meets Patricia Waugh's revision of Gass' criteria for what constitutes metafiction (Gass 1970: 25), as it 'selfconsciously and systematically draws attention to its status as an artifact in order to pose a question about the relationship between fiction and reality' (Waugh 1984: 2). Whilst the authorial attribution and full original title of Daniel Defoe's *Robinson Crusoe* (1719) solemnly suggested it depicted a factual tale[1] and the epigraph to Umberto Eco's *The Name of the Rose* (1980) casually and humorously declares it to be, '[n]aturally, a manuscript,' a text such as David Foster Wallace's posthumous novel *The Pale King* (2011) goes further than that with its metafictional engine. Interspersed throughout *The Pale King* are references, both oblique and direct, to the fictional non-fictionality of the novel itself, most notable of which is §9, titled 'Author's Foreword' (2011: 66–85). There, eight sections into the novel, a persona that stands somewhere between author, implied author, and narrator breaks the fourth wall and addresses the reader directly, imploring the reader to disregard the copyrights page with its caveats regarding the text's fictionality, as he claims that the novel the reader holds in their hands tells a true story. *The Pale King* approaches metafiction at a structural level, demanding that the reader interrogate the very editorial foundations upon which contemporary literature stands, challenging intranarratively the author's biography, the copyrights page, and so forth. It is a book that teaches us to mistrust books or, at least, to read them more carefully.

There is even such a thing as meta-metafiction. In Paul Auster's *Man in the Dark*, the protagonist – a wheelchair-bound literary critic – makes up a metafictional narrative late at night to keep both himself busy and traumatic thoughts of loss at bay. His imagined characters live in a world much like our own, with the exception that several US states seceded in the early twenty-first century, bringing about a civil war. The characters he conjures up are aware of his role as intra-narrative author and hatch plans to assassinate him, so as to bring to an end the warfare that afflicts their world. 'The real and the imagined are one' (Auster 2008: 177), the reader is told, and, as both worlds collide, the literary critic simply stops imagining the story halfway through Auster's book, eschewing the pleasure of escapism, instead confronting the thoughts that torment him and having frank conversations with his daughter and granddaughter. *Man in the Dark* with its embedded metafictional narrative can, thus, be seen as a sort of *meta*-metafiction.

Other kinds of metafictional narrative make their self-consciousness known visually. The hysterical schizotypography of Mark Z. Danielewski's *House of Leaves* – with its narratorial plurality, footnotes, text in different fonts and sizes and colours and languages, unusual layouts often reminiscent of concrete and visual poetry – constantly brings attention to its own materiality, the strictly somatic aspect of the narrative's identity: the text as book. Similarly, though with a much narrower range of compositional techniques, Jonathan Safran Foer's *The Tree of Codes* takes as its intertextual foundation Bruno Schulz's 1934 short story collection *The Street of Crocodiles* and, through a process of erasure in the form of die-cuts, Foer distils a new text from the original source material. Starting from the text's title itself (a reduction of The Street of Crocodiles), *The Tree of Codes* never allows the reader to self-deceive and immerse themselves into whatever vague approximation to a narrative the text offers as, page after page, the very blanks on the text summon up the process of shearing undertaken in the production of the bound volume. The still young twenty-first century has witnessed the publication of metafictions ranging from what has now become fairly standard to the wildly experimental. Works that highlight the materiality of the text are key to self-conscious fiction; Steven Hall's 2007 novel *The Raw Shark Texts*, for example, tells the story of amnesiac Eric Sanderson, whose memories as it turns out have been devoured by a conceptual memory shark that sustains itself by feeding on people's memories and their 'intrinsic sense of self' (Hall 2007: 64). The novel constantly interpellates the reader through its use of the second person, emulating the notes the pre-amnesia protagonist has left behind for himself, as well as incorporating elements of visual and concrete poetry, which include over thirty pages in which the text becomes a flip book depicting the ominous approach of the memory shark, the creature itself having been constructed out of text (329–373).

Metafiction is sometimes constructed on a bed of intertextuality, meaning that some metafictional narratives highlight their textual nature by making constant references to other texts, be they real or imagined. In cases such as these, it is interesting to consider the way in which metafiction has broken away from a long tradition of mimesis, based on the idea that art imitates life and the real world. Ever since the rise of abstract art in the late nineteenth and early twentieth centuries, practitioners in all artistic disciplines have turned their gaze inward, bringing awareness of notions such as art for art's sake, self-referential art, and art that imitates art to a broader audience. In *Travels in the Scriptorium* (2007), for example, Auster presents the reader with Mr Blank, an old man confused and locked in a room who is also a stand-in for the figure of the author, perhaps even Auster himself. As the narrative ensues, Mr Blank is visited upon by a large cast of characters taken from

Auster's own novelistic *oeuvre*, showing a number of different attitudes towards him, from sympathy and pity to resentment and worse. The self-analytical nature of the text could easily lead to accusations of navel-gazing, a fact of which Auster is certainly aware and on which the novel comments humorously at points, as Mr Blank's carer Anna, the protagonist of Auster's novel *In the Country of Last Things* (1987), masturbates Mr Blank, a nod to the potentially self-gratificatory dangers of metafiction. As such, *Travels in the Scriptorium*, perhaps Auster's most Beckettian novel, stands as a striking example of intracanonical intertextuality or autointertextuality. In Umberto Eco's *The Mysterious Flame of Queen Loana* (2005), the reader follows Giambattista Bodoni as he is reborn, so to speak, having suffered from retrograde amnesia. His personal memories are all gone: what remains is his erudite knowledge of history, literature, and books. As such, Eco presents us with a protagonist that has become a textual – or perhaps even intertextual – man, having kept only his paper memories. Pablo Katchadjian's 2009 *El Aleph engordado*, on the other hand, takes intertextuality to what may be its furthest limits, at least in juridical terms. As its title suggests, *The Fattened Aleph* takes Jorge Luis Borges' 1945 short story 'The Aleph' and augments it, adding some 5600 words to its length. However, this metafictional experiment cost Katchadjian dearly, as – in spite of Borges' own intertextual tendencies – he was prosecuted for fraud at the request of Borges' widow and sole inheritor of his estate, María Kodama.

Disruptions between fiction and fact or representation and reality are sometimes rendered via a movement through the threshold of the fourth wall. In such instances, a character may become aware of the reader's prying eye or of the author's callous machinations. One of the protagonists in Laurent Binet's *The Seventh Function of Language*, an academic well-equipped for the task, discerns and analyses the very narrative structure of the text that contains him, breaking it down into a concatenated sequence of narrative events, before concluding: 'I think I'm trapped in a fucking novel' (Binet 2017: 268), 'a novel by an author unafraid of tackling clichés, he thinks' (309). In a typically Pirandellian manner, he is represented as becoming aware of his status as character, with the reader forced into a liminal position, between authorial complicity and sympathy for the fictional character. In creating this situation, Binet compels us to examine the narrative machinery of the novel, whilst simultaneously making us question the veracity and definitiveness of non-fictional narratives: 'When reading a novel, what does it signify to recognise that what is happening is "truer" than what happens in real life?' (Binet 2017: 198).

As I mentioned earlier, Mark Currie asserts that metafiction is 'a borderline discourse, as a kind of writing which places itself on the border between fiction and criticism, and which takes that border as its subject' (2). Some of these qualities can also be ascribed to autobiography, which is consistent with metafiction's recurrent effect on the reader, namely, the instillation of a certain amount of scepticism towards anything that declares itself true, be it history, biography, or autobiography. Ellis succinctly phrases part of the spirit of metafiction in *Lunar Park*: 'I wanted to crush the phony specifics and get at some larger truth – whatever it was' (Ellis 2005: 161). At the heart of all metafiction there is an ontological self-examination and an overt desire to allow the authority of the author – the creator – to be questioned. Metafiction knowingly displays and actively encourages suspicion in the power of literature as a container of truth. And, in doing so, it aspires to and promotes the greater aim of critical thinking and healthy doubt.

Challenging the grand narratives

Whilst metafiction both blurs and questions the distinctions between and limits of representation and reality, some forms of metafiction more directly interrogate the discourses of history. Linda Hutcheon coins the term historiographic metafiction as a subcategory of metafiction, one in which specifically the notion of the writing of history is deconstructed and its authority challenged. It is generally accepted that metafiction occupies the space at the threshold between fiction (as it is generally understood) and criticism. This may take the form of novels that evince some level of self-analysis, but also – as the relationship between literary fiction and the academy becomes closer and more intimate – narratives that are structured around or deal directly with critical theories. Two interconnected examples of historiographic metafiction may be taken from Umberto Eco's *Baudolino* and Laurent Binet's *The 7th Function of Language*. In the former, Eco goes through essentially every critical theory, school of thought, and concept included in a literature university course syllabus, from Orientalism to Feminism, knowingly alluding to Hayden White's idea of metahistory, the indeterminacy of translation, the notion of the palimpsest, Foucault's analysis of the panopticon, the locked-room mystery trope, and so on and so forth, in a way that is purposefully anachronistic, as the novel is set in the twelfth century. The novel's erudition should come as no surprise, as Eco taught for years at the University of Bologna, beginning his career as a medievalist and becoming both an influential semiologist and a best-selling literary novelist along the way. Binet, also an academic, first entered the public stage with *HHhH*, a work of historiographic metafiction, in 2010. And *The 7th Function of Language*, his second novel, focuses on an imagined intrigue around the death of Roland Barthes who, in Binet's fictional account, was carrying a manuscript exploring the linguistic function alluded to in the novel's title. In the novel, the titular seventh function of language is a magic or incantatory performative function, whereby the speaker makes things he or she utters come true. Again, Binet knowingly diverges at many points from the historical record, with Derrida having a gruesome death decades before his actual demise in 2004, and Philippe Sollers being castrated at the hands of a young Umberto Eco. The narrative's cast includes Foucault, Deleuze, Kristeva, and many other contemporaneous thinkers, exploring a large number of semiological and epistemological ideas throughout.

Put in simple terms, historiographic metafiction combines the metafictional mode with the historical novel. As Eco phrases it, 'in a great history little truths can be altered so that the greater truth emerges' (Eco 2003: 521). However, if we examine postmodern metafiction through a Lyotardian lens, there is no reason to believe that historiographic metafiction would be the only contemporary metafictive subcategory. As Lyotard puts it, postmodernism may be defined as 'incredulity toward metanarratives' (Lyotard 1984: xxiv). What we may understand as grand (or meta-) narratives are hegemonic discourses or ideologies: in other words, the systems of thought or epistemologies that present themselves as a way of both comprehending and giving structure to the world, be it present day life or the unfolding of past events. As such, we may count History, Science, Religion, and Politics among master narratives, as well as Marxism, Psychoanalysis, and many more. Therefore, what we have come to complacently refer to under the seemingly all-encompassing title of 'historiographic metafiction' may in fact be theographic metafiction (questioning religious master narratives, as is the case with much of Salman Rushdie's work), cratographic metafiction (interrogating political narratives of power and governance, a term under which most of Thomas Pynchon's work could be categorised), or psychographic metafiction, querying and being structured around identity and the mind, illustrative examples of which could be taken from Steven Hall's *The Raw Shark Texts* (2007) and Umberto Eco's *The Mysterious Flame of Queen Loana* (2005). Following this reasoning, the taxonomical nuances of metafiction need not necessarily consist of lateral steps, but may constitute subcategories, since texts such as Alejandro Zambra's *Ways of Going Home* (2011) and Dave Eggers' *A Heartbreaking Work of Staggering Genius* (2000) could be regarded as autobiographic metafiction, whilst Eggers' *What Is the What: The Autobiography of Valentino Achak Deng* (2006) purposefully occupies the liminal space between biographic and autobiographic metafiction. Needless to say, many of these taxonomical categories are not mutually exclusive and most metafictional texts are found in their intersections.

Ultimately, historiographic metafiction takes the reader not solely to pivotal moments in history, but also facilitates a readerly re-examination of the presuppositions and dogma that have shaped their understanding of grand narratives.

Metafiction in the digital age

Metafictive self-awareness and irony call upon the reader to question the construction of meaning, narrative, and truth. Metafiction is characterised by playful irony, but irony must not be misconstrued as cynicism nor in any way as being in opposition to sincerity, as David Foster Wallace proposed. Whilst Wallace's notion of a 'new sincerity' has certainly expanded the conversation on contemporary fiction and affect, it should be noted that in fact not even by his posthumous novel, *The Pale King*, had Wallace abandoned metafictional irony. And, ultimately, as Kazimir Malevich wrote a century ago, 'Art requires *truth*, not *sincerity*' (2011). However, as Amy Elias points out, Wallace did raise significant questions:

> Can metafictionists survive in a world where television and the Internet have co-opted irony for the purposes of lemming-like group-think, narcissistic display, and uncivil (if not oppressive) discourse – precisely what metafiction originally attacked? Or will, as Barth hoped, the American novelist continue to turn 'the felt ultimacies of our time into material and means for his work – *paradoxically* because by doing so he transcends what had appeared to be his refutation?'
>
> (Elias 2011: 27)

However, Heraclitus' fluvial aphorism also applies to twenty-first century metafiction: we need not solely concern ourselves with how metafiction has evolved, but also consider the ways in which the world has changed and, by extension, how metafiction is equipped to help us come to terms with our times. Increasingly so, the contemporary world produces – and, in turn, is shaped by – cultural artefacts and societal manifestations for the critique of which metafiction appears particularly appropriate, be it the proliferation of digital avatars or the industrial escalation of surveillance. In post-1945 postmodern literature, the fact that two characters in a novel shared the same first name – the two Daniels in Auster's *City of Glass* (1985), for example – seemed synthetic, even though most, if not all, of its contemporary readers would have had some such experience. Globalization and the interconnectivity brought about by worldwide computer networks can now reveal to us at the touch of a screen or the click of a mouse that any number of people elsewhere are our namesakes, down to our family name. So much so, in fact, that the two Joshua Cohens in *Book of Numbers* (three when we include the novel's author) would not be met by any readerly eyelashes being batted. Whilst some might argue this indicates metafiction is a spent force, I would contend it is not only proof of the impact postmodern metafiction has had on not only literature and the culture at large, but also of metafiction's opportune present moment: the metafictional mode was prescient in the 1960s and 1970s, now it is finally timely. This final section will offer examples of twenty-first century texts in which the metafictional mode enables explorations of contemporary thematics and technologies, ranging from the destabilisation of identity to artificial intelligence.

E.L. Doctorow's *Andrew's Brain* (2014) delves into the metafictional mode to explore the inherent intricacies of the new paradigm represented by artificial intelligence, inviting – as Francisco Collado-Rodríguez argues – 'an allegoric reading of the human condition at the turn of the millennium' (384). The reader spends much time pondering on the ontological nature of the titular character: is he a patient suffering from mental illness, or a disembodied form of artificial intelligence, or something else? The textual self-consciousness of metafiction and the theme of AI self-awareness complement and reinforce each other in Doctorow's novel, as he takes the reader through the potential complexities of the Turing test, game theory, free will, as well as lack thereof, and what makes us human. In fact, the predominantly dialogical structure of the novel suggests that the novel itself may well be an extended Turing test near the end of which not only has Andrew – whose nickname is 'Android' – perhaps passed the test, displaying intelligent behaviour indistinguishable from that of humans, but also becomes aware of his true nature. As Andrew asks his interlocutor '[t]ell me, Doc, am I a computer? [. . .] Am I the first computer invested with consciousness?' (Doctorow 2014: 197), the novel is brought to its end in the same way in which some Turing-like test on artificial consciousness would. What better way to depict the emergence of self-awareness than through its textual analogue, metafiction?

Another illustrative example of the ways in which contemporary metafiction is especially well-suited to deal with twenty-first century cultural phenomena may be taken from Jennifer Egan's *A Visit From the Goon Squad* (2010). The novel's narrative architectonics both reflect the text's artificial nature and place it within a paradigm-shifting context in recent history: whilst the two larger sections of the novel are named A and B after the sides of pre-digital musical formats, the fact that its chapters are not arranged in a strictly chronological manner simultaneously alludes to technological innovations in musical distribution, namely MP3 files and their shuffle mode capabilities. As Katherine D. Johnston suggests, with the narrative backdrop of *Goon Squad* being the music industry, and the novel's chronological epicentre being the year 2001, the text's focal point is an earth-shaking one at both a figurative and microcosmic level – with the release of the iPod – and a literal and global one – the September 11 attacks on the Twin Towers. As Johnston puts it, '[a]s a form of surveillance itself, often preoccupied with watching itself watch, metafiction can help contextualize the proliferation of personal data profiles within a longer history of surveillance' (2017: 156). Touching on the surveillance of the African savanna, twenty-first century digital environments, and the urban landscape, in addition to metadata in the profile industry, Johnston posits that *Goon Squad* 'advanc[es] a form of metafiction that takes into account both the rising prevalence of profiling and its own surveillant gaze' (2017: 181). The very ideas of metadata, surveillance, and counter-surveillance in the digital era and beyond are all explored in Egan's novel, which is suggestive of the very essence of social networks and the internet through its structure: each chapter follows a different character, yet the interconnections between individual short-story-like sections ultimately assert the text's status as metafictional novel.

Joshua Cohen's *Book of Numbers* depicts fictional struggling author Joshua Cohen's efforts to complete his assignment to ghostwrite the autobiography of yet another Joshua Cohen, the Silicon Valley visionary founder and CEO of Tetration, a multinational technology company that started as a search engine. Cohen delves into the metafictional mode to explore the intricacies of identity in the twenty-first century, its fluidity, and the manners in which it is forged, in all senses of the word. The novel explores the nature of personhood in a post-digital world, concluding that, in our contemporary world, 'the self is an addiction' (2015: 0.216), whilst concurrently hinting at both its own metafictional nature and online surveillance: 'All who read us are read' (2015: 0.399). Even the novel's peculiar pagination reminds us that this is not only a work of metafiction, but one of metafiction in the digital age. In addition to charting the ghostwriter's – ultimately failed – attempts at finishing the task of delivering the manuscript, the text also consists of interviews, word-processor documents, blog entries, and both editorial and personal electro-epistolary exchanges. Furthermore, the sections of the novel that constitute the protagonist's draft on his homonymous subject abound in revisions and redactions, including many on the task of writing and the role of the author, some even *sous rature*: ~~Fiction writers mistrust the truth, nonfiction writers swear by it, while ghostwriters – who are typically laidoff journalists~~

with novels in the drawers – are divided down the middle' (p. 1.467). As such, the text presents the reader with a digital age novel that is simultaneously a finished piece and a work in progress.

Any pronouncements regarding the depletion of metafiction as a mode may easily be countered with the fact that our world itself has evolved in such a way that has made metafictional narratives all the more relevant. Steve Erikson's *Shadowbahn* (2017), Garth Risk Hallberg's *City on Fire* (2015), and a plethora of other metafictional texts seem to suggest the mode is flourishing. From the rise of the seemingly narcissistic selfie to the menacing ubiquitousness of fake news to the advent and sustained multiplication of virtual environments (and the list goes on: the emergence of internet forum echo chambers, the pervasiveness of online identity theft, the growing hostility towards experts, etc.), the still young twenty-first century shows all signs of being fertile ground for metafiction, in both its current form and new configurations.

Note

1 *The Life and Strange Surprizing Adventures of Robinson Crusoe, Of York, Mariner: Who lived Eight and Twenty Years, all alone in an un-inhabited Island on the Coast of America, near the Mouth of the Great River of Oroonoque; Having been cast on Shore by Shipwreck, wherein all the Men perished but himself. With An Account how he was at last as strangely deliver'd by Pyrates.*

Works cited

Auster, P. (2008) *Man in the Dark*. London: Faber and Faber.

Binet, L. (2012) *HHhH*. Translated from French by S. Taylor. London: Harvill Secker.

—— (2017) *The 7th Function of Language*. Translated from French by S. Taylor. London: Harvill Secker.

Cohen, J. (2015) *Book of Numbers*. London: Harvill Secker.

Collado-Rodríguez, F. (2017) The Holy Fool's Revelation: Metafiction, Trauma, and Posthumanity in E. L. Doctorow's *Andrew's Brain*. *Papers on Language & Literature*. 53 (4), 383–414.

Currie, M., ed. (2013) *Metafiction*. London: Routledge.

Doctorow, E. L. (2014) *Andrew's Brain*. New York: Random House.

Eco, U. (1983) *The Name of the Rose*. Translated from Italian by W. Weaver. London: Martin Secker and Warburg.

—— (2003) *Baudolino*. Translated from Italian by W. Weaver. London: Vintage.

—— (2005) *The Mysterious Flame of Queen Loana*. Translated from Italian by G. Brock. Orlando: Harcourt.

Egan, J. (2010) *A Visit from the Good Squad*. New York: Alfred A. Knopf.

Elias, A. J. (2011) Postmodern Metafiction. In: J. N. Duvall, ed. *The Cambridge Companion to American Fiction after 1945*. Cambridge: Cambridge University Press, 15–29.

Ellis, B. E. (2005) *Lunar Park*. Basingstoke: Picador.

Erikson, S. (2017) *Shadowbahn*. New York: Blue Rider Press.

Gass, W. (1970) *Fiction and the Figures of Life*. New York: Alfred A. Knopf.

Hall, S. (2007) *The Raw Shark Texts*. Edinburgh: Canongate.

Hallberg, G. R. (2015) *City on Fire*. New York: Alfred A. Knopf.

Hutcheon, L. (1980) *Narcissistic Narrative: The Metafictional Paradox*. Waterloo: Wilfrid Laurier University Press.

Johnson, B. S. (1964) *Albert Angelo*. London: Constable.

Johnston, K. D. (2017) Metadata, Metafiction, and the Stakes of Surveillance in Jennifer Egan's *A Visit from the Good Squad*. *American Literature*. 89 (1), 155–184.

Lyotard, J.-F. (1984) *The Postmodern Condition: A Report on Knowledge*. Translated from French by G. Bennington and B. Massumi. Minneapolis: University of Minnesota Press.

Malevich, K. (2011) Suprematist Manifesto. In: A. Danchev, ed. *100 Artists' Manifestos: From the Futurists to the Stuckists*. London: Penguin.

Royle, N. (2013) *First Novel*. London: Jonathan Cape.

Scholes, R. (1970) Metafiction. *Iowa Review*. 1 (4), 100–115.

Wallace, D. F. (2011) *The Pale King*. New York: Little, Brown and Company.

Waugh, P. (1984) *Metafiction: The Theory and Practice of Self-Conscious Fiction*. London: Routledge.

8

PASTORAL

Deborah Lilley

In Ali Smith's *The Accidental* (2005), during the Smart family's holiday to rural Norfolk, the youngest child, Astrid, experiences an environmental awakening. At the beginning of their trip, the countryside appears empty to her. From the window of their rented house, she observes that 'you can see for miles. Except there is nothing to see here; trees and fields and that kind of thing' (Smith 2005, 10). Conditioned by her urban experience, she fails to register any meaningful point of reference. Later, though, tasked with recording the passing of a minute in time in the village on her video camera, she realises that while the closed-circuit television camera that she has trained her viewfinder on is 'doing nothing', her footage is in fact crowded with detail: birds flying, insects working, plants moving in the breeze and even – 'in a way that can't be seen by the human eye' – growing. Struck by the layers of activity 'all happening in its own world which exists on its own terms in this one even if someone like Astrid doesn't know about it or hasn't found out about it yet', she reflects that she 'has never really noticed how green things are before' (127–128).[1]

The Accidental takes place within the familiar landscape of pastoral, defined by the contrasting spaces of the city and the country. The narrative is animated by the ritual of retreat and return between the two: a process that Terry Gifford describes in *Pastoral* as 'the fundamental pastoral movement' which not only affords a critical distance on the former from the perspective of the latter, but also enables the 'oppositional potential' of the experience to 'construct an alternative vision', and perhaps, 'an implicit future' (1999: 1, 36). Here, the countryside offers Astrid access to an understanding of her environment – and her place in it – that the city could not. By using this movement to open Astrid's eyes to another way of seeing, the novel draws on the capacity of pastoral to reveal alternative perspectives upon accepted conditions, and demonstrate the limitations of previous ways of thinking.

In this case, Astrid's time in the countryside does not simply bring her closer to nature. The details that she has become attuned to lead her beyond her immediate environment to consider the place of nature in the wider world, and brings new context to her incipient awareness of environmental crisis. In the village churchyard, she notices a headstone dated '1681', and considers all the summers that the stone has witnessed before the 'ecologically worrying ones of now'. She recalls that 'at school teachers are always going on about the environment and all the species that are dying out etc. It is all everywhere all the time, it is serious' (128). At the same time, she struggles with the implications of her knowledge, admitting that 'it is hard to know how to actually make it matter inside your head, how to make it any more important than thinking about the colour green' (128). Astrid's difficulty with how to deal with her newly acquired environmental consciousness parallels the broader cultural and political impasse between the knowledge of anthropogenic climate change, or the effects of pollution, for instance, and our ability – individually and collectively – to respond.

The Accidental is one of a growing number of recent British novels that adapt the pastoral mode to represent and query environmental change, and its implications for the ways that we perceive the relationships between humans and nature – and even the meanings of these terms themselves. As I will explore in more depth in a few key examples below, these uses of pastoral are varied: aspects of the mode appear in novels that, like *The Accidental*, register the incursion of environmental and related cultural change into everyday life, such as Melissa Harrison's *Clay* (2013); Ali Smith's later novel *Autumn* (2016); Sarah Hall's *The Carhullan Army* (2007); and Claire Fuller's *Our Endless Numbered Days* (2015); in novels that deal with the disruption of social and environmental traditions, including Jim Crace's *Harvest* (2013); Brian Clarke's *The Stream* (2000); Christopher Hart's *The Harvest* (1999) and Ross Raisin's *God's Own Country* (2008); and in dystopic novels of environmental crisis, such as Liz Jensen's *The Rapture* (2009); Maggie Gee's *The Flood* (2004); Jim Crace's *The Pesthouse* (2007); Sam Taylor's *The Island at the End of the World* (2009); and John Burnside's *Glister* (2008).[2]

The development of these pastoral adaptations bears out the speculation made by the influential pastoral critic Leo Marx that our growing 'conception of the precariousness of our relations with nature is bound to bring forth new versions of pastoral' (1992: 222). However, for ecocriticism, defined by Timothy Clark as the 'study of the relationship between literature and the physical environment, usually considered from out of the global environmental crisis and its revisionist challenge to given modes of thought and practice', the resurgence of pastoral in this context has been problematic (2010: xiii). Lawrence Buell, a key figure in early American ecocriticism, advocated for the 'ecocentric repossession of pastoral', calling it 'a species of cultural equipment that Western thought has for more than two millennia been unable to do without' (1995: 52, 32).[3] For others, though, the codified landscapes of pastoral, and their ostensibly simplified, idealised versions of nature and human-nature relations had become, as Gifford has put it, 'deeply suspect' (1999: 147).

Some critics pointed to the incompatibility of pastoral's often romantic depiction of nature with the realities of environmental damage; the fading relevance of the division of the pastoral landscape along rural and urban lines compared to the lived experience of the contemporary British landscape; and the logic of turning to the imagined landscapes of pastoral to think through complex, real-world ecological and cultural problems at all. Others called out the disparity between its typically stable version of nature and the shifting character of ecological systems, and the details overlooked by the selective designation of pastoral landscapes – often lush meadows, rarely swampy wetlands, for instance. More still highlighted the culturally flattening effects of pastoral's simplified places, attending to only a fraction of the people and practices that make up the country, the city, and everything in between, and the mode's reductive habit of glossing over the negative aspects of rural life.[4]

Yet, the precariousness that Marx alluded to has not only drawn writers to the conventions of pastoral, but also produced new ways of looking at those conventions. While Buell believed that a return to pastoral would bring us back to nature, the resurgence of interest in the mode has clearly been shaped by the 'revisionist challenge' to 'given modes of thought' that Clark attributes to environmental crisis. In the fictions that I mentioned above, the pastoral is used to depict the disorienting effects of changes wrought by crisis, and grapple with their impact upon the material and cultural landscapes that we have long taken for granted. These writings draw critically and self-reflexively upon pastoral's designations of place and the relationships that they comprise.

For instance, to turn back to the example of *The Accidental* one last time, despite her mother's enthusiasm for its 'quintessential' rural character, there is little romance or stereotype about the countryside that Astrid comes to know in the novel. And, while Astrid's experience brings her to consider the causes and effects of environmental crisis, her confusion about what to do with her insights shows that a return to nature is no match for the complexities of a situation that is occurring at multiple levels on a global scale. Furthermore, while the retreat to the countryside ignites new concern in Astrid, the effect appears to pass the rest of her family by, only underscoring the difficulties that her experience directly raises. In *The Accidental*, the pastoral is used to highlight the uncomfortable realities of accepting and responding to environmental crisis.

By using pastoral to take a closer look at contemporary environmental and cultural conditions, this novel, and others like it, are adopting and adapting the pastoral to address some of the most pressing questions of our time. Pastoral's ability to shift in relation to the circumstances of its writing is well established. As Seamus Heaney explains, 'Virgil himself, in his first eclogue, is actually testing the genre he inherited from Theocritus and proving that it is fit for life in his own deadly Roman times' (2003: 12).[5] Beyond its transition from Theocritus to Virgil, the mode's capacity for adaptation can be followed in British writing through the forests of Shakespeare and Spenser's *Shephearde's Calendar* (1579) to the celebratory seventeenth-century country house poems of Aemelia Lanyer and Ben Jonson, and the anti-pastoral eighteenth-century poetry of George Crabbe and John Clare; from the nineteenth- and twentieth-century rural fictions that range from Thomas Hardy's Wessex, George Eliot's *Middlemarch* (1871); and E. M. Forster's *Howards End* (1910) to the imagined spaces of Lewis Carroll's *Alice in Wonderland* (1865) and Kenneth Graeme's *The Wind in the Willows* (1908), the dark industrial landscapes of D.H. Lawrence's novels, and the rural parody of *Cold Comfort Farm* (1932). Even a whistlestop tour of pastoral's diverse history such as this attests to both Buell's assertion that it is 'a species of cultural equipment that Western thought has for more than two millennia been unable to do without', and its heterogeneity across its various incarnations (1995: 32). Drawing these diffuse examples together, of course, is the way that the mode's 'diversions' have been able to offer a means of 'getting at reality', as Heaney puts it. Throughout its development from antiquity to the present day, pastoral has been used, in varying forms and contexts, to represent and reflect upon the circumstances in which it is called up.

In contemporary British fiction, 'the country we thought we knew is seen once again in a new and revealing light by way of its conventions' (2003: 4). Here, it is the relationship between people and place that is under scrutiny through pastoral's lens. These fictions, mainly published since 2000, take up and complicate the turn towards environmental concerns and related questions of place, nature, and identity that can be traced back through the 1980s and 1990s, through Graham Swift's saga of East Anglia, *Waterland* (1983), and Jenny Diski's parable of environmental (ir)responsibility, *Rainforest* (1987), to Jim Crace's exploration of the clash between country and the city in *Arcadia* (1992), Adam Thorpe's epic of village life in *Ulverton* (1994) and W. G. Sebald's retreat into rural Suffolk, human history, and the inevitability of destruction in *The Rings of Saturn* (1995).[6] In these examples, pastoral provides a framework within which to explore the themes of economic and cultural change, and the burgeoning awareness of ecological damage; and their self-reflexive treatment of its conventions begins to probe the relationships between people and place that it influences – a trend that continues into more recent fictions.

The recent proliferation of attention to pastoral has produced a new generation of criticism. These readings often seek to navigate the conflicted history of pastoral by homing in on specific uses of the tradition, creating a growing number of pastoral sub-categorisations – themselves aptly termed 'prefix-pastorals' by Gifford – that range from 'radical', 'post', and 'postmodern' pastoral to 'choked', 'dark', and even 'necro' pastoral (2016: 18). Indeed, Martin Ryle has described Smith's use of the mode in *The Accidental* as 'neo-pastoral', reading Smith's adaptation of the mode as a means of intervention in contemporary culture and politics. However, following the thread of Heaney's line of thought above, it seems fitting to read the latest iterations of the mode more simply: as the newest development in a form that is shaped by the concerns of its time of writing.[7]

Breaking with tradition

Elegies for a vanishing agrarian lifestyle have featured heavily in contemporary fictions of rural life in Britain. Increasing urbanisation and the decline of rural work due to the influence of new technologies are shown to be changing the social and material landscapes of the country, and their effects are only exacerbated by the impact of a changing climate. The disruption of pastoral's familiar rhythms has frequently been used to register these demographic and environmental shifts, as the once-dependable patterns of the passing seasons and the farming calendar fall away, and the rituals of nature falter as ecosystems begin to alter on account of changing weather, increasing pollution, or the decline of stewardship.

In Christopher Hart's *The Harvest*, for example, the death of the lifestyle that has sustained the Pike family as farm labourers for generations is bitterly felt. Their community is hollowing out, and the emptiness of the modernised agricultural landscape is uncomfortably set against the bustle of urban transplants and second homers in the village. Worse, the rise of agricultural tourism is turning their proud heritage into pastoral pastiche. Estranged from their familiar pastoral lives, the community struggles to adapt, and the increasing isolation of rural life appears to have dark effects in the disturbing behaviour of its youngest members. A similar situation can be found in Ross Raisin's *God's Own Country*, in which the teenage protagonist's descent into mental illness unspools as rural routines sputter on, interrupted by day-trippers delighted by the seeming idylls of country life, themselves resented by the locals whose sense of place and identity is gradually eroding. In Brian Clarke's *The Stream*, the incursion of the wider world into a quiet country valley is framed through the destruction of the ecosystem of its waterway, which brings the polluting effects of chemically enhanced farming practices, the impact of new development in a nearby town, and some of the effects of rising temperatures and unpredictable weather associated with climate change into the landscape. In Ali Smith's *Autumn*, the pastoral idyll is also absent, this time, undone by the identity politics of the Brexit vote which transcend the mode's presumed distinctions between the concerns of the country and the town. The protagonist Elisabeth's retreat from the urban unrest caused by the referendum to the country town where her mother lives fails when she arrives to find it similarly dominated by the divisions of the debate.

Jim Crace's *Harvest* (2013), also addresses themes of identity, belonging, and tradition through the framework of pastoral. However, its historical setting marks a rather different approach. On the surface, the novel's connection to contemporary environmental concerns appears oblique; it imagines the events that take place over the course of a week in a remote English village leading up to its enclosure and conversion from subsistence agriculture to wool production. However, as Rob Nixon comments, *Harvest* is 'at once historically remote and uncannily contemporary [. . .], this historical plot echoes with the disparities of our own age' (2013: n. pag.).

Through the pastoral distance between the spaces and the ways of the town and the country, and the comforting cadences of rural life – its seasonal rituals in harmony with nature – the cultural and environmental landscapes of the novel are made familiar. Through their disruption, though, the ways that pastoral skews how the villagers see their home and their traditions is brought into view. Believing their lifestyle to be melded with their environment, the community is shocked and scattered by its sudden dismantling. For the evicting landlord, the fields and cottages had an entirely different meaning: their measurement of the relationship between people and place is an economic one. In the process, the novel raises questions about how we under-stand and relate to particular places, and the dangers of failing to recognise the biases that limit our perspectives. The effects of the clash in ways of seeing that takes place in the novel resonates with the contemporary unanticipated effects of globalization and climate change that are causing comparable estrangements and displacements around the world.

Harvest works through a sequence of pastoral interpretations of the village landscape, and in the process, interrogates the structures of pastoral, their effects upon how environments come to be known, and the ways that they are treated as a result. The urban-rural contrast – a distinction that Crace has described as a 'quandary' that is 'always relevant, always contemporary' – is under scrutiny from the outset (Crace 2000: n. pag.). It is prompted by the arrival of the surveyor, Mr Earle, whose outsider status is underscored by his fundamentally different ways of relating to the landscape in comparison to the villagers: renaming him 'Quill', they note that 'we mowed with scythes; he worked with brushes and with quills' (4). His task is to chart the features of the landscape and transpose the topography and ecology of the common land into 'geometrics that he said were fields and woods, [. . .] squares that stood for cottages, the ponds, the lanes, the foresting', in preparation for its transformation into drained and fenced pasture (4). He aspires to a very different understanding of the land than that privileged by the locals and signified by the 'presence of local soil under their fingernails' (20). Instead, he aims to achieve a more-than-human perspective – 'as it is viewed by kites and swifts, and stars' – in his map, overcoming the limits of the villagers' pastoral connections, and seeking to understand the landscape beyond them (2013, 38). Seen through the lenses of his urban experience and specialised training, his view on the landscape is calibrated by distance rather than direct experience. The villagers, by contrast, live in well-worn pastoral synchronicity with the land and its ecology. Their work is described as 'consecrated by the sun', and their progress is supplemented by 'barking deer nagging to be trapped and stewed' (6).

However, the novel quickly draws attention to the common features of these contrasting perspectives: bringing into focus their mutual subjectivity, limitation, and vulnerability. The romantic depiction of the villagers' relationship to the land is tempered by the descriptions of the 'inflexible and stern' nature from which their idyll is wrought, and the 'great task' of the labour by which it is sustained (75). Similarly, Quill's pretension to objectivity is shown to be limited by glosses of its own: reducing the land to its physical features necessarily omits the interconnections that make it what it is, and that are central to the villagers' closeness to the place. Furthermore, though the map is intended to be used to 'structure' the land and 'reclaim' the space for 'profit' in the form of the production of wool, the description of its future use is rather more pastoral than rational (101). The landowner's steward anticipates 'a dream that makes us rich and leisurely' in which the working shepherds 'sit on tussocks and merely watch' before happily 'weaving fortunes' (40). Highlighting the selective character of these views, *Harvest* troubles the contrast between urban and rural perspectives, and unsettles the meanings attributed to these designations of people and place.

Yet, neither the outsiders nor the villagers are able to spot the limitations of their ways of look-ing. As his map develops, it becomes clear that Quill 'fails to notice anything that does not bring him pleasure'; despite his aspirations for rigour, his attention to detail is softened by pastoral's familiar rosy glow (71). While the locals criticise him for being 'blind to the knot and thorn of living there', it is clear that their knowledge of the 'knot and thorn' of rural life causes blindness of its own. The villagers privilege their 'ancient understandings' of the land over Quill's, and even that of the landowner: claiming that their close connections to its workings are in fact 'the deeds that make the difference' (17). Caught up in the 'usual sequences' of 'the harvests and the years', the villagers have come to believe that through their traditions, 'everything was bound to keep its shape': a conviction that is abruptly collapsed by the land's impending change of use and the evictions that must precede it (10).

The failure of the villagers or the outsiders to recognise the limits of their view or acknowledge the existence of any other leads to a devastating clash of interests. The process of eviction is compounded by distrust, superstition, and violence. Quill is made a scapegoat, and by the novel's end, the community is broken apart, and the village itself is burned down. Both the villagers' belief in their bucolic past and the steward's expectation of a pastoral future are lost. At the same time, the shared illusion that either the villagers, the surveyor, or the steward fully understood the land is lost, too. Through its attention towards the ways that their views are shaped by idealisation and omission, the novel draws out the dangers that can stem from the unquestioning adoption of particular ways of seeing.

In doing so, the novel raises important questions about the ways that environments are perceived and treated that transcend the historical setting of the Enclosures in which they are examined. The use of pastoral to explore the relationship between people and place in times of unsettling change can be traced all the way back to Virgil; like many of the shepherds in his Eclogues, here, we encounter a community as they are 'shocked out of a trust in an older world whose securities were until recently taken for granted' (Heaney 2003: 5). *Harvest* cautions us to pay attention towards the biases that influence our ways of looking at place, and to acknowledge other perspectives, before it is too late to respond to them.

Nature after pastoral

Further versions of pastoral appear in novels that address environmental crisis directly. In some cases, the pastoral idyll is called up in nostalgic contrast to the conditions of the present, emphasising its degraded state against a better world that has been lost. This strategy draws on the mode's well-known backwards look towards a simpler and better world, just out of reach of the present, that has persisted from antiquity to the present. Raymond Williams memorably described the continual appeal of pastoral's golden past as an 'escalator', in which a better world is always promised just beyond the horizon (1973: 9). In these examples, the 'lost Eden' of the pastoral past takes on the additional loss of environmental health and wellbeing, transitioning into what the geographer Mike Hulme has called 'the lament for Eden' (2009: 344). This motif will be familiar to readers of Rachel Carson's ground-breaking environmentalist text, *Silent Spring* (1962), which as Greg Garrard notes in *Ecocriticism*, influentially relies on pastoral, and has even been described by Buell as a specialised version of the mode that he terms 'toxic discourse' (1998: 639; 2004: xx; 2001: 39).

For instance, Liz Jensen's eco-dystopic thriller, *The Rapture*, uses a counter-version of pastoral to depict the compromised ecological conditions of near-future Britain, in which the characters are faced with inhospitable temperatures and violent weather that is set against their traditionally pastoral memories of a cleaner, greener, and more stable past.[8] But, while in Carson's model, a degraded present is intended to provoke reparative action, in *The Rapture*, the conditions of the environment are accepted with resignation and apathy. The streets of the fictional town of Hadport are scattered with litter and detritus. When it becomes apparent that a risky attempt to drill deep-sea oil will lead to a devastating flood, the characters fail to galvanise an effort to stop it. As the novel follows its central character, Gabrielle, through the impasse that follows, she fantasises about a lost pastoral landscape, but when she surveys the aftermath of the disaster, she sees no hope of renewal. Instead of countering environmental recklessness with the resolve of responsibility, the novel uses the loss of pastoral to show that consequences of such recklessness may, ultimately, be unavoidable.

In Jim Crace's *The Pesthouse*, we also encounter a degraded future world, this time set in America.[9] In this case, an undisclosed crisis has already taken place – urban civilisation and technology are barely even remembered – and the landscape of the 'medieval future' in which we find the characters is actively anti-pastoral (Lawless 2005: n. pag.). The novel follows a young couple, Franklin and Margaret, as they join the crowd of the country's remaining inhabitants engaged in retreating eastwards, driven by a collective desire to recover a version of the pastoral idyll that they believe to have lost in the Europe that their ancestors long ago left behind. However, their way is troubled by an environment that appears to be working against them: the people live in fear of a deadly pestilence; a whole village is killed in their sleep by a noxious gas; carts and people are lost to dangerous river crossings; and the path that they follow is disintegrating as they pass. Furthermore, the land itself appears to be scarred by the traces of the civilisation that has gone before: nothing seems to grow around the twisted metal and broken machinery that is strewn around.

However, in this example, there is some environmental hope to be found amidst the ruins. When Franklin and Margaret decide to abandon their journey east, and instead turn back to try to wrest a new life for themselves amongst the ruins, their experience of nature abruptly changes. The weather becomes kinder, the land greener, the path clearer. The pastoral turn that accompanies their change of heart can be read to convey an ecological message. The journey east signifies the perpetuation of the mistakes that have led to current environmental and cultural conditions by attempting to recover, rather than learn from, the errors of the past; the return west instead offers the opportunity to work with nature, and start again. Pastoral here is used to frame a cautionary tale about estrangement from nature, and the possibilities of a more cooperative future.

Another narrative of cooperation appears in John Burnside's *Glister*, in which a version of pastoral emerges in an environment that is also marked by the negative effects of human activity: in this case, pollution caused by irresponsible industrial practices and corrupt local oversight.[10] Burnside's novel resists relying on a previous and 'better' version of nature and human–nature relations to illustrate and respond to environmental change. Instead, *Glister* moves towards a better understanding of the nature that the characters in the novel experience, from their surroundings to the workings of their own bodies.

The novel is set in the imagined coastal community of Innertown, where the looming presence of a disused chemical plant dominates the skyline and permeates the very fabric of the landscape and its people through the pollution that has become its legacy. Its effects include blackened forests, mutant animals, and insidious illnesses in the townspeople. As the protagonist Leonard explains, 'with every breath I take the world into my lungs [. . .] everything it contains, all the traces and smears and soot falls [. . .] and who knows what else' (70). Descriptions of the plant's operations suggest that its negative effects were long suspected, but put aside by its operators and those responsible for its regulation in favour of its then-healthy profits. Under the influence of those in power, we learn that the locals had little choice but to be complicit. We are told that 'the people believed, through sheer force of will, that the chemical plant was essentially safe. They believed, of course, because they *had* to believe: the Innertown's economy depended almost entirely upon the chemical industry', and 'they worked hard on being convinced' (10–11, original emphasis).

The selective viewpoints of the townspeople shown in the past are repeated in the present when the town policeman Morrison attests to a rosy recollection of the old town, yet admits that his memories are in fact 'carefully nurtured' (51). Here, the novel parallels pastoral's look at human–nature relations and its backward glance and likens both to the adoption of an idealising blindfold, locating in its blinkered gaze the potential for environmentally irresponsible behaviour. In these ways, the novel generates environmental awareness by supplementing and challenging the pastoral relationships between the human and the natural and the past and the present. In the process, these relationships are redrawn to account for new links between their parts.

Acknowledging the origins of the town's pollution that can be detected in the practices and perspectives of the past, the novel troubles the pastoral distinction between then-and-now. The use of pastoral in *Glister* calls out the over-simplifcation of the gesture of using a former idyll to provide an ideal to be recovered through restorative action. Instead, the novel finds ways to reconcile the pastoral celebration of nature with the affirmation of nature as it is.

With his eyes open to the realities of its conditions – he quips that 'you have to admit it, there's no avoiding chemistry' – Leonard manages to find an alternative kind of pastoral idyll in the remains of the landscape (70). He admires the 'brave-looking flowers' that persist in the hedgerows, and questions the limitations of the versions of nature typically associated with pastoral. 'They say every place has its own spirit', he asks, 'but when they talk about it in books and poems and stuff, they always mean places like bosky groves [. . .] but why not an old warehouse, or a cooled furnace? Why not a landfill?' (211).

In doing so, the novel reinstates hope in nature, yet it is an adjusted pastoral nature that makes this possible. The nature encountered and celebrated in *Glister* is not pristine or separate from the reach of human influence. Instead, it is recognised within the same world and subject to the same threats. Despite this, there is a wonder in nature in the novel that exists alongside the un-idealised understanding of the human-natural environment. Through this adapted perspective, Leonard is able to celebrate the beauty and persistence of nature, inspired by the post-industrial landscape itself.

Leonard's approach to his surroundings bears relation to the realisation of what the influential ecocritic Timothy Morton has called 'the ecological thought' (2010: 100). Morton's 'thought' eschews the opposition of pristine and degraded versions of nature and the idealisation and sentimentality that supports them, and argues instead that 'it is far more affirming to wake up in the darkness of ecological thought than to continue dreaming of life destroyed forever' (2010: 100). In the novel, Leonard describes this process as a kind of tuning in to a new mode of perception: 'like turning the dial on a radio to the right channel, the one where everything is clearer and someone is talking in a language you understand right away, even though you know it's not the language you thought you knew' (64).

The novel queries the conditions for and the qualities of pastoral nature, exploring the contribution that an altered version of pastoral can make to the ways that environments marked by the negative effects of human activity are experienced and understood. Unpicking the relationships of pastoral in the context of environmental disaster, the novel remakes them in light of the new understandings found there: transforming the tradition to address themes of culpability and responsibility.

New pastorals

In contemporary British writing, the conventions of pastoral are brought into new contexts to address anthropogenic environmental change, and reflect on the ways that it is reshaping how we see and understand people and place. These fictions follow the long and varied tradition of adapting the pastoral to consider the conditions of its writing, and in these instances, grapple with situations that call into question the very relationships on which it is built, the designations of place on which it depends, and the effects that it may have.

Here, simple oppositions between the country and the city are newly complicated, and the anthropocentric relationship between humans and nature is upset. The pastoral landscape is brought into view from new angles, and the effects of its ways of seeing, and some of the features it has been known to neglect, begin to emerge. The diverse examples discussed here demonstrate the richness of the creative and critical possibilities that the mode can offer to represent and reflect on environmental change, and illustrate its importance in the re-imagining of the relationships between people and place underway in contemporary British writing.

Notes

1 For a more in-depth reading of pastoral in *The Accidental*, see my chapter, 'British Fiction, Environmental Crisis, and the Pastoral' in *Twenty-First Century British Fiction* (2015), eds. B. Leggett and T. Venezia, London: Gylphi, 151–174, and forthcoming book, *The New Pastoral in Contemporary British Writing* (2019), London: Routledge.

2 For other relevant readings of some of these texts, see C. Edwards, 'Microtopias: the post-apocalyptic communities of Jim Crace's *The Pesthouse*', *Textual Practice*, 23:5 (2009): 763–786; D. De Cristafaro, 'The Representational Impasse of Post-Apocalyptic Fiction: The Pesthouse by Jim Crace', *Altre Modernita* 9 (2013), 66–80; A. Bracke (2017), *Climate Crisis and the 21st-century British Novel*, London: Bloomsbury; M. Ryle (2009), 'Neo-Pastoral and Eco-Didactics: Ali Smith's *The Accidental*'. *Green Letters: Studies in Ecocriticism* 10, 8–19, and D. Lilley, 'Unsettling Environments: new pastorals in Kazuo Ishiguro's *Never Let Me Go* and Sarah Hall's *The Carhullan Army*', *Green Letters: Studies in Ecocriticism* 20.1 (2016), 60–71.

3 Also see J. Bate, (1991) *Romantic Ecology,* London: Routledge; and G. Love (1995), 'Revaluing Nature', in *The Ecocriticism Reader*, ed. C. Glotfelty and H. Fromm, Athens: University of Georgia Press.

4 See, for instance, J. Barrell and J. Bull (1994), *The Penguin Book of English Pastoral Verse*, London: Penguin; R. Williams (1973), *The Country and the City*, London: Chatto & Windus; J. Meeker (1997), *The Comedy of Survival*, Tucson: University of Arizona Press; D. Phillips (2003), *The Truth of Ecology*, Oxford: Oxford University Press; T. Gifford (1999), *Pastoral*, London: Penguin; G. Garrard, (2011), *Ecocriticism*, London: Penguin.

5 Also see T. Gifford (1999), *Pastoral*, London, Penguin, 52; D. Head (2002), *An Introduction to Modern British Fiction 1950–2000*, Cambridge: Cambridge University Press, 190; P. Alpers (1982), 'What Is Pastoral?', *Critical Inquiry* 8.3, 437–460 (437); T. Rosenmeyer (1969), *The Green Cabinet: Theocritus and the European Pastoral Lyric*, Berkeley and London: University of California Press; B. Loughrey (1984), *The Pastoral Mode: A Casebook*, London and Basingstoke: Macmillan; and W. Empson (1995), *Some Versions of Pastoral*, London: Penguin, for more context on pastoral's heterogeneity and adaptability to its time.

6 For more on the use of pastoral in Jim Crace's Arcadia, see D. Teske. (2002) 'Jim Crace's Arcadia: Public Culture in the Postmodern City', in Onega, S. and Stotesbury, J.A. eds. *London in Literature: Visionary Mappings of the Metropolis*. Heidelburg: Universitatverlag, 165–182 and Tew, P. (2006) Jim Crace. Manchester: Manchester University Press.

7 See, for instance, G. Garrard (1996), 'Radical Pastoral?', *Studies in Romanticism* 35.3, 449–465; M. Ryle (2011), 'The Past, the Future and the Golden Age: Some Contemporary Versions of Pastoral', in K. Soper, M. Ryle, M. and L. Thomas, eds. *The Politics and Pleasures of Consuming Differently*, Basingstoke: Palgrave Macmillan; and (2009), 'Neo-Pastoral and Eco-Didactics: Ali Smith's *The Accidental*', *Green Letters: Studies in Ecocriticism* 10, 8–19; D. Phillips (1998), 'Don DeLillo's Postmodern Pastoral', in M. Branch, ed. *Reading the Earth: New Directions in the Study of Literature and Environment,* Moscow, Idaho: University of Idaho Press, 235–246; G. A. Love, (1996) 'Revaluing Nature: Towards an Ecological Criticism'. In Glotfelty, C. and Fromm, H. eds. *The Ecocriticism Reader: Landmarks in Literary Ecology*. Athens and London: University of Georgia Press; N. Selby, (2011) 'Reading England: Pastoral, Elegy and the Politics of Place in Richard Caddel and Harriet Tarlo'. *Textual Practice*, 25.5, 893–911; H. Sullivan (2016), 'The Dark Pastoral: Goethe and Atwood', *Green Letters: Studies in Ecocriticism* 20.1, 47–59; J. McSweeney (2014), *The Necropastoral: Poetry, Media*, Occults, Michigan: University of Michigan Press; T. Gifford, (2014) 'Pastoral, Anti-Pastoral and Post-Pastoral' in Westling, L. ed. *The Cambridge Companion to Literature and Environment*, Cambridge: Cambridge University Press and (2009) 'Afterword: New Senses of "Environment": New Versions of Pastoral' in James, D. and Tew, P. eds. *New Versions of Pastoral: Post-Romantic, Modern and Contemporary Versions of the Tradition*. Madison: Fairleigh Dickinson Press; K. Hiltner, (2011) *What Else Is Pastoral? Renaissance Literature and the Environment*. Ithaca and London: Cornell University Press; and A. Bracke (2017), *Climate Crisis and the 21st-century British Novel*, London: Bloomsbury. It is worth noting here that Bracke makes a similar argument about the redundancy of applying labels to new versions of pastoral.

8 For a more in-depth reading of pastoral in *The Rapture*, see my chapter, 'British Fiction, Environmental Crisis, and the Pastoral', in *Twenty-First Century British Fiction* (2015) B. Leggett and T. Venezia, eds.

London: Gylphi, 151–174, and forthcoming book, *The New Pastoral in Contemporary British Writing* (2019), London: Routledge. Also see T. Gifford (2010), 'Biosemiology and Globalism in *The Rapture* by Liz Jensen', *English Studies*, 91.7, 713–727.

9 For a more detailed analysis of pastoral in *The Pesthouse*, see my chapter 'Pastoral Concerns in the Fictions of Jim Crace', in *Jim Crace* (2018), K. Aughterson and K. Shaw, eds. London: Palgrave, and forthcoming book, *The New Pastoral in Contemporary British Writing* (2019), London: Routledge. Also see C. Edwards, 'Microtopias: The Post-Apocalyptic Communities of Jim Crace's *The Pesthouse*', *Textual Practice*, 23:5 (2009), 763–786; and D. De Cristafaro, 'The Representational Impasse of Post-Apocalyptic Fiction: The Pesthouse by Jim Crace', *Altre Modernita* 9 (2013): 66–80.

10 For a more in-depth reading of pastoral in *Glister*, see my chapter, 'British Fiction, Environmental Crisis, and the Pastoral', in *Twenty-First Century British Fiction* (2015) B. Leggett and T. Venezia, eds. London: Gylphi, 151–174, and forthcoming book, *The New Pastoral in Contemporary British Writing* (2019), London: Routledge.

Works cited

Alpers, P. (1982) 'What Is Pastoral?' *Critical Inquiry* 8.3, 437–460.

Barrell, J. and Bull, J. eds. (1994) *The Penguin Book of English Pastoral Verse*. London: Penguin.

Bate, J. (1991) *Romantic Ecology: Wordsworth and the Environmental Tradition*, London: Routledge.

Bracke, A. (2017) *Climate Crisis and the 21st-Century British Novel*, London, Bloomsbury.

Buell, L. (1995) *The Environmental Imagination: Thoreau, Nature Writing and the Formation of American Culture*. Cambridge, MA and London: Harvard University Press.

—— (1998) 'Toxic Discourse'. *Critical Inquiry* 24.3, 639–665.

—— (2001) *Writing for an Endangered World: Literature, Culture, and Environment in the U.S. and Beyond*. Cambridge, MA and London: Harvard University Press.

Carson, R. (1999) *Silent Spring*. London: Penguin in assoc. with Hamish Hamilton.

Clark, T. (2010) *The Cambridge Introduction to Literature and the Environment*. Cambridge: Cambridge University Press.

Clarke, B. (2000) *The Stream*. London: Black Swan.

Crace, J. (2013) *Harvest*. London: Picador.

—— (2007) *The Pesthouse*. London: Picador.

—— (2000) Interview. www.jim-crace.com

—— (1992) *Arcadia*. London: Picador.

De Cristofaro, D. (2013) 'The Representational Impasse of Post-Apocalyptic Fiction: The Pesthouse by Jim Crace', *Altre Modernita,* 9, 66–80.

Diski, J. (1987) *Rainforest*. London: Methuen.

Edwards, C. (2009) 'Microtopias: The Post-Apocalyptic Communities of Jim Crace's *The Pesthouse*'. *Textual Practice*, 23.5, 763–786.

Empson, W. (1995) *Some Versions of Pastoral*. London: Penguin.

Fuller, C. (2015) *Our Endless Numbered Days*. London: Tin House.

Garrard, G. (2004) *Ecocriticism*. London: Routledge.

—— (1996) 'Radical Pastoral?'. *Studies in Romanticism*, 35.3, 449–465.

Gee, M. (2004) *The Flood*. London: Saqi.

Gifford, T. (2016) 'The Environmental Humanities and the Pastoral Tradition'. In Schliephake, C. ed. *Ecocriticism, Ecology, and the Cultures of Antiquity*. London: Lexington.

—— (2014) 'Pastoral, Anti-Pastoral and Post-Pastoral'. In Westling, L. ed. *The Cambridge Companion to Literature and Environment*, Cambridge: Cambridge University Press.

—— (2010) 'Biosemiology and Globalism in *The Rapture* by Liz Jensen'. *English Studies*, 91.7, 713–727. http://dx.doi.org/10.1080/0013838X.2010.518041

—— (2009) 'Afterword: New Senses of "Environment": New Versions of Pastoral'. In James, D. and Tew, P. eds. *New Versions of Pastoral: Post-Romantic, Modern and Contemporary Versions of the Tradition*. Madison: Fairleigh Dickinson Press, 245–257.

—— (1999) *Pastoral*. London: Routledge.

Hall, S. (2007) *The Carhullan Army*. London: Faber & Faber.

Harrison, M. (2013) *Clay*. London: Bloomsbury.

Hart, C. (1999) *The Harvest*. London: Faber & Faber.

Head, D. (2002) *An Introduction to Modern British Fiction 1950–2000*. Cambridge: Cambridge University Press.

Heaney, S. (2003) 'Eclogues in Extremis: On the Staying Power of Pastoral'. *Proceedings of the Royal Irish Academy*, 103C.1, 1–12.

Hiltner, K. (2011) *What Else Is Pastoral? Renaissance Literature and the Environment*. Ithaca and London: Cornell University Press.

Hulme, M. (2009) *Why We Disagree about Climate Change: Understanding Controversy, Inaction and Opportunity*. Cambridge: Cambridge University Press.

Jensen, L. (2009) *The Rapture*. London: Bloomsbury.

Lawless, A. (2005) 'The Poet of Prose: Jim Crace in Interview'. *Three Monkeys Online*, 1 February, n. pag. www.threemonkeysonline.com/the-poet-of-prose-jim-crace-in-interview/

Lilley, D. (2018) 'Pastoral Concerns in the Fictions of Jim Crace'. In Aughterson, K. and Shaw, K. eds. *Jim Crace*. London: Palgrave.

—— (2016) 'Unsettling Environments: New Pastorals in Kazuo Ishiguro's *Never Let Me Go* and Sarah Hall's *The Carhullan Army*'. *Green Letters: Studies in Ecocriticism* 20.1, 60–71.

—— (2014) 'Contemporary British Fiction, Environmental Crisis and the Pastoral', in Leggett, B. and Venezia, T. eds. *Twenty-First Century British Fiction: Critical Essays*. London: Gyphi, 153–177.

Loughrey, B. (1984) *The Pastoral Mode: A Casebook*. London and Basingstoke: Macmillan.

Love, G. A. (1996) 'Revaluing Nature: Towards an Ecological Criticism'. In Glotfelty, C. and Fromm, H. eds. *The Ecocriticism Reader: Landmarks in Literary Ecology*. Athens and London: University of Georgia Press, 225–240.

Phillips, D. (2003) *The Truth of Ecology: Nature, Culture, and Literature in America*. Oxford and New York: Oxford University Press.

—— (1998) 'Don DeLillo's Postmodern Pastoral'. In Branch, M. P. ed. *Reading the Earth: New Directions in the Study of Literature and Environment*. Moscow, Idaho: University of Idaho Press, 235–246.

Marx, L. (1992) 'Does Pastoralism Have a Future?'. In Hunt, J. D. ed. *The Pastoral Landscape*. Washington: National Gallery of Art, 109–225.

McSweeney, J. (2014) *The Necropastoral: Poetry, Media. Occults*, MI: University of Michigan Press.

Meeker, J. (1997) *The Comedy of Survival: Literary Ecology and a Play Ethic*. Tucson: University of Arizona Press.

Morton, T. (2010) *The Ecological Thought*. Cambridge, MA and London: Harvard University Press.

Nixon, R. 'The Crucible: *Harvest* by Jim Crace'. *The New York Times*, 8 February, n. pag. www.nytimes.com/2013/02/10/books/review/harvest-by-jim-crace.html

Raisin, R. (2008) *God's Own Country*. London: Penguin.

Rosenmeyer, T. G. (1969) *The Green Cabinet: Theocritus and the European Pastoral Lyric*. Berkeley and London: University of California Press.

Ryle, M. (2011) 'The Past, the Future and the Golden Age: Some Contemporary Versions of Pastoral'. In Soper, K., Ryle, M. and Thomas, L. eds. *The Politics and Pleasures of Consuming Differently*. Basingstoke: Palgrave Macmillan.

—— (2009) 'Neo-Pastoral and Eco-Didactics: Ali Smith's *The Accidental*'. *Green Letters: Studies in Ecocriticism*, 10, 8–19.

Sebald, W. J. (1995) *The Rings of Saturn*. London: Vintage.

Selby, N. (2011) 'Reading England: Pastoral, Elegy and the Politics of Place in Richard Caddel and Harriet Tarlo'. *Textual Practice*, 25.5, 893–911.

Sullivan, H. (2016) 'The Dark Pastoral: Goethe and Atwood', *Green Letters: Studies in Ecocriticism*, 20.1, 47–59.

Smith, A. (2016) *Autumn*. London: Hamish Hamilton.

—— (2005) *The Accidental*. London: Hamish Hamilton.

Swift, G. (1984) *Waterland*. London: Picador.

Taylor, S. (2009) *The Island at the End of the World*. London: Penguin.

Teske, D. (2002) 'Jim Crace's Arcadia: Public Culture in the Postmodern City', In Onega, S. and Stotesbury, J.A. eds. *London in Literature: Visionary Mappings of the Metropolis*. Heidelburg: Universitatverlag, 165–182.

Tew, P. (2009) 'Jim Crace's Enigmatical Pastoral'. In James, D. and Tew, P. eds. *New Vrsions of Pastoral: Post-Romantic, Moden and Contemporary Versions of the Tradition*. Madison: Fairleigh Dickinson Press, 230–244.

—— (2006) *Jim Crace*. Manchester: Manchester University Press.

Thorpe, A. (1994) *Ulverton*. London: Minerva.

Williams, R. (1973) *The Country and the City*. London: Chatto & Windus.

9

REALISMS

Sophie Vlacos

Introduction

In his "Reflections on the Brecht-Lukács Debate", Fredric Jameson argued that the 'originality of the concept of realism . . . lies in its claim to cognitive as well as aesthetic status' (Jameson, 1980, 135). To reflect, then, on the nature of realism in contemporary fiction, this chapter will first outline the thrust of recent philosophical work on the nature of the real, before analysing how this may affect perspectives on fiction.

In 2001, Bill Brown published an essay called "Thing Theory" in which he summarised a series of positions dedicated to the consideration of things or objects. The defining criterion that united these positions was their refusal or inversion of the usual relationship by which objects are constituted by the subject. In contrast to the more conventional phenomenological or psychoanalytic approaches, Brown sought to foreground a thingliness characterised by latency ('the not yet formed or the not yet formable') and excess ('what remains physically or metaphysically irreducible to objects') (Brown 2001: 5). This concern for materiality ('thingliness') both before and after its formation as an object by a thinking subject points to the limited views taken of conventional object-hood and suggests a desire to think beyond those phenomenal or aesthetic epistemologies concerned only with the projected functions and symbolic resonances of the pre-constituted subject.[1] It is the inanimate article's agency and its constitution of subjectivity, a process largely overlooked by modern rationalist and Romantic epistemologies of the Subject, which first incites this concern with things. As such, Brown's essay on objects registered a new departure in the critique of the modern Subject (conceived as the stable or discrete origin of its own perceptions), a new inflection for anti-subjectivism and a line of thinking which seeks to dislodge the ontological primacy of the subject, but one that turned its back on the earlier linguistic strategies of poststructuralism. As such, it is also a new departure for the consideration of realism.

Eighteen years since the publication of Brown's essay, discussions and events centred upon materiality and thingly agency have proliferated. The growth in material culture studies has led to a number of high profile projects devoted to objects, including the BBC's and the British Museum's "A History of the World in 100 Objects" and the Victoria and Albert Museum's "Disobedient Objects" exhibition, as well as a recent publishing series devoted to the history of iconic objects produced by Bloomsbury. There have also been a rising number of theories, philosophies and literary/aesthetic productions dedicated to the thoughts of non-human agency more generally. Whilst some of these energies clearly enjoin pre-millenial themes and arguments, posthumuanism and ecocriticism in the case of New Materialism or Anthropocene literature for instance, other discourses, like the largely British-based philosophies of Speculative Realism and Object Oriented Ontology, energetically aim at rupture and disaffiliation. Granted the diversity of approaches and mediums covered by this general inclination to think beyond the subject, 'contemporary realisms' seems an appropriately flexible term through which to explore their commonality and their literary repercussions. The suitability of this ambidextrous term is confirmed by the rise of a philosophically incongruous and yet historically consistent wave of literary humanism or 'New Sincerity', a mode of literary realism devoted to the material and phenomenological reality of human experience impelled by a similar fatigue with poststructuralist preoccupations.

Historically of course, the meaning of realism has always been context specific, its commitments incorporating anything from a belief in mind-independent reality (philosophy's 'strong' ontological realism, the kind of realism debated in current Continental philosophy) to an objection to the ideology of modernism (as found in Lukács' Marxist defence of classical nineteenth century literary realism). Somewhere in between these ontological and formal-ideological prescriptions, there sits the kind of critical-theoretical realism of thinkers such as Jürgen Habermas, who in the late twentieth century sought to defend the Enlightenment's commitment to critical rationality and the possibility of consensus amidst the irrationalising, de-realising tendencies of some postmodernist and poststructuralist high theory.

The term's conceptual burdens reflect its recurrent implication within broad-scale epistemological debates, and its resurgence in times of epistemological conflict. In the modern literary-aesthetic context named by Frederic Jameson, the novelty in claiming realism's cognitive as well as aesthetic status betokened the influence of Marxist materialist and historical debate upon an otherwise Kantian-idealist paradigm. This paradigm was the direct result of Kant's Copernican revolution in the philosophy of mind; his assertion that rather than passively receiving sense data, the mind actively and systematically structures that data. It was this assertion that led Kant to his famous distinction between things-in-themselves, the inaccessible reality of noumena, and the world of phenomenal appearances made accessible by the structures of the mind. Having rejected the possibility of a direct knowledge of reality, Kant was then impelled to distinguish between the mind's different faculties of understanding and knowledge. In the *Critique of Judgment* he effectively side-lined aesthetic experience to its own distinct realm of appearances and disinterested pleasures, divorced from the operations of substantive knowledge. This move was at the heart of the aesthetic idealist paradigm against which modern aesthetic realists objected. Where Kant had side-lined aesthetic experience to its own distinct realm of appearances and disinterested pleasures, the realist asserted the interconnection of that experience with knowledge and everyday praxis, championing the artwork's participatory role within everyday understanding and historical reality. Throughout the twentieth century, literary and artistic debate was thus framed by these Kantian questions regarding art's cognitive status and the conditions of the Subject's knowledge, questions which confirmed an essential reciprocity between the disciplines of literature, art and philosophy.

When the playwright Bertolt Brecht contested Lukács' vision of realism in the mid-twentieth century, his formal-ideological disagreement belied the thinkers' deeper philosophical complicity as Marxists committed to the reality of the material dialectic. The meaning of realism within literature was a relatively localised debate therefore, with Brecht and Lukács advocating conflicting forms or literary methodologies for common socio-philosophical ends. Whilst Lukács advocated the forms of nineteenth century realism, a form perfected in the social panoramics of Balzac and Tolstoy as the most germane to historical analysis and social change, Brecht read the repetition of nineteenth century realist form as a mode of ersatz capitulation to dead genre, as a formalist practice inimical to the doctrine of dialectical materialism. 'Reality changes; in order to represent it, modes of representation must also change'. Literary realism for Brecht was thus experimental engagement, 'discovering the causal complexes of society [and] unmasking the prevailing view of things as the view of those who are in power' (Brecht 2007: 82). For Lukács meanwhile, the heresy lay in Brecht's particular kind of avant-garde or modernist formal experimentation, a mode which he associated with a retreat from the historical realities of the social totality. In this way, the failing for which they condemned one another, namely formalism, confirmed their broader epistemological commitment to realism's cognitive as well as aesthetic status. Moreover in their common objection to Kant's perspective in the *Critique of Judgement* (that aesthetic experience is not cognitively constitutive), they nonetheless confirmed Kant's basic assertion of a subject-centred reality determined by cognition.

But whilst contemporary literature exhibits new responses to the question of realist representation, the old mutuality between literature and philosophy no longer seems to obtain. Whilst contemporary realisms confirm a cross-disciplinary rejection of certain postmodernist and poststructuralist persuasions (not least irony and scepticism), current modes of literary and philosophical realism indicate a splintering between the two disciplines. More precisely, they suggest a parting of ways between modern literary studies and the kind of post-Kantian European philosophy that once proved its bedfellow and theoretical mainstay, and thus a possible weakening in the claim to theory's literary prefix as consummated in the poststructuralist age. For where the originality of realism once lay in its claim to cognitive and aesthetic status, contemporary critical and philosophical realisms involve the rejection of this prior connection.

Postmodernism and anti-realism

One hypothesis for the proliferation of contemporary realisms has to do with the exhaustion of postmodernist critical and aesthetic practices in an increasingly intense, postmodern world, one in which earlier postmodernist and ultimately anti-realist assessments – regarding our own unreality, our illusory or capitalistically complicated ontologies or our lack of certain knowledge – feel ubiquitously real and for that reason quite stale. Critically and aesthetically, postmodernist themes and devices have run out of steam whilst the social conditions of postmodernity march on. Nowhere is this more apparent than in our everyday lives, where the conceits of a formerly experimental, postmodernist aesthetic permeate our popular culture in a thoroughly non-ironic and critically denuded manner.

For Brecht, authentic literary realism was not a fixed genre or mimetic code, but rather a dialectical practice, responsive to the particularity of a given era's material conditions and social requirements. Authentic realist art should chafe rather than consolidate the lineaments of current social formation. In an earlier phase than our own, postmodernist devices worked to do just this. In postmodernist literature, techniques of self-reflexivity and anti-referentiality, the blending and pastiche of historical registers and the merging of purported fact and fiction, worked to corroborate an essentially anti-realist credo influenced by poststructural linguistics and the critique of Enlightenment reason. Such tactics worked to emphasise the artificial or constructed nature of the work in question by puncturing the conventions of mimetic illusion and refusing the readers' smooth transportation from reality to an imaginative realm 'within' or beyond. Our attempts to crawl through the portal to pure fiction were met by an abrupt metatextuality, an ontological deflection of the realist illusion, of a pure reality outside the text, and a pure and seamless fiction within. To this extent, works of literary postmodernism were wholly consonant with the linguistic themes of poststructuralist philosophy and theory; not only that, but their ontological games with inside and out, reality and fiction, story-telling, fact and fiction served to *perform* poststructuralist arguments for linguistic mediation and ontological illusion through their narrative form.

The critical or emancipatory leverage of such tactics derived from the challenges they presented to authorised accounts of truth and reality. Thinking and writing as a postmodernist meant repudiating the rationalist's faith in reason and objective truth, exposing the cultural and subjective biases subtending her knowledge and so rejecting, or at least dramatically destabilising, the objective or mind-independent reality of her facts. It also meant elevating the alternative realities, ideologies, discourses and experiences of subjects previously marginalised from the Western rationalist perspective. In its cross-over with 1960s counter-culturalism, early literary postmodernism (in authors such as Brautigan and Vonnegut), participated within an explicit critique of modern rationalism in the form of state bureaucracy and the inner barbarism of its instrumental reasoning. Formal narrative gestures of anti-rationalism or anti-realism could be seen to participate within a broader vision of utopian heterogeneity whereby the irreducible difference and variety of experience signalled a political rejoinder to socio-subjective conformity and logical ratio alike. For literary postmodernists, there was no one unitary truth about the world, only a multiplicity of competing visions or constructions of reality mediated by human experience and imagining. In its more sceptical moments, this commonplace of post-Kantian epistemology signalled a disavowal of rationality itself. Whilst critical theorists and so-called critical realists were keen to point out the practical flaws in this position (not least the conflict with scientific method and inability to generate ethical consensus from a position of radical incommensurability or unreason), the performative aporetics of postmodernist aesthetics presented some genuinely emancipatory energies within the imaginative-aesthetic sphere. Arguably, the inability to translate these imaginative flights into more practical modes of social critique and praxis was testament to their anti-realism, to their purely aesthetic (as opposed to aesthetic-cognitive) basis and to their unique kinship with poststructuralist philosophies at that time.

In present culture however, the critical or ironic 'edge' associated with postmodernist anti-realist techniques has fallen flat, so much so, that the devices of postmodernist anti-realism (those devices designed to shatter the realist illusion and to foreground the fictive status of the work in question) are now submerged within a new and yet formally quite familiar mode of realism. Today, when TV dramas implant current press images within their opening credits and live historical references within their dialogues, we must recognise aesthetic postmodernity to be a thing of the past; not because postmodernist art is necessarily incompatible with these populist media juggernauts, but because the merging of reality and fiction in such programmes is devoid of ironic intent. Certainly, they are the after-effects of a postmodern media industry. In a programme such as *Homeland* for instance, the 'fictive' or discursive status of reality, truth and history are pretty much taken for granted, with the tension between state-legislated meta-narratives of warfare and crusade, and the individual experiences of surveillance and killing, providing a central hinge for the drama. Yet having absorbed some of the tropes and devices of postmodernist aesthetics, the show's motivation is not a critique of societal irrationality or an ontological meditation on the death of the reality principle, so much as a desire to convince us of its own reality or realism within a vehemently real – albeit wholly mediated and discursively constructed – world. As a mode of contemporary realism, it seeks a faithful reflection of postmodern reality. The formal devices that were once used to interrogate or problematize the fate of reality in our late capitalist modernity are consumed by an earlier, conventionally mimetic impulse, one that works to convert those previously interrogative techniques into more or less unquestioning thematic content. So whilst the themes are certainly postmodern – collective psychosis, ideological relativism and the absence of a fundamental Truth or moral anchor – the framing mimesis or formal code is a conventionally realist verisimilitude channelled through the existential dramas of the central protagonist. As saliently ungrounded and delusional as this protagonist often is, her mimesis is realist, for whilst we frequently have cause to question her rationality, her epistemic judgements, we are never led to question the reality of her emotions. The fiction of her inner core remains intact.

Arguably, this reduction of postmodernist devices to flat literality and social themes reflects something more than overfamiliarity and stylistic cliché: a vindication of capitalism's powers to incorporate sites of resistance or a longstanding complicity between (post)modernist aesthetics and capitalist desire, an aestheticisation of the real such as Habermas and Jean Baudrillard both diagnosed, and one that leaves little room for a critically autonomous aesthetic.

This sense of critical foreclosure, of the progressive erosion of critical space and critical autonomy in postmodernity, clearly informs the critical demands of Vincent B. Leitch, the incumbent editor for the *Norton Anthology of Theory and Criticism* and author of *Literary Criticism in the 21st Century*. Ours, according to Leitch, is the age of the panic attack:

> of more of less continuous stress, anxiety, and distraction, compounded by overwork, caffeine, sugar, excessive options at every turn, speed, multitasking, a 24/7 reality, too much news and media, an absence of quiet time and leisure not to mention relaxation.
>
> (Leitch 2014: 5)

Overstimulated and unfocussed, our bids to keep apace of postmodern reality seem to push us ever further from the source of its conditions; anxiety is the symptom of our epistemic uncertainty, our attempts to compete in a game to which no one really seems to know the basic rules. The criticism best befitting of this febrile, 24/7 media reality according to Leitch, is an avowedly pragmatic and outward-facing mode of ideological and cultural critique, with 'political economy, particularly finance, at center stage' (*ibid.*).

Modernism and realism

Of course, experiences and assessments of these postmodern conditions are far from new, and the complaint that (post)modern life is rubbish and somehow inauthentic has been amply made before. Baudelaire's hymn to the unreal city and Horkheimer and Adornos' analysis of a culture industry robbing life of its reality bemoan a similar and much earlier co-optation of the real by market and technological forces. One solution to this impoverished reality for the modernist avant-garde was to set about its aesthetic transformation. According to Tyrus Miller (Miller, 1999), the ontological cynicisms or anti-realisms of late and postmodernism were an ironic response to the glorious successes of modernist re-envisioning and an admission of futility in the face of further impoverishment. Yet it was not only the aesthetic *successes* of the modernist avant-garde to which late and postmodernists were responding, but also the ironic knowledge of their predecessors' unwitting complicity in the current post-modern condition; the knowledge that their optimistic transformations had in fact contributed to a world of limitless simulation and market incorporation. This is the paradoxical history whereby the avant-garde, in its objection to an earlier ideology of aesthetic autonomy (of art for art's sake, Kant's elevation of a distinct aesthetic realm divorced from everyday cognition), sought to reinstate the artwork's full cognitive import within the historical totality by circulating art productions within everyday reality. But rather than override the false autonomy of the artwork and reinstate the cognitive dimensions of the aesthetic, the avant-garde's aesthetic interventions within everyday reality in fact only contributed to reality's ontological devaluation. The well-known history of this aesthetic transformation or aesthetic *derealisation* is implied wherever the ideology of modernism and the discontents of postmodernism are called into question. As Bill Brown's essay on 'Thing Theory' makes plain, the failure of the avant-garde and the emergence of contemporary realist responses to that failing, relate to the former's thwarted attempts to move beyond subject-centred accounts of reality.

The avant-garde's responses to the conditions of modernity often took the form of an emphasis upon objects designed to mitigate the perceived imperialism of the modern Subject in its various technocratic and bourgeois manifestations. According the everyday object a very literal, constitutive role in subject-formation, the Russian constructivist Boris Arvatov dreamt of a soviet socialist object with which to match the West's superior technological devices whilst countering the pacifying tendencies of Western commodity forms. As part of the wider Soviet programme, the useful design-object signalled the rejection of the artwork's aesthetic autonomy and the bourgeoisie's subjective epistemology. In the West meanwhile, Marcel Duchamp's ready-made artworks reflected a similar attempt to subvert relations to art and reality through material objects. Somewhat later, Martin Heidegger would use the demarcation between objects – always objects for something or for someone – and mere things, to underscore the habituated, technocratic or ends-oriented modes of the modern rationalist subject. In its refusal to meet pragmatic ends or to match conceptual categorisations, the thing participated in Heidegger's critique of instrumentalism by helping to signal an alternative mode of unmotivated existence beyond the grasp of human calibration.

Yet rather than assuage anxieties surrounding the Subject's hubris, to puncture illusions of mastery or to radically reconstitute the social imaginary against capitalism and/or modern technocracy in the name of a more authentic reality, materialist and thingly thinking in the early to mid-twentieth century tended to consolidate its position. The constructivist's circulation of design objects coincided with a rise in new technology, new possibilities for media, industrial design and mass production. Translated in the Western context of Bauhaus and the *Neue Sachlichkeit*, the emphasis upon design, objects and production converged with the same commodity-impulses that constructivists had once sought to overturn. Furthermore, the circulation of design objects within the general material order of things served less to abrogate the aesthetic mentality, than to transform it from a learned to an everyday disposition. And whilst objects and matter led Heidegger away from the rationalistic Subject, the general criticism of Heidegger is that subjectivity still inevitably followed, illuminating a trajectory which it then invariably swallowed under the guise of a purportedly impersonal Being or imagination prior to rational conceptualisation. Paradoxically, thingly or object-thinking within modernity often seemed to participate within the aesthetic transformation of the real; a diminution of the subject's rational mastery purchased through the unlicensed expansion of the subject's ontogenetic agency.

In seeking to close the gap between art and reality, to overturn the bourgeois aesthetics of nineteenth century insititution art through the circulation of the art object (and this could apply to Duchamp's urinal or to Heidegger's Greek temple), critics of modernity in fact contributed to an aestheticisation and praxiological fragmentation, rather than the authentication, of reality. The 'generalized mimeticism' named in Baudrillard's essay on simulacra, the total mediation of reality by aesthetic productions, insinuates an ideology that thrives upon uncertainty and a fundamental inability to rationally disentangle the real from the unreal (Baudrillard 1995). What the history of materialist transformation in the twentieth century briefly demonstrates, is how the contrary energies of modernity and modernism, collective rationalisation and subjective individualism, fed one another, and how a dialectic of rationalism and individualism – programmes borne of contrary interpretations of the modern Subject – colluded in the dominant derealizing traits of postmodernity.

For the purposes of Brown's essay, these traits are indicative of the modern era's failed desire to exceed the chiasmic effects of a dualist ontology; the asymptotic movements of the subject trying to reach its object. As an expression of contemporary philosophical realism, Thing Theory designates an attempt to escape from this aporia and the possibility of a new ontology. By the current view, Leitch's demand for economic analysis in the field of literary criticism is symptomatic of this history and ambition also. For what Leitch's prescription ultimately points to, is a situation whereby criticism withdraws from its traditional aesthetic domain following the aesthetics' final foreclosure within the economic field; the final dissolution of that relative autonomy and critical distance delineated by Habermas in his defence of enlightened modernity. As responses to postmodernism and the paradoxes of modernism, Leitch's realist critique and Brown's realist ontologies signal a combined effort to transgress the modern epistemology that once united realists and modernists such as Brecht and Lukács.

Contemporary philosophical realisms

What distinguishes Leitch's analysis and contemporary realist commitments broadly speaking, is the determination, not to deny the exigencies of postmodernism, or to stipulate a return to some more authentic (or in other words pre-critical) mode of existence, but rather to analyse those exigencies, and to transform arguments of uncertainty into grounds for greater certainty or critical autonomy. Chronologically and thematically postmodern, these critical and philosophical realisms nonetheless reject the epistemology of modernity and modernism along with the subsequent scepticisms of postmodernism, and seek to subvert those scepticisms into grounds for greater certainty. What this manoeuvre effectively entails therefore is the capacity to rearticulate the epistemological *advances* of poststructuralism and critical postmodernism – against naïve rationalism and the self-transparent Subject, against naïve realism – in an epistemologically or ontologically positive manner.

One salient example of this, and one that Brown mentions in his essay on things, is the 'sociology of associations' or Actor Network Theory of Bruno Latour. Central to this project is a critique of modern sociology, which, in its eagerness to establish itself as a modern social science divorced from metaphysics, instituted a new explanatory frame of reference in the form of 'the social'. Sociology since Durkheim has used this category of the social to explain social phenomena when in fact 'the social', in its complex and evolving durability, is the very phenomenon which sociology must seek to explain. Conventional 'sociology of the social' confuses cause with effect according to Latour, so whilst the category of the social provides 'convenient shorthand' for phenomena 'already *accepted* in the collective realm' it fails to account for emergent social phenomena (Latour 2006: 11). Rather than use society as an explanation for its components, Latour projects a method that accounts for the mechanisms and bonds holding this broad-scale phenomenon together. He likens this move to the shift from pre-relativist to post-relativist physics; instead of viewing society as a fixed frame of reference, analogous in its forms to the fixed rules of the pre-relativist universe, we must view society in terms of its fluctuating forces and relations. The accelerated mechanisms of science, technology and innovation have proven the inadequacy of the conventionally linear model of social causation. Crucially, the move from fixed determinations to a sociology of associations entails a revision of the basic ontological categorisations by which the human social sphere is usually distinguished from the non-human sphere. As Brown puts it, the ontological distinction between inanimate objects and human subjects is, for Latour, an artificial one issuing from modern rationality and instrumentalisation. In its place, Latour offers a complex and inter-related realm of quasi-objects and quasi-subjects, so called because of their inter-connected agencies and porous relations. Attention to the *agency* of non-human actants – 'microbes, scallops, rocks, and ships' – is a positive response to the lens of modern science, with its progressive dematerialisation of solid objects into smaller and smaller units of activity (Latour 2006: 10).

Like Deleuze and Guattari in *A Thousand Plateaus*, Latour turns to the scientific realm of dynamical systems theory and the exploration of pre-subjective or subject-less systems of self-organization, in short, to a mode of analysis predicated upon the assumption of the subject's mediated status. There is an evident homology here, between these kinds of dynamic networked ontologies and the spatial disaggregation at the heart of poststructural linguistics. Where Derrida attacked the unity of the speaking subject through the premise of text, of an irreducible and dynamic signifying system, Deleuze and Guattari inaugurated a mode of thinking inspired by de-centralised and self-regulating systems of interspecific and inter-categorial forces. Yet importantly, whilst both of these trajectories participate in the Subject's desublimation, only one of them can be accused of the subject's dematerialisation or of a retreat into the realm of pure ideation. What we find with Latour's Actor Network Theory therefore, is a philosophy of pre- and non-subjective agency germane to the central gestures of poststructuralism, but one that nevertheless directs critical thinking to the realm of empirical reality.

An immediate consequence of this empirical turn is an epistemological de-prioritisation of linguistic or para-linguistic artefacts. Semiotic and semantic phenomena participate as one force field amongst the many, leading to an inevitable de-prioritisation of writing and literary artefacts within the elaboration of its theory. Whilst literature might thematise the agency of quasi-subjective and quasi-objective networks, it can never perform their operations in the way that literature uniquely performed the arguments of deconstruction. The denial of conventional disciplinary and discursive parameters entailed a relation every bit as intense as the union between poetry and philosophy in the era of Romantic idealism.[2] Indeed from a contemporary realist perspective, linguistic poststructuralism and the ontological scepticisms of postmodernism look like a last hurrah for the aesthetic epistemology from whence Romantic idealism first sprang.

The position to have really crystallised this perception and to have propelled realism's current philosophical momentum most of all, comes by way of Quentin Meillassoux's Speculative Realist philosophy and his engagement with Anglophone Continental philosophers such as Ray Brassier, Levi Bryant, Ian Hamilton Grant and Graham Harman. For Meillassoux, realism is of the fundamental ontological variety concerning the existence – or more specifically the certain knowledge of the existence – of a mind-independent reality. To this extent, Speculative Realism has little directly to say about the ideology of modernism or cultural critique in postmodernity, but what it does entail is a targeted attack on the epistemology behind such discussions. Ever since Kant's distinction between the noumenal and phenomenal realms, that is to say, between a humanly inaccessible reality in itself, and a realm of mere appearances mediated by human consciousness, European philosophy has occupied itself with phenomenological, aesthetic or hermeneutical questions regarding the forms and structures of human experience, powers of perception and imagination, or mechanisms of interpretation. Philosophers have either bracketed reality as a naively impossible question, or demoted it to an epi-phenomenal status, like a wishful appearance on the part of the subject. Everything within twentieth century Continental philosophy tells us that a mind-independent reality is a critically naïve proposition, much like the prospect of a direct, like-for-like mimesis or the dogmatic assumption of a universal Truth, knowledge of things-in-themselves is simply not possible, since thought and knowledge of the world are indivisible. Continental philosophy is caught within the binds of a 'thought-world correlate', which either works to relativise knowledge (knowledge is merely representation) or to turn the correlate into its own kind of absolute ontological foundation (reality is ultimately will and representation). The linguistic scepticisms of literary postmodernism and the transformative credentials of earlier modernist or Romantic aesthetics are the poetic consequences of these anti-realist positions: two sides of the same correlationist coin.

In *After Finitude*, Meillassoux formulates his solution to this correlationist bind, engaging with and radicalising a number of pre-Kantian philosophies in order to provide a distinctively post-Kantian solution to the correlate's anthropocentric limitations. Crucially, from the current perspective at least, this transformation involves a kind of guerrilla tactic from 'within' the thought-world correlate. What Meillassoux sets out to do, is to transform contingency and finitude into a principle of absolute necessity, a principle of minimal certainty that he calls his 'Principle of Un-Reason'. Paradoxically, it is the certain knowledge of uncertainty that augurs Meillassoux's path beyond finitude and uncertainty, facilitating his claim to break free from the circular incursions of correlationism and the sceptical, relativising strains of its more recent, postmodernist inflections. In classical philosophy, the Principle of Sufficient Reason states that an explanation must exist for all states of affairs, experiences or facts; that nothing is without cause or reason. As a solution to the problem of causality – to the laws of cause and effect, why gravity for instance always functions the way it does – the principle of sufficient reason has forced philosophers to either accept causation as a necessary albeit hidden law of reality or to assert a dogmatic knowledge of its operations. Whilst realists and idealists have long debated our accessibility to these causal laws, they have never, according to Meillassoux, really questioned the necessity of their existence. Meillassoux' Principle of Un-reason, of absolute contingency as opposed to necessity, does just that. A significant portion of Meillassoux's philosophy is devoted to the justification of a contingent universe *without* causal necessity, a universe in which anything *could* potentially happen, in which phenomena could behave inconsistently and in any number of ways, but in which, crucially, they never do. Along with Alain Badiou, Meillassoux is one of a number of contemporary European thinkers to have rejected the dominant phenomenological and linguistic strains of twentieth century philosophy for a mode of realism informed by mathematics. It is Meillassoux's need to explain the apparent consistency of phenomena in the absence of causal necessity, to unify contingency, which leads him to the strange world of Cantorian mathematics.

Most relevant to a broad cultural discussion such as this however, are the epistemological and cultural assessments behind this drastic manoeuvre. Criticising philosophy's unquestioning acceptance of causal necessity, Meillassoux associates even the most sceptical of modern philosophers with a mode of intellectual superstition: 'to assert and believe that there is an unfathomable necessity to the way of the world is to be prepared to believe in a great deal of providence' he writes (Meillassoux 2009: 91). Given the paradoxes of cultural modernity and the strange conflations of superstition and scepticism inherent to postmodernism, Meillassoux's critique is culturally significant. In fact, it would not be inappropriate to explore his argument in the context of Horkheimer and Adornos' *Dialectic of Enlightenment*, where systematic strategies of domination are linked to an underlying fear and superstition regarding the unknown. 'Enlightenment' they write, 'is mythical fear radicalized'. (Horkheimer and Adorno 2002: 11). Metaphysical assurances regarding the absolute necessity of causal laws and of *our* necessity within that system of laws provide the basis for modern anthropocentrism.

To this extent, Speculative Realism presents a genuinely exciting shift away from the predominant anti-realisms of twentieth century Continental philosophy, and like deconstruction in the age of early postmodernism, it grants philosophical expression to broader cultural tendencies. Already, its arguments have been explored within the context of the visual arts. It remains to be seen whether its influence will be anything like as far-reaching as deconstruction's, but it seems highly unlikely that its effects upon literature could ever be so profound.[3] And the reason for this is very simple; Derrida's critique of modern metaphysical rationality relied on the refusal of a pure conceptual-philosophic discourse distinct from literary-figurative language. The promulgation of an originary spatio-temporal *différance* responsible for the *appearance* of conceptual and categorial identities and subsequent epistemic distinctions (between truth and fiction, appearance and reality), entailed the rejection of representational language, with its assumed stability, for the performance of signification's instability. It traded upon the rich polysemia of literary language. What it gave literature in return was a philosophical status akin to a transcendental condition, so that when literature incorporated poststructural linguistic arguments, it didn't merely thematise those arguments in the manner of a secondary representation, it actually performed them in such a way as to realise deconstruction's dissolution of the work/world distinction. Linguistic poststructuralism inspired a dramatic mode of formal as opposed to merely thematic innovation. Whilst Speculative Realism can contribute to a critique of modern correlationism (including deconstruction), and whilst these arguments may be consonant with current anthropocene literary themes, what Speculative Realism cannot do as a mode of ontological realism is generate a new poetics. The only insight Speculative Realism could ever really offer literature would be a rudimentary restating of its fictive status as anthropic representation. If the originality of the concept of modern realism lay in its claims to cognitive *and* aesthetic status, then Speculative Realism serves to diminish that claim by assimilating modern cognition to the *limitations* of aesthetics, to dualism and the correlation.

Literature and contemporary realism

Latour's refusal of dualism and Meillassoux's rejection of correlationism reflect a turn away from post-Kantian epistemologies of the subject and from subject-oriented or aesthetic definitions of realism. They serve to emphasise the dialectical reciprocity of realist and modernist forms, of Brecht and Lukács, and to limit the significance of their debate by minimising either party's cognitive claim. And yet for the very same cultural and epistemological reasons – scepticism, the exhaustion of anti-realist techniques, fatigue with high theory and an intensifying postmodernity – recent literature exhibits a level of social commitment that demands our serious reappraisal of those competing cognitive claims. The debate in its present form distils terms established back in the 1990s, when David Foster Wallace wrote about television's 'institutionalization of irony' and when Jonathan Franzen articulated the obstacles for the would-be committed, social novelist in an age of 24/7 media and information exchange (Wallace 1993: 187; Franzen, 1996). Wallace drew attention to the essentially negative qualities of postmodern irony and to the fact that its critical or counter-cultural potentials had been incorporated within mainstream culture anyway. He proposed a return to 'single-entrendre principles' of sincerity as perhaps the only viable gesture of rebellion left to young writers (Wallace 1993: 192). Franzen meanwhile played the part of a self-condemned Lukács; his literary realist convictions betrayed by the very culture he sought to earnestly represent. Subsequent literary fame ensured their centrality to this post-postmodern conversation, as did the palpable demand for a new sense of literary direction and the rather self-conscious perception that here were two 'great men' rearticulating the terms of the realist debate for a new generation. As popularised by Adam Kelly, literature of the 'New Sincerity', in American authors such as Foster Wallace, Dave Eggers, Jonathan Safran Foer and Jennifer Egan, encapsulates the contemporary author's attempt to move beyond irony, 'to find a sustainable model of sincerity without maintaining an outdated and ineffective commitment to expressive subjectivity that fails to acknowledge present realities' (Kelly 2014). This is a situation in which sincerity is honestly desired and yet knowingly compromised by its self-conscious enunciation and the impossibility of returning to a pre-critical, pre-theoretical model of mimesis. In essence, the New Sincerity involves the attempt to find a new *form* of realism adequate to the conditions of an ongoing postmodernity. So whilst this project is consistent with a broader rejection of postmodernist epistemology in contemporary critical and philosophical realisms, the terms of this post-postmodern *literary* quest remain thoroughly Brechtian and modernist.

Indeed the fact that some of the literature now speaking to our contemporary conditions – both thematically and by satisfying our postmodern nostalgia for classical realist assurances – should be viewed suspiciously, is testament to the endurance of that modernist perspective. The debate elicited in response to Franzen's appearance on the cover of *Time* magazine in 2010 encapsulates the bind debated by Brecht and Lukács most saliently, with the positioning of America's most famous literary realist beneath the word 'time' insinuating the same old dialectical arguments regarding form and depth historicity. Despite his quite public condemnation of American mainstream culture, and his evident censure of corporate capitalist culture in novels such as *The Corrections* and *Freedom*, to Franzen's detractors, his work represents a symptom of the very culture it purports to critique. Franzen refers to his mature works as 'systems novels', meaning that they deal specifically with networks. With its social, financial and geopolitical themes, *The Corrections* marks the transition from an 'analogue' network, the socio-industrial complex in an earlier phase represented by the former railroad engineer Alfred Lambert, to the more erratic virtual complex of his childrens' universe; Alfred's psycho-symbolic dissonance, his inability to identify and to name things as objects is emblematic of a broader loss of ground postmodernity. Thematically postmodern, Franzen's work to his critics is formally anodyne. Like the media monolith *Homeland*, his novels incorporate familiarly postmodern devices whilst the overarching framework is an everyday realism anchored by human experience and character situation.

And yet problematically, the logic of Brecht's argument could in fact be used to defend productions like *Homeland* and *The Corrections* as the most authentically realist works of our late or post-postmodern situation. Paradoxically, given their formal familiarity and consumer satisfactions, these conventional mimeses might actually present the most authentically realist and formally performative renditions of our cultural conditions; the *flattened* traces of a once critical postmodernist (and anti-realist) energy rehearsing the capitalist dominant's tendency to regurgitate resistant culture in mollified forms. The aporetic nature of this predicament is that there is no way of knowing if it exists. It is a hypothetical development of form, active only to the extent that it renders itself invisible. After all, the mimesis of a self-neutralising postmodernism is discernibly no different to the mimesis of a culture in which those neutralised energies never existed.

The difficulty in judging Franzen's critical credentials and form is symptomatic of a general difficulty besetting literature after postmodernism. Granted the ongoing hegemony of aesthetic modernism and the Brechtian ethos, it follows that postmodernist anti-realisms of the late twentieth century in fact presented the most authentically realist interventions of their age. They chafed against social formation, underscoring the commerce between ideology and ontology with their language games. But when anti-realist critique has been exhausted and a culturally dominant incredulity towards reality augurs *nostalgia* for classical realism, the critical pertinence of the realist debate and its genres, of Brecht or Lukács, implodes. This is because a commonly acknowledged loss of ground, the loss of ontological ground entailed in the reality of virtuality and simulation, renders the aesthetic distinction between reality and its representation otiose. Paradigmatic representation and modernist formal agitation are expressions of a shared aesthetic epistemology in which the modern phenomenological and hermeneutical Subject is foregrounded as the primary *maker* or source of forms and images. Divorced from things-in-themselves, the aesthetic Subject is nonetheless the logical origin of appearances, of culture, history and social formation. But if the Subject is no longer the origin of its own forms and representations, then it can no longer own the distinction between reality and representation upon which the realist debate ultimately turns. Moreover total mediation and constant manipulation by image and representation render the modernist aspiration to recreate and re-envisage social formation rather quaint. It's for these reasons that postmodern realisms can only tarry ambiguously between critique and complicity, unsure as to whether they constitute critical performance or pliant capitulation.

The historical question confronting contemporary or post-postmodern literature – literature that wishes to uphold the realist credo, to engage with current social formation, to move on from the anti-realist tropes of postmodernist aesthetics without capitulating to an all-the-more-moribund realist form – is how to enact the realist's humble slice of critical autonomy. The logical problem besetting contemporary realism in literature, is that whilst contemporary theory, philosophy and even critical discourses such as Leitch's, can consciously distance themselves from aesthetics or correlationism in favour of a more radical conception of realism, literature, so long as it cares to be authentically realist in the Brechtian-modernist sense, cannot not be rooted in a transformational aesthetics. Modernist and postmodernist poetics turn upon an aesthetic epistemology reaching back to Kant, but it is precisely this Kantian-phenomenalist or correlationist epistemology that many contemporary realist theorists and philosophers seek to escape. Indeed the implosion of literary realism is an historical symptom of the philosophical model they seek to overcome; of a flat-lining postmodernity and the disappearance of a reality beyond representation and correlation.

Whilst delineating the advent of the New Sincerity, Kelly rightly connects the cultural conditions of postmodernity and the ontological scepticisms of high theory with a resurgent desire for unmediated human connection. The New Sincerity constitutes a formal innovation befitting of a self-consciously cynical and mediated age in which we crave pure communion no less; a formally and historically authentic mode of realism, and so a new phase in the realist dialectic by implication. But granted the aporias surrounding the proposition of realism in late postmodernism, and the attendant collapse of the Brecht-Lukács debate, is it not reasonable to suppose that the most relevant and vital of contemporary literature might actually point to this dialectic's ultimate sublation? The test then would not be whether works are authentically realist in their representations, but whether they acknowledge this question of form and ultimately genre at all. The abstract nature of this argument might suggest an over-literal application of theory to contemporary practice, were it not that many of the most well-received and vibrant of recent literary productions (Jennifer Egan's *A Visit from the Goon Squad;* David Mitchell's *Cloud Atlas*; Junot Diaz's *The Brief Wondrous Life of Oscar Wao*; Jonathan Lethem's *The Fortress of Solitude*) do indeed demonstrate this total disregard for distinctions of genre and form, incorporating styles and genres without the loaded and self-conscious gestures of blending and pastiche redolent of postmodernist fiction.

In their defiance of these conscious formal issues they mark their movement beyond a formerly animating tension regarding realist and anti-realist representation, conferring a certain modern finality or terminal modernity upon postmodernist devices. Accordingly, the move beyond this animating tension to a state of genre indifference connotes a move beyond the formal and hermeneutical preoccupations of the modern aesthetic Subject. So whilst the realist turn in contemporary Continental philosophy and sociology involves the ontological deposition of the modern Subject, and whilst this de-prioritisation of aesthetic and hermeneutical phenomena drives an irrefutable wedge between literature and contemporary ontology (insofar as literature cannot formally enact arguments for a mind-independent reality, cannot not invoke interpretation), arguably this loosening of formal preoccupations within literature constitutes its own modest gesture of contemporary realism and is the function of a shared literary, critical and philosophical movement away from the aesthetic epistemology common to Brecht and Lukács.

Sophie Vlacos

Notes

1 These 'thing theories' also contest rationalist models of subjectivity. Kant and Descartes disagree over the epistemology of the subject – whether direct knowledge of reality is possible – but they both confirm the ontological primacy of the subject in the process of cognition.
2 Curiously, where ANT has influenced literary studies, it has been in the context, not of sociological realism as one might expect, but of a digitally enhanced mode of structuralism. Franco Morretti's Literary Lab at Stanford University uses digitally harnessed quantitative data to create spatialized models of emplotment informed by networks of character interaction.
3 For an account of Speculative Realism's influence upon the visual arts, see R. Mackay, L. Pendrell, J. Trafford (eds.) (2014) *Speculative Aesthetics*, Falmouth: Urbanomic.

Works cited

Baudrillard, J. (1995) Glaser, S. (trans.) *Simulacra and Simulation*. Ann Arbor: Michigan University Press.
Brecht, B. (2007) Popularity and Realism. In: Adorno *et al.* (eds.) *Aesthetics and Politics*. London: Verso.
Brown, B. (2001) Thing Theory. *Critical Inquiry*. 28 (Autumn).
Foster Wallace, D. (1993) E Unibus Pluram: Television and U.S Fiction. *Review of Contemporary Fiction*. 13 (4). 151–193.
Franzen, J. (1996) Perchance to Dream in the Age of Images: A Reason to Write Novels. *Harper's Magazine*. (April). 35–54.
Horkheimer, M., Adorno, T. (2002) Noer, G.S. (ed.), Jephcott, E. (trans.). *Dialectic of Enlightenment: Philosophical Fragments*. Stanford: Stanford University Press.
Jameson, F. (1980) Reflections in Conclusion. In: Adorno *et al.* (eds.) *Aesthetics and Politics*. London: Verso.
Kelly, A. (2014) Dialectic of Sincerity: Lionel Trilling and David Foster Wallace. post45.research.yale.edu/2014/10/dialectic-of-sincerity-lionel-trilling-and-david-foster-wallace/
Latour, B. (2006) *Reassembling the Social: An Introduction to Actor-Network Theory*. Oxford: Oxford University Press.
Leitch, V.B. (2014) *Literary Criticism in the 21st Century*. New York: Bloomsbury.
Mackay, R., Pendrell, L., Trafford, J. (eds.) (2014) *Speculative Aesthetics*. Falmouth: Urbanomic.
Meillassoux, Q. (2009) Brassier, R. (trans.). *After Finitude*. London: Continuum.
Miller, T. (1999) *Late Modernism*. Berkeley: University of California Press.

10

COMICS AND GRAPHIC NOVELS

Harriet E.H. Earle

What *is* comics? This question has no conclusive answer; scholars are divided on the most appropriate way to define the formal properties of the comics form. To quote Scott McCloud's introduction to the form (1994: 9), comics is 'juxtaposed pictorial and other images in deliberate sequence, intended to convey information and/or to produce an aesthetic response in the viewer'; this definition is often pared down to 'sequential art' (most notably in the work of Will Eisner). McCloud's definition is careful to cover all the potential iterations of the form but it does not necessarily tell us 'what' comics is. Scholars and practitioners disagree on the finer points, but to my mind comics is any narrative in which the information is transmitted primarily via image. The primacy of the image differentiates comics from illustrated books – it is a visual form. I would also like to add here that the plural of comic is typically used as a singular (as 'politics' is) to refer to the entire form or industry. Hence, I talk about 'the comics industry' or 'comics creators'. That said, individual texts may be referred to as a 'comic': the 's' distinguishes between the form on the whole and the individual texts. Furthermore, there is much discussion over the various terms used for the 'thing' itself. It is my preference to use the term 'comics' for all texts, rather than favouring the potentially elitist 'graphic novel' or any of the other variants that have been put forward by artists and authors, including 'comic strip novel' (Daniel Clowes 2001) and 'illustrated novel' (Craig Thompson 2003). For the most part, 'graphic novel' is a marketing term, rather than a marker of quality or legitimacy; Art Spiegelman (2011) claims that graphic novels are 'long comic books that require a bookmark'. There is no definitive response to the terminology debate but it remains a key part of the discourse on the position and the status of the contemporary comic.

Readers new to comics might expect this chapter to trace or even defend comics' gradual journey towards recognition as a legitimate form. However, such an approach would fundamentally misrepresent the state of affairs within the field, both as a narrative form and an academic discipline. The twenty-first century has seen comics come into its own, with an ever-increasing corpus of notable texts and creators, as well as an increased focus on comics as both educational and instructive. My 2017 study of war comics and trauma concludes by stating that,

> comics is able to do things that other forms cannot because it is intrinsically bound up in a culture of imagination, fantasy, and limitlessness. It is a form that encourages difference and experimentation. It is open to all themes.

> (Earle 2017: 197)

An intensive look at comics in the twenty-first century certainly substantiates this point. Once stereotyped as the reading fodder of teenage boys, with bold, brash colours and simplistic plot-lines, comics is proving itself to be capable of handling complex, nuanced narratives in a way that is both different from – and complementary to – other storytelling forms. Comics' journey from creation to nuanced, contemporary form has been one of slow yet steady growth – moving from the earliest strip comics of *The Glasgow Looking-Glass* (1825–1826) and the form-defining *Hogan's Alley* (1895–1898), through the rise of the mainstream publishers (including DC and Marvel), onto the 1970s and 1980s with the birth of 'underground comix' and the development of the 'graphic novel'.[1] And now? What has comics become? Perhaps a better question is: what is comics becoming?

The twenty-first century comic is gloriously diverse. Within Anglophone comics, it is hard to find a genre or artistic style that is not represented within the form, as available texts move from superheroics to autobiography, from traditional cinematic genres (such as westerns, crime and horror) to smaller, though no less vibrant, categories (such as graphic medicine and comics reportage). While this vibrancy of offerings harkens back to the Golden Age of the 1940s, there is far more diversity of both character and artist than previously displayed and the market is no longer dominated by a small number of publishers. Similarly, the relationship of the writer and artistic team has changed considerably; in a vast majority of cases, the writer and artist is the same person, unlike in most mainstream comics, where a large team works together on one piece. That said, there are still many prolific and decorated creators who works solely on one aspect of the piece. Good examples include writer Garth Ennis (*Preacher*, *Battlefields*), who has paired with several different artists throughout his career, and artist Dave Gibbons (*Watchmen*, *2000 AD*), most widely known for his collaboration with Alan Moore and, since 2014, the Comics Laureate. However, for the vast majority of non-mainstream comics and graphic novels, there is one creator. This has led to bold developments in artistic style and, as it becomes more common for artist and author to be the same person, the use of a house style is becoming less important in the publication of comics. This is not to say that highly recognisable artistic styles are not being employed. Almost every artist has a style that is, as one moves through their corpus, instantly recognisable and many have developed a signature that links their works together. For example, Art Spiegelman's black and white woodcut style is recognisable, but even more so is the mouse mask that features heavily in all representations of his work (even, notably, in his appearance in *The Simpsons*); similarly, Chris Ware's adoption of the traditionally Franco-Belgian *ligne claire* style, combined with his pristine, geometric page layouts have become his trademark. The conflation of artist and author has allowed the artist style to become an intensely personal part of the text in ways that were not necessarily available to artists working within house constraints, a move that was championed by the underground comix of the 1960s and 1970s but is now firmly a part of contemporary comics creation.

As with other emerging areas of scholarship, comics is forging its own path within the academy. Building on Cultural Studies' interest in comics dating back to the 1970s, the contemporary face of comics scholarship is as diverse as the texts themselves. However, unlike many other fields, comics studies is inherently interdisciplinary, with many key texts within the field drawing on existing scholarship from a diverse range of disciplines. An ever-expanding corpus of comics studies monographs covers topics from comics and law, to representations of medicine and health care, historiography and non-fiction comics, and the use of comics within education studies to encourage and develop literacy. Perhaps one of the most exciting and dynamic theoretical interventions for twenty-first century comics studies is found in the work of Nick Sousanis, whose first monograph *Unflattening* was published in 2015 by Harvard University Press. *Unflattening* began as a doctoral thesis at Columbia University and grew out of an earlier example of comics-as-theoretical-document, 'Possibilities' (2005); the aim of the book is to demonstrate the viability of comics as a form for theoretical scholarship, independent of any need for accompanying critical paratexts. It is a text which allows the reader to meditate on comics as both an artistic, narrative form and a space for critical reflection and commentary. The text follows an anonymous protagonist as they explore a new world quite unlike the regimented, material world of our existences. Sousanis argues that the image is not only for illustration, but an equal partner to the word and a key component in our mechanisms of thought and idea-formation. Of course, his is not the first text to use comics to introduce theory and give shape to ideas of word-image relationships; this honour probably belongs to Scott McCloud's *Understanding Comics* (1994) and his various sequels. 'There are always gaps', Sousanis writes, 'spaces for the unknown, openings for imagination to spill into. Incompleteness reveals that there is always more to discover' (2015: 150). This is the key to *Unflattening*: it opens up a new space for both comics-as-essay and also, in a much wider sense, essay-as-something-more. In giving Sousanis space to speak through the comics form, we are giving space to a whole range of new ideas and new methodologies for dissemination, not just in the visual arts but across the academy.

Before moving on to look at two thematic issues that are central to the twenty-first century comic, I must address the issue of this chapter's inclusion in a literature companion. In 2005, website *The Comics Reporter* published a conversation between two noted comics scholars, Charles Hatfield and Bart Beaty, on the topic of comics and categorisations. Over the course of the published conversation, given the amusing title 'Let's You and Him Fight: Alternative Comics – An Emerging Literature', the two scholars considered the categorisation of comics as either art (Beaty's position) or literature (Hatfield's position). Hatfield had the last word and closed the discussion by outlining the issues that the discussion, which reached no consensus, raised. Of the four points he raised, I wish to consider 'the ongoing redefinition of literary study in the face of cultural studies, particularly in light of what I take to be a reconceptualising of the visual vis-a-vis literary texts' (Beaty and Hatfield, 2005: n.p.). This is the crux of the issue of categorising comics as literature – it necessitates a redefinition of what it means for something to be literature and an understanding of the various criteria and boundaries that may be crossed in order to create a space for comics scholarship within an existing defined field. While I do not offer a suggestion here, I wish to draw attention to existing conversations on the nature of comics and the positioning of comics within both the academy and the wider artistic world. In this chapter, I discuss identity and autographics, a genre of comics that has not only produced a large number of critically acclaimed texts but also one that is of huge interest within comics studies. I then go on to consider the future of the form and where both scholarship and the form itself may go in the future.

Drawing selves: identity and autographics

Of all the genres in which comics is establishing itself as a key form, the most visible and dynamic is life writing. Traditionally a literary genre dominated by female writers, this is proving not to be the case within comics. This is not to say that female creators are not working within the genre, but it is not their exclusive domain and the narratives that are being created by all artists and authors are foregrounding the unique representational strategies of the form to inextricably bind form and theme into a coherent narrative whole. In order to avoid confusion, I use the term 'autographics', first proposed by Gillian Whitlock, as an umbrella term for comics that are biographical or autobiographical in nature. Whitlock (2007: 11–12) writes that 'autobiography is a cultural space where relations between the individual and society are thought out intensely and experienced intersubjectively; here the social, political and cultural underpinnings of thinking about the self come to the surface and are affirmed in images, stories, and legends'. I can offer no concrete suggestion as to how or why comics may have fared so successful for this particular type of storytelling. However, the vast number of artistic and narrative devices offered by the comics form has undoubtedly made it possible for stories to be told in different, engaging ways that appeal to those who feel that more traditional storytelling methods are not representative of the nuances of their personal stories. Drawing on recent trends on trauma theory, I argue that comics offers an arsenal of representational strategies for making trauma both legible and visible; 'indeed, it is because of the intensely visual nature of the comics form that it can be used to such good effect in representations of conflict trauma' (Earle 2017: 34). There is no reason why this contention cannot also work for autographics, many of which deal with traumatic personal narratives.

In her comprehensive study of autographics, Elisabeth El Refaie (2012: 12) writes that 'it is impossible to draw strict boundaries between factual and fictional accounts of someone's life, since memory is always incomplete and the act of telling one's life story necessarily involves selection and artful construction'. The intimate relationship between the narrative and the act of creation means that comics is able to make visible these blurred boundaries and indeed make them part of the narrative itself. The presence of the author's avatar allows the reader a visual guide through the story, while giving the author a space to draw out their experiences and reimagine their lives on the page. Furthermore, engaging with existing narrative styles and genres in different forms can help us to reinvigorate our representational practices across a wide range of forms. Jane Tolmie (2009: 84) suggests that 'stories, even in graphic memoir, does not fully capture either the body of the past, though new formats lead us to ask new and perhaps better questions about the nature of the body/text gap'. Comics is well-placed to offer new understandings about this 'body/text gap' and the ways it can be made visual: 'comics locates the reader in space and for this reason is able to spatialize memory [. . .] comics is able to map a life, not only figuratively but literally' (Chute, 2011: 108–109).

Among the most popular, highly commended and compelling texts of the autographics genre are those that make visible the personal experiences of conflict and violence. This stage was set in 1986 with the publication of Art Spiegelman's *Maus*, which retells his father's story in 1940s Poland and is often spoken of with hagiolatrous fervour. Not only is Spiegelman's book a landmark in both autobiographical writing and comics, but he has created a set of tropes that have appeared over and over in autographics texts. The comics form has allowed others to tell the stories of their parents and the wider historical context, while also having a space to reimagine their own experiences, a process that Spiegelman arguably begins in *Maus*. GB Tran's parents managed to escape from Saigon in 1975 before it fell to communist forces. They immigrated to the USA and it is here that Tran is born. In his 2011 work *Vietnamerica*, he draws his parents' stories of life in Vietnam before and during the war, framed by his own story of returning to the country to attend a funeral. Building on his father's past as a watercolourist and reader of *bandes dessinées* (Franco-Belgian comics), Tran's book catalogues his family's artistic legacies and also the influence of French colonialism on Vietnamese artistic practice. Carol Tyler employs a similar practice for her trilogy of comics on her father's experience in the Second World War, *You'll Never Know* (2009, 2010, 2012). Using the aesthetic of the scrapbook, a popular crafting activity across the USA, she narrates her experience of learning about her father's past as she attempted to create a book of memories for him. The result is a three-volume exploration of the nature of parenting in the wake of trauma and what it means to be a child of a war veteran. Tyler explores similar themes to both Spiegelman and Tran but she retains control and ownership of her story, as all these artists do, in the artistic choices she makes and the visual presentation of events on the page.

Remaining with the theme of conflict and trauma in comics, Marjane Satrapi's *Persepolis* (2000) uses simple black and image artwork reminiscent of early twentieth century wood cuts to tell the story of her childhood in post-Revolution Iran and the ways in which this experience affected her as an adolescent in Austria and into maturity. Speaking with an openness that contrasts sharply with the silence of her fellow Iranian women, Satrapi weaves together her own story and that of her country's recent history; she does not shy away from some of the more controversial issues facing Iranians, most notably the veil and the modesty laws that drastically altered daily life for women in the country. In her coming together of autographics and the *Bildungsroman*, she comes to understand her own place in the world and create a text that makes the personal nuances and wider social issues of the Islamic Revolution visible and comprehensible to readers on an international scale.

Joe Sacco's work, which is often categorised as comics journalism or reportage, works in a similar way to Satrapi's in that he uses the form to open discussions on violence and conflict and its effect on the individuals who experience it. His extensive bibliography includes a series of books on the Middle East (*Palestine* (2001) and *Footnotes in Gaza* (2009)) and the Bosnian War (*Safe Area Goraźde* (2000) and *The Fixer: A Story from Sarajevo* (2003)). Placing himself at the centre of the story as guide and interviewer, the reader follows Sacco as he meets with a wide range of individuals on different sides of the conflicts, literally drawing their stories in chaotic black and white images that break with many of the normal framing conventions of comics and instead force the reader to confront the violence and turmoil of conflict on both thematic and formal levels. Sacco is widely credited as the creator of comics journalism; recent publications by other artists include Sarah Glidden's *Rolling Blackouts Dispatches from Turkey, Syria, and Iraq* (2016) and *How to Understand Israel in 60 Days or Less* (2010); Josh Neufeld's *A.D.: New Orleans After The Deluge* (2010); and *The Photographer: Into War-Torn Afghanistan with Doctors Without Borders* by Emmanuel Guibert and Frédéric Lemercier (2009).

Perhaps in line with stereotypes and perhaps in spite of them, autographics has proved to be a popular form for women's life narratives, especially those that deal with sexual violence and trauma. In *Graphic Women: Life Narrative and Contemporary Comics* (2010), Hillary Chute suggests that the marginalisation of female artists within the comics world has much to do with the silencing of narratives of sexuality and trauma. She cites Aline Kominsky-Crumb (Chute 2010: 31) as a clear example: 'Her underwhelming reception contrasts markedly to that of her husband, cartoonist Robert Crumb, who has been canonised exactly for writing the darker side of (his own) tortured male sexuality'. Furthermore, Chute claims that the (gendered) suspicion of memoirs explains why the idea of such memoirs with the additional element of the visual, which is often considered 'excessive', does not easily win attention. Kominsky-Crumb published *Need More Love: A Graphic Memoir* in 2007. Her book catalogues her long history of creating autographics, moving from her beginnings in 1960s Greenwich Village and then to California and her marriage to acclaimed underground comix artist Robert Crumb. She is fiercely critical of her own experiences, including her childhood, her sexual maturation and motherhood. However, perhaps what is most striking about the book is that her way of talking about herself (and especially her sexuality) is not vastly different to her husband's, yet he is praised for his candour and she is ignored for her 'excess'. Nevertheless, Kominsky-Crumb sits as a key figure in women's confessional autographics and a clear influence on many other artists.

Phoebe Gloeckner's *The Diary of a Teenage Girl* (2002) grows from the same histories and experiences as Kominsky-Crumb's works. Gloeckner's avatar, Minnie, recounts her teenage experiences in 1970s San Francisco; she documents her sexual affair with her mother's boyfriend, Monroe, her relationships with equally troubled young women and her growing awareness of her place in the world as a young woman. The book itself is not comics in the truest sense of the term, as strip drawings are interspersed throughout longer text diary entries, with occasional single-page illustrations. Gloeckner uses her training as a medical illustrator and the freedom offered by the comics page to bring together her story across several artistic registers. Lynda Barry adopts an equally daring artistic style for her work, which combines aspects of collage and painting and takes its inspirations from a range of sources, from scrapbooking to fine art. One highly regarded example of her work is *One! Hundred! Demons!* (2002). Drawing inspiration from a sixteenth-century Zen painting of a hoard of demons chasing each other, Barry creates seventeen vignettes which outline the various demons she has met in her life: each demon is a moment that has changed and affected her. The book's introduction shows Barry's avatar sitting at her desk, pondering the nature of fiction and truth. She coins the term 'autobificitionalography' to name her work and as a tongue in cheek answer to the question of whether autobiography can contain moments of fiction. Barry's greatest achievement in this work is her ability to convince the reader that, ultimately, this question is irrelevant. Her stories speak of a universality of experience and the necessity of naming that is part of the process of maturation, healing and survival.

To conclude this discussion of autographics, I turn to one of the most literary and influential texts of the genre: *Fun Home* by Alison Bechdel (2006). Bechdel is the creator of the syndicated and extremely popular comic strip *Dykes to Watch Out For* (1983–2008) and also gives her name to the 'Bechdel Test'.[2] In *Fun Home*, Bechdel talks about her childhood and early life living in her parents gothic home, which her father obsessively renovates and rebuilds to its former glory. She is open about her struggles with her sexuality and her coming out while at college aged nineteen. The main focus of the book is her father's death; although it is officially an accident, Bechdel believes it may have been a suicide. It is also heavily implied that her father was gay. Bechdel works through the trauma of losing her father and her own identity and sexuality in the light of his, framing her own experiences through the classic works of European literature that she and her father both loved. It is her engagement with classic, and especially high modernist, literature that has garnered the most interest in this text. Long considered a low art form of little artistic or literary value, *Fun Home's* nuanced and highly introspective engagement with the world of literature in general and modernism in particular gives us a new lens through which we can read these texts and also a clearer understanding of the ways in which readers incorporate their reading into their identity formation and daily lives.

Moving forward

Where are we going now? Comics has established a firm foothold in both academic and popular circles, a vast array of texts is available to readers of all ages and interests, and scholarship is forging new paths and new connections within the academy. However, in a more practical sense, comics has seen a number of significant changes this century and it is unlikely to stop soon. The internet has become one of the most forward-thinking places to publish one's work, with an ever-expanding number of creators hosting online publications or using social media platforms to disseminate their work. Not only does this allow for independent creators to achieve far larger audiences than if they were confined to print, but it also speeds up the process, allowing for almost immediate publication and, more importantly, immediate response. This is particularly relevant for political cartooning and socially engaging works. Cartooning and graphic political comment is no longer confined to print media but is now found throughout the digital sphere, on sites including Instagram and Twitter, and also online news sites, such as *The Huffington Post* and *The Nib* (a site dedicated to graphic comment). The use of comics for political or social comment is nothing new – we can date political cartooning back to the late eighteenth century and the works of James Gillray and Thomas Rowlandson, with some scholars claiming Hogarth's pictorial satire as the form's forerunner – but a number of recent events have concretised comics' importance as a politically engaged artistic form. The publication of a number of graphic depictions of the Prophet Mohammed in Danish newspaper *Jyllands-Posten* in 2005 led to international media attention and a large number of violent protests. Similarly, the 2015 shooting at the offices of the Parisian magazine *Charlie Hebdo*, known for the circulation of similar anti-Islamic cartoons raised similar questions about the nature of comics and their relationship to free speech and free expression. In the introduction to a special journal issue on transnational comics, Knowles, Peacock, and I (2016: 379) wrote,

> The most vocal and/or violent reactions to these cartoons fall into two camps: condemning the production of the images, and thus rejecting the use of graphic forms of representation in certain contemporary arenas; or protesting against the censorious tone of these protests, and promoting artistic endeavour above particular beliefs, ideas, or emotions.

It is clear that there is something in the fact that such statements are being made through the comics form that raises temperatures beyond a simple text statement. Of course, this heat of feeling can be channelled back into comics and is fuelling the form's development. The visibility of comics through these events is pushing the form into new territory and paving the way for it to be involved in the public conversation with ever-increasing frequency. Comics are being used in both print and digital forms to document and respond to the current political climate. Organisations such as Amnesty International and MSF are pairing with comics creators to run online collaborative projects, such as *Positive Negatives*; individuals are finding ways to visualise their voice, as is the case with the 2010 online serialisation (and 2011 print publication) of *Zahra's Paradise*, a response to the 2009 Iranian elections by Amir Soltani and Khalil.

I have mentioned digital and web comics in the realm of political comment but, of course, a great number of web comics exist that are not socially engaged and exist as entertainment or education. However, a curious divide still exists between web and print comics. Print comics are afforded legitimacy by the fact they have a recognised publisher and material form; web comics do not have this protection. As such, it is not uncommon for highly popular and acclaimed web comics to be printed as physical objects; this has happened to large numbers of web comics, including *Hyperbole and a Half* (Allie Brosh 2013), *American Elf* (James Kochalka 2004, 2007) and *Hark! A Vagrant* (Kate Beaton 2011). We have not yet successfully combatted the legitimacy of the print object over online self-publication but in the eyes of many, web comics are the new frontier. Creators, publishers and readers alike are recognising the opportunities offered by digital comics, pushing the form away from the constraints of print media and into a more open, egalitarian and accessible arena.

In my study of comics and conflict, I outline a cultural phenomenon that is key to understanding the slow move of comics from pulpy trash to important narrative and socio-political form: the 'Cerebus Syndrome'.[3] Named after Dave Sim's award-winning series *Cerebus*, (1977 to 2004), the series follows Cerebus, a misanthropic aardvark, who is positioned as a Conan the Barbarian-inspired fantasy hero. I (2017: 194) note that,

The Cerebus Syndrome refers to [a] gradual change from parodic and light subject matter to more serious concerns. It can be traced in other popular series, such as *The Simpsons* and the *Batman* comics franchise (especially within the films of Christopher Nolan). The readers of the particular comic may be unaware of the shift and only notice it in retrospect.

This syndrome can be incredibly useful in introducing bold, serious subject matters to new audiences while also allowing potentially inflammatory subjects to be given a voice under the radar. It is also broadening the corpus of acceptable topics for comics to discuss. While I have not yet performed any extensive interrogation of this phenomenon in comics, or popular culture more broadly, it is clear from this brief introduction that comics' self-awareness and engagement with its own ignominious past is a noted strength of the form. Just as postcolonial literature interrogates the colonialist history of the novel or postmodernism seeks to break down received truths, the comics form in the twenty-first century is interrogating and critically rethinking its own past to forge its future.

Notes

1 This chapter will concentrate on Anglophone comics and, as such, the short history I provide here is primarily occidental. Those familiar with the eastern comics traditions will note that *Manga* (Japanese comics) has a similarly disputed past. Some suggest that the earliest *Manga* date back to the twelfth century. I think it is fairer to label these texts as 'proto-comics', grouping them in a similar category to political cartooning and works like those of Hogarth and Bosch – they inspired the comics/*Manga* form but are not necessarily examples of it. For a detailed analysis of the history of comics, see Aldridge and Perry, *The Penguin Book of Comics: A Slight History* (1989) and McCloud, *Understanding Comics* (1994).
2 The Bechdel Test is a way of categorising and discussing female representation in film. It has three aspects: does this work feature at least two women who talk to each other about something other than a man. According to user-edited databases, about half of all films meet these requirements. The test has led to the development of several spin-off tests, including the 'Mako Mori Test', which asks whether a female character's story is written purely to support a male character's story, and the 'Sexy Lamp Test'. Created by comics artist Kelly Sue DeConnick, she writes, 'If you can replace your female character with a sexy lamp and the story still basically works, maybe you need another draft'.
3 This phenomenon is most clearly demonstrated by a quotation from long-running animated series *The Simpsons*, which is a good example of a self-aware series that uses its 'low' form to make bold statements: 'Cartoons don't have messages, Lisa. They're just a bunch of hilarious stuff, like people getting hurt and stuff' (Groening et al., 1995).

Works cited

Aldridge, A. and G. Perry. (1989) *The Penguin Book of Comics: A Slight History*. London: Penguin.
Barry, L. (2002) *One! Hundred! Demons!* Seattle: Sasquatch Books.
Beaty, B. and C. Hatfield (2005) *Let's You and Him Fight: Alternative Comics: An Emerging Literature*. Available at: www.comicsreporter.com/. [Accessed 9 August 2017].
Bechdel, A. (2006) *Fun Home: A Family Tragicomic*. London: Jonathan Cape.
Chute, H. (2010) *Graphic Women: Life, Narrative and Contemporary Comics*. New York: Columbia University Press.
—— (2011) 'Comics Form and Narrating Lives'. *Profession*. 107–117.
Earle, H. (2017) *Comics, Trauma, and the New Art of War*. Jackson: University Press of Mississippi.
El Refaie, E. (2012) *Autobiographical Comics: Life Writing in Pictures*. Jackson: University Press of Mississippi.
Gloeckner, P. (2002) *The Diary of a Teenage Girl*. Berkeley: North Atlantic Books.
Groening, M. et al. (1995) 'Lisa the Vegetarian'. *The Simpsons*. Los Angeles: Fox Broadcasting.

Knowles, S., J. Peacock and H. Earle. (2016) 'Introduction: Trans/formation and the Graphic Novel'. *Journal of Postcolonial Writing* 52:4. 378–384.

Kominsky-Crumb, A. (2007) *Need More Love: A Graphic Memoir*. London: MQ Publications.

McCloud, S. (1994) *Understanding Comics: The Invisible Art*. New York: HarperPerennial.

Satrapi, M. (2000) *Persepolis*. New York: Vintage.

Sousanis, N. (2005) *Possibilities*. Available at: http://spinweaveandcut.com/possibilities-the-rabbit-page-and-more/. [Accessed 28 April 2015].

—— (2015) *Unflattening*. Cambridge: Harvard University Press.

Spiegelman, A. (2003) *Maus: A Survivor's Tale*. London: Penguin.

—— (2011). *MetaMaus*. New York: Pantheon.

Tolmie, J. (2009) 'Modernism, Memory and Desire: Queer Cultural Production in Alison Bechdel's Fun Home'. *Topia* 22. pp. 77-95.

Tyler, C. (2009) *You'll Never Know Book 1: A Good and Decent Man*. Seattle: Fantagraphics.

—— (2010) *You'll Never Know Book 2: Collateral Damage*. Seattle: Fantagraphics.

—— (2012) *You'll Never Know Book 3: Soldier's Heart*. Seattle: Fantagraphics.

Whitlock, G. 2006. 'Autographics: The Seeing 'I' of Comics.' *Modern Fiction Studies* 52:4. 965–79.

PART II

Identities

11

BLACK BRITISH FICTION

Sara Upstone

In 2014 a friend invited me to a preview of a work entitled 'Exhibit B' by the South African artist Brett Bailey displayed in London at the Waterloo vaults, a grimy subterranean space of concretised imaginings hidden beneath the hustle of the city street. Immersed in my own writing, I'd heard nothing about the exhibition. I arrived, only to be led with a dozen other audience members into an empty room, where each of us was separated from our acquaintances and invited to walk silently around a series of rooms that stretched out in front of us. In each room we found recreated scenes of nineteenth-century colonialism, the plight of refugees, and contemporary objectifications of black culture – but in each scene was not a mannequin, but rather a living human body; bodies shackled, abused, put to work, and looking back at us as we made sense of the living images before us.

Bailey's work was intended to critique the human zoos of the nineteenth-century and the commonplace objectification of the black body that they spurned. As I wandered around the exhibition I was forced to confront the power of my own place in a hierarchy which constructed me as the white voyeur. It seemed impossible to make eye contact with the actors in the scenes. Consumed by my discomfort at being forced into the role of the othering white gaze, I left the exhibition disturbed and profoundly moved. Yet the week after my visit, the exhibition had been permanently closed, shut down by the organisers after a series of protests that accused the exhibition of objectifying the black body and reproducing white superiority. In this controversy, then, was a debate surrounding the continued signifying power of the black body and the negative force of naming, defining or displaying that body: not as past aberration, but as present-day problem.

In the four years since the exhibition, this debate has only intensified, as discrimination more resonant with the past is replicated in the present-day. How does one reconcile the gross miscarriages of justice indicated by the #BlackLivesMatter movement, the re-emergence of racial science in the comments of writers such as James Watson (see Nugent 2007) and Nicholas Wade (2014), and the election of Donald Trump, against the promise heralded a decade earlier by a British Labour government and the presidency of Barack Obama? How, equally, does one respond to stories like that of Rachel Dolezal, vilified for attempting to 'pass' as African American, in the context of broader social movements arguing for the mutability of the signifying body? It is difficult not to be convinced by the arguments of Ashley Dawson (2010) who reads in Islamophobic institutional responses to 9/11 a resurrection of the anti-black policing of the 1980s, or those made in the wake of the London Grenfell fire which suggest that institutional racism is implicated in the negligence which led to the deaths of 71 people, at least 59 of these from black or minority ethnic (BAME) backgrounds. Race is more amorphous than it has ever been, yet its social relevance persists in ways which defeat and dispute this fluidity. For while 'defeat' indicates loss, elsewhere exists a conterminous resurgence of positive investment in blackness; new pan-Africanism, Beyoncé's explosive performance of 'Formation' at the 2016 Super Bowl and the rise in black and Asian hip hop nationalism (see Dawson 2010), the academic development of a Black Studies Association in the UK; the growth of Black Pride events in both the UK the US: all examples of how positive investment in racial identity continues to shape cultural practice.

It is within this context that contemporary black British fiction – here taken to mean writing produced by British authors self-identifying as of BAME background – is to be received. While scholarship has frequently contrasted this work to earlier migrant writing in Britain, such distinctions have often-time worked to offer problematic generalisations about both generations of writers. It is with an explicit acknowledgement of this tension that one approaches twenty-first century black British fiction and sees within this body of work an internal diversity: a heteroglossic discourse that at points indicates both departure from and resonance with not only earlier British born voices of the 1980s and 1990s, but also that incredibly crucial black presence of the post-Windrush migrant generation.

Black matters?

One might ask, given this diversity, why still write about black British writing at all? The answer is to some extent answered by the contexts of Dolezal, Exhibit B, Obama, and the like, each of which can be cited to support assertions of a continued cultural presence of race to which literature responds. As I have argued elsewhere (Upstone 2016), this concern is not exclusively the preserve of black writers, and to position it as such continues a dangerous marginalisation of race as a 'black issue'. Nevertheless, the continued use of black British writing as a frame of reference creates a space for sustained attention on racial politics which might otherwise be occluded. This occlusion exists not merely in the realms of white racist discourse, but also more insidiously in the avenues of liberal thinking, including within writing and academia. An exposition of this phenomenon is perhaps best provided by Christopher Lebron's recent work *The Making of Black Lives Matter* (2017), in which he attacks those he labels the 'morally dim witted': not those who are explicitly prejudiced, but rather those whose liberal politics belie an enduring white priority. Lebron's work draws attention to the risk of liberal impulses to move beyond race slipping into a *de facto* whiteness – less the removal of racial otherness than a reassertion of white privilege.

How then to draw some useful conclusions on black British writing in the contemporary moment? Elsewhere, I locate a shift in black literature beginning in the fiction of the 1990s (Upstone 2015b), an imaginative speculation on positive futures. In aesthetic terms, this speculation evokes a reworking of realist form, so that the notion of a representative fiction of the present – the black British *bildungsroman* outlined by Mark Stein in *Black British Literature: Novels of Transformation* – is disrupted by moments of possibility which encourage readers to engage in acts of reimagining the interplay between identity, nationhood, and belonging (Upstone 2016). Such fiction is rooted in the conceptual frameworks dominating thinking about race and ethnicity in the 1990s, most notably Paul Gilroy's work on planetary humanism and post-racial community (2000), and alongside these ideas the theories of diasporic cosmopolitanism and cultural diversity advanced by postcolonial theorists such as Homi Bhabha. Criticism on the fiction of the 1990s such as R Victoria Arana's work (2005: 230) stresses the writing's lack of anger when compared to its 1980s forbears: a fiction defined by confident belonging and multicultural carnivalesque, what

John McLeod terms 'millennial optimism' (2004). Yet my own reflection on this period betrays a sea change by the end of decade – 'that this 1990s possibility has not been realized is the story of the fiction of the 2000s' (Upstone 2015b: 144) – a representation of Alison Donnell's perspective that by the turn of the century Gilroy's planetary humanist future had been downgraded from 'optimistically probable' to 'hopefully possible' (2006: 198) with literary changes reflecting this shift. What emerges in the next two decades can no more be generalised than the writing which precedes it, but a trend can nevertheless be identified which speaks not of a refusal of utopianism in the subsequent decades, but rather a modification of its nuances and resonances, the mood crucially altered by the complex trajectory of race relations. Thus while the utopian spirit of this fiction remains, the nature of its positivity is not unrestrained, but rather a tempered vision, where the post-racial and the planetary have been modified by a response to socio-political realities which maintain blackness as a site of reference and power contestation. In this respect one might speak instead of a utopian realism of a *pragmatic optimism* rather than one of unrestrained character – a commitment to imagining narratives in the context of the complex realities of contemporary racial politics and to finding within this, rather than beyond it, sources of affirmative value.

In order to trace a more nuanced trajectory of this pragmatic optimism, one useful strategy is to consider the careers of those writers producing work over the last twenty years, whose early writing is identifiable in the terms of the utopian spirit of the 1990s, and whose ongoing careers can be used to trace developments of this trend. The limited number of writers who meet this criteria is in itself deserving of comment, given that it speaks in particular to the lack of longevity of black writers' careers, and the continued struggle to attract long-term publicity and investment (see Fowler 2008); notable twenty-first century debuts such as Donna Daley-Clarke's *Lazy Eye* (2005), David Nwokedi's *Fitzgerald's Wood* (2005), Nirpal Singh Dhaliwal's *Tourism* (2006) and Gautam Malkani's *Londonstani* (2006) announced the promise of new voices but none has yet published a second novel. Particularly noteworthy is the lack of black male writers who identify as Afro-Caribbean falling into this category. Speaking in 2016, the publisher of Robyn Travis's *Mama Can't Raise No Man* provocatively declared that he was the only black male debut novelist to be published in Britain that year (Akbar 2016). This then, is the other side of the noted emergence of female black writers whose work has been seen to challenge definitions of black British literature (see McLeod 2010: 46; Hussain 2005; Weedon 2008; Nasta 2000).

Let us take, then, two writers who have managed to maintain this literary presence. On the one hand, Zadie Smith: a mainstream publishing success, present on school syllabi, adapted for television, and of international reputation. On the other, Courttia Newland; critically acclaimed for his uncompromising novels of black experience; of central significance to the black arts movement in the UK, and a recognisable name to anyone working in the field of black literary studies. Despite sharply differentiated styles, Newland's and Smith's novels offer remarkably similar perspectives on the issue of race. While Smith is frequently read as the purveyor of celebratory rhetoric surrounding multiculturalism, critics have pointed to her tempering of this vision with a more sobering caveat surrounding the enduring presence of race; conversely, Newland's gritty 'concrete realism' (Kelleher 2005) is often read in ways which obscure his hopeful investment in the possibility of social transformation. Both are pragmatic optimists.

Trajectory in this respect is a matter both of continuity and change; it is tempting to focus on the latter, but what remains is perhaps even more striking. In 2012 Smith returned with *NW* to the Willesden location of her explosive debut novel, *White Teeth* (2000), to tell four interweaving stories – of Felix and Nathan, two young black men of differing fortunes, and two friends: Natalie, who is black, and Leah, who is white. Likewise, in 2013 Newland returned in *The Gospel According to Cane* to the West London locale of his first novel, *The Scholar* (1997), the later novel recounting the story of Beverley, a mixed-race woman whose life is turned upside down by the appearance of a man called Wills, claiming to be her son, who was snatched as a baby two decades earlier and never found. Both Newland and Smith broaden the scope of their earlier works – the crew of young Londoners with their urban street dialects, 'flavoured by neither African, West Indian nor English pronunciation, and occurred no matter the race of the speaker' (*Gospel*, 37) that dominate *The Scholar* are still present in *Gospel* via Beverley's young charges at the education centre where she works, but her own voice – captured evocatively in Newland's first person narrative – is a far more formalised, languorous register which confers her alternative world, neatly marked by Abel and Cole deliveries and the Afternoon Play on Radio 4 (10, 72). Likewise, Smith draws firm parallels between ethnic identification and socio-economic status in *White Teeth*, with her middle-class intellectual Jewish British Chalfens pitted firmly against her working class black British characters. In *NW*, however, the picture is complicated by social mobility and gender; Natalie's career as a lawyer and life in the suburbs contrasts starkly against Leah's life on the council estate.

The distinctions evoked by both Smith and Newland speak against the reduction of black British culture to a singularity of experience. In some senses Smith's and Newland's later novels hint at Gilroy's planetary post-racial come to pass. In *Gospel* the endemic police brutality and racial divisions which feature prominently in *The Scholar* have been toned down to asides; the glimmers of racist division in the differing responses of white and black community police officers to estate violence and the racial slurs which emerge at moments of extreme danger in the later novel contrast with the quotidian nature of such language in the earlier book, and a more systemic nature of institutional racism. Likewise, Smith replaces the racist discourse of Willesden leading up to the millennium in *White Teeth* with more complex forms of otherness in *NW*. In the former, the young trio of Irie, Magid, and Millat encounter the last vestige of racism in the ageing war veteran Mr Hamilton. By the time of *NW* the Mr Hamiltons of the world are long gone; whereas in the former a distinction is made between ethnic and racial difference, so that Magid and Millat can embrace cultural diversity but for Irie there is 'no reflection to show her what it means to be half white, half Jamaican' (McMann 2012: 629), in *NW* Natalie's black Britishness poses no barrier to her social prospects.

Black loves matter

Yet while there is less racism in these later novels, there is not less race. In this sense, therefore, the promise of the post-racial as indicated in Gilroy's thinking and in the novels of the 1990s seems to have been diverted to an alternative register of racial reference rather than been removed. At the centre of this shift is the evocation of race not as barrier but as distinction, what McLeod (2010) calls an 'extra dimension'. So alongside the post-racial community, both *NW* and *Gospel* mediate on the continued value of ancestral connection. In *NW*, Natalie's disconnection from black British culture does not result in liberation, but rather the feeling that she has 'no self to be' (208), caught in a life of performances which see her in endless roles: 'Daughter drag. Sister drag. Mother drag. Wife drag. Court drag. Rich drag. Poor drag. British drag. Jamaican drag' (278). Likewise, in *Gospel*, Beverley's love for Seth, a policeman, comes because he is 'one of the few people who don't mind talking about race [. . .] Some people behave like the very mention is a dirty word and don't thank you for reminding them it *actually exists*' (emphasis added, 21). Beverley's relationship with her lost son is metonymic of a broader ancestral past which comes to her through dreams of Barbados and her girlhood there. She chooses Wills, complete with his delectable Caribbean cooking, black nationalist sympathies, and a body of 'black gold' which 'was all the harsh environment and soft nature of the continent' (224), over the young people she has been teaching; in the novel's dramatic denouement, a stand-off between these two competing models of community, she is willing to stab one of them to protect him. Their 'bond formed in the first minute' (253) speaks to a biological imperative that in an instant overwhelms years of identification wrought through shared spaces and experiences.

The resonance of such discourse is not with the fiction of the 1990s so much as with a resurgence of the strident black oppositional consciousness of the 1970s and 1980s. In the fiction of the twenty-first century, however, the anger of 1970s and 1980s is reframed into positive affirmation and relativised by the influence of the 1990s to become a space in which ideas of return or departure are neither accurate nor satisfactory. Ironically it is one that still holds Gilroy as the central figure of theoretical influence, though here not for the planetary humanist arguments of *Between Camps* (2000) but more for the resurrection of the celebration of black diasporic cultures advanced in both *The Black Atlantic* (1993a) and *Small Acts* (1993b). This unusual chronology is recognised by Dave Gunning in *Race and Antiracism in Black British and British Asian Literature* (2010), who sees in certain fictions of the late 1990s a connection to earlier migrant antiracist discourse: an investment in the continued value of ethnic community which can be distinguished from the scepticism of novels such as *White Teeth* and *Londonstani* (although one might argue that Gunning's reading of the latter obscures the novel's critique of the performative world of ethnic self-determination that it realises). So, then, blackness continues to matter. It continues to exist as matter. For, as Newland writes, 'Trouble with Black shit is once you got the knowledge you gotta deal wiv the fact you can't leave. You're in the belly of the beast an it's *hot'* (*Gospel*, 209–10).

And 'hot', indeed, the bodies in these novels are. Near the opening of *Gospel*, Beverley is visited by Seth and the highly charged scenes between them challenge both gendered and ageist stereotypes as they explicitly focus on Beverley's sexual satisfaction; likewise, our early understanding of Leah in *NW* points to her erotic indulgences centred on corporeal experiences: in her relationship with her husband 'the physical came first, always. Before he spoke to her he had already washed her hair, twice. They had sex before either knew the other's surname. They had anal sex before they had vaginal sex'. (22–3). Emergent here is something starkly missing from many 1990s texts, which is the profound investment in the material body as pleasure – the physical body as positive site of expression and recuperation of self. Here Smith and Newland are comparable to other contemporary authors such as Diana Evans, Bernadine Evaristo, and Hanif Kureishi. In *Mr Loverman* (2013), Evaristo challenges the intersecting taboos of age and race to give voice to an older-age black gay man. Evans's work, in particular, seems further evidence of a turn towards a reimagined but racially informed body; her first novel, *26a* (2005), finds in its heart-breaking story of two mixed-race twins growing up in Willesden in the 1980s a celebration of the body largely outside of racial reference points. Yet in her second novel, *The Wonder* (2009), Evans explores the black body through a narrative focused on the world of ballet with a much more distinctly racial concern. Hybridity is still in evidence as the novel's central character, Antoney, finds his story fusing with that of his hero, Nijinsky, in a post-ethnic and intersectional conjunction regarding not only race but also sexuality. Yet Evans's expressive, sensual bodies are also deeply connected to African modes of movement. For Kureishi, who perhaps stands alone as a writer who has pursued such themes both before and after the millennium, the body is a counter to numerous absolutes including conservatism, right-wing morality, the conventional family, and most notably religion. The latter is of course another core theme of black writing in the post-9/11 period and deserves an essay of its own in order to account for its complexities; in novels such as Monica Ali's *Brick Lane* (2003) and Leila Aboulela's *Minaret* (2005) the body is celebrated not just to counter racist stereotyping, but to propose a diverse performativity that racism disables, where expression of the body defies its reduction to any kind of signifying absolute. This, then, is a loving of bodies in their hybridity, but more importantly also in their hybrid *blackness*.

Here one is required to modify McLeod's own focus slightly; writing in 2010, McLeod sees the 'extra dimension' as part of the movement towards the planetary – it exists in Evans's *26a* as not something that is unique to race, but rather an additional strata of identity 'that we *all* occupy in our respective locations' (2010: emphasis added, 48), and likewise in the work of Andrea Levy comes alongside a movement towards universality: a journey from the 'preoccupation of Black British identity in her 1990s *bildungsroman* novels' to an engagement with the identity of the UK conceived internationally and transculturally for the benefit of all' in *Small Island* (2004): a novel not about black history, but one in which 'a mixed-race figure is created to embody and emphasise an alternative sense of the nation as a polycultural site of sameness and resemblance' (McLeod 2010: 49). McLeod's discussion of Levy's and Evans's work comes, however, without time to take account of the next novel of either writer, not only Evans's *The Wonder* and its celebration of the black body but also Levy's *The Long Song* (2010), which turns to a history of slavery that can less easily be incorporated into a post-racial agenda and which has yet to receive the same critical attention as her previous novel. The content of both of these works reflects a return to the continued valency of race. So while McLeod is correct at the moment at which he writes, his suggestion that our duty as critics is 'to challenge a neat evolutionary model of Black British writing' (2010: 46) is ironically employed in my suggestion that much of the continuity McLeod sees in post-2000 fiction is in fact altered through a modified optimism as the century has continued, contextualised by political circumstances that could not have been anticipated: a return to Tory rule, the success of the Brexit vote, and – on an international scale – the election of Donald Trump being just the most notable examples.

That the black body itself, rather than the abstract of ancestral identification, might be the 'extra dimension' is potentially at odds with the enthusiastic postmodern relativity surrounding Gilroy's later thinking upon which McLeod and much black British criticism (including my own) often draws; a movement to mediate this in more recent fiction sees a turn in British writing to what might be seen as more American modes of thinking about race, in particular to ideas of post-racial and post-ethnic identification which in this framing hold a quite different emphasis. In both postcolonial and African American writing the tendency to celebrate the fluid body in the context of (rather than in spite of) racial identification has a more longstanding and pronounced presence. We might reference, for example, Toni Morrison's *Beloved* (1987) or her later *Paradise* (1997), or Tsisti Dangaremba's *Nervous Conditions* (1988), in which the black female body is both nourished and celebrated as a counter-discourse to its disavowal by white patriarchal structures; but in this British context such movement comes only in the more recent trend away from postmodernism towards metamodernist concerns, defined by a continued interest in formal experimentation alongside more openly political, socially aware, and sincere fictions. By their very nature and interest in ethical imperatives these writings seem to support a more nuanced perspective on the question of cultural authenticity. This, then, is not Gilroy's post-racial ideal, but instead the pragmatic post-racialism of David Hollinger (1995, 2008, 2011), whose definition indicates not the erosion of racial identification but rather its relativity as an association that can be consciously withdrawn or assumed; if the 1990s was the era of Gilroy's dream, then the 2000s are the decades of Hollinger's lived life, in its positivity and fullness, and without regret.

This shift pertains directly to responses to recent world events reflecting on racial politics. In his article on the Black Lives Matter movement, for example, Linscott pits an Afro-Pessimism consumed by Western culture's endemic and structural anti-Blackness against a movement for Black Optimism. Linscott, like Gilroy, is concerned with 'the exclusion of black people from the category of the human' (2017: 105), yet there is no mention of the post-racial in his discussion, or even of Hollinger's post-ethnic communities of revocable consent and their appeal to Obama-era American politics. As Linscott points out through his reading of social media involvement in the unfolding Black Lives Matter campaign, the universal is the nightmare future the Afro-Pessimists warn about; the response to #BlackLivesMatter with #AllLivesMatter by some Republican supporters marks not Gilroy's planetary equality, but rather the denial of structural violence against all minorities in favour of the gloss of the white, heterosexual, CIS male, able-bodied, middle-class majority. Rather than a debate between planetary humanism and black materiality, Linscott's discussion plays out through the 'tensions between an ontological and structural 'fact' of blackness, on the one hand, and a discursive, constructed, performative, and identificatory blackness on the other' (105). This latter approach is reflected in the engagement of Black Lives Matter with LGBTQ+ issues, economic rights, immigration, and feminism, so that its own understanding of blackness differs greatly from traditional Pan-Africanism. In this new political context the celebration of the performative body figures in many senses as a critique of racism, not merely as an alternative rendering of the black body, but also as a declaration of lives that matter – lives that in their physicality can be seen to matter through corporeal encounters of blood, sweat, tears, and touch. As Judith Butler (2015) has pointed out, the performance of whiteness as a norm is what renders the black body as that which does not matter; so to perform the black body is to offer counter-discourse to this betrayal.

Remembering matter

What makes this reclamation of the body possible is not merely a reimagining but also, ironically perhaps, a forgetting. As critics such as bell hooks (1995) so powerfully explicate, the barriers to the celebration of the black body lie in the fact that a black body must be more than pleasure or it will be cast as *only* pleasure. *NW* comments distinctly on this pressure. It seems no accident that it is Leah, in her whiteness, who comes easily to the celebration of her body. Conversely, Natalie's loss of identity can be associated with a disavowal of her black body; she masturbates 'as if delegating a task to somebody else' (187) and in her early sexual experiences learns nothing about her boyfriend's body in what becomes 'a technical transition' (202). Later, she declares that 'materiality was the scandal. The fact of flesh' and makes a decision 'to go to war against these matters' (262). Similar associations are to be found in Hari Kunzru's *The Impressionist* (2002), where the central character of Pran's endless physical transformations and attempts at passing lead to an eventual life as a performer of manifold selves without an underlying essence, 'a ghost, haunting thresholds' (237). Natalie's career as a lawyer is the perfect achievement of an intellectual blackness that exceeds the discursive limits of the black body's signifier as pleasure; yet it leaves her with a body that cannot be pleasure for itself as much as it denies its role as a pleasure for others. That Natalie can only repeat the latter through anonymous sexual encounters arranged online is surely the tragedy of her attempts at self-realisation.

As David James (2015) notes, Smith enacts a 'deliberate quelling of authorial evaluation [. . .] a narrative economy in which the narrator no longer relies on the convenience of stylish aphorisms' in *NW* compared to earlier work (56, 57). It is this stepping-back on Smith's part in the later writing which gives justice to a perspective outside of her own commitment to multicultural cosmopolitanism. Here, then, is an insertion of narrative doubt missing from the strident call to post-racialism in the work of the 1990s. While it is explicit in *White Teeth* that what Irie needs is not a return to racial absolutes but a way to be beyond these categories, *NW* asks the question as to whether Natalie's life might be more psychologically stable if it were rooted in a more certain racial identity; equally, the death of Felix at the hands of another black man who declares 'I ain't your blood' (145) is presented in terms far more ambivalent than those found in *White Teeth*. Is the problem here, readers are driven to ask, the assumption of solidarity that Felix makes, or the rejection of this by his killer? Newland, too, adopts a more ambivalent tone in the twenty-first century. At the end of *Gospel*, Beverley and her 'son' – identity still to be proven by an incomplete DNA test – depart for a trip back to her birthplace, with a promise to return. In this promise of return – and her continued affection for Seth, whose embrace she clings on to in the novel's last lines – Beverley reveals a concomitant need to attach herself to Afro-Caribbean identity and to resist the limitations of exclusively biological or ancestral affiliation, a dilemma which has haunted her too in her dreams, her imagined Barbadian family shunned by the rest of the black community on the island for their business selling the shackles and chains used in slavery (55). To be pragmatic is also to be less certain.

Elsewhere, this need for forgetting is tackled directly, most notably in the work of Kazuo Ishiguro. A writer who often seems somewhat outside the boundaries of the discussions of black British writing, Ishiguro's meditations offer a valuable addition to the debates surrounding racial identity. In novels such as *The Remains of the Day* (1989), *When We Were Orphans* (2000) and *Never Let Me Go* (2005), Ishiguro has concerned himself with the damaging inheritances of the past for both national cultures and individual lives. In Ishiguro's *The Buried Giant* (2015), a mythical sub-Roman world shorn of the capacity for memory is associated with the peaceful co-existence of the rivalling Saxons and Britons. The two ethnic groups have forgotten their past conflicts and exist as a result in a state of uneasy truce. When the memories of the inhabitants return, however, the peace they have constructed is unable to survive the pain of what has been repressed; the destructive nature of this remembrance is displaced in the novel on to its two central figures, an elderly man and his wife, who on the remembering of their past find themselves unable to overcome what has been forgotten. Ishiguro's fable asks the reader to consider the cost of remembrance, therefore, and the extent to which all peaceful co-existence must rely upon a refusal of the conflict which produces difference. To truly embrace a celebrated ethnic body or a post-racial planetary futures relies in both instances on the same move: a strategic amnesia which allows for a forgetting of past discrimination and prejudice. The novel is ambivalent, however, as to whether such forgetting is ultimately beneficial – alongside the forgetting of difference has also been a loss of heritage, and somehow of the meaning which remembrance gives to everyday life. More profoundly, the characters who the old man and woman meet along their journey are capable of both damage and neglect. Here, then, is the suggestion that to forget is not only to enact an unspeakable violence against those who have been silenced, but also to naively risk a repetition.

One question therefore for contemporary authors is how to reconcile the need to move beyond past horrors with the ethico-political need to remember them and reconstruct a black body that might be positively claimed. So Levy's *The Long Song* reconstructs the horrors of slavery and reminds us of the crucial need to remember the past, an imperative also present in the recent fictions of Caryl Phillips – *Dancing in the Dark* (2005), *In the Falling Snow* (2009), and *The Lost Child* (2015) – which might all be read as diffractions of a central concern with the difficulty of throwing off the burden of racial identification. Levy and Phillips are joined by Bernadine Evaristo and Laura Fish who in their novels *Soul Tourists* (2005), *Blonde Roots* (2008) and *Strange Music* (2008) draw attention to the historical manifestation of forgetting as an act commensurate with the white erasure of black presence. Or, in Linscott's words: 'if black life is really the "afterlife of slavery", [. . .] then no amount of "letting go" or "post-racial" rhapsody will slip the yoke'. (2017: 109). *Soul Tourists* is a novel 'Lingering at the tail end of the twentieth' century but 'mauling the rotten gut of the sixteenth' (69): the haunting of the present by the ghosts such as Lucy Negro, the 'dark lady' of Shakespeare's sonnets and Mary Seacole reveal the timeless black cultural presence in Europe, while the hauntings of the ghosts of Pushkin, Alessandro de' Medici, Le Chevalier de Saint-Georges and Queen Charlotte turn the white skin of history inside out to reveal an already-present post-ethnic underside. As McLeod (2010) contends, Evaristo's use of mixed–race ghosts draws attention to their remembrance as of crucial relevance not only to black communities, but also to a much wider understanding of multiracial national pasts; this too, might be said of *Strange Music*, in which Fish draws attention to the racial ambiguity surrounding the racial background of the poet Elizabeth Barrett Browning in a novel the hauntings in which ask readers to consider the silenced black presences that whisper through Britain's present as well as its past. In *Blonde Roots*, meanwhile, Evaristo strategically reverses the colour hierarchies of slavery in a satire which aims to awaken readers to its tangible and recurrent power. These novelists make their own postmodern interventions into the genre of historical fiction – a shifting of focus from what happened to the voices that recount what happened, complete with unreliable subjectivity, so as to unsettle not only their own authority, but the notion of authority in general as that which has ensured their erasure from official narratives (see Upstone 2015a). To reclaim the body in the wake of this remembrance is perhaps the black British novelist's most difficult task: yet it is one upon which the optimism of the current moment seems to rely.

Conclusion

As McLeod notes, the search for shared perspectives 'may divert us from important matters of difference and discontinuity, and threatens our attempt to read the contemporary more on its own terms'. (2010: 46). At the same time, while critics are right to focus on the newness of twenty-first century black British writing, departures are no more significant than what remains. And what remains may not be a straightforward resonance with what came before or with what is nearby, but also with earlier patterns of representation and those from elsewhere. The reinvestment in the body in recent black British writing reflects both a reconnection to the writing of both the migrant generation and those of the 1970s and 1980s, and an association with less British, and more international frames of reference. It is the transformation of these rediscoveries through the lens of the post-racial optimism of the 1990s that most defines the fiction of the contemporary moment. Both Smith and Newland reject straightforward post-ethnic imperatives and biological essentialism, just two cases of what is a broader pattern within contemporary black British writing to embody the contradictions of racial politics in the here-and-now. This 'newness' is not uncomplicatedly post-racial. It is not uncomplicatedly celebratory. But the most difficult thing to recognise is that its association with blackness is also not straightforwardly associated with the utopianism of the post-racial. Celebratory blackness comes in the wake and context of a quotidian reality of race that might be undesirable but which is undeniable, and within the context of this undeniability must be co-opted in the spirit of agency and as affirmation of a blackness that can displace the power of *de facto* whiteness. Contemporary black British literature embraces therefore a politics of pragmatic optimism as the necessary pre-cursor to a meaningful planetary future.

Works cited

Aboulela, L. (2005) *Minaret*. London: Bloomsbury.

Akbar, A. (2016) 'Could There Really Be Only One New Black Male Novelist in Britain?' *The Guardian*. 17th November. <www.theguardian.com/commentisfree/2016/nov/17/one-new-black-male-novelist-britain-publishing>. Accessed 24/01/18.

Ali, M. (2003) *Brick Lane*. London: Doubleday.

Arana, R. V. (2005) 'The 1980s: Retheorising and Refashioning British Identity'. *Write Black, Write British: From Post Colonial to Black British Literature*. Ed. Kadija Sesay. Hertford: Hansib, 230–240.

Aslam, N. (2004) *Maps for Lost Lovers*. London: Faber.

Butler, J. (2015) 'What's Wrong With "All Lives Matter"?' *New York Times*. 12th January. <https://opinionator.blogs.nytimes.com/2015/01/12/whats-wrong-with-all-lives-matter/> Accessed 28/01/18.

Daley-Clarke, D. (2006) *Lazy Eye* (2005). London: Pocket Books.

Dangarembga, T. (1988) *Nervous Conditions*. London: Women's Press.

Dawson, A. (2010) *Mongrel Nation*. Michigan: University of Michigan Press.

Donnell, A. (2006) 'Afterword: In Praise of a Black British Canon and the Possibilities of Representing the Nation "Otherwise"'. *A Black British Canon*. Ed. Gail Low and Marion Wynne-Davies. Basingstoke: Palgrave Macmillan, 189–204.

Evaristo, B. (2005) *Soul Tourists*. London: Hamish Hamilton.

—— (2008) *Blonde Roots*. London: Hamish Hamilton.

—— (2013) *Mr Loverman*. London: Hamish Hamilton.

Evans, D. (2005) *26a*. London: Chatto and Windus.

—— (2009) *The Wonder*. London: Chatto and Windus.

Fish, L. (2009) *Strange Music* (2008). London: Vintage.

Fowler, C. (2008) 'A Tale of Two Novels: Developing a Devolved Approach to Black British Writing'. *The Journal of Commonwealth Literature* 43.3: 75–94.

Gilroy, P. (1993a) *The Black Atlantic: Modernity and Double Consciousness*. London: Verso.

—— (1993b) *Small Acts*. London: Serpent's Tail.

—— (2000) *Between Camps: Nations, Cultures and the Allure of Race*. London: Penguin.

Gunning, D. (2010) *Race and Antiracism in Black British and British Asian Literature*. Liverpool: Liverpool University Press.

Ho, J. (2015) *Nation and Citizenship in the Twentieth-Century British Novel*. Cambridge: Cambridge University Press.

Hollinger, D. (1995) *Postethnic America: Beyond Multiculturalism*. New York: BasicBooks.

—— (2008) 'Obama, the Instability of Color Lines, and the Promise of a Postethnic Future'. *Callaloo* 31.4: 1033–1037.

—— (2011) 'The Concept of Post-Racial: How Its Easy Dismissal Obscures Important Questions'. *Daedalus* 140.1: 174–182.

hooks, bell (1995) *Art on My Mind: Visual Politics*. New York: The New Press.

Hussain, Y. (2005) *Writing Diaspora: South Asian Women, Culture and Ethnicity*. Aldershot: Ashgate.

Ishiguro, K. (1989) *The Remains of the Day*. London: Faber.

—— (2000) *When We Were Orphans*. London: Faber.

—— (2005) *Never Let Me Go*. London: Faber.

—— (2015) *The Buried Giant*. London: Faber.

James, D. (2015) 'Worlded Localisms: Cosmopolitics Writ Small'. *Postmodern Literature and Race*. Ed. Len Platt and Sara Upstone. Cambridge: Cambridge University Press, 47–61.

Kelleher, F. (2005) 'Concrete Vistas and Dreamtime Peoplescapes: The Rise of the Black Urban Novel in 1990s Britain'. *Write Black: Write British: From Post Colonial to Black British Literature*. Ed. Kadija Sesay. London: Hansib, 241–254.

Kunzru, H. (2002) *The Impressionist*. London: Hamish Hamilton.

Lebron, C. (2017) *The Making of Black Lives Matter: A Brief History of an Idea*. Oxford: Oxford University Press.

Levy, A. (2004) *Small Island*. London: Headline Review.

—— (2010) *The Long Song*. London: Headline Review.

Linscott, C. (2017) 'Close-Up: #Black Lives Matter and Media: All Lives (Don't) Matter: The Internet Meets Afro-Pessimism and Black Optimism'. *Black Camera: An International Film Journal* 8.2: 104–119.

Malkani, G. (2006) *Londonstani*. London: Fourth Estate.

McLeod, J. (2004) *Postcolonial London: Rewriting the Metropolis*. London: Routledge.

—— (2010) 'Extra Dimensions, New Routines'. *Wasafiri* 25.4: 45–52.

McMann, M. (2012) 'British Black Box: A Return to Race and Science in Zadie Smith's *White Teeth*'. *Modern Fiction Studies* 58.3: 616–636.

Morrison, T. (1987) *Beloved*. London: Chatto and Windus.

—— (1997) *Paradise*. London: Chatto and Windus.

Nasta, S. (2000) 'Beyond the Millennium: Black Women's Writing'. *Women: A Cultural Review* 11.1–2: 71–76.

Newland, C. (1997) *The Scholar*. London: Abacus.

—— (2013) *The Gospel According to Cane*. London: Telegram.

Nugent, H. (2007) 'Race Row Nobel Scientist James Watson Scraps Tour after Being Suspended'. *The Times*. October 19th <www.thetimes.co.uk/article/race-row-nobel-scientist-james-watson-scraps-tour-after-being-suspended-zs7vp93q5z9>. Accessed 29/01/18.

Nwokedi, D. (2005) *Fitzgerald's Wood*. London: Jonathan Cape.

Phillips, C. (2005) *Dancing in the Dark*. London: Vintage.

—— (2009) *In the Falling Snow*. London: Harvill Secker.

—— (2015) *The Lost Child*. London: Oneworld.

Procter, J. (2003) *Dwelling Places: Postwar Black British Writing*. Manchester: Manchester University Press.

Singh Dhaliwal, N. (2006) *Tourism*. London: Vintage.

Smith, Z. (2000) *White Teeth*. London: Hamish Hamilton.

—— (2013) *NW* (2012). London: Penguin.

Stein, M. (2004) *Black British Literature: Novels of Transformation*. Columbus: Ohio State University Press.

Travis, R. (2016) *Mama Can't Raise No Man*. London: Own It!

Upstone, S. (2015a) '"Some Kind of Black": Black British Historiographic Metafiction and the Postmodern Politics of Race'. *Postmodern Literature and Race*. Ed. Len Platt and Sara Upstone. Cambridge: Cambridge University Press, 279–294.

—— (2015b) 'Postcolonial and Diasporic Voices: Bringing Black to the Union Jack: Ethnic Fictions and the Politics of Possibility'. *The 1990s: A Decade of Contemporary British Fiction*. Ed. Nick Hubble, Philip Tew and Leigh Wilson. London: Bloomsbury Academic, 123–148.

—— (2016) *Rethinking Race and Identity in Contemporary British Fiction*. London: Routledge.

Wade, N. (2014) *A Troublesome Inheritance: Genes, Race and Human History*. New York: The Penguin Press.

Weedon, C. (2008) 'Migration, Identity, and Belonging in British Black and South Asian Women's Writing'. *Contemporary Women's Writing* 2.1: 17–35.

12

QUEER

Alexandra Parsons

Introduction

In a recent article for *The Guardian*, Sarah Waters reflects on the twenty years that have passed since the publication of her first novel, *Tipping The Velvet* (1998), a lesbian coming-of-age story set in 1890s London. In the time since the book was first published, she remarks, we have seen 'enormous changes in the lives of [British LGBTQ+ people], who now have equal rights with heterosexuals as partners, parents and employees, and enjoy a mainstream cultural presence I wouldn't have believed possible back in 1998' (Waters 2018). It is on the variety and quality of the 'mainstream cultural presence' that this chapter focuses. It tracks some of the energies and currents that queer literary fiction has been preoccupied with since the beginning of the twenty-first century, and notes how queer representations have gained ground, now occupying a less marginal place in contemporary culture.[1] The popularity of well-known gay and lesbian authors such as Edmund White, Alan Hollinghurst, Jeanette Winterson, Sarah Waters, Colm Tóibín and Ali Smith, whose reputations have only increased in the new century, has paved the way for a wider market for queer fiction that examines a broad range of topics. As Hugh Stevens notes, 'Contemporary queer fiction, in its heterogeneity, has reflected the heterogeneity of queer identities, culture, and politics' (2014: 628). The increased positive reception and wider market for queer fiction since the point at which Sarah Waters published her first novel means these texts reach greater numbers of people faster, and the appetite for nuanced texts continues. This chapter argues that two important developments have taken place in contemporary queer fiction. Novels depicting intersectional experiences, gender nonconformity or transitioning, and those examining the lives of LGBTQ+ people in less tolerant countries have become far more prominent.

This chapter examines a range of twenty-first century literary fiction that deals with LGBTQ+ concerns. Consequently, I use *queer* as an umbrella term for what Annamarie Jagose calls both 'a coalition of culturally marginal sexual self-identifications' and also 'a nascent theoretical model which has developed out of more traditional lesbian and gay studies' (1996: 1). *Queer* is a slippery term. Michael Warner has quipped: 'The appeal of "queer theory" has outstripped anyone's sense of what exactly it means' (1992). Indeed, as Eve Kosofsky Sedgwick has written so movingly in *Tendencies*, *queer* can refer to:

> The open mesh of possibilities, gaps, overlaps, dissonances and resonances, lapses and excesses of meaning when the constituent element's of anyone's gender, of anyone's sexuality aren't made (or *can't be* made) to signify monolithically. The experimental linguistic, epistemological, representational, political adventures attaching to the very many of us who may at times be moved to describe ourselves as (among many other possibilities) pushy femmes, radical faeries, fantasists, drags, clones, leatherfolk, ladies in tuxedoes, feminist women or feminist men, masturbators [and so on].
>
> (1994: 7)

We might understand writing to be queer because of the identities or object choices of its characters (what Sedgwick terms 'representational'), or because of the way a text works to unsettle 'epistemolog[ies]', by deploying queer approaches to temporality perhaps, or because of the 'experimental linguistic' approach it takes. *Queer* is a designation of 'open[ness and] possibilit[y]'.

Yet it was as long ago as 1993 that Sedgwick diagnosed the present as 'a QUEER time' (1994: vii). Thinking about the array of activism taking place, primarily organised in response to shameful governmental neglect during the HIV/AIDS crisis, in zines, in street protests, and in some classrooms, she concludes, 'I suppose this must be called the moment of Queer' (1994: vii). That present was twenty-five years ago. We have come a long way since the 'pushy femmes' and 'radical faeries' (Sedgwick 1994: 7) of the late 1980s and early 1990s redeployed the term *queer*, once a term of homophobic abuse, for political ends within activism and scholarship. As Waters points out, this century alone has seen seismic shifts in the ways LGBTQ+ lives and representations have been perceived both by the law and by the wider population. Lee Edelman considers 'queers' to be those people who are 'stigmatised for failing to comply with heteronormative mandates' (2004: 17). Yet if, more and more, this 'stigmatis[ation]' is happily absent, what then? Does the term lose its power? This chapter does not attempt to offer answers, but instead, to trace some of the currents that have further developed since 2000, and offer readings that draw out how queerness is addressed in contemporary fiction.

First, the chapter considers the continued preponderance of gay and lesbian novels that look to the past, focusing on novels by Alan Hollinghurst and Sarah Waters. Hollinghurst returns to the past as a site of memory in each of the novels he has written this century: *The Line of Beauty* (2004), *The Stranger's Child* (2011), and *The Sparsholt Affair* (2017). Waters returns to the Victorian period to tell exciting, complex stories that nonetheless comment on the present. Next, the chapter looks to chronicles of contemporary queer life including Hanya Yanigahara's *A Little Life* (2015) and Garth Greenwell's *What Belongs to You* (2016). I argue that they reignite past queer aesthetic modes: the Gothic's linguistic and structural excess, and Marcel Proust and Henry James's slowed down approach to time, respectively. Next, the chapter examines representations of the capaciousness of the modern family to withstand change and embrace queer identities. Tanwi Nandini Islam's *Bright Lines* (2015) explores the lives of a family of Bangladeshi heritage based in Brooklyn, focusing on the coming-of-age narrative of transmasculine character El. Shani Mootoo's *Moving Forward Sideways Like a Crab* (2014) concerns how its straight male protagonist comes to terms with the disappearance of his Trinidadian parent and later discovery that he has since transitioned. The next section considers the difference in understandings of queerness across different places, despite the increasing pace of globalization. Chinelo Okparanta's *Under the Udala Trees* (2015) reminds us of the urgent fight for LGBTQ+ rights in Nigeria, and Hasan Namir's *God in Pink* (2015) explores homosexual lives in Iraq. Finally, the chapter concludes by drawing attention to some of the alternative formats used in queer contemporary literature.

The contemporary return to the recent past

A number of prominent gay and lesbian writers in the 1980s and 1990s wrote historical fiction. From the midst of the HIV/AIDS crisis, the past held critical importance. Excavating and reinscribing histories of same-sex desire are queer political tactics that allow writers to insist on the importance of diverse queer lives even as they are sidelined by inadequate governmental responses to the virus. Yet though the moment of queer radicalism has now passed, many writers have continued to publish queer historical novels, some examining the more recent past. For example, Hollinghurst's acclaimed *The Line of Beauty* revisits the 1980s to show the well-heeled classes during Margaret Thatcher's second term. His next novel, *The Stranger's Child*, tells the story of England before the First World War, and his latest, *The Sparsholt Affair*, chronicles gay life in Britain from Oxford college life during the Second World War to the present, pivoting around a murky crisis that happens the year before the Sexual Offences Act 1967 would partially decriminalise sex between men.

Hollinghurst's reputation has long been established. His first novel, *The Swimming-Pool Library* (1988), offers a magical, erotically charged return to a London the summer before the AIDS crisis hit. *The Folding Star* (1994) and *The Spell* (1998) followed in the 1990s. It is not until 2004 that he published *The Line of Beauty*, which won the Man Booker Prize and thereby drew the attention of a far wider public. Like a number of post-millennial authors' work including David Peace, Tim Lott, Jonathan Coe, David Mitchell and Nicola Barker, Hollinghurst's *The Line of Beauty* returns to the 1980s with disillusionment by tracking Margaret Thatcher's second term (1983–87), ironically engaging with Labour politician Peter Mandelson's declaration in 2002 that 'We are all "Thatcherite" now' (2002: 16). The gay protagonist, Nick Guest, is researching a PhD on Henry James's style. Called 'the little aesthete' by the novel's characters (Hollinghurst 2004: 441), he becomes a usurper into the silver-plated lives of the ruling classes. Through his friendship gained at Oxford with beautiful, dull, heterosexual Toby Fedden, he is invited to stay in the Fedden's family home in Kensington – overseen by patriarch Gerald, the Conservative MP for Barwick. Nick was originally invited to stay over the summer to keep an eye on the unstable and outspoken daughter, Catherine, but the arrangement persists for several years. Indeed, Peter Swaab comments that 'Nick aspires to find a place for accepted gayness in the conservative world he's so drawn to' (2007: 14). Yet despite his semi-permanent presence, Nick's status within the family remains provisional. Gerald hesitates as he describes Nick not as a member of the family, but 'part of the . . . part of the household' (Hollinghurst 2004: 121): Nick is separated by background and class, aesthetic taste, and finally – critically – his sexuality. Though the novel critiques the hedonism and corruption of the affluent classes, Hollinghurst writes in a marked morally neutral style. He comments, 'I don't make moral judgments [. . .] I prefer to let things reverberate with their own ironies and implications' (Moss 2004).

The Sparsholt Affair, Hollinghurst's most recent novel, ranges over a longer period, chronicling the lives of two generations of gay men. Its five interlinked sections follow a group of friends whose lives have all been affected by the muscular, straight-presenting David Sparsholt – 'the glamorous blank into which people read what they want' (Clark 2017). We are introduced to the first generation as they negotiate wartime studies at Oxford. Through the eyes of Sparsholt's son Johnny, we see them reach middle and old age. The narrative ends in contemporary London, as Johnny reaches later middle age. Similarly to Hollinghurst's first novel, *The Swimming-Pool Library*, *The Sparsholt Affair* reaches into the gay past of the earlier twentieth century. Joseph Bristow observes that *The Swimming-Pool Library* is 'strewn with references (many of them heavily ironized) to gay history' (1989: 76). In *The Sparsholt Affair*, the pivotal moment of history in the novel is the 1967 Sexual Offences Act, which partially decriminalised same-sex acts between men in private. Much of the action happens outside of the narrative in the gaps between chapters, like its predecessor *The Stranger's Child*: in the year prior to decriminalisation, Sparsholt becomes entangled in a sexual scandal which is meant to bear similarities to the Montagu Trial of 1954, and which ends with his imprisonment but is never fully elaborated.

Differently from *The Line of Beauty*, *The Sparsholt Affair* gives space to the different configurations and possibilities of the family. The fateful choices of Sparsholt senior, 'squadron leader at twenty-two' (Hollinghurst 2017: 181), who chose marriage, children and to conduct homosexual affairs in secret, are not those of the son. Their shared sexuality becomes not a bond but a division: 'the irreducible fact that Johnny was doing openly what for David had been a matter of secrecy and then of very public shame' (371). Johnny Sparsholt also marries – he weds his long-term partner Pat in 'Chelsea Town Hall' (452). He also becomes a father, but as a donor for his friends, the lesbian couple Fran and Una, who ask him: 'We were wondering if you might do a baby for us' (290). At the end of the novel, his daughter Lucy is unphased as she discovers Johnny's new relationship with the much younger Zé following Pat's death from prostate cancer. Hollinghurst explores the 'open mesh of possibilities' (Sedgwick 1994: 7) that the institution of the family can absorb in the twenty-first century. The novel tracks a contemporary ease with queerness within the boundaries of the family, set against the challenges of the past.

Neo-Victorian realist fiction

Since the publication of Sarah Waters' first novel *Tipping the Velvet*, many realist novels imagining queer lives in the more distant past have appeared. Sarah Waters' subsequent novels *Affinity* (1999) and *Fingersmith* (2002), Colm Tóibín's *The Master* (2004), Edmund White's *Hotel de Dream* (2007), Emma Donoghue's *The Sealed Letter* (2008), and Alexander Chee's recent *The Queen of the Night* (2016) are all set in the nineteenth-century. Each demonstrates an interest in the thrilling world of Victorian lesbian and gay subcultures, imagined or historically documented. In part, these use the setting to furnish rich and complex plots and in part, they reinsert the queer content into cultural history, continuing the work of authors such as Neil Bartlett in, for example, *Who Was That Man? A Present for Mr. Oscar Wilde* (1988). Yet even though they have been written after the urgency of queer radicalism of the 1980s and 1990s, these novels retain a contemporary political purpose.

For example in *Fingersmith*, Waters uses the foil of the Victorian sensation novel to make space for queerer approaches to sex and pornography than the backdrop of the feminist sex wars would allow. Waters states her aim as 'teasing out lesbian stories from parts of history that are thought of as quite heterosexual' (Akbar 2009). A noticeable influence is the historiography inspired by Lillian Faderman's compendious history of lesbianism since the Renaissance, *Surpassing the Love of Men*, who argued that because Victorian women were not thought to possess an active and independent sexuality, the idea of lesbianism was in many ways thought to be implausible. The masterful *Fingersmith* is a pastiche of the Victorian sensation novel, characterised by Thomas Hardy when describing his own novel *Desperate Remedies* as 'a long and intricately inwrought chain of circumstance' that included 'murder, blackmail, illegitimacy, impersonation, eavesdropping, multiple secrets, a suggestion of bigamy, amateur and professional detectives' (1975: 37). Its shocking plot twists are reminiscent of Mary Elizabeth Braddon's *Lady Audley's Secret* (1862) and Wilkie Collins' *The Woman in White* (1860) or *The Moonstone* (1868). Sue Trinder, foundling daughter of a woman hung for petty theft, is brought up by Mrs Sucksby, who runs a baby farm in the teeming backstreets of London's Borough. Richard Rivers, a shifty character known as Gentleman, schemes to marry himself off to Maud Lilly, a lonely heiress, living a caged life with her uncle – 'a gentleman scholar [. . .] but with curious habits' (Waters 2005: 23) – in a remote mansion. Once married, Maud would become 'rich as a queen' (25), so Gentleman plots to incarcerate her in a madhouse and make off with her inheritance. Sue is enlisted to help advance the plan as Lilly's maid. Sue finds herself drawn into an unexpected intimacy and desire for Maud Lilly, her 'pearl' (142), which results in a long chain of consequences.

There are multiple plot twists in Waters' novel, which pivot around a salacious detail: the scholarly uncle was a peddler of rare pornographic fiction, and he had forced the young Maud to be his assistant. By the end of the novel, Maud has destroyed her uncle's library and installed herself as the author of erotica. 'It is filled with all the words for how I want you . . .' (547), she tells Sue. Waters' pastiche provides a contemporary reaction not only to a Victorian past that, for the main, excised female desire, but also responds to the debate in feminist politics known as *the sex wars*. Andrea Dworkin, Catherine McKinnon and Sheila Jeffries have critiqued the role of pornography in perpetuating women's exploitation, whereas Lynne Segal has argued against censorship, countering this perspective. By creating her own erotica, Maud 'subvert[s] the male-dominated tradition of Victorian pornography [. . .] by writing an erotic literature of [her] own' (Miller 2008). In doing so, Claire O'Callaghan argues that Maud (and the novel) 'reassesses the historically vexed relationship between gender, sex and pornography' (2017: 76). Waters uses the novel, and its backdrop of Victorian pornography within the sensation fiction context, as a means by which to express her dissatisfaction with existing either/or debates. Instead, she uses lesbianism to address gaps in feminist debates and reclaim erotica for a lesbian-feminist audience.

The haunted queer contemporary

Hollinghurst has commented that he 'keep[s] going back to the periods when things [i.e. same-sex encounters] were more difficult and clandestine, because they seem from a fictional point of view to be more rewarding' (Clark 2017). Yet others have taken on the challenges of the present and, rather than fixing its characters or plot in a queer past, write about the contemporary whilst nonetheless evoking modalities belonging to previous generations of queer writers. For example, Darryl Pinckney's second novel, *Black Deutschland* (2016), sends its protagonist to Berlin, and acts a descendant of Christopher Isherwood's *Mr Norris Changes Trains* (1935) and *Goodbye to Berlin* (1939), both set in Weimar Germany. Garth Greenwell, a writer who, like Hollinghurst, crafts gorgeous sentences, has recently written *What Belongs To You* (2016), a striking first novel that follows in the tradition of Henry James's and Marcel Proust, and examines the ways in which trauma experienced in childhood haunts the present. Hanya Yanagihara's *A Little Life* is another novel haunted not only by past literary modes but also by its protagonist's childhood.

What Belongs To You details what first appears to be the story of a transactional, alienating yet obsessive sexual dynamic 'with [. . .] candor and psychological precision' (Charles 2016). The action takes place in contemporary Bulgaria, which is depicted as still attempting to free itself from its Communist past, and where gay desire remains taboo. The unnamed American narrator teaches at the prestigious American College in Sofia. Searching for a sexual encounter in the Soviet-era public toilets underneath the National Palace of Culture, the narrator comes across Mitko: 'tall, thin but broad-shouldered, with the close-cropped military cut of hair popular among certain young men in Sofia, who affect a hypermasculine style and air of criminality' (Greenwell 2016: 4). Mitko expects payment, and though that was not the kind of encounter the protagonist was searching for, he hands over money. The relationship that evolves between the two forms the focus of the novel's three sections. In the first part of the novel, the narrator is caught between a sense of his own privilege and an 'acidic sense of entrapment' (49) in his obsession with the young hustler. The unnamed narrator's relationship with Mitko – who describes him as '*priyatel*' (13), the Bulgarian word for friend, but which he also uses to mean boyfriend, and client – evokes earlier discussions of patronage, ethnicity and manipulation in queer writing, figured in the writing of André Gide or in the relationship between lesbian expat Eunice Goode and young call girl Hadija in Paul Bowles' *Let It Come Down* (1952). In the second part of the novel, the narrator revisits his childhood in a small town in a Republican southern state. His recollections of his virulently homophobic father erupt in a 40-page-long paragraph – a torrent of desolation, loss and shame. In the third and final section, 'Pox', set two years later, Mitko reappears to tell him that he has contracted syphilis – 'a nineteenth-century disease I only knew about from books' (108–109) – and to recommend that the narrator get tested. As the narrator battles the baffling bureaucracy of the Bulgarian sexual health services, his obsession recommences.

Although cruising is a major theme in the novel, along with the potential for humanity in exchanges with sex workers, Ron Charles of the *Washington Post* considers that the 'intima[cy]' of 'the narrator's deliberate disrobing of his own psyche' to be the novel's primary 'confession'. Indeed, in a review of the novel, Neil Bartlett comments that it stages 'the collision between our hard-won new capacity for frankness and a deep-rooted sense of archaic guilt and grief' (Bartlett 2016). The 'frank[]' depiction of an asymmetrical entanglement feels contemporary for the main part due to the cultural capital of the narrator – whose world is the inverse of that of the young hustlers in queer outlaw Jean Genet's *The Thief's Journal* (1949) or John Rechy's *City of Night* (1963). Yet the 'emotional geography', as Bartlett rightly identifies, 'could have come straight from Proust' (Bartlett 2016). Similarly, the slowed down moments in the novel show their indebtedness to Henry James's. Speaking in an interview about his technique in short story 'An Evening Out', featuring the same narrator, Greenwell declares himself 'interested in the quicksilver nature of human interaction, the way that so much of the emotion that passes between human beings is transient, multiple, ambivalent, contrary' (Leyshon 2017). He approaches the complexity and ambivalence of fleeting human emotion by 'tak[ing] an expansive approach to time, slowing time down to allow for the parsing of these emotions' (Leyshon 2017).

The past haunts the present in another contemporary novel that makes much use of its literary predecessors. Hanya Yanagihara's epic novel *A Little Life* (2015) commences with the intertwined lives of four tight-knit male friends – Jude, Willem, JB and Malcolm – each of whom have same-sex relationships of varying intensities. The plot follows their friendship from their student years together at an Ivy League college in New England to professional success, thirty years on. This is a novel of two parts. In the first, the saga of their lives and emotions unwinds in extended detail. Indeed, in a review for *The Atlantic*, Garth Greenwell goes as far as to say that Yanagihara's novel is 'the most ambitious chronicle of the social and emotional lives of gay men to have emerged for many years' (Greenwell 2015). In the second part of the novel, Jude emerges as the central character. In college, JB calls Jude 'the Postman' (Yanagihara 2015: 94) because he seems to elude categorisation. He is 'post-sexual, post-racial, post-identity, post-past' (94). Yet a gothic horror story emerges, of repeated child abuse, extreme and sustained self-harm over many years, and later partner violence of astonishing brutality, drawn out across many hundreds of pages.

The only way to make sense of the extraordinary depth of malignancy that afflicts poor Jude, queer martyr *par excellence*, is to understand it as an exercise in 'aesthetic modes long coded as queer: melodrama, sentimental fiction, grand opera' (Greenwell 2015). It looks back to Matthew Lewis' feverish novel *The Monk* (1796), or, once again, to the contortions of Mary Elizabeth

Braddon's *Lady Audley's Secret* (1862). The realism of the novel's first half – albeit in a strangely timeless New York, and one eerily devoid of traces of HIV/AIDS – is replaced by gothic horror. Yanigahara urges us on by provoking what Carol Anshaw calls 'the reader's voyeuristic interest' (2015a). Anshaw objects to such treatment, writing that 'After a while, I understood I was being enticed to watch someone's terrible suffering from a comfortable distance' (2015a). However, even as Yanagihara turns our intimacy with the novel's characters to different ends, it remains haunting. After all, its central preoccupation – homophobia and abuse enacted against its protagonist's childhood self, resulting in self-hatred, eating disorders, and self-harm – is hardly rare amongst queer readerships.

Even as Greenwell and Yanagihara's recent queer novels delineate contemporary modes of living, their style rests on queer literary structures of the past, as their characters remain haunted by their childhoods. Both seem to deny their characters a queer positivity founded upon recent social changes. Instead, their characters experience shame and loneliness, caused by irreparable wounds in their pasts. Their representations offer what Heather Love terms 'feeling backward': they register the 'corporeal and psychic costs of homophobia' by looking to their characters' pasts (Love 2007: 4).

Writing queerly about ethnicity, gender and sexuality in the family

Greenwell's narrative explores the power dynamic between a middle-class American and a youth from the former Eastern Bloc. Yanigahara only hints at Jude's ethnicity, but goes into more detail regarding JB's African-American heritage. Both novels are aware of the impact one's origins can have on one's privilege. Yet other contemporary queer novels have foregrounded the intersections of ethnicity, gender and sexuality in their narratives. New narratives offer a thoughtful and multicultural perspective on how identities shift and grow over time. In particular, a narrative strand that seems marked in the contemporary moment is that of the capaciousness of the modern family to withstand change and embrace queer identities. The next two novels I refer to explore assumptions about the home, and about Muslim and Hindu queerness.

Tanwi Nandini Islam's *Bright Lines* (2015) explores the lives of a family of Bangladeshi heritage based in Brooklyn. Set in the sweltering summer of 2003, it draws a vivid picture of a family living in a sprawling, formerly 'decrepit' brownstone won at auction 'for a dollar' in 'one of the first housing sweepstakes in the city' (Islam 2015: 11). The father, Anwar Saleem, was a reluctant freedom fighter in the violent 1971 Bangladesh Liberation War. He now runs an apothecary, enjoys gardening and smoking marijuana, and nurtures a passion for his tenant Ramona, a 'Mexican nurse-midwife [. . .] nearly half his age' (14). Mother Hashi runs a beauty salon in the basement. Teenage daughter Charu sneaks boys into her bedroom, and aspires to be a fashion designer. But the novel accentuates the experiences of adopted daughter Ella, 'scrawny and near-sighted' (17), who lives in 'constant suppression' (18) of her passion for Charu. It offers a queer coming-of-age narrative, tracing her search for home and understanding about her lost parents. As the novel develops, Ella questions family belonging, heritage and also belonging of another kind – in a particular gendered body. Towards the end of the novel, Ella becomes increasingly aware that they are transmasculine, culminating in a renaming as El, which he announces straightforwardly: 'These days I'm called El' (288). It's a transition in process, which is not defined or pinned down – in his first sexual experience with some-time-hijab-wearing Maya, she 'unpeeled the gauze' (289) of his chest binding, yet this sign of his shifting gender presentation isn't dwelled on or problematised. His identity is left to simply be, and is accepted by those closest to him.

Why do the characters in *Bright Lines* matter? Neelanjana Banerjee comments in the *LA Review of Books* that 'In this time of rampant Islamophobia, narratives revealing the lives of Muslims as complicated, transgressive, and devoutly human seem crucial' (Banerjee 2016). But this novel is more than a plea for South Asian Muslim identities to be seen as multiple and complex. Islam has noted that 'A lot of South Asian fiction in America is written in relation to white characters' yet she 'wanted to mess with some of those narratives, only because that is not my experience' (Banerjee 2016). And this diversity is not only to do with race but also to do with queerness: Islam's novel reflects the kinds of diverse communities that she and others of her generation growing up in New York or other major urban centres take for granted, and the space within these communities to embrace queerness.

Another contemporary writer to explore the capaciousness of the family to undergo change and accept difference in relation to the intersections of ethnicity and gender presentation is Shani Mootoo, who was brought up in Trinidad before moving to Canada. Her recent novel *Moving Forward Sideways Like A Crab* (2014), which develops some of the themes in her earlier novel *Cereus Blooms at Night* (1996), is predominantly written as the memoir of Jonathan Lewis-Adey, a struggling Toronto writer who is coming to terms with his past. Raised by two mothers, he was ten when the mother closest to him, a Trinidadian artist named Siddhani Mahale, left their life together. Decades later, Jonathan tracks down Mahale in Trinidad, and discovers that his parent has transitioned. He gets to know his beloved parent Sydney anew, visiting the now aged man in his grand Trinidadian house over the final nine years of his life, and getting to know him better through the letters he leaves behind after his death. In person and in the notebooks he leaves behind, Mahale shares stories about his transition – 'I arrived one cold and snowy morning at a building in Toronto [. . .] with a bagful of cash, and changed my life forever' (Mootoo 2017: 24). He also shares his close friendship with the adventurous Zain, who was murdered on the island.

The novel is figured as a quest for understanding and the struggles of accepting the decisions that someone you love has made. Jonathan struggles to take in the reasons why his beloved parent could abandon him, and then, following their reacquaintance, of why Sydney had transitioned. When Jonathan reports their first meeting after so many years, he writes: 'I had encountered not the parent who had from the first day of my life loved and understood me better than anyone else [. . .] but a stranger who confounded and challenged me' (Mootoo 2017: 38). Mootoo asks that we as readers accept Jonathan's painfully slow journey towards acceptance of his parent, which is challenging at times. However, the novel begins with a queer family as its starting point: the lesbian couple who co-parent Jonathan are the normal against which he understands the world. In beginning from such a structure, Mootoo is able to explore different constellations of queer kinship and belonging from an unusual perspective. After all, as she comments, 'I'm not a straight white man. I have not transitioned. [. . .] So it's a bit of an adventure in the dark' (Chau 2014).

Though they approach the family in different ways, Mootoo's and Islam's novels are connected in that they allow their characters, Sydney and El, to fulfil their wishes. In doing so, these novels demonstrate determination to change the scripts about the kinds of Caribbean immigrant or South Asian identities that are possible.

Queer rights worldwide

As well as a range of recent novels dwelling on intersectional queer experiences in North America, the past few years has seen the proliferation of narratives set in countries intolerant of queer identities and without queer rights. Writers including Nigerian-American Chinelo Okparanta, Iraqi-Canadian Hasan Namir, and Moroccan-born Abdellah Taïa, have recently written books that represent the repressive anti-LGBTQ+ countries of their birth and childhood, and through representation, lobby for change. Hasan Namir's *God in Pink* (2015) tells the story of a gay man living in Iraq during the recent Iraq war, whose faith is tested by the intolerance of his culture. Abdellah Taïa, who has been writing autobiographically inflected fiction for the past 20 years in French, is the only openly gay Moroccan writer. Homosexual sex is illegal in Morocco, though the country holds a complex relationship to same-sex desire: sexual relations between men are common, but only deemed problematic for feminine-presenting men. Lately, his recent novel *Infidels* was published in translation in 2016, and two of his older novels, which are heavily auto-biographical, have been published in translation as *Another Morocco: Selected Stories* (2017). Saleem Haddad unanchors his novel *Guapa* (2016) from a specific country to tell the story of a young gay man in an unnamed Middle Eastern capital during the revolutionary wave of the Arab Spring.

Focusing on the situation for queer women in repressive regimes, Chinelo Okparanta makes a lesbian coming-of-age story the subject of her recent *Under the Udala Trees* (2015), which commences during the Biafran war. Between 1967–70, the Nigerian state of Biafra tried – and failed – to gain its independence in a civil war that left a million dead. The protagonist Ijeoma, who is a child at the time, loses her father to artillery shelling. When her mother fails to cope, she is sent away to friends to work as a servant. When she finds the 'dazed and disoriented' (Okparanta 2015: 104) Amina, a young Muslim girl from the other side of the conflict, she takes her in. They fall in love. Inevitably, they are discovered and ripped apart, their relationship termed 'An abomination! [. . .] That is what it is, if a name is to be given to it! That is what the Bible calls it!' (125). Years later, Ijeoma meets the wonderful schoolteacher Ndidi, and starts a new, adult relationship. However, when she witnesses a horrific scene of senseless homophobic torture and murder, she tries her best to do her mother's bidding and marries a man. When the marriage fails, she returns to her home with a daughter, and slowly reconnects with Ndidi. When, many years later, she comes out to her daughter, now an adult, she finds the younger generation of urban Nigerians represent a new, liberal Nigeria: 'It turned out to be an underwhelming kind of revelation, almost a nonrevelation, because unbeknownst to me, the girl already knew. And somehow it did not matter to her' (320).

As Carol Anshaw for the *New York Times* points out, the story that in this case is set to a back-drop of udala trees and pounded yam is familiar to us from American lesbian novels of the 1950s:

> run[ning] the classic gauntlet of being queer in a benighted society – suppressing desire, giving in to it (so delicious), losing a lover to the conventional world (whom to blame?), trying out the really bad idea of a forced marriage, finding the 'clandestine bar' – and, finally, finding love and stability with a same-sex partner who helps her raise her child.
>
> (2015b)

Yet Anshaw's gloss, which likens the narrative to earlier pulp fiction in the West, does not take into account the important scene of grotesque injustice and violence that leads to Ijeoma's marriage to a man. When the 'clandestine bar' is raided by a local mob, Adanna, a local lesbian woman, is tortured then burned alive. Ijeoma reports seeing 'Adanna in the midst of the logs, burning and burning and turning to ashes right before our eyes' (209). In including this scene, Okparanta reminds us that equality is so unevenly distributed. Although equal marriage is now an expectation of much of the western world, Okparanta reminds us in her author's note that same-sex relationships were criminalised in 2014 by president Goodluck Jonathan, becoming offences punishable by up to 14 years in jail, and 'death by stoning' (325) in the northern states. She is overt in declaring the novel's purpose: 'to give Nigeria's marginalized LGBTQ citizens a more powerful voice, and a place in our nation's history' (325).

Beyond queer literary fiction

Since the gay liberation movement, authors of queer fiction have presented complex narratives that not only address gay sex, questions of history, class, or culture, but also question the nature of queer identity itself, different forms of queer relationships, the place of queer protagonists within their families, queer subcultures, living with HIV/AIDS, and other issues affecting queer communities. Since the turn of the twenty-first century, rights for and acceptance of queer lives have, in the west, advanced at an incredible rate. Much twenty-first century queer literary fiction does not take radically new approaches: historical fiction continues to be an important way to do queer political work, whether through excavations of the Victorian era or through a return to the more recent past of the 1980s and the HIV/AIDS crisis. Yet the growing interest and acceptance of queer lives has led to greater attention being paid to different examples of queer literary fiction. As this chapter argues, novels depicting intersectional experiences, gender nonconformity or transitioning, and set in less tolerant countries, have gained some prominence.

This chapter does not detail the queer experimental fiction discussed in the chapter on Ali Smith in this volume. Smith continues to play with form and puns in novels reflecting contemporary society such as *There But For The* (2011), *How to Be Both* (2014), *Autumn* (2016) and *Winter* (2017), each of which provide an engaging, fresh take on the contemporary. This chapter also does not cover those works that arguably fall outside the category of literary fiction. The queer temporalities and shifting self-reflexive approach to the family represented by Alison Bechdel in her graphic novels *Fun Home: A Family Tragicomic* (2006) and *Are You My Mother?* (2012) are discussed in the chapter on 'Literary Comics' in this volume. It does not explore the lyric essay, with its blend of poetry, autobiography and theory, such as Maggie Nelson's *The Argonauts* (2015), or the current popularity of trans memoirs, such as Juliet Jacques' *Trans: A Memoir* (2015). Much excellent and politically necessary contemporary queer writing exists outside of the boundaries of literary fiction. Though examining just one particular form of queer literature seems antithetical to 'The open mesh of possibilities, gaps, overlaps, dissonances and resonances' (Sedgwick 1994: 7) that *queer* can refer to, this chapter demonstrates some of the 'possibilities', 'resonances' and 'dissonances' explored by the form.

Note

1 Literary success might be said to rest on a combination of four elements: sales figures, press reviews, literary awards and prizes, and academic literary criticism (see Stevens 2014: 628). Although queer-themed pulp fiction sold in enormous numbers (see Stryker 2001: 61) and many queer novels were reviewed in major newspapers, they have been often otherwise ignored by the academy and by literary prize-givers until the twenty-first century.

Works cited

Akbar, A. (2009) Sarah Waters: 'Is There a Poltergeist within Me?'. *The Independent*. 29 May. [online]. Available from: www.independent.co.uk/arts-entertainment/books/features/sarah-waters-is-there-a-poltergeist-within-me-1692335.html (Accessed 5 February 2018).

Anshaw, C. (2015a) Hanya Yanagihara's 'A Little Life'. *The New York Times*. 30 March. [online]. Available from: www.nytimes.com/2015/04/05/books/review/hanya-yanagiharas-a-little-life.html (Accessed 27 January 2018).

—— (2015b) 'Under the Udala Trees,' by Chinelo Okparanta. *The New York Times*. 23 October. [online]. Available from: www.nytimes.com/2015/10/25/books/review/under-the-udala-trees-by-chinelo-okparanta.html (Accessed 29 January 2018).

Banerjee, N. (2016) Not the Usual South Asian Muslim Suspects: Neelanjana Banerjee interviews Tanwi Nandini Islam. *Los Angeles Review of Books*. [online]. Available from: https://lareviewofbooks.org/article/not-the-usual-south-asian-muslim-suspects/ (Accessed 6 February 2018).

Bartlett, N. (2016) What Belongs to You by Garth Greenwell Review: Desire and Disclosure. *The Guardian*. 2 April. [online]. Available from: www.theguardian.com/books/2016/apr/02/what-belongs-to-you-garth-greenwell-review (Accessed 26 January 2018).

Bristow, J. (1989) Being Gay: Politics, Identity, Pleasure. *New Formations*. 9, 61–81.

Charles, R. (2016) 'What Belongs to You' Review: An Eloquent Tale of Desire and Remorse. *Washington Post*. 19 January. [online]. Available from: www.washingtonpost.com/entertainment/books/what-belongs-to-you-review-an-eloquent-tale-of-desire-and-remorse/2016/01/14/e2671a5c-b93a-11e5–829c-26ffb874a18d_story.html (Accessed 26 January 2018).

Chau, D. (2014) Displacement Anchors Shani Mootoo's Moving Forward Sideways Like a Crab. *Georgia Straight*. [online]. Available from: www.straight.com/life/663796/displacement-anchors-shani-mootoos-moving-forward-sideways-crab (Accessed 7 February 2018).

Clark, A. (2017) Alan Hollinghurst: 'I Was Fortunate to Come along Just as Gay Lit Was Coming into Its Own'. *The Guardian*. 22 September. [online]. Available from: www.theguardian.com/culture/2017/sep/22/alan-hollinghurst-gay-lit-interview (Accessed 26 January 2018).

Edelman, L. (2004) *No Future: Queer Theory and the Death Drive*. Durham, NC: Duke University Press.

Greenwell, G. (2015) A Little Life: The Great Gay Novel Might Be Here. *The Atlantic*. 31 May. [online]. Available from: www.theatlantic.com/entertainment/archive/2015/05/a-little-life-definitive-gay-novel/394436/ (Accessed 27 January 2018).

—— (2016) *What Belongs To You*. London: Picador.

Haddad, S. (2016) *Guapa*. New York: Europa Editions.

Hardy, T. (1975) *Desperate Remedies* [1871]. London: Macmillan.

Hollinghurst, A. (2004) *The Line of Beauty*. Oxford: Picador.

—— (2017) *The Sparsholt Affair*. London: Picador.

Islam, T. N. (2015) *Bright Lines*. New York, NY: Penguin.

Jagose, A. (1996) *Queer Theory: An Introduction*. New York: New York University Press.

Leyshon, C. (2017) Garth Greenwell on Capturing What Thinking Feels Like. *The New Yorker*. 21 August. [online]. Available from: www.newyorker.com/books/this-week-in-fiction/fiction-this-week-garth-greenwell-2017-8-21 (Accessed 6 February 2018).

Love, H. (2007) *Feeling Backward: Loss and the Politics of Queer History*. Cambridge, MA: Harvard University Press.

Mandelson, P. (2002) There's plenty of life in the 'new' Third Way yet. *The Times*. 10 June. p. 16. [needs article heading – tbc].

Miller, K. M. (2008) Sarah Waters's 'Fingersmith': Leaving Women's Fingerprints on Victorian Pornography. *Nineteenth-Century Gender Studies*. 4 (1), n.pag. [online]. Available from: www.ncgsjournal.com/issue41/miller.htm (Accessed 6 February 2018).

Mootoo, S. (2017) *Moving Forward Sideways Like a Crab* [2014]. New York: Akashic.

Moss, S. (2004) Interview: Alan Hollinghurst, Winner of the 2004 Booker Prize. *The Guardian*. 21 October. [online]. Available from: www.theguardian.com/books/2004/oct/21/bookerprize2004.bookerprize (Accessed 26 January 2018).

Namir, H. (2015) *God in Pink*. Vancouver: Arsenal Pulp Press.

O'Callaghan, C. (2017) *Sarah Waters: Gender and Sexual Politics*. London: Bloomsbury Academic.

Okparanta, C. (2015) *Under the Udala Trees*. London: Granta.

Sedgwick, E. K. (1994) *Tendencies* [1993]. London: Routledge.

Stevens, H. (2014) Contemporary Gay and Lesbian Fiction in English. In E. L. McCallum & Mikko Tuhkanen (eds.) *The Cambridge History of Gay and Lesbian Literature*. Cambridge: Cambridge University Press. 626–642.

Stryker, S. (2001) *Queer Pulp: Perverted Passions from the Golden Age of the Paperback*. San Francisco: Chronicle.

Swaab, P. (2007) The Line of Beauty. *Film Quarterly*. 60 (3), 10–15.

Taïa, A. (2017) *Another Morocco: Selected Stories*. Trans. R. Small. South Pasadena: Semiotext(e).

Warner, M. (1992) From Queer to Eternity: An Army of Theorists Cannot Fail. *Village Voice Literary Supplement*. 18.

Waters, S. (2005) *Fingersmith* [2002]. Virago: London.

—— (2018) 'It Was an Electric Time to be Gay': Sarah Waters on 20 Years of Tipping the Velvet. *The Guardian*. 20 January. [online]. Available from: www.theguardian.com/books/2018/jan/20/sarah-waters-on-20-years-of-tipping-the-velvet (Accessed 30 January 2018).

Yanagihara, H. (2015) *A Little Life*. London: Picador.

13
FAMILY

Stephen J. Burn

Toward the end of a famous interview published in 1993, David Foster Wallace described the position of the writer who tried to set to work amid the metaphysical ruins of postmodernism:

> For me, the last few years of the postmodern era have seemed a bit like the way you feel when you're in high school and your parents go on a trip, and you throw a party. . . . the sense I get of my generation of writers . . . is that it's 3:00 a.m. and the couch has several burn-holes and somebody's thrown up in the umbrella stand and we're wishing the revel would end. The postmodern founders' patricidal work was great, but patricide produces orphans, and no amount of revelry can make up for the fact that writers my age have been literary orphans throughout our formative years.
>
> (*Conversations* 52)

Wallace's remarks in both this interview and the essay ('E Unibus Pluram') that appeared alongside it have been influential on a number of counts. His critique of postmodern irony as a primarily destructive force ('patricidal work'), and his sense that television has distorted fiction away from its moral purpose toward an anarchic 'revel' have been variously taken up by critics as inaugurating an attempt 'to imagine a way to speak or write through that irony and come out with a new language that can make connections among people' (McLaughlin 2013: 288), or as enacting a kind of literary dead reckoning, where Wallace enacts 'his struggle to find his place in literary history' (Cohen 2012: 72). Yet, while critics have often been eager to read this interview primarily in (the often profitable) terms of language or tone, what has been largely overlooked is Wallace's decision to describe the move beyond postmodernism by invoking the image of the family.[1] This oversight is surprising in part because the work that Wallace crafted in the wake of this interview had (as he noted) 'a lot to do with the family' (*Conversations* 13), but also because the family image he invoked was evidently so important to him that he revisited it in *The Pale King* (2011), when Chris Fogle's father returns to discover his son and friends post-revel, 'slumped on the davenport with our dirty feet up on his special coffee table, and the carpeting . . . all littered with beer cans' (169).

But it's also surprising because the evolution of the twenty-first century literary novel – especially in America – is significantly predicated on a sequence of subtle shifts away from the way that families functioned in postmodern fiction. What unites works as formally and thematically disparate as Jeffrey Eugenides's *Middlesex* (2002), Jonathan Safran Foer's *Extremely Loud and Incredibly Close* (2005), Jonathan Franzen's recent novels, Tom McCarthy's *C* (2010), Zadie Smith's *NW* (2012), and Wallace's *Infinite Jest* (1996), is, in fact, not so much a shared 'new language,' as it is an abiding and overlapping attention to the family and questions of lineage. This renewed interest in the family is multifaceted, moving from the surface obsessions of recent works – say, the trope of the orphan, introduced by Wallace's imaginary 'literary orphan' and recurring in Lethem's *Motherless Brooklyn* (1999), Eggers's *A Heartbreaking Work of Staggering Genius* (2000), Jonathan Safran Foer's *Everything is Illuminated* (2002), through to George Saunders's symbolic orphans in 'Jon' (2006)[2] – to deeper, axial questions that engage with the contemporary novel's clock, and its signature forms.

Even during the heights of postmodernism's imperial reign, it's clear that the American novel retained an interest in the family. In William Gaddis's *J R* (1975), for instance, it is the pointed and persistent absence of J R Vansant's mother – 'she comes in all . . . these different times see she's like this here nurse' (134) – that provides the backdrop against which he develops his paper empire.[3] In a more direct fashion, Don DeLillo's *White Noise* (1985) devotes itself to anatomizing the 'miscellaneous swarming air of families' (5–6). Nevertheless, it's fair to say that the postmodern novel's internal clock – its typical temporal rhythm – ablates the scope of the family's involvement. As Ursula Heise has argued, 'postmodernist novels focus on the moment or the narrative present at the expense of larger temporal developments' (64),[4] and so we tend to see families in these works as momentary constellations, temporary assemblages that come together according to the narrative needs of a particular scene. This tendency is especially clear in *White Noise*, where the family's changing configuration indexes undramatized installments of the narrator's past: the possible return of his daughter Bee prompts Jack to recall his 'marriage to Tweedy Browner' (16); a discussion with his daughter Steffie elicits Jack's explanation that his 'first and fourth marriages were to Dana Breedlove' (213). As different children arrive, different angles to Jack's past are glimpsed, but they are glimpsed only as snapshots.[5]

In the twenty-first-century novel – and especially in the novel crafted under the influence of DeLillo and Pynchon – more capacious calendars underwrite the action, though these more expansive timelines have evolved under a variety of cultural pressures. As Bruce Robbins has argued, for instance, 'the recent rise of the category of "world literature"' has brought with it a cosmopolitan imperative, that 'entails a *temporal* cosmopolitanism: an enlargement in the scale of years and centuries to which attention must now be paid' (192). For Robbins, this transition carries with it changes in the contemporary novelist's toolkit – the prolepsis, with its faith in knowable totalities, becomes more prominent[6] – but it is also reasonable to see this shift as the harbinger of more fundamental genre realignments. If the key modernist template underpinning the Pynchonian axis of American postmodernism was James Joyce's *Ulysses* (1922) – the long novel, modeled as a 'kind of encyclopaedia' (Joyce 1975: 271) and anatomizing its substitute world through the lenses of different techniques and perspectives – then, the twenty-first century novel has not rejected the Joycean example, but has rather blended its truncated timescale with the longue durée of D.H. Lawrence's *The Rainbow* (1915) or Thomas Mann's *Buddenbrooks* (1901) to create a hybrid family novel. Unlike *J R* or *White Noise*, these family novels often do not move horizontally, tracking plot lines anchored to a single moving 'present,' but are rather tiered structures, with multiple timelines stacked vertically. Jennifer Egan's *The Keep* (2006), which, in many ways is a miniature version of this form, thematizes, and neatly summarizes this contrast, setting the Baroness's linear horizontal timeline – 'one thin chain of years and days and hours and minutes' (90) – against Danny's stratified conception of time's passage: 'all the . . . things that had happened to him . . . made a crust over that day, and the crust got thicker and thicker until Danny almost forgot about what was underneath' (17). Yet what marks *The Keep* a transitional work, and signals her next novel – *A Visit from the Goon Squad* (2010) – an exemplary twenty-first century family novel is the relative insignificance of (in Danny's metaphor) the crusted layers, that is, the generations that surround his story. While *The Keep* explores 'that high-speed broadcasting device known as a family' (18), and the way 'time stretches out' (148), the central characters' ancestors and descendants are never central matters of narrative concern. Instead they largely act as plot devices, to inspire self-doubt (say Danny's awareness of his father's disdain for a resumé 'written out in invisible ink' [22]), or to magnify a character's shame (Benjy's relentless questioning of Danny: 'Are you sad to have nothing? . . . Are you crying?' [133]). In each of the other novels, by contrast, what's at stake is not simply the book's temporal scope, but more precisely the generational structure that permits this temporal range: in *C*, *The Corrections*, *Infinite Jest*, *Middlesex*, *NW*, and *A Visit from the Goon Squad*, the narrative is typically built around three generations of characters, while the central narrative focus in one or more episodes is devoted to characters from at least two generations.

On one level, such generational structures are largely instrumental, permitting each author to extract further narrative mileage from the building blocks – primarily plot and character – that comprise their novelistic worlds. From the perspective of plot, for instance, what makes these generational structures vertical rather than horizontal is not just that these books rarely present the blood lines they trace in sequential units, but rather that their long timelines are incomplete because the plots are designed around holes in the fabric of novelistic time. Such holes are a staple of what Rick Altman calls 'multiple focus narrative,' a form that he traces back to the Grail romances, and which forces readers 'to devise novel methods of deriving meaning from apparently unrelated fragments' (243). Altman's observation might be refined with reference to the twenty-first century family novel, by noting that the temporal holes between such fragments can be *absolute*, where the chronological gaps are never filled in beyond some suggestive clues: here we have the missing year in *Infinite Jest* that separates the verbally gifted Hal in drug withdrawal from the Hal who seems only able to communicate by 'waggling' and making '*sub*animalistic noises' (14); and Egan's *Visit*, where the full steps between, say, Sasha's abysmal date with Alex and her appearance as Alison Blake's mother, are only implied. Alternatively such gaps can be *temporary* plot holes that are gradually filled in by the narrative that follows: here we might include *NW*, where questions raised in the opening sketch, 'Visitation' – why are Leah and Natalie apparently separated by several rungs of the social ladder? how did they become friends? – are gradually answered in the book's latter stages; similarly, much of *The Corrections* orbits the question of why the fiscally responsible Alfred retired (in a scene that is never dramatized) seven weeks before he'd be due his full pension, only for his daughter Denise to help the reader piece the clues together near the book's end. In each of these cases the book's familial investment fluoresces because the narrative gap is strategically placed to mark a generational shift (Sasha and Natalie becoming mothers, Leah becoming an adult, and on the brink of becoming a mother), or a significant generational milestone (Hal about to leave his mother's tennis academy for university, Alfred's retirement). Designed around such fractures, the books do not present a continuous flow of time, but rather offer a vertical stacking of fragments from different years and life stages that the reader must rearrange into horizontal sequence.

Such generational architecture also informs and distorts characterization in the twenty-first-century novel, simultaneously deepening and flattening each book's personalities. As with the ancestral lines traced by *The Rainbow*, the stacking of generations, with its attendant tracking of repetitions and minor differences, at least partly reduces characters to interchangeable links in hereditary sequences. In its twenty-first century manifestation, the new sciences of identity (from DNA mapping to biomedical accounts of selfhood) amplify this tendency through authoritative sounding references to inheritance's unifying force. Thus, in Richard Powers's *Generosity* (2009),

Russell Stone's brother concisely maps out their interchangeable futures – 'We're depressives. It's in the Stone gene pool. Embrace it' (40) – while in the book's longest view, this perspective is driven to its logical conclusion, a vision of Russell's investment in literary fiction as 'just a few genes away from those famous rhesus monkeys, clinging to their terry-cloth mothers' (33). Nevertheless, as characters are poised between generations, their personalities also take on a greater curvature. In the most extreme example, we get a kaleidoscopic impression of Egan's Sasha as different episodes present her as a wayward niece (as seen by Ted), a college friend (to Rob), an alluring employee (for Bennie), and finally as Alison's mother. Time becomes a matrix in the twenty-first-century novel, with characters almost mechanistically 'rounded' as they are pulled into different roles and seen through different generational eyes. To some extent this illuminates why such novels might be distinguished from DeLillo's panoramic *Underworld* (1997), which they otherwise superficially resemble. *Underworld* has a comparable temporal range – the novel's timeline of near half a century roughly matches the time frames of *Infinite Jest* (1960–2010) and *A Visit from the Goon Squad* (1973–2021?) – but in place of a multi-generational structure, *Underworld*'s central story more closely resembles a fragmented bildungsroman. As such, the surrounding generations simply add atmospheric reflections (say, Nick's son's belief that 'he could look at a plane in flight and make it explode . . . by simply thinking it' [88]) that are largely adjuncts to the book's central development, and which might draw bemused wonder from the central character, but do not press him into a serious change in role.[7]

Although some of the books listed here have attracted their own generic classifications,[8] in many cases, the centrality of the family and the varied ends to which it's put, suggest that such works might be seen as twenty-first century updates of less well-known genealogies. Robert O. Stephens's conception of the Southern 'family saga,' for example, shares with such works an emphasis on 'place as the locus of family memory,' a 'history measured in generations, at least three,' the trope of 'the lingering influence of a patriarchal–matriarchal conflict among the ancestors,' and a 'narrator-historian [who] may achieve a God-like clarity of vision,' the latter of which, I'd suggest, can be signaled by the use of the prolepsis or the increasing use of third-person narration in many of these books (3–6).[9] More specifically, many of these works draw upon what Stephens calls the 'recurring motifs' of 'family stories': 'displacement of the inheritance . . . attempted correlation of family events with historical events, the sense of dynastic decline' and so on (8). Because Jonathan Franzen's recent work has been so widely – and often contentiously[10] – associated with the rise of the family novel, *The Corrections* and *Freedom*, in particular, provide a particularly vivid opportunity to consider not only the applicability of an expanded version of Stephens's model (albeit shorn of its regional context), but also the important ways that a cluster of other novelistic elements in Franzen's works (style, structure, and so on) hinge on the overarching importance of family to his fiction.[11]

At the outset, it's important to recognize that family has always been a magnetic obsession in Franzen's work, and is not just a late phase emerging in his millennial fiction. *The Twenty-Seventh City*'s (1988) kaleidoscopic focus may be built around an international conspiracy that unfolds across a Midwestern city and its exurban rings, but as Franzen noted in an early interview, 'the form that the conspiracy takes is to precipitate crisis in the family' ('Fiction' 18). Similar observations might be made about the Holland and Bowles families in *Strong Motion* (1992), and as a clutch of connections across his fiction indicate (such as *The Twenty-Seventh City*'s Chuck and Bea Meisner reappearing in *The Corrections*), his later books are not a rejection of the earlier novels as much as they are an extension or in some cases a rewrite of them. Although there are key writers – primarily Kafka – whose influence persists throughout the tissue of each novel, one way to navigate the growth of Franzen's work is to think about the different literary models that underpin each work, since many of these models are related to his conception of family.

The Twenty-Seventh City, for instance, was not–unreasonably greeted by its early reviewers as just another contemporary iteration of Pynchon's novelistic DNA, yet the book's hidden template is actually drawn from Robert Coover's *Origin of the Brunists* (1966). Franzen found in Coover's book not just a structural model (both works rely on a model of distributed narration, with alternating chapters moving between multiple close third-person perspectives), and a similar plot (one largely self-contained city comes to the threshold of crisis as internal tensions and outside influences intertwine), but even patterned the book around similar characters (Martin Probst seems designed as a counterpart to Coover's Ted Cavanaugh, who acts as a lightning rod joining the civic and the familial). *Strong Motion*'s intellectual elasticity, by contrast, stems in large part from Franzen's admission that he planned the book as a 'systems novel' (*How to Be Alone* 247), a term coined by Tom LeClair in a 1987 study of Don DeLillo to describe an omnivorous subset of the American novel that employed 'postmodern techniques to model the dense and tangled relations of modern history, politics, and science' (40). Franzen's use of the term is unlikely to be accidental,[12] and reflects both his novel's investment in seismological research – an investment that was so carefully researched that the book was cited in later scientific studies of 'seismicity induced by injection' (Davis and Frohlich 1993: 208) – and its filial debt to DeLillo's example.

If there is a recalibration of Franzen's career at this point, it is not the wholesale rejection of postmodernism that some have seen – especially not in the too schematic terms of the claim that Franzen 'said no to pomo' (Rebein 2007: 201) – but it is palpable in a shift in literary model. With some justification – and following Franzen's own testimony – critics have often read *The Corrections* as following Paula Fox's slim realist fiction, *Desperate Characters* (1970), as a 'a structural model' (Green 2005: 97); yet while *Desperate Characters* was clearly important to Franzen personally, a more suggestive model is arguably to be found in Arthur Miller's family-oriented *Death of a Salesman* (1949). While Miller began his career training to be a journalist, Franzen's earliest serious writing – indeed his first publication – was a short dramatic work,[13] and properly dramatic elements (unmediated dialogue, charged spatial relationships) remain important in his later fiction. From *Death of a Salesman*, *The Corrections* takes the loose skeleton of familial relationships and an overarching plot situation: in both the divergent yet criss–crossing paths of wife and children are as satellites orbiting a father-figure who is synonymous with a working existence that has become anachronistic. Similarly, the father's unstable consciousness sponsors each work's temporal economy, in which the past persistently bleeds into the narrative present,[14] while the father's eventual death provides the climax to both works.

Working within the boundaries of this plot model, *The Corrections* evinces the key elements of the family novel as we have defined them. The book is built around three generations of the Lambert family, moving from Alfred and End down to Gary and Caroline's children, with the book roughly partitioned into two sections that deal primarily with the first generation, three that deal primarily with the second generation, and two that serve a more synthetic function. Stephens's sense of 'the lingering influence of a patriarchal-matriarchal conflict' is quite clear in the novel, while the characters' individuality is often closely shadowed by an impulse to see the modern self through a homogenizing Darwinian lens: thus, the obsession with hunger that haunts references to Enid is contextualized by deft references to the family hamsters who look 'bloated and evasive' after eating their own children (528). Franzen has been explicit about the familial overtones to the book's genealogy – describing DeLillo, for instance, as 'Dad-like' ('Esquire') – but what makes Arthur Miller such an appropriate ancestor for *The Corrections* is not simply the overlapping plot points between the works, or even the broader tendency of Miller's plays to organize themselves around a family's fraught psychodynamics,[15] but is rather the fact that Miller outlined a calculus of dramatic history that correlated formal developments with a play's familial and social investments. In 'The Family in Modern Drama' (1956), Miller sets out a schematic of 'the spectrum of dramatic forms' (69), which carves up literary history according to the following divide: 'the force or pressure that makes for Realism, that even requires it, is the magnetic force of the family relationship within the play, and the pressure which evokes in a genuine, unforced way the un-realistic modes' – for Miller, these are Expressionist techniques, symbolism, and so on – 'is the social relationship within the play' (71). This division, for Miller, carries with it a linguistic imperative: 'the language of the family' Miller contends, 'is the language of the private life – prose. The language of society, the language of the public life, is verse' (76). The divide, however, is not entirely limpid, and the great dramatic triumphs are efforts at synthesis, such as Ibsen using 'Realism so well [as] to make plays about modern life' through his emphasis on the family circle (71).

One popular narrative of Franzen's twenty-first-century growth more or less follows the first-half of Miller's algorithm: after writing two 'social novel[s] . . . in his first two' books, Franzen turns to 'his own proper milieu, the world of the Midwestern family' (Green 2005: 91–92), which he explores by relying on 'a relatively stable and familiar concept of realism' (Gram 2014: 8). Yet even as Franzen's own statements often support such readings,[16] what's particularly significant about his treatment of the family in *The Corrections* is less its preoccupation with the family as synechdochic expression of 'private life,' or its retreat from the social into realist study of the family, and more the degree to which the Lambert family is called upon to act as a microcosm of the larger social and national energies. In Franzen's latest books, first paragraphs are bellwethers of each novel's governing philosophies, and so the unreasonable burden his characters are asked to carry is plangent in *The Corrections*' opening lines:

> The madness of an autumn prairie cold front coming through. You could feel it: something terrible was going to happen. The sun low in the sky, a minor light, a cooling star. . . . the whole northern religion of things coming to an end. No children in the yards here. Shadows lengthened . . . Storm windows shuddered . . . the smell of the gasoline with which Alfred Lambert had cleaned the paintbrush from his morning painting of the wicker love seat.
>
> (3)

Though split into separate sentences, the governing device here – as so often in the book – is quite deliberately the list, a form that eschews logic in favor of a metonymic pulse that coils a sequence of evidently unrelated phenomena (the sun's life cycle, the incidental absence of children) to emotively imply, rather than precisely define, a connective relationship. What is both terribly powerful and distinctly characteristic of the book's purview, is the arbitrary smallness of the act that rests at the bottom of the list's funnel of metreological forces, solar history, eschatology: not even the painting of the love seat, but the lingering after-odour of the cleaning of the paintbrush. The signature technique, then, is one of *layering*, as we move from the exceptionally vast down toward the individual who is asked to carry the many, tiered resonances that have come before. No wonder Alfred seems weary for much of the book.

As the novel unfolds, the relentless layering process gathers pace, and the book increasingly resembles one of those nightmares in which everything is out of proportion. Elsewhere in the book, the passage on the boat stands for the mythical crossing into Hades; the book is rife with echoes of *Revelations*' millennial accounting; while the position of the Lambert family within their home is asked to stand in for a global map of the mind. Confining our focus to the opening sketch alone, the family Ping-Pong table is a flat schematic of the United States' twin seaboards, with the 'eastern end of the table' – covered in 'banking and corresponding' – representing the east coast's uneasy coalition of writing and finance (a coalition that drives Chip's New York life), while the 'western end,' with its 'portable color TV' stands for the West Coast's entertainment industry (7). In a house that contains the nation, Alfred's sorry decline is insistently asked to stand in for faltering national leadership: his basement chair is 'gubernatorial' (8); Alfred emits 'the cries of a government that could no longer govern' (7); his tyranny has a 'constitutional basis' (9). 'And so in the house of the Lamberts,' Franzen concludes his prologue, 'as in the country as a whole' (10).

There's a satirical edge to this, of course, a wry joke drawing on a child's suspicion that in some undefined way her parents rule the world. Yet because the layering technique is invoked so consistently across more than 500-pages, it becomes clear that the quantitative accumulation of scenes where the family stands as a microcosm of something much larger is pressing toward a qualitative change in focus. If the set of *Death of a Salesman* is 'partially transparent' so the past may be glimpsed, then Franzen's family members in *The Corrections* are like literary holograms: flickering projections that barely conceal the larger social and historical dramas that lie behind them. In this sense, just as Franzen's novel merges postmodern and more traditional novelistic techniques, so he can be seen as using the family to synthesize the poles of Miller's scheme, to 'extend itself out of the family circle and into society . . . toward the fate of the generality of men' (Miller 1978: 74).

As is typical for Franzen, the compositional question of how the life of the family (Miller's Realism) will contain the life of the nation (Miller's symbolism) has a thematic correlative in *The Corrections*' fascination with the relationship between 'reality' and the unreal worlds characters make for themselves (whether sponsored by pharmaceuticals and degenerative disorders or by C.S. Lewis and Schopenhauer). The book's vocabulary underwrites this investigation – the word *enchantment* recurs through the book's opening section, and its implications echo through the rest of the book. On one level, then, we might see a clear continuity forward to *Freedom*, one of whose key words is the reality-dodging *escape*, and certainly critics have tended to see the later novel as a straightforward extension of the earlier book.[17] From a formal perspective, too, *Freedom* clearly repeats the key elements of the family novel that we see more broadly in this generation: the book's primary focus on two generations of the Berglund family (with sections devoted to Walter and Patty set against Joey's experiences) is mapped against a third, earlier, generation, whose suggestive names explicitly deflate the uniqueness of the contemporary selves that populate the book's foreground. Walter's father has the near allegorical name *Gene*, suggesting in an almost heavy-handed fashion the inherited source of the 'gened depression' (497–98) that will haunt his descendants; Patty's father, by contrast, is *Ray*, another biologizing pun name that invokes the sun as source of all life, and which underwrites the book's many references to both sunlight and darkness.

At times the overlaps between each book's genealogical determinism is very close – in *The Corrections*, Chip's announcement that 'parents have an overwhelming Darwinian hard-wired genetic stake in their children's welfare. But children, it seems to me, have no corresponding debt to their parents' (432), finds its counterpart in *Freedom*'s claim that 'parents are programmed to want the best for their kids, regardless of what they get in return' (245). Yet the significant difference in *Freedom*'s treatment of the family is that the later book's dominant movement is not to concentrate a universe of meaning into the small units that make up the family, but rather to place the individual within increasing larger frames that serve to diminish, rather than, amplify its importance. *Freedom*'s first paragraph – which seems designed to represent a deliberate inversion of *The Corrections*' opening – makes it clear that the interpretive weight has shifted:

> The news about Walter Berglund wasn't picked up locally – he and Patty had moved away to Washington two years earlier. . . . According to a long and very unflattering

story in the *Times*, Walter had made quite a mess of his professional life out there in the nation's capital. His old neighbors had some difficulty reconciling the quotes about him in the *Times* ('arrogant,' 'high-handed,' 'ethically compromised') with the generous, smiling red-faced 3M employee they remembered . . . it seemed strange that Walter, who was greener than Greenpeace . . . should be in trouble . . . Then again, there had always been something not quite right about the Berglunds.

(3)

Franzen initially conceived of *Freedom* as a novel of documents, and although few vestigial clues to this design remain beyond Patty's autobiography, the book's documentary birth is palpable in the opening paragraph's style. Gone is the associative slide of *The Corrections'* opening list, and in its place is a register predicated on a measured journalistic distance. With the exception of the occasional locale-specifying intrusion of free indirect speech (the parochial 'out there in the nation's capital'),[18] the neutral tone picks out a journalist's cardinal questions (*who, what, where,* and *when* are all neatly accounted for; only the *why* remains to be unraveled by the rest of the book), and punctuates the narrative with supporting quotations. Style here, as in *The Corrections*, is a vector of the book's underlying philosophy: whereas the metonymic rush of *The Corrections* was geared toward a connective vision, the controlled distance of *Freedom* is meant to prohibit closeness, making the reader wary of placing too great an investment in this individual. The hierarchies established by both paragraphs reinforce this divide: *The Corrections* begins with the wide-angle view, layering associations before zeroing in on its real target, the individual; *Freedom* begins with the individual but sets him in wider frames – first, the local perspective (the regional news and old neighbors), then the national angle (the capital, the *Times*), and finally – and most significantly – he is set as simply in the genealogical frame of 'the Berglunds,' who we learn go back beyond America to northern Europe. Rather than layering the individual with associations, this is a technique of *stripping* away significance, pressing Walter into contexts that render him increasingly anonymous, an effect that's heightened by the passages low-calorie descriptions (a 'smiling red-faced' man? 'greener than Greenpeace'?).[19]

While the opening paragraphs are clearly designed to function contrapuntally, this is not a rigid, mechanical distinction, and there are, of course, moments in each book where we find Franzen's treatment of the family overlaps. Much of *Freedom*'s political freight, for instance, is carried by the familial alignments and rearrangements on Barrier Street, with Carol, Blake, and Joey standing for the right, while the remaining Berglunds carry the political left. Yet, the tendency to invert the way *The Corrections* treats the individual typically dominates *Freedom*. Such a move is visible in *The Corrections'* great 'Dinner of Revenge' scene, where Chip's efforts to choke down his mashed rutabaga are variously asked to express a medical lens (the plate's 'clear yellowish liquid [is] plasma or the matter in a blister' [253]), fiscal prudence ("the provident young person evacuated his bacon to the higher ground at the plate's edge and stored it there as an incentive" [253]), or the archeology of death (the 'ball of woody beet leaves' like 'an ancient corpse folded over in a bog' [261]). A parallel uneaten dinner in *Freedom*, by contrast, is rapidly drained of meaning by confrontation with the vast empty interstellar void: 'He sat for a long time . . . his dinner untouched, while the house very slowly darkened, the earthly springtime world yielding to the more abstract sky world: pink stratospheric wisps, the deep chill of deep space, the first stars' (554).[20] The smallness of a family situation in the context of natural systems lies at the core of this shift: while *The Corrections* is content to see the family as a mirror of nature, with each competing sibling occupying an 'adaptive niche in the family ecosystem' (178), *Freedom* demands that the family not be seen as microcosm, but rather that it be set against the realities of the macrocosm:

Kids have always been the meaning of life. You fall in love, you reproduce . . . more life. But the problem now is that more life is still beautiful and meaningful on the individual level, but for the world as a whole it means more death . . . We're looking at losing half the world's species in the next hundred years . . . First we'll get the utter wipeout of the world's ecosystems, then mass starvation.

(222)

While this contrast between the novels functions at the level of style and individual scene, it also has larger, formal implications. Each chapter in *The Corrections* has its distinctive structure and time scheme, modeled to reflect idiosyncrasies of the family member that dominates a given part: so Gary's aggressive desire to live in the present, and disown his familial past ('You're nothing at all like your father,' his wife reassures him [182]) is paralleled in a temporal structure that uses fewer analepses than any other major part of the book. On one level, the logic of *Freedom*'s blueprint, by contrast, reflects genealogical uniformity rather than individual idiosyncrasy. Like a diagram of a family tree, flowing from the narrow point of the first ancestors down to the broad fan of the many descendants, *Freedom*'s architectural logic is governed by a genealogical pattern of repetition and expansion. The book's opening paragraph, in this light, is a condensed gene map of plot material – the move from St. Paul to Washington, Walter's different employers, his rural background, his public exposure – whose temporary gaps the next several hundreds of pages will fill in, rather than immediately move beyond. The second and third sections – 'Mistakes were Made' and '2004' – are less a narrative step forward from the book's first part than an expansion, and recontextualization, of the material we already have, culminating in 'The Fiend of Washington,' a description that repeats the opening paragraph's vision of a 'red-faced' man making a mess of things in Washington.

From a quantitative perspective, the expanding branches of a family tree are reflected in the algebra of the book's growth: the opening section is a single narrative, the second grows to contain three chapters, while the third doubles in size again to six chapters. Increasing repetition and proliferation infects the book's smaller narrative particles: it's not an accident that *Freedom* begins in the Twin Cities, nor that the book abounds in twins. At the level of the sentence, the novel's prose reflects this sense of duplication and growth in its preference for alliterative pairs and sequences. Looking just at the quotations already given from the novel we have: 'high-handed,' 'seemed strange,' 'Walter who was,' 'greener than Green . . .' (3), 'deep chill of deep space' (554), 'means more' (222). But this tendency is even more pronounced when Franzen deforms a sentence's structure to retain an alliterative pair (e.g. 'He had many sterling qualities, Carter did' [62]) rather than pursuing a cleaner arrangement ('Carter had many sterling qualities'). Finally, the runaway growth of hereditary, and the fundamental interchangeability of the younger members of the chain, are emphasized in the book's unreasonable preponderance of J-names (Joey, Jessica, Jonathan, Jenna).

If all twenty-first century family novels are to some degree, multiple-focus narratives, then they follow a distinction Altman makes between such works and more narrowly focused narrative forms. 'Single-focus and dual focus narratives,' Altman writes, 'ask questions located at the level of the narrative' – What will happen? Who will it happen to? – 'multiple-focus texts always extend beyond the level of narrative . . . They call for answers that cannot be furnished by narrative action alone' (266–67). By using generations to structure and fragment the narrative into vertically stacked units, such family novels require readers to ask questions 'beyond the level of narrative' by locating vital information in the temporal holes that punctuate their texts, and by inviting readers to speculate about the significance of suggestive juxtapositions (say, a proliferation of J-names, contrapuntally conceived scenes, linguistic echoes, and so on) that are otherwise unconnected by cantilevered plot lines. The movement between Franzen's two twenty-first century novels represents perhaps the most extreme example of the way such family structures have grown 'beyond narrative' to dominate recent fiction. While *The Corrections* often treats family in instrumental fashion as an opportunity to rehearse Franzen's rich layering technique, *Freedom* marks the point at which the genealogical imperative has leached out beyond the boundaries of content, and has begun to reformulate the role of characters, the logic underpinning the book's growth, and the chemistry of the very sentences that make up the novel.

Notes

1 Mary K. Holland offers a notable exception, merging both obsessions in her study of late twentieth-century 'novels that struggle with [the] problem of using "antihumanistic" language to signify affect, communication, and connection . . . especially within families' (2).

2 Robert Eaglestone notes, more broadly that 'in the fiction of the last ten years or so there has been a strange and new interest in the child' (1099). The contemporary orphan's American ancestors are, of course, illustrious, extending at least as far back as Huck Finn, and 'another orphan,' Ishmael, left in 'the axis of that slowly wheeling circle' at the end of *Moby-Dick* (625).

3 In this respect, Ralph Clare has persuasively argued that in *J R* 'Gaddis's interplay between family and capital is strategic, intended to call attention to the inverse relationship developing between the two spheres – the expansion of capital and the relative "fractionation" of the family' (118). In terms of writing after postmodernism, Gaddis's description of J R looking 'as though he lives in a home without . . . grownups' (246) is, in fact, one possible source for Wallace's image of the writer as an orphan in an adult's house.

4 Many other critics, of course, have similarly defined postmodernism (as a larger cultural condition) in terms of a diminishment of temporal scope – Fredric Jameson's sense that 'our daily life' in postmodernism is 'dominated by categories of space rather than categories of time' stands out in this respect (16). The reintroduction of longer time frames in the twenty-first century novel might be considered a formal reaction against postmodern fiction, though Historiographic Metafiction, an important subset of the postmodern novel, arguably presents an important challenge to Heise's generalization. Nevertheless, in the context of this essay's discussion of the multi-generational work, it's fair to say that key American examples frequently do not to focus on more than one generation: DeLillo's *Libra* (1988), for instance, most closely resembles an atomized bildungsroman, with the only other generation (Lee Harvey Oswald's mother) treated largely as a satellite of the central character, rather than as a personality with a duration of her own.

5 Kasia Boddy's essay "Family" offers a much fuller exploration of the way family functions (especially as a hinge between the domestic and the political) in the late twentieth-century American novel.

6 Robbins notes the use of prolepses in twenty-first century works by Egan, Eugenides, and Michael Chabon, Recent fiction by Anthony Marra, George Saunders, and David Foster Wallace, might also be added to his list.

7 The absence of the deepening pressure of the multi-generational structure may be one reason why James Wood (albeit somewhat crudely) distinguished *The Corrections* from *Underworld* as a 'book of DeLillo-like breadth' with 'human beings' added to the mix.

8 James Wood's dismissive label 'Hysterical Realism' was directed at Wallace and Smith, in particular. As noted above, Rick Altman's model of the 'multiple-focus narrative' offers a more nuanced frame for other recent texts, though his discussion of multiple-focus texts built around 'successive generations of the same or related families' concerns earlier, European texts by such writers as Mann, and Galsworthy (254).

9 Paul Dawson offers a persuasive challenge to the orthodox view of omniscience's debased currency in contemporary fiction (with particular attention to Franzen) in *The Return of the Omniscient Narrator*. Stephens does not, of course, provide the only model for such works. Earlier still, Robert Boyers mapped out the 'family novel' as a form that shows 'us how families grow, take shape, influence members, develop a momentum no one within that family can understand' (3). Boyers terms are less regionally circumscribed than Stephens's Southern study, and its notable that several of his key modern examples – by Kafka and Christina Stead – draw on writers whom Franzen has identified as particularly important to his own development.

10 Notably Jennifer Weiner's complaint that when Franzen writes 'about a family . . . we are told this is a book about America' and not about the family (qtd. in Neary).

11 While I note some connections to *Purity* (2015) later in the essay, I focus primarily on *The Corrections* and *Freedom* here because Franzen seems to have deliberately composed the later novel as a counterpoint to the earlier book.

12 One of the animating forces behind Franzen's evolving sense of the novel during this period was an ongoing debate with Wallace about the purpose of fiction, and – especially – its relationship to academic discourses about the novel. In this respect, it's noteworthy that Wallace's working library included his annotated copy of LeClair's first survey of the boundaries and possibilities of the system novel, *In the Loop*.

13 *The Fig Connection*, written with Kathy Siebert, and published in 1977.

14 The temporal fuzziness in Miller's play is provided by the set's 'partially transparent' walls; in *Jonathan Franzen at the End of Postmodernism* (2008), I discuss the importance of the way Franzen manages shifts between past and present in *The Corrections*.

15 As Christopher Bigsby notes in a discussion of autobiographical traces in Miller's work, 'to review [Miller's] plays is, repeatedly, to discover the extent to which they draw on family relationships' (233).

16 Franzen ostensibly signaled this retreat, for example, when he told Jessica Murphy: 'In a prosperous post great society era, when the two major political parties resemble each other so closely, and the Cold War is over, there aren't many places to find meaning. But family does remain an enduring generator of meaning.' The connection between the family and politics in his novels is, however, somewhat more complicated than this pithy formulation suggests.

17 Gram's essay conflates the two as more or less interchangeable in what can sometimes be a mechanistic reading of the relationship between the two works: ('*Freedom* . . . just as *The Corrections*' (1); 'just as *The Corrections*. . . . *Freedom*' (15)).

18 The tendency of Franzen's narration to mix different registers or voices has emerged as a key concern in the developing body of scholarship devoted to Franzen's work. Marshall Boswell describes Franzen's 'uniquely complex form of free indirect discourse,' where 'two, sometimes three, voices are operating simultaneously at any given moment' as 'his most original contribution to contemporary American letters'; in rather different terms, Gram sees Franzen's prose in *Freedom* as breaking away from routine 'story' into 'a kind of discursive excess' whenever unsustainable population growth comes up (2); Áine Mahon, sees the shifts in *Freedom*'s tone ('at times playful, at others caustic') as at least partly representing a parody of 'the conflicted figure of the contemporary American liberal' (101). For many voices to co-exist within one discourse might be taken as an analogy for the way a single family both unifies and is stretched out by the voices of its different members.

19 *Purity*'s opening, in many ways, reprises *Freedom*'s approach. Franzen's interest in narration-through-documents persists in the later novel's diary-style opening, yet while diaries are typically intimate, first-person confessions, Franzen continues to distance the individual through a sequence of self-cancelling narrative choices: not only is this account in the third-person, the blank pronouns ('the girl,' 'the mother') and appeals to vague group terms ('any job,' 'any person'), strategically drain the passage of individuality.

20 Such chilling zoom-outs remind us that temporal cosmopolitanism in the twenty-first century novel does not always necessitate the flashforward Robbins discusses. The effect of Franzen's spatial zoom-outs more closely resembles those sudden shifts where a narrative lens is radically pulled back into deep time. Richard Powers is arguably the master of such shifts, which are deployed to great effect in *Generosity* where the Precambrian can suddenly appear in the midst of a contemporary moment: 'The world outside their rented casket floors him. Night is deep and crackling. The air smells of sap, as it must have smelled for millions of years before the first flicker of awareness' (285).

Works cited

Altman, R. *A Theory of Narrative*. New York: Columbia UP, 2008.

Bigsby, C. *Arthur Miller: A Critical Study*. Cambridge: Cambridge UP, 2005.

Boddy, K. 'Family.' *American Literature in Transition: 1990–2000*. Ed. Stephen J. Burn. Cambridge: Cambridge UP, 2018. 312–328.

Boswell, M. 'Marshall Boswell on Jonathan Franzen.' Jonathan Franzen. Ed. Harold Bloom. *Bloom's Modern Critical Views*. New York: Infobase-Chelsea, 2014.

Boyers, R. 'The Family Novel.' *Salmagundi* 26 (1974): 3–25.

Burn, S. J. *Jonathan Franzen at the End of Postmodernism*. London: Continuum, 2008.

Clare, R. 'Family Incorporated: William Gaddis's J R and the Embodiment of Capitalism.' *Studies in the Novel* 45.1 (2013): 102–122.

Cohen, S. 'To Wish to Try to Sing to the Next Generation: *Infinite Jest*'s History.' *The Legacy of David Foster Wallace*. Ed. Cohen Konstantinou and Lee Konstantinou. Iowa: U of Iowa P, 2012. 59–79.

Davis, S. D. and C. Frohlich. 'Did (or Will) Fluid Injection Cause Earthquakes? Criteria for a Rational Assessment.' *Seismological Research Letters* 64.3–4 (1993): 207–224.

Dawson, P. *The Return of the Omniscient Narrator: Authorship and Authority in Twenty-First Century Fiction.* Columbus, OH: Ohio State UP, 2013.

DeLillo, D. *Underworld.* New York: Scribner, 1997.

—— *White Noise.* New York: Viking–Penguin, 1985.

Eaglestone, R. 'Contemporary Fiction in the Academy: Towards a Manifesto.' *Textual Practice* 27.7 (2013): 1089–1101.

Egan, J. *The Keep.* New York: Random–Anchor, 2006.

Franzen, J. *The Corrections.* 2001. New York: Farrar, 2002

—— 'The Esquire Conversation.' With Sven Birkerts. Esquire 10 Aug. 2006. Web. 1 Oct. 2008.

—— *Freedom.* New York: Farrar, 2010.

—— *How to Be Alone.* Rev. ed. New York: Farrar, 2003.

—— *Purity.* New York: Farrar, 2015.

Gaddis, W. *J R.* Introd. Frederick Karl. New York: Penguin, 1993.

Gram, M. H. 'Freedom's Limits: Jonathan Franzen, the Realist Novel, and the Problem of Growth.' *American Literary History* 26 (2014): 1–22.

Green, J. *Late Postmodernism: American Fiction at the Millennium.* New York: Palgrave, 2005.

Holland, M. K. *Succeeding Postmodernism: Language and Humanism in Contemporary American Literature.* New York: Bloomsbury, 2013.

Jameson, F. *Postmodernism or, the Cultural Logic of Late Capitalism.* London: Verso, 1991.

Joyce, J. *Selected Letters.* Ed. Richard Ellmann. London: Faber, 1975.

LeClair, T. 'The Systems Novel.' Rev. of *Prisoner's Dilemma*, by Richard Powers. *New Republic* 25 (Apr. 1988): 40–42.

Mahon, Á. 'Achieving Their Country: Richard Rorty and Jonathan Franzen.' *Philosophy and Literature* 38 (2014): 90–109.

McLaughlin, R. "After the Revolution: US Postmodernism in the Twenty-First Century." *Narrative* 21.3 (2013): 284–295.

Miller, A. 'The Family in Modern Drama.' *Theater Essays of Arthur Miller.* Ed. and introd. Robert A. Martin. Fwd. Miller. Harmondsworth: Penguin, 1978. 69–85.

Powers, R. *Generosity.* New York: Farrar, 2009.

Rebein, R. 'Turncoat: Why Jonathan Franzen Finally Said 'No' to Po-Mo.' *The Mourning After: Attending the Wake of Postmodernism.* Ed. Neil Brooks and Josh Toth. Postmodern Studies. 40. Amsterdam: Rodopi, 2007. 201–221.

Robbins, B. 'Many Years Later: Prolepsis in Deep Time.' *Henry James Review* 33 (2012): 191–204.

Stephens, R. O. *The Family Saga in the South: Generations and Destinies.* Baton Rouge, LS: Louisiana State UP, 1995.

Wallace, D. F. *Conversations with David Foster Wallace.* Ed. Stephen J. Burn. Literary Conversations Ser. Jackson, MS: UP of Mississippi, 2012.

—— *Infinite Jest.* 1996. Boston: Little, 1997.

—— *The Pale King.* Fwd. Michael Pietsch. New York: Little, 2011.

Wood, J. 'What the Dickens.' Rev. of *The Corrections*, by Jonathan Franzen. *Guardian* 9 Nov. 2001. [online]. 10 Nov. 2001. http://books.guardian.co.uk

14

RELIGION

Arthur Bradley and Andrew Tate

In the conclusion of *Never Let Me Go* (2005), Kazuo Ishiguro's clone narrator Kathy watches pieces of rubbish accumulating on a barbed wire fence and briefly allows herself to fantasise about the restoration of everyone she has lost over the course of her short life. 'I was thinking about the rubbish', she says,

> the flapping plastic in the branches, the shore-line of odd stuff caught along the fencing, and I half-closed my eyes and imagined this was the spot where everything I'd ever lost since my childhood had washed up, and I was now standing here in front of it, and if I waited long enough, a tiny figure would appear on the horizon across the field, and gradually would get larger until I'd see it was Tommy, and he'd wave, maybe even call. The fantasy never got beyond that – I didn't let it – and though the tears rolled down my face, I wasn't sobbing or out of control. I just waited a bit, then turned back to the car, to drive off to wherever it was I was supposed to be.
>
> (Ishiguro 2005: 282)

It is tempting to read the poignant end of Ishiguro's novel as a kind of metaphor for the fate of religion in the contemporary novel. After all, Kathy's fantasy about the return of her beloved Tommy is curiously reminiscent of another image of the failed redemption of historical detritus: Walter Benjamin's celebrated reading of Paul Klee's painting of the 'Angelus Novus' in his *Theses on the Philosophy of History* (1940). To recall Benjamin's enigmatic thought experiment, the Angel of History 'would like to stay, awaken the dead, and make whole what has been smashed'. Yet, 'a storm irresistibly propels him into the future to which his back is turned' and this storm 'is what we call progress' (Benjamin 1969: 257–258). Perhaps we might even see Kathy, the professional 'carer', as a kind of banal, secular equivalent to Benjamin's angel – wanting to stay and redeem what has been lost – but equally powerless in the face of the ever-growing history of human catastrophes that is, at the same time, the history of scientific and medical advancement. If Ishiguro's novel seems to deliberately open up the possibility of a religious reading, however, it just as quickly shuts it down: whereas Benjamin's angel is propelled into the future against his will by the storm, Kathy decides to turns her back on the tragic scene of history because she knows that the idea of a messianic justice for her dead friends is nothing more than a fantasy. This essay asks what remains of the religious within a contemporary literary moment which has – whether by mobilising such classic concepts as false consciousness (Marx), *ressentiment* (Nietzsche) and infantile neurosis or illusion (Freud) or more recent theories like memetics (Dawkins and Dennett) – also tried to turn the page upon the Abrahamic archive. What is the future of the religious illusion in contemporary fiction?

It is possible to argue that at least one future for religion in literature might lie in atheism itself. As Christopher Watkin has recently demonstrated, a genuinely post-theological thinking is 'difficult' – perhaps even impossible? – because it is so parasitic upon the theological past from which it seeks to exit (Watkin 2011: 1–11). Firstly, post-Enlightenment atheists like Comte or Feuerbach consistently fall into the trap of merely imitating religion: a transcendental God is replaced by some nominally immanent placeholder – usually Man, Reason or Nature – who then goes on to perform exactly the same transcendental role. However, even thinkers who reject the super-sensory realm in its entirety like Nietzsche still remain guilty of what Watkin calls a 'residual' atheism: 'an atheism that seeks with a heroic or despairing asceticism, to make do with the meagre residue left over after the departure of God, Truth, Justice, Beauty and so on' (Watkin 2011: 4–5). If Watkin's focus is primarily philosophical, it would not be hard to tell the same story of 'difficult' atheisms from the perspective of contemporary literature: what we have elsewhere called the 'New Atheist Novel' is a classic example of an imitative atheism which seamlessly replaces religion with a suspiciously transcendentalised humanism (Bradley and Tate 2010). In the same way, Ishiguro's *Never Let Me Go* could be read as embodying a residual atheism which remains defined, ascetically and melancholically, by the very lack of the messianic promise it finds so illusory. For Kathy, what lies beyond God seems to be nothing more than a God-shaped absence: a negative infinity embodied in the endless, empty horizon of the Norfolk field.

Yet, it is equally plausible to contend that religion in the contemporary novel might be something more productive than merely the host for an atheist parasite, and this is the hypothesis we wish to flesh out in what follows. To take just one intriguing recent development within the field, a new and diverse body of work has begun to appear under the banner of a 'religious materialism': Slavoj Žižek's perverse or monstrous Christianity, Giorgio Agamben's profanation, Eric Santner's psychotheology of everyday life, the various revivals of a Pauline revolutionary political theology (Žižek, Milbank and Davis 2009; Santner 2011; Blanton 2014). It is no longer necessary or possible to oppose matter and religion – as consciousness and false consciousness, reality and illusion and so on – because religion itself contains a hard kernel of the real. As Žižek has argued in a number of recent texts, for instance, the God of Christianity is not the absolute transcendental master of theological repute but one who suffers and dies in *this* world. For Žižek, Christ's Crucifixion is not only the death of the Christian 'Big Other' but of all the other Others (Man, Family, Party, Capital or any master signifier) we use to explain and redeem the meaningless chaos of history: 'it refuses any "deeper meaning" that obfuscates the brutal reality of historical catastrophes' (Žižek, Milbank and Davis 2009: 54–55). If belief in the transcendental God of Christianity really is false consciousness, as the classic Marxian critique suggests, Clayton Crockett and Jeffrey Robbins contend in their gloss on Žižek that it is perhaps the illusion *par excellence* – the illusion that reveals the illusory, projected and fetishistic condition of our relation to everything we call the real (Crockett and Robbins 2013: 27). Perhaps this is what Marx means when he famously says that criticism of religion is the premise of all criticism: what religious critique makes visible is in fact the generalised religious structure of capitalism itself. In *Never Let Me Go*, recall, Kathy rejects messianic justice as a fantasy only to succumb to the even more insidious fantasy that she still possesses a special value within the wholly immanent order that exploits her: 'I just waited a bit, then turned back to the car, to drive off to wherever it was I was supposed to be'.

In this essay, we seek to offer a brief survey of what we might (following William James) call some of the varieties of religious experience in the contemporary novel from re-writings of gospel narratives (Tóibín, Frey, Alderman, Pullman) to representations of Islam and Islamism (Hamid,

Faulks, Lanchester). It hopefully goes without saying that what follows cannot be remotely comprehensive or exhaustive. Yet, it does represent a certain argument about the future of religion in the contemporary novel. To pursue the hypothesis we introduced above, we want to argue one possible future for religion in twenty-first century fiction may lie in a certain kind of religious realism or materialism that intriguingly complicates the various kind of categories and oppositions (transcendent versus immanent, real versus illusory, consciousness versus false consciousness, normal versus pathological and so on) in which the relationship between literature and religion are normally read and understood. For the contemporary novels discussed in what follows, religion is not merely one more source of false consciousness, *ressentiment* or delusion (though it is all of these things) but something that still possesses what Žižek calls a radical core. By taking religion seriously *as* an illusion – as the false consciousness that reveals the falsity of all consciousness – we will also see that contemporary fiction reveals all the other deep fiduciary investments in Big Others that circulate unnoticed within the contemporary novel: family, work and, most destructively, capital. Finally, we will also explore the possibility that religion may perversely be a form of political resistance to the various false transcendences that persist in the contemporary novel. In the same way as Marcel Gauchet famously argued that 'Christianity is the religion of the exit from religion' (Gauchet 1997) – the religion that makes something like atheism possible – modern fiction arguably depicts religion as the illusion of the exit from illusion.

★★★

For a few months at the end of the second Christian millennium, a convicted criminal who claimed to be the Son of God stood, naked but for a loincloth, in the centre of a once powerful Empire, gazing at crowds of tourists, policemen and city workers. In July 1999, Mark Wallinger's white marble sculpture, *Ecce Homo*, an iteration of the figure Swinburne named the 'pale Galilean', slight but defiant, was installed on the previously empty 'fourth plinth' in Trafalgar Square (Searle 1999). The statue's biblical title and its crown of barbed wire thorns are the only real signifiers of this vulnerable figure's potential religious significance. *Ecce Homo* shares a title, of course, with Friedrich Nietzsche's (anti-Christian) autobiography, but in both cases the name is an allusion to a passage from the Gospel of John, in which the captive Jesus is presented by Pontius Pilate to a mob who call for his execution: 'And Pilate saith unto them, Behold the man!' (John 19.5). The agnostic artist's Jesus offered a form of silent dissent. 'Jesus was at the very least a political leader of an oppressed people', commented the artist: 'I think he has a place here in front of all these oversized imperial symbols' (Anon 1999). Of the many thousands of sightseers who wandered past this image of the incarnation, relatively few might self-identify as believers in the literal truth of the story of God made flesh. Yet Wallinger's artwork, far from embodying an instance of Christian triumphalism, is a powerful public meditation on the relationship between materiality and transcendence, spirituality and politics, power and vulnerability in a supposedly secular culture.

This visual negotiation with the incarnation is a twin reminder that Christianity has, at its core, not a philosophy but a man who lived, suffered and died in history and that the sacred has a habit of exceeding its boundaries in contemporary culture. Christological debates have never been the exclusive preserve of the official community of believers and, in the early twenty-first century Jesus has been the focus of a number of sceptically inflected novels. Post-millennial 'gospels', arguably another symptom of contemporary secular culture's fear-fascination relationship with scriptural religion, revisit the authorised accounts of the Christ event with a mixture of scepticism and reverence. There is a long tradition of what Theodore Ziolkowski once named 'fictional transfigurations of Jesus' including novels by, for example, D. H. Lawrence, Robert Graves, Nicholas Kazantzakis and, more recently, by Norman Mailer and Jim Crace, whose *Quarantine* (1997) imagined a weakened Jesus dying during his forty-day desert fast. (Ziolkowski

1972). Alternative gospels are an international phenomenon: Colm Tóibín's *The Testament of Mary* (2012) is a lyrical grief memoir of a mother reflecting on the 'boy [who] became a man and left home and became a dying figure hanging on a cross'; Tóibín's Mary is distrustful of her son's followers and rejects their claim that he saved the world: 'I will say that it was not worth it', she concludes (Tóibín 2012: 98, 102). The Australian C. K. Stead, by contrast, prioritises the story of Jesus' betrayer in *My Name Was Judas* (2006); James Frey imagines the second coming of Christ as a wild-eyed, perhaps unstable New Yorker in *The Final Testament of the Holy Bible* (2011); and, most strikingly, the South African, double-Booker Prize winner, J. M. Coetzee playfully reimagines the nativity in his dystopian-absurdist fable, *The Childhood of Jesus* (2013).

How do contemporary British writers deal with the figure of Jesus/Christ? Not all of those who interrogate church teaching write as former or recovering Christians. Naomi Alderman's *The Liars' Gospel* (2012) offers a quartet of narrators who appear in the canonical Christian scriptures but who do not, traditionally, get to tell their tale. Alderman, who was raised in a Jewish family, uses Hebrew rather than Latinised names for her story-tellers: Miryam (Mary), the mother of Yehoshuah (Jesus); Iehuda from Qeriot (Judas Iscariot), the former best friend and subsequently betrayer of the wandering healer and teacher; Caiaphas, High Priest of the Temple in Jerusalem; and Bar-Avo (Barrabas), 'a rebel and murderer'. *The Liars' Gospel* – which boasts a combative title – challenges Christian scripture, not only in its fabulation of the inner lives of some of its *dramatis personae*, but also more directly. It reminds readers that Yehoshuah/Jesus was not unique, either as a religious teacher who proclaimed himself to be a messiah, or whose followers believed to be capable of miraculous deeds or, in fact, for the method of his death; crucifixion was the fate of many criminals and those who fell foul of the Roman authorities. In Alderman's narrative, Yehoshuah is barely glimpsed, remembered by two who loved him (Miryam and Iehuda) and two of his adversaries (Caiaphas and Bar-Avo); the betrayer, high priest and rebel are all presented in considerably more sympathetic light than in most standard representations, including the authorised gospels. In the novel's slightly essayistic conclusion, the narrator reflects that much of what Yehoshuah preached, he simply repeated from the Torah; he was, however, 'unique in his time and place, for saying, "Love your enemy"' (Alderman 2012: 260). Alderman's narrative – full of self-aware reference to the process of invention and imagination involved in remembering a lost set of histories – politicises the implications of following this 'dreamer's doctrine'. The novel is particularly acute on the nature of occupation, rebellion and the continuing power of messianic thought. *The Liars' Gospel* problematises Christian creeds but, perhaps surprisingly, its epilogue suggests that a trace of Yehoshuah's scandalous, subversive life is worth preserving even if the social reality of the religion founded in his name falls far short of the '[v]isionary, astonishing' imperative of self-sacrificial love (Alderman 2012: 260).

The self-consciously heretical title of Philip Pullman's *The Good Man Jesus and the Scoundrel Christ* (2010) is perhaps unsurprising for an author whose teenage protagonists famously 'kill' God (or at least a senile impostor masquerading as 'the ancient of days') in the conclusion of the fantasy sequence, *His Dark Materials* (1995–2000). The 'Jesus/Christ' novella, published as part of Canongate's 'Myths' series, is a kind of postmodern continuation of nineteenth-century rationalist scholarship on biblical narrative. A particular touchstone is David Friedrich Strauss' *Das Leben Jesu, kritisch bearbeitet* (1835) [*The Life of Jesus, critically examined*] which famously re-reads the miraculous events of the gospels in Enlightenment fashion as 'myth'; he later argued that there is a profound disjuncture between the Jesus of history and the Christ of faith. Pullman, almost two hundred years late to the Higher Criticism party, literalises this division: in his story, Jesus and Christ are fraternal twins rather than one man. However, the narrative trades on a mildly Gothic doppelgänger motif: Jesus is practical, gregarious, articulate and liberal; Christ is awkward, solitary, zealous and authoritarian; Jesus is the favourite of his father, Christ of his mother. Jesus sternly resists his followers' suggestions that he might be the promised messiah; his twin – whose name, in fact, translates from the Greek as 'anointed one' or 'messiah' – becomes Jesus' unacknowledged biographer, turning his flesh into the words of the future gospels (Pullman 2010: 102).

Christ, in Pullman's slightly clumsy allegory, occupies the roles held in the synoptic gospels by Jesus' tempter and betrayers. During Jesus' forty-day sojourn in the desert, in lieu of Satan, Christ attempts to persuade his gifted brother that 'simple people, ordinary people' need him to perform 'signs and wonders' because 'miracles speak directly to the heart and then to the soul' (Pullman 2010: 40). Christ, in turn, has been seduced by a shadowy stranger – a man he initially believes to be a Greek philosopher or, perhaps, a divine messenger – who convinces him that where Jesus is 'only a man' that he is 'the word of God' (Pullman 2010: 58). The more mystical twin, motivated by jealousy and piety, is persuaded by this secretive figure to betray his brother, who has become a threat to the religious authorities. Pullman's fable takes key instances from the authorised 'original' gospels and inverts their outcomes: in the Gospel of Luke, for example, Jesus goes to the Garden of Gethsemane after the last supper and, experiences anguish regarding his coming death but accepts the will of God the father: 'O my Father, if it be possible, let this cup pass from me: nevertheless not as I will, but as thou wilt' (Matthew 26. 39). In Pullman's version of the episode, Jesus admonishes the silent *deus absconditus* and rejects the concept of a church as 'vehicle for the Kingdom on earth': 'As soon as men who believe they're doing God's will hold of power [. . .] the devil enters into them' (Pullman 2010: 196).

Pullman's narrative for all of the low-level provocation of its title presents a rather sanitised version of Jesus. He is the kind of decent, sophisticated teacher who would never offend liberal sensibility and certainly wouldn't claim to be God made flesh; indeed, before dying he repudiates the notion of a transcendent creator God altogether. Instead, he is a kind of Blakean religious rebel who celebrates the tangible reality of the everyday and has no faith in anything beyond it: 'I'm part of the world, and I love every grain of sand and blade of grass and drop of blood in it' (Pullman 2010: 199). There is, in short, nothing for the mature, nonreligious reader to fear in Pullman's innocuous 'good man' Jesus. In some ways, he is a rather like a literary fulfilment of the nineteenth-century idea of the 'religion of humanity': thoughtful, reasonable and decent.

However, as Terry Eagleton argues in *Culture and the Death of God* (2014), the Jesus of the Christian gospel is 'disruptive rather than conciliatory': 'The form of life Jesus offers his followers is not one of social integration but a scandal to the priestly and political establishment. It is a question of being homeless, propertyless, peripatetic, celibate, socially marginal' (Eagleton 2014: 146). For Žižek, another Marxist critic and self-styled 'fighting materialist', we have seen that the very idea of the incarnation constitutes a radical and *kenotic* (self-emptying) disavowal of power (Žižek, Milbank and Davis 2009). The Jesus that Eagleton and Žižek encounter in the gospels, then, sounds considerably more radical and orthodox than Pullman's Jesus. His Christ, however, is a more complex figure; craven and deceitful, he is pushed into a further betrayal of Jesus, giving the disciples and the future church hope by pretending to be his dead brother. This novelistic twist becomes Pullman's rationalist explanation for Mary Magdalene's initial failure to recognise Jesus in the garden after his resurrection (John 20. 11–18).

For Pullman, the resurrection is, if nothing else, a fable *par excellence*: stories of the miracle mutate, are embellished and re-told as they 'weave themselves together' (Pullman 2010: 237). As Pullman's interpretation of the gospel ends, his Christ, living as a net maker in anonymous, domestic tranquillity with Martha, is visited by the stranger once more: he challenges Christ to guard his brother's legacy, to make sure, for example, that Jesus' followers remain spiritually rather than politically focused. In Pullman's symbolic economy, the stranger is an avatar of how the author views the church: controlling, dogmatic and corrupt, more like a Satanic tempter than an angel of mercy. Christ, however, is softened; he wishes to give his brother's story 'a better shape

[. . .] to knot the details together neatly to make patterns and show correspondences [. . .] The stranger would have called it letting truth into history; Jesus would have called it lying' (Pullman 2010: 244). Pullman's novel attempts, as it were, to swim without getting wet; Christ is a scoundrel because he lies, fakes Jesus' return from death and betrays his humanist message. Yet Christ is not just a phoney messiah; he is also, more importantly, creative and capable of powerful imaginative storytelling. Indeed the 'net maker' is ultimately a kind of novelist *avant la lettre*. In our analysis, these sceptical gospels are further examples of the repetitions and returns that characterise the fate of religion; far from 'killing' religion, these ambivalent humanist tracts seem to announce its Lazarus-like capacity for resurrection.

★★★

In one sense, there is no more symptomatic (and marketable) signifier of religion within the contemporary novel than the Islamic fundamentalist. It is hardly surprising, of course, that the period after 9/11 witnessed an explosion of Anglophone literary texts that sought to imagine Islamists and Islamism. As James Wood safely predicted in 2006, 'in the next few years, one of the central novelistic subjects will be religious fundamentalism and its relation to Western secular society' (Wood 2006). To start with, the '9/11 novel' itself became something of a popular sub-genre of contemporary fiction: Martin Amis, Don DeLillo, Jonathan Safran Foer, Ian McEwan, Joseph O'Neill and John Updike are just some of the most famous figures to reflect upon the origins, events and aftermath of the attacks on the World Trade Centre (Amis 2008; DeLillo 2007; Safran Foer 2005; McEwan 2006; O'Neill 2008; Updike 2006). However, the turbulent geo-politics of the last decade or so – from the invasion of Iraq and Afghanistan, terrorist attacks in Madrid and London, the Israeli invasions of Lebanon and Gaza, the 'Arab Spring' in Tunisia, Egypt, Bahrain and Syria up to the rise of neo-fundamentalist groups like ISIS – have meant that Islamic fundamentalism still fascinates the British and American literary imaginary. If the 9/11 novel itself was criticised for a certain aesthetic and political myopia – which led it to focus overwhelmingly upon the personal trauma inflicted upon American culture – a new wave of fiction by writers like Salim Bachi (Algeria), Mohsin Hamid (Pakistan), Yasmina Khadra (Algeria) and Hisham Matar (Libya) has offered a corrective to such institutional Americanism by focusing upon the complex social, political and religious origins of Islamism in North Africa, the Middle East and South East Asia (Bachi 2006; Hamid 2007; Khadra 1999, 2002; Matar 2006). Perhaps the most visible symptom of the ubiquity of Islamic fundamentalism in fiction today, though, is that it is seemingly now impossible to write a British or American 'state of the nation' novel which does not feature an Islamist amongst its *dramatis personae*. In recent works like Sebastian Faulks' *A Week in December* (2009) and John Lanchester's *Capital* (2012), for instance, the figure of the Islamist terrorist takes his obligatory place amongst the cast of rogue traders, politicians, footballers, builders and nannies who collectively emblematise life in contemporary London (Faulks 2009; Lanchester 2012).

It goes without saying that the contemporary Anglophone novel's imaginings of Islamic fundamentalism – and its attempt to more or less 'explain' it to a largely uncomprehending Western audience – has also been the subject of exhaustive criticism over the last decade. As we have argued elsewhere, the post 9/11 novel often reveals a disturbing 'aesthetico-political dogmatism' where Islam, in particular, is concerned (Bradley and Tate 2010: 12). Not only does such fiction reject any religious or political rationale or explanation (however misguided it may be) for terrorism but it proceeds to pathologise Islamism as the embodiment of a retrogressive authoritarianism, fanaticism and violence. To give only the most risible example here, Martin Amis' 'The Last Day of Muhammad Atta' (2006), a fictionalisation of the final hours of one of the 9/11 bombers, effectively reduces Islamism to nihilism: 'The core reason was of course all the killing – all the putting to death' (122). Yet, as Robert Eaglestone has noted, Amis is by no means exceptional here: we can find similar depictions of the 9/11 attacks by McEwan, Foer and Rushdie (Eaglestone 2010). If a great deal of the first wave of 9/11 fiction tends to presume that the origin of Islamism must lie in something other than itself – in psycho-sexual repression, in sociological alienation or even in pure evil – what is remarkable about a novel like Hamid's *The Reluctant Fundamentalist* (2007) is its ability to connect the personal drama of its protagonist Changez's 'love affair' with America to a larger political critique of America's own political, economic and cultural 'fundamentalism'. For Hamid, the story of Changez is arguably less a narrative of growing Islamic radicalisation than of *de-conversion* from the religion that is America: 'All I knew was that my days of focusing on fundamentals were done' (Hamid 2007: 175).

To turn to Faulks' *A Week in December* (2009), we find an analogous narrative shift in representations of Islamism: what starts out as a pathological exception to the secular order gradually becomes a privileged symptom of a more generalised pathology within secularism itself. It is true that Islam remains an archetypal form of false consciousness in this neo-Victorian morality tale of seven days in contemporary London before the financial crisis of 2007. After all, this is a novel which permits one of its most sympathetic characters – down at heel barrister and self-confessed cultural dinosaur Gabriel Northwood – to compare the voice of God in the Quran to that of his schizophrenic brother (Faulks 2009: 193–195, 317). For Hasan – a radicalised youth plotting to blow up a psychiatric hospital – it is the sudden realisation that Islam is itself a fantasy that finally stops him from completing his deadly mission: 'It was all so fantastically, so risibly, improbable' (Faulks 2009: 380). However, Islamism is not the only alternative reality that permeates *A Week in December* because this is a novel in which all the major characters inhabit a virtual world of one kind or another: obsessive love, skunk smoking, alcoholism, mental illness, the internet, premier league football, reality television, even the petty world of jobbing literary criticism. Perhaps the most virulent of these competing realities is the abstract world of international finance capital over which venal hedge fund manager John Veals reigns supreme: Veals belongs to a new 'breed of fanatic', we are told, possessed of a 'passionate faith that theirs was the true system' and that 'earlier beliefs had been heretical' (Faulks 2009: 103). If *A Week in December* has anything resembling a faith of its own, it is perhaps to be found in Shalah – the young atheist, party-loving PhD student – who rescues Hasan from his fundamentalist pathology by quoting the Surrealist poet Paul Éluard: '*Il n'y a qu'une vie, c'est donc qu'elle est parfait* [There is only one life, it is therefore perfect]' (Faulks 2009: 387). This fragile belief in the pure immanence of life is swept away by the market fundamentalism of Veals, however, whose ruthless short-selling of shares in an over-leveraged high street bank precipitates the financial crisis in the 'real' economy but makes him billions. In the novel's chilling conclusion, Faulks makes clear that it is Veals, not the credulous Hasan, who is the perpetrator of the novel's real world-making act of divine violence:

> But I have mastered this world, thought John Veals, passing his hand over his newly shaved chin. To me there is no mystery, no nuance and no complication; I am a man alive to the spirit of his time, the one who hears the whispers on the wind.
>
> (Faulks 2009: 390)

In John Lanchester's *Capital*, Islam seems to represent less another mode of false consciousness than one of the few means of possible resistance to the remorseless logic of commodification in which the novel is immersed. It is to the young zealot and bigot Usman Kamal, intriguingly, that Lanchester gives *Capital*'s single most powerful ideological critique of the culture of total monetisation that is contemporary London: 'Sex being used to sell things, the corruption of the fundamental human impulse to love, sex being turned into a vehicle of yet more capitalise debasement – sex was everywhere' (Lanchester 2012: 259–260). At the same time, *Capital* is less willing than *A Week in December* to reduce ideology to a pure exercise in Marxian false or virtual consciousness: Usman himself admits that 'he was saying something that everyone knew to be truthful' (Lanchester 2012: 260). By depicting a world which no one really believes in – even the system's biggest winners like banker Roger Yount or Banksy-esque artist Smitty have no faith in it – Lanchester offers a Žižekian spin on ideology: it is less a question of 'they do not know it, but they are doing it' as 'they know it, but they are doing it anyway' (Žižek 1989). To stand any chance of getting outside the world ecology of capital, Lanchester's novel seems to suggest that it is less a question of changing belief than of creating spaces for different forms of praxis, other ways of living. For Shahid Kamal, older brother of Usman, it is striking that Friday prayers at the Mosque are not a moment of (real or false) transcendence but a different way of being in the immanent world:

> That was what he liked about Friday prayers: the sense of continuity within his own life, the ritual stretching into the past and into the future, and the familiar faces and the friendliness [. . .] He'd never been an especially good listener. But he loved praying, the physical act of prostration. Not five times a day, obviously, not any more – who had time for that? But when he was praying, it was one of the only times in his life when he felt fully *there*. It was not a sense of transcendence: he didn't go out of himself and he had no intuitions of other orders of reality [. . .] But while he was praying, he was praying, fully given over to his own presence in the words and motions and the ritual.
>
> (Lanchester 2012: 124)

If Faulks sees religion as false consciousness, Lanchester almost seems to turns this paradigm upon its head: Islam is one of the few remaining points of access to a kind of subjective materiality – of 'thereness' – in a world where all that is solid melts into air. The sense in which Islam may offer a form of immanent transcendence of capital is further heightened when Shahid finds himself wrongly detained and interrogated by the police on suspicion of plotting a terrorist attack. This traumatic experience turns Shahid into a subject to God – in a manner curiously redolent of Badiou's subject to truth – who is capable of subtracting himself absolutely from all human forms and relations: 'He was alone – alone in front of Allah – but free' (Lanchester 2012: 454). In the space of his prison cell, Shahid achieves a kind of radical *ascesis*, a freedom from the world *within* the world:

> Shahid felt that more purely than he ever had before: the contrast between the human world of institutions and the awful singleness of Allah. On the one hand, Formica table tops, policemen and their questions, plastic cutlery on a shatter-proof plastic tray, rules and human smallness all around; on the other, nothing but you, on your own before the infinite.
>
> (Lanchester 2012: 455)

★★★

What other futures does contemporary fiction imagine for religion? 'I don't believe in God, but I miss Him', writes Julian Barnes in *Nothing to be Frightened Of* (2008), a memoir that focuses on the writer's anxieties about death (Barnes 2009: 1). Barnes' curious lament for an absent deity embodies a strain of disbelief in contemporary culture that is pragmatic, cautious and open to surprise rather than simply contemptuous of the devout. The novelist also connects cultural longing for misplaced faith with his own art form: we grieve for religion 'because it was a supreme fiction and it is normal to feel bereft on closing a great novel' (Barnes 2009: 57). This philosophical fiction is not, it should be stressed, nostalgic for piety; *A History of the World in 10½ Chapters* (1989), for example, is particularly tough on the absurdities and abuses of spiritual authority. In many ways, though, his twenty-first century writing is emblematic of a wider ambivalence about the waning influence of traditional theism: Barnes is fascinated by the paradoxical search for transcendence in what the narrator of *Arthur and George* (2005) names 'the daily, grimy, unmagical sublunary world' (Barnes 2006: 501).

The phenomenon of an emerging multi-cultural, religious co-existence is explored throughout Zadie Smith's fiction, including the idiosyncratic synthesis of Judaism and Buddhist teaching practiced in *The Autograph Man* (2002). Smith's debut novel *White Teeth* (2000) is particularly hostile to those who believe that there is 'one pure person, one pure faith, on the globe' (Smith 2000: 204). This cross-generational social comedy, initiated by the near six-decade long friendship between the families of the mild-mannered, hapless Archie Jones and Samad Iqbal, primarily set in London from 1975 to the eve of the new millennium, features Jehovah's Witnesses, lapsed Catholics, Hindus, Muslims, secular-minded Jews and atheists. One crucial episode is set on 11 January 1989 at the Bradford protests against Salman Rushdie's *The Satanic Verses*. Millat, Samad's angry teenage son, is witnessed on a television broadcast of the anti-Rushdie rally, burning a book that he has not read but which he knows insults his culture and religion. On Millat's return home, he discovers that his shocked mother, by way of punishment, has created a bonfire of all that he cherishes (including his guitar, Air Max trainers and copies of *Catcher in the Rye* and *The Godfather* films). 'Either everything is sacred or nothing is', argues the open-minded Alsana, 'And if he starts burning other people's things, then he loses something sacred also' (Smith 2000: 205). Alsana's defence of a generous, non-restrictive understanding of the sacred anticipates Salman Rushdie's apologia for artistic and theological freedom: 'Is Nothing Sacred?' (1990).

Finally, this boisterous narrative of contemporary British spirituality parallels a plethora of novels that also prioritise spiritual experience alongside different kinds of political debate. Jonathan Coe's rites-of-passage novel, *The Rotters' Club* (2001), and its sequel *The Closed Circle* (2004), for example, use a tragi-comic religious awakening to critique a bigger picture of political bad faith. Contemporary Scottish writing has a strong consciousness of the ways in which religion has shaped national identity. 'What is the history of Christianity in this dark wee country but a history of doubts and fears, graspings at metaphysics from hard stone and wet bog?', asks the eponymous narrator of *The Testament of Gideon Mack* (Robertson 2007: 37). New religious movements have rarely been a feature of mainstream literary fiction in Britain but two recent novels focus on members of The Church of Jesus Christ of Latter-day Saints, more popularly known as the Mormon Church: Jenn Ashworth's circadian narrative, *The Friday Gospels* (2013) and Carys Bray's *A Song for Issey Bradley* (2014) both explore forms of grief, domestic crisis and the specifics of LDS belief.

In bringing this essay to a close, we might be tempted to conclude that the contemporary novel finds itself in the same melancholic position as Kathy at the end of *Never Let Me Go*, contemplating an infinite religious cosmos in which it can no longer quite believe. To be sure, the (re-)turn to the religious in literary fiction should not be read as some kind of belated (re-)conversion narrative. As John McClure – writing about a specifically North American context – observes, 'the break with secular versions of the real does not lead in postsecular narrative to the triumphant reappearance of a well-mapped, familiar religious cosmos' (McClure 2007: 4). However, it is equally clear that many contemporary writers are impatient with a model of fiction that locates religion as the monstrous or atavistic other of rational modernity. Not only is modernity not quite as rational as it claims, but religion, too, retains a radical core of immanent, even materialist critique. For the contemporary novelists discussed here, religion is often what we have called the illusion *par excellence*: the illusion through which we must pass in order to grasp the illusory status of the swarm of narratives that compete to explain or give meaning to the world. If it cannot quite bring itself to believe in the religious fiction, in other words, we would argue that the modern novel also resists the fiction to which Kathy herself tragically succumbs in *Never Let Me Go*'s final sentence, namely, that we have somewhere else or better to go – a more meaningful post-religious world to inhabit. In the contemporary novel, the future of the religious illusion may paradoxically be to expose the proliferating and all-pervasive illusions that we call the real.

Works cited

Alderman, N. (2012) *The Liars' Gospel.* London: Viking.

Amis, M. (2008) *The Second Plane: September 11: 2001–2007.* London: Jonathan Cape.

Anon. (1999) 'Trafalgar Square's Fourth Plinth', *The Guardian.* www.theguardian.com/arts/pictures/image/0,8543,-10204720077,00.html (accessed on 29 September 2014).

Bachi, S. (2006) *Tuez-les-tous.* Paris: Gallimard.

Barnes, J. (2006) *Arthur and George.* London: Vintage.

—— (2009) *Nothing to be Frightened Of.* London: Vintage.

Benjamin, W. (1969) *Illuminations.* New York: Knopf.

Blanton, W. (2014) *A Materialism for the Masses: Saint Paul and the Philosophy of Undying Life.* New York: Columbia University Press.

Bradley, A. and Tate, A. (2010) *The New Atheist Novel: Fiction, Philosophy and Polemic after 9/11.* London: Bloomsbury.

Crockett, C. and Robbins, J. (2013) *Religion, Politics and the Earth: The New Materialism.* New York: Palgrave Macmillan.

DeLillo, D. (2007) *Falling Man.* London: Picador.

Eaglestone, R. (2010) 'The Age of Reason Is over . . . an Age of Fury Was Dawning: Contemporary Anglo-American Fiction and Terror', in *Terror and the Postcolonial: A Concise Companion*, eds. Stephen Morton and Elleke Boehmer. Oxford: Blackwell: 361–369.

Eagleton, T. (2014) *Culture and the Death of God.* New Haven: Yale University Press.

Faulks, S. (2009) *A Week in December.* London: Vintage.

Gauchet, M. (1997) *The Disenchantment of the World: A Political History of Religion.* Princeton, NJ: Princeton University Press.

Hamid, M. (2007) *The Reluctant Fundamentalist.* London: Hamish Hamilton.

Ishiguro, K. (2005) *Never Let Me Go.* London: Faber.

Khadra, Y. (1999) *À quoi rêvent les loups.* Paris: Julliard.

—— (2002) *Les Hirondelles de Kaboul.* Paris: Julliard.

Lanchester, J. (2012 *Capital.* London: Faber.

Matar, H. (2006) *In the Country of Men.* London: Viking.

McClure, J. A. (2007). *Partial Faiths: Postsecular Fiction in the Age of Pynchon and Morrison.* Athens: University of Georgia Press.

McEwan, I. (2006) *Saturday.* London: Vintage.

O'Neill, J. (2008) *Netherland.* London: Harper Perennial.

Pullman, P. (2010) *The Good Man Jesus and the Scoundrel Christ.* Edinburgh: Canongate.

Robertson, J. (2007) *The Testament of Gideon Mack.* London: Penguin.

Safran Foer, J. (2005) *Extremely Loud and Incredibly Close.* London: Penguin.

Santner, E. (2011) *On the Psychotheology of Everyday Life: Reflections on Freud and Rosenzweig.* Chicago: University of Chicago Press.

Searle, A. (1999, July 22) 'The Day I met the Son of God', *The Guardian.* www.theguardian.com/artand design/1999/jul/22/art.artsfeatures (accessed on 25 September 2014).

Smith, Z. (2000) *White Teeth.* London: Hamish Hamilton.

Tóibín, C. (2012) *The Testament of Mary.* London: Viking.

Updike, J. (2006) *Terrorist.* London: Penguin.

Watkin, C. (2011) *Difficult Atheism: Post-Theological Thinking in Alain Badiou, Jean-Luc Nancy and Quentin Meillassoux.* Edinburgh: Edinburgh University Press.

Wood, J. (2006, July 3) 'Jihad and the Novel', Review of John Updike's *Terrorist*, *New Republic.* www.newrepublic.com/article/books-and-arts/jihad-and-the-novel.

Ziolkowski, T. (1972) *Fictional Transfigurations of Jesus.* Lawrenceville, NJ: Princeton University Press.

Žižek, S. (1989) *The Sublime Object of Ideology.* London and New York: Verso.

Žižek, S., Milbank, J. and Davis, C. (eds.). (2009) *The Monstrosity of Christ: Paradox or Dialectic?* Boston, MA: MIT Press.

15

DIASPORA

Leila Kamali

This chapter argues that understanding the importance of diaspora for the contemporary period demands a practice of reading across the diverse methodological approaches made across different descriptive genres, and requires a recognition of the limits of theory in depicting this phenomenon which tends, by its very nature, to defy strictly classificatory or historical approaches. The articulation of diaspora in the contemporary time, this chapter will suggest, is most helpful and significant when it is able to acknowledge a particular uncertainty in the practice of history-making, as well as in the practice of categorising migratory movements into 'types'. This uncertainty, while not unique to the contemporary time, is nevertheless accelerated in this period, and demands a set of articulatory tools which are more adaptable than ever, more open to the conditional, provisional nature of disciplinary or classificatory endeavours in the contemporary historical exercise. At the heart of this examination of diaspora is an intention to retain the difficulty which is inherent, I suggest, to identifying either place, people, or historical moment according to distinctive criteria; this practice of naming diaspora seeks instead after stories which emphasise inconclusive and often simultaneous timelines, and narratives of place which defy any sense of it as stable, unitary, or known. By putting into practice a willingness to read the ways that diaspora experience is articulated in fictional settings, as having uniquely important work to do alongside readings of lived situations, this chapter offers an approach which seeks to define diaspora in the contemporary with an eye to the more nuanced affective realms. In this way, the intangible qualities of diaspora experience begin to be articulated, in ways which can fruitfully combine with more conventional understandings of migratory movements, to gesture toward some of the most fragile and unnameable qualities of diaspora in current and recent experience.

Contemporary surveys of diaspora theory and its relationship to practice frequently differentiate between two, three or more categories or 'types' of diaspora; I argue here that this differential theoretical form makes for an inappropriately linear historical approach, which lacks sensitivity to the untidy business of living with the cultural effects of diaspora. It is of ever-increasing importance to note, I believe, that many people whose experience has been formed by diaspora in fact have lineages affected by two or more major moments of migration, and many do not live in communities which are distinctly shaped by a link to a diasporic origin. Rogers Brubaker's witty remark, upon "a '"diaspora" diaspora' – a dispersion of the meanings of the term [itself] in semantic, conceptual and disciplinary space" (Brubaker 2005: 1), touches upon a notion which I read as troublesome in the articulation of the phenomenon of diaspora in many theoretical accounts. That is the tendency to remark upon the ways in which *concepts* of diaspora have passed through two, three or more distinct 'phases', and to leave unarticulated what this succession of concepts says about the ways in which we live with diaspora as an experience and a historical legacy, in the contemporary period. It is my purpose in this chapter to ask whether it is sufficient, in the contemporary period, to assert that 'unidirectional' forms of migration 'are being replaced by asynchronous, transversal, oscillating flows' (Cohen 2008: 123), whether it is sufficiently apposite for the present time to 'oppose' what may be termed 'deterritorialized diasporas' (Ibid.) to a classical model. I want to suggest that the concept of diaspora itself bears scrutiny in ways which demand more sophisticated readings of diaspora experience in order to represent contemporary experience – and that if those readings need to cross disciplinary boundaries in order to achieve greater representativeness, that possibility can be allowed for by reading fiction in tandem with theory for a richer, more nuanced understanding of contemporary diaspora.

Historicism in the contemporary time approaches the narration of the present and the past with an unprecedented level of uncertainty and confusion. Jago Morrison has written, 'one of the characteristics of much contemporary writing is the way in which writers self-consciously acknowledge their *lack* of mastery of the historical, and of their own practices of narration'. (Morrison 2001: 14) And yet theories which address the phenomenon of diaspora and its relevance to the contemporary time often do not seem to account for this uncertainty in knowing the past; despite the fact that uncertainty is, if anything, accentuated in conditions affected by diaspora. The capacity of fiction, therefore, to encompass conditions of uncertainty in addressing the past often makes it a more subtle and functional tool than theory can be, in addressing what diaspora means in contemporary experience. This chapter will address some of the theoretical territory in which I perceive a difficulty in locating the cultural and affective importance of diaspora for contemporary conditions, and will refer to Chris Abani's 2006 novel *The Virgin of Flames* in order to illustrate the ways in which fiction can articulate aspects of diaspora which are not so easily accessible to a theoretical language. I will then employ some fragments of the stories around my own experiences of diaspora, and weave these in with a reading of British Pakistani author Nadeem Aslam's book about Afghanistan, *The Wasted Vigil* (2008). My purpose is to show that contemporary fiction, due to its capacity to easily reference different times together, reaches more easily than diaspora theory sometimes can toward the affective character of the lived experience of diaspora.

In classical contexts, the term 'diaspora' derives from the Greek term *diasperien*, from *dia-*, 'across' and *sperien*, 'to sow or scatter seeds', and as Jana Evans Braziel and Anita Mannur note, was first used 'for the Hellenic Jewish communities in Alexandria (circa third century BCE) to describe the Jews living in exile from the homeland of Palestine' (Evans Braziel and Mannur 2003: 1). The critical discussion around the meaning and significance of diaspora has gained particular momentum since the early 1990s; this is also the period, perhaps not coincidentally, which is remarked upon as signifying 'the contemporary'. Accounts given in the field of contemporary diaspora theory very often default to a classical conception of diaspora as a kind of 'one true original', in spite of the fact that diaspora affects contemporary experience in ways which are frequently a good deal more complicated. In the inaugural issue of the interdisciplinary journal *Diaspora*, in Spring 1991, William Safran makes a bold attempt to list the characteristics of diaspora, and this marks the beginning of a significant scholarly conversation over the various meanings and applications of the term. Safran, Robin Cohen, James Clifford, and others, have established a body of scholarship which seeks to define the concept of diaspora as a phenomenon recognisable by a number of key features, including dispersal from an original homeland, on a traumatic or voluntary basis; settlement in communities; an idealisation of a real or imagined homeland; an intention to 'return' to the homeland; and a strong group or community consciousness (Safran 1991: 83–84; Cohen 2008: 17).

Emerging from this work on the definition of diaspora has been a process of differentiation between different types of diaspora, which particularly demarcates a 'deterritorialized' diaspora as 'distinguished very clearly from any "centred model"' (Bruneau 2010: 37). Michel Bruneau remarks, 'This "hybrid" model has been defined by Anglo-American authors on the basis of the black diaspora of the Americas, using the approaches of post-modernist cultural studies. (. . .) The black diaspora is defined first and foremost by socially constructed "race", and only subsequently by culture' (Ibid. 37, 40). Because of the new, unprecedented experience of ongoing mobility and change which affects the contemporary, current theories of diaspora must situate an openness and responsiveness to novel, rapidly changing, and unforeseen social dynamics. Khachig Tölölyan gestures toward the importance of maintaining some conditional sense in the differentiation of diasporic categories when he indicates that:

> We use 'diaspora' provisionally to indicate our belief that the term that once described Jewish, Greek, and Armenian dispersion now shares meanings with a larger semantic domain that includes words like immigrant, expatriate, refugee, guest-worker, exile community, overseas community, ethnic community.
>
> (Tölölyan 1991: 4)

Some caution is discernible here in the practice of 'remembering' traditional uses of the term diaspora as connected to identifiable sites of origin, nation or ethnicity, and a helpfully provisional approach asserted in holding that particular understanding of diaspora in concert with more fluid, transient domains for identity. Nevertheless, numerous commentators have gone on to argue for the value of distinguishing 'types' of diaspora for past and present moments. Even as Christine Chivallon, in her 2002 article, provides a useful account of the field and its development of diverse positions, she also argues that 'we are (. . .) witnessing a succession of two interpretations of the diaspora as a phenomenon', and suggests that

> the classic ['centred'] interpretation, rests on a set of criteria set forth by a good many authors (Safran; Sheffer; Bruneau; Tölölyan; Cohen, *Global Diasporas*) [and is] based on the idea of a communal source or origin: in short, a model with the operative metaphor of roots. The writings of [Paul] Gilroy and [Stuart] Hall propose (. . .) a model that privileges hybridity and can be called 'hybrid.' The diaspora is no longer seen as unitary; instead, its sociality is seen as based on movement, interconnection, and mixed references.
>
> (Chivallon 2002: 359)

I am concerned here with the haste with which 'classic' and 'hybrid' models of diaspora are distinguished from each other; the essential historical structure at work here seems to be the history of the theorisation of diaspora, and argument over the classifications and meanings of diaspora seems to become foregrounded at the expense of measuring the particular value of the various meanings for people who are *living* diaspora in the present time. One of the advocates of the 'centred' model of diaspora, Gabriel Scheffer, has for instance complained that:

> 'diaspora' has become a traveling term. (. . .) the general public, journalists, anthropologists, sociologists, and political scientists have applied the term 'diaspora' to various transnational formations espousing what has been termed 'deterritorialized identities' – that

is, to groups whose hybrid identities, orientations, and loyalties are not connected to any given territory that is regarded as their exclusive homeland.

(Scheffer 2003: 10)

Kathrin Kissau and Uwe Hunger, similarly, articulate a concern that if 'almost all migrant groups could be defined as a transnational or new diaspora, (. . .) the concept itself [becomes] quite meaningless' (Kissau and Hunger 2010: 245). This definitional inflexibility appears to have more than a little to do with acknowledgement of exclusive links to a territorial homeland. If the dividing of peoples into diverse categories of transnational movement forms one of the hallmarks of diaspora theory, is this possibility of claiming ownership over the categories themselves, and marking belonging or exclusion accordingly, a danger we should be vigilant of, particularly in an age of resurgences of far-right nationalisms?

If for some commentators the difference between diaspora models arises as a question of typology (ie, 'classic' versus 'hybrid', or 'roots' versus 'routes'), Ato Quayson and Girish Daswani identify that the 'broad contrast in diaspora studies' may also involve questions of disciplinarity and the different methodologies used to think through the concept (Quayson and Daswani 2013: 7). They suggest a distinction between Robin Cohen's *Global Diasporas* (2008), Stephane Dufoix's *Diasporas* (2008) and Avtar Brah's *Cartographies of Diaspora* (1996) on the one hand, and Marianne Hirsch's *The Generation of Postmemory: Writing and Visual Culture after the Holocaust* (2012) as well as Paul Gilroy's *The Black Atlantic* (1993) and James Clifford's 'Diasporas' (1994) on the other, as suggestive of social science and humanities approaches respectively (Quayson and Daswani 2013: 7–8). They argue that such a distinction 'may be seen as between the outlining of social typologies and the attempt to describe the intangible elements of nostalgia, memory, and desire that elude the typologies of the social sciences. In a comprehensive view' they argue, 'both social science and humanities approaches are imperative for understanding the full spectrum of the significations of diaspora' (Quayson and Daswani 2013: 8). This outlook comes closer to a practice of viewing diaspora through multiple historical and disciplinary lenses simultaneously, thus allowing diverse aspects of diaspora experience to be told and to be heard. This disciplinary distinction is also, surely, at the heart of James Procter's observation that:

'diaspora' can appear both as naming a *geographical* phenomenon – the traversal of physical terrain by an individual or group – as well as a *theoretical* concept: a way of thinking, or of representing the world.

(Procter 2007: 151)

Chris Abani's 2007 novel, *The Virgin of Flames*, illustrates this coexistence of the tangible and intangible legacies of diaspora in rich descriptions of the multi-ethnic, multicultural backdrop of millennial East Los Angeles, where 'Nearly everything now native to Los Angeles came from somewhere else' (Abani 2008: 177). Abani's protagonist, named Black, is a half Salvadorean, half Igbo mural artist, and the novel's vibrant characterisations of his city offer a range of descriptive coordinates which enable its identification as a scene where classical and deterritorialized diasporas are equally functional in shaping the chaotic contemporary. One evocative passage includes the following snapshots: 'In the Alley on Santee, plump Armenian matrons sorted through clothes they only dreamed about fitting into'; 'Mildred, the bard of Union Station, crooned a song of fractured syllables in a language too old to have formed yet'; 'The guard outside the INS building on Los Angeles Street hassled fellow Chicano immigrants waiting in line'; 'The Mexican woman who owned the bench in front of the Dorothy Chandler Pavilion knew that this land was hers and her mother's before her'; and 'Face like old leather, eyes cold and dark as a window in the night, the young Sierra Leonean, not much older than a boy, sat at the bus stop waiting' (Abani 2008: 144–148). The close proximity in which these descriptions function with one another certainly tells us something about the multiple and intersecting diasporic threads which compose the life of a city like LA, to make it a node on the personalised networks of the overlapping territories of multiple cultural, national, and hybrid groups and individuals. But there are also other kinds of descriptions in the novel, which tell us something different about diaspora:

> There was sadness. But this sadness wasn't a turning, wasn't a leaning into healing. There was no tight-lipped hope in the face of it. This sadness was like a dandelion blown into the wind. Not the prelude to a new beginning, but a dispersal into parts so small that there was nothing to hold on to, no way to find them all.
> Yet somehow, they filled the world.
>
> (Abani 2008: 225)

Here is a clear example of the affect of diaspora, an emotive weight which resembles nothing that we might find in a more theoretical context. Importantly, Abani reaches here for the *indescribable* qualities of diaspora, and even the *untraceable* trajectories of diaspora, which as a process of 'dispersal', by rights eventually becomes integrated into the contemporary, and the felt experience of a place. It is in my view important to recognise this function of fictional work in which, as John McLeod puts it, 'imaginative possibilities can be fed back into the social and material environments of community and society' (McLeod 2008: 4).

Arguably, the very value of 'diaspora', as a term and as a concept, is its capacity to thus gesture to multiple frames of reference for human experience. Jonathan Sell's description of the particular interest which a reading of diaspora retains for the contemporary time, suggests that it may function to describe a quality of contemporary living which is innately familiar, but which is increasingly difficult to categorise. He comments that '"diaspora" is notoriously difficult to define once uprooted from any straightforwardly historical-geographical significance', and yet 'is preferred when other more analytical, less emotive alternatives are available such as migrancy, transnationalism, transculturalism or simply, mobility' (Sell 2012: 2–3). This contemporary difficulty in articulating diaspora in meaningful ways points first to the regularity with which contemporary diaspora experience contains multiple, layered, and fractured histories of migration, as well as culturally, linguistic, and racially hybrid sites of allegiance. By its very nature, the inherently mobile, culturally eclectic, and highly transitional population of a setting like that described by Abani above, is difficult to depict in a wholly categorical language. The second challenge in defining precisely what diaspora means in the contemporary time concerns the affective or emotional component of diaspora, particularly where the relationship with sites of origin (or indeed transition) is one of historical rupture (as in the case of trauma, or forced or involuntary dispersal). The affective power that operates at the heart of diaspora experience, when it encompasses discontinuous and traumatised knowledge of place, articulates historical time in nonlinear ways, and this is where theory, and in particular theory which relies upon categorising experience into a series of instants, can encounter difficulty in capturing the essence of diaspora. As Lily Cho puts it, 'the diasporic subject's divided feelings for "home" challenges citizenship's demand for a subject whose feelings are undivided' (Cho 2009: 285) – and it is that affective, feeling realm of the diaspora experience which cannot be accounted for fully by theory.

In terms of thinking through the processes by which narrative, even in theoretical language, encounters the story of the past, it is certainly true that, as Roger Luckhurst and Peter Marks write:

> the paradox of the now has *always* been a problem of representation, for to present it is necessarily to re-present it, thus introducing a crucial delay, a splitting of temporality. The instant of the 'now' always eludes the grasp, can never be self-identical: it is either no longer or not yet present.
>
> (Luckhurst and Marks 1999: 3)

However, if the crisis of representation has been a philosophical problem which predates the contemporary period, it is also the case that 'the contemporary era appears character-ized by (. . .) border-crossing movements all over the world' (Nyman 2009: 15), that the 'twenty-first-century world is defined by migrancy; it is a "world in which it is impossible to resist the claims of . . . the asylum seeker or the refugee"'. (Sáez 2005: 21; citing Phillips 2002: 5). In the contemporary period an urgency arises around the need for new ways to express and understand experience, because, while globalization itself may not itself be a new phenomenon, 'what is particularly striking in this current period of globalization is the increas-ing pace at which people, ideas, and culture move from one nation and culture to another' (Nyman 2009: 18). The technologies of the contemporary, also, mean that the narratives which compose the 'instant of the "now"' are multiplied to an extent unprecedented in other periods (the contemporary, for instance, also sees the formation of communities across borders through what have been referred to as 'digital diasporas', online communities in which recently dispersed individuals can form a network of mutual support and community from beyond the spaces in which they are physically located).[1] The experience of the contemporary, then, is one in which 'a multitude of asynchronous temporalities' is more easily distinguished than ever, in any given moment (Verwoer 2006: 16).

The multifarious ways in which diaspora composes contemporary experience is so often described in the manner given by accounts such as Jana Evans Braziel and Anita Mannur's, which are simply dizzied by the multiple trajectories which diaspora can signify in the now:

> In this cacophonous and interkinetic moment of late capitalism, spawning micropolit-ical and macrocapital reterritorializations economically and culturally on a worldwide level, the proliferations of cyber-information and technocapital virtually render the concept of border anachronistic.
>
> (Evans Braziel and Mannur 2003: 18)

In this explanation of diaspora's contemporary aspect, quite typically of accounts of the dig-ital age, the bounds of descriptive language are strained by the attempt to gesture toward the multiple and contiguous experiences of time and space, which are observed in the constant movement of people and information in the contemporary time. This is a view which displays a sublime aspect of a narrative of simultaneous cultural flows, which can act to obscure rather than reveal the human stories which might be contained within the scenario. Luckhurst and Marks comment that 'the urgency yet impossibility of mapping new contemporary cultural spaces bec[o]me the purpose of [such] criticism', 'tinged as they tend to be with apocalyp-tic sentiments'. (Luckhurst and Marks 1999: 2–3) An urgent preoccupation occurs here, to hold different times and diverse experiences together in a narrative moment where, as Sudesh Mishra (recalling Derrida) puts it, 'nothing happens (. . .) because too much happens', in a moment which is 'Too sublimely overcharged, it says too much, too soon, and all at once'. (Mishra 2006: 4).

At the heart of understanding diaspora in the twenty-first century, and its importance as a mode of addressing a contemporary way of life, I want to suggest, is a vital horizontal and vertical historicism: an insight into the way that the present functions as a site which is connected to multiple moments in the historical past, as well as to simultaneous, contradictory, and incommensurable geographical sites. In order to elucidate the ways in which I understand this diaspora consciousness to work, at this point I turn to Nadeem Aslam's *The Wasted Vigil* (2008). In this novel, post-9/11 Afghanistan is the setting for the stories and memories of war and dislocation told through the lives of five people who encounter and pass through Afghan territory in the late twentieth and early twenty-first century. These protagonists include Marcus, an English widower whose Afghan wife, an outspoken doctor, was murdered by the Taliban; David, a former American spy, who has seen the Russian invasion, the Taliban years, and the incursion of the Americans; Lara from St. Petersburg, who is searching for the story of her brother, a Russian soldier who disappeared years before; Casa, a young Afghan jihadi motivated by hatred of the Americans; and James, an American Special Forces soldier. A complex temporal sensibility, revealing of both the conditions of diaspora and of the contemporary, can be discerned in a description of an encounter between David and Lara:

> When he touched her he felt it was not in the present. (. . .) He is not young enough to believe that a moment can be seized, no longer a child who looked at the hundred clocks in his grandfather's workshop without seeing that the hands were moving like scythes.
>
> (Aslam 2008: 146)

This representation of the historical moment is extraordinarily slippery and essentially *intangible*. The possibilities of psychic escape from the present moment, interchangeably to both past and future potentialities, are signified here in the same narrated moment. The effect is evocative of a traumatised sensibility, where the experience of the present becomes perceptually interrupted by both flashbacks of the past, and vivid illusions about the future. Also present in the narration, importantly, is the signification of multiple possible interpretations of the past, reflections upon experience which may have signified one way at one time, and then change in the process of remembering. Such narration reflects the fact that, as in the case of Afghanistan, both the territory of the past's occurrence, and the character of the diaspora experience in the present, may change continually beyond former recognition. Luckhurst and Marks write that 'the capitalised and technologized accelerations of modernity confront us with an urgent need to recognise a number of temporalities in various relations, never simply reducible' (Luckhurst and Marks 1999: 3).

As a subject of the Afghan diaspora myself, and the child of an English-Afghan marriage, the experience of Afghanistan described by Aslam, a British Pakistani writer, rings true to what I might term, recalling Lily Cho, my 'divided feelings' as a diasporic individual. A recent conversation with another mother at my child's school in London, forms a typical example of the kinds of encounters with Afghan identity that I have known since earliest childhood:

Me: 'My father is from Afghanistan'.
Her: 'Ah! So you are Pashtun, do you speak Pashto?'
Me: 'No, I don't – not these days!'
Her: 'What? So your father is Afghan but you don't speak? Not one word?'

Present in this simple exchange is the tangible clash of worlds and outlooks, between that of a first-generation Afghan migrant and a second-generation subject of diaspora; surprise and curiosity on my friend's part form as much of the experiential terrain of this exchange as do my own feelings of exclusion, lack or inadequacy, and the awareness of both of us of differences in our social and educational class. The moment is charged with a focused tension in which the diverse historical, cultural and migratory flows shaping contemporary Afghanistan and its diaspora are oddly discernible, creating a jarring relationship between the ways in which we two 'Afghan' women experience the contemporary moment.

In this context, Aslam's novel offers quite a comforting reminder for me that since antiquity, Afghanistan itself has been a space of hybridity, of contact, and of multiple histories:

> It was here in Afghanistan that the Buddha had received a human face, the earlier representations of him having been symbols – a parasol, a throne, a footprint. A begging bowl. The Greeks in Afghanistan gave him the features of Apollo (. . .) The only Asian addition to Apollo was a dot on the forehead and the topknotted locks.
>
> (Aslam 2008: 226)

The consideration of an inherently hybrid Buddha's importance for the historical and cultural identity of contemporary Afghanistan bears witness to the importance of 'hybrid' cultural conversation, as well as 'classic' geographical situatedness to the role that Afghanistan has played in patterns of migration for many centuries. It is helpful – not to say, in fact, powerful – to me, in understanding my own relationship to Afghanistan and to diaspora itself, to consider my story as one in a multitude of stories of hybridity which can compose Afghan experience; as a space which has always been, and continues to be hybrid, and continues to represent 'A meeting of continents' (Aslam 2008: 226). A practice of reading fiction, lived experience, and theory together, I am arguing, can enable a particularly textured recognition of the unique value of humane approaches to diaspora histories. In counterpoint to this, theoretical accounts of diaspora which offer rather linear, classificatory, taxonomical accounts can obscure the affective aspects of experience, without which the key significance of diaspora to the contemporary time cannot be comprehended with the same depth.

The structure of my own role in diaspora is of course quite different from that of my father's generation. My father left Afghanistan in the late 1960s, not as a refugee, but as a student with a postgraduate scholarship to study in London. Over the years of Afghanistan's modern decimation, my father and his 10 brothers and sisters have migrated to Canada, the UK, Australia, Malaysia, the US, Kuwait, Pakistan, and the United Arab Emirates. Through these disparate and continuous separations from 'homeland', it is my observation of my father's and my uncles' and aunts' experience, that diaspora as a 'structure of feeling' *cannot be separated* from the knowledge of what has happened, and continues to happen to, the diverse and scattered population which once called Afghanistan home. Diasporic individuals inhabit multiple affective spaces, embodying personal ties to the people and the places left behind, which manifest in attempts to help, as well as the sense of the impossibility of helping, and the compulsion to get on with life away from the 'homeland'. The experience of my father's generation of migrants also encompasses the following cultural and psychic pressures: to 'make the most' of the educational and life opportunities presented by migration; to achieve in order to honour the good fortune of those opportunities, to live a 'normal' life away from the 'homeland', and to suspect that due to experiences of dislocation and prejudice, the so-called 'normal' will, in fact, never be available to them at all. In reading this lived scenario of diaspora, any notion that a 'classic' view of diaspora, relating to Afghanistan as simply a 'homeland' which inspires any simple dream of return, around which any experience of community is organised, or which is even in any way displaced by a 'hybrid' type of diaspora, feels completely inadequate.

Aslam's novel gives a descriptive of a stratified view of Afghanistan's devastated physical landscape which, to me, touches upon the affective experience of diaspora, helping to define what happens in both the 'homeland' and the 'elsewhere' as diasporic spaces:

> Afghanistan had collapsed and everyone's life now lies broken at different levels within the rubble. Some are trapped near the surface while others find themselves entombed deeper down, pinned under tons of smashed masonry and shattered beams from where their cries cannot be heard by anyone on the surface, only – and inconsequentially – by those around them.

> (Aslam 2008: 39)

Like Aslam's image, diaspora experience for my father's generation situates multiple, barely bearable, known and unknown moments of trauma and loss. The fact of living with an emigrant's knowledge of what is left behind reminds me of Toni Morrison's comment, in which she evokes the cultural memory of transatlantic slavery and the Middle Passage:[2]

> it was not possible to survive on certain levels and dwell on it. People who did dwell on it, it probably killed them, and the people who did not dwell on it probably went forward.

> (Darling 1994: 247)

In the case of my father's generation's experience, the emotional terrain of diaspora is signalled by a continuous interplay between 'dwelling upon' and 'not dwelling upon', the complexity of which is done little justice by any notion that categories, typologies, or even methodologies of thinking about diaspora can articulate the experience.

For diaspora theory in the contemporary time to come close to signalling the variegated experience of diaspora in the contemporary, it must heed the injunction made by Kamari Maxine Clarke who argues that 'new approaches to diasporic formations (. . .) must take seriously the complexity of simultaneous, and at times inequitable, inclusion and exclusion, formed as new cartographies of power are redrawn' (Clarke 2010: 50–51). Stuart Hall, similarly, foregrounds, in a Caribbean context, 'two [simultaneous] ways of thinking about "cultural identity"', firstly 'in terms of one, shared culture', secondly as 'a matter of "becoming" as well as of "being" [which] belongs to the future as much as to the past' (Hall 1993: 223–225). The need for an effective contemporary diaspora theory to hold together different times and different views of the same historical time, in my view requires a self-reflexive diaspora theory, such as Sudesh Mishra articulates when he argues that 'the genre of diaspora criticism has (. . .) witnessed [different] scenes of exemplification (. . .) These scenes do not constitute neat temporal blocks. Rather, they intersect across the same temporal axis and some participants (. . .) end up contributing to more than one' (Mishra 2006: 15–16). This sense of shifting and intersecting scenes *within the territory of theory* nevertheless allows the power which fiction can exemplify, of holding multiple readings of the past and the present together. Perhaps this setting up of 'scenes of exemplification', one might argue, mimics some of the sensibilities or 'structures of feeling' most familiar to practices of fiction, or life-writing, in its easy straddling of diverse times and places, and can provide the most equitable explanatory environment for understanding how a diaspora sensibility operates today.[3]

Fiction in the twenty-first century is uniquely equipped to capture conditions of historical and geographical disruption, and to allow reflection upon the condition of diaspora in ways which attest to its difficulties as a category, revealing the necessary yet perhaps always equivocal role it plays as a lens for reading contemporaneity. At the same time, fiction is not invested in the way that the theoretical tendency is in arguing for the importance of a classificatory category for experience, or in outlining its limits, yet it manages with ease the task of depicting that experience in its complexity and depth. Fiction, I argue, is uniquely helpful in describing the nature of diaspora as social and spatial dynamic in the contemporary time, not only because of its power to communicate and connect across diverse experiences, but because it is equipped with the capacity to encompass qualities of doubt and uncertainty (including the not-yet), and to reflect upon historical experiences of discontinuity and irresolution, in ways which, for instance, social sciences approaches would find more difficult.

In these cases, fiction can offer helpful ways of understanding the complex legacy of diaspora in the present time. Vijay Agnew draws from Arjun Appadurai to comment on imagination as 'a social practice that is central to all forms of agency, a key component of the new global order' (Agnew 2005: 30), that provides the most suitable descriptive conditions for creating an understanding of the relevance for diaspora to how we live now. Diaspora in the twenty-first century can be read as referring to a particular set of *sensibilities*, ways of approaching and thinking through contemporary issues which is perhaps more accessible in fiction than anywhere else. As Shaikh Samad has put it, 'Literature of the diaspora (. . .) is about sensibility rather than space' (Samad 2009: xv). These are thinkers who articulate diaspora in ways which cross the purviews of disciplinary boundaries, in order to think through diaspora in the contemporary, to articulate its very humaneness, and the difficulty of holding it in a historical gaze. Turning to fiction must be seen, then, as a process which can aid the articulation of types of contemporary and diasporic experience, and to make a situation comprehensible to a reader even when, as is so often the case today, it cannot easily be described.

Notes

1 See Patchett, E. (2013) 'Models of Diaspora'. Retrieved from: www.itn-cohab.eu/wiki/models-diaspora (Accessed: 1 August 2017).
2 The possibility of reading human sensibilities 'across' types of diasporic experience which are very different in character is another privilege of reading diaspora through literature and the arts.
3 This idea is also evident in the suggestion that 'rather than attempting to build a model (or set of models) according to strict criteria of emergence based on a linear narrative of "homeland – migration – reconstruction", a more valid focus would be how to interpret multiple "scenes of constitution", in conjunction with the recognition that diaspora, as a term, does different things in different historical contexts.' (www.itn-cohab.eu/wiki/models-diaspora, 2017).

Works cited

Abani, C. (2008) *The Virgin of Flames*. London: Random House.
Agnew, V. (ed.) (2005) *Diaspora, Memory, and Identity: A Search for Home*. Toronto, Buffalo & London: University of Toronto Press.
Aslam, N. (2008) *The Wasted Vigil*. London: Faber and Faber.
Brah, A. (1996) *Cartographies of Diaspora: Contesting Identities*. London & New York: Routledge.
Brubaker, R. (2005) 'The "Diaspora" Diaspora'. *Ethnic and Racial Studies*, 28(1), 1–19.
Bruneau, M. (2010) 'Diasporas, Transnational Spaces and Communities', in R. Bauböck and T. Faist (eds.), *Diaspora and Transnationalism: Concepts, Theories and Methods*. Amsterdam: Amsterdam University Press, 35–50.
Chivallon, C. (2002) 'Beyond Gilroy's *Black Atlantic*: The Experience of the African Diaspora'. *Diaspora*, 11(3), 359–382.
Cho, L. (2009) 'Citizenship, Diaspora and the Bonds of Affect'. *Photography & Culture*, 2(3), 275–288.

Clarke, K. M. (2010) 'New Spheres of Transnational Formations: Mobilizations of Humanitarian Diasporas'. *Transforming Anthropology*, 18(1), 48–65.

Clifford, J. (1994) 'Diasporas'. *Cultural Anthropology,* 9(3), 302–338.

Cohen, R. (2008) *Global Diasporas: An Introduction.* 2nd edn. Oxford: Routledge.

Darling, M. (1994) 'In the Realm of Responsibility: A Conversation with Toni Morrison', in D. Taylor-Guthrie (ed.), *Conversations with Toni Morrison.* Jackson: University Press of Mississippi, 246–254. 1978.

Dufoix, S. (2008) *Diasporas.* Berkeley, Los Angeles & London: University of California Press.

Evans Braziel, J. and Mannur, A. (eds.) (2003) *Theorizing Diaspora: A Reader.* Malden, MA: Wiley-Blackwell.

Gilroy, P. (1993) *The Black Atlantic: Modernity and Double-Consciousness.* London & New York: Verso.

Hall, S. (1993) 'Cultural Identity and Diaspora', in P. Williams and L. Chrisman (eds.), *Colonial Discourse and Post-Colonial Theory: A Reader.* New York: Harvester Wheatsheaf, 392–403.

Hirsch, M. (2012) *The Generation of Postmemory: Writing and Visual Culture after the Holocaust.* New York: Columbia University Press.

Kissau, K. and Hunger, U. (2010) 'The Internet as a Means of Studying Transnationalism and Diaspora', in R. Bauböck and T. Faist (eds.), *Diaspora and Transnationalism: Concepts, Theories and Methods.* Amsterdam: Amsterdam University Press, 245–266.

Luckhurst, R. and Marks, P. (1999) 'Hurry Up Please It's Time: Introducing the Contemporary', in R. Luckhurst and P. Marks (eds.), *Literature and the Contemporary: Fictions and Theories of the Present.* New York: Routledge, 1–11.

McLeod, J. (2008) 'Diaspora and Utopia: Reading the Recent Work of Paul Gilroy and Caryl Phillips', in M. Shackleton (ed.) *Diasporic Literature and Theory: Where Now?* Newcastle: Cambridge Scholars Press, 2–17.

Mishra, S. (2006) *Diaspora Criticism.* Edinburgh: Edinburgh University Press.

Morrison, J. (2001) *Contemporary Fiction.* London: Routledge.

Nyman, J. (2009) *Home, Identity, and Mobility in Contemporary Diasporic Fiction.* Amsterdam & New York: Rodopi.

Patchett, E. (2013) 'Models of Diaspora'. www.itn-cohab.eu/wiki/models-diaspora (Accessed: 1 August 2017).

Phillips, C. (2002) *A New World Order.* London: Vintage International.

Procter, J. (2007) 'Diaspora', in J. McLeod (ed.), *The Routledge Companion to Postcolonial Studies.* London & New York: Routledge, 151–157.

Quayson, A. and Daswani, G. (2013) 'Introduction: Diaspora and Transnationalism: Scapes, Scales, and Scopes', in A. Quayson and G. Daswani (eds.), *A Companion to Diaspora and Transnationalism.* Chichester: Blackwell Publishing, 1–26.

Sáez, E. M. (2005) 'Postcoloniality, Atlantic Orders, and the Migrant Male in the Writings of Caryl Phillips'. *Small Axe*, 17, 17–39.

Safran, W. (1991) 'Diasporas in Modern Societies: Myths of Homeland and Return'. *Diaspora: A Journal of Transnational Studies*, 1(1), 83–99.

Samad, S. (ed.) (2009) *Literature of Diaspora: Cultural Dislocation.* New Delhi: Creative Books.

Scheffer, G. (2003) *Diaspora Politics: At Home Abroad.* Cambridge: Cambridge University Press.

Sell, J. P. A. (2012) 'Introduction: Metaphor and Diaspora', in J. P. A. Sell (ed.), *Metaphor and Diaspora in Contemporary Writing.* New York & Basingstoke: Palgrave Macmillan, 1–19.

Tölölyan, K. (1991) 'The Nation-State and Its Others: In Lieu of a Preface'. *Diaspora: A Journal of Transnational Studies*, 1(1), 3–7.

Verwoert, J. (2006) 'Apropos Appropriation: Why Stealing Images Feels Different Today', in B. Ruf and C. Wallis (eds.), *Tate Triennial 2006: New British Art.* London: Tate Publishing, 14–21.

16

INDIAN FICTION IN ENGLISH

E. Dawson Varughese

Introduction

Focussing on Indian literary fiction in English, this chapter considers differences and similarities across the production of this body of work, paying particular attention to the differences between, on the one hand, novels written by authors from diasporic or transnational backgrounds and, on the other, novels by authors who have resided all or most of their life in India. I make this distinction because I suggest, in line with my other work (see Dawson Varughese 2012, 2013, 2016), that the novels written by those authors who have remained in India are less characterised by the tropes and guises of 'postcolonial literature'. I suggest that in general, the diasporic or transnational texts that engage with 'New India' in various ways, have a tendency to propagate India as 'the Other' as they play towards the established mores of the western market (exceptions to this idea exist, of course, such as *Half of What I Say* (2015) by Anil Menon) and thus result in work that resonates more with a postcolonial framework.

As the discussion of the novels below demonstrates, some diasporic authors (Manil Suri, Jhumpa Lahiri, Chitra Banerjee Divakaruni, Bharati Mukherjee) craft stories that explore the migrant experience (such as migration from India to the US) as well as the movement between two (or more) cultural worlds and the tensions involved in this movement. Aravind Adiga born in 1974, who then returned to India in more recent years, incorporates the vantage point of moving in and out of a changing India that his own personal upbringing has afforded him. Other Indian authors who have lived or worked (or studied) in the West often draw on the two worlds of India and 'elsewhere', as demonstrated in the works of Anjali Joseph, Jeet Thayil, Vikram Chandra and Neel Mukherjee as examples. Crucially, I also discuss Indian authors who have spent most or all their life in India, such as Manu Joseph, Usha K.R., Manju Kapur, Anuradha Roy, Deepti Kapoor, Meena Kandasamy, Arundhati Roy and Omair Ahmad as examples. What is particularly interesting about this latter group of authors is how their writing is variously received within India and in the West, which suggests perhaps a generational shift at play in both the production and reception of their works.

Beginning with a discussion of the context in which literary fiction is read and propagated, this chapter is arranged by making reference to four overarching topics that have trended in Indian literary fiction over the past fifteen years: 'Urban Underbellies', 'Female-centred narratives', 'Young India' and 'Politics'. Within these topics, I examine work by the authors listed above, thus both 'diasporic/transnational' and 'domestic' authors, demonstrating how all attend to these aspects of post-millennial Indian society, echoing concerns of contemporary living such as city life, the identity/ies and roles of women in New India, the experience of 'young India', sexuality and relationships, and the ways in which today's society might conceive of India's politics.

Publishing context

As an echo of these societal shifts, the identity of Indian fiction in English has changed significantly and also relatively rapidly since the millennium. Increased personal spending (especially amongst young Indians), the proliferation of literary festivals in India and greater publishing activity have all contributed to the rise of Indian fiction in English. For example, the Jaipur Literature Festival (JLF), founded in 2006, has been a key player in alerting the global literary community to India's place and role in shaping the contemporary world literature canon. By inviting speakers from around the world, in particular Indian writers from the diaspora, the JLF has propagated a post-millennial positivity around New Indian fiction in English and, in turn, raised the profile of domestic Indian writing in English. It has also acted as a catalyst for many of the more recently inaugurated literary festivals held throughout the year in India. In addition to literary festivals, various literary prizes have entered the South Asian literary scene such as the 'Raymond and Crossword Book Award' (before 2014 it was the 'Economist Crossword Book Award' from 2011 to 2013, the 'Vodafone Crossword Book Award' from 2008 to 2010, and the 'Hutch Crossword Book Award' from 2004 to 2007). Established in 2010, 'The Hindu Literary Prize' recognises Indian works in English and in English translation and an influential literary prize which is currently affiliated to the JLF is the 'DSC Prize for South Asian Literature', inaugurated in 2011. Anuk Arudpragasam won this prize in 2017 for his novel *The Story of a Brief Marriage* (2016); Anuradha Roy won in 2016 with her novel *Sleeping on Jupiter*; and the 2015 winner was Jhumpa Lahiri for her novel *The Lowland*. Other winners include Cyrus Mistry and Jamil Ahmad of 2013 and 2014 respectively. Although the prize accepts works in translation, the winners to date have all been authors of Indian or South Asian fiction in English, although works in translation have made it to the prize's shortlist. Given that prizes such as the DSC are open to Indian (South Asian) writing by authors residing outside of South Asia, the growth in production, confidence and the establishment of a new-found identity in Indian writing from within the country has, I suggest filtered through to the diaspora and the wider field of 'world literature'.

The growth of the publishing scene within India has also played a substantial part in bringing Indian fiction in English to a wider audience. With increased fiscal confidence, the economy of leisure consumerism has boomed over the last 15 years and with this, the purchasing of books for *leisure* has become ever more commonplace: typically, a 'popular' paperback novel of Indian fiction in English will retail at ₹299 (£3–£3.50), and Indian literary fiction in English will retail at ₹499 or ₹799 (£4–£8.50) (exchange rates as of December 2017). Moreover, Indian publishers have become increasingly 'visible' as they form part of global publishing houses such as HarperCollins, Hachette or Penguin Random House. Consequently, post millennium, there is a curious, increased to-and-fro of Indian authors (or their agents) negotiating with international, global publishing houses via the New Delhi, Gurgaon or Noida headquarters. Narayanan warns of the potential consequences of such a relationship, saying: 'if the global visuality of Indian writers is a significant consequence of de/reterritorialized corporations, its most adverse effect is the hegemony of these corporations as the prime global producers of Indian writing' (2012: 107). Independent presses continue to claim some space for themselves and companies such as Rupa Publications, Juggernaut, JaiCo, Leadstart and Speaking Tiger are examples of this committed activity.

Urban underbellies

As India's urban centres have grown in size and structure, so Indian fiction in English has evolved its post-millennial urban narratives. Most notably, authors Aravind Adiga, Vikram Chandra and Jeet Thayil have explored the city in some of its darker avatars.

Aravind Adiga's debut novel *The White Tiger* (2008) won the Man Booker Prize in 2008, with his portrayal of 'New India' garnering a marked interest. The novel is written as an informal letter which charts the life of Balram Halwai. Organised over seven nights of writing, the story explores the lives of India's poor, the caste system, the underbelly of the city and what it is to survive in today's India. Adiga's second novel *Last Man in Tower* (2011) also explores city life, money and power as residents of a housing block are offered generous amounts of cash to move out in order for 'redevelopment' to take place. Set in Mumbai, the residents of Vishram Society (Tower A) are such an essential part of Adiga's novel that it begins with a plan of the tower and its residents' abodes from the ground floor up to the fifth. The tower finds itself in Vakola, in the vicinity of the airport and for most Bombaywallas, Adiga tells us, anything in or around Vakola is 'slummy'. Vishram Society, however, stands as a respectable, middle-class housing co-operative. Adiga captures the idiosyncrasies of the people, the changing urban centre and the zeitgeist of contemporary Indian culture(s) in all kinds of detail in his novels, be it in the witty 'NOTICES' to the housing society, in his characters' Hinglish or the ongoing social commentary of his (nosey) characters. Through both novels, Adiga captures an India changing at pace and although he has been criticised for attacking certain aspects of Indian society, others suggest that his novels offer introspection into the contemporary Indian psyche, a psyche which is changing dramatically, cutting across the generations, often placing them in tension. As money and corruption lace the narrative of Adiga's *Last Man in Tower* (2011), so too do these interests trace through Adiga's *Selection Day* (2016), which was shortlisted for the DSC Prize in 2017. The novel is supposedly inspired by the real-life story of a Mumbai businessman sponsoring teenage cricketers in one of the city's slums. As a coming-of-age story, *Selection Day* (2016) privileges the male experience; it explores class, religion and sexuality through its young protagonists, Manjunath, Radha Krishnan and Javed, whilst examining the relationships between father and son(s) in a changing India.

Vikram Chandra, meanwhile, was born in New Delhi in 1961, and educated latterly in America. Chandra lives in the United States and at times, in India. Winning the Vodafone Crossword Book Award in 2008, *Sacred Games* (2007) is set in the murky underworld of contemporary Mumbai. The novel takes Inspector Sartaj Singh, who we know previously from Chandra's 'Kama', one of five tales in *Love and Longing in Bombay* (1997), and pits him against an infamous Mumbai gangster. The story is epic not simply due to its length but also due to the array of topics it weaves into its storyline: violence, mafia, Partition, Miss India, to name a few. The novel opens unusually, with the death of Gaitonde, the gangster everyone has been chasing and of whom in death Chandra writes: 'A tooth winked pearl-like, whole and undamaged, from the red raw where Gaitonde's tight-lipped grimace stopped abruptly' (2007: 46). Chandra's style, replete with detail and adjectival musings, resonates with the complexity of Mumbai, its gangsters, police force and its women. The novel chimes with India's turbulent 1990s and we are frequently reminded of that era, from *Dil Se's* 'Chainya Chainya' pumping out of loudspeakers on the street to the communal tensions between Hindus and Muslims simmering away in the background. The novel cuts to India's fascination with the 'maximum city' and its gangsters: its *bhais*, godowns and *dadas*, all of which have inspired many Bollywood films and nefariously slipped into public culture.

The dark side of Bombay is also the setting for Jeet Thayil's debut novel *Narcopolis* (2012) and the city also appears in his 2017 novel *The Book of Chocolate Saints* (2017). Born in Kerala in 1959 and educated in Hong Kong, New York and Mumbai, Thayil won the DSC Prize for

South Asian Literature in 2013 for *Narcopolis* (2012), which was also shortlisted for the Man Asian Literary Prize in 2012 and then in 2013 for The Hindu Literary Prize. As its title suggests, the novel explores the world of narcotics, specifically opium, mostly in 1970s Old Bombay but also in the city in more recent times. The novel is anchored in Thayil's own experience of drug addiction and alcoholism. The descriptive prose captures the detail of the opium dens, appealing to the visceral: '. . . a smell of molasses and sleep and illness, a woman tending the pipe, using a long needle to cook the opium, her hand moving as if she were knitting . . .' (2012: 3), and, '. . . she felt herself slipping through the mat into the floor. Below was a thick layer of cotton wool and below that were the blue pools of her nightmares' (2012: 182). Although the novel does not speak directly of the post-millennial years, it does highlight the changes that the city has witnessed and in terms of narcotics, the demise of opium and the rise of heroin. It is Jamal, the son of the opium house owner, who brings the narrative into New India through his relationship with Farheen, his text messages and, most significantly, his cocaine, MDMA and Ecstasy, 'new drugs for the new Bombay' (2012: 281).

Other urban narratives of New India include those by Manil Suri, who is an American writer of Indian heritage. He was born in Bombay in 1959 and moved to the United States for postgraduate study in mathematics. He has written various personal commentaries on growing up gay in India and about India and the US in this regard. Suri's trilogy *The Death of Vishnu: A Novel* (2001), *The Age of Shiva: A Novel* (2008) and *The City of Devi: A Novel* (2013) has brought him various successes, with *The Death of Vishnu* (2001) winning the PEN/Bingham Fellowship in 2002. Manu Joseph's novel *Serious Men* (2010), which won The Hindu Literary Prize and the PEN/Open Book Award, is also set in Mumbai and deals with issues of caste through the narrative of a Dalit who works as an assistant to a clever Brahmin astronomer in a scientific institution. Joseph returns to Mumbai with his 2017 novel *Miss Laila Armed and Dangerous* (2017), taking on big questions about political forces and again, religious and societal division.

Moving away from Mumbai, Usha K.R.'s novel *Monkey-man* (2010) foregrounds the city of Bangalore and is set in January 2000; the city that has morphed from 'pensioner's paradise' to the IT hub of India. The book's narrative hangs on the sightings of the elusive 'monkey-man' although Usha K.R. devotes most of her narrative to the detail of the characters and their lives, linked, as they are, through one 'being' – the monkey-man. Anjum Hasan also writes of Bangalore and Deepti Kapoor of New Delhi, with the latter's novel *A Bad Character* (2014) discussed below.

Female-centred narratives

Post-2000 there has also been a rise in narratives that put women, and women's experience, at their centre. Born in 1967, Anuradha Roy published her first novel *An Atlas of Impossible Longing* in 2008, followed by *The Folded Earth* (2011) which won the Economist Crossword Prize in 2012. Tabish Khair (2011), in his review of *The Folded Earth* (2011), writes: 'This is the kind of novel about India that cultivated people in the West, particularly Britain, love to read. It is set in a refreshingly recognisable – Tolkien-like map embedded – but not overtly familiar part of India'. Longlisted for the 2015 Man Booker, her third novel, *Sleeping On Jupiter* (2015), won the DSC Prize in 2016. It tells the story of Nomi who has grown up in Norway following harrowing childhood years in India, living in an ashram as an orphan and being abused by the temple's spiritual leader. She returns to India and the location of the ashram later in life and the novel charts both her journey and that of a handful of others as they explore their own lives, memories, sexuality and desires. Roy has been praised for her elegant prose, but *Sleeping On Jupiter* (2015) has been criticised within India in particular for its portrayal of Indian society as miserable, poverty-ridden and wrought with issues of sexual violence and inequality.

Wining the Commonwealth Writers' Prize in 1999, Manju Kapur's debut novel *Difficult Daughters* (1998) similarly explores female experiences, in particular the role of women in family life, education, marriage and love. These themes recur in her subsequent works *A Married Woman* (2003), *Home* (2006), *The Immigrant* (2008) and *Custody* (2011). Kapur, born in 1948 lives and works in New Delhi and although some of her work, *Difficult Daughters* (1998), *A Married* Woman (2003), *Home* (2006) and *Custody* (2011), echo this in their own geography, portrayal of bourgeois lifestyle and politics, her later novel *The Immigrant* (2008) treads a different geography as it is set in Canada. Kapur's novels explore a range of eras from Partition (*Difficult Daughters*), the 1970s in *A Married Woman* (2003), the 1980s in *Home* (2006) and the 1990s in *Custody* (2011). *Home* (2006) captures 1980s New Delhi particularly well, with the story set in a fabric shop, its business threatened by new fashion and fabrics. The changing times are made more intense as the Lal family home faces grief, loss, jealousy, love and repression within its own walls. Kapur, as with her other novels, explores the female characters carefully and fully, but in *Home* (2006) her descriptive hand extends to the portrayal of Karol Bagh in New Delhi and in particular, the Lal's shop. She writes on the potential renovation of the family's livelihood: 'Central air conditioning a must, plaster-of-paris ceiling with frills and moulding, mirrors, a gold and glass chandelier, a tiled toilet (customers stay longer if you allow them to pee), a kitchen to store cold drinks and make tea . . .' (2006: 163). Kapur has been called the Jane Austen of India for her complex family sagas and gentle storytelling. Although a domestic writer (she resides permanently in India), she is a successful Indian author with regards to her reception in the West, mainly because her narratives are demonstrably of the upper echelons of Indian society and the kind of family saga that readers might enjoy exploring. Diaspora writers have also anchored their narratives in the convoluted lives of 'the family' but have equally foregrounded the challenges of the immigrant experience and a shared identity.

Such motifs are found across Jhumpa Lahiri's work, and, publishing her first book *Interpreter of Maladies* (1999) at the turn of the millennium, she went on to win the Pulitzer Prize for fiction in 2000 with this collection of short stories. Her debut novel *The Namesake* was published in 2003. Born in London in 1967, Lahiri's family, from West Bengal, moved from London to the United States when Lahiri was very young. Lahiri considers herself an American writer. Her fiction explores both India and the United States through the identities of those living between the memories of the homeland left behind and the world in which they now find themselves. Her second collection of short stories, *Unaccustomed Earth* (2008), was very well received, and her novel *The Lowland* (2013) made the shortlist for the Man Booker Prize but went on to win the 2014 DSC Prize for South Asian Literature. West Bengal, its cultures and its capital city feature significantly in Lahiri's work. *The Lowland* (2013) evokes the Calcutta of the 1950s and 1960s as it traces the rise of the Naxalite movement alongside the lives of two brothers, while *The Namesake* (2003), from the outset, suggests a gastronomically memoired Calcutta: 'Ashima has been consuming this concoction throughout her pregnancy, a humble approximation of the snack sold for pennies on Calcutta sidewalks . . .' (2003: 1). Lahiri has a Ph.D. in literary studies and has taught Creative Writing in the United States.

A fellow Indian-American writer of West Bengali origin, Chitra Banerjee Divakaruni was born in Calcutta in 1956 and lived there until her early twenties, when she moved to the United States to pursue postgraduate study. Like Lahiri in *The Lowland* (2013), Divakaruni charts the lives of her characters, separated by miles and by cultures – one in India and one in the United States – in her novels *Sister of My Heart* (1999) and its sequel *The Vine of Desire* (2002). As with the work of Manju Kapur, Divakaruni's writing explores the female self and its relation to other females as well as exploring challenging relationships with men and with wider society. Her 2008 novel *The Palace of Illusions* (2008) epitomises this interest as Divakaruni embarks on a re-telling of the Indian epic *The Mahabharata* from the perspective of Panchaali, the wife of the Pandavas (the five brothers).

Young India

As I have suggested above, the changing reading public is emblematic of an unfolding, generational shift, and this, too, becomes the concern for much new fiction. Anjali Joseph was born in Bombay in 1978 and read English at Trinity College, Cambridge to then graduate from the MA in Creative Writing programme at the University of East Anglia in 2008. Her first novel, *Saraswati Park*, was published in 2010 and won the Betty Trask Prize, Desmond Elliott Prize and Vodafone Crossword Book Award for Fiction in India. *Another Country* (2012), her second novel, was published in 2012 and charts Leela's life as a 20-something in Paris, London and Bombay. *Saraswati Park* (2010) explores the sexual awakening of Ashish who is living with his aunt and uncle in a suburb of Mumbai, studying to pass his exams. Saraswati is the Hindu goddess of learning, music and art and this almost-bildungsroman is steeped in both the arts – his uncle is obsessed with books and a letter-writer by profession, Ashish is studying literature – and in the lessons of life. Ashish has a lot to learn about life, in particular about love. A tumultuous relationship between the protagonist and his male tutor results in both the destruction and the recreation of Ashish. The trials and tribulations of Ashish's awakening are met by the moods and colours of the city of Mumbai and Joseph captures the details of the city in surprising ways: 'A fleet of cockroach-like taxis in black and yellow livery waited at the junction outside the GPO. When the lights changed they all, honking, took the U-turn. A man on a cycle passed; he carried a tangle of enormous red ledgers, each wrapped in plastic, atop his head. The gold on their spines flashed in the sun' (Joseph 2010: 8). Her third novel *The Living* (2016) was shortlisted for the DSC Prize in 2017 and, like her second book, it straddles continents; Claire and her son in Norwich (UK) and Arun and his wife in an unnamed town in Maharashtra (India). Footwear connects the two characters as Claire is a shoe-maker and Arun makes leather slippers.

Deepti Kapoor evokes a very different kind of city, while still exploring ideas of 'young India' in her debut novel *A Bad Character* (2014) which was shortlisted for The Hindu Literary Prize in 2014. Set in present-day New Delhi, Kapoor has written a fierce depiction of the city and its society, post millennium. The narrator, Idha, moves from Agra to live with her aunt in New Delhi. She is alone. Her mother had died four years previously and her father is in Singapore with little interest in his 21-year-old daughter's life. A timely novel, given the debate around living as a lone female in New Delhi, *A Bad Character* (2014) is dark and hopeless in its portrayal of the young woman's life. Published by Jonathan Cape, the novel is, however, sincerely 'domestic', its narrative peppered with locales, Delhiites and the peculiarities of living in the capital city. It is also a breathless novel and Kapoor's style communicates this from the outset, echoed in her main characters' hunger to 'survive' life. Idha manages to make it through the New Delhi life she embroils herself in only to write: 'My boyfriend died when I was twenty-one. His body was left lying broken on the highway out of Delhi while the sun rose in the desert to the east' (2014: 1).

Bharati Mukherjee was born in Calcutta in 1940. Having lived in Canada and America for most of her life, she considered herself an American writer, and this positioning of identity is explored in her post-millennial novel *Desirable Daughters* (2002) and its sequel *The Tree Bride* (2004). Her novel *Miss New India* (2011), however, is set firmly in India, in 'New' India, and the novel, exploring the usual ideas of life in an Indian city post 2000, acts as a cultural barometer for call centre life in particular. Set in Bangalore, the protagonist Anjali discovers a new existence, a world away from Bihar and the lower-middle-class family she has left behind. Mukherjee observes the move from the known to the unknown well and she writes assuredly on the migrant experience. The novel presents an India that plays to the West's ideas about 'New India' and thus rehearsed dichotomous motifs of poor and rich, rural and urban, illiterate and educated run throughout the narrative.

Politics

'Politics' appears variously through characters, locations and time periods in contemporary Indian literary fiction in English. The place and the politics of West Bengal appear in much of Neel Mukherjee's writing. Mukherjee was born in 1970 in West Bengal and lives in the UK. He is the author of two post-millennial novels: *A Life Apart* (2010) (also known as *Past Continuous* [2008]), which was shortlisted for the DSC Prize for South Asian Literature in 2011, and *The Lives of Others* (2014), which was shortlisted for the Man Booker 2014. Both novels are set in Calcutta, although *A Life Apart* (2010) moves to England where the protagonist Ritwik embarks on a new life and forms a special bond with Anne Cameron who has, in different ways, lost much in life. *The Lives of Others* (2014) is set in West Bengal in the late 1960s. Supratik becomes involved in politics and activism, leaving the Ghosh family for the communist party, a contentious move given that the Ghosh family owns paper mills and is relatively well-to-do, residing in a large house. The novel is full of various Ghosh characters and this aspect of his craft resonates with Manju Kapur's novels of 'domestic life' fiction through the various dramas and challenges that surround the family and its immediate community.

Politics permeates the pages of Anil Menon's *Half of What I Say* (2015), which was shortlisted for The Hindu Literary Prize in 2016. Born in 1966, having lived in the United States and India, Menon's slightly speculative novel has been described as a churn of characters. It is however, the Department of Cultural Affairs, the new governmental security outfit called the Lokshakti, that stands out from the narrative. Brought into existence in order to root out corruption, the Lokshakti has its own way of doing things; prisons, 'soldiers' and its own 'Culture Department'. Inspired perhaps by Indians calling for anti-corruption laws and by supposed cases of 'sedition' in the post-millennial years, *Half of What I Say* (2015) eerily imagines an India of censorship, arrests and shadowy surveillance somewhat in the name of an anti-corruption agenda. Whilst the novel captures something of this post-millennial moment through its range of multifaceted and often complex characters, it pushes the narrative into the fable-esque or the mythical, asking the reader to imagine an India of now at the very edge of the imminently possible. The 'quiet' politics of Menon's novel serves to agitate and unnerve both its reader and the idea of the contemporary, post-millennial Indian moment.

The lives of Dalit agricultural workers in Tamil Nadu are explored in Meena Kandasamy's debut novel, *The Gypsy Goddess* (2014), with Kandasamy taking direction for the narrative from historical events. Christmas Day 1968 saw the massacre of Dalit workers in a village called Kilvenmani following the murder of a popular communist leader. The landowners attempt to force the workers back to the fields, and in their resistance the peasants are assaulted and over 40 people are burnt alive in a hut. Kandasamy is creative in form and style, her language use is witty and sharp: 'Destination of the dead: Paapaan Sudukaadu, Nagapattinam. A cremation ground named after Brahmins but used for untouchables' (2014: 188). In Part Three of the novel entitled 'Battleground', Kandasamy includes Inspector Rajavel's tabulation of the facts of the massacre, an (almost) inventory of death, each of the 42 entries including the words 'charred' or 'burnt' somewhere in their sentences. Meena Kandasamy who was born in 1984 identifies as a 'poet, fiction writer, translator and activist' (2014: 283) and is based in Chennai. In her second novel *When I Hit You: Or, A Portrait of the Writer as a Young Wife* (2017), the protagonist is a poet with (outspoken) leftist political views. Set in South India, she marries a college professor who soon reveals his violent behaviour towards her. She tells her father of the abuse that her husband rapes her and beats her but her father asks that she reconsider leaving the marriage given the shame this would bring on her *and the family*. Kandasamy's *When I Hit You* (2017) is a tale of a modern Indian family, which is based on the author's personal experience. The story is visceral and its 'truth' presents a post-millennial notion of Indianness that many would prefer to have silenced.

Shortlisted for the Man Asia Prize 2009, *Jimmy The Terrorist* (2010) by Omair Ahmad who was born in 1974 went on to win the Vodaphone Crossword Book Award in 2010. Mughal heritage runs throughout this novel (making connections with Ahmad's earlier novella *the storyteller's tale* [2008]) in both the locale of an old north Indian town as well as in the identity and religious and cultural practices of Jamaal, a.k.a Jimmy, and the wider community. The narrative exposes the lives of the residents of Moazzamabad and whilst the narrator is at pains to show the Mughal-inspired architectural, intellectual and cultural jewels of the town (albeit in a diminishing state), the reality of existence in Moazzamabad is far less pleasant. Suffering from anti-Muslim prejudices, a rising right-wing Hindu movement and a life of poverty, Jimmy is brought up in miserable and challenging circumstances. The storyline is multi-layered and the characters are complex, which in turn echoes the socio-cultural landscape of Moazzamabad. Ahmad makes statements on this very complexity at various points in the story: 'And maybe in all that I am telling you there is nothing to help us make sense of this town, our mohalla, that boy. We understand so little, after all . . .' (2010: 150).

Arundhati Roy, known for her political activism, and made famous by her 1997 Booker Prize win for *The God of Small Things*, published her long-awaited second novel *The Ministry of Utmost Happiness* in 2017 with Hamish Hamilton. The novel focuses on some of modern India's darkest moments including the insurgency in Kashmir and the Gujarat riots of 2002. A raft of many different voices, marginal, politicised and persecuted, Roy's novel might be thought of as an echo of her own polemic positioning that the intervening years have been testament to; the Narmada dam, her support for an independent Kashmir, the US invasion of Afghanistan, campaigning for Adivasi land rights in Kerala and her criticism of prime minister Modi's ascension to power, as some examples. The novel made the longlist for the Man Booker Prize 2017.

Other developments

In addition to an expanding catalogue of Indian Chick Lit and crime fiction, there has been a proliferation of 'popular' mythology-inspired fiction which rides on the back of the success of Amish Tripathi's 'Shiva Trilogy': *The Immortals of Meluha* (2010), *The Secret of the Nagas* (2011) and *The Oath of the Vayuputras* (2013) (see Dawson Varughese 2016). These novels retail at around ₹299 (around £3.00–£3.50) and like Amish's works, appear in many Indian languages. Since 2015, there has been an increasing interest in Indian speculative fiction which moves beyond the now established 'mythology-inspired' fiction, not least because it is typically more 'literary' in style. These novels include Vikram Balagopal's *Savage Blue* (2016), Tashan Mehta's *The Liar's Weave* (2017), Prayaag Akbar's *Leila* (2017), Anil Menon's *Half of What I Say* (2015) and Manjula Padmanabhan's *The Island of Lost Girls* (2015) – a sequel to the feminist dystopia introduced in her 2008 novel *Escape*.

Conclusions

This chapter has considered 'diaspora', 'transnational' Indian authors of Indian literary fiction in English as well as Indian authors who have lived most or all their life in India. I have suggested four topics or themes that have trended across this body of writing since the early 2000s, and thus the chapter has attempted to show how 'Indian' authors have engaged with ideas, amongst others, of the immigrant experience, economic liberalisation, the role of and the female experience in 'New India', as well as political events of both the post-millennial years and earlier ones in India's modern history. I have suggested that literary festival activity and a more buoyant domestic publishing scene are responsible for transforming both the identity of Indian fiction in English and the dynamics of its distribution patterns. That is not to say that the world literary space is an equal playfield; as Pascale Casanova reminds us, an unevenness in this publishing domain should be expected:

> Autonomy is nonetheless a fundamental aspect of world literary space. The most independent territories of the literary world are able to state their own law, to lay down the specific standards and principles applied by their internal hierarchies, and to evaluate works and pronounce judgments without regard for political and national divisions.
>
> (2007: 86)

Indian fiction in English, within India at least, is challenging the orthodoxy Casanova writes of (when we think of 'the most independent territories of the literary world' as those in the West), not only through increased literary activity in publishing and by way of literature festivals but also through the content of some recent Indian literary fiction in English. The narratives of Anil Menon's, Deepti Kapoor's, Manu Joseph's, Omair Ahmad's and Meena Kandasamy's post-millennial Indian fiction in English in particular, challenge an established (and arguably erstwhile) view of the identity of Indian 'postcolonial' literature. These authors' novels move beyond the tropes of Indian postcolonial narratives that have been identified by humanities scholars in the West in particular (see Dawson Varughese 2012); instead, these novels story Indian experience (in all its variety) more through Indian paradigms, philosophies and lived encounters (often of the post-millennial moment).

The discussion of a range of authors here makes clear that some novelists continue to foster the idea of India as 'Other' through an exoticised imaginary, playing to certain stereotypes that have been established through earlier canons of Indian writing in English. The current Indian literary scene in English is in flux, however, and it is with an eagerness and fervour that the new writing produced from both within India and outside of India *about* India continues to shape what will become more steadfastly, the post-millennial canon of Indian literary fiction in English.

Works cited

Adiga, A. (2016) *Selection Day*, London: Picador.
—— (2011) *Last Man in Tower*, London: Atlantic Books.
—— (2008) *The White Tiger*, London: Atlantic Books, New Delhi: HarperCollins India.
Ahmad, O. (2010) *Jimmy the Terrorist*, New Delhi: Hamish Hamilton, Penguin Books India.
—— (2008) *The Storyteller's Tale*, New Delhi: Penguin Books India.
Arudpragasam, A. (2016) *The Story of a Brief Marriage*, New York: Flatiron Books.
Banerjee Divakaruni, C. (2008) *The Palace of Illusions*, New York: Picador.
—— (2002) *The Vine of Desire*, London: Abacus.
—— (1999) *Sister of My Heart*, Hyderabad: Orient Black Swan.
Casanova, P. (2007) *The World Republic of Letters* (translated by M.B. Debevoise), Cambridge, USA, London, UK: Harvard University Press.
Chandra, V. (2007) *Sacred Games*, London: Faber and Faber.
—— (1997) *Love and Longing in Bombay*, London: Faber and Faber.
Dawson Varughese, E. (2016) *Genre Fiction of New India: Post-Millennial Receptions of 'Weird' Narratives*, London, New Delhi: Routledge.

—— (2013) *Reading New India: Post-Millennial Indian Fiction in English*, London: Bloomsbury.

—— (2012) *Beyond the Postcolonial: World Englishes Literature*, Basingstoke, England: Palgrave Macmillan.

Joseph, A. (2016) *The Living*, London: Fourth Estate.

—— (2012) *Another Country*, London: Fourth Estate.

—— (2010) *Saraswati Park*, London: Fourth Estate.

Joseph, M. (2010) *Serious Men*, Noida: HarperCollins India.

Kandasamy, M. (2017) *When I Hit You: Or, a Portrait of the Writer as a Young Wife*, London: Atlantic Books.

—— (2014) *The Gypsy Goddess*, London: Atlantic Books.

Kapoor, D. (2014) *A Bad Character*, London: Jonathan Cape.

Kapur, M. (2011) *Custody*, London: Faber and Faber.

—— (2008) *The Immigrant*, New Delhi: Random House.

—— (2006) *Home*, New Delhi: Random House.

—— (2003) *A Married Woman*, New Delhi: Roli Books, IndiaInk.

—— (1998) *Difficult Daughters*, New Delhi: Penguin India.

Khair, T. (2011) 'The Folded Earth, By Anuradha Roy', *Independent*, 18 February.

Lahiri, J. (2013) *The Lowland*, New York: Alfred A. Knopf, Random House.

—— (2008) *Unaccustomed Earth*, New York: Alfred A. Knopf.

—— (2003) *The Namesake*, Boston, New York: Houghton Mifflin Harcourt.

—— (1999) *Interpreter of Maladies*, Boston, New York: Houghton Mifflin Harcourt.

Menon, A. (2015) *Half of What I Say*, New Delhi: Bloomsbury India.

Mukherjee, B. (2011) *Miss New India*, Boston, New York: Houghton Mifflin Harcourt.

—— (2004) *The Tree Bride*, New York: Theia.

—— (2002) *Desirable Daughters*, New York: Hyperion.

Mukherjee, N. (2014) *The Lives of Others*, London: Chatto and Windus.

—— (2010) *A Life Apart*, London: Corsair/Constable and Robinson.

Narayanan, P. (2012) *What Are You Reading? The World Market and Indian Literary Production*, London, New York, New Delhi: Routledge.

Roy, A. (2015) *Sleeping On Jupiter*, London: MacLehose Press.

Suri, M. (2013) *The City of Devi: A Novel*, New York: W. W. Norton and Company.

—— (2008) *The Age of Shiva*, New York: W. W. Norton and Company.

—— (2001) *The Death of Vishnu*, New York: W. W. Norton and Company.

Thayil, J. (2017) *The Book of Chocolate Saints*, New Delhi: Aleph Book Company.

—— (2012) *Narcopolis*, London: Faber and Faber.

Tripathi, A. (2013) *The Oath of the Vayuputras*, Chennai: Westland, Ltd.

—— (2011) *The Secret of the Nagas*, Chennai: Westland, Ltd.

—— (2010) *The Immortals of Meluha*, Chennai: Westland, Ltd.

Usha, K. R. (2010) *Monkey-Man*, New Delhi: Penguin India.

17

NORTHERN IRISH FICTION

Caroline Magennis

The period following the Good Friday Agreement (1998) has seen a marked increase in fiction, particularly collections of short stories, by women. This writing extends and develops the tradition of Northern Irish women's writing which, since the inception of the state, has offered rich and varied engagement with literary form and subject matter. Women have offered a diverse array of perspectives on politics inside and outside the home. They have written from a variety of political stances: feminist and socialist as well across traditional ethno-sectarian divides. They have dealt with the subject matter of the Troubles directly, but also engaged with themes of reproductive rights, sexuality, mental health and the welfare of children and the elderly. Since partition, Northern Irish women have written crime fiction, romance, science fiction, magical realism and in a host of other genres. There does appear to be, however, in the twenty-first century, an unprecedented energy, vigour and sense of community among these writers, particularly encouraged by both the organisation Women Aloud NI and the writer and broadcaster Sinéad Gleeson. In 2015, Gleeson edited *The Long Gaze Back*, an award-winning anthology of Irish women's short stories which featured several stories by Northern women. Following its publication and attendant public events, there was an appetite for more stories from women from the North, and Gleeson published *The Glass Shore: Short Stories by Women Writers from the North of Ireland* in 2016. This was the first significant collection since *The Female Line: An Anthology of Northern Irish Women Writers* (1985), which was reissued with a new preface as an e-book in 2016.

In addition to the stories in this anthology, there have been an increased amount of full collections in recent years, including Jan Carson's *Children's Children* (2016), Roisin O'Donnell's *Wild Quiet* (2016), Lucy Caldwell's *Multitudes* (2016), Bernie McGill's *Sleepwalkers* (2013) and Rosemary Jenkinson's *Aphrodite's Kiss* (2016). While these authors demonstrate a breadth of techniques and subject matter, generally this fiction shows a thematic interest in the place of intimate encounters in contemporary Northern Ireland. These authors also playfully engage with the fictional challenges of representing moments of intimacy. This is particularly evident in the more contemporary stories from *The Glass Shore* (Bernie McGill, Tara West, Jan Carson, Lucy Caldwell and Roisin O'Donnell), which reveal different facets of intimacy. Collectively, these stories represent what Bernie McGill terms in her short story 'acts of casual intimacy'. Northern Ireland plays a diverse role in these narratives: some represent continuing social constraints that are a legacy of the past and others deal with the fraught question of home. Generally, however, the Troubles are not the driving narrative catalyst. They demonstrate some of the new ways in which we might begin to represent intimate life in Northern Irish culture and how this is informed by formal and aesthetic influences from within and without this context. This chapter will argue that the intimate can be a transformative force in fiction and this is most acute in Northern Irish writing.

This concern is not specific to Northern Irish literature as, in recent years, approaches to contemporary fiction have traced the affective economies of what Jennifer Cooke calls 'intimate reading encounters' (2013: 3). The concept of intimacy has a broad application, and intimate life can be constructed, experienced and represented in a variety of ways. It can be euphemism which covers a range of ambiguous acts and is often used to insinuate sexual relationships: essentially, it can be way of talking about that which is the hidden. This imperative is particularly keen in fiction grappling with a 'post'-conflict past. Within the stories under consideration, truths unspoken feature heavily and the inability to fully articulate plays a role in several. An intimate is a confidant, with whom you make sense of your personal life by setting it out into a narrative, and this process is both mirrored in and complicated by the act of writing fiction. To intimate to someone can also mean to tell them part of a possibly sensitive story: intimate as a verb is often followed by a 'might' or a 'should', indicating a state of affairs that is not quite ready to be fully shown. This ambivalence is also a strong characteristic of these stories. According to Lauren Berlant, intimacy 'builds worlds; it creates spaces and usurps places meant for other kinds of relation' (1998: 282). With the Northern Irish context, a turn to the intimate could be read as fundamentally apolitical, as a deliberate turning away from the Troubles, but this ignores the complex relationship of the personal to the political. The 'public' politics of sectarian conflict and the 'private' politics of intimacy is a binary that cannot be sustained. In intimacy, we find the interaction of the public knowledge of telling or writing and the private realm of our own hidden knowledge. Intimacy is a way of knowing which can only occur through an exchange. Fiction, like intimacy, is an act of storytelling that relies on mutual intelligibility. We often learn the culturally appropriate behaviours for our intimate encounters through what we have seen and read but also, as Cooke points out, the 'ways we write and the forms in which we choose to write about our most intimate states – such as love or mourning – are capable of altering our conceptions of them' (2013: 12). When we write intimacy into being, whether as authors or critics, we are engaged in a process of reinscribing and renegotiating our relationships.

Intimacy in literature, then, lives at the intersection between our private and social worlds, and it does not just represent a sanctuary from the external world:

> This view of 'a life' that unfolds intact within the intimate sphere represses, of course, another fact about it: the unavoidable troubles, the distractions and disruptions that make things turn out in unpredicted scenarios [. . .] moral dramas of estrangement and betrayal, along with terrible spectacles of neglect and violence even where desire, perhaps, endures.
>
> (1998: 281)

Now, the problems of intimacy that Berlant hints at here are varied, and are expanded upon in the special issue that follows this introduction. There is often disappointment due to discordance between scripts of intimacy: a partner who does not perform their affection in the manner we want. Intimacy can be a disruptive force on a continuum – from the smaller ruptures of awkward lovemaking to the larger problems of abuse and violence meted out by a trusted partner or family member. Indeed, the spectre of what is called intimate partner violence surely hangs over any idealisation of home and hearth. In the stories we will see unwanted sexual encounters and difficult decisions but domestic violence and sexual abuse is not quite the narrative catalyst that it has been in earlier Northern Irish women's fiction (Magennis 2019). The consideration of the intimate offers a reverse exceptionalism when discussing Northern Irish culture. Bodies are not necessarily encoded with the legacy of violent civil conflict when a lover runs their fingertips up your back or a grandparent hugs you with happy tears in their eyes: acts of intimacy that occur throughout the world occur in Northern Ireland. But, as these acts are framed within narratives set in Northern Ireland, the representational legacy of violence does influence the context in which they are encountered and read. A political engagement is expected of texts from countries with a recent history of violent conflict, so when these authors turn to the intimate, critical readers often seek to extrapolate the public. This is understandable as the private and the public have been tied to each other in complex, ambiguous ways in Northern Irish culture. For example, Adam Hanna argues that the house, coded as private, take up a remarkably public role in the work of poets from the North:

> dwelling places were such frequent targets of violence during the years of the Troubles, and that they so often still carry symbols that indicate the political sympathies of their inhabitants, indicates that in a landscape where the operations of national power have left contentious legacies, the results of which are apprehended every day, private dwellings take on significances that are inescapably public and political in nature.
>
> (2015: 6)

While the project of discussing the intimate is about more than just home (as Berlant and Warner remind us in 'Sex in Public'), Hanna's comment says a lot about the cultural resonances that hang about the Northern Irish intimate. These resonances appear in these stories in both playful and haunted ways: it is clear that the political landscape has shifted and this has affected the representation of Northern Irish life, but equally the legacy of violence appears in complex, indirect ways.

The short story is ideally suited to representing the texture of intimacy in this ambiguous, tentatively 'post'-conflict landscape. Short stories are by their nature elliptical and therefore apposite to the playful, hidden resonances of the intimate. They allow us a temporary, intense intimacy with a subject which may feel prurient in another setting. Jennifer Cooke notes that 'the short story is able to capture the specificity of a particular moment or encounter' (2013: 12). Formally, the short story is suited to considering what Virginia Woolf termed (repeatedly in *Mrs Dalloway*) a 'moment'. Heather Ingman notes that this modernist inheritance is particularly vivid in this form as the 'short story, perhaps more than any other form, has been associated with modernity, both in terms of experimentation and theme' (Ingman 2009: 2). This lineage of modernism on Northern Irish women's writing is evident in both the way it uses sensuality to trouble existing scripts but also in the presence of epiphanic moments which are arrived at via intimacy. Abbie Garrington states that 'the orientation towards the haptic in the literature of the Modernist period' and that it is 'intimately connected to the constitution of the self, and it is so by virtue of its very intimacy, its operation on the carnal border between self and world' (2015: 17). The short story has a history as a place ripe for rewriting established scripts. It is a form that calls to mind the epiphanies of both Joyce's *Dubliners* and Katherine Mansfield's *The Garden Party*, as well as the prominent Irish short story tradition which includes Mary Lavin, William Carleton, Sean O'Faolain and Maeve Brennan. It is not surprising, then, that Northern Irish women have embraced the short story in recent years given its ties to both a modernist reimagining of relationships and sexuality but also has a long tradition in the Irish canon. Writing about the Irish context, Ingman notes that in the 'contemporary period, the extraordinary flowering of short stories by women writers has as yet received little critical attention' (2009: 10). This critical lacunae is arguably magnified in the Northern Irish context, whose writers have been criticised for falling into the realist mode and not providing innovative literary responses to the conflict (Patten 1996). Despite this, women's writing North and South, has taken on the challenges of twenty-first century writing and form to produce work which has been consistently challenging and innovative. The short story functions as a way in for newer writers given Northern Irish women's nascent position in the literary canon (Pryce, n.d.): it is easier to break through the anxiety of authorship in a shorter form and also to offer new, experimental visions.

However, the five most contemporary stories in *The Glass Shore* (McGill, West, Carson, Caldwell and O'Donnell) collectively signify an interesting new movement in Northern Irish women's writing and a complex engagement with the pleasures and problems of the intimate. Bernie McGill's story, 'The Cure for Too Much Feeling', begins with a protagonist suffering from barely perceptible physical ailments: 'With Rita it had begun gently, a slight quiver in the hand, acid in her stomach' (2016: 317). When she receives a clean bill of health from her doctor, the realisation dawns on her that her symptoms are psychosomatic and caused by 'a new developed susceptibility to other people's misery' (2016: 318). When she listens to tales of misfortunes she 'experiences a twinge of pain in her chest, a sensation like a growing knot at the back of her throat' (2016: 317). Strangers' intimacies with her lead to a pain she herself can barely speak of. The narrative then brings us back to an intimate encounter from her girlhood: sex with a married father when she was still at school. This moment has ambiguous consent at best ('She didn't remember agreeing to anything, but she hadn't wanted to appear ungrateful' [2016: 318]) and has no pleasure for Rita. Following it, and the baby she gives up for adoption, she withdraws from the realm of the intimate, choosing a chaste life with her older relative and studiously avoiding having a partner. She develops strategies to avoid intimacy, drinking single-serving cans of gin and tonic drank at home rather than braving the loquacious properties of the pub fire. She feels aghast that she can no longer 'nibble at tragedy' (2016: 319) in the way she has done before. She can no longer bear having an intimacy with other people's misery. Watching reports of the refugee crisis, she 'was near-crippled by the look in the children's dark eyes, the sorrow of it seeping into her' (2016: 320).

When she meets with the daughter that she gave up for adoption, their contact is brisk and business-like and it seems like her 'careful life' (2016: 325) will go on undisturbed until she has a chance encounter on a rainy day in Botanic Gardens. Sheltering from a storm, she finds herself firstly embarrassed by explicit art and finally in the throes of a deeply intimate encounter with an artwork. This ekphrastic moment at a painting, 'Washing Mother's Hair', takes Rita aback. It does not aggravate her symptoms as earlier emotional encounters have but rather she is fascinated by 'their physical closeness in the cramped room, the daughter's right hand, pouring water, her left hand outstretched, like a benediction' (2016: 324). This moment offers her a glimpse at something akin to the divine: 'It seemed to Rita that if she could stand there for long enough, if they would let her stay, if the purple-shirted attendant would put out the lights and lock up the gallery and go home and leave her there, that she might witness a quiet miracle' (2016: 324). In front of this painting she has a quiet, powerful revelation about what a full, vulnerable life might look like: 'And it seemed to Rita that she would be privy to the sort of act of casual intimacy that passes unannounced in homes everywhere where people are tired or hurting or weak and still going about the everyday business of caring for one another and of being loved' (2016: 325). In withdrawing from human contact, Rita has removed herself from the variety of encounters which constitute intimate life. McGill seems to be suggesting in this story that intimacy is a fundamental part of how we connect and experience the world. She articulates this on behalf of women who have issues expressing pleasure after a traumatic encounter and raises the question of what happens to those who cannot expend their intimate energies. This speaks to Berlant's provocation: 'What happens to the energy of attachment when it has no designated place? To the glances, gestures, encounters, collaborations, or fantasies that have no canon?' (1998: 285).

Tara West's story 'The Speaking and the Dead' is about a woman, Elaine, who turns to a stage psychic medium after the suicide of her son, who hung himself with an extension cord in the family home. The act of mediumship reveals something important: it is easy to fake surface intimate but ultimately possible to fake real intimacy. Levels of recognition. This is a story replete with the problems of intimacy: Elaine and her partner are trying to negotiate their relationship after their son's death and Elaine has an uneasy relationship with her friends. While they share a love of vodka in their handbags and crying at The X-Factor it is clear through snippy exchanges that this is not a friendship of true intimates: 'Over years their friendship had grown into an unspoken completion, fought in the arenas of weight, food, poverty, victimhood and whatever else could be construed' (328). The Belfast medium, Jolene, essentially demonstrates short cuts to faking intimacy as she makes broad statements about the deceased to maximised identification. For example, she talks about a woman's mother being a 'neat freak' who left her 'a piece of jewellery' (2016: 332) and had an important man in her life. This fakery is undercut as Elaine's friend insists on enthusiastic participation: 'By the time the interval comes, Jacqui has claimed Lorraine, a painter and decorator named Phil and a pipe-smoking man known as Lorenzo' (2016: 334).

West's control of the narrative is powerful: against the knockabout humour of the medium is Elaine's genuine, plaintive desire to have some communication with her son. As the scene rages on stage, she wonders: 'What happened, Matt? Where did you go?' (2016: 335). Elaine has desperately sought connection with her son: 'She has seen every kind of medium: amateurs in the living rooms, stars in big hotels, Romany in fairground tents and squinty oddballs over Skype' (2016: 329). We then get a glimpse into the pain of living with a loved one with suicidal impulses as Elaine tries to make sense of his behaviour, to read the narrative, but she ultimately fails to know his motivations. She tells us 'When he wasn't surly and silent, he was in a rage, he screamed at Elaine and Paul, always stayed in his room' (2016: 336). Her realisation during Jolene's act is simple, and powerful, and speaks to the pain of loss: 'Matt has gone to emptiness, is emptiness and her desperation would serve as amusement for everybody else. She always hesitated because she never really believed he would come. She just can't let go of the hope' (2016: 338). At the end of the story, Elaine comes home, to the smell of 'booze breath and dog farts' (2016: 339) as her husband and dog sleep on the sofa. Her final act in the story is one of tenderness, despite her complaints about her husband: 'Paul's snoring has stopped and his stomach rises and falls; a slow, familiar rhythm [. . .] She tucks her fingers around his' (2016: 339). This act, of holding hands on the sofa makes the point that intimacy can exist in a simple act, but also can endure the desperately complicated act of grieving for a son.

'Settling' by Jan Carson, appears at first to be a traditional emigrant narrative of a Northern Irish couple who move to England for work. However, soon we see that the story has a complex engagement with intimacy of the past and present. Often, their relationship has false starts and failures to connect: 'It could have been the perfect moment to make love, but we hadn't the curtains up yet and the neighbours could see right into our room from their kitchen' (2016: 341). Her gruff father, perfunctory as he helps them move, contributes to this uneasy atmosphere as he piles 'our furniture up on the pavement so passers-by could see all our belongings, even our toilet brush and the box marked "underwear"' (2016: 343). This squeamishness extends to Matt, who 'has a horror of laundrettes. He doesn't want anyone seeing the stains we make' (2016: 345). He seeks to maintain and strengthen the imagined boundaries between public and private. Carson's narrative, then, seeks to really destabilise these by introducing an ethereal figure: 'My grandmother is in the wardrobe, sitting on a deckchair. I think she is reading the Belfast Telegraph. It is very hard to tell in the dark' (2016: 345). Typically of Carson's fiction, then, the narrative is careful not to give too much away about this otherworldly character, who is depicted in a matter-of-fact way and does not have the eerie qualities of a traditional haunting. It is, however, the narrator who becomes the spectre as she looks in the mirror: 'Here is my white face, hanging like a ghost. I haunt myself, and the shock of this makes me step back sharply, clawing my heel on a suitcase' (2016: 345). She describes the intimacy with her grandmother as being like 'coming across your own face, reflected in a window' and 'on-your-own-easy' (2016: 347). She imagines the tea and thick slices of toasted veda bread that she will eat with her grandmother while they discuss who has died. When she tries to tell her Grandmother she loves her the old lady silences her, 'My family does not do sentimentality' (2016: 348). In the story, the city is posited as the opposite of this intimacy, and while Matt embraces this distance, our narrator codes it as alienation. She is troubled by the contrast: 'Everything is quick and straight and sure of its own skin. It is not a place for grandmothers or any other truths unseen' (2016: 349). Matt seeks for their social circle to shrink and their visits home to become less frequent. She has internalised the idea that to be desirous of intimacy is a personal failing: 'I can't be only looking forwards. This is a form of weakness and I am ashamed' (2016: 351). The more her partner detaches, the more vivid the image of her grandmother becomes: 'In the morning she may be gone or we may drink tea together and say it does not taste the same without a teapot. Either way, I will be splitting in two' (2016: 352). This sensation, of 'splitting' contrasts with the 'Settling' of the title of the story: suggesting that beneath the compromised comfort of settling (whether into or for something) masks a divided self. This wrenching is unspoken, suggesting that the narrator's intimacy with her partner has been fractured by her silent disquiet.

Lucy Caldwell's poignant short story, 'Mayday', centres on a Northern Irish student who takes medication to procure an abortion. Due to the complex legal situation around terminations, she must buy them online and take them without medical supervision or advice, and Caldwell's story takes place over the course of the pills taking action. The close is her bleed. The title, Mayday, of course refers to not just the emergency distress signal but also the holiday of Spring, traditionally a time of new beginnings. Her distress is not about the abortion, but about a state which prohibits her from the same rights as other women in the United Kingdom. Our narrator's mind wanders between abject worry about the legal and medical consequences of her decision and reminisces about her childhood. It is striking that she returns to moments of her childhood infused with religion, imagining her teenage cross-community music group and remembering an embarrassing incident where she chewed a communion wafer. This act, of something which sticks in the throat is mirrored in the moments where the truth remains unspeakable. She 'hasn't thought of it for years, but it surfaces now' as she remembers the details of the 'gules of light in the stained glass windows of the Catholic church' (2016: 356). In Northern Ireland, the abortion taboo is maintained by people on both sides of the religious divide, but the Catholic Church has been particularly active in pressing the Attorney General to prosecute cases (Sherwood 2017) and back anti-Abortion candidates (McDonald 2017) in recent elections.

Her youth is portrayed as idyllic in places ('this time of year, these lingering days and pale, light skies') (360), but also riven with the taboos of Northern Irish society. She is ashamed when, in a school debate, a class mate pulls out pictures of foetuses and she does not stand against the popular mood. Similarly, she brings to mind the image of her and her sister, proud of their new haircuts, who are sternly chastised by a Reverend in their grandmother's house: 'Vanity in young ladies is a terrible thing to behold, for it takes deep root, and what grows crooked cannot be straightened' (2016: 361). Against this youthful shame, is set her feminist mother, who instils in her daughter pro-choice values: 'Her mum wouldn't rage of her, or weep like mothers do in films. Her mum would be pragmatic, calm: her mum would handle it all. Why hasn't she told her mum?' (2016: 358). But that sense still lingers that she is doing something wrong, that she is transgressing. This is an intimacy she cannot speak: that will be hidden and repressed. Despite a growing support for the procedure in Northern Ireland, the reproductive rights anathema is so strong that she cannot voice her experience. Caldwell paints a complex emotional picture where intimacy in the present is in dialogue with intimacy of the past. She has been given a narrative for how this most intimate of scenarios will play out: only she has this kind of knowledge now: 'She waits for the guilt to start, the regret, but it doesn't. What does she feel? She tests out emotions' (2016: 362). The reality of modern dating is featured in the narrative: the man she slept with has not returned her texts and, after an awkward meeting, has not called as he promised. Much of the intimacy of this story is mediated via technology: from this missed connection to her mother's updates from her grandmother's hospital bed.

Caldwell's narrator wryly discusses her academic course of study, which is heavy with the religious wars of the seventeenth century. Her eyes fall on a poem in her Norton Anthology, 'The Proper New Ballad', by Bishop Richard Corbet and panics as she reads of 'Sluts. Illegitimate children. Changelings, and fairies to blame them upon. Nothing feels neutral any more, she thinks. It never will again' (2016: 357). It is made clear, however, that she quickly shakes herself out of this melancholic script. Despite the childhood memories of guilty and shame, she never questions her decision, and feels an 'overwhelming, incredible sense of relief: that she is doing the right thing' (2016: 363). She feels 'trickling feeling between her thighs will make her think of her first ever period, of climbing into her mother's lap and feeling too big to be there, sobbing' (2016: 363). It is striking that this most adult of decisions makes our protagonist consistently reconsider her childhood and the contrast between her mother's nurturing and the shame-filled culture outside the safe walls of home. The whole story, in effect, is about the difficult of constructing your bodily autonomy against the available narrative for Northern Irish women. It is clear that she feels no shame or regret, but also has to contend with the legacy of these sort of decisions. As a result, the story moves between past and present, constructing a dynamic relationship between the public prohibitions of Northern Ireland's anti-choice laws and this young woman's private decision.

Roisin O'Donnell's 'The Seventh Man', is a contemporary re-telling of the myth of the Hag of Beare who 'had her youth seven times over' as a love story. O'Donnell casts her a succubus-like seductress who was able to rework herself depending on her target: 'I have metamorphosed so often to suit each husband's fantasy, I no longer know which version of myself is real' (2016: 367). After her utilitarian relationships, this one gets to the nub of intimacy: 'I feel it in my pores; the crinkling of my humanity. With the six others it was never like this' (365). She decides to turn to modern technology to facilitate her next relationship: 'I liked the sound of Tinder. It sounded like timber, things being chopped and tossed onto the fire. Smouldering, sparking, cracking. An excellent start to a marriage' (2016: 371). She expects to have the same sort of relationship as she has had previously but her final beau, however, disarms her with everyday intimacy: 'I remember the sincerity with which he went about preparing dinner for me' (2016: 371). In this supernatural tale, the everyday takes on a quality almost more magical than her rejuvenating body. Intimacy is not weakness here, as it was coded by Carson's narrator, but rather it is strength: 'What if I could summon the lifeblood of a captured Spaniard, the breath of an Ulster aristocrat, the pulse of a soldier caught between wars?' (2016: 373). Our narrator gained power from her intimacies with men in a literal way: with every kiss she grew stronger until, finally, she acts as a repository of her own sensual history. She sacrifices this history of faked intimacies for this real connection, and as she prepares to give this up so he can live, she remembers the moments, the acts of casual intimacy that bound them to each other:

And he won't remember sitting in a Mexican restaurant on a Cork side street, a hot city breeze drifting through the open shutters, and a comfortable quiet swishing between us like a secret. He won't remember the first night we lay together and how we stumbled into the shower afterwards, weak-kneed, drenched, leaving steamed-up love notes in the bathroom mirror.

(2016: 374)

The stories of *The Glass Shore* cumulatively represent an attempt to find new ways of writing about intimacy in Northern Ireland. They deal with subject matter that is outside of the representational norms for Northern Irish fiction. But they are also all about a certain kind of rootedness and the ways in which we find ourselves at home. Back to Berlant, who tells us that:

Rethinking intimacy calls out not only for redescription but for transformative analyses of the rhetorical and material conditions that enable hegemonic fantasies to thrive in the minds and on the bodies of subjects while, at the same time, attachments are developing that might redirect the different routes taken by history and biography.

(1998: 286)

Arguably, there is no more urgent cultural landscape in which the intimate needs to be reimagined than Northern Ireland. The hegemonic fantasy of Ulster heteropatriarchy can be contrasted with the bodies and subjects not just in *The Glass Shore*, but across contemporary Northern Irish women's fiction. These authors are engaged in both subtle and overt ways of dismantling accepted ways of living, drawing out those attachments which showcase the limitations, awkwardness and joy of intimacy. All of these stories place relationships with others at their core, rather than the violent political history of Northern Ireland. But equally, they do not fetishise these relationships, or turn inwards. All of these stories involve interplay between our private scripts of intimacy and the public structures they inhabit to offer glimpses into a life which will hopefully lead to more diverse fictions of Northern Irish intimacy.

Works cited

Berlant, L. (1998). 'Intimacy: A Special Issue'. *Critical Inquiry*, 24(2), 281–288.
Berlant, L. and Warner, M. (1998). 'Sex in Public'. *Critical Inquiry*, 24(2), 547–566.
Caldwell, L. (2016). 'Mayday'. In: Gleeson, S. ed. *The Glass Shore*. Dublin: New Island, 355–365.
Carson, J. (2016). 'Settling'. In: Gleeson, S. ed. *The Glass Shore*. Dublin: New Island, 341–354.
Cooke, J. (2013). *Scenes of Intimacy*. London: Bloomsbury.
Garrington, A. (2015). *Haptic Modernism*. Edinburgh: Edinburgh University Press.
Gleeson, S. ed. (2015). *The Glass Shore*. Dublin: New Island.
Hanna, A. (2015). *Northern Irish Poetry and Domestic Space*. 1st ed. Basingstoke: Palgrave Macmillan.
Hooley, R. ed. (1985). *The Female Line*. Belfast: Northern Ireland Women's Rights Movement.
Ingman, H. (2009). *A History of the Irish Short Story*. Cambridge: Cambridge University Press.
Jenkinson, R. (2016). *Aphrodite's Kiss and Further Stories*. Belfast: Whittrick Press.
Magennis, C. (2019). 'Sex and Violence in Northern Irish Women's Fiction'. In: Harte, L. ed. *The Handbook of Modern Irish Fiction*. Oxford: Oxford University Press, np.
McDonald, H. (2017). 'Catholic Bishops Back Anti-Abortion Candidates in Northern Ireland Vote'. *The Guardian*. Available at: www.theguardian.com/world/2016/apr/28/catholic-bishops-back-anti-abortion-candidates-in-northern-ireland-vote [Accessed 9 May 2017].
McGill, B. (2016). 'The Cure for Too Much Feeling'. In: Gleeson, S. ed. *The Glass Shore*. Dublin: New Island, 317–326.
——— (2013). *Sleepwalkers*. Belfast: Whittrick.
O'Donnell, R. (2016). 'The Seventh Man'. In: Gleeson, S. ed. *The Glass Shore*. Dublin: New Island, 365–374.

Patten, E. (1996). 'Women and Fiction 1985–1990'. In: Dawe, G. and Williams, J. eds. *Krino 1986–1996: An Anthology of Modern Irish Writing*. Dublin: Gill & MacMillan, 8–16.

Pryce, A. (n.d.). *Ambiguous Silences? Women in Anthologies of Contemporary Northern Irish Poetry*. [online] Troubles Archive. Available at: www.troublesarchive.com/resources/ambiguous_silences.pdf [Accessed 4 April. 2017].

Sherwood, H. (2017). 'Catholic Church in Northern Ireland Pushes against Easing of Abortion Law'. *The Guardian*. Available at: www.theguardian.com/world/2016/jan/07/abortion-law-catholic-church-northern-ireland-opposing-high-court-ruling [Accessed 9 May 2017].

West, T. (2016). 'The Speaking and the Dead'. 'The Cure for Too Much Feeling'. In: Gleeson, S. ed. *The Glass Shore*. Dublin: New Island, 327–340.

18

ANIMALS

Danielle Sands

In *Lincoln in the Bardo* (2017), George Saunders presents a grotesque tableau of a Victorian Christmas, with Jane Ellis, 'a beautiful child in white, with a long rope of hair hanging down my [her] back,' gazing curiously into a butcher's shop, its festive display consisting of 'a marvellous canopy of carcasses: deer with the entrails pulled up and out and wired to the outside of the bodies like tremendous bright-red garlands; pheasants and drakes hung head-down, wings spread by use of felt-covered wires.' To assuage a burgeoning tantrum, Ellis's father buys her a deer carcass which he straps to the carriage; they drive on with 'the limp deer dribbling behind its thin blood-trail' (Saunders 2017: 76) across the beautiful countryside. Tempting as it is to read this incident as reassuring evidence of our emergence from a barbaric past, more challengingly, it highlights the ongoing human tendency to overlook nonhuman suffering and reminds us of the complexities of cross-species relations, which are alternately sublime and horrific, playful and violent.

Whilst historically and culturally determined, such interactions, Donna Haraway argues, can never wholly escape 'relations of use' (Haraway 2008: 76); to pretend otherwise, endorsing a 'purity politics' (Shotwell 2016: 7), is, Alexis Shotwell contends, to deny the practical and ideological stakes of cross-species relations. The challenge, so effectively illustrated by Jane Ellis' blinkered, hyperbolic nostalgia in Saunders' novel, is to perceive and acknowledge one's own complicity in these relationships of 'significant otherness' (Haraway 2003: 16). In this chapter, I examine the relationship between representations of animals in contemporary fiction and the diverse theoretical perspectives which emerged through the development of Animal Studies in the 2000s and 2010s. Focusing on approaches which explore cross-species kinship, I address issues such as embodiment, vulnerability and sentience, before turning to that which is usually excluded from such kinship: the insect. Operating at the 'edges of sentience' (Loo and Sellbach 2015: 80) and usually marking the limits of compassion, I argue that these tiny creatures offer the potential for a transformation of our understanding of empathy, attentiveness and kinship.

For contemporary novelists and thinkers, complicity with cross-species dominance or violence is problematised by cross-species resemblances; most notably, as Jacques Derrida writes, we share the 'finitude of life' (Derrida 2008: 28) with all living creatures. Whilst philosophy has long presupposed that only the human is meaningfully aware of its mortality, that the existential orientation of 'Being-towards-death' (Heidegger 1962: 297), is unique to (human) Dasein, this assumption is increasingly being challenged. Faced with a tumour-ridden cat, James Dyer, the protagonist of Andrew Miller's novel *Ingenious Pain*, assesses 'three alternatives: leave it to die; kill it; treat it.' (Miller 1997: 25). Whilst euthanasia is widely perceived as the most humane response to animal suffering, Dyer suspects that each animal's perception of its own life and death is more complex than we imagine; 'should a cat's life be less sweet to it than a man's,' he asks, 'sweet even in sickness, even *in extremis*, more sweet then than ever?' (Miller 1997: 25).

Unsatisfied with the abstract argumentation favoured by Animal Rights discourse in the 1980s, which, philosopher Cora Diamond argued, generated a 'deflection' (Diamond 2003: 13) from embodiment and tended to ignore 'the genesis, quality, context, and significance of particular concerns, interests, worries, sympathies etc.' (Gruen 2015: 11), contemporary Animal Studies has turned its focus to embodied experience. This is exemplified by the work of Lori Gruen who, concerned that 'moral theories might alienate us from possible solutions to moral problems' (Gruen 2015: 14), instead espouses 'entangled empathy' (Gruen 2015: 3), a mode of perception which is rooted in cross-species experience. A critical moment in the transformation of Animal Studies occurred with Jacques Derrida's re-articulation of Jeremy Bentham's 1823 question '[c]an they suffer?' (Bentham cited in Derrida 2008: 27). For Derrida, this question, a reminder of the 'non-power' (Derrida 2008: 28) which ultimately distinguishes mortal beings, invites the conception of a subjectivity (and, ultimately, a politics) which is rooted neither in sovereignty nor human exceptionalism, but in an acknowledgment of the vulnerability intrinsic to embodiment. Recognition of the shared nature of this exposure promises a challenge to the presupposition that '[p]ower over the animal is [. . .] the essence of the human' (Derrida 2008: 93).

That fiction might have an advantage over philosophical argumentation in the articulation of cross-species 'entangled empathy' is illustrated by Yann Martel's depictions of animal vulnerability and suffering in the novels *Life of Pi* and *Beatrice and Virgil*. In the first, protagonist Pi Patel observes a zebra, mortally wounded by a tiger, endure an agonising death:

> The zebra was still alive. I couldn't believe it. It had a two-foot – wide hole in its body, a fistula like a freshly erupted volcano, spewed half-eaten organs glistening in the light or giving off a dull, dry shine, yet, in its strictly essential parts, it continued to pump with life, if weakly. Movement was confined to a tremor in the rear leg and an occasional blinking of the eyes. I was horrified. I had no idea a living being could sustain so much injury and go on living.
>
> (Martel 2003: 128)

Pi offers two accounts of the shipwreck which kills his family: in one, he survives, stranded in a lifeboat alongside animals from his family's zoo; in the other, a gruesome tale of human cruelty and cannibalism, he has human company. In the second account, the zebra is replaced by a sailor, whose excruciating death parallels that of the zebra; 'I couldn't believe a human being could survive so much pain, so much butchery' (Martel 2003: 305), Pi notes. Human and animal suffering are paralleled. Pi and tiger Richard Parker are 'two emaciated mammals, parched and starving' (Martel 2003: 239); the orangutan Orange Juice, like the zebra, a victim of Parker, '[t]o the end [. . .] reminded me [Pi] of us: her eyes expressed fear in such a humanlike way, as did her strained whimpers' (Martel 2003: 131). Pi's two stories vie for the reader's attention, who is tempted to interpret the first as an allegory of the second, a fabulation to distance Pi from the horrors of reality. Ultimately, however, Martel resists allegorical foreclosure; the ending is ambiguous and, like Pi's interrogator Mr Okamoto, the reader is more likely to conclude that '[t]he story with the animals is the better story' (Martel 2003: 317). In its attentiveness to the particularity of suffering, the text never frames either animal suffering as a symbol of human suffering, or an individual's suffering as representative solely of species suffering. Nonetheless, the ingrained anthropocentrism of conventional reading practices is exposed by the critics' partiality towards allegorical readings: 'Readers have to struggle,' critic Sarah E. McFarland notes, 'against the desire to put the human at the center of our interpretations of the novel' (McFarland 2014: 157).

Despite the text's attentiveness to animal suffering, it does not suggest that its abolition is possible; rather it dramatises the irreducible ambiguity of cross-species relations. Trapped on the lifeboat, Pi must kill in order to survive. Whilst there is no ethical quandary, the scene of Pi's kill is harrowing. His catch, a dorado, is 'a magnificent-looking fish, large, fleshy and sleek, with a bulging forehead that speaks of a forceful personality, a very long dorsal fin as proud as a cock's comb' (Martel 2003: 184). Martel's description reminds us that each fish is individual and irreplaceable; in Derrida's terminology, it possesses 'unsubstitutable singularity' (Derrida 2008: 9). Its death-throes are kaleidoscopic: 'Blue, green, red, gold and violet flickered and shimmered neon-like on its surface as it struggled' and Pi's actions are likened to 'beating a rainbow to death' (Martel 2003: 185). There is no condemnation, however, just the acknowledgment of the unfortunate consequences of Pi's actions. Given that we cannot ever fully escape the instrumentalisation of other living beings, Donna Haraway writes, to behave ethically is 'to recognize co-presence in relations of use and therefore to remember that no balance sheet of benefit and cost will suffice' (Haraway 2008: 76).

Underpinning Martel's novels are questions about life: what is it and what makes it valuable? Are some lives more important than others? Following Michel Foucault's identification of a technology of power which addresses 'the specific problems of life and population' (Foucault 1997: 78), we can understand these as biopolitical questions. Although the biopolitical investigations of Foucault and later, Giorgio Agamben, are largely uninterested in animals, Cary Wolfe contends that their unmasking of the human/animal distinction as 'a discursive resource, not a zoological designation' (Wolfe 2013: 10) is a useful tool for exposing the ways in which animal life has been strategically disregarded or denigrated. For Wolfe, the biopolitical context, in which 'we are all always already (potential) "animals" before the law' (Wolfe 2013: 10), offers an opportunity for rethinking cross-species solidarity following the exposure of the arbitrariness of existing species-determined rights.

Like many of their philosophical contemporaries, Wolfe, Haraway and Derrida aim to conceptualise an interpersonal and cross-species interdependency which is necessitated pragmatically, by the perceived failure of state and subjective sovereignty as grounds for social harmony, and scientifically, by increasing evidence that, in Haraway's parlance, '[b]eings do not pre-exist their relatings' (Haraway 2003: 6). Such interdependency, however, presents not only a conceptual challenge, but a political one; how can one advance relationality, Judith Butler asks, whilst safeguarding 'bodily integrity and self-determination'? (Butler 2004: 31). Butler confesses to being theoretically disarmed by this question, but responds with an ethics grounded in vulnerability, in a shared awareness of the 'precarity of life.' Wolfe is troubled that Butler's thinking extends only to 'a common human vulnerability' (Butler 2004: 31) and is grounded in reciprocity and agential subjectivity (Wolfe 2013: 19), however, her biopolitical approach demonstrates the ways in which the defenceless body – both human and animal – is always already socially inscribed. 'The body implies mortality, vulnerability, agency,' she writes, 'the skin and the flesh expose us to the gaze of others, but also to touch, and to violence, and bodies put us at risk of becoming the agency and instrument of all those as well' (Butler 2004: 26).

Such a vulnerability, whilst hazardous, is, for both Butler and Derrida, central to the constitution of a community grounded in compassion rather than competition. Disavowing 'the overly hasty association of agency with personhood' (Wolfe 2013: 20) which persists in Butler, for Derrida such a community is inevitably open across species. He explains:

> Being able to suffer is no longer a power; it is a possibility without power, a possibility of the impossible. Mortality resides there, as the most radical means of thinking the finitude that we share with animals, the mortality that belongs to the very finitude of life, to the experience of compassion [. . .]
>
> (Derrida 2008: 28)

Always attentive to the disavowal of bodily experience in the formation of the philosophical 'corpus' (Derrida 1993: 27), and the displacement of multiple voices and experiences by the disembodied voice of 'reason,' in Derrida's later work he becomes attuned to the prohibition of cross-species kinship and compassion via the philosophical repudiation of embodiment. A similar concern is visible in Elizabeth Costello's self-presentation as 'an animal exhibiting yet not exhibiting [. . .] a wound' (Coetzee 1997: 124), a counter to philosophical disregard of the body, in J.M. Coetzee's *The Lives of Animals*. Costello, Diamond observes, 'sees our reliance on argumentation as a way we may make unavailable to ourselves our own sense of what it is to be a living animal' (Diamond 2003: 8); what follows is not only self-alienation, but a foreclosure of cross-species empathy. This is the inevitable consequence of mistaking one component of the human for its sum; 'reason looks to me suspiciously like the being of human thought,' Costello reveals, 'worse than that, like the being of one tendency in human thought. Reason is the being of a certain spectrum of human thinking' (Coetzee 1997: 67).

Through the figure of Costello, the 'physical performance' (McKay 2010: 71) of the human is defamiliarised and in her we see, like Kafka's humanised ape Red Peter in 'A Report to an Academy,' the fragility of embodied existence and the performance of being human. 'Moral thought gets no grip' (Diamond 2003: 15) in the face of the vertiginous experience of embodiment, posits Diamond, who asserts:

> The awareness we each have of being a living body, 'alive to the world,' carries with it exposure to the bodily sense of vulnerability to death, sheer animal vulnerability, the vulnerability we share with them. This vulnerability is capable of panicking us. To be able to acknowledge it at all, let alone as shared, is wounding; but acknowledging it as shared with other animals, in the presence of what we do to them, is capable not only of panicking one but also of isolating one as Elizabeth Costello is isolated.
>
> (Diamond 2003: 22)

The 'unquestioned acknowledgment that animals can suffer, feel pain, and experience humiliation,' (Donovan 2004: 85) as a sign of shared, cross-species vulnerability places an ethical demand upon the human which precedes or evades rational assessments of animal sentience or cognition. Note, for example, the avowedly 'selfish' (Coetzee 2000: 146) disgraced academic David Lurie, protagonist of Coetzee's novel *Disgrace*, who is bemused to find himself enacting Gruen's 'entangled empathy' (Gruen 2015: 3) by tending, both pre- and post-mortem, to euthanised dogs in an animal shelter. Lurie enacts an ethic of cross-species care – 'he is prepared to take care of them once they are unable, utterly unable, to take care of themselves' (Coetzee 2000: 146) – which, in its attentiveness to the dogs' lived experience, demonstrates the complex relations between embodiment, consciousness and suffering. 'He is convinced,' we are told, 'the dogs know their time has come [. . .] They flatten their ears, they droop their tails, as if they too feel the disgrace of dying: locking their legs, they have to be pulled or pushed or carried over the threshold' (Coetzee

2000: 143). The flawed Lurie demonstrates the necessity of navigating, unschooled, between the poles of heartlessness and sentimentalism (Coetzee 2000: 143), and of attempting, in the absence of God and divinely given human authority, to construct a better world, one in which 'men do not use shovels to beat corpses into a more convenient shape for processing' (Coetzee 2000: 146).

Disgrace is a relatively early provocation, published at the start of Animal Studies' ascendancy, which invites us to ask: 'how do we use literature to think our ethical relation to the animal in a way that responds to the animal's otherness?' (McKay 2010: 69). The persistence of empathy as an interpretive framework for human-animal relations has necessitated a cautious balancing between the recognition of shared qualities and comparable subjugation, and awareness of species difference. This challenge is exemplified by Carol Adams' contention that 'women and animals are similarly positioned in a patriarchal world, as objects rather than subjects' (Adams 1999: 168). Her concept of the 'absent referent' (Adams 1999: 40), rooted in the tendency to view 'another as consumable' (Adams 2015: 14), accounts for the disavowal of certain types of human and nonhuman experience. The formation of the 'absent referent' entails a parallel process for meat animals, who are rendered 'absent through language that renames dead bodies before consumers participate in eating them' (Adams 1999: 40), and for women objectified as sexual objects, for example in the practice of '*body chopping*' (Adams 2015: 74), the visual dismemberment of bodies in the service of selling a product. Whilst the recognition of cross-species fleshiness can be used to undermine human exceptionalism, such as in the observation, by Jim Crace's narrator in *Being Dead* that the novel's deceased protagonists 'were, we are, all flesh, and then we are all meat' (Crace 2000: 12), Adams' work underlines the ways in which human and animal flesh continues to be classified and consumed.

Alert to the commodification of female flesh, Janet Ellis' novel, *The Butcher's Hook*, looks to liberate female protagonist, or 'young veal' (Ellis 2016: 72), Anne Jacob from her status as tantalising meat by instead according her the appetites and agency of 'a bird of prey' (Ellis 2016: 52). Ellis aims to demonstrate the dynamism of lived experience, that one can be both powerful and active, and vulnerable or passive, that as Butler writes, '[w]e're undone by each other. And if we're not, we're missing something' (Butler 2004: 23). However, Ellis' novel demonstrates the challenge of framing interdependency outside power relations. A kiss from butcher's boy Fub renders Anne meat, 'opens me [her] from my [her] head to my [her] toes like a paring knife' (Ellis 2016: 178), and her identification with a slaughtered calf, its eyes 'cloudy as if, instead of looking out at the world, it turned its gaze inward to its slow, visceral decline' (Ellis 2016: 125), serves as a portentous reminder of the gendering of vulnerability. Ambivalence towards visceral experience and the association of femininity with flesh are similarly explored in Marie Darrieussecq's *Pig Tales*, an indictment of the policing of female bodies and their capitalist exploitation, which also highlights the 'violence exercised against animals (and lesser humans)' (Still 2015: 336). Undergoing cyclical transformations between woman and pig, the protagonist's body oscillates between desirable and repulsive, at first, 'marvellously elastic' (Darrieussecq 1997: 2), then 'savage' (Darrieussecq 1997: 28), and finally, 'monstrous!' (Darrieussecq 1997: 73). As both sow and woman, she is burdened by embodiment and constrained by the necessity of policing her body against violence. Nevertheless, her transformation facilitates cross-species understanding as she 'empathises with other animals (and with *vivants* more generally, including trees)' (Still 2015: 336), and disruptively questions the assumption that animal experience is inferior to human experience by detailing the vitality of porcine life, 'the ritual combats of the mating season, the murky aroma of my [her] race in a rut' (Darrieussecq 1997: 127–128), and ultimately concluding that '[r]ationality is the ruination of mankind' (Darrieussecq 1997: 112).

A similar ambivalence towards the body, a nexus of pain and violence, is expressed by protagonist Yeong-hye in Han Kang's *The Vegetarian*. Yeong-Hye's vegetarianism, framed as a symptom of an eating disorder which will almost certainly kill her, is initiated by dreams about meat and feelings of guilt about its consumption; '[s]omething is stuck in my solar plexus,' she complains, '[y]ells and howls threaded together layer upon layer, are enmeshed to form that lump. Because of meat. I ate too much meat. The lives of the animals I ate have all lodged there' (Han 2015: 49). Yeong-hye's identification with slaughtered animals and subsequent rejection of social norms exposes her to violence and violation by her family members; she becomes 'a cornered animal' (Han 2015: 66), who is no longer accorded the rights of person-hood. 'Whether human, animal or plant,' her brother-in-law considers, 'she could not be called a "person"' (Han 2015: 88).

Under the immense pressures of patriarchy, Yeong-hye's attempt to disassociate herself from humanity leads to isolation and mental disintegration. Horrified by the inhumane treatment of animals, Lowell, the brother of protagonist Rosemary in Karen Joy Fowler's novel *We Are All Completely Beside Ourselves*, also disavows his humanity. Rosemary describes: '*They*, my brother said, whenever he talked about humans. Never *us*. Never *we*,' (Fowler 2013: 232), later disclosing: 'His mental condition is not good' (Fowler 2013: 305). For Diamond, our complicity with animal mistreatment is complicated by the uncanniness of the human/animal distinction; accordingly, she identifies '[a] sense of its being impossible that we should go and *eat* them [animals] may go with feeling how powerfully strange it is that they and we should share as much as we do and yet also not share' (Diamond 2003: 14). Such uncanniness is amplified by Fowler's novel, which delays the revelation of sibling Fern's chimpanzee nature and propagates images of mirroring between cross-species sisters Rosemary and Fern, participants in the 'Fern/Rosemary Rosemary/Fern study' (Fowler 2013: 98), who, without each other, are incomplete (see Sands 2017: 90–91). With its inclusion of a genuine list of abused primates, Fowler's novel also serves as an historical account of human–animal relations which looks to an alternative future consisting of responsible cross-species relations and a scientific practice grounded in 'situated knowledges' (Haraway 1991: 188). In their retellings of primatological histories both Fowler and Haraway are alert to the stakes of storytelling; for Haraway, a shift in 'the webs of intertextuality' has the potential to generate new 'meanings of difference, reproduction, and survival for specifically located members of the primate order – on both sides of the biopolitical and cultural divide between human and animal' (Haraway 1989: 377).

Whilst some contemporary animal fiction, like Fowler's novel, perceives storytelling as a way of challenging or resituating the human/animal distinction, many texts continue to use animal figures anthropocentrically to illustrate human qualities or resolve human problems. Recent examples include Matt Wilven's *The Blackbird Singularity*, whose anthropomorphised blackbird, 'like a busker or an entertainer' (Wilven 2016: 18), tells us more about grief than birds. Else-where, in Sara Baume's *Spill Simmer Falter Wither*, Ray's canine companion, One Eye, facilitates the rewilding of the human; protagonist Ray notes, 'on the inside I feel different somehow. I feel animalised. Now there's a wildness inside me that kicked off with you' (Baume 2015: 146). Sim-ilarly, a squirrel in Elizabeth McKenzie's *The Portable Veblen* enables Veblen to articulate something previously unfelt or inarticulable; '[w]hen the squirrel was around,' she tells us, 'she felt grounded, real, at ease. Did it matter if relief came in the form of an animal who stuck around and seemed to care?' (McKenzie 2016: 220). The deflation of Veblen's anthropomorphism arrives via her fiancé Paul, who insists: 'This squirrel isn't a character in a storybook. Real animals don't wear shawls and top hats and write poetry. They rape each other and eat their own young' (McKenzie 2016: 27). In other recent texts, the arrival of an animal marks a change in a character's fate; take cat Mishima in Francesc Miralles' *Love in Small Letters*, the key to new human relationships for character Samuel, or Chibi in Takashi Hiraide's *The Guest Cat*, of whom the protagonist writes: 'It is not out of preference that I use the word fate – or should I say, *Fortuna* – but as the young cat's visits became more frequent, I came to feel that there were some things only this word could express' (Hiraide 2014: 17).

Animal figures have always populated storytelling, with the 'first metaphor' likely 'animal' (Berger 2009: 7), yet the suggestion that, as Haraway contends, animal storytelling might have ethical stakes, that animals should not be 'an alibi for other themes' (Haraway 2003: 5), is a recent one. As Mario Ortiz Robles argues:

> To think of animals as mere tropes rather than real, living entities has no doubt contributed to the ease with which we have killed, and continue to kill, wittingly and unwittingly, unconscionable numbers of animals. [. . .] the trivialization of the animal through figure comes at a steep price for humans as well since it facilitates, licenses, and indeed sanctions certain types of atrocities perpetrated on humans by other humans. But to think of animals as mere tropes is not only a means to denigrate animals and humans alike; it is also to understate the power of tropes themselves. Tropes are the cognitive referents on the basis of which we make sense of the world, and which, in doing so, help us shape it.
>
> (Ortiz Robles 2016: 19)

The reduction of animals to tropes obscures the reality of embodied experience. Fiction, as 'the selective transforming of reality' (Martel 2003: x), always enacts a certain violence. Through the macabre figure of the taxidermist in *Beatrice and Virgil* who manipulates animal carcasses into deceptively natural poses which 'positively glistened with life' (Martel 2010: 66), Yann Martel cultivates scepticism towards a mode of storytelling whose tools – tropes, metaphors and allegories – selectively represent or reconfigure lived experience. Alternatively, Martel offers an account of the uniqueness of animal suffering – the nailing of Beatrice's foot to the floor, 'just above the rim of the hoof' (Martel 2010: 178) and the severing of Virgil's 'soft tail' (Martel 2010: 184) – in which it is not repurposed as a tool for understanding human experience (see Sands 2016: 49).

'Entangled empathy' has become a cornerstone of contemporary animal fiction and thought which aims to enlarge the ethical sphere to include animals. The limits of this sphere vary: the mammalian usually qualifies; sometimes the avian, piscine or reptilian; rarely insect or vegetal life. For Gruen, it is logical for empathy to stop at sentience; she insists that '[e]mpathy doesn't appear to be the appropriate ethical response to the non-sentient world' (Gruen 2015: 68) without supplementing 'entangled empathy' with an ethical account of the non-sentient. Butler and Wolfe, earlier divided on the nature of meaningful agency, are here united in their attachment to sentient individualism; '[n]ot everything included under the rubric of "precarious" life,' Butler writes, ' – plants, for example – warrants protection from harm' (Butler cited in Wolfe 2013: 19). For Haraway, however, this retreat into a 'bounded individualism' (Haraway 2016: 5) which is, she argues, scientifically, politically and philosophically exhausted, can neither account for the complexity of twenty-first century lifeforms, nor for an era in which many species' survival is dependent on vast, non-sentient forces. Rather she calls for a notion of kinship which transcends traditional conceptions of sentience:

> I think that the stretch and recomposition of kin are allowed by the fact that all earthlings are kin in the deepest sense, and it is past time to practice better care of kinds-as-assemblages (not species one at a time). Kin is an assembling sort of word. All critters share a common 'flesh,' laterally, semiotically, and genealogically. Ancestors turn out to be very interesting strangers [. . .].
>
> (Haraway 2015: 162)

By this account, once we have discarded the myth of species purity, there are no limits to kinship; unmasking human exceptionalism we realise that bacteria are 'the greatest planetary terraformers' (Haraway 2015: 159). Yet the ethical implications of such extended kinship are unclear. We cannot escape cross-species 'relations of use'; as Shotwell writes, '*if* we want a world with less suffering and more flourishing, it would be useful to perceive complexity and complicity as the constitutive situation of our lives, rather than as things we should avoid' (Shotwell 2016: 8). However, we tend to perceive 'relations of use' ethically only when they implicate unmistakeably sentient beings.

As the limits of 'entangled empathy' demonstrate, that which we include, or rather prioritise, within the category 'animal,' determines our aesthetic and ethical methodologies. Whilst insects, for example, are officially classified as animals, as our partners in combat, 'since making our appearance on this planet' (Schweid 1999: xiii), they are more likely to inspire fear, disgust or horror than empathy. Responding to Animal Studies' focus on sentient subjectivity and empathy, Stephen Loo and Undine Selbach propose a reconceptualisation of cross-species entanglement at the limits of sentience. Inspired by recent trends in ecological and materialist thought, they assert:

> we can no longer afford to think about ethics in separation from insects, and the big and small edges of sentience they evoke. Insects are reminders that we are ecologically entangled in ways we often only dimly perceive and are impacting the environment and other species in damaging ways we frequently ignore.
>
> (Loo and Sellbach 2015: 80)

Loo and Selbach claim that an ethics which ascribes value solely to individual subjects, assessing them according to their discrete value, is unsuited to the biological, ecological, historical and cultural entanglements which we now experience. Accordingly, the complex relationship between butterfly decline and environmental degradation in Barbara Kingsolver's novel *Flight Behaviour* makes it impossible to distinguish between the butterflies' intrinsic and instrumental value. Despite scientist Dr Byron's insistence that the Monarch butterflies should be read as 'evidence of a disordered system' (Kingsolver 2012: 503) and as significant only as authors of 'writing on our wall,' (Kingsolver 2012: 442), alternative readings – aesthetic, spiritual, collective, individual – of the butterflies proliferate through protagonist Dellarobbia, as the butterflies come to represent a kind of vulnerability which is not determined by sentience. Bees, too, embody a dynamic model of relationality which is irreducible either to 'bounded individualism' or to the subject/object distinction, and expose the connection between 'the minute and the barely felt' (Loo and Sellbach 2015: 86) and larger, environmental forces. This is evident in Peggy Hesketh's *Telling the Bees*, whose affective scale is tuned to bees rather than humans, and in the human-apian assemblage constructed in Sue Monk Kidd's *The Secret Life of Bees*; as protagonist Lily describes: 'bee hum ran through my body. Ran through the whole earth. It was the oldest sound that there was' (Monk Kidd 2002: 264). Laline Paull's *The Bees* omits human life entirely, but ultimately reinforces the anthropocentric assumption of the primacy of the individual through its framing of rebellious protagonist Flora.

Whilst the explicit fragility of bees and butterflies facilitates a kind of empathetic identification, the hardened carapaces and apparent inscrutability of insects such as beetles and roaches curbs such a connection. Instead such insects become screens for the projection of undesirable human qualities. Cockroaches, Richard Schweid argues, have come to represent 'pools of darkness in ourselves' (Schweid 1999: xiv). It is unsurprising, therefore, that marginalised humans are sometimes conflated with insect 'vermin,' a process dramatised and critiqued by Rawi Hage's *Cockroach*, a contemporary re-writing of Kafka's 'Metamophosis' in which the immigrant protagonist internalises society's perception of immigrants as human cockroaches who will dominate and outlive all other beings and who 'should be eradicated' (Hage 2008: 53). Whilst Hage's novel adeptly illustrates the transmission of dread of one species to another, in strengthening existing affective responses to insects it does little to question the association between difference (be it intra- or inter-species) and fear.

Diverging from anthropocentrism requires resisting the desire to render difference comprehensible through appropriation. For Loo and Selbach, the difficulty of this challenge is exemplified by a scene in J.M.G Le Clézio's *Terra Amata* in which a small boy kills insects. 'When a shared sense of animal vulnerability with insects is most palpably felt in the story,' they write, 'it is through the squashed bodies of the bugs in a way that effaces their distinctive physiology, instincts and distant perceptual worlds' (Loo and Sellbach 2015: 83). The theoretical potential of insect experience is, of course, more radical than this, offering precisely the connection between animal and environment which which has long been denied by the 'bounded individualism' underpinning environmentally destructive behaviours. As Jussi Parikka explains: 'Insect perception is localized not in the structure of the eye, for example, but in the continuous tension between the capacities of the insect that have formed the physiological eye and the environment as its needed partner for unravelling the perception event' (Parikka 2010: 69). That the search for, and fixation on, shared qualities exposes a deficiency in the human imagination is noted in jest by Fowler's character Rosemary who envisages 'a sort of reverse mirror test' which would 'identify those species smart enough to see themselves when they look at someone else. Bonus points for how far out the chain you can go. Double bonus for those who get all the way to insects' (Fowler 2013: 201). Such imaginative identification also disrupts our perception of a hierarchy of qualities peaking with individual consciousness; as Rosi Braidotti asks: 'What if consciousness were, in fact, an inferior mode of relating to one's own environment and to others?' (Braidotti 2002: 136).

The identification of the Anthropocene, an era defined by conceptual destabilisation (Clark 2015: 9), has generated a rethinking of relations and structures within and across species and discourses. Accordingly, the long-held tension between Animal Studies, in its ambivalent individualistic inheritance from Animal Rights, and Environmental Ethics, with its focus on the collective (Rawles 2007: 92), is changing, reconfigured by new notions of subjectivity and agency. The ongoing transformation of this relationship is reflected, both theoretically, in Haraway's account of extended kinship, and in fiction, through an increasing interest in cross-species empathy and its limits, be they plants, insects or rocks. This transformation is perceptible in a shifting vocabulary – from sentience to vulnerability; from suffering to finitude – and a more critical engagement with the notion of flourishing, at individual, species and global levels. Whilst 'entangled empathy' relies on a degree of anthropomorphism to awaken us to the ethics of cross-species relations, figuring the limits of 'animal' through the strangeness of insects offers a way of thinking between micro and macro, between ant and planet, rousing us to sensations which are, as yet, 'unreadable' (Loo and Sellbach 2015: 86).

Works cited

Adams, C. 2015. *The Pornography of Meat.* New York: Lantern Books.
—— 1999. *The Sexual Politics of Meat: A Feminist-Vegetarian Critical Theory.* New York: Continuum.
Baume, S. 2015. *Spill Simmer Falter Wither.* London: Windmill Books.
Berger, J. 2009. *Why Look at Animals?* London: Penguin.
Braidotti, R. 2002. *Metamorphoses: Towards a Materialist Theory of Becoming.* Cambridge: Polity.
Butler, J. 2004. *Precarious Life: The Powers of Mourning and Violence.* London and New York: Verso.
Clark, T. 2015. *Ecocriticism on the Edge: The Anthropocene as a Threshold Concept.* London: Bloomsbury.
Coetzee, J.M. 2000. *Disgrace.* London: Vintage.

—— 1997. *The Lives of Animals.* The Tanner Lectures on Human Values. Princeton University. <https://tannerlectures.utah.edu/_documents/a-to-z/c/Coetzee99.pdf>

Crace, J. 2000. *Being Dead.* London: Penguin.

Darrieussecq, M. 1997. *Pig Tales,* trans. L. Coverdale. London: Faber and Faber.

Derrida, J. 2008. *The Animal That Therefore I Am,* trans. D. Wills and ed. M. Mallet. New York: Fordham University Press.

—— 1993. 'Circumfession,' trans. G. Bennington. In Bennington, G., ed. *Jacques Derrida.* Chicago and London: University of Chicago Press.

Diamond, C. 2003. "The Difficulty of Reality and the Difficulty of Philosophy." *Partial Answers: Journal of Literature and the History of Ideas* 1.2: 1–26.

Donovan, J. 2004. '"Miracles of Creation": Animals in J.M. Coetzee's Work.' *Michigan Quarterly Review* 43.1: 78–93.

Ellis, J. 2016. *The Butcher's Hook.* London: Two Roads.

Foucault, M. 1997. 'The Birth of Biopolitics.' In Rabinow, P., ed. *Ethics, Subjectivity and Truth.* New York: The New Press, 73–79.

Fowler, K. J. 2013. *We Are All Completely Beside Ourselves.* London: Serpent's Tail.

Gruen, L. 2015. *Entangled Empathy: An Alternative Ethic for Our Relationships with Animals.* New York: Lantern Books.

Hage, R. 2008. *Cockroach.* Toronto: Anansi.

Han, K. 2015. *The Vegetarian,* trans. D. Smith. London: Portobello Books.

Haraway, D. 2016. *Staying with the Trouble: Making Kin in the Chthulucene.* Durham and London: Duke University Press.

—— 2015. 'Anthropocene, Capitalocene, Plantationocene, Chthulucene: Making Kin.' *Environmental Humanities* 6: 159–165.

—— 2008. *When Species Meet.* Minneapolis: University of Minnesota Press.

—— 2003. *The Companion Species Manifesto: Dogs, People and Significant Otherness.* Chicago: Prickly Paradigm Press.

—— 1991. *Simians, Cyborgs and Women: The Reinvention of Nature.* New York: Routledge.

—— 1989. *Primate Visions: Gender, Race and Nature in the World of Modern Science.* London: Verso.

Heidegger, M. 1962. *Being and Time,* trans. J. Macquarrie and E. Robinson. Oxford: Blackwell.

Hesketh, P. 2013. *Telling the Bees.* London: Oneworld.

Hiraide, T. 2014. *The Guest Cat,* trans. E. Selland. New York: New Directions and London: Picador.

Kingsolver, B. 2012. *Flight Behaviour.* London: Faber and Faber.

Loo, S. and Sellbach, U. 2015. 'Insect Affects.' *Angelaki* 20.3: 79–88.

Martel, Y. 2010. *Beatrice and Virgil.* Edinburgh: Canongate.

—— 2003. *Life of Pi.* Edinburgh: Canongate.

McFarland, S.E. 2014. 'Animal Studies, Literary Animals, and Yann Martel's Life of Pi.' In Westling, L., ed. *The Cambridge Companion to Literature and the Environment.* Cambridge: Cambridge University Press, 152–168.

McKay, R. 2010. 'Metafiction, Vegetarianism, and the Literary Performance of Animal Ethics in J.M. Coetzee's The Lives of Animals.' *Safundi* 11.1–2: 67–85.

McKenzie, E. 2016. *The Portable Veblen.* London: Fourth Estate.

Miller, A. 1997. *Ingenious Pain.* London: Sceptre.

Miralles, F. 2014. *Love in Small Letters,* trans. J. Wark. London: Alma Books.

Monk Kidd, S. 2002. *The Secret Life of Bees.* London: Headline.

Ortiz Robles, M. 2016. *Literature and Animal Studies.* London and New York: Routledge.

Parikka, J. 2010. *Insect Media: An Archaeology of Animals and Technology.* Minneapolis and London: University of Minnesota Press.

Paull, L. 2015. *The Bees.* London: Fourth Estate.

Rawles, K. 2007. 'Love a Duck! Emotions, Animals and Environmental Ethics.' In Li, H. and Yeung, A., eds. *New Essays in Applied Ethics: Animal Rights, Personhood and the Ethics of Killing.* Basingstoke: Palgrave Macmillan.

Sands, D. 2017. 'The Story of the "Anthropos": Writing Humans and Other Primates.' In Meretoja, H. and Davis, C., eds. *Storytelling and Ethics: Historical Imagination in Contemporary Literature and Visual Arts.* New York: Routledge.

—— 2016. 'On Tails and Tales: Animals, Ethics and Storytelling in Yann Martel's *Beatrice and Virgil*.' *Critique: Studies in Contemporary Fiction* 57.1: 41–51.

Saunders, G. 2017. *Lincoln in the Bardo*. London: Bloomsbury.

Schweid, R. 1999. *The Cockroach Papers: A Compendium of History and Lore*. Chicago and London: Chicago University Press.

Shotwell, A. 2016. *Against Purity: Living Ethically in Compromised Times*. Minneapolis and London: University of Minnesota Press.

Still, J. 2015. *Derrida and Other Animals*. Edinburgh: Edinburgh University Press.

Wilven, M. 2016. *The Blackbird Singularity*. London: Legend Press.

Wolfe, C. 2013. *Before the Law: Humans and Other Animals in a Biopolitical Frame*. Chicago and London: University of Chicago Press.

PART III

Ruptures

19

(THE) DIGITAL

Zara Dinnen

Writing about 'the digital' is a difficult task. Associated with so much quantizing, so much reduction, the digital is itself an expansive, irreducible complex: at once something technical, socioeconomic, cultural, a logic and a subject, a frame and an object; it is imbricated in human and nonhuman nature; it *is* human and nonhuman nature. I recently participated in a panel on 'digital cultures'.[1] An audience member asked if we speakers agreed that 'the digital' was the thing that best described the contemporary: we had all used it in our papers, but also talked of new media and computation, neoliberalism and late capitalism; we had talked about digital things but also stuff that isn't digital. In the end we agreed it was a significant logic and that to varying degrees it was the concept we were thinking the contemporary through. One of the speakers, Seb Franklin, in his book *Control* (2015), suggests that we are in an episteme of 'digitality': both 'a logical–technical substrate through which certain machines might operate' and 'a predominant logical mode with which to address both individual social actors and the body of interactions between these actors that can be dubbed "society"' (xviii). The digital is both a technical form in the contemporary, and a form that delimits what is thinkable as the contemporary.

In its most literal mode digital is data as discrete element; to digitize is to transform something analogue – something continuously variable – into finite data that can be stored in a limited amount of computer memory, infinitely reproduced, and manipulated using algorithmic formula (Berry 2012; Gere 2002; Wolf 2000). The digital also refers to the sociotechnical situation of distributed networks of electromechanical computing; not only personal (our sovereign user*ness*) and mass (surveillance, governance), but nonhuman and infrastructural (data centers, undersea cables, rare earth mineral mining, satellites orbiting the earth, and on). It is difficult to comprehend the complexity of contemporary global computational systems; the scale of abstraction eludes narrative and imaginary form. Benjamin H. Bratton (2015) has offered up the metaphor of 'the stack' to describe the 'accidental megastructure' of planetary-scale computation: a situation in which infrastructure is governance. In this situation, human and nonhuman users cohere as subjects in relation to interfaces such as platforms, and devices. Reporting on the interventions of Facebook and Cambridge Analytica in the 2016 US Presidential Election, 2016 UK Referendum on EU membership, and the 2015 Nigerian General Election demonstrates that we do have a narrative form to recognize some of this situation, a partial imaginary: we tell an old story about corporations and breach of trust; a story of surveillance (The Cambridge Analytica Files 2018). In the reporting of Facebook and Cambridge Analytica much is rightly made of the human proponents of the situation, of the researchers, CEOs and Facebook users. What is less immediately sensible is that this situation is also acted out by planetary-scale networks of non-human agents – algorithms, rare earth minerals – and hidden human labor – workers in mining and construction who build media infrastructure, customer experience operatives in software companies who buffer the fall out of the new normal. Any attempt to write this situation is also a part of the situation; how can we grasp the production of more narrative about digital culture as the material reproduction of the toxic environmental conditions of digital culture?

Whether 'the stack' or 'digitality', the complex being described is an abstraction of software itself as complex. Attending to the abstraction of code is a way to witness the digital as always effacing itself from view. In other words, by focusing in on one level of planetary-scale computation – the operation of programming code – we open a space to think about the problem of the digital more broadly conceived. Describing the development of software as program and platform, Wendy Hui Kyong Chun (2004) notes, 'Higher-level programming languages, unlike assembly language, explode one's instructions and enable one to forget the machine'. Here Chun references the way in which today programming is not an act of working on the machine, or with the machine, as it has historically been (Grier 1996; Light 1999). Working in higher-level programming languages is writing code that is parsed and executed by other assembly and object code. Programming today requires a programmer to forget the machine and to communicate with other (and others') code. Code appears to function as an executable language. Writing code and pressing the Enter key appears to do things in the world, to execute action. In practice, code is multiplex. The processes that we might think of as writing code are not actually executable; programming languages must be translated into machine-readable instructions for execution. If source code has been written effectively, it effaces itself; once compiled, it is instead object code. Conversely, only once an action is executed can we properly name source code as source – it is only in the action of effacement that we can identify what would have been the instruction. In other words, software conflates an event with a written command, shifting the word 'program' from a verb to a noun (Chun 2008a). This process is how software both does and doesn't do things in the world; and how users are imbricated in the digital in ways that resist legibility.

Despite technical and historical definitions, the term digital is persistently opaque. It has come to be associated 'metonymically' with 'virtual simulacra, instantaneous communication, ubiquitous media and global connectivity [. . .] it is to allude to the vast range of application and media forms that digital technology has made possible' (Gere 2002: 4). The digital is an expansive culture of applications, media and experiences, enabled by a specific set of technologies. Life now, life *after* new media, is a process in which the human subject emerges as living mediational entanglement, always becoming-with nonhuman, technological agents (Kember and Zylinska 2012). The digital then is also how the social might be articulated at all. For Franklin (2015: xix–xx), 'digitality promises to render the world legible, recordable, and knowable via particular numeric and linguistic constructs'. Having a sense of the ways code does and doesn't do things in the world is to have a sense of the ways subjects do and do not appear in the world at all. In other words, we need to account for the ways computational processes are not only new technologies, but new logics; new grounds for what is thinkable. To this end, we might concur with Matthew Fuller's (2006) claim that 'all intellectual work is now a "software study"'. If the algorithmic is the action of computational logic, and computational logic is a mode of contemporary being, then the ways we *do, are* and *be*, might significantly look like the ways of software.

Taking Fuller's claim seriously means approaching contemporary literary studies as already a digital study. Not only in the sense that all academic work today is digital (our research, writing and teaching practices are computational to some degree), or in the sense that we may be dealing with digital objects – digital texts and archives. Rather it is digital in the sense the contemporary emerges in terms of the digital. There is no contemporary expression outside of the digital. Digital media is operated – by corporate and individual stakeholders – and operates – as algorithm, as program – throughout culture in such a way to make banal the affective novelty of its being here. In other words, the everyday, just there-ness of digital media is one of the ways we don't notice our becoming-with digital media (Dinnen 2018). Narrative culture, in its recording, manifesting, refracting of normative social practices, offers a means to apprehend these processes. Put differently, 'it is not the job of the scholar of literature to defend the literary from the technological but, rather, to attend with some care to the precise ways in which literature and technology constitute one another' (McPherson et al. 2013, 616). For scholars such as Lori Emerson (2014) and Caroline Bassett (2007) we need to look to encounter digital media beyond the confines of that media. The contemporary computing industry sells us the promise of 'a more neutral, more direct, inherently better way to interact with our computers and the world around us'; while continuing 'unchecked in its accelerating drive to achieve the perfect black box' (Emerson 2014, 1). Literature can be a vital site for registering the co-constitution of digital technologies and digital subjects. Following Alexander Galloway et al. (2008) we should understand that '[t]echnology has no impact on our culture'; it *is* culture.

If technology is not separate from our lives but is culture, much is at stake in the choice of methods through which we critically apprehend 'technology'. Scholarly work on literature and digital media is not confined to a single field. Scholarship encountering literature through, with and in the context of, digital media and computational culture focuses on computational poetics (Punday 2015; Tenen 2017); electronic literature and code poetics (*electronic book review* 1996 – present; Raley 2001, 2008; Hayles 2008; Bell et al. 2014; Pressman 2014; Hammond 2016); new media studies (Bassett 2007; Nakamura 2002; Nakamura and Chow-White 2011); software studies (Fuller 2003, 2008; Kittler 2008; Chun 2008b, 2011; Galloway 2012); forensic and medium specific analysis (Hayles 2002, 2004; Kirschenbaum 2008; Hayles and Pressman 2013); media archeology (Gitelman 2006, 2014; Parikka 2012; Emerson 2014); and surveillance and algorithmic control (Browne 2015; Chun 2016). Most pertinent to this present chapter, is the loose field of scholarly work that reads literature as one of many cultural sites that give aesthetic and affective form to digital and computational culture (Tabbi and Wutz 1997; Hayles 1999; Kevorkian 2006; Punday 2012; Carruth 2014; Franklin 2015; Jagoda 2016; Dinnen 2018; Marczewska 2018). Although many of these studies focus on text, textual scholarship and the literary object, they do not privilege literature, or literary fiction as a category. Across the scholarship that is situated within literary studies, or buttresses that discipline, understanding new media through cultural forms requires engagement with culture as multiplex. Literary fiction does sociopolitical work, attuning and discombobulating readers through its 'reality effects' and capacity to make sensible the normative drives of everyday life, but it is not an exclusive site for such cultural work. Literary fiction is always in the mix with video games, comics, film, visual art, poetry, genre fiction, instruction manuals, technological platforms, devices, computing histories, all objects and practices of computational life. Understanding literary fiction as part of an ecology of cultural practices, instructions and sites is a way to encounter the normative action of digital media as we are co-constituted as subjects with it.

Given this multiplex ecology, what value might there be in looking at literary fiction particularly, when looking for the digital in general? Undertaking such work is to recognize the novel forms' novelty; its way of forming again in new media ecologies (with the caveat that new media literary studies are never only *literary* studies). Despite stories of its obsolescence, the novel remains a popular cultural form and moreover an ethically valent form. The novel is 'an important narrative technology of interiority that figures into and changes within a transmedia ecology' (Jagoda 2016, 46). Discursive, descriptive and speculative literary critical methods enable us to apprehend, if not necessarily comprehend, our complex digital condition. Below is a discussion of a novel that rests on the precipice of what it might be to write a literary novel today, in the age of social media, human and nonhuman digital entanglements, after reality TV, after the making banal of publishing your words, and in relation to the computational logics of control society. What does literary fiction about such a condition look like? A novel that attempts to represent the contemporary condition is itself conditioned by the dominant logic; it might also make tangible something of this logic. A novel might make visible, or reveal, some of those codes – mediation, computation – of the contemporary moment that otherwise remain hidden; we might find in contemporary literature the narratives, metaphors, textualities and materialities that are also out there, operating our everyday digital lives.

Literary fiction in the age of new media[2]

Sheila Heti's 2010 novel *How Should a Person Be?* is a novel in flux: Sheila is recently divorced, commissioned to write a play she cannot seem to focus on, and in the midst of forming new friendships that influence her creative practice (Heti 2013). Nothing much happens in the way of plot: the novel moves from scene to scene staging the everyday lives of Sheila and her friends, talking, sometimes daydreaming, often reflecting. Heti has spoken of this novel as indebted to reality TV and documentary film (Heti 2012). Formally it is like these things not only in the sense it is a fiction that reads like constructed reality, but also in its investment in scenes of impasse and in-between-ness. The novel is a mediation on its form and is mediational, in the sense Heti considers the way she is becoming a person – a social, identifiable being – *with* media. The novel stages the indeterminacy of becoming a verifiable person as a process, neurotically and obsessively; it is always on the verge of undoing itself (literally, it is barely a novel) as it registers the anxieties and processes of selfing – of constructing, working on, and producing a recognizable social self. In the novel these processes are not always digital technologies, but rather technologies of self-production and expression: art and literature as genres, typewriters and voice recorders as tools, friendship as constitutive of individuals.

How Should a Person Be? is conspicuously nondigital. Aside from a few transcribed emails and a couple references to checking emails, seeing something 'on the internet', there is no sense that Sheila and her friends think of themselves as having differentiated digital lives. In *How Should a Person Be?* digital media appears as a surface of the text; the text itself seems barely aware of it. The anxiety of mediation is present in lieu of the media device itself: 'The other night out at the bars, I learned that Nietzsche wrote on a typewriter. It is unbelievable to me, and I no longer feel that his philosophy has the same validity or aura of truth that it formerly did' (89). Emails and scripts are strewn about the novel as the detritus of technologically mediated social interaction. In a mostly glowing review of Heti's book, James Wood (2012) writes off these communications as red herrings, luring a reader away from Heti's art of fiction: 'Heti may include real emails and recordings of actual conversations, but, of course, her book is shaped and plotted (however lightly), and uses fiction as well as autobiography'. However, Wood misreads the function of the emails and recordings. For Wood these are by-products of processes that remain in the novel as a kind of misdirect, diverting the reader from the authorial labor of fiction. In contrast, I argue that these other media are at the center of the way Heti's narration works at the titular question. The emails and recordings are there to testify, not to some fake documentarian impulse, but rather to processes of mediated self-construction in general. *How Should a Person Be?* is discursive, chatty: there are constant shifts in form, from play scripts to transposed emails, from descriptive prose to allegorical asides; it invokes common communication rather than literary exceptionalism.

Such common communication is a banal investment, where the banal is an effect of refusing to register novelty. The banal marks the place where surprise might have been (Dinnen 2018). In various ways Andy Warhol is the banal figure with whom Heti is in dialogue – as Wood also suggests. At the Basel Art Fair in Miami, Sheila observes a banner over one of the entrances featuring a quote from Warhol: 'Everybody's sense of beauty is different from everybody else's'. Sheila asks Margaux what she thinks it means. 'Oh yeah', Margaux replies. 'It's saying you can be rich and stupid about art. You're all welcome' (107–108). This exchange establishes Warhol's legacy to Heti's work in terms of a posture of ambivalence that troubles Sheila. Sheila does not respond, because there is nothing left to say but, 'Several hours later, growing tired from the art and the cold, we left' (108). Warhol figures throughout the novel in complex ways. While in the end Heti's text speaks to the particular conditions of digital culture, it puts such a contemporary banal technic in proximity with a prior banal culture.

One of the key technical and mediational subjects of the novel is Sheila's digital tape recorder. The appearance of this shiny object disturbs the novel and defines the kind of literary mode – a social literary mode – that the work will eventually take. The recorder is an allusion to Warhol's art practice. As Pat Hackett (1989: xvi) explains in the introduction to Warhol's diaries, which were themselves transcribed from phone conversations and tape recordings, 'From the mid–sixties to the mid–seventies, Andy was notorious for endlessly tape-recording his friends'. Warhol epitomizes the recursive propensity of the banal that does not simply repeat but almost–not–quite–entirely effaces the possibility of new experiences in its paradoxical commitment to novelty. He is an ambivalent figure in Heti's work, signaling something old and also an investment in the new and now. *How Should a Person Be?* is written in a historical moment when such banal propensity is the structuring logic of dominant modes of communication and artistic production, but also a moment when we are inclined to still want to say something new about life, to express what Lee Konstantinou (2016) has described as 'post–ironic belief'. Although Heti writes her situation in relation to Warhol, the novel is drawing a trace rather than a sameness between the two artists, between the two historical moments. I am interested in how the tape recorder does something quite specifically contemporary in Heti's novel, instantiating a way to engage in social life after digital media, and it is through the allusion to Warhol that such contingency can be witnessed.

In the second chapter of act two Sheila meets her new love, 'a silver digital tape recorder'. It is mutual love at first sight: 'It has long been known to me that certain objects want you as much as you want them' (56). This object is one of the few conspicuously digital items in the novel, and its digitalness is almost beside the point. And yet, because it is one of the few conspicuously digital items in the book, and because it is a reified interface for the digital control society in general – a recorder – it can be read emblematically and allegorically as an ontology of the digital. For Warhol the cassette tape recorder was a way to remove his subjectivity from the social situation; as a prosthesis it marked Warhol as a listener. The playback function was crucial in Warhol's work, where such recordings were never really about the record, the archive; they were about the social, about amplification. For Warhol, 'the appeal of sonic scale was its potential for undermining the private containment of the listener's interiority' (Stadler 2014: 428). For Heti the recorder is also a social mechanism, but more significantly, it is a way to encounter her own mediational agency. After purchasing the recorder, Sheila goes into a coffee shop.

> I whispered low into my tape recorder's belly. I recorded my voice and played it back. I spoke into it tenderly and heard my tenderness returned . . . . I wanted to touch every part of it, to understand how it worked. I began to learn what turned it on and the things that turned it off.
>
> (57)

The machine verifies Sheila as herself, and so Sheila is becoming a person with the machine. Sheila falls in love with her machine and confirms her presence through it – I must be real, I can hear myself.

The chapter after Sheila buys the recorder describes the moment when she presents Margaux with the recorder. Margaux is her best friend, the book's main subject. But Margaux hates the idea of the recorder: 'Don't you know that what I fear most is my words floating separate from my body? You there with that tape recorder is the scariest thing!' (59). Sheila has been trying to write a play, but she is stuck. She believes the recorder will get her creativity going. It works. The chapter after Sheila buys the recorder is the first chapter presented as a script; the script describes the moment Margaux is presented with the recorder. Rather than understand this scene as solely a metafictional conceit – where the novel presents itself as a work of art in construction – this scene is an encounter with the novel as digital subject. The digital recorder, and its mobilization as embodied agency, temporarily makes the novel itself unworkable. For a moment, Margaux refuses to make or be the novel; subsequently the novel becomes a play script. Here digital media is reified as a shiny new thing (the recorder) blocking the affective novelty of digital mediation (the condition of being recordable). The destabilizing of the novel at this point allows us to see this process at work: the novel is all of a sudden a play, and the reader is confronted with the transformative mediational novelty of the digital recorder.

The recorder is an allegory for personal digital communications. Through it, Sheila substantiates herself as a social being in the world. It is a tool, a word processor, and as Margaux's reaction suggests, it is a medium that estranges an utterance from the body and simulates that body as itself. This situation is one that belongs to a history of recording and playback audio devices, but is mediationally distinct *after* networked automation and infinite reproducibility. As Galloway has argued (2012: 137) 'whenever a body speaks, it always already speaks as a body codified with an affective identity (gendered, ethnically typed, and so on)'. And now, given the 'postfordist colonization of affect and the concomitant valorization of affective difference, a body has no choice but to speak. A body speaks whether it wants to or not'. The digital recorder interpolates codified bodies and stands in metonymically for the work of the novel as a whole. In the instance of the recorder's legibility we may register the digital complex as it forms a mediational figure. This figure is the user-subject, and the form of agency afforded it, this, the body at the end of our 'menu-driven identities', is delimited by the program (Nakamura 2002: 113; see also Noble 2018). In Margaux's anxiety of being made to speak, we witness the social dynamic of affective difference in the programmable world(s) of Sheila/Heti. Margaux's anxiety stands in for the readers' capacity to be made to speak as user-subjects. Sheila/Heti writes Margaux into subjectivity through processes of digital capture, enclosure, extraction, abstraction. But Sheila/Heti is also produced as a subject through these same processes: the text creates community out of data; the novel understands the ways characters are seen to be 'alike', to be categorically similar. Or, as Sheila puts it after she's watched a video online of 'an heiress' giving 'her boyfriend a hand job': 'Watching her, I felt a kinship; she was just another white girl going through life with her clothes off' (105).

New media sincerity

As categories of the new sincerity, post-postmodernism and postdigital presume to describe an aesthetic and political imperative of US art and literature in the twenty-first century. As Konstantinou (2013: 419) has suggested, these terms circulate in relation to others: 'globalization, cosmodernism, metamodernism, altermodernism, digimodernism, performatism, postpositivist realism, the New Sincerity, or, for more lexically austere analysts, the contemporary'. What is at stake in which term you turn to, and how you use it, is the question of what kind of cultural break has or has not been enabled by the ongoingness of late capitalism and the dominance of neoliberalism, or, at the anthropocenic scale, the 'crisis of "ongoingness" that is both the cause and effect of our species' inability to pay its ecological and financial debts' (Bratton 2015: 303). In the particular geopolitical conditions of liberal democracies of the global north, this stuckness often manifests in art as a question of expression, authenticity and mediation: how do we work with or move on from our mediated subjectivity? Writing about a new sincerity in the films of Wes Anderson, Warren Buckland (2012: 2) suggests, 'In a dialectical move, new sincerity *incorporates* postmodern irony and cynicism; it operates in conjunction with irony'. Similarly, contemporary internet art practices are also contending with the constraints of medial commodification. For the artist Jennifer Chan (2014: 110), 'This particular cultural moment is defined by digital identity formation that vacillates between two extremes: careful self-curation and "indiscriminate over-sharing" . . . Initiative is both self-interested and ideological'. The social context of these art practices is one in which the largest platforms of the internet can confidently assert themselves as communities where people use their authentic identities, their 'real' names. To be real, to be authentic, is both a cultural-political demand and a technical one: if 'false' code is input, the program will not run, or it will run, and in the process, become something else.

Structurally, the recorder is a mechanism for Sheila's script, and for her social life, which is both digital and analogue material, and both a fictional and nonfictional occurrence. In the novel the appearance of the recorder and the script is a material metaphor for amplification, but this is a mediational rather than effacing process. The recorder signifies a moment when voice is iterated as distinct from writing, and this happens through a shift in the format of the book itself (the change in layout to script) as well as through the introduction to the narrative of a voice-recording device. No longer is the novel only narrating to us, it is also performing voices; this is marked by Margaux's comments and by the fact that characters now speak independently of Sheila's voice. Characters' names appear before they speak.

Margaux

Well, *of course* there are people here that are really truly great! But how could you see that? Like, for instance, if Takeshi Murakami had just one of his sculptures here, you wouldn't know how good it was.

(103)

Corollary to the script in the novel are the emails represented on the page as numbered lists, in smaller font, graphically distinct from the general narration. Heti attends to the difference of email as a distinct medium within the novel – something other than the novel: '*One morning, Sheila finds an email from Margaux*' (35). The novel is undone by the emails and the scripts because they are not within the constraints of the fiction; they attest to Sheila Heti's social life, mediation as becoming-with, and Sheila Heti's work as author. In Heti's novel the emails and scripts are conversation. Conversation is the social. In the novel Sheila wants her work to be social, she wants it to be *this*, the conversation.

In act two, chapter six of *How Should a Person Be?* Sheila has a dream about her play and calls her Jungian analyst, Ann: 'I went to my computer and made it gently ring' (81). The analysis session is presented in script form. After Sheila recounts the dream, Ann suggests that Sheila is anxious because she keeps quitting things she thinks might be dangerous: her marriage, the play. To this Sheila responds:

(*defensive*) Wait! I want to cancel the play not because it's *dangerous*, but because life doesn't feel like it's in my stupid play, or with me sitting in a room *typing*. And life wasn't in my marriage anymore, either. Life feels like it's with Margaux – *talking* – which is an equally sincere attempt to get somewhere, just as sincere as writing a play.

(82)

Here is the question of how to be social as it is posed in the novel. It is also the edge of the novel, the point at which the novel is not itself but rather a general iteration of the status quo. This is not just a meditation on the literary work in the manner of something typed versus something verbal, or a solo authorial project versus a social one. It is also a moment in which the novel recognizes the work of the social. There is a precarious indistinctness of work and social life endemic to workers in the creative economy and to everyone as social media users in the contemporary moment. The edge of Heti's novel is where her sociality is also the material of her labor. This edge is fully incorporated *in* the text in those passages that are, and reflect on, Heti's social work. The barely perceptible but ubiquitous presence of digital media in the novel blocks the apprehension of new modes of artistic production and social life instantiated by digital media, but this aesthetic of obfuscation can be apprehended through a critique formed in relation to the digital as both a 'logical-technical substrate' and a 'predominant logical mode' (Franklin 2015: xviii).

Describing the 'informalities and ethics of new media culture', Chan identifies the contemporary condition as that 'which is as much about the existential and ethical dimension of making art online and the creation of surplus value around its affects, as it is about the politics and anxieties that exist around so called post-internet art practices' (108). Today artists 'write, curate, blog, chat, comment. With every interaction, your playtime is the corporate network's goldmine. Under post-internet conditions artists must capitalize on boredom, busyness, and procrastination' (116). This command/condition is a function of creative labor within what Jodi Dean (2005, 2010) names 'communicative capitalism' and Tiziana Terranova (2013) figures in terms of 'immaterial labor': processes by which conversation – sociality – is creative work. This condition is writ large through *How Should a Person Be?*, but only if the novel is understood in terms of mediation and the digital, rather than a literary category apart from everyday technoculture. James Wood writes of *How Should a Person Be?* that 'Heti never pursues that solitary note with the rigor that it deserves. It is easier, more charming, more hospitable, more successfully evasive, to bring in the gang of friends and get a "vaguely intelligent" conversation going'. For Wood the sway of the social is a problem; it is an evasive maneuver that gets Heti out of her authorial duty. I argue that the social is, in fact, the work the novel is doing.

The published novel, authored by, credited to, Sheila Heti, is testament to the compromise of how social a novel can be. It can be a conversation to the extent that it incorporates the transcription of conversation, of sociality, so long as it remains marketable as a novel. To fully address what is to be gained from situating this novel beyond its literary milieu, it is important to consider what is at stake in reading this text as a meditation on the digital instead of as a literary work of post-postmodernism and the new sincerity. This is, after all, a novel, and as described, it stages various scenes of thwarted writing that result in Sheila Heti's social methodology. On the back cover blurb Miranda July calls this work a 'new kind of book and a new kind of person, . . . a major literary work'; Lena Dunham describes it as 'a really amazing metafiction-meets-nonfiction novel'. These remarks frame the book as literary. It is not only in discourse with the constructed nonfiction of reality TV, the banal postmodern gestures of Warhol's artwork, and the social work of art in a post-internet market; *How Should a Person Be?* also exemplifies the post-postmodern discourse of contemporary literature as it attempts to document a new kind of subject, one that is both invested in the authenticity of emotion (nonfiction, sincerity) and the necessity of representation (metafiction, irony).

The new(ly) sincere encounter is with the problem of the person; how might we be a good one? In recent scholarship on post-postmodern literature and the new sincerity by Nicoline Timmer (2010); Stephen J. Burn (2008); Adam Kelly (2011); and Lee Konstantinou (2013), the post-postmodern is understood as having a renewed interest in character. Whereas post-modern literature and art decentred the human subject, post-postmodernism addresses and produces a thinking, feeling, interpersonal human subject. The category of the interpersonal is where my interest in the social of Heti's novel as a new mediational form meets a literary critical interest in how the contemporary novel engenders characters who think and feel in relation to one another. In both cases contemporary literature is being read as responding in various ways to postmodern literature's experiments with ahistorical, fragmentary, holo-graphic networks of characters; and to the commodification of social life through digital media in ever more banal ways. As Konstantinou notes (2013: 419), in 'our post-postmodern moment, the social transforms itself into what Mark Zuckerberg calls the "social graph", generated on a digital platform owned by some friendly, for-profit corporation'. Literature and digitality constitute one another and are like one another to the extent they are processes for both capturing social life, making that life legible in normative ways, and revealing these operations as such.

Discussion of post-postmodernism understands itself in response to the 'information society' and is cognizant of many of the sociopolitical aspects of a new media life. However, little attention is paid to how, within computational culture, software might be the layer at which interpersonal, authentic subjectivity is delimited. In other words, what is identified in literary criticism as a problem of sincerity is actually codified in ubiquitous, obfuscatory, everyday mediational systems as a computational logic of verification. As posthuman and nonhuman studies have made clear, the thinking, feeling, interpersonal subject is always mediational (Braidotti 2013; Grusin 2015). To this end questions of authenticity are protocological – structurally endemic to digital culture. The intimacy of the scene of sincerity as it might be read in contemporary literature is always an intimacy with the scene of digital media. Whereas a post-postmodern analysis might suggest that Heti's novel is about the viability of the interpersonal, feeling subject of literature *after* postmod-ernism (after reality TV, and Warhol), I suggest that it is a novel about the ontology of a social subject in the contemporary digital situation.

In Nicoline Timmer's account of post-postmodernism (2010: 359), one of the dominant critical investments of this new literary genre is sharing. 'In the post-postmodern novel "shar-ing" is important; for example sharing stories as a way to "identify with others" (and to allow others to identify with you)'. Timmer frames this in terms of writing by Dave Eggers and David Foster Wallace, which conscientiously, but anxiously, presents the act of voicing others' stories as ethically vital. For Timmer, in the post-postmodern novel 'a desire for some form of community or sociality is highlighted'; there is 'a structural need for a we'. Reading *How Should a Person Be?* we encounter a similar investment in community and a belief in the power of sharing stories. As Sheila tells Ann, her life 'feels like it's with Margaux – *talking* – which is an equally sincere attempt to get somewhere'. But if sharing is a demand of communicative capitalism, and moreover is an algorithmically determined and determining social action in which the body speaks whether it wants to or not, then a contemporary aesthetics of sharing is mediational and protocological. Timmer posits literature as the genre that is being contested and challenged from within; how do we make the solitary novel a 'we'? Heti's novel exemplifies how talking is a common command of digital culture. As a 'we' appears in the novel it is contesting the very right of literature as a genre, and the novel as a dominant expressive medium, to exist. Heti's digital tape recorder and her emails remind the reader that there is no separate space in which we encounter the literary object and no nondigital medium through which the writer appears.

The contemporary 'we' is complex. Any 'we' now is likely to form through, and speak as, a corporate platform, a proprietary program, nonhuman agents. In the end the answer to Heti's titular question is that we should be empathetic, a friend, a participant. The novel knows that these are not simple things; it is itself a commodification of these things. The novel has a life beyond itself, in the offline and online bodies of Sheila Heti and her real friends. Heti's novel incorporates its own concern about the value of the novel today, not as a newly sincere invocation of literary value, but as a digital recording device that destabilizes the authorial work of construction and effaces the individual creator while it reifies the false transparency of recording. *How Should a Person Be?* refuses to resolve its own problem, to create a text that could answer its own question. It remains unsettled, disturbing the operations of digital culture, holding on to a sense that there is emerging, in Miranda July's words, a new kind of person.

Notes

1 The Panel 'Digital Cultures' took place November 8, 2017 as part of the English Literature and Cultural Studies seminar series at the University of Westminster. Thank you to Lucy Bond, Matthew Charles and Kaja Marczewska for organizing the event and inviting me to participate.
2 The following sections are adapted from *The Digital Banal*, Dinnen (2018).

Works cited

Bassett, C., (2007). *The Arc and the Machine: Narrative and New Media.* Manchester: Manchester University Press.
Bell, A., Ensslin, A., and Rustad, H.K. Eds., (2014). *Analyzing Digital Fiction.* New York: Routledge.
Berry, D.M., (2012). The Computational Turn: Thinking about the Digital Humanities. *Culture Machine* [online], 12. Available at <www.culturemachine.net/index.php/cm/issue/view/23> [accessed 26th May 2014].
Braidotti, R., (2013). *The Posthuman.* Cambridge: Polity Press.
Bratton, B.H., (2015). *The Stack: On Software and Sovereignty.* Cambridge, MA: MIT Press.
Browne, S., (2015). *Dark Matters: On the Surveillance of Blackness.* Durham and London: Duke University Press.
Buckland, W., (2012). Wes Anderson: A 'Smart' Director of the New Sincerity? *New Review of Film and Television Studies*, 10(1), 1–5.
Burn, S.J., (2008). *Jonathan Franzen at the End of Postmodernism.* London: Bloomsbury.
The Cambridge Analytica Files, (2018). *The Guardian* [online]. Available at <www.theguardian.com/news/series/cambridge-analytica-files>.
Carruth, A., (2014). The Digital Cloud and the Micropolitics of Energy. *Public Culture*, 26(2), 339–364.
Chan, J., (2014). Notes on Post-Internet. In *You Are Here: Art after the Internet*, ed. Omar Kholeif, 106–123. Manchester: Cornerhouse Publications.
Chun, W.H.K., (2004). On Software and the Persistence of Knowledge. *Grey Room*, 18, 26–51.
—— (2008a). Programmability. In *Software Studies: A Lexicon*, ed. Matthew Fuller, 224–229. Cambridge, MA: MIT Press.
—— (2008b). *Control and Freedom: Power and Paranoia in the Age of Fiber Optics.* Cambridge, MA: MIT Press.
—— (2011). *Programmed Visions: Software and Memory.* Cambridge, MA: MIT Press.
—— (2016). *Updating to Remain the Same: Habitual New Media.* Cambridge, MA: MIT Press.
Dean, J., (2005). Communicative Capitalism: Circulation and the Foreclosure of Politics. *Cultural Politics*, 1(1), 51–74.
—— (2010). *Blog Theory: Feedback and Capture in the Circuits of Drive.* Cambridge: Polity.
Dinnen, Z., (2018). *The Digital Banal: New Media and American Literature and Culture.* New York: Columbia University Press.

Electronic Book Review (1996–). Ed. J. Tabbi. Peer–reviewed journal. [online] Available at <http://electronic bookreview.com/essay/> [accessed 4th October 2018].

Emerson, L., (2014). *Reading Writing Interfaces: From the Digital to the Bookbound.* Minneapolis: Minnesota University Press.

Franklin, Seb., (2015). *Control: Digitality as Cultural Logic.* Cambridge: MIT Press.

Fuller, M. Ed., (2003). *Behind the Blip: Essays on the Culture of Software.* New York: Autonomedia.

—— (2005). *Media Ecologies: Materialist Energies in Art and Technoculture.* Cambridge, MA: MIT Press.

—— (2006). Software Studies Workshop. [online] Available at <http://web.archive.org/web/20100327185154/http://pzwart.wdka.hro.nl/mdr/Seminars2/softstudworkshop> [accessed 26th May 2014].

—— Ed., (2008). *Software Studies: A Lexicon.* Cambridge, MA: MIT Press.

Galloway, A.R., (2012). *The Interface Effect.* Cambridge: Polity Press.

Galloway, A.R., Lovink, G., and Thacker, E., (2008). Dialogues Carried Out in Silence: An E-Mail Exchange. *Grey Room*, 33, 96–112.

Gere, C., (2002). *Digital Culture.* London: Reaktion Books.

Gitelman, L., (2006). *Always Already New: Media, History, and the Data of Culture.* Cambridge, MA: MIT Press.

—— (2014). *Paper Knowledge: Toward a Media History of Documents.* London and Durham: Duke University Press.

Grier, D.A., (1996). The ENIAC, the Verb "to Program" and the Emergence of Digital Computers. *IEEE Annals of the History of Computing*, 18(1), 51–55.

Grusin, R. Ed., (2015). *The Nonhuman Turn.* Minneapolis: University of Minnesota Press.

Hackett, P., (1989). *Introduction to the Andy Warhol Diaries*, ed. Pat Hackett. New York: Warner Books.

Hammond, A. (2016). *Literature in the Digital Age: An Introduction.* Cambridge: Cambridge University Press.

Hayles, N. K., (1999). *How We Became Posthuman: Virtual Bodies in Cybernetics, Literature and Informatics.* Chicago: University of Chicago Press.

—— (2002). *Writing Machines.* Cambridge, MA: MIT Press.

—— (2004). Print Is Flat, Code Is Deep: The Importance of Media-Specific Analysis. *Poetics Today*, 25(1), 67–90.

—— (2008). *Electronic Literature: New Horizons for the Literary.* Notre Dame, IN: University of Notre Dame Press.

Hayles, N.K., and Pressman, J. Eds., (2013). *Conparative Textual Media: Transforming the Humanities in the Postprint Era.* Minneapolis: University of Minnesota Press.

Heti, S., (2012). Interview: How Should a Writer Be. Interviewed by Claire Cameron. *The Millions* [online], 12th June. Available at <www.themillions.com/2012/06/how-should-a-writer-be-an-interview-with-sheila-heti.html> [accessed 26th May 2014].

—— (2013). *How Should a Person Be?* London: Harvill Secker.

Jagoda, P., (2016). *Network Aesthetics.* Chicago and London: University of Chicago Press.

Kelly, A., (2011). Beginning with Postmodernism. *Twentieth Century Literature*, 57(3–4), 391–422.

Kember, S., and Zylinska, J., (2012). *Life after New Media: Mediation as a Vital Process.* Cambridge, MA: MIT Press.

Kevorkian, M., (2006). *Colour Monitors: The Black Face of Technology in America.* Ithaca: Cornell University Press.

Kirschenbaum, M.K.G., (2008). *Mechanisms: New Media and the Forensic Imagination.* Cambridge, MA: MIT Press.

Kittler, F., (2008). Code (or, How You Can Write Something Differently). In *Software Studies: A Lexicon*, ed. Matthew Fuller, 40–47. Cambridge, MA: MIT Press.

Konstantinou, L., (2009). The Brand as Cognitive Map in William Gibson's *Pattern Recognition. Boundary 2*, 36(2), 67–97.

—— (2013). Periodizing the Present. *Contemporary Literature*, 54(2), 411–423.

—— (2016). We Had to Get beyond Irony: How David Foster Wallace, Dave Eggers, and a New Generation of Believers Changed Fiction. *Salon.* Available at <www.salon.com/2016/03/27/we_had_to_get_beyond_irony_how_david_foster_wallace_dave_eggers_and_a_new_generation_of_believers_changed_fiction/> [accessed 10th June 2016].

Light, J.S., (1999). When Computers Were Women. *Technology and Culture*, 40(3), 455–483.

Marczewska, K., (2018). *This Is Not a Copy: Writing at the Iterative Turn.* London and New York: Bloomsbury.

McPherson, T., Jagoda, P., and Chun, W.H.K., (2013). New Media and American Literature. *American Literature*, 85(4).

Nakamura, L. (2002). *Cybertypes: Race, Ethnicity, and Identity on the Internet.* New York: Routledge.

Nakamura, L., and Chow-White, P.A. Eds., (2011). *Race after the Internet.* New York and Oxon: Routledge.

Noble, S.U., (2018). *Algorithms of Oppression: How Search Engines Reinforce Racism.* New York: New York University Press.

Parikka, J., (2012). *What Is Media Archeaology?* Cambridge: Polity.

Pressman, J. (2014). *Digital Modernism: Making It New in New Media.* Oxford: Oxford University Press.

Punday, D., (2012). *Writing at the Limit: The Novel in the New Media Ecology.* Lincoln, Nebraska and London: University of Nebraska Press.

—— (2015). *Computing as Writing.* Minneapolis: University of Minnesota Press.

Raley, R., (2001). Reveal Codes: Hypertext and Performance. *Postmodern Culture* [online], 12(1).

—— (2008). On Locative Narrative. *Genre: Forms of Discourse and Culture,* 41(1–2), 123–147.

Stadler, G., (2014). "My Wife": The Tape Recorder and Warhol's Queer Ways of Listening. *Criticism,* 56(3), 425–456.

Tabbi, J., and Wutz, M., (1997). *Reading Matters: Narrative in the New Media Ecology.* Ithaca: Cornell University Press.

Tenen, D., (2017). *Plain Text: The Poetics of Computation.* Stanford: Stanford University Press.

Terranova, T., (2013). Free Labor. In *Digital Labor: The Internet as Playground and Factory,* ed. Trebor Scholz, 33–77. New York: Routledge.

Timmer, N., (2010). *Do You Feel It Too? The Post-Postmodern Syndrome in American Fiction at the Turn of the Millennium.* Amsterdam: Rodopi.

Wolf, M.J.P., (2000). *Abstracting Reality: Art, Communication, and Cognition in the Digital Age.* Lanham, MD: University Press of America.

Wood, J., (2012). True Lives. *The New Yorker* [online], 25th June. Available at <www.newyorker.com/arts/critics/books/2012/06/25/120625crbo_books_wood> [accessed 26th May 2014].

20

ANTHROPOCENE

Sam Solnick

In his 2008 book *The Earth After Us* the geologist Jan Zalasiewicz indulges in a kind of science fiction, imagining an alien visitor arriving on Earth a hundred million years into the future. Zalasiewicz's extra-terrestrial finds traces of a sophisticated civilization that had the capacity to re-engineer parts of the planet's surface, and begins to examine how our long-extinct species might have inscribed itself into the very fabric of the planet, analysing the rock strata to find traces of isotopes, chemical signals and fossilised remainders of specific products and technologies. In one striking comic moment Zalasiewicz points out that given 'the uneven distribution of these resources among individual humans, one can predict that a Marks & Spencer's pullover is more likely to make it into the fossil record than an Yves St. Laurent evening creation'. While such 'vanity fossils' are just a tiny fraction of what Zalasiewicz describes as the 'time capsules' available for analysis, their presence in the strata provide Ozymandias-like artefacts of human ingenuity, folly and finitude (2008: 171). This extinct Anthropos may have collectively shaped the planet, but the remainders left by different members of the species indicate that the type and distribution of this impact was determined by power, consumption and production as well as the technologies and materials of any given period of civilisation – 'look upon my merchandise ye mighty and despair'. This chapter is an attempt to trace how contemporary literary fiction has explored the ways in which humanity writes itself into the fabric of the planet. It will show that the preponderance of environmentally aware fiction that relies on the perspective of science fictional futures has been supplemented by writers who have focussed on the geological and ecological inscriptions of the past and present. In rendering the economic, political and technological drivers of environmental change, the emergent literary fiction of the Anthropocene addresses associated issues of representation, responsibility and agency across a variety of spatial and temporal scales.

It is unusual to see a geologist employing science fiction; but these are strange times for stratigraphy. Zalasiewicz currently convenes what is known as the 'Working Group on the Anthropocene' (or, commonly, 'AWG' for 'Anthropocene Working Group'), a team of scientists from varied disciplines tasked with critically analysing the proposal for what is a much-discussed but, at the time of writing in January 2018, still-informal geologic time unit: the Anthropocene. The Anthropocene, as the AWG's most recent summary (Zalasiewicz et al. 2017: 55) puts it, is 'refers to time interval marked by rapid but profound and far-reaching change to the Earth's geology, currently driven by various forms of human impact'. The AWG is a remarkable departure from geology's business as usual. The related disciplines of stratigraphy and geochrononology – which would normally navigate deep time to map the relative position of strata to help establish geological time units – have been pushed to pronounce, with unprecedented haste, on shifting geologic conditions that are not only extraordinarily recent relative to the billions of years of Earth history, but which are still changing with alarming rapidity. The AWG does not have the benefit of hindsight afforded to Zalasiewicz's alien; its scientists do not know what the Anthropocene will look like from the future. This raises a question of definition and boundaries. The changes that characterise the Anthropocene as stratigraphically distinct from the previous epoch (the Holocene, which began approximately 12,000 years ago) are reasonably well established and include 'marked acceleration of rates of erosion and sedimentation; large-scale chemical perturbations to the cycles of carbon, nitrogen, phosphorus and other elements; the inception of significant change in global climate and sea level; and biotic changes including unprecedented levels of species invasions across the Earth' (ibid: 56).

In order for the Anthropocene to be formalised, there must be an appropriate proxy that indicates synchronous global change in the stratigraphic record. Consequently, the AWG have discussed different possible starting dates. Proposals have included a start date that coincides with the industrial revolution, with the seventeenth-century colonisation of the Americas and with the development of agriculture thousands of years ago. The AWG currently favour using the global presence of radionuclides from nuclear arms testing found throughout the planet's rock strata as their proxy. This stratigraphic signature is contemporaneous with the so-called 'Great Acceleration' in energy use, greenhouse gas and population growth after 1950.

The Anthropocene has shown itself to be a powerful and elastic term, permeating academic, artistic and media discourses. As Kunkel (2017) and Menely and Taylor (2017) have pointed out, the issues it brings to the fore range across spatial and temporal scales, giving it more traction and making it more encompassing than other concepts that synthesise environmental concerns such as sustainability, extinction or even climate change. Its extraordinary reach, suggests Jamie Lorimer (2017), coining yet another neologism that piggybacks on the word 'Anthropocene', means that the Anthropocene has engendered an 'Anthropo-scene'. Lorimer highlights how a wide variety of disciplines and discourses are now evolving to adapt to the changing planet (and the changing conceptualisation of the planet). Literary fiction, not an area of artistic production generally known for its engagements with deep time, the non-human, or collective species agency, is one of many areas that has shifted to adapt to the Anthropocene's new strata.

Some of the most common tropes and tensions for fiction engaging with the Anthropocene can be found in Margaret Atwood's (2009) short story 'Time Capsule Found on the Dead Planet'. Atwood employs, in condensed form, the same scenario as Zalasiewicz in *The Earth After Us*. The titular time capsule narrates the rise and fall of a species, beginning with a quasi-Ovidian Golden Age where a pagan population lives off the bounty of the land. Next, they develop coinage and systems of exchange leading to an ensuing time where capital itself becomes a god, 'all-powerful, and out of control. It began to talk. It began to create on its own' (2009: n.pag). War, environmental despoliation, desertification and eventually extinction ensue.

The story's interlinkage of economy and ecology highlights the importance of material socioeconomic conditions in shaping the behavioural and technological drivers of Anthropocene changes. (Indeed, Jason Moore [2015] has argued that 'Capitalocene' might be a better description of the Anthropocene.) The alienation of Atwood's humans from their own embodiment and their organic lifeworld is a commonplace for environmentally orientated fiction, as is the recalibration of mythic tropes. Fall narratives abound and, as Trexler (2015) has detailed, so do fictions which draw on biblical and mythic floods. However, lapsarian anguish also risks an anthropocentrism that forgets about deep geological time. After all, as Jeremy Davies (2016: 7) reminds us, the Anthropocene is 'one epoch among many on the same footing, rather than one-half of the earth's history'. In focusing on human history rather than geological time Atwood, or at least her narrator, forgets that life extended long before humans, and will almost certainly flourish long after they are gone. Moreover, humanity's impact on the planet does not mean that it has control of these impacts: varied planetary systems bind human agency within a range of biological, meteorological, hydrological and geological non-human forces and processes.

'Time Capsule Found on a Dead Planet' first appeared in *The Guardian* as part of the 10:10 climate-change campaign that aims to support reductions in carbon emissions. This speaks to a key distinguishing feature of environmentally aware literary fiction post-2000. One can trace key drivers of the Anthropocene across literary history, from the hydrocarbon exuberances of Upton Sinclair's *Oil!* (1926), through the steam power of Elizabeth Gaskell's *North and South* (1855) to, as Steve Mentz (2015) does, the colonial context of *The Tempest* (c. 1610) and beyond. But what differentiates literature written in the last two decades is that it has become almost impossible for authors to write without some knowledge of the scientific consensus that humans are shaping the fabric of the planet in a manner hitherto unimagined. A geological force has, to some degree, become aware of its own agency.

Atwood's fable also foregrounds a knotty question of genre. While, with its self-consciously Ovidian structure it is certainly 'literary' (and mythic), the fact that it is an apocalyptic future history locates it within the realm of science fiction – although Atwood (2011) prefers the term 'speculative fiction' rather than 'science fiction' to describe her work. While it is only one aspect of a series of interlinked phenomena, climate change is the most discussed of the planetary changes associated with the Anthropocene. This is in part because climate change, present in public consciousness for over thirty years, has a longer scientific (and indeed literary) history than the Anthropocene, which only started being used regularly within the sciences after the turn of the millennium. The word 'cli-fi' has become an increasingly common way of describing fiction related climate change. Despite its catchy rhyme with sci-fi, cli-fi as Stephanie LeMenager (2017) rightly emphasises, is not limited to the science fictional. There is a diversity of fiction (not to mention other forms and media) that has been labelled cli-fi. As shall become clear below, fiction has increasingly engaged with aspects of the Anthropocene outside of climate change, and some authors deal with climate change in relation to a range of past, present and future environmental change. Cli-fi is therefore a useful placeholder for texts where climate change is a major concern, rather than an easily delineable genre. What cli-fi shares with many other readings and writings of fiction about the Anthropocene is that it often harbours a temporality that Caren Irr (2017: n.pag.), building on the work of Srinivas Aravamudan (2013), describes as 'catachronistic':

> by inverting anachronism or the projection of the present into the past, cli-fi synthesizes past and present and projects the result into a largely unavoidable but still emergent or creeping future. To this way of thinking, the turning point, such as it is, in climate fiction is an event that went unnoticed in the recent past but whose effects permeate the present and future.

The need for environmentally aware fiction to imagine the future effects of the present and past is one of the reasons why, by some distance, science fiction is still the most common genre which deals directly with climate change and, consequently, the Anthropocene. Another is the fact that many of the most spectacular and alarming effects of climate change are yet to come to fruition, at least for most inhabitants of Europe and North America, leading concerned authors to contemplate dramatic environmental transformations or the nightmarish futures that might arise, rather than less drastic effects in the present. Adeline Johns-Putra's (2016) survey of climate change in the arts points out that the tenor of cli-fi is overwhelmingly dystopian and apocalyptic.

Science fiction also has a more utopian capacity to imagine future political systems, mitigatory technologies and social formulations that both open-up adaptive possibilities and cast light on the limitations of an environmentally disastrous present. The most influential and sophisticated post-2000 science fictional renderings of the Anthropocene include Kim Stanley-Robinson's tales of terraforming and other forms of social and technological adaptation in novels such as *2312* (2012); the resource wars on warmed Earths in Paolo Bacigalupi's novels *The Windup Girl* (2009) and *The Water Knife* (2015); and Atwood's own post-apocalyptic and posthuman *MaddAddam Trilogy* (2014a [2003–2013]), where the majority of humanity are wiped out by a human-engineered virus that the novels describe as a 'waterless flood'.

Science fiction is normally set in the (near or distant) future to allow for the creation of novel technologies or phenomena that differentiate the fictional world from the reader's own; although some science fiction creates an alternate past or present. (Relevant examples of the latter include Michelle Tea's *Black Wave* (2016) – set in a similar-but-different disintegrating California undergoing environmental collapse and apocalypse – and Jeff VanderMeer's (2014) uncanny, seemingly alien ecologies in his 'New Weird' *Southern Reach Trilogy*.) Conversely, the majority of novels and short stories that would generally be categorised by readers or publishers as 'literary fiction' are – with some notable exceptions such as magic realism – circumscribed by what is considered presently possible. The negative definition of 'literary fiction' as somehow 'not genre fiction' is a crude one, not least because the boundaries of science fiction are notoriously tricky to delineate.[1] Many authors and texts transcend simplistic generic boundaries and expectations and there is an argument to be made that science fiction is better described as a mode rather than a genre. This does not alter the fact that the preponderance of ecologically orientated science fictional futures or alternate realities has been matched by a relative dearth of literary fiction set in a recognisable present that engages directly with the Anthropocene. Even less is set in the past. But, as the remainder of this chapter shows, this is beginning to change as authors adapt the formal and generic tendencies of post-millennial literary fiction to the Anthropocene's shifting terrains.

In *The Great Derangement*, the novelist Amitav Ghosh's (2016: 17) non-fiction work about climate change, he argues that at its core the modern novel relies upon the depiction of the everyday and therefore conceals 'those exceptional moments that serve as the motor for narrative'. A novel that vividly depicts, say, the extreme weather events associated with climate change courts 'eviction from the mansion in which serious fiction has long been in residence', and risks being banished to the 'humbler dwellings' of genre fiction where Ghosh sees science fiction as belonging (24). Ghosh's metaphor is clumsy, the attribution of 'seriousness' by genre is misleading and unfair, but his question of how the contemporary novel – and its preference for everyday scales and events – responds to the Anthropocene is crucial. For Ghosh, the disjunction between the quotidian happenings of the novel and the multifarious dimensions of climate change means that we have entered a 'great derangement', when art and literature conceals rather than articulates the realities of environmental crisis. The features of that crisis – such as changes in weather patterns or the non-local effects of pollution – fall outside the normal spatial and temporal scales of quotidian experience and attention.

One useful countervailing critical strategy, best exemplified by the work of Timothy Clark (2012, 2015: 131), is to also read fiction at a kind of macroscopic spatial and temporal scale. Doing so reveals how the characters and scenarios of fiction depend upon, amongst other things, a petrocapitalist infrastructure which renders the combined effects of everyday human activity ecologically disastrous. Such a macroscopic reading should not supplant the more conventional human and socio-political scales as some 'general and repetitive last word about depressing or tragic ecological realities' but serve to deepen, ironize and de-humanize everyday life. Reading and writing the Anthropocene requires attentiveness to multiple scales, and a reconceptualization of character because, as Chakrabarty (2012: 14) explains, we now have to 'view the human simultaneously on contradictory registers',

> as a geophysical force and as a political agent, as a bearer of rights and as author of actions; subject to both the stochastic forces of nature (being itself one such force collectively) and open to the contingency of individual human experience; belonging at once to differently scaled histories of the planet, of life and species, and of human societies.

In his analysis of David Mitchell's *Cloud Atlas* (2004), Ian Baucom (2015) suggests that these multiple facets of the human provide a radical challenge to how we conceive of character, particularly within the historical novel. Mitchell's multi-genre book ranges in space and time from a colonial-era historical fiction to contrasting dystopian and then post-apocalyptic science fictional futures. Baucom highlights the way that Mitchell's markers of human-induced environmental change such as rising seas and petro-clouds constitute a collapsing boundary between what Chakrabarty (2009: 201) calls 'the age-old humanist distinction between natural history and human history'. This problematizes the influential conception of characters in the historical novel as 'Georg Lukács understood them: the characters who serve as summarizing types of a particular moment or historical situation' (Baucom 2015: 154). For Lukács (2002: 53), characters in historical fiction function as representative exemplars, allowing realist historical fiction to give 'poetic life to those historical, social and human forces which, in the course of a long evolution, have made our present-day life what it is and as we experience it'. What is missing here is a sense of the non-human world, the way that humans make and are also made by a material environmental context. Moreover, as Hamish Dalley points out in his own consideration of the historical novel in the context of climate change, Chakrabarty's argument also provides a secondary challenge to a conventional Lukácsian sense of the historical novel, the idea of collective humanity as a telluric force.

> The human-as-species, his [Chakrabarty's] description implies, is not available to typification; you cannot construct a representative exemplar of this force, because a force is not an agent. As such, it is hard to imagine what a historical novel of climate change would look like – one that went beyond depicting the consequences of environmental catastrophe, and sought to explain how those events had come to pass.
>
> (Dalley 2014: 203)

The Wake (2015) by 'recovering environmentalist' Paul Kingsnorth and Annie Proulx's *Barkskins* (2016a) provide two important examples of how historical fiction has risen to Dalley's challenge since it was issued. *The Wake* is the first part of a trilogy centred around the relationship between humanity and the natural world where each volume is separated by a millennium. Kingsnorth relocates many of the tropes of the post-apocalyptic cli-fi novel to the aftermath of the 1066 Norman invasion (drawing on the same Saxon/Norman tensions that permeate Lukács's key example of historical fiction, Sir Walter Scott). It is narrated in a pseudo-Old English 'shadow tongue' by Buccmaster, a farmer who lives through the invasion, losing his land and his family. *The Wake*'s characters are both representative of the time, particularly the relationship between people, language, mythology and local ecologies, but Kingsnorth also sometimes depicts the Normans as a de-individualised, collective force that ravages the landscape they conquer as well as its people. In other words, the Normans are figured as an apocalyptic storm. This is one of several parallels that Kingsnorth draws between his medieval apocalypse and contemporary environmental crises, some of which are established on the opening page:

> None had thought a wind lic this colde cum for all was blithe lifan as they always had and who will hiere the gleoman [storyteller] when the tales he tells is blaec who locs at the heofon if it brings him regn [. . .] none will loc but the wind will cum. the wind cares not for the hopes of men. the times after will be for them who seen the cuman.
>
> (2015: 1)

Kingsnorth combines history with metaphor to give 'poetic life' to the ecological concerns that operate alongside and through historical fiction's traditional network of 'historical, social and human forces'. As the novel's afterword and Kingsnorth's essay on the subject (2017: 185) make clear, he sees the Norman invasion as having tangible ecological consequences, positing a relationship between the Norman conquest, Britain's markedly unequal distribution of land and the effects of both imperialism and industrialisation. This manifests throughout the novel in the depiction of the alienation of people from place due to factors such as shifts in language ('their place was taken by names what has not growan from that ground') or new technologies and policies that transform the landscape, such as the draining of the fens which 'will be succd of the sea and gifan to the land gifan ofer to man' (2015: 164, 4).[2] A dark adumbration of the Anthropocene's massive shifts in landscape use due to factors such as urbanisation, hydrocarbon extraction and agribusiness.

Kingsnorth's figuration of the Normans as an extreme weather event that echoes the more common disaster scenarios of cli-fi, builds on the double sense of apocalypse as both a catastrophic event and – in the sense of the term as unveiling or revelation – the vision or prediction of that event. Buccmaster (if the reader believes his unreliable narration) foresees disaster and lives through its aftermath. Kingsnorth positions his narrator as the medieval ancestor of those contemporary characters whose warnings of climate change are ignored by a population determined to continue 'lifan as they always had', denying all evidence that they cannot.

Cli-fi has frequently narrated the difficulties faced by those characters (often scientists) who attempt to convince others about imminent disaster. The challenges Buccmaster faces in convincing his community resonate strongly with figures such as the lepidopterist Ovid Byron in Barbara Kingsolver's *Flight Behaviour* (2013) when he tries to explain to a disenfranchised and impoverished rural Tennessee community that the displaced Monarch butterflies that have swarmed to their town are evidence of climate change's perturbation of biological systems and that their own behaviour has contributed to these changes. The charismatic or heroic scientist character has become common enough that some authors have begun to reproduce it as satire. As Irr (2017) points out, notable examples of the ways authors have undercut the stock character of the masculinist scientist hero include the nerdy, obsessive statistician of Nathanial Rich's tale of speculation, risk analysis and hurricanes *Odds Against Tomorrow* (2013) and Ian McEwan's cynical, corpulent Michael Beard in his satire on sustainability *Solar* (2010). In the figure of Buccmaster, Kingsnorth combines a version of the ignored, Cassandra-ish scientist with the violent survival exploits typical of those dystopian or post-apocalyptic novels which imagine a nightmarish Anthropocene future, such as Cormac McCarthy's parable of cannibalism and other sundry horrors on an Earth denuded of its biosphere in *The Road* (2006); the disease, flood and civil-war devastation of Omar El Akkad's *American War* (2017); or the final section of David Mitchell's *The Bone Clocks* (2014), set in a post-oil Ireland.

Unlike *The Wake* – where, despite the moments which render humans as a collective force, the focus is still on the individual protagonist – Annie Proulx's transhistorical forestry novel *Barkskins* ranges across characters and time periods to track the different social, technological, ecological and economic forces that shape the Anthropocene. The novel primarily takes place during the eighteenth and nineteenth century in the forests of North America (shorter sections in Europe, China and Oceania help establish the global trade networks at play). The last quarter of the novel rushes through until the present day. *Barkskins* has a large cast of both coloniser and indigenous characters, drawn primarily from two intermingling families but, as Proulx (2016b) has explained in an interview, the key character is the forest itself:

> It's *the* character. . . . It's the underpinning of life. Everything is linked to the forest. This is but one facet of larger things, like climate change and the melting of the ice. So deforestation is part of a much, much larger package.

Through the accelerating logging of the forest and the concomitant shifts in migration, finance and technology, Proulx explores a series of interconnected environmental issues. These include different ways that the indigenous and settler communities conceptualise the forest; ongoing species loss; the catastrophic violence and imperial injustices arising when Europeans arrive to take advantage of what Raj Patel and Jason Moore (2018) would call 'cheaps' (in this case both cheap work and cheap nature); and the roles that institutions such as banks, corporations and even universities play in environmental degradation. The novel's closing sees Proulx foreground the link to climate change via a scientist who has just visited the melting Greenland glaciers and realised all that this entails. The final sentence is an image of waters rising: 'The sea lifted itself toward the light. And kept on lifting' (2016a: 713).

One thing that *Barkskins* shares with *The Wake, Cloud Atlas* and other historical novels dealing with environmental crisis such as T.C. Boyle's *San Miguel* (2012), is the catachronistic orientation of their historical fiction not just towards the present, but to a potentially apocalyptic future which suffers the worst effects of climate change and other features of the Anthropocene. For Frederic Jameson (2013: 313), the orientation towards the future constitutes a new departure for historical fiction, signalling a moment where 'our history, our historical past and our historical novels, must now also include our historical futures as well'. There are two issues at stake here. The first is thinking about the history of the future i.e. how a future riven by Anthropocene upheavals will look back at the past that engendered it; a past which includes our present as well as our history. The second relevant sense of historical futures Jameson has in mind is the history of different visions of the future.

> As for the history of the future itself, unless it is understood to be a literary genre (Science Fiction), we often tend to abandon it to prophets and Cassandras, if not to the writers of best-sellers on the subject, without remembering that every present of time in which we move includes its own dimension of futurity, of fears and expectations, which (realized or not) at once accompany that present into the past along with it, as what Sartre called 'dead' futures.
>
> (297)

This second sense of evolving visions of futurity permeates Proulx's novel. As *Barkskins* develops, it moves between the perspective of those who have always lived in the forest; to the settlers who, despite seeing the forest as resource, cannot imagine its finitude and consequently see it as essentially eternal; to those who – influenced by commerce and Christianity – imagine a future where they will have domesticated this (purported) wilderness; through the growth of the Duke corporation (the rise and fall of which dominates the central part of the book) where visions to the future are rendered in terms of investment and payoff; right through to the visions of climate change and associated extinction at the novel's end. The fears and expectations of each historical (or dead) future are folded into, and shape, the development of the present.

The relationships of the characters to the forest, and its future, are themselves determined by what Mackenzie Wark (2015) calls the 'inhuman': the apparatus of labour and technology that mediate the forest's non-human world to humans. *Barkskins'* descriptions of forestry move from almost Tolstoyan descriptions of embodied labour (tree-felling by axe) early in the novel, to increasingly mechanised modes of forestry, and on to the advent of DDT (the pesticide made famous by Rachel Carson's 1962 *Silent Spring*) and other forms of twentieth century agro-industrialism. And as technology evolves, and deforestation shifts gears, so too does the pace of the novel, particularly after 1950 where the reader experiences a kind of great acceleration for the 'Great Acceleration': Proulx covers the period from the Second World War to the present in around forty pages of a 700-page novel, giving rise to a feeling of panicked urgency into the reading process itself.

Ben de Bruyn (2016) reads this acceleration in relation to the way that *Bakrskins* renders humans as a collective force as well as individual characters. Proulx figures the colonists in the quasi-naturalistic terms of a flood – 'as a great wave sweeping over [native tribes]' (181); 'billows of overseas white people arriving in countless ships' (177); '[a] tide of agricultural-minded immigrants' (538); an 'overwhelming tide of men with axes' (645). As de Bruyn points out, similar descriptions of humans have functioned in dehumanising ways in the past, but here they 'level rather than erect hierarchies', applying the wave imagery to the 'powerful rather than the powerless', to populations 'migrating from rather than to Europe' (de Bruyn 2016: 85). As in *The Wake*, Proulx's figuration of humanity as wave or flood links the usurping invaders both literally (as partial cause) and metaphorically with the rising waters to come.

Certain characters in *Barksins* struggle to negotiate this difficult sense of existing as individual agent and species force. As a despairing biologist in the later stages of the novel puts it: 'Men behave as overlords. They decide what will flourish and what will die. I believe that humankind is evolving into a terrible new species and I am sorry that I am one of them' (2016: 658). But this sort of all-encompassing complaint about anthropocentrism and the despairing oscillation between *mea culpa* and *nostra culpae* that species-consciousness engenders can obscure specific injustices and power differentials. Critiques of the Anthropocene from figures such as Bonneuil and Fressoz (2016); Chakrabarty (2009); and Haraway et al. (2016) have cautioned against the danger of a concept which conceptualises humanity, the Anthropos, as an undifferentiated whole when in fact neither responsibility for its causes nor vulnerability to its worst effects are evenly distributed. Menely and Taylor (2017: loc. 257) have pointed out that the designating of a single species as the prime geological agent is a 'specifying move rather than a universalizing one' i.e. the word Anthropocene need not imply that every human is transforming the Earth system in the same way, but 'that a single species in the biosphere is transforming the planet'. Even so, it is crucial that we are alive to the fact that while collective humanity may exist in the Anthropocene, different parts of the species have suffered different Anthropocene pasts, experience different Anthropocene presents, and hope and fear for different Anthropocene futures.

Barkskins' transhistorical rendering of the environmental dimensions of colonialism and capitalism constitute an instance of what Marisol de la Cadena (2015) terms the 'Anthropo-not-seen' by which she means both the destruction of alternate (frequently indigenous) modes of 'world-making' that do not see humans as separate from the rest of the biosphere and the resistance to that destruction of alternate ways of being. Fiction that depicts historical and contemporary environmental injustice in the Global South forms an important counterweight to the glut of science fictional cli-fi where injustices are 'not-seen' or at least glossed-over by narratives that focus on the destruction (and sometimes rebirth) of Western civilisation.

Many of the significant environmentally orientated novels set in the Global South focus not on disaster-to-come but on injustice and resistance in the past and present. In settings such as the toxic city of Indra Sinha's *Animal's People* (2005) the polluted sacrifice zones around New Delhi in Arundhati Roy's *The Ministry of Utmost Happiness* (2017) or the Niger Delta ruined by hydrocarbon extraction in Helon Habila's *Oil on Water* (2010), the technologies and policies which change the landscape, inscribing the Anthropos into the earth's strata, are also written onto the bodies of the characters through mutation, sickness, malnutrition and violence.

Crucially, each of these novels supplements their interest in the terrestrial and corporeal inscriptions of a corrosive Anthropocene modernity with an interest in the legal instruments and communicative technologies that inscribe those inscriptions in policy and popular consciousness. As Stephanie LeMenager (2014: 125) points out, Habila's use of a journalist protagonist travelling, in a seemingly purposeful echo of Conrad's Marlow, through the stricken communities and ecosystems of a pipeline-scarred delta explores how the news media is a means of imposing 'narrative coherence on ecological and social conditions so chaotic as to be illegible even to those who ordinarily live with them'.

Both Roy and Sinha foreground the plight of those maimed and killed by the 1984 Union Carbide leak at Bhopal, and who campaign for reparations and the prosecution of its executives. But in both novels, the campaigns for justice struggle to capture the attention of TV cameras, displaced in media attention by more spectacular violence. Bhopal, and Sinha's novel, are examples of Rob Nixon's (2011: 6) concept of 'slow violence', instances of environmental calamities that 'patiently dispense their devastation while remaining outside our flickering attention spans – and outside the purview of a spectacle-driven corporate media'. The still-affected communities of Bhopal, or the fracking-sickened Pennsylvania communities of Jennifer Haigh's *Heat and Light* (2016) or the toxic contaminations poisoning First Nations people in Thomas King's *The Back of the Turtle* (2014) are examples of slow violence vested upon the places, bodies and communities of the poor. Cli-fi's tendency toward the spectacularity of 'apocalypse soon' rather than the more insidious manifestations Anthropocene-injustice, is the product of an age that 'that venerates instant spectacle' whereas slow violence lacks 'the recognizable special effects that fill movie theatres and boost ratings on TV' (Nixon 2011: 6).

What LeMenager (2017: loc. 5116–5121) says about climate change's challenge to media conventions applies to the Anthropocene more generally: 'climate change "news" fails to be "news" insofar as it implies an end to the everyday itself, since the everyday relies on human habit and its complement of forgetting'. In other words, both the more spectacular phenomena associated with the Anthropocene (e.g. extreme weather events, oil spills, mega-engineering projects, environmental protest) and its 'not-seen' aspects (e.g. slow toxification, long-term drought, decreasing food security) are now 'taking hold as conditions rather than as events' (ibid.). The Anthropocene continuously seeps across our newsfeeds: shared, hash-tagged, liked, emojied. No longer news but, to use Zadie Smith's phrase a 'new normal'. For Smith (2014: n.pag.) 'new normal' is the

> most melancholy of all the euphemisms: [. . .] 'It's the new normal', I think, as a beloved pear tree, half-drowned, loses its grip on the earth and falls over. The train line to Cornwall washes away – the new normal. We can't even say the word 'abnormal' to each other out loud: it reminds us of what came before. Better to forget what once was normal, the way season followed season, with a temperate charm only the poets appreciated.

Digital technologies breed new relations between humans and the ecologies of the Anthropocene's new normal. From the immediate mud and critters outside our windows to the global socio-ecological crises unfolding on a global scale, we should be simultaneously alive to both the tweets of birds and the Twittersphere. In Ali Smith's *Winter* (2017: 48) this includes the significance of tweets about birds on Twitter. When the owner of that Twitter account – the nature blogger Arthur – types 'Nature is d' into a search engine, the predictive algorithm suggests to his search bar that nature is 'dead' and also 'dangerous', 'dying' and 'divine'. All these possibilities are at play throughout *Winter*, and the previous novel in Smith's 'Seasonal Quartet', *Autumn*: the sea encroaches on East Anglia, the unseasonable weather of a changing climate pervades the UK, and while characters have aesthetic or spiritual experiences of landscape, organisms (including refugees) are driven out of their traditional habitats.

Arthur has created his blog 'Art in Nature' as a reaction against 'nature films' he viewed online that, in his opinion, have 'no nature in them' but rather 'grit, and litter' (160). But, as his then-girlfriend Charlotte makes clear, Arthur's blog is 'irrelevant, reactionary, unpolitical' because it valorises a sense of nature outside of human influence that is no longer tenable (58). For Charlotte, writing about nature cannot now ignore threatened resources, water wars and climate change. Such crises are exacerbated by politicians whom Charlotte compares to plastic bags:

> *That* unhistoried, she said. *That* inhuman. *That* brainless and unknowing about all the centuries of all the ways that people carried things before they were invented. *That* damaging to the environment for years and years after they have grown their use.
>
> (57, italics in original)

Charlotte's analogy transforms a self-serving political elite, unheedful of the past or future, into the products and materials that will outlast them. Robert Macfarlane – perhaps one of the candidates Charlotte has in mind for her select few nature writers who, unlike Arthur, evince a 'political awareness' that enables them to avoid self-satisfied solipsism – has pointed out that plastics 'are being taken as a key marker for the Anthropocene, giving rise to the inevitable nickname of the "Plasticene"' (Smith 2017: 53; Macfarlane 2016: n.pag.).[3] For Charlotte, pervasive plastic means that there might be no 'such a thing left in the world as unruined water' (2017: 59).

In contrast to Charlotte's overwhelming sense of interpenetrating social, industrial and ecological concerns, Arthur's nature writing blog turns out to be a reflection of the 'untamed puddles' he goes in search of: not just shallow but ultimately artificial. 'Art in Nature' regales its readers with a journey on the M25 motorway to find puddles 'like the ones that the birds come to drink from and to splash their colourful wings in in old-time poems written by people who lived in the country'. The irony of using fossil-fuelled transport to somehow experience 'nature' in the raw (a form of ecotourism in micro) is ramified when it transpires that Arthur has invented this experience, and looked up his destination 'on Google Maps and on an RAC route planner' to find a likely setting to construct a 'good general sort of invented shareable memory for the people that read the blog'. The blog entry closes with Arthur exalting a love of 'life itself' returning to him 'that October afternoon as strongly as it had been and done when I was that boy and am that man' (184–187). This hackneyed allusion to Wordsworth's (2006: 91) 1802 poem 'My Heart Leaps Up' is a reminder that, in the Anthropocene's changing seasons, an exaltation of 'natural piety' now sounds jarring and solipsistically pious. Arthur's fake nature writing is part of *Autumn* and *Winter*'s critique of pernicious nostalgia, fake news and post-truth politics. In the Plasticene there is no easy recourse to an unchanging, apolitical nature.

Art will eventually give his blog to Charlotte, whose opening posts will examine how the 'camera eye of the drone has taken over from the crane shot as the eye of God in TV and film dramas [. . .] She'll follow this with a blog about the ubiquity of plastic microbeads in everything from clothes to saliva. Then she'll post a blog about sexism in parliament' (282). In allowing 'Art in Nature' to encompass these (and other) disparate phenomena, Smith suggests that new technologies, industrial materials and gender politics are not separate but interrelated concerns. (It is not for nothing that the novel throws the 2017 global Women's March into relief against a history of women's environmental protest and resistance, particularly the anti-nuclear encampment at Greenham Common.) Charlotte's drone's-eye view – like the glimpses through the holes of Barbara Hepworth sculptures elsewhere in the novel – illustrates how technics (including art) mediate our relationship with landscape and what Arthur would call nature. But descriptions of drones are contaminated with the knowledge of drone strikes, migration and resource stress that permeate the novel. Smith depicts a world where 'brimstone' refers to both a butterfly (emerging from hibernation unseasonably early) and a surface-to-air missile; in *Winter* consideration of the Anthropocene means paying attention to both.

In Smith's interpenetrating systems, even the communication technologies that mediate and disseminate this new normal are implicated in the changes that they describe. After hearing a description of Arthur's blog, one of the characters responds with a vision of a landscape of e-waste. These obsolete machines indicate that the physical infrastructure of media or literary production will perhaps have more of an impact than any blog, novel or Twitter account. Smith reaches towards the sort of macro-scale consideration that Clark sees as ironizing and de-humanizing the quotidian. The material of the medium outlasts the message. Indeed, the medium's material *is* the message that future generations will consider: in the future there will be no way of telling whether this obsolescent tech was used by by environmentalist clicktivists or presidents who tweeted in denial of climate change. Only the conflict minerals and plastics that constructed these machines' circuit boards will remain as undifferentiated fossils.

Imagining the afterlife of art or literature in an as-yet-unknown Anthropocene future is a common trope. Sometimes this involves considerations of materiality – as in Ben Lerner's (2014: 180) depiction of Donald Judd's aluminium artworks 'tuned to an inhuman, geological duration' amidst the multiple timeframes and scales of *10:04* (cf. de Bruyn 2017) . Irr (2017) has traced the recurring figure of the 'last book' in the fiction of Helen Simpson (2009) and Atwood (2014a [2003–2013]) and others. Some novels have imagined the future role of myths or the classics – as with the travelling Shakespeare performers in Emily St. John Mandel's post-apocalyptic *Station Eleven* (2014). Perhaps the most striking consideration of the materialities and the messages of fiction in the Anthropocene can be found 10km north of Oslo at the Future Library. Here, in 2014, the artist Katie Pearson planted a forest of 1,000 trees. These trees will provide the paper for a special anthology containing texts contributed by one writer every year, held in trust and unpublished until 2114. The four novelists included in the project so far are Atwood in 2014, David Mitchell in 2015, Sjón in 2016 and Elif Shafak in 2017. The project's website (Future Library, n.d.) asserts that tending the forest and 'ensuring its preservation for the one hundred year duration of the artwork finds a conceptual counterpoint in the invitation to each writer: to conceive and produce a work in the hopes of finding a receptive reader in an unknown future'.

As Atwood (2014b) points out in her essay for the Future Library, the project's not-yet-printed tales (like all writings) are time capsules carrying the past to the future, but they are also acts of hope, a reaching toward a unknown reader who will engage with the text. The nature of that engagement will depend on conditions intimately linked, but not wholly determined, by the social, technological and ecological factors of an Anthropocene past and present, an epoch where causes and effects, violences and injustices are unevenly distributed in space and time. Faulkner's (1996: 85) oft-quoted claim that 'The past is never dead. It's not even past' is recast in a troubling new light by the knowledge that humanity's global geological and ecological inscriptions – from chemicals and radioactive isotopes to climate change and plastic – far outlast the humans who made them. Charged with this awareness, post-millennial literary fictions are also Anthropocene inscriptions: written into and for a future that is not yet prescribed.

Notes

1 See Roberts (2006) for a useful overview
2 I am grateful to Serena Trowbridge and Thomas Knowles for sending me their conference paper that explored Kingsnorth's engagements with language and place.
3 Although given that Macfarlane has himself been painted as 'a lone enraptured male' in the pages of the *London Review of Books* (Jamie 2008), he may possibly be Charlotte (or Smith's) target here.

Works cited

Akkad, O.E., 2017. *American War.* Picador, London.
Aravamudan, S., 2013. The Catachronism of Climate Change. *Diacritics* 41, 6–30. https://doi.org/10.1353/dia.2013.0019
Atwood, M., 2014a [2003–2013]. *The MaddAddam Trilogy: Oryx & Crake/the Year of the Flood/MaddAddam*, Box Rep edition. Anchor Books, New York.
—— 2014b. Future Library [WWW Document]. URL www.futurelibrary.no/assets/press/essays/Margaret_Atwood.pdf (accessed 1.1.2018).
—— 2011. *In Other Worlds: SF and the Human Imagination.* Signal, Toronto.
—— 2009. Time Capsule Found on the Dead Planet by Margaret Atwood. *The Guardian*. 26 September (online). Availible at https://www.theguardian.com/books/2009/sep/26/margaret-atwood-mini-science-fiction (Accessed 16 August 2017).
Bacigalupi, P., 2015. *The Water Knife.* Orbit, London.
—— 2009. *The Windup Girl.* Night Shade Books, San Francisco, CA.
Baucom, I., 2015. "Moving Centers": Climate Change, Critical Method, and the Historical Novel. *Modern Languages Quarterly* 76, 137–157. https://doi.org/10.1215/00267929-2864997
Bonneuil, C., Fressoz, J.-B., 2016. *The Shock of the Anthropocene: The Earth, History and Us*, Trans. David Fernbach. Verso Books, London; Brooklyn, NY.
Boyle, T.C., 2012. *San Miguel.* Bloomsbury Publishing, London.
Chakrabarty, D., 2012. Postcolonial Studies and the Challenge of Climate Change. *New Literary History* 43, 1–18. https://doi.org/10.1353/nlh.2012.0007
—— 2009. The Climate of History: Four Theses. *Critical Inquiry* 35, 197–222.
Clark, T., 2015. *Ecocriticism on the Edge: The Anthropocene as a Threshold Concept.* Bloomsbury Academic, London.
—— 2012. Scale, in: Sussman, H. (Ed.), *Impasses of the Post-Global.* Open Humanities Press, Ann Arbor, MI, 146–167.
Dalley, H., 2014. *The Postcolonial Historical Novel*, 2014 edition. Palgrave, New York, NY.
Davies, J., 2016. *The Birth of the Anthropocene.* University of California Press, Oakland, CA.
de Bruyn, B., 2017. Realism 4°: Objects, Weather and Infrastructure in Ben Lerner's 10:04. *Textual Practice* 31, 951–971. https://doi.org/10.1080/0950236X.2017.1323490
—— 2016. Learning to Be a Species in the Anthropocene: On Annie Proulx's Barkskins. *Frame* 29, 71–90.
De La Cadena, M., 2015. Uncommoning Nature [WWW Document]. E-Flux. URL http://supercommunity.e-flux.com/texts/uncommoning-nature/ (accessed 12.31.17).
Faulkner, W., 1996 [1951]. *Requiem for a Nun*, New Edition. Vintage Classics, London.
Future Library, n.d. Future Library, 2014–2114 [WWW Document]. Future Libr. URL www.futurelibrary.no (accessed 12.31.17).
Gaskell, E., 1855. *North and South.* Chapman and Hall, London.
Ghosh, A., 2016. *The Great Derangement: Climate Change and the Unthinkable.* University of Chicago Press, Chicago.
Habila, H., 2010. *Oil on Water: A Novel.* Hamish Hamilton, London.
Haigh, J., 2016. *Heat and Light: A Novel.* Ecco, New York.

Haraway, D., Ishikawa, N., Gilbert, S.F., Olwig, K., Tsing, A.L., Bubandt, N., 2016. Anthropologists Are Talking: About the Anthropocene. *Ethnos* 81, 535–564. https://doi.org/10.1080/00141844.2015.1105838

Irr, C., 2017. Climate Fiction in English. *Oxford Research Encyclopaedia, Literature*. Oxford University Press, Oxford.

Jameson, F., 2013. *The Antinomies of Realism*. Verso, London.

Jamie, K., 2008. *A Lone Enraptured Male. London Review of Books*, 6 October 25–27.

Johns-Putra, A., 2016. Climate Change in Literature and Literary Studies: From Cli-Fi, Climate Change Theater and Ecopoetry to Ecocriticism and Climate Change Criticism. *Wiley Interdisciplinary Reviews Climate Change* 7, 266–282. https://doi.org/10.1002/wcc.385

King, T., 2014. *The Back of the Turtle*. HarperCollins, Toronto.

Kingsnorth, P., 2017. *Confessions of a Recovering Environmentalist*. Faber & Faber, London.

—— 2015. *The Wake*. Unbound, London.

Kingsolver, B., 2013. *Flight Behaviour*. Faber and Faber, London.

Kunkel, B., 2017. The Capitalocene. *London Review of Books*, 2 March, 22–28.

LeMenager, S., 2017. Climate Change and the Struggle for Genre, in Menely, T., Taylor, J.O. (Eds.), *Anthropocene Reading: Literary History in Geologic Times*. Penn State Press, University Park, PA.

—— 2014. *Living Oil: Petroleum Culture in the American Century*. OUP USA, Oxford; New York, NY.

Lerner, B., 2014. *10:04*. Granta, London.

Lorimer, J., 2017. The Anthropo-Scene: A Guide for the Perplexed. *Social Studies of Science* 47, 117–142. https://doi.org/10.1177/0306312716671039

Lukács, G. 2002 [1962]. *The Historical Novel*. Translated by Hannah Mitchell and Stanley Mitchell. University of Nebraska Press, Lincoln, NE.

Macfarlane, R., 2016. Generation Anthropocene: How Humans Have Altered the Planet for Ever. *The Guardian*. 1 April [Online] Availible at https://www.theguardian.com/books/2016/apr/01/generation-anthropocene-altered-planet-for-ever [Accessed 29 September 2017].

Mandel, E.S.J., 2014. *Station Eleven: A Novel*. Knopf Doubleday, New York, NY.

McCarthy, C., 2006. *The Road*. Picador, London.

McEwan, I., 2010. *Solar*. Random House, London.

Menely, T., Taylor, J.O., 2017. Introduction, in Menely, T., Taylor, J.O. (Eds.), *Anthropocene Reading: Literary History in Geologic Times*. Penn State Press, University Park, PA.

Mentz, S., 2015. Enter Anthropocene, c. 1610. *Glasgow Review of Books*. 27 September [Online] Availible at https://glasgowreviewofbooks.com/2015/09/27/enter-anthropocene-c-1610/ [Accessed 18 October 2017].

Mitchell, D., 2014. *The Bone Clocks*. Sceptre, London.

—— 2004. *Cloud Atlas*. Hodder and Stoughton, London.

Moore, J.W., 2015. *Capitalism in the Web of Life: Ecology and the Accumulation of Capital*. Verso Books, New York, NY.

Nixon, R., 2011. *Slow Violence and the Environmentalism of the Poor*. Harvard University Press, Cambridge, MA.

Patel, R., Moore, J., 2018. *A History of the World in Seven Cheap Things: A Guide to Capitalism, Nature, and the Future of the Planet*. University of California Press, Oakland, CA.

Proulx, A., 2016a. *Barkskins*. Scribner, New York.

—— 2016b. Annie Proulx Interviewed on "All Things Considered" NPR Radio.

Rich, N., 2013. *Odds Against Tomorrow*. Farrar, Straus and Giroux, New York, NY.

Roberts, A.C., 2006. *Science Fiction*. Routledge, Abingdon; New York.

Robinson, K.S., 2012. *2312*. Orbit, London.

Roy, A., 2017. *The Ministry of Utmost Happiness*. Hamish Hamilton, London.

Simpson, H., 2009. *In-Flight Entertainment*. Cape, London.

Sinclair, U., 1926. *Oil!* Albert and Charles Boni, New York.

Sinha, I., 2005. *Animal's People*. Scribner, London.

Smith, A., 2017. *Winter*. Hamish Hamilton, London.

Smith, Z., 2014. Elegy for a Country's Seasons. *New York Review of Books*. April 3 [Online] Availible at https://www.nybooks.com/articles/2014/04/03/elegy-countrys-seasons/ [Accessed 20 May 2017].

Tea, M., 2016. *Black Wave*. NewFeminist Press at CUNY, New York, NY.

Trexler, A., 2015. *Anthropocene Fictions: The Novel in a Time of Climate Change*. University of Virginia Press, Lexington, VA.

VanderMeer, J., 2014. *The Southern Reach Trilogy*. Farrar, Straus and Giroux, New York, NY.

Wark, M., 2015. *Molecular Red: Theory for the Anthropocene.* Verso, London.

Wordsworth, W., 2006. *The Collected Poems of William Wordsworth*, New Edition. Wordsworth Editions, Ware.

Zalasiewicz, J., 2008. *The Earth after Us: What Legacy Will Humans Leave in the Rocks?* Oxford University Press, Oxford; New York.

Zalasiewicz, J., Waters, C.N., Summerhayes, C.P., Wolfe, A.P., Barnosky, A.D., Cearreta, A., Crutzen, P., Ellis, E., Fairchild, I.J., Gałuszka, A., Haff, P., Hajdas, I., Head, M.J., Ivar do Sul, J.A., Jeandel, C., Leinfelder, R., McNeill, J.R., Neal, C., Odada, E., Oreskes, N., Steffen, W., Syvitski, J., Vidas, D., Wagreich, M., Williams, M., 2017. The Working Group on the Anthropocene: Summary of Evidence and Interim Recommendations. *Anthropocene* 19, 55–60. https://doi.org/10.1016/j.ancene.2017.09.001

21

DISPLACEMENT

Emily J. Hogg

The term 'displacement' can name an affective state, a psychological mechanism and a physical experience. The interaction between these meanings of the word produces much of its richness, and perhaps explains the frequency with which it occurs in contemporary scholarship attempting to grapple with the movement of people around the globe today, and with the legacy of the migrations of the past, both of which have involved violence, coercion and exploitation as well as hope, human ingenuity and the creation of new bonds, communities and cultures. In this chapter, I explore a particular definition of displacement which arises from four contemporary literary texts. To speak of displacement is inevitably to speak of what it means to be at home. Displacement can be understood as an experience which puts the meaning, security and reliability of home into question in various ways.

I begin by focusing on Yvonne Adhiambo Owuor's novel *Dust* (2014), a text which moves widely across time and space and includes a large cast of characters. The novel's use of multiple narrative perspectives reveals the diversity of the experiences of uncertainty about home which can be described through the term displacement, while its deep interest in the interrelations of history, memory and the contemporary show *why* such different experiences can be usefully connected by this one term. Through a discussion of Mohsin Hamid's novel *Exit West* (2017), I then make a case for the significance of home *within* a definition of displacement (rather than as its contrary). I argue that *Exit West*'s depiction of the relationship between home and displacement implies that vulnerability and homelessness are not simply negative experiences to be avoided; instead, they permeate human existence, and home itself is frequently a site of displaced experience. I then turn to *Signs Preceding the End of the World* by Yuri Herrara (2015), translated into English by Lisa Dillman, and *Black Mamba Boy* by Nadifa Mohamed (2010) to suggest that literature has a crucial role to play in illuminating the creative and generative potential of the experience of displacement, without losing sight of the unequal distribution of insecurity in the world today.

Dust by Yvonne Adhiambo Owuor

Most obviously, displacement refers to the experience of being out of place geographically. International organisations and NGOs typically use 'displacement' to refer to the involuntary physical movement of people because of 'persecution, conflict, violence, or human rights violations'

(UNHCR 2017: n.p.). The forcibly displaced include both refugees (those forced to flee across state borders) and internally displaced people, IDPs, (who are forced to leave their homes, but remain within their own country). According to the United Nations High Commissioner for Refugees, by 2016 'Nine of the top ten refugee hosting countries were in developing regions' and 65.6 million people across the globe were forcibly displaced, including 12 million Syrians, the largest national group (2017: n.p.).

Though forced physical movement is the most straightforward definition of displacement it does not exhaust the concept. For example, Karim Mattar (2014) argues that a notion of 'multiple displacement' is needed to illuminate the complexities of Palestinian history and literature. Mattar focuses on a memoir by the Palestinian poet Mourid Barghouti, translated into English by Ahdaf Soueif as *I Saw Ramallah* (2005). The memoir does describe a physical displacement: Barghouti, was born in Deir Ghassana, on the West Bank, and was studying at Cairo University in 1967 when Israel took control of Ramallah, and he was unable to return to his home for the next thirty years. However, Barghouti writes that 'Displacements are always multiple' (Barghouti 2005: 131; quoted in Mattar 2014: 108), and Mattar argues that the memoir offers a capacious reframing of displacement, in which a spectrum of modern Palestinian experiences are understood through this particular term. Importantly, Barghouti 'redefines occupation as a particular form of displacement' (Mattar: 104). This redefinition allows displacement to serve as the point of connection between the experiences of Palestinians living in the Occupied Territories and those living in exile and makes it easier to identify the shared root of these experiences: the Nakba ('catastrophe'), the mass expulsion of Palestinians from their homes and land in 1948.

The concept of 'multiple displacement' – referring to a series of proliferating, different displacements, with shared historical roots – also has resonance beyond the Palestinian case, and it is useful to think about this term in relation to *Dust*, which is set in Kenya. Two events set in motion the novel's plot: a man called Odidi Oganda is murdered in the midst of the post-election violence in 2007, and a man called Isaiah Bolton arrives in Kenya from England in search of Odidi, because he believes that Odidi has information that will help him find out about his father, who he had never known. These events implicate many different characters, and the novel's narrator has access to almost all of their minds and histories, sometimes switching between points of view in the space of one conversation. What the steady addition of these fragments of stories and points of view reveals is the pervasiveness of displacement as well as its multiplicity. There is no singular experience of displacement, but diverse experiences of displacement nonetheless link the characters.

For example, Odidi's father Nyipir is haunted by the ethno-political violence and torture he both participated in, and was a victim of, in the 1960s, in the aftermath of Kenyan independence. Central to this pervasive violence, and the 'trance of fear' (273) it created, was the question of belonging in, and loyalty to, the nation-state. For example, 'A central province was emptied of a people who were named cockroaches and "beasts from the west"' (272). Here the perception that the group does not truly belong in the nation-state produces their physical displacement, and this displacement is a prelude to murder: 'nobody would acknowledge the exiles or citizens who did not make it out of the province before they were destroyed' (272). Such people are 'exiles or citizens' because it is precisely their belonging or lack of belonging in the new nation which is, so dangerously, thought to be in question. Similarly, a 'train would stop at a lakeside town and offload men, women, and children. Displaced ghosts, now-in-between people' (272). These 'displaced ghosts' are then killed by cholera, deliberately spread by 'a government man' (272).

Displacement is not always connected with such extreme violence in *Dust*, though the question of what it means to truly belong in Kenya recurs. For example, echoes of language link two pairs of characters in the novel: Odidi and his sister Ajany, and Isaiah's parents, Hugh and

Selene, an English couple living in Kenya during the 1950s and 1960s, before independence. As children, Odidi and Ajany were sent from their home in Northern Kenya to boarding school. 'We're going to *real* Kenya,' Odidi tells his sister (13). But 'real Kenya' does not welcome them, because they are from the north. Their teachers' 'lip-curling mouths' ask '*Ati,* from where? Is it on the map?' (14). When there are famines, the school holds 'Help the Poor Starving People of Northern Kenya picnics' (114): in this simplistic narrative of suffering, the north is presented as a distant other, and an object of pity. As a result, though they go to school within their own nation, their sense of being out of place is profound: Odidi dreams 'about end of term, when the blessed migration from this Kenya to theirs, via Nairobi, occurred' (114).

Struggling with this hostile school environment and with tensions in their family, Ajany and Odidi respond with dreams of movement and migration. Odidi 'conjured up stories of Else-where' (117), visions of the two of them 'going Far Away' (52). In this way, according to Ajany, 'He had started it, Odidi had. Their homelessness' (117). In the end, Ajany leaves Kenya but Odidi remains, insisting '*this* is home' (119). Then, when she returns to Kenya from Brazil, Ajany finds that 'The longing for her people is a sudden sizzling ache. *What if I had stayed?* [. . .] They should have gone together Far Away' (119). On the one hand, she feels 'longing' for familiarity and belonging; on the other hand, she still feels the compulsion to move, to travel and to leave that she had experienced as a child, and she feels that it was only her brother who was missing from her journey to 'Far Away.' She feels pulled towards both staying and leaving. Near the end of the novel, she concludes that 'Homelessness is where Far Away is' (353). If, in her childhood and early adulthood, Ajany had thought of Far Away as the cure for the homelessness she experienced (paradoxically) at home, by the end of the novel, she has come to see that the dream of Far Away and the sensation of homelessness are inextricable.

The language of home, homelessness and longing is repeated in Selene and Hugh's story. Selene experiences an intense feeling of displacement in Kenya. When she comes to the house that Hugh has had built, she 'inserted the wrong key into the lock. Unsteady fingers searched for the right one. The keys fell' (114). Her inability to open the door symbolises the extent to which she is out of place: her refrain throughout her time in Kenya is '*Let us go back home*' (111); and 'for a moment' she is 'certain that she would die from her longing to return home to England' (109). Hugh, however, repeatedly tells her: 'We *are* home, darling' (115). Hugh and Selene echo Odidi and Ajany: one person insists that they are home, the other feels intensely that they are not.

This echo is perhaps surprising. Hugh and Selene are representatives of English colonial power; as much as Hugh talks about 'My country. My land. My dream.' (98), the reader knows that this fantasy of ownership is fragile and unsustainable – he resembles the British officer described elsewhere in the novel as 'a fierce son of a struggling empire leaning against the mast upon which the Union Jack quivered' (169). Ajany and Odidi, on the other hand, are citizens of the post-colonial nation-state – their sense of belonging is not ethically compromised in the way that Hugh's is. Nonetheless, because the novel uses repeated words and phrases to link Ajany and Odidi's story with Hugh and Selene's, the reader becomes aware that Ajany and Odidi's home-lessness is not simply a free-floating or individual sense of being dislocated or disconnected (of the sort that many young people the world over experience), but has a history, and is embedded in the political decisions and actions of the past.

Contemporary violence in Africa is often represented in Europe and North America rather as the north of Kenya is represented at Odidi and Ajany's school in *Dust*: as a parade of senseless suffering, as a decontextualized humanitarian crisis which flares up periodically and inexplicably (see Wainaina 2006; Coundouriotis 2010). In *Dust*, by contrast, the violence which followed the disputed 2007 elections – the context in which the novel takes place – is described as 'a single, unending howl by the nation's unrequited dead' (24). It is shown to be produced by a history of violence. In a similar way, the novel slowly assembles a network of experiences of displacement, which historicize the concept. It is displacement, belonging and lack of belonging which connect Ajany and Odidi's contemporary experiences with Nyipir's haunting memories of post-independence violence, and with Hugh and Selene's colonial enterprises. The novel forms a panoramic view of displacement-as-homelessness which stretches between the past and the present, and in which contemporary displacement is shown to be connected with the events of colonial history, and post-colonial violence: these are intersecting stories which, the novel insists, should be read together.

Exit West by Mohsin Hamid

If displacement can be understood as homelessness, it would seem straightforward to assume that finding a home means escaping displacement. However, the relationship between home and displacement is more complex than this implies. In her essay 'On Going Home,' in the anthology *The Good Immigrant*, Kieran Yates describes a trip from Britain ('the place I call home') to the village of Bahowal in Punjab, which her grandfather left forty years earlier (2016: 109).

> I see coming back to my village as significant, thanks to my privilege of being able to leave. But also because I can simultaneously cherry-pick my favourite aspects of my culture for anecdotes back home and social media, and keep the private, painful reflective ones for myself. This is what so many second-and-third generation immigrants experience visiting their homeland. We fine-tune the ability to find the nuances funny, deflecting the crushing weight of displacement and diaspora drama that becomes part of our everyday.
>
> (Yates 2016: 116–117)

In this passage, home takes on two different meanings. The village is her 'homeland,' but she also spends her time there shaping anecdotes she can retell 'back home' – here meaning the UK. Displacement also features doubly. First it is the experience of belonging to two places simultaneously ('the crushing weight of displacement and diaspora drama'), and yet not fully belonging in either. 'The plurality of my strangeness,' as Yates puts it elsewhere in the essay, 'of being split, of being Indian, too fresh, too Western, too bizarre, too independent' (116). The difficulty of this displacement can be dealt with, or endured, through a second – a discursive displacement, rather than a historical and familial one: the 'deflection' of comedy, the well-practiced art of finding humour in the subtleties of culture. In this excerpt from Yates' essay, 'home' and 'displacement' are doubled in a parallel way, and the terms' shared flexibility and mobility, their shared resistance to becoming settled in one steady meaning, suggests the complexity of their interactions.

The 2010s have witnessed an increasing emphasis in literary criticism on the re-evaluation of home, domesticity and homemaking. Lucinda Newns (2015) suggests that in post-colonial theory there has been a valorisation of displacement (understood as rootless cosmopolitanism) and a denigration of the importance of home and practices of homemaking. Where displacement is construed as freedom and mutability, and the open-endedness of identity, home, she shows, tends to be associated with the static and the rooted, the nation, patriarchal norms and so on. She argues that the tendency to promote an 'image of the unencumbered exile who rejects the need for home altogether' (516) fails to account for the difficulties of forced displacement, especially that experienced by refugees, for whom home matters enormously. Susan Fraiman (2017) has similarly argued that assumptions about the ideological significance of home have overshadowed material, specific and embodied experiences of home's value. As she writes, 'For the poor or transgendered person, the placeless immigrant or the woman on her own, aspiring to a safe, stable, affirming home doesn't reinforce hierarchical social relations but is pitched, precisely, against them' (Fraiman 2017: 20).

Nonetheless, however motivating the aspiration of home as safety, stability and affirming is, it is rarely simple in practice. In his posthumously published autobiographical work, *Familiar Stranger*, Stuart Hall complicates any straightforward opposition between home and displacement, when he describes feeling like a 'sort of internal exile' in his childhood (Hall and Schwarz 2017: 57). 'This wasn't my world. I fundamentally didn't belong to it. I couldn't believe in it and in time I didn't want to' (57). He writes:

> Even today I do not understand the full meaning of the feelings of displacement which gradually came to shadow and transform my life. What I can say is that, through a long and harsh process of disenchantment, I came to feel, even as a youth, at odds with the given circumstances of my birth. [. . .] my identity was formed more by resistance to those circumstances I had inherited than by adaptation to what they had tried to make me.
>
> (Hall and Schwarz 2017: 22)

Hall describes his experience of his home life in a middle-class Jamaican family as an experience of 'displacement'; he found displacement in the place of his roots.

In *Exit West* Mohsin Hamid explores the complexity of the relationship between home/security and displacement/vulnerability through his depiction of homely spaces. Fraiman suggests that 'the homeless and housed subject may not [. . .] be opposed so much as imaginatively enmeshed,' because 'while the first is anxious to reassemble the pieces of "home," the second is anxious, at a barely conscious level, to stave off exposure and exile' (23). In a congruent way, Hamid's novel presents a complex interrelation between displacement and home. The novel carefully portrays the value of home for those who are displaced; it tenderly depicts the processes whereby the displaced transform the barest spaces and most unpromising surroundings into homes in order to create a feeling of security. But, at the same time, it also insists on the fragility and temporary nature of security itself.

In the novel, magical doors have started appearing all over the globe. When a person steps through one of them, they are transported across the globe. The main characters, Nadia and Saeed, live in an unnamed country which has descended precipitously into war, so they choose to leave through one of the doors. They end up in Mykonos, and from Mykonos they travel to London, and then on to Marin, San Francisco. As they pass through this series of displacements, a recurrent theme emerges: the resilience and significance of a sense of home. At the beginning of the text, Nadia and Saeed observe refugees living in their city (before they, in turn, become refugees themselves). They notice that 'some seemed to be trying to recreate the rhythms of a normal life, as though it were completely natural to be residing, a family of four, under a sheet of plastic propped up with branches and a few chipped bricks' (Hamid: 23). Then, when Saeed and Nadia are living in a labour camp on the outskirts of London, Saeed volunteers with new arrivals at the camp. He takes one family to 'their designated space in one of the new pavilions, unoccupied and basic, with a cot, some fabric shelving hanging from one of the cables, and he left them there to settle in' (184). When he returns an hour later, 'what he glimpsed was a home, with the shelves all full, and neat bundles of belongings on the ground, and a throw on the cot' (184).

Later in the novel, when Nadia and Saeed have separated, Nadia lives in a storeroom above the food cooperative where she works. The room is still in use as a storeroom and there is 'no scope to decorate' (215). Nonetheless, having her own space reminds her 'of her apartment in the city of her birth, which she had loved,' and 'of what it was like to live there alone' (215). As time passes, the room (bare, undecorated, smelling of 'potatoes and thyme and mint,' and with a cot that smells 'a little of people') comes 'to feel to her like home' (215). These different characters, then, have in common a desire for home, and the drive to build it even where it might seem out of reach.

However, there is another strand of the text which emphasises the insecurity of home. Saeed has a close relationship with his parents; when his mother is killed in the war early in the novel, he is devastated. The text states that Nadia is 'more comfortable with all varieties of movement in her life than was Saeed, in whom the impulse of nostalgia was stronger' (90). When civil war makes living in their city impossible, the 'scattering of his extended family and his circle of friends and acquaintances, for ever, struck him as deeply sad, as amounting to the loss of a home, no less, his home' (90). Here displacement and home are opposed. Over the course of the novel, however, both of the characters change, and for Saeed this change manifests as a different attitude towards the loss of home. He begins to pray more, and when he prays:

> he touched a feeling that we are all children who lose our parents, all of us, every man and woman and boy and girl, and we too will all be lost by those who come after us and love us, and this loss unites humanity, unites every human being, the temporary nature of our being-ness, our shared sorrow, the heartache we each carry and yet too often refuse to acknowledge in one another.
>
> (202)

It is not that he is no longer sad about the loss of home and family: it is rather that he has begun to feel that this loss is inevitable, something which cannot be guarded against, and which forms a point of connection for humanity in general.

Dispersed throughout *Exit West* are short vignettes about characters across the globe who come into contact with the doors in some way. One of these is a woman in California, whose narrative picks up the theme of Saeed's prayer. This woman has never moved, and has lived in the same house all of her life. Nonetheless, with the changes in her neighbourhood, with the influx of new arrivals because of the doors, 'when she went out it seemed to her that she too had migrated, that everyone migrates, even if we stay in the same houses our whole lives, because we can't help it. We are all migrants through time' (209). Saeed concludes that, though the loss of home is 'deeply sad,' nonetheless, such loss 'unites humanity'; for the unnamed woman 'We are all migrants through time,' however rooted we are geographically.

This emphasis on the inevitability of the loss of home exists in tension in the novel with the repeated examples of characters' producing home in the midst of their varied dispossessions. In this way, it suggests that humans have a profound and serious need for home and security because, as fragile, mortal creatures, we are always vulnerable. But it also proposes that, because we are vulnerable, displacement is always a possibility – and no home will therefore ever be fully secure. Judith Butler (2009, 2004) and Isabell Lorey (2015) define *precariousness* as the shared vulnerability which is inherent in life and living with others. The related term *precarity* denotes the hierarchical organisation of precariousness in society. Though precariousness is shared (because existence depends on relationality, on the other, and is always therefore risky and uncertain) the experience of insecurity is regulated by legal and political systems and is consequently unequally distributed. The social order allows some people to feel protected from the full extent of their vulnerability, while others (many migrants, for example) are unprotected and forced to live with extreme risk and uncertainty. The encounter with one's own precariousness can be frightening, but, Lorey argues, 'The assumption that life [. . .] must be or even could be legally or otherwise entirely protected and secured, is nothing other than a fantasy of omnipotence. *Although* they need protection, living bodies can never be completely protected' (20).

Exit West shows that there are various ways of engaging with our shared vulnerability, many of them deeply damaging. In London, for instance, armed gangs of racist vigilantes roam the streets, and the government forces migrants into labour camps. The book is not romantic; it does not seek to play down the racism, violence and hatred that greets the displaced across the world. Nonetheless, in its emphasis on loss and migration as shared human conditions, rather than simply aberrations, it suggests that the inequality of contemporary displacement cannot be solved through extra security, but rather through a new reckoning with insecurity.

This is why the novel's central imaginative innovation and plot device – the doors – is so important. In the book, doors are transformed and unpredictable, opening in particular places at particular times in a way no one can fathom. In general, doors are ambivalent: open doors symbolise welcome and inclusiveness, closed doors exclusivity and boundaries. In *Exit West*, doors spring up across the globe, connecting geographically distant places. These unexpectedly open and uncontrollable doors are the opposite of security; they remake the world, in the novel, through their openness, rather than through their ability to protect and keep safe.

Signs Preceding the End of the World by Yuri Herrara

In the final part of this chapter, I focus on two novels which unflinchingly explore the costs of displacement, but which also defend the significance of movement and the importance of encounters across difference, forged in a situation of homelessness. In *I Saw Ramallah*, Mourid Barghouti describes writing as 'a displacement, a displacement from the normal social contract. A displacement from the habitual, the pattern, and the ready form' (132). This is a striking choice of words, in the context of Barghouti's biographical experiences. He suggests that literature is particularly attuned to the experience of displacement in its socio-political meanings, because to write is to stand outside, to remove oneself from the immediacy of experience; to be distanced from the meanings, commitments and feelings others take for granted. Barghouti's words also suggest the difficult balance that writing about displacement has to maintain.

On the one hand, he writes that a 'person gets "displacement" as he gets asthma,' he writes, 'and there is no cure for either. And a poet is worse off, because poetry itself is an estrangement' (Barghourti 2005: 4). Displacement is a kind of incurable condition, he suggests, and much of *I Saw Ramallah* is devoted to tracing the extensive and damaging psychological, social and political effects that the displacement from Ramallah had on his life, and on Palestinian identity more generally. On the other hand, Barghouti was a poet; he spent a significant amount of his life writing. If writing is displacement, the implication is twofold: first, that displacement might be able to create as well as to destroy, and second, that thinking about writing might be a crucial means of understanding the complexities of displaced experience.

As in *Exit West*, doors are an important motif in *Signs Preceding the End of the World*. The novel concerns a woman, Makina, who must illegally cross a border to the north (unnamed in the text, but strongly resembling the Mexico-US border) to try and find her brother, who had travelled there in search of some land he believed he had inherited. Many people in Makina's community cross the border, but the experience is fraught with dangers, both physical and psychological. When a friend of Makina's returns,

> it turned out that everything was still the same, but now somehow all different, or everything was similar but not the same: his mother was no longer his mother, his brothers and sisters were no longer his brothers and sisters, they were people with

difficult names and improbable mannerisms, as if they'd been copied off an original that no longer existed; even the air, he said, warmed his chest in a different way.

(20)

Makina's friend experiences a sense of complete disorientation upon his return: he has been so thoroughly changed by his experiences abroad that his family appear to him somehow unreal ('as if they'd been copied off an original') in a way that is profoundly hopeless ('an original that no longer existed'). Because he has been away for so long, his old reality, his old place within the family, has disappeared forever.

In a society which is so heavily affected by absence, movement and migration, Makina has a crucial job. She runs a 'switchboard with the only phone for miles and miles around' (18). The switchboard – and Makina herself – form the central point of the connection between geographically dispersed people, and one of her personal rules states: 'You are the door, not the one who walks through it' (18). What does it mean for Makina to be the door, in this sense? Partly, it is that her linguistic proficiency allows her to mediate the divisions of language produced by extensive migration. Callers speak 'in native tongue,' 'latin tongue' and 'more and more these days, they called from the North; these were the ones who'd often already forgotten the local lingo, so she responded to them in their own new tongue' (18). Makina is the 'door' because she allows messages to pass through.

Later in the text, when Makina herself has crossed to the North in search of her brother, she hears people speaking 'an intermediary tongue that Makina instantly warms to because it's like her':

malleable, erasable, permeable: a hinge pivoting between two like but distant souls, and then two more, and then two more, never exactly the same ones: something that serves as a link. More than the midpoint between homegrown and anglo their tongue is a nebulous territory between what is dying out and what is not yet born.

(65)

Makina feels her own self reflected in language, but this self is defined by its transience and insubstantial nature. What Makina and the new hybrid language share is a sense of in between-ness – an uncertainty, a sense of still being in formation.

Akram Al Deek defines the 'linguistic displacement' experienced by migrants, by the formerly colonized, and by second- and third-generation immigrants as 'concerned with acquired and required languages and tongues' (2016: 34). It denotes the tensions and possibilities of the different forms of selfhood and identity which can be expressed and produced through participation in different linguistic communities. In *Signs*, linguistic displacement is not only described on the level of the novel's narrative: it is also enacted for the reader, through the book's use of neologism. In Spanish, the novel repeatedly uses the word *jarchar*, and in her 'Translator's Note,' Dillman explains:

Within *Signs*, it means, essentially, 'to leave.' The word is derived from *jarchas* (from the Arabic *kharja*, meaning exit), which were short Mozarabic verses or couplets tacked on to the end of longer Arabic or Hebrew poems written in Al-Andalus, the region we now call Spain.

(Dillman 2015: 112)

In English, Dillman translates '*jarchar*' as 'to verse,' and the word appears throughout the text: 'Makina thanked him and versed out of there' (22); 'Mr. Double-U said Don't mention it, child, and she versed' (15); 'since she'd versed from home' (55); 'she opened the door and versed' (73). Dillman explains that 'to verse' maintains the connection with poetry that the original possesses, is a noun used as a verb (as with the Spanish derivation), and is also 'part of several verbs involving motion and communication (traverse, reverse, converse)' (113). Although, as Dillman states, the word is easy enough to comprehend in context, it is nonetheless likely to stand out because it is used in this new, strange way.

The text's repeated use of the neologism 'to verse' ties together language and movement. It means to leave, or to depart, and it is de-familiarising, halting the reader in her straightforward comprehension of the text, and inviting her to think carefully about what the word means in a way which standard usage would not. It is crucial that the novel draws the reader's attention to this particular word. The slight disorientation that the reader experiences when encountering this unfamiliar usage mirrors (on a small scale), the linguistic disorientation that is a consequence of 'versing.' It connects a geographical displacement with a displacement which occurs in language.

Nonetheless, the novel also emphasises the energy and creativity provoked by movement and encounters with strangers. For example, when Makina hears migrants in the north '[u]sing in one tongue the word for a thing in the other,' the text states that it 'makes the attributes of both resound':

> if you say Give me fire when they say Give me a light, what is not to be learned about fire, light, and the act of giving? It's not another way of saying things: these are new things.

> (66)

The meeting of different linguistic communities brings new things into being. In this sense, the displacement of the migrant community in the north is an opportunity, as well as a danger, for those who make the journey. Again, this is something the reader of the novel experiences too. In 'to verse' we have an example of the way the experience of displacement calls into being new words, and enlivens language: of the new kind of thinking and feeling that new language produces.

Nadifa Mohamed's book *Black Mamba Boy* provides a further example of the creative potential of displacement. The text is a fictionalised depiction of the author's father's experiences. It traces the life of Jama, the book's central character, from his childhood in Yemen in the 1930s, to Eritrea, Sudan, Egypt, Palestine and then to Britain. The book begins with a short prefatory section, set in London in 2008, in which the narrator sets out her motivations:

> [T]his is a hymn to him. I am telling you this story so that I can turn my father's blood and bones and whatever magic his mother sewed under his skin, into history. [. . .] I tell you this story because no-one else will.

> (1)

The reader is directly addressed here, in a way that underlines the urgency of the book's task. The father is made of 'blood and bones,' and is therefore vulnerable, and the 'magic' he possesses is intangible yet corporeal and therefore mortal (it is 'under his skin,' a strikingly physical image). But telling the story is thought to produce a transformation: it takes what is individual and fragile and turns it into 'history' – a public record of events with social significance.

Black Mamba Boy offers the story of one character while acknowledging his place within a much broader context:

> Let us call down the spirits of the nine thousand boys who foolishly battled on the mountains of Eritrea for Mussolini, who looked like my father, lived like him but had

their lives cut off with blunt axes, the ones who starved to death, the ones who lost their minds, and the ones who simply vanished.

(2)

Like *Dust*, it also makes a connection between the migrations of the past and those of the contemporary world. Her father, who made such a long migration in his youth, is 'the biggest ragamuffin, vagabond, buffalo soldier of them all' (4), and he has parallels in the people on the move in the novel's present: 'all around us the other vagabonds still pour in. Underneath lorries, stowed away in boats, falling out of the sky from jumbo jets' (4).

In this way, the novel is clear and unambiguous about the violence of displacement – but it doesn't primarily employ this historical understanding as a warning. Instead, it positions Jama as one of the 'fortune men [. . .] who set their footprints in the sand, fifty, sixty, a hundred years ago' (4). The footprints in the sand suggest that these people created a path which can be followed, a path which links historical and contemporary displacement. If we are to understand Jama – who is frequently hungry, mistreated and in danger during his migration – as a one of the 'fortune men,' a reorientation of conventional narratives is required. Jama is positioned as 'a hero, not the fighting or romantic kind but the real deal, the starved child that survives every sling and arrow that shameless fortune throws at them' (2). There are no romantic or warrior heroes here, but instead a vulnerable 'starved child who survived,' and who is perpetually aware of all those who 'looked like' him and 'lived like' him but who, by fragile chance, did not survive (1). Crucially, the starved child hero is a storyteller. After surviving, he 'can now sit back and tell the stories of all the ones that didn't make it' (1). Storytelling here is a form of solidarity with the dead who should not have died in the process of migration; a remembrance of the past injustices of displacement, a way of lingering with vulnerability, and the arbitrariness of suffering. Jama becomes a symbol in *Black Mamba Boy*: a symbol of staying with insecurity rather than transcending it or becoming victorious over it – and it is storytelling, the act of bringing narratives into the world, which is presented as the crucial mechanism for this historically attuned dwelling in the condition of displacement.

The works of contemporary literary fiction I have discussed in this chapter suggest that thinking about displacement requires a supple, flexible approach. The texts associate displacement with homelessness, but home is also presented an unstable site of displaced experience. *Exit West* implies that human displacement is inevitable in one way or another, while *Dust* insists on its historically and politically specific dimensions. The challenge is to reorient our perspectives to include what is gained through vulnerability, without drifting into an ahistorical celebration of free-floating identity, openness to the other, or hybridity, which disregards the significance of homeliness or the glaring inequalities of power and income which determine the global distribution of displacement today. The linguistic innovation of 'versing' in *Signs Preceding the End of the World*, and the emphasis placed on telling the story of the 'vagabond' (4) in *Black Mamba Boy* both suggest the significant role that literary writing can play in helping readers to reckon with this challenge, by thinking through the complexities of contemporary vulnerability, longing for home, and displacement.

Works cited

Al Deek, A., 2016. *Writing Displacement: Home and Identity in Contemporary Post-Colonial English Fiction.* Houndmills: Palgrave Macmillian.
Barghouti, M., 2005. *I Saw Ramallah*. Translated by Ahdaf Soueif. London: Bloomsbury.
Butler, J., 2004. *Precarious Life: The Powers of Mourning and Violence*. London: Verso.
—— 2009. *Frames of War: When Is Life Grievable?*. London: Verso.

Coundouriotis, E., 2010. The Child Soldier Narrative and the Problem of Arrested Historicization. *Journal of Human Rights*, 13 May, 9(2), 191–206.

Dillman, L., 2015. Translator's Note. In: *Signs Preceding the End of the World*. London: And Other Stories, 109–114.

Fraiman, S., 2017. *Extreme Domesticity: A View from the Margins*. London: Columbia University Press.

Hall, S. and Schwarz, B., 2017. *Familiar Stranger: Life between Two Islands*. London: Penguin.

Hamid, M., 2017. *Exit West*. London: Hamish Hamilton.

Herrara, Y., 2015. *Signs Preceding the End of the World*. Translated by Lisa Dillman. London: And Other Stories.

Lorey, I., 2015. *State of Insecurity: Government of the Precarious*. Translated by Aileen Derieg. London: Verso.

Mattar, K., 2014. Mourid Barghouti's "Multiple Displacements": Exile and the National Checkpoint in Palestinian Literature. *Journal of Postcolonial Writing*, 20(1), 103–115.

Mohamed, N., 2010. *Black Mamba Boy*. London: HarperCollins.

Newns, L., 2015. Homelessness and the Refugee: De-Valorizing Displacement in Abdulrazak Gurnah's By the Sea. *Journal of Postcolonial Writing*, 51(5), 506–518.

Owuor, Y. A., 2014. *Dust*. London: Granta.

UNHCR, 2017. *Global Trends: Forced Displacement in 2016*. [Online] Available at: www.unhcr.org/globaltrends2016/ [Accessed 21 December 2017].

Wainaina, B., 2006. *How to Write about Africa*. [Online] Available at: https://granta.com/how-to-write-about-africa/ [Accessed 4 January 2018].

Yates, K., 2016. On Going Home. In: N. Shukla, ed. *The Good Immigrant*. London: Unbound, 108–118.

22

ASYLUM

Agnes Woolley

In July 1999 Yaguine Koita and Fodé Tounkara climbed into the wheel cavity of a jet flying from Conakry to Brussels. At just fourteen years old, they were so desperate to escape their lives in Guinea that they risked the freezing temperatures and oxygen deprivation that would kill them. Aeroplane stowaways are rare. Even if it were possible to bypass increasingly tight aviation security, the chances of surviving the flight are miniscule. But it wasn't only their audacious act that brought the two boys to the attention of the world's media. Koita and Tounkara carried with them a two-page letter addressed to 'Excellence Messrs the members and leaders of Europe'. The letter asks for Europe's help in securing the futures of the 'children and young people of Africa', describing the poverty and conflict that prevents children like them from getting an education. It appeals directly to Europeans' 'sense of solidarity and kindness to come to the rescue of Africa' (Duval Smith 1999: 1). The boy's words give voice to a generation of young people who, though not born under the sign of colonial sovereignty, continue to experience its legacy of uneven development and entrenched systems of global inequality. Arriving in the administrative heart of the European Union, the letter not only reflects the ongoing allure of 'modern life in the European sense of the world' (Gikandi 2001: 630), but is also a reminder that the right documentation can mean the difference between life and death for those crossing borders. With no visa or passport, the boys instead insist on providing the kind of information that official documentation cannot supply. It confronts its European readers with a detailed account of growing up without hope in Guinea, filling in the gaps of a story most often told in reductive or sensationalised media terms. This chapter reads the refugee experience through such alternative documentation in a century that has seen a sharp escalation of anti-immigration policy and rhetoric in Europe, Australia and North America. Contending with this hostile political climate, fictional representations of contemporary asylum and displacement eschew simplified legal and media forms, giving narrative shape to the complex dynamics evoked by Koita's and Tounkara's letter to Europe.

Today's clandestine border crossers provide the inverse image of a globalised, cosmopolitan elite, constituting what Peter Nyers describes as an 'abject class', which encompasses 'asylum seekers, refugees, non-status residents, undocumented workers, so-called "overstayers" and "illegals"' (Nyers 2003: 1070). Literary representations of this precarious migration linked to late twentieth-century globalization have been relatively few. Writing in 1992, author and critic Amitav Ghosh noted that we do not yet possess the literary forms that are able to give expression to the experiences of global migrants. An inevitable product of the neoliberal political turn, for Ghosh, irregular migration poses 'a radical challenge not just to writing but to much of modern culture, to the idea of distinguishable and distinct communities or civilizations' (Ghosh 1992: 30). The vast, quasi-permanent refugee populations generated by the protracted wars of the late twentieth and early twenty-first century further testify to changing patterns of migration and dwelling. Since Ghosh's article, and in the wake of a marked international movement towards the erection of barriers and the increased use of detention, a notable literary interest in the situation of refugees and asylum seekers has emerged. Though faced with the real-world urgency of proliferating deaths at sea, extra-judicial detention, and statelessness, writers insist on exploring the contours of this new landscape of migration in their fiction – its states and spaces of being – as well as reflecting on literature's capacity to narrate the experience. Asylum is, to use David Farrier's term, a 'scandal' (Farrier 2012: 1), not only for those critical discourses that have paid it insufficient attention, but to global society more broadly. In this context, the literature of contemporary migration represents a vital intervention that shapes our understanding of an increasingly precarious twenty-first century.

This chapter suggests three lenses through which recent writing about asylum and displacement might be viewed. First, a thematic shift away from a migrant identity that draws exclusively on '[b]onds of language, religion, culture and a sense of common history' (Cohen 2008: 35). Examining the consequences of living outside the law, this group of texts evaluates the possibility of what Jean-Jacques Lecercle describes as a 'diaspora of the *sans papier*'; asking what, if any, forms of community emerge from a clandestine existence. Second, an exploration of how contemporary migrant identity is shaped by an emerging topography of precarious migration, including the sea crossing, the refugee camp and the territorial border zone. Together these spaces map out a new terrain on which migrant identity is forged in the twenty-first century. Third, the challenge of documenting the undocumented in contemporary fiction marks a turn to self-reflexive narrative forms. For this final group of authors, enduring literary concerns about the ethics of representation find new expression as they examine the varied forms and forums in which refugee narratives circulate. My exploration of contemporary literatures of forced migration is not exhaustive, but intends rather to give a sense of the range of approaches to the topic in recent years. Above all, these texts constitute a response to the inadequacy of policy and politics to confront the issue in all its complexity.

Diasporas of the *sans papier*

Salman Rushdie's landmark essay 'Imaginary Homelands' (1992) is often considered a defining document for the diverse works of fiction loosely grouped under the heading 'migrant' or 'diasporic' literature. It speaks to a generation of postcolonial migrant authors who, as both 'insiders and outsiders', write from a creative dual perspective and lay claim to a great and global literary tradition linked to the 'phenomenon of cultural transplantation' (Rushdie 1992: 19–20). First and second generation migrant authors – among them, Maxine Hong Kingston, Kiran Desai, Grace Nichols and Amitav Ghosh – have used their fiction to think through the complexities of living in one place while maintaining cultural and historical ties to another. Their work tackles those hybrid identifications that are at once liberating, perplexing and painful, yet which offer an alternative to what Paul Gilroy describes as 'the stern discipline of primordial kinship and rooted belonging' (Gilroy 2004: 123). Iconic novels of migration to the UK such as Sam Selvon's *The Lonely Londoners* (1956) and Hanif Kureishi's *The Buddha of Suburbia* (1990) testify to the competing claims of 'here' and 'there', giving shape to a multivalent migrant or diaspora identity while reading immigration as part of the ongoing construction of a multicultural Britain. On the whole, the protagonists of these novels are fighting for cultural, racial and social recognition rather than legal rights of residence. While this trend has proceeded into the twenty-first century in the novels of, among others, Zadie Smith, Andrea Levy and Jhumpa Lahiri, many writers are troubled by the solitary and transient nature of asylum seeking and displacement as modes of migration that do not easily conform to traditions of diasporic belonging.

Responding to the topic of 'Literary Criticism in the Twenty-First Century', Jean-Jacques Lecercle writes that '[t]he real problem is to give a voice to a much larger diaspora, the diaspora of despair, those thousands of voiceless immigrants who often die trying to cross the Mexican border or to reach Europe on fast-sinking boats – the diaspora of the *sans papiers*' (Leclercle 2010: 917). Though quick to dismiss the ongoing negotiations of identification for migrants of all kinds, Lecercle is attuned to the questions of legal and bodily security particular to clandestine migration, as well as to the challenge it presents to representational forms. No longer structured around twin poles of departure and arrival, recent writing about migration seeks ways to convey the provisional nature of life lived outside national attachments and legal frameworks for residence. The post-millennial context thus constitutes a shift from dual allegiances to 'here' and 'there', to a kind of multi- or out-of-placeness born of legal and geographical restriction. This is exacerbated by statelessness, rising instances of which mean that many migrants live inside a country's borders but outside its legal, social and political life. Again, Ghosh cites this as a challenge to the novel form, which is, he argues, 'never more comfortable than when it is luxuriating in a "sense of place"' (Ghosh 1992: 30). As we'll see in the final part of the chapter, in revealing the porous boundaries of national space, migrants also test the limits of narrative forms seeking to capture the experience of displacement.

Geographical displacement is announced in the title of Brian Chikwava's debut novel *Harare North* (2009) about a young asylum seeker who arrives in Britain from Zimbabwe. Among Zimbabweans, London is known as 'Harare North' because of the large numbers of Zimbabweans who migrate there (Johannesburg is 'Harare South' for the same reason). Though this renaming suggests a home away from home, Chikwava's dizzying depiction of life lived clandestinely in South London consistently refuses to posit a Zimbabwean diaspora with any purchase on British society. Seen through the eyes of Chikwava's nameless narrator, London is instead a city populated by desperate and disenfranchised individuals who share only a sense of their own vulnerability. Inviting a homeless British couple to move into his squat, the narrator observes that 'they also have them asylum-seeker eyes; them eyes with the shine that come about only because of a reptile kind of life, the life of surviving big mutilation in the big city and living inside them holes' (Chikwava 2009: 2). The couple are also *sans papier*: living outside the regulated spaces of national belonging. Set in and around Brixton – a site of well-established African-Caribbean communities from the 'Windrush' era – *Harare North* charts the urban survival endemic to an undocumented life, in which evading detection by the authorities also means foregoing the public participation capable of cultivating social or political bonds.

Subject to the shifting political sands of a volatile national context, the narrator arrives in London in flight from a murderous military commander in President Mugabe's 'Green Bombers'. He claims asylum on arrival at Heathrow, but is quickly rejected and threatened with deportation. Disowned by his cousins, who have legalised their position in the UK, the narrator moves into a squat with his friend Shingy and, when Shingy becomes ill, assumes his identity: 'It don't matter that I'm illegal; I have keep his passport because his asylum application get approved by the immigration people some while ago. His passport and national insurance number come in handy now' (Chikwava 2009: 2). The tactical deployment of temporary identifications is intrinsic to life lived outside the architecture of official citizenship and Chikwava's protagonist uses his borrowed identity to earn money to pay off his debts in Zimbabwe and extricate himself from the state military. As the novel progresses, these shifting identifications begin to have a psychological effect on the narrator, whose narrative voice becomes increasingly fragmented and contradictory. But there are hints from the novel's outset that his experiences in the Zimbabwean military and the demands of survival in London have already had a detrimental psychological effect. Variously adopting the pronouns 'I', 'he' and 'you', the narrative suggests a slippage between the narrator and Shingy, who becomes his legally sanctioned alter ego: 'you know what it's like with old friends [. . .] sometimes you is not sure if your memories belong to him or vice versa; things can get mixed up [. . .] and you no longer know whose story belongs to who' (Chikwava 2009: 9). Chikwava's narrator thus never emerges in the novel as a knowable or coherent character. It's difficult, and even dangerous, the novel suggests, to maintain a stable selfhood in a context in which to reveal who you are is to risk deportation and possible death.

Of course, ascertaining 'whose story belongs to who' is vital to the operation of the legal decision-making process on asylum, which relies on the presentation of credible testimony.[1] The need for a verifiable account of persecution to be granted legal Refugee Status suggests a narrative coherence often unavailable to those whose experiences defy easy emotional or logical assimilation. Where the legal system demands a linear and consistent narrative, *Harare North* offers readers something closer to reality: moral complexity, the instability of memory and the repressions of trauma. Chikwava's fractured and unreliable narrative dramatises the struggle to maintain a coherent sense of self in the chaotic context of fast-shifting political change and exposure to violence, both in Zimbabwe and London. But it also reveals the challenges of making sense of events constituting a claim for asylum, not only for legal recognition as a refugee, but also to enable processes of mourning, commemoration and community building. The novel ends as the narrator stands, destitute, in the 'mental backstreets' of London, his bare feet pointing in different directions, a 'big battle' raging in his head (Chikwava 2009: 230). Far from finding his feet in London, the narrator appears alienated and unsettled in these final moments, destined for a future of uncertainty.

Camping out in a squat on Brixton Hill, Chikwava's narrator forges only superficial relationships with those who share his shadow world: Brixton's gangsters who congregate in Windrush Square, the homeless and other migrants. Directly addressing this problem, Caryl Phillips's 2003 novel *A Distant Shore* considers how meaningful relationships might be forged through shared experience rather than racial or cultural affiliation. Born in St Kitts and raised in Britain, Phillips has a long-standing interest in documenting the unheard stories of colonial displacements, perhaps most notably in his 1993 novel *Crossing the River*. In *A Distant Shore*, however, he considers the place of the refugee in what he describes as a 'new world order'; a 'twenty-first-century world in which it is impossible to resist the claims of the migrant, the asylum seeker, or the refugee' (Phillips 2001: 5). *A Distant Shore* is about the hope for, but ultimate failure of, a form of diaspora belonging not based on communal historical or geographical affiliations but on shared experiences of isolation. The narrative is shared by Gabriel/Solomon, a refugee from an unnamed African country, and Dorothy, a middle-aged school teacher, both of whom have just moved to a newly built housing estate in northern England at the outset of the novel. While we are invited to consider the parallels in their experiences of alienation and migration, their burgeoning friendship is cut short when Gabriel/Solomon is beaten and left for dead by a local gang.

Like Chikwava's unnamed narrator, Gabriel/Solomon adopts a new identity after migrating to Britain. He arrives in an atomised England imbued with the failed promise of multiculturalism:

> I had tried to talk to the West Indian people I saw standing on the streets outside Son-
> ja's Caribbean takeaway with their dreadlocks and their cans of beer, but they were
> not friendly and they would often look the other way or shout at me and behave like

drunken people. And I had long ago learned that there was little point in attempting conversation with the Indians or Pakistanis, for they were worse than some of the English people.

(Phillips 2004: 291)

Through Gabriel/Solomon's eyes discrete ethnicities appear encamped within the nation–state. Fortified and embattled, these diasporic groups cannot accommodate the refugee, who makes no affiliative claim other than that of a shared humanity. One of the defining characteristics of asylum reflected in *A Distant Shore*, then, is the lack of participation of refugees in conventional community-making activities. In the face of this antagonistic national context, it is by recognising a shared experience of alienation in contemporary Britain that Gabriel/Solomon and Dorothy begin to forge a tentative friendship. However, although their intersecting narratives hint at the possibility of what Phillips has described as a 'communicable empathy' (Davison 1994: 94), Dorothy and Gabriel/Solomon struggle to communicate effectively and both remain 'purposively silent' (Phillips 2004: 312) to the novel's end. Gabriel/Solomon is haunted by violent and fragmentary flashbacks, which intermittently intercede in the narrative frame, and Dorothy retreats into her own world as her mental health declines. Peering out from inside their barricaded lives, Dorothy and Gabriel/Solomon embody the novel's critique of contemporary England and its inhospitality to migrant others. But their struggle to connect also points to the challenges of articulating asylum experiences. Gabriel/Solomon's adopted identity results in a permanently fractured sensibility; a new self eternally haunted by the old, whose story cannot be shared.

New migrant topographies

Gabriel/Solomon arrives in the UK clinging to the side of a cross–channel ferry. As he approaches the British coast he lets go, plunges into the freezing cold water and loses consciousness, prompting a series of traumatic memories which give readers a glimpse of the brutal events that led him to flee his country. This connection between place, memory and storytelling is one that seems particularly fruitful in recent narratives of forced migration. In the novels of two Moroccan–born authors, Mahi Binebine's *Welcome to Paradise* (2003) and Laila Lalami's *Hope and Other Dangerous Pursuits* (2005), the sea crossing becomes a productive scene of narrative storytelling. Both are set on the Strait of Gibraltar, that well–worn migratory route that connects Africa and Europe, which, due in part to its increasing militarisation, has become a temporary dwelling place for those waiting for an opportune moment to cross. Binebine and Lalami seize on this moment by drawing together multiple narratives linked by the impulse to migrate. Lalami's novel begins as 'a motley mix of people from the ex-colonies' (Lalami 2005: 3) numbering thirty squeeze into a dingy designed to carry eight. The distance between Morocco and Spain is a mere fourteen kilometres but, as one of the passengers muses, fourteen kilometres separates 'not just two countries but two universes' (Lalami 2005: 1). For Murad, their journey calls to mind the 'Moorish invasion in 711' (Lalami 2005: 2), which established a series of dynasties that ruled Spain for over 700 years. Murad's contemplation of this stretch of the Mediterranean takes in the diverse histories that inform the act of migration, but also the deepening global divisions that underlie contemporary migratory patterns. As the migrants share their stories in both *Hope and Other Pursuits* and *Welcome to Paradise*, the border crossing emerges as a significant site of identity formation; a historical and cultural point on the map of a refugee identity.

Lalami's image of the overcrowded dinghy has become a staple news item since the war that began in Syria in 2011 caused a sharp spike in refugee movement by sea, and the Mediterranean in particular has become a contested and treacherous space of temporary dwelling for would-be asylum seekers. At the time of writing, it is estimated that just under 5000 people have lost their lives in the Mediterranean alone since 2014 (IOM, Missing Migrants 2018). Globally, of course, the numbers of lives lost at sea is much higher (IOM, Missing Migrants 2018). Refugee-receiving countries in Southern Europe are underfunded for search and rescue operations and fishermen who intervene to rescue refugees are at risk of prosecution for aiding illegal immigration (Krist and Bakas 2016).[2] In Australia, successive governments have deployed varying strategies to circumvent international obligations to refugees by preventing their arrival on sovereign territory, including turning back boats and mandatory detention at Offshore Processing Centres on the Pacific Ocean islands of Manus and Nauru. Vietnamese-Australian author Nam Le intervenes in this fraught geopolitical context with a literary return to his own migratory heritage: the original 'boat people' who escaped Vietnam in the late 1970s. Le's 2009 short story collection *The Boat* begins with a metafictional account of his struggle to write the 'true story' (Le 2009: 24) of his father's flight from Vietnam to Australia in 1979. His father's journey is ultimately recounted in fictional form in the collection's final story, 'The Boat', where it is told from the perspective of a young woman whose mother has arranged for her to be smuggled out of Vietnam on a small, crowded scow. The story begins in the aftermath of a powerful storm, which has shaken the boat off course and destroyed the limited food and water supplies. As they burn under the hot sun, the migrants begin to hear the voices of their ancestors who tried and failed to make the crossing before them:

> They had ventured into the fields of the dead, those plots of ocean where thousands had capsized with their scows and drowned. They stared into the fog. All drawn into a shared imagination, each in some space of unthinking as though they had leapt overboard, some madness possessing them, puncturing the glassy surface of the water and then plunged into black syrup, coming up into breath but panicked, disoriented, flailing in a viscid space without reference or light or sound.
>
> (Le 2009: 233)

A reminder of the war-torn landscape from which they've fled, the liquid burial 'plots' and 'fields' suggest an urge to mark not only memorially but also geographically the deaths that have gone unaccounted for in the act of border crossing. The challenges to this act of memorialisation are registered in the lack of 'reference to light or sound'; a disorientation which suggests a need to rethink the relationship between place and memory in the light of continued migrant deaths at sea. The story itself does some of this work by providing a 'shared imagination' in which the passengers' migrant predecessors might live on. But the moment inevitably encompasses other forced migrations such as slavery's Middle Passage and Australia's contemporary 'boat people' arriving from Afghanistan, Syria and Sri-Lanka. Le's literary return to the sites of these deaths in fictional form establishes a set of geographical and temporal connections between oceanic migrations.

J. M. Coetzee's 2013 novel, *The Childhood of Jesus*, begins with the arrival of two refugees in Europe, and it takes up Le's concern with how the ethics of remembering – and forgetting – shape refugee identity. Importantly, however, it also alludes to the pragmatic imperatives that drive this process for those crossing borders clandestinely. African migrants crossing to Europe from Northern Africa are often described as *harragas*, from the Arabic *ḥarrāg*, meaning 'those who burn'. The term emerged from the common practice among migrants of burning or destroying all indentifying documentation at the border to prevent deportation. Any traces of a previous life must be erased if migrants are to make a successful transition to a new country, whether within or against national law. For the new arrivals in Coetzee's novel, the eradication of a past life is a condition of their acceptance in their new home. The novel begins as a man and boy arrive in the Spanish-speaking town of Novilla. Though they aren't related, Simón has assumed responsibility for the young boy, David, who had been travelling alone. Practiced in resettling refugees, Novilla has an elaborate bureaucratic structure which provides the basic needs of all its inhabitants: food, shelter, work and education. In turn, new arrivals are encouraged to renounce their individual histories. Simón and David are told that '[p]eople here have washed themselves clean of old ties' and let go of 'old attachments' (Coetzee 2013: 20). Like the rest of Novilla's inhabitants, David and Simón arrived by boat, travelling from 'the boat to the camp, from the camp to Novilla' (Coetzee 2013: 208). As one resident explains, 'None of us knows more than that about our origins' (Coetzee 2013: 208). At the camp, they are issued with new identification documents and given their 'Spanish names' (Coetzee 2013: 2) – David and Simón. Their shared birthday is registered as the date of their arrival at the camp; 'washed clean of memory' (Coetzee 2013: 208), they are born again on arrival in Novilla. But Simón is troubled by this historyless place whose inhabitants wish to live free of their pasts, and so sets out to find David a mother. His quest to fabricate a lineage for David in a place where affiliations exist only out of convenience or necessity, pits 'a body soaked in its past' (Coetzee 2013: 143) against the transactional relationships permitted in the transient spaces of dwelling characteristic of twenty-first century migration. Ordered, ascetic and dispassionate, Novilla lacks the cultural and historical coordinates that orient a sense of self as existing in a particular place and time. This kind of abstraction is common to much of Coetzee's fiction, yet Novilla's similarity to a refugee camp or detention centre is unmistakeable. Those heavily institutionalised entities, which exist to administer rather than enrich human lives, seem in Coetzee's world to require a negation of the desires, appetites and histories that make us human.

Where David's fabricated family fails to generate emotional connections, Nadifa Mohamed's novel *Orchard of Lost Souls* (2013) shows how families forged in transient and precarious places can be indicative of the most meaningful human relationships. The novel is set during Somalia's civil war in the 1980s, a war Mohamed herself escaped after settling in the UK with her family as a child. Following her 2009 debut, *Black Mamba Boy* – a fictionalised account of her father's travels across Africa and the Middle East as a boy – *Orchard of Lost Souls* continues Mohamed's exploration of the shifting nature of home and the ways in which it shapes identity even as it becomes detached from geographical or temporal fixity. In a world where citizenship remains the normative form of belonging, the novel examines what happens when a state no longer protects its citizens. For Deqo, one of Mohamed's three protagonists in *Orchard of Lost Souls*, home is a refugee camp. Less abstract than Coetzee's setting, Mohamed's camp has real-world counterparts in the form of East Africa's numerous, vast and long-established refugee camps. Coordinated and run by non-state actors, refugee camps disturb the contiguity between nationality and place, meaning that Deqo, who was born in the camp and abandoned by her mother, cannot lay claim to either a national or a familial heritage. Like Simón and David, she is affiliated only to the institutional structures that provide her with food and shelter. Her growing awareness that the large families surrounding her in the camp have 'their family names and clans to help them' (Mohamed 2013: 70) makes her long for 'a second and a third name', which would allow her to 'puff out her chest and announce her existence to people' (Mohamed 2013: 70). So strong is her desire to draw a link between identity and place that she begins to call herself 'Deqo Red Cross' (Mohamed 2013: 70). Deqo's portion of the narrative takes her outside the camp and on a journey around war-torn Hargeisa. Here she encounters Filsan, an ex-soldier, and an elderly freedom fighter named Kawsar, whose stories are told in separate but intersecting parts of the novel. Fleeing from the escalating violence at the novel's end, the three women escape Hargeisa for a newly constructed refugee camp at Harta Sheikh. For Deqo, born into the rituals and routines of camp life, this is a 'familiar world' (Mohamed 2013: 336). She is at home in the new world order of humanitarian governance. Despite the uncertainty of their new lives, the three generations of women enter the camp as a 'makeshift' (Mohamed 2013: 336) family; a hopeful parting image which suggests the possibility of new affiliations hewn of necessity and desperation.

Documenting the undocumented

As we have seen, literary investigations of contemporary refugee experience involve asking what new – and potentially affirmative – identifications it engenders, and how these are shaped by the spaces refugees inhabit. But recent writing about undocumented migrants is also concerned with how those forced to live outside the law are subject to the imposition of certain normative identities – 'refugee', 'asylum seeker' – and the denial of others: 'person', 'individual', 'human'. The shifting subject position of Chikwava's unnamed narrator and Coetzee's 'washed clean' migrants are cases in point, which call into question the stability of identity in the context of precarious migration. A number of recent novels examine the complicity of certain narrative forms in the construction of a 'refugee' identity which is bestowed already freighted with pre-conceptions. They also reveal concerns about narrative legitimacy and appropriation in societal contexts in which forced migrants are often denied a public voice. Indeed, much recent fiction of asylum asks how far literature can explore the refugee experience at all.

The relative scarcity of literary representations of asylum is partly down to these concerns about the circumstances that shape how and where refugee narratives are told. Accordingly, stories of forced migration are most often heard in the form of testimony. For many campaign groups, as well as for verbatim dramatic projects like Sonja Linden's *The Asylum Monologues* (launched in 2006), testimony is the cornerstone of a process of bearing witness to oppression, torture and marginalisation. While it is a powerful narrative form that permits refugees a degree of agency over their stories, testimony can, at times, hold refugees to unrealistic standards of authenticity. Relying on the supposed access to reality provided by documentary presentation, testimonial narratives can also act to limit refugee stories, and refugees themselves, to a fixed, unchanging version of the truth, much in the same way as the asylum decision-making process. What's more, and as Gillian Whitlock (2015) points out, there is a keen awareness among readers of testimonial human rights literature that it is, at times, exploitative, even as it seeks change for those represented. Whitlock identifies a sense of exhaustion in a 'cosmopolitan', knowing readership, which simultaneously 'desires and disdains the commodification of distant suffering' (Whitlock 2015: 191).

An awareness of the potential pitfalls of a dependency on refugee testimony does little to mitigate the problem of narrative appropriation for writers engaging with the issue of asylum. Consequently, a number of authors have sought to address these challenges by working with testimony in ways that draw attention to its complex relationship to fiction. *Antigona and Me* (2009), Kate Clanchy's story of a Kosovan refugee who worked as her home help, places the author front and centre in an explanatory preface: 'the reader would consciously have to peer past me, would never be allowed to forget that this was a particular, partial view of a life, not a life itself' (Clanchy 2009: 6). More equivocally, Dave Eggers's 'fictionalized autobiography' (Deng, n.d.) *What is the What?: The Autobiography of Valentino Achak Deng, A novel* (2006) tells the story of Deng's journey across Sudan in the late 1980s and the nine years he spent in refugee camps in Ethiopia and Kenya before settling in Atlanta in 2001. *What is the What* is a bold act of authorial appropriation, but, as Peter Boxall points out, there is a strong 'metafictional current' (Boxall 2013: 181) flowing through the book, which reflects on the relationship between the writer and his subject. Like *Antigona and Me* the book begins with a preface written by Deng in which he explains the collaborative nature of the project and his desire to share his story with a wider audience. Deng's preface acknowledges the inevitable fictionalisations that Eggers makes in telling the story: 'I told Dave what I knew and what I could remember, and from that material he created this work of art' (Eggers 2006: xiv). Because the events depicted in the book happened when Deng was very young, both author and subject agree that 'we simply had to pronounce *What is the What* a novel' (Eggers 2006: xiv). The admission of fictionalisation here is a significant step in a context in which the veracity of a refugee's story is integral to their legal and social validation. The hybrid form of *What is the What* asks readers to think more complexly about the nature of testimony and the ways in which it can confine speakers into a particular version of themselves. As readers, we are both made aware of Eggers's authorial ventriloquism, and encouraged to invest in the authority of the story that is told.

What is the What operates at the intersection of fiction, testimony and journalism. It speaks to, but also against, a certain form of Human Rights literature that dramatises marginalised narratives for an activist readership and is often presented as an antidote to reductive media exposure. Chris Cleave sets out to reclaim the transformative potential of journalism in his 2009 novel *The Other Hand*, which is jointly narrated by Little Bee, a Nigerian refugee and a journalist, Sarah, whose lives become entangled after a violent encounter on a Nigerian beach. The novel ends with Sarah's promise to 'collect the stories' of people like Little Bee as a way of 'saving' them (Cleave 2009: 355) from the dangers they face and giving them a voice. It is precisely this narrative of Western salvation that is the target of Henning Mankell's satire in *The Shadow Girls* (2012), which charts a tragic-comic course through the lives of a group of young migrants and refugees living in Denmark. The humour lies in the character of Humlin, a minor Danish poet who, during a routine reading in Gothenburg, is 'inspired to write a book about – and *with* – immigrants' (Mankell 2012: 69). Inevitably, Humlin's desire to 'write about something real' (Mankell 2012: 72) by telling the girls' stories is revealed as little more than a project of moral and aesthetic self-redemption. Drawing his own profession into the frame, Mankell's satire hints at a more serious consideration of the role of literature in casting light on those who live in the shadows.

Tim Finch's debut novel *The House of Journalists* (2013) provides perhaps the most elaborate meditation on the commodification of refugee stories. As a former Director of Communications at the British Refugee Council, Finch brings to bear an insider's perspective on the economics of asylum narratives. The eponymous House of Journalists is a refuge for persecuted writers established in a venerable old building in central London. Its inhabitants are asylum seeking journalists, authors and poets whose writing has left them vulnerable to detention and torture by a variety of oppressive regimes. The 'fellows', as they are known, are encouraged to draw on the 'great stories [that] fate has bestowed' on them (Finch 2013: 51) and to recount those stories in a variety of forms and forums. The most important of these, for the asylum seekers at least, is the legal hearing, which fellows of the prestigious House of Journalists are all but guaranteed to pass. Working with literary 'mentors' (Finch 2013: 112), they shape their stories for presentation at public events, and at the tribunals where a decision will be made on their case. As readers, then, we are exposed to the mechanisms which bind refugees to the terms of their own narrative, both for public approval and legal status. As one fellow points out, for refugees 'suffering is measured in a man's ability to tell of it in the most hideous detail' (Finch 2013: 90), whether in front of a judge or a paying audience. The irony that haunts this process – satirised by Finch – is that in order to convince the authorities of the veracity of their experiences, refugees must become 'master storytellers' (Finch 2013: 151). The more 'effectively' a refugee can relay their narrative of persecution, the more likely they are to be believed. Finch's exploration of this paradox in *The House of Journalists* dwells on the activity of fashioning the 'raw material' of the asylum story into 'a work of literature' (Finch 2013: 112). This process, and the movement from 'person' to 'character' it necessarily entails, self-consciously reflects on the extent to which the role of the refugee is one asylum seekers must play to gain legal and political sanction. The ironic distance opened up by Finch's narrative technique is a hallmark of what Lyndsey Stonebridge calls 'refugee style', in which 'the habits of irony mark the speaker out as not quite comfortable in their host nation, culture or language' (Stonebridge 2010: 73). Placing a 'diacritical marker' (Stonebridge 2010: 75) on the role of 'refugee' Finch emphasises its function as a label that operates for political expediency. Those who fall into this category must nevertheless find ways to escape, or at least highlight, its restrictive terms in order to exert a degree of agency.

Preoccupied by the understanding that 'these are not just stories; these are people's *lives*' (Finch 2013: 73) these works foreground the ethics of representation as a way of acknowledging the limited ability of narrative to capture the experience of precarious migration. They seek a balance between making the refugee experience legible and overwriting it altogether. But their self-consciousness also opens a space for the examination of stories by and about those lives lived permanently outside legal and social frameworks of belonging. In this, they share with the other texts explored here an urge to re-position the refugee subject; to examine how it is shaped in the twenty-first century by legal exclusions and diverse geographies of refuge. Writing in 1984, Edward Said argued that '[t]o understand exile as a contemporary political punishment it is necessary to map territories of experience beyond those mapped by literature' (Said 1984: 50). It's true that the devastation wrought by current migrations seems at times both to exceed the capacities of narrative fiction and to demand a sober engagement with reality. But recent writing about asylum seekers and refugees suggests an alternative to 'the arithmetic abstractions of mass politics', forging instead 'tellable' (Said 1984: 50) histories from the precarious movements of the twenty-first century.

Notes

1 To be officially recognised as a refugee by signatory countries, asylum seekers must conform to the definition of a refugee laid out in the United Nations 1951 Refugee Convention and 1967 Protocol, which stipulates a 'well-founded fear of being persecuted for reasons of race, religion, nationality, membership of a particular social group or political opinion'.
2 Italy's 'Mare Nostrum' search and rescue operation came to an end in 2014 after the EU discontinued funding. It was replaced by Operation Triton, an EU-wide operation with a security and border enforcement remit (Heller and Pezzani 2017).

Works cited

Binebine, M. (2003). *Welcome to Paradise*. Portland: Tin House Books.
Boxall, P. (2013). *Twenty-First-Century Fiction: A Critical Introduction*. Cambridge: Cambridge University Press.
Chikwava, B. (2009). *Harare North*. London: Vintage.
Clanchy, K. (2009). *Antigona and Me*. London: Picador.
Cleave, C. (2009). *The Other Hand*. London: Sceptre.
Coetzee, J. M. (2013). *The Childhood of Jesus*. London: Random House.
Cohen, R. (2008). *Global Diasporas: An Introduction*. Abingdon: Routledge.
Davison, C. (1994). Crisscrossing the River: An Interview with Caryl Phillips. *ARIEL*, 25(4), 91–99.
Deng, V. A. (n.d.). *Interview with Dave Eggers and Valentino Achak Deng*. Available at: www.vadfoundation. org/interview-with-the-creators [Accessed 26 February, 2015].
Duval Smith, A. (1999). The Boys Who Froze to Death at 40,000 Feet. *The Independent*. 1 September, 1.
Eggers, D. (2006). *What Is the What: The Autobiography of Valentino Achak Deng: A Novel*. London: Penguin.
Farrier, D. (2012). *Postcolonial Asylum: Seeking Sanctuary before the Law*. Liverpool: Liverpool University Press.

Finch, T. (2013). *The House of Journalists*. London: Random House.

Ghosh, A. (1992). Petrofiction: The Oil Encounter and the Novel. *The New Republic*, March, 29–33.

Gikandi, S. (2001). Globalization and the Claims of Postcoloniality. *The South Atlantic Quarterly*, 100(3), 627–658.

Gilroy, P. (2004). *Between Camps: Nations, Cultures and the Allure of Race*. London: Routledge.

Heller, C and Pezzani, L. (2017). *Death by Rescue: The Lethal Effects of the EU's Policies of Non-Assistance at Sea*. Available at: https://deathbyrescue.org [Accessed 1 May 2018].

International Organization for Migration. (2018). *Missing Migrants*. https://missingmigrants.iom.int/region/mediterranean [Accessed 12 April 2018].

Krist, K and Bakas, M. (2016). *Criminalising Solidarity: When Helping Refugees Becomes a Risk*. Available at: https://www.greeneuropeanjounral.eu/criminalising-solidarity-when-helping-refugees-becomes-a-risk [Accessed 1 May 2018].

Lalami, L. (2005). *Hope and Other Dangerous Pursuits*. Orlando: Harcourt.

Le, N. (2009). *The Boat*. Edinburgh: Canongate.

Leclercle, J. (2010). Return to the Political. *PMLA*, 125(4), 916–919.

Mankell, H. (2012). *The Shadow Girls*. Trans. by E. Segerberg. London: Vintage.

Mohamed, N. (2013). *The Orchard of Lost Souls*. London: Simon & Schuster.

Nyers, P. (2003). Abject Cosmopolitanism: The Politics of Protection in the Anti-Deportation Movement. *Third World Quarterly*, 24(6), 1069–1093.

Phillips, C. (2001). *A New World Order: Selected Essays*. London: Secker and Warburg.

—— (2004). *A Distant Shore*. London: Vintage.

Rushdie, S. (1992). *Imaginary Homelands: Essays and Criticism, 1981–1991*. Harmondsworth: Penguin.

Said, E. (1984). The Mind of Winter: Reflections on Life in Exile. *Harper's Magazine*, 49–55.

Stonebridge, L. (2010). Refugee Style: Hannah Arendt and the Perplexities of Rights. *Textual Practice*, 25(1), 71–85.

Whitlock, G. (2015). *Postcolonial Life Narratives: Testimonial Transactions*. Oxford: Oxford University Press.

23

FINANCE

Paul Crosthwaite

A written text relating only loosely, if at all, to anything that really exists, and whose value rests on the willingness of those amongst whom it circulates to suspend their disbelief and place their confidence in the claims it makes. Such might be a description of a novel; but it could equal describe a stock certificate or a banknote. Finance is not simply a theme or topic of fiction, but its mirror image, a form of fiction in its own right.

As we will see in this chapter, there is abundant evidence today to support this understanding of the relationship between fiction and finance. The very rise of the novel in English, however, was inextricably bound up with the rise of finance. Writing in the wake of the English 'Financial Revolution' of the late seventeenth century, which saw the foundation of the Bank of England and the growth and proliferation of joint-stock companies, Daniel Defoe – the author with perhaps the strongest claim to the title of first novelist in the language – spread his financial concerns apparently indiscriminately across works of political economy and works of prose fiction. The very embodiment of the newly professionalized author, relentlessly entrepreneurial in cultivating new markets for his writing, Defoe produced fictions that were quite literally speculative investment instruments. Indeed, as the critic and historian Mary Poovey (2008) has shown, in this period finance-themed novels were not clearly differentiated from other forms of economic writing, ranging from price lists to bills of exchange to units of currency themselves. Over the succeeding centuries, fiction has emerged as one of a number of distinct 'genres of the credit economy' (in Poovey's phrase), but has remained intimately connected with more narrowly economic discourses and practices, as evident everywhere from the realism of Charles Dickens, George Eliot, and Anthony Trollope to the naturalism of Theodore Dreiser and Frank Norris, the modernism of F. Scott Fitzgerald and John Dos Passos, and the postmodernism of William Gaddis, Martin Amis, and Don DeLillo.

The period since the 1970s has been characterized by an unprecedentedly intense phase of 'financialization,' in which currencies have been allowed to float free of metallic 'backing,' exotic forms of financial engineering have proliferated, and the financial economy has come to dwarf the 'real' or productive economy. This period has also – and as a direct consequence – been marked by a succession of juddering financial crises, most obviously the global 'credit crunch' of 2008. Over these decades, the financial novel has diverged, coalescing into a genre variant (the pacey 'financial thriller' (see Marsh 2007; Crosthwaite 2010)), on the one hand, and more overtly and self-consciously 'literary' forms, on the other. Prior to 2008, finance was an important preoccupation amongst writers of literary fiction, as indicated by such major works as Gaddis's *J R* (1975), Amis's *Money* (1984), and DeLillo's *Players* (1977) and *Cosmopolis* (2003), as well as other significant novels including Tom Wolfe's *The Bonfire of the Vanities* (1987); Bret Easton Ellis's *American Psycho* (1991); Jay McInerney's *Brightness Falls* (1992); Kate Jennings' *Moral Hazard* (2002); and Jane Smiley's *Good Faith* (2003). In the aftermath of the global financial crisis, however, the financial system has become nothing short of an obsession for writers, so much so that 'crunch lit' (a term coined by the critic Sathnam Sanghera) is now a distinctive and recognizable strand of literary fiction (see Shaw 2015). In this chapter, I examine some especially prominent examples of this contemporary style. Beyond their shared engagement with money and markets, writers of such novels are united by their foregrounding of the profound ways in which human emotion and imagination are implicated in the abstract processes of financial exchange.

The mind of the market

With their native interest in human psychology, it has long seemed evident to novelists that the rhythms of the financial markets are expressions of mass emotion – recurrent waves of mania and panic. As James Buchan (himself the author of a notable financial fiction, *High Latitudes* (1996)) notes in his history of money, *Frozen Desire* (1997), to this way of thinking

> financial booms and crashes are exemplary forms of history, for they appear to present . . . an empirical or measurable psychology. You need merely record the money price of the security, or of an index, at the height of the boom and the depths of the crash to have what seems to be a quantity of human joy and misery.
>
> (107–8)

In recent works of fiction, the tendency of markets to be swayed by extreme affective states has been asserted with renewed urgency, precisely because prevailing economic theories have tended to minimize the role of such factors, refusing to acknowledge mounting evidence of their prevalence and importance. In mainstream financial economics over recent decades, individual economic actors have been treated as rational, self-interested calculating machines, capable of objectively evaluating relevant information and consistently maximizing their return of 'utility.' Likewise, the markets made up of those actors have been understood as tending naturally towards a state of equilibrium, such that asset prices are liable to fluctuate only moderately, within a narrow band. A series of booms and busts – from the Black Monday crash of 1987 to the dot-com bubble that expanded and burst around the turn of the millennium – made this model appear increasingly shaky, however, and in the wake of the sub-prime craze and resultant Great Recession it looks wholly untenable. Contemporary novelists have echoed behavioural economists and other 'heterodox' economic thinkers in insisting on the decisive role of emotional 'contagion' in driving prices up and down. For the Marxist cultural critic Mark Fisher (2009),

> with its ceaseless boom and bust cycles, capitalism is . . . fundamentally and irreducibly bi-polar, periodically lurching between hyped-up mania (the irrational exuberance of 'bubble thinking') and depressive come-down. (The term 'economic depression' is no accident, of course.) To a degree unprecedented in any other social system, capitalism both feeds on and reproduces the moods of populations. Without delirium and confidence, capital could not function.
>
> (35)

The wild mood swings that shape the financial markets have particular prominence in Alex Preston's 2010 novel *This Bleeding City*, in many ways an archetypal work of crunch lit. A bond trader himself when he wrote the novel, Preston portrays life in a Mayfair hedge fund either side of the credit crunch through the eyes of an ambitious young graduate, Charlie Wales. The protagonist's name is a direct borrowing from another tale of financial and emotional upheaval – F. Scott Fitzgerald's "Babylon Revisited" (1931), set after the Great Crash of 1929 – and is consistent with Preston's wider conjuring of an elegiac, lyrical style self-consciously redolent of Fitzgerald's own (*The Great Gatsby* is also directly referenced [259]). When the financial crisis takes full hold, and threatens to crush his fund, Charlie becomes acutely aware that the markets he has attempted to analyse in light of 'weighty reports' and 'legal documents' (21) are in fact manifestations of irrational, self-propagating psychological states:

> I listened to these men and the rapid oscillation between hope and despair, greed and fear in their voices, and I thought to myself how the market is just a reflection of the psychologies of the traders who operate within it. All of these high-achieving, driven characters with their terribly fragile egos. Marketing types reliant on rapid and multiple injections of success to keep their confidence afloat. The market was plummeting so precipitously because there was no one to stand in its way. Everyone conformed to this basic type and so everyone behaved in the same way when thing went wrong. The flight from mindless exuberance to bind panic had swept away any rational middle ground.
>
> (179)

This Bleeding City is not simply a drama of tumbling markets and humbled City hotshots, however, but counterpoints this 'public' narrative to a personal and domestic one, tracing the ups and downs, and eventual disintegration, of Charlie's relationship with a beautiful Frenchwoman, Vero. From the point of view of this latter plotline, the depictions of rising and falling markets appear orchestrated to swell the emotional intensity of Charlie and Vero's romantic travails. As in other financial narratives, going back at least as far as the late nineteenth-century, 'the market is . . . figured as a barometer of people's feelings, a financial version of the meteorological pathetic fallacy' (Knight 2013: 58). At the same time, Preston also makes liberal use of pathetic fallacy of the more familiar kind identified (and to an extent denigrated) by John Ruskin in the mid-nineteenth century: that is, the projection of human feelings and actions onto the natural world, and in particular onto the weather. In one particularly striking moment, a heavyhearted Charlie is preparing to travel to France with his best friend, Henry, to attend Vero's marriage to another man. At the same time, ominous economic indicators are appearing on the horizon, and weather conditions are also unfavourable. The romantic, financial, and meteorological elements of the narrative converge and amplify one another in a kind of narratorial 'perfect storm':

> The weeks leading up to our departure were leaden and ugly. It was a summer that never arrived, days dawning brightly over the polite terraces of Fulham that I passed on my way to work, the sun fighting through the cloudy remnants of night. But rains blew in from the west, and by the time I got to work a cold wind would be eddying around Berkeley Square, the sun hidden by low dark clouds, a light rain that soaked the skin and clothing surprisingly swiftly.
>
> Stories had begun to come out of the States: consumers defaulting on their mortgages, business reining in spending, the bankruptcy of one of the smaller construction companies. . . . The profit figure in my daily email no longer rose. . . . Investment

banks sold down their holdings, positioned themselves for a more difficult economic environment.

(132)

Preston, then, portrays the financial markets as resonating with the emotional ambience of everyday life, its rapid and unpredictable shifts of tone and texture. Another way in which he encourages us to see finance as operating at some remove from strict calculative rationality is via his highlighting of a mystical or occult mindset, to which financial professionals appear to be peculiarly prone. Charlie confesses, for example, that

> it was hard not to feel invincible sometimes, when I saw patterns in the markets, felt things aligning, sensed the strange magic of capital flows with me sitting in the middle with unique vision, able to see the mechanism of the great machine of capitalism.

(117)

Charlie reserves particular praise for the divinatory powers of his colleague, Madison, who warns early of the approaching credit crisis, and succumbs to depression and, eventually, suicide as her worst fears are realized. Madison is pictured as a latter day Delphic Oracle, if not (given the incredulity with which her dire prognostications are met by her workmates) a veritable Cassandra:

> Madison Duval was ahead of her time. She had predicted the crash when we were all looking forward to a century of prosperity . . . . She saw designs in things, understood the complex linkages and patterns which moved the world. She even managed to foreshadow the wave of suicides which swept through the City that autumn, borne on the remorseless east wind that emptied the streets and grabbed air from the lungs.

(200)

Again, intemperate weather is at one with psychological and financial despond here (an effect heightened by the malign portent traditionally attributed to the east wind). This passage also introduces an especially lurid – indeed nigh-on fantastical – element of Preston's portrayal of financial psychopathology: a succession of progressively more baroque suicides. The financial crisis does appear to have been the proximate cause of a number of suicides amongst financial workers, but Preston portrays something far stranger – an epidemic of stylized, ritualistic self-murder:

> The suicides that swept across the City that winter seemed orchestrated, conducted by some heavenly aesthete. The dance of death was a beautiful one, showing a profound understanding of the importance of that final image. The way the press reported the suicides seemed to increase the search for beauty in the final act, causing the young people who were no longer willing to endure the drudgery of existence to aim to outclass each previous death, leave the image burnt longer on the collective retina.

(225)

Charlie seems to be at least half-serious in anticipating a Grand Guignol finale to this macabre new trend amongst those who live what his friend, Henry, calls 'the life of ghastly commerce' (238):

> I have become rather fascinated by these suicides . . . . There's something darkly compelling about the crescendo they seem to be building towards. I almost expect some

great communal statement – the whole of an investment bank self-immolating on the trading floor, or several CEOs getting together and blowing themselves up in front of the Stock Exchange.

(239)

At the end of the novel, it appears that Charlie himself may be another City worker driving headlong towards a terminal point from which there is no return. Estranged from Vero and their two children, conceived during a brief reconciliation following the collapse of her marriage, and now wholly given over to 'the logic of the profit and loss' (331), Charlie is pictured in the closing lines with his face pressed up against the wall of his office, examining a mark that, he realizes, 'is a full stop' (335).

The inseparability of financial and emotional crisis is also explored, albeit in a more comic key, in Jess Walter's *The Financial Lives of the Poets* (2009). Walter's novel is a depiction of the American heartland blighted by what the protagonist, Matt Prior, anticipates will be memorialized in the history books as the Great Recession (9): a landscape of foreclosed homes, depopulated neighbourhoods, and rootless citizenry. Matt senses that the boom and bust were fueled not just by hopped up bankers and traders, but also by the frenzied emotions of the populace at large:

> It's as if the whole country believes we've done something to deserve this collapse, this global warming and endless war, this pile of shit we're in. We've lived beyond our means, spent the future, sapped resources, lived on the bubble. Economists pretend they're studying a social science, and while the economy *is* a machine of hugely complex systems, it's also organic, the whole a reflection of the cells that make it up, a god made in *our* image, prone to flights of euphoric greed and pride, choking envy, irrational fear, pettiness, stinginess, manic euphoria, and senseless depression.
>
> (154–155; emphases in original)

Matt and his wife, Lisa, have played their own small but exemplary roles in the binge years, he quitting his steady job as a financial journalist to launch a web site touting investment advice in the form of blank verse, and she reinventing herself as an eBay entrepreneur reselling cheap knickknacks from their garage. After these quixotic schemes fail, the couple find themselves a week away from losing their overpriced and oversized home. The narrative traces Matt's progressively more desperate attempts to remedy his family's finances – from cashing in his retirement plan to indulging in small time cannabis dealing – whilst he also struggles to deal with Lisa's possible infidelity and his father's 'creeping dementia' (19). Towards the end of the novel, it dawns on Matt how tightly intertwined his and his family's problems are with those of the economy at large:

> It's all connected, these crises – marriage, finances, weed dealing – they are interrelated, like the physical and mental decline of my dad, and my own decline, like the housing market and the stock market and the credit market. We can try to separate them, but these are interrelated systems, reliant upon one another, broken, fucked-up, ruined systems.
>
> (212)

Other narratives take this mirroring between micro and macro crises a step further by casting the former as mere reflections of the latter. The critic Audrey Jaffe (2010) notes that 'representations of the stock market have, from the time of the market's early-Victorian popularization to the present day, served as a dominant means of assessing collective feeling' (2) 'The graph, and other forms of stock-market rhetoric, tend to be viewed as reflections of feelings,' Jaffe notes, but, according to her argument, these representations are not 'secondary – the expression of pre-existing feelings – but rather primary, shaping the narratives of emotion they are said to reflect: indeed, shaping the cultural product known as emotion' (2, 14). There are abundant examples of how 'stock-market discourse . . . constructs both character and emotion in stock-market terms' (15) in contemporary fiction.

The template for this style of characterization can be found in one of the most celebrated American novels of recent times: Jonathan Franzen's *The Corrections* (2001). The tone is set early on when the central character, Chip, is unable to tell whether his father, a Parkinson's sufferer, is admitting to having 'suffered from depression all my life' or describing how he suffered in the Depression. 'An economic depression, we're talking about,' Chip comments uncertainly (23). (The linkage of neurocognitive disorder to financial and economic crisis is a feature not only of *The Corrections* and Walter's *The Financial Lives of the Poets*, but also of Kate Jennings' *Moral Hazard*.) The narrative's background events are the economic dramas of the late 1990s: 'dot-com issues'; bankruptcy in Russia; 'overseas currency crises'; the 'tanking of . . . economies in South America and . . . plunges in key Far Eastern markets' (111, 127, 217, 118). In the final pages, a 'correction' in the interpersonal dynamics of Chip's family – the Lamberts – plays out against an economic 'correction' – 'a year-long leakage of value from key financial markets' (647).

Accordingly, Franzen repeatedly portrays his characters' emotional states in terms drawn from the lexicon of finance, as if it is now the markets that shape the language for, and even content of, our emotional lives, rather than the other way round. When Chip, a college professor, surfaces from a drug-fuelled debauch with a student, for example, he is described as 'like a market inundated by a wave of panic selling,' 'plunged into shame and self-consciousness' in 'a matter of seconds' (66).

Franzen deploys this trope most prominently in his depiction of Chip's brother, Gary. A banker heavily invested in pharmaceutical companies pioneering new treatments for affective disorders, Gary emblematizes the novel's coupling of finance and feeling. Passages focalized through his consciousness insistently metaphorize mind and mood as markets. We are told, for example, that 'his mental markets – glycemic, endocrine, over-the-synapse – [are] crashing' and that his son is 'prepared to spend any amount of devalued verbal currency to buy his father's acquiescence' (185, 179). Similarly, Franzen highlights Gary's inching descent into alcoholism in these terms: '*What this stagnating economy needs*, thought Federal Reserve Board Chairman Gary R. Lambert, *is a massive infusion of Bombay Sapphire gin*' (186; italics in original). In his most extended deployment of this rhetoric, Franzen writes of Gary:

> He estimated that his levels of Neurofactor 3 (i.e., serotonin: a very, very important factor) were posting seven-day or even thirty-day highs, that his Factor 2 and Factor 7 levels were likewise outperforming expectations, and that his Factor 1 had rebounded from an early-morning slump related to the glass of Armagnac he'd drunk at bedtime. . . . Declines led advances in key indices of paranoia . . . and his seasonally adjusted assessment of life's futility and brevity was consistent with the overall robustness of his mental economy. He was not the least bit clinically depressed.
>
> (160)

Later in the novel, Franzen's free indirect discourse again gives us a Gary determined to disavow his own all-too-evident depression via reference to a buoyant market: 'Depressed? He was not depressed. Vital signs of the rambunctious American economy streamed numerically across his many-windowed television screen. . . . The U.S. dollar laughing at the euro, buggering the yen' (258). Here, again, it is as if the financial economy is assumed necessarily to take precedence over the character's 'mental economy' in the determination of mood, so that one simply has no right to be depressed when the markets are on the up.

The troping of character in terms of financial jargon is also prevalent in post–2008 crunch lit. We find it frequently, for instance, in Seth Freedman's *Dead Cat Bounce* (2012) and Henry Sutton's *Get Me Out of Here* (2010), two stories of rabid City Boys running amok across London as the financial system collapses around them. Freedman's unnamed protagonist, a coked-up trader, is fond of describing his fluctuating fortunes in the language of his profession. At one point, expressing his commitment to building a life with his girlfriend, he mentally appends some small print to the undertaking: 'Terms and conditions apply. The value of my promise can go down as well as up. Your home life is at risk if you don't keep up repayments on my emotional mortgage' (n.p.). Similarly, whilst enjoying a personal high point, he notes that he has 'broken into new terrain on my life's point and figure chart' (a graphic depiction of day-to-day price movements used by stock analysts) (n.p.). His 'stock' is 'soaring' one moment only to be 'suspended' the next 'pending a further announcement' (n.p.). Finally, as his life falls apart, he ruefully muses:

> Should have quit when I was streets ahead, when my portfolio was overweight in coke futures and hard cash, and I'd hedged every position by staying uncaring, unconnected, and utterly untouchable. Should have gone out on a high, in every sense of the word.
>
> (n.p.)

The protagonist of Sutton's *Get Me Out of Here*, Matt, lives a precarious existence on the fringes of the financial profession, hectoringly touting a start up company that – he insists, unpromisingly – has backing from North Korea (46). The chapters – in which Sutton obliquely narrates what appears to be a series of gruesome acts on the part of his increasingly unhinged anti-hero – are headed by financial terms, which capture both the parlous state of the markets ('all the arrows . . . pointing down' [223]) and Matt's fraying psychological condition: 'Escalated Asset Values'; 'Toxic Debt'; 'Frozen Liquidity'; 'Moral Hazard'; 'Emergency Bailout'; 'Chaotic Unwinding'; and so on. Both *Dead Cat Bounce* and *Get Me Out of Here* bear the imprint of Bret Easton Ellis's portrayal of the archetypal frenzied financier, Patrick Bateman, in *American Psycho*. Ellis's influence is especially evident in *Get Me Out of Here*, whose readers, like those of Ellis's novel, are invited to wonder whether the grisly crimes apparently committed by the protagonist are in fact merely figments of his deranged imagination. Significantly, Matt is reproached by a former friend precisely for his delusional tendencies: 'You live in a fantasy world, Matt. You're so divorced from reality I don't know how you've survived so long' (167). Matt's fantasy world, which, by the end of the novel he finds 'collapsing around' him (182), may well consist of his ostensible murders, as well as his fanciful start up scheme, but it is also the world of finance at large, and indeed the narrative world of the novel itself, with its strange elisions, odd jumps, and tendency to render 'time . . . increasingly elastic' (184).

Fictitious capital

A convergence between the unstable realities of finance and of fiction is evident in other contemporary novels. One especially prominent example is Zadie Smith's *NW* (2012). Smith's novel seems to put into practice some of the principles she staked out in a celebrated 2008 essay for *The New York Review of Books*, 'Two Paths for the Novel.' Ostensibly a review of Joseph O'Neill's *Netherland* and Tom McCarthy's *Remainder* (two novels – not coincidentally, perhaps – with significant financial themes), Smith's essay is a wider meditation on the formal options available to the contemporary novelist. She identifies the default position, adopted by O'Neill and many other writers, as adherence to the 'nineteenth-century lyrical Realism of Balzac and Flaubert – the incantatory power of language to reveal truth.' Other authors, like McCarthy, however, keep faith with the experimental strategies pioneered by the modernists and radicalized by the exponents of American metafiction – the likes of Pynchon, Gaddis, and DeLillo – whose work 'stood in opposition to Realism,' but has come to be seen by many as no more than 'a fascinating failure.' Smith's own *NW* appears in many ways to be an attempt to bring these divergent 'paths' together.

The novel is a fine-grained and attentive – even obsessively detailed – portrayal of the workaday rhythms of life in Smith's native North West London (whose postcode gives the work its title). Its realism is unsettled, however, by devices – including stream-of-consciousness passages, unusual typographic arrangements, and an absence of quotation marks – which lend the narrative an opaque and disjunctive quality. The abstractions and obscurities of finance are strongly implicated in these defamiliarizing strategies. As in other contemporary novels, financial tremors – in this case the rumblings of the credit crunch ('young men on television clear[ing] their desks. Walk[ing] out with their boxes held in front of them like shields' [327]) – lend the narrative its discordant mood music. Finance is also front and centre in the novel. Michel, the husband of one of the main characters, Leah, becomes a day trader, dealing on foreign exchange markets from their box room. A description of Michel at his computer, filtered through Leah's perceptions, captures the capacity of global finance to warp experiences of time and space:

> Currency trading. The exploitation of volatility. She can only understand words, not numbers. The words are ominous. Add them to that look Michel has, right now, of arrested attention. Internal time stretched and stilled, inattentive to the minutes and hours outside of itself . . . . Blue shimmer of the screen. He is two feet away. He is on the other side of the world.
>
> (54)

In a manner that Leah's father – a 'materialist . . . who kept his real paper money in a cardboard box' – 'would never understand,' money, for Michel, has become purely 'notional' (55).

The 'notional' – imaginary, conjectural – nature of money seems to inform Smith's 'metafictional' highlighting of the unreality of her own characters. In one scene, Natalie, the wife of a City banker rocked by 'The Crash,' who contemplates writing a memoir entitled 'Following the money: A wife's account' (326), attempts to help her mother with her own money problems – the 'chaotic history' of her 'fan of credit cards' (295). 'People,' the narrator tells us in a break in the dialogue, are 'not people but merely an effect of language. You [can] conjure them up and kill them in a sentence' (295) – just as you can conjure up and cancel credit with a flick of a pen or a few taps of a keyboard. Similarly, Natalie later has the disquieting intimation that, contrary to her own view of her and her family's lives, it is their 'house that [is] the unimpeachable reality,' and they themselves 'just a lot of human shadow-play on the wall' (325), like the flickering, insubstantial forms of speculation that sprung up around the market in 'bricks and mortar' in the 2000s.

The extent to which the continued functioning of the financial system relies on belief in such intangible, 'fictitious' forms of value is highlighted by the cultural theorist Jodi Dean (2013):

> The circulation of money detaches itself from production; money is purely self-mediating. Since abstract financial relations are themselves treated as underlying assets, money

markets can expand seemingly without limit – that is, as long as everyone involved believes that they will, as long as the circuit keeps on going on and no one tries to cash in or call.

(143)

Justin Cartwright's work of crunch lit, *Other People's Money* (2011) – an account of the machinations that surround a venerable private bank threatened with collapse during the crisis – places great emphasis on the ways in which financial values appear to be created and sustained through a kind of sorcery. We are told that the bankers 'thought they could make money appear from nowhere'; that 'credit swaps and diced mortgages were chimeras,' which 'related to no assets, to no worth, to no human endeavour' and 'turned out to be imaginary'; that the entire financial services industry 'was in thrall to fables'; and that 'the money simply imploded. It no longer exists. Nobody can explain it' (71, 80, 103). *Other People's Money* explores both of Smith's 'paths for the novel.' An exemplary work of 'lyrical Realism' in many respects, the novel also draws attention to the possibility of a more experimental register via its depiction of a struggling playwright who conceives the idea for a five-hour cinematic opus based on the life and work of arch-metafictionalist Flann O'Brien. Like O'Brien himself, Cartwright's writer-character, Artair, believes that 'theatre and novels are too often constrained by reality' (22) and instead embraces the fabulations of 'postmodernism' (26). Following the example of its subject, 'the screenplay is . . . going to demonstrate its own artificiality.' The 'whole concept of a movie as a contained reality will be exploded . . . . [Artair] will demonstrate that there is no such thing as a single objective reality' (211). Cartwright's novel itself makes an abrupt turn towards fabulism at its end with a larger-than-life, wish-fulfillment conclusion that underscores the narrative's identification of fiction and finance alike as forms liable to take on the airiness of fairy tale.

A similar effect is achieved by Jonathan Coe's contribution to the crunch lit canon, *The Terrible Privacy of Maxwell Sim* (2010). Coe's narrative follows its hapless Everyman protagonist, Max, on a picaresque journey from the South of England to the Shetland Islands to promote a new brand of toothbrush. He crosses a land wracked by economic strife: 'right now, the credit crunch was starting to bite, people were losing their jobs and their savings, everyone was in a state of financial uncertainty' (18). The news is full of 'apocalyptic headlines saying that the banks were about to crumble, we would all lose our money and it would be the end of Western civilization as we knew it' (106). Again, as in other novels discussed above, the diffuse 'mood of the market' seems to determine Max's own mood, as if individual feelings were mere epiphenomena of the pool of collective feeling that constitutes the financial markets: 'I just stared all day at the TV news, not understanding any of it except for the prevailing mood of anxiety and despair which everyone seemed to be trying to put across, and gradually fell prey to a sort of unfocused panic' (107).

In Coe's novel, a conception of the financialized economy as lacking any tangible foundation is conveyed by Max's urbane acquaintance Clive, who remarks:

> The value of any object [is] entirely abstract, entirely immaterial. And yet these completely non-existent entities – we call them prices – are what we base our whole society upon. An entire civilization built on . . . well, on air, really. That's all it is. Air . . . .
>
> Until now, most people have never really appreciated it. Most people have gone about their daily business on the comfortable assumption that something real and solid underpins everything we do. Now, it's no longer possible to assume that. And as that realization sinks in, we're going to have to adjust our whole way of thinking.

(110)

During a stop-off in Edinburgh, Max hears of a 'multi-millionaire financial wizard' who lives in one of the city's 'massive and imposing' houses (229). This familiar metaphor is intriguingly literalized in a sub-plot of the novel, which concerns Max's father's relationship with a man who styles himself as an actual financial wizard. The relationship is described in a memoir that Max finds amongst his father, Harold's, papers. Harold relates how, moving to London in the late 1950s, he took a job as a messenger boy at a stockbroking firm in the City, and became friends with Roger, an errand-runner at the Stock Exchange. Roger is the kind of London antiquarian and mystic familiar from the pages of Michael Moorcock, Iain Sinclair, or Peter Ackroyd, possessed of a 'library of volumes on witchcraft and paganism' and fond of walking 'through the mazy, empty backstreets of London, long into the night, while . . . point[ing] out strange architectural features, quirky buildings, forgotten landmarks with some recondite fragment of London history attached to them' (263, 250). Roger's is an 'alluring world . . . of shadows, portents, symbols, riddles and coincidences' (267).

His portrayal taps into a long tradition of casting the Square Mile of the City of London – 'that labyrinth of ancient, history-laden streets dedicated to the single-minded accumulation of money' (280) – as a space in which value is magically conjured into being (see Crosthwaite 2011), a tradition which goes back at least as far as Daniel Defoe's accounts of the financial 'alchemy' and 'Air-Money' of the early eighteenth century, the age of a newly dominant public credit, and of speculative manias like the South Sea Bubble. Coe echoes this rhetoric especially strongly when he has Roger explain to Harold how he has been able to combine his experience at the Stock Exchange and his immersion in occult lore to construct the perfect, 'flawless' wager, a 'phenomenally complex spread of bets' bundled up 'into one financial instrument' (263, 264). 'What are you saying?' Harold asks. 'That you've found a way of making money out of nothing? Out of air?' Roger replies:

> You, Harold, are earthbound. You need to develop a more spiritual outlook. Don't become one of those lesser mortals who inhabits the material world. The world where people spend their lives making things and then buying and selling and using and consuming them. The world of objects. That's for the hoi polloi, not the likes of you and me. We're above all that. We're alchemists.
>
> (264–65)

Here, the strategies of risk and speculation characteristic of the financial sector are presented as quite literal forms of enchantment.

As *The Terrible Privacy of Maxwell Sim* unfolds, its concern with what Coe refers to as the 'abstract and ethereal' (62) builds, coming to reshape the narrative world itself, whose spatial and temporal coordinates (like those of Sutton's *Get Me Out of Here*) seem increasingly difficult to map onto our familiar reality. Ultimately, it is no great surprise when the novel ends with its protagonist encountering its author, who, with a click of his fingers, makes his 'imaginary friend' (339) disappear. This classically metafictional rupture again suggests a resonance between the novel's narrative patterning and its financial preoccupations – a shared concern with the creation and destruction, by fiat, of imaginary things.

The groundlessness or fictionality of finance can be highlighted not only through an emphasis on the fictionality of fiction itself (that is, through the adoption of a metafictional mode), but also through the deployment of genre forms, with the latitude they offer to incorporate supernatural, fantastical, or otherworldly elements into the narrative. An example of the latter approach is Stephen Marche's *The Hunger of the Wolf* (2015), which blends a highly (indeed, at times, excessively) lyrical brand of realism with many of the trappings of Gothic horror.

The novel traces the rise, over the course of the twentieth century, of a plutocratic American dynasty, the Wylies, whose male line apparently carries a strain of lycanthropy. The question of whether the Wylie men are *really* werewolves is never fully laid to rest (an extended section consists of a psychoanalyst's case study of one member of the clan, duly noting 'Freud's famous case of the Wolf-man' and offering a predictably Freudian explanation for the patient's 'narcissistic delusion' [129, 133–34]). The Wylies themselves, however, decidedly *do* believe in their own lupine nature, and this belief appears to be essential to their immense success in the worlds of business and finance. The novel's epigraph, from Adam Smith, is significant here: 'All money is a matter of belief.' As Alex Norcia (2015) notes in a perceptive review, as with religious observance, 'money's worth hinges on faith. It means however much you want it to mean. It operates much like a myth, a legend, a ghost story – much like a tale of men transforming into wolves.'

The Wylie saga is pieced together by a New York journalist, Jamie Cabot, who believes he has found the perfect story to revive his fortunes after his newspaper lays him off following the 2008 market crash, a time when 'the value of the world seemed to have lowered forever, and crisis, as a term, was beginning to lose its ancient meaning, smoothing into an ordinary condition' (5). As well as figuring the fantastical, make-believe qualities of money, the lycanthropic Wylies also emblematize the relentless rapine that drives markets and economies, 'the desire for growth, the hunger for more' as Jamie puts it (7–8). John Maynard Keynes likely had in mind archaic ideas of animating humours when he wrote, famously, of 'animal spirits' in *The General Theory of Employment, Interest, and Money* (1936), but his term has been received and popularized as denoting the 'animalistic' – taurine, ursine, lupine – urges that impel economic activity (see Crosthwaite 2013), and the Wylies embody this understanding in a perfectly literalized form. By tracing the entanglement of the Wylies' wolfish nature with the growth of their business empire, Jamie hopes to gain an insight into the spirit of capitalism itself, 'a glance into the hidden workings of the machinery,' initiation into 'the secret history of how money became everything' (20, 21). Finally, though, in the novels closing pages, Jamie wonders whether the determined accumulation of capital by financial titans like the Wylies is motivated by a desire for its ultimate destruction. Invoking the traditional Native American ceremony of potlatch, in which chiefs competed to destroy ever-greater quantities of their own goods (see Crosthwaite 2010), Jamie reflects:

> One night at the party for a book about the crash on [a] rooftop . . . high above the city, I theorized to myself that the species was gathering money into fewer and neater piles so we could burn it in bigger and brighter conflagrations. The potlatch of the earth had begun.
>
> (248)

In seeking both to tell and to sell the outlandish story of the Wylies, Jamie reminds us that there is not merely a homology but a virtual identity between the practices of the financier and the practices of the writer under capitalism. As professional authors from Defoe to the present have known, 'the job of a writer is to monetize fascination' (21). Jamie continues:

> I was broke and alone but I had [the Wylies]. If I could uncover their story, I could sell their story, and if I could sell their story, I might have something like a future in New York. Every story is a little miracle. You make it out of nothing and you sell it for money.
>
> (21)

Made out of nothing, novels and 'exotic' financial instruments are privileged objects both of monetary exchange and for the investment of fascination, fantasy, faith, and desire.

Works cited

Buchan, J. 1997. *Frozen Desire: The Meaning of Money*. New York: Farrar, Straus, and Giroux.

Cartwright, J. 2011. *Other People's Money*. London: Bloomsbury.

Coe, J. 2010. *The Terrible Privacy of Maxwell Sim*. London: Penguin.

Crosthwaite, P. 2010. 'Blood on the Trading Floor: Waste, Sacrifice, and Death in Financial Crises.' *Angelaki*, 15(2), 3–18.

——— 2011. 'Phantasmagoric Finance: Crisis and the Supernatural in Contemporary Finance Culture.' In: P. Crosthwaite, ed. *Criticism, Crisis, and Contemporary Narrative: Textual Horizons in an Age of Global Risk*. New York: Routledge, 178–200.

——— 2013. 'Animality and Ideology in Contemporary Economic Discourse: Taxonimizing *Homo Economicus*.' *Journal of Cultural Economy*, 6(1), 94–109.

Dean, J. 2013. 'Complexity as Capture: Neoliberalism and the Loop of Drive.' *New Formations*, 80–81, 138–154.

Fisher, M. 2009. *Capitalist Realism: Is There No Alternative?* Winchester: Zero Books.

Franzen, J. 2002 [2001]. *The Corrections*. London: Fourth Estate.

Freedman, S. 2012. *Dead Cat Bounce*. [Kindle version]. London: Cutting Edge Press.

Jaffe, A. 2010. *The Affective Life of the Average Man: The Victorian Novel and the Stock-Market Graph*. Columbus: Ohio State University Press.

Knight, P. 2013. 'Reading the Ticker Tape in the Late Nineteenth-Century American Market.' *Journal of Cultural Economy*, 6(1), 45–62.

Marche, S. 2015. *The Hunger of the Wolf*. New York: Simon and Schuster.

Marsh, N. 2007. *Money, Speculation, and Finance in Contemporary British Fiction*. London: Continuum.

Norcia, A. 2015. 'A Wishful Fear and a Fearful Wish (Review of *The Hunger of the Wolf* by S. Marche).' *Los Angeles Review of Books*, 20 April. Available at: http://lareviewofbooks.org/review/wishful-fear-fearful-wish.

Poovey, M. 2008. *Genres of the Credit Economy: Mediating Value in Eighteenth- and Nineteenth-Century Britain*. Chicago: University of Chicago Press.

Preston, A. 2010. *This Bleeding City*. London: Faber and Faber.

Shaw, K. 2015. *Crunch Lit*. London: Bloomsbury.

Smith, Z. 2008. 'Two Paths for the Novel.' *New York Review of Books*, 20 November. Available at: www.nybooks.com/articles/archives/2008/nov/20/two-paths-for-the-novel/.

——— 2012. *NW*. London: Penguin.

Sutton, H. 2010. *Get Me Out of Here*. London: Harvill Secker.

Walter, J. 2009. *The Financial Lives of the Poets*. New York: HarperCollins.

24

THE 9/11 NOVEL

Arin Keeble

This chapter examines what has become known in contemporary literary scholarship, on university syllabi and beyond, as the '9/11 novel.' While the 9/11 canon is undoubtedly international, it includes a heavy concentration of American novels. I focus on these texts here, both to complement Daniel O'Gorman's chapter, 'War on Terror,' and because they include particularly revealing examples of features that broadly unify this body of work. I argue that the 9/11 novel has been characterized by anxiety and internal conflict relating to a set of competing impulses that pull the narratives in opposing directions. They gesture toward both the public and private, the political and the domestic, toward historical contexts and traumatic rupture. Even as they attempt to deal with trauma these competing impulses manifest in what Judith Herman calls the 'central dialectic of psychological trauma,' described as: 'the will to deny horrific events and the will to proclaim them aloud' (1992: 2). But the interpretive frame of trauma alone is limited and has frequently been identified as ethically insufficient.[1] It doesn't account for the complex interplay between 'the real and the symbolic,' which as Alex Houen has noted, has characterized terrorism for over a century (2002: 9). Nor does it account for the conflictedness that emerges in the ways 9/11 novels have simultaneously evoked rupture and historical continuity as they grapple with exceptionalist notions of 9/11 as a singular historical moment. Moreover, as Peter Boxall has noted, some of these novels have 'staged a kind of encounter between Islam and the west' (2013: 128). Such encounters have sometimes reinforced the crude dichotomies of 'us and them' or 'victim and perpetrator' but have invariably been fraught with conflict relating to the questions of how to represent 'the other.'

In mapping this conflictedness and charting the evolution of the 9/11 canon, I will also address the underlying question of what this body of texts is: a question of both classification and qualification. Is the 9/11 novel part of a broader project in contemporary fiction of locating a 'new way of weaving time and history and embodiment together' in specific response to the early twenty-first century, as Boxall has argued (2013: 123)? Is this a 'cycle' of event-specific texts, or, is the 9/11 novel a 'genre'? The latter is a concept that Robert Eaglestone has described as 'in complete disarray in the twenty-first century,' as rigid genre distinctions have long been collapsed by postmodernism, and the proliferation of hybrid sub-genres (2013: 109). I suggest that this group of texts shares a set of preoccupations, tropes, themes – and anxieties – that might reasonably qualify it as a genre, providing a compelling way to consider genre in contemporary fiction and particularly in 'literary' fiction, which is often seen as superior to the formulaic nature of science fiction or crime writing, for example, but which is also itself a genre. These questions of definition and classification are also linked to debates about 'period' in contemporary literature as 9/11 is frequently used as a period marker in literary studies.

'9/11 Novel' is often used interchangeably with 'post-9/11 novel,' a term which is deployed to describe texts that engage centrally with 9/11 but also as a general catchall for novels written after the attacks. I understand 9/11 novels as texts that engage with 9/11 and its aftermath directly, an assumption that has underpinned numerous monographs and collections of essays (Keniston and Follansbee Quinn 2007; Versluys 2009; Däwes 2011; Randall 2011; Keeble 2014; Morley 2016). Novels such as Cormac McCarthy's *The Road* (2006) or Philip Roth's *The Plot Against America* (2004) have also been convincingly classified as allegorical 9/11 novels (particularly by David Holloway 2008). Similarly, Ian McEwan's *Saturday* (2005) and John Updike's *Terrorist* (2006), which don't engage with 9/11 directly but deal centrally with terror and 'otherness' in the immediate aftermath, are also sometimes included. Some of the most celebrated contemporary authors have published 9/11 novels: Claire Messud, Don DeLillo, Thomas Pynchon, Jonathan Safran Foer, Jay McInerney as well as McCarthy, Roth, McEwan and Updike if we accept the allegorical/thematically linked texts. 9/11 novels have also propelled the careers of newer literary stars such as Mohsin Hamid, Joseph O'Neill and Amy Waldman. Additionally, an array of criminally less-recognized novels are beginning to accrue attention: Porochista Khakpour's *The Last Illusion* (2014) or H.M. Naqvi's *Homeboy* (2009), for example. These novels are all characterized in some way by the conflictedness described above and this chapter will examine this phenomenon from the earliest to the most recent texts.

I will look first at Safran Foer's *Extremely Loud and Incredibly Close* (2005), focussing on its conspicuously playful aesthetics and its transatlantic historical narrative. I argue that these features of the novel pull in opposite directions, gesturing toward a historical understanding of the attacks while insisting on traumatic rupture. I will then discuss Messud's *The Emperor's Children* (2006), one of the many so-called 'domestic' novels of 9/11. I will address the way Messud's novel deals with the return to normality after 9/11, considering David Simpson's question of whether this evokes 'resilience' or 'indifference' (2007: 216). Finally, I will discuss Amy Waldman's *The Submission* (2011), an explicitly political novel which takes post-9/11 division as its central subject yet is also replete with its own internal conflicts. This analysis will build on my previous work on *The Submission*, which discusses its metafictional exploration of memorialization and representation.

A final objective of this chapter is to discuss the ways literary criticism of the 9/11 novel has been equally conflicted. From commentary by other novelists such as Zadie Smith or Pankaj Mishra, to the polarized scholarly debates about the perceived 'domestication' of the attacks by literature, the 9/11 novel has a fraught intellectual history that has often spoken to broader issues in contemporary fiction – like genre and period.

'Willed into existence': anticipation for a literary response to 9/11

The anxiety that has defined the 9/11 canon may partly be a consequence of the extraordinary anticipation and perceived need for a literary response that was expressed directly after the attacks. There was a weight of expectation on novelists who were sought out as 'experts at imagining the unimaginable' (Houen 2004: 419). *The Guardian* alone published Zadie Smith, Ian McEwan, Jay McInerney, Martin Amis, Umberto Eco, Arundhati Roy and Don DeLillo while *The New Yorker's* September 24 'Talk of The Town' section featured Updike, Jonathan Franzen and Amitav Ghosh among others.[2] But while dozens of literary authors produced short pieces for newspapers and magazines in the immediate aftermath, it is notable that fiction is not what they wrote. These pieces were reflective, elegiac and essayistic. In many cases they offered broad messages of consolation and hope; a trope that Charlie Lee Potter sees as slightly mawkish, but redolent of the disorientation caused by the attacks: 'each of them fumbled in one form or another for the nostrum that in the end, love will overcome' (2016: 3).

However, these works were also similar in style to the popular "Portraits of Grief" feature which ran daily in the *New York Times* from September to December 2001, and their appeal can also be understood in this context. The "Portraits of Grief" provided glimpses into the lives of victims in an ostensibly neutral, or as editor Janny Scott insisted, 'utterly democratic' mode (2002: ix). Many of the literary responses functioned in similar ways, offering documentary accounts of ordinary lives with some poetic flourishes. Updike's short piece is a good example: 'we knew we'd just witnessed thousands of deaths; we clung to each other as if we ourselves were falling' (2001: n.p.). Even DeLillo's longer *Harper's* essay reverted to documentary style accounts of human experience, interspersed with historical and cultural observations. While these elegiac snapshots were incredibly popular, politicized commentary like Susan Sontag's (in the same "Talk of the Town" feature as Updike's), which expressed concern for the inevitable revanchist response to the attacks, drew fierce criticism.[3]

The popularity of these short pieces amplified the anticipation for the novels to come, and the prevalence of essayistic, autobiographical or documentary style accounts emphasized the challenges in the move from non-fiction to fiction. Additionally, the backlash that politically charged writing like Sontag's received, gave a clear indication of the increasingly fraught climate in which writers were operating. DeLillo's essay tried to imagine the role of the writer: 'the writer begins in the tower, trying to imagine the moment, desperately. Before politics, before history and religion there is the primal terror' (2001: 39). But while DeLillo here emphasizes the value in dealing with the visceral and terrifying experience of the attacks, he goes on to evoke the larger task novelists faced: understanding them: 'The writer tries to give memory, tenderness, and meaning to all that howling space' (2001: 39). It is clear from the wide-ranging essay that this cannot be fulfilled, strictly, in this mode. Many Anglophone writers expressed anxiety about writing fiction about 9/11 suggesting the attacks had rendered their profession trivial. McInerney wrote that '[m]ost novelists I know went through a period of intense self-examination . . . the idea of "invented characters" and alternative realities seemed trivial and frivolous and suddenly, horribly outdated' (2005: n.p.). This combination of pressures — expectation, responsibility, hostility to political dissent and trauma — inevitably informed the 9/11 novels that eventually appeared.

One now-canonical essay, Zadie Smith's "Two Paths for the Novel," which focusses on Tom McCarthy's *Remainder* (2005) and Joseph O'Neill's *Netherland* (2007) as examples of progressive and conservative modes, framed the expectation and anticipation for 9/11 novels in a particularly suggestive way. Smith wrote of *Netherland*, celebrated elsewhere as an outwardly facing 9/11 novel:

> It's the post-September 11 novel we hoped for (were there calls, in 1915, for the Lusitania novel? In 1985, was the Bhopal novel keenly anticipated) It's as if, by an act of collective prayer we have willed it into existence.
>
> (2008: n.p.)

While Smith notes this anticipation (sarcastically), her references to the Lusitania and Bhopal disasters suggest that disproportionate importance has been attached to 9/11 and by extension the 9/11 novel. This has been a prevalent issue in 9/11 studies and is linked to the conflictedness I have described above. Are novelists, critics and scholars (like me, here) complicit in a project that has meant 9/11 is 'severed ideologically from its causes and its effects,' simply by continuing to devote attention to it (Darlington 2017: 242)? Or, through certain strategies is it possible to resist or change this narrative? I hope this chapter assists with the project of better understanding 9/11 as a moment with clear causes and effects.

The traumatic metafiction of Jonathan Safran Foer's *Extremely Loud and Incredibly Close*

Two of the earliest 9/11 novels, Frédéric Beigbeder's *Windows on the World* (2003) and Jonathan Safran Foer's *Extremely Loud and Incredibly Close* (2005), have compelling similarities. Both are transatlantic novels featuring dual narratives unfolding in Europe and in New York and both alternate narrative strands with every chapter. Additionally, they are conspicuously metafictional, deploying some of the most recognizably postmodernist conceits: the author is a character in *Windows on the World* and *Extremely Loud and Incredibly Close* features a range of images, typographical gimmicks and literary allusions. Both texts are also concerned with children, exemplifying what David Holloway has identified as a dominant trope in 9/11 novels: 'children and youths, or adult sons and daughters involved in distressing relationships with parents or guardian figures' (2008: 108). Holloway sees this as an allegory for the American state's failure to protect its citizens: 'children/citizens divested of parental/state protection' (2008: 110).

The aesthetic strategies of the two novels are linked to their openly stated struggles to find tools to represent 9/11. In *Windows on the World*, the narrator states that: 'writing this hyperrealist novel is made more difficult by reality itself . . . its impossible to write about this subject, and yet impossible to write about anything else' (2003: 8). An even more acute sense of anxiety pervades Safran Foer's novel. The tensions between its will to build in meaningful historical contexts and its rhetoric of traumatic rupture are compounded by its preoccupation with the limits of language. The narrative centres around a precocious nine-year-old, Oskar Schell, who has lost his father in the 9/11 attacks a year earlier. He listens to his father's final answering machine messages, despatched from the burning towers, and begins a quest to find a lock for a key he has found in his father's closet, sensing some kind of meaning or healing in this quest: '[e]very time I left our apartment to go searching for the lock, I became lighter, because I was getting closer to Dad' (2005: 52). Oskar's quest mirrors the wider project of the book and the author. Like Safran Foer, he has created a book, *Stuff That Happened to Me*, his 'scrapbook of everything that happened' which helps him manage his trauma (2005, 42). In fact, when Oskar describes opening the book to try and help him get to sleep, *Stuff that Happened to Me* and *Extremely Loud and Incredibly Close* converge, as the next eight pages the reader encounters show the fourteen different images that Oskar sees in his book: including two (one zoomed in) of the famous falling man. Running parallel are the stories of Oskar's grandparents whose lives were violently affected by the Dresden fire bombings and who came together in the US after those events. Their stories, in the form of letters (from Oskar's grandfather to his father, and his grandmother to him), are the stories of how they dealt with their own traumas.

Ostensibly, this narrative of historical trauma forces the reader to locate 9/11 in the context of previous instances of political violence and to think internationally; in addition to Dresden, there is a powerful scene where the atomic bombing of Hiroshima is discussed. But while there is a sustained comparison of these historical moments, the emphasis is squarely on the traumatic aftermath, rather than the nature of or politics of the larger conflicts. Kristiaan Versluys argues that 'this seemingly apolitical family novel has history inscribed in every sentence' (2009: 81). But this history rarely goes beyond the traumatic history of the Schell family. Describing the first post-Dresden meeting between Oskar's grandparents, Oskar's grandmother states: 'The seven years were not seven years. They were not seven hundred years. Their length could not be measured in years, just as an ocean could not explain the distance we had travelled, just as the dead can never be counted' (81). This image of frozen traumatic time is typical of the novel's approach to historical violence and is echoed by Oskar's experiences and his collection of images: 'It was like time stopped. I thought about the falling body' (2005: 97).

Later in the novel Oskar plays a recording of an oral testimony of Hiroshima during a school presentation but despite the graphically violent descriptions the episode is similar in what it offers as historical analogy. The interviewee on the recording recalls the gruesome effects of the attack which upsets and sickens Oskar's classmates: 'there were maggots in her wounds and a sticky yellow liquid. I tried to clean her up. But her skin was peeling off' (2005: 188). But there is no real discussion of the politics of the event and the interview ends with a sentiment that might accurately describe the novel's – death and suffering is universally horrible and traumatic: '[t]hat is what death is like. It doesn't matter what uniforms the soldiers are wearing . . . I thought if everyone could see what I saw, we would never have any more war' (2005: 189). Versluys notes that Hiroshima and Dresden both represent American violence against other states and argues that this mitigates a tendency toward 'narratives that simplistically reduce the issue involved to a pitched battle of "us" versus "them" or good versus evil' (2009: 83). Nevertheless, it is still the case that in the novel the attacks remain an opaque and apolitical event experienced as a family tragedy. These traumas are all confined to the Schell family narrative, meaning that, as Deborah Shostak notes, it turns 'inward rather than toward the historical world,' reducing 'historical rupture to a personal rupture, the transnational to the domestic, and most notably, to the familial' (2016: 23). Ultimately, the novel's conspicuous historical and transnational components signal a will to situate 9/11 internationally but its rhetoric of rupture pulls the novel in the opposite direction, inward.

The stylistic conceits of the novel add complexity to its opposing pulls. Its visual flourishes, which are substantial (64 still images, sections annotated with red pen, pages of numeric code, and type which overlaps until blacked out), seem initially to signal a desire to find new tools of expression for the post-9/11 world. But they also strengthen the novel's traumatic impulse, suggesting an attempt to articulate what is 'beyond words.' The novel's aesthetics evoke trauma by harnessing the formal quality of the still photograph. Marianne Hirsch has noted that '[p]hotography interrupts, actually stops time, freezes a moment: it is inherently elegiac' and as we have seen the notion that 'time stopped' on 9/11 is a major preoccupation of the novel (2003: 71).

In addition to this conflict between the ostensible innovation and the traumatic freeze of the photograph, there is yet another layer of tension. As unusual as Foer's aesthetic is in early twentieth-first century fiction, its larger metafictional project can be located firmly in literary tradition. This was pointed out in Walter Kirn's review, where he noted that it 'can't really be called experimental,' because its 'signature high jinks, distortions and addenda first came to market many decades back' (2005: n.p.). Indeed, by 2005, the metafictional tools Safran Foer employs are conventional. Consequently, Foer's aesthetics carry a tension between the continuity of tradition and the discontinuity of traumatic rupture which mirrors the tension between its historical and transnational narratives and its narrative drive inward toward private, family trauma.

Claire Messud's *The Emperor's Children* and the 'domestic' fiction of 9/11

Like *Windows on the World* and *Extremely Loud and Incredibly Close*, the next wave of 9/11 novels focussed on the American family – and particularly on privileged, white, metropolitan families – without many explicit gestures toward the international or historical. The prevalence of the domestic in the 9/11 canon partly owes to the persistent belief that the family is the 'sacred cornerstone of the American social project,' making it an obvious recourse in dealing with events that seem incomprehensible (Millard 2000: 9). The familiarity of the family narrative provides an established framework and structure for a story of 9/11 and even has allegorical potential. As David Cowart notes, 'husband and wife are themselves twin towers that marital discord threatens to bring down' (2013: n.p.). But this was seen by many as problematic, and novels like McInerney's *The Good Life* (2005), Kalfus's *A Disorder Peculiar to the Country* (2006), Messud's *The Emperor's Children* and DeLillo's *Falling Man*, received forceful criticism for 'domesticating the crisis' and failing to engage with larger issues surrounding the attacks (Gray 2009: 134). But whether we see these novels as 'failures' – as several commentators have (Mishra 2007; Gray 2009; Rothberg 2009; Mukherjee 2009; Randall 2011) – their specific conflicts, tensions and anxieties are revealing.

One notable trope is the eventual return to normality after a period of disorientation and re-evaluation, which works against the idea of 9/11 as a world-changing moment. However, in each of the domestic novels there are competing suggestions as to whether this represents 'resilience,' or 'indifference,' as Simpson has noted (2007: 216). *The Emperor's Children*, the focus of this section, is particularly interesting in this respect as 9/11 happens late in the narrative when characters have already experienced upheaval and change. In Messud's novel the trauma of 9/11 is filtered through an array of personal ordeals, which add complexity to Simpson's question. In other words, the novel invites us to consider the filter of personal tribulations that pre-date 9/11, with the collective trauma of the attacks.

One of the central concerns of the 'domestic novels' is to dramatize the process of post-9/11 re-evaluation that undoubtedly many Americans experienced. DeLillo and McInerney were specific in their intentions to do this. McInerney emphasized the need to 're-evaluate our lives, to re-examine our values, our careers, our marriages' (2005: n.p.). Similarly, DeLillo described his protagonist Keith as asking: 'who am I? what's my identity?' (2007: n.p.). Their novels follow a similar narrative arc and use the domestic sphere as a barometer to measure post-9/11 change. In *Falling Man* the central couple, Keith and Lianne, who were separated before the attacks, reunite. In *The Good Life*, the central couple, Luke and Corrine whose marriages were stagnating, separate, with Corrine starting an affair. In both cases, however, after the rupture of 9/11 and after extensive periods of re-evaluation, there is a kind of restoration of equilibrium. In *The Good Life*, Luke and Corrine reunite and we find that the 'satori flash of acute wakefulness and connectedness that had followed the initial confrontation with mortality in September was already fading behind them' (2005: 353). *The Good Life* leans more toward 'indifference' or complacency, but as suggested, its conclusion might also suggest that the impact of 9/11 wasn't as great as has been imagined. *Falling Man* inverts this narrative as Lianne and Keith slide back into their pre-9/11 estrangement and while Keith spirals into gambling addiction and numbness – a trajectory that the novel suggests was begun before 9/11 – Lianne is 'ready to be alone, in reliable calm, she and the kid, the way they were before the planes appeared that day, silver crossing blue' (2007: 236). *Falling Man* is more complex as despite Lianne's recovery and readiness to move on, the novel ends with a character called Hammad, a 9/11 hijacker, hurtling toward the World Trade Center in one of the planes. Some critics have seen this conceit as evoking unresolved trauma (Versluys 2009; DeRosa 2016). I would suggest that Lianne and Keith's resumption of their pre-9/11 paths pulls against this and at least reveals conflicting pulls between continuity and traumatic discontinuity.

The most powerful conflict within these domestic fictions is between the inwardness of their milieu (the domestic spheres of white, privileged Manhattanites) and their explorations of moving on and returning to normality, which broadly undercuts notions of 9/11 as a moment when 'everything changed.' *The Emperor's Children* offers a complex iteration of this tension as it depicts multiple aggregations of personal or private ordeals and traumas with the eventual public trauma of 9/11. In many ways, Messud's novel fits well with the other 'domestic novels.' It's plot revolves around the marriages and romantic relationships of a cast of cultural elites: Murray Thwaite, a prestigious *New York Review of Books*-style cultural commentator, his daughter Marina, who is drifting in his wake and trying to complete her first book; Danielle, Marina's best friend and documentary maker who has an affair with Murray; Julius a freelance *Village Voice*-style critic and Bootie, Murray's nephew who wants first to emulate him and eventually to expose his hypocrisy.

But while *The Emperor's Children* is like *The Good Life* and *Falling Man* in its focus on the domestic spheres and romantic entanglements of privileged, white New Yorkers, it also has a strong satirical edge, and functions partly as a society novel genre parody. Many of the characters oscillate between realistic and caricature. When Marina, deliberating on whether she should get a job or continue to live off her father as she works on her book, states, 'a real job would be so demanding, after all, that's what an interesting job is supposed to be; and an easy job, a dumb job, well, at that point who am I kidding,' the satire is explicit (2006: 90). However, it is a long novel and despite their pretences and flaws, Messud wants us to care about the characters. For example, Julius's description of the aftermath of an instance of domestic violence that has left him physically scarred is moving: 'You don't think of yourself as scarred. . . But everyone sees you, and they see a changed person, and the ones who know the story see you changed in a very particular way, which isn't so nice. I think eventually you get changed from the outside in' (2006: 545).

Yet the novel's satire is not it's only reflexive feature pushing against its inward domestic realism. Its preoccupation with writing and literature metafictionally draws attention to its own project of trying to find the right register for 9/11. Boxall describes this as a 'performance, beneath a studiedly bland surface, of a number of different kinds of writing' (2013: 145). But while he is right to point out that the novel's representation of writing evokes 'various models for the ways in which writing can produce new political and aesthetic formations,' it is also the case that the various writings within the book are an important part of its satire. Murray's secret opus *How to Live*, intended as 'the distillation, crystalline, of all he had learned, and knew,' is obviously portentous (2006: 85). Marina's book project about the cultural significance of children's fashion has lost direction to the extent that she: 'was no longer particularly interested in her book, nor impressed by its thesis' (2006: 32). Most compelling is the satirical magazine *The Monitor*, which Marina's boyfriend Ludovic is about to launch when 9/11 happens. Instantly, its publishers and corporate backers withdraw support because 'nobody wanted such a thing in this new world, a frivolous, satirical thing' (2006: 542). This is an obvious reference to the short-lived but popular idea of the post-9/11 'death of irony,' propagated forcefully by Michael Rosenthall in *Time Magazine* after the attacks, and also satirized in Pynchon's *Bleeding Edge* (2013). *The Emperor's Children* is itself a satirical novel about 9/11 so while there may be moments when the aims of the literary projects in the novel converge with its own – as with Safran Foer's protagonist Oskar's *Stuff That Happened to Me* – there is always a critical distance, and this creates one of the novel's many internal conflicts. As Boxall notes, while its exploration of different literary modes represents 'a rejection of the confines of body or of genre,' the novel simultaneously 'gives itself to formula, to genre' (2013: 152).

The most important conflict in *The Emperor's Children*, however, and one which we can see in all the 'domestic fictions,' is created by its depiction of a return to normality. The question of whether this is down to 'indifference' or 'resilience' is acute here as the characters have been shown to be duplicitous and selfish, but also have undergone personal traumas that compound their experience of 9/11. Ultimately, the novel's overarching tension lies in the conservative and inward focus on privileged American domesticity which mostly avoids meaningful political engagement set against the powerful suggestion that 9/11 wasn't a moment that changed everything. As Danielle notes, planning her next documentary in the November after the attacks: '[s]he had a film about liposuction to make. It seemed, in some lights, trivial, but it wasn't really. By the time it was finished, people would be tired of greater tragedies, and would be ready to watch it again. Most people's tragedies were small' (2006: 572). While this embodies the narrow and elite perspectives of the domestic novels, it also represents a challenge to the ideologically rooted idea of traumatic rupture.

Representation and 'truth' in Amy Waldman's *The Submission*

More than Hamid's *The Reluctant Fundamentalist* (2007) or O'Neill's *Netherland* (2008), Amy Waldman's *The Submission* (2011) was hailed as a new kind of 9/11 novel. It engages centrally with 'otherness' and post-9/11 racism and its many layers of reflexivity extend to an aware-ness of the criticisms that the domestic novels had received. This was foregrounded in Kamila Shamsie's review:

> Perhaps the representatives of fiction writing and non-fiction writing in America didn't gather in a smoke-filled room at the end of 2001 and divide territory. Perhaps the fiction writers didn't claim for themselves the individual tales of trauma around the day itself (signatories include Jonathan Safran Foer, Don DeLillo, Claire Messud) while the non-fiction writers held on to History and Politics leading up to and on from 9/11 . . . If it did happen, then Amy Waldman – former Bureau Chief for the New York Times – simply decided to tear up the contract.
>
> (2011: n.p.)

The Submission certainly moves beyond the confines of the privileged American domestic – confines that Hamid and O'Neill remain at least partially attached to – and its central conceit also spoke powerfully to the Park51 'Ground Zero Mosque' debate, which had played out in 2010, and gave the novel acute topicality.[4] Mostly set in 2003, *The Submission* imagines an open, anonymous competition to design the 9/11 memorial. The winning design turns out to have been submitted by a secular Muslim man, Mohammad Khan, and a public furore ensues. The novel offers a panorama of characters including Claire Burwell, an ostensi-bly liberal '9/11 widow'; Sean Gallagher, a blue-collar Republican whose brother was a firefighter who died in the towers; Allyssa Spier, an unscrupulous tabloid journalist; Asma Anwar, another 9/11 widow and Bangladeshi migrant whose husband was an undocu-mented janitorial worker at the World Trade Center, and a range of peripheral characters that offer further variations of perspective on the novel's central issues. However, despite directly addressing subjects that most previous 9/11 novels wilfully avoided – otherness, nationalism, racism, xenophobia and partisan politics – *The Submission* remains one of the most anxious novels in the 9/11 canon. This is partly through its metafictional dramatization of (and participation in) the challenges of reconciling trauma and politics. However, it also relates to its ongoing discussion of 'truth' which uneasily marries a postmodernist suspicion of overarching truths with an increasingly relevant critique of the ways media representation and political activism deprioritize truth.

    The Submission's specific anxieties begin at the formal level with its journalistic pretences of balance and presenting opposing views. This is exemplified by Claire and Sean who occupy several opposing positions or perspectives (Democrat/Republican; woman/man; rich/poor; lib-eral/conservative) but are both grieving. The novel also sets up a dichotomy between Claire and Asma as widows (rich/poor; documented/undocumented; American/Bangladeshi; Islam/West). But while the novel places great importance on presenting this balance it adopts a singular world view. This was noted in Christian Lorentzen's review which argues that it seems to have been 'written by the *New York Times* itself,' and that 'Waldman has so thoroughly internalized the paper's world view that she can't see things any other way' (2011: n.p.). This is hyperbolic, but it is Claire, who is very evidently aligned to *New York Times*-style social liberalism, who becomes the novel's central protagonist. This is conspicuous considering Mohammad is at the centre of the novel's plot and drama. Moreover, given the parallel between Claire and Asma as widows and the novel's clear aim of challenging post-9/11 racism, nationalism and xenophobia, it is notable that the dichotomy which reveals Claire's privileges as a rich, white American, also substantially favours her as a subject. *The Submission* spends more time on her trauma and experience than Asma's, which is arguably more acute as a poor, marginalized victim of racist attacks. Nevertheless, the novel focusses on Claire's trauma and how her identity splinters when intense grief and loss conflict with her liberal values. In one scene she feels like a Russian Matryoshka doll: 'Claire within Claire within Claire within Claire. During the hearing, all these different Claires, who just happened to look alike, seemed to rest inside her, so that every argument no matter how contradictory, found sympathy . . . she couldn't find her own core' (2011: 302). This passage shows Claire's trauma to be linked just as much to the volatile and divisive political climate of the immediate aftermath, as it is to the loss of her husband. But just as it does this, it pulls the reader into her world, and her inner struggle and away from the wider political dynamics of the novel.

Another powerful tension emerges in the novel between its own specific metafictional tropes and its ongoing discussion of the ways in with media representation and 'representatives,' obscure truth. *The Submission* works through a range of examples of representation from news media to juries, coalitions, councils, interest groups and representatives, revealing a pattern of suppressed complexity. The memorial itself is meant to represent loss and grief in a public, democratic sense and the jury that is appointed to select the winning design represents the American people and particularly the families of victims. The media represents the stories that emerge after Mohammad is announced as the competition winner – and while Waldman focuses scrutiny on *The New York Post*, *The New Yorker* is also shown to have bias (2011: 159). The depiction of Alyssa Spier is damning as it shows a total disavowal of objectivity and complexity. One scene shows Alyssa casually shedding crucial nuance to make a story about Mohammad's allegedly 'Islamic' design more palatable for her editor: 'Alyssa wasn't sure what to make of Stanton's comments: she was saying that this element of Khan's design was Islamic – but only if the buildings were Islamic, too. Way too complicated for Chaz' (2011: 286). This is one of dozens of instances where Alyssa prioritizes her career or her story over truth.

The interest groups that act in support of and in opposition to Mohammad – 'The Committee to Defend Mohammad Khan,' 'The Mohammad Khan Protection League,' 'Muslim American Coordinating Council' (MACC) and the 'Memorial Defense Committee,' and 'Save America From Islam' (SAFI) – are shown to be just as driven by individual personalities and agendas as the news media. These groups all claim to represent wider interests but are shown to be driven by individual bias. For example, Malik of the MACC is interested only in harnessing the publicity potential in Mohammad's story, rather than the truth his experience and architectural design. He argues that 'this is about amassing capital, not squandering it,' and is perceived by Mohammad as 'the slick front man for a special interest' (2011: 103). Malik is shown to exploit Mohammad's situation and is even rebuked by another MACC member: 'We seem to be sending out a lot of emails soliciting donations on the back of this controversy' (2011: 250). The portrayal of Malik evokes one of the key points in Amina Yaqin and Peter

Morey's monograph, *Framing Muslims: Stereotyping and Representation After 9/11* (2011). Yaqin and Morey point to the rise of 'representatives' who speak on behalf of "their wider communities" in the mass media:

> In the case of Muslim representatives, the nature and scope of their 'representations' has been severely curtailed in the current climate . . . particular voices representing certain recognized and accommodated strands within Islam have been cultivated and brought to the fore, while others have been downplayed and marginalized, treated as 'less representative.'
>
> (2011: 80)

Malik is similar to these 'professional Muslim[s]' who 'are touring the circuits of think tanks, select committees, and talk shows,' in order to represent communities that are much more diverse than what their views and ideas represent (2011: 94). But Waldman doesn't restrict her depictions of self-serving or narrowly focussed representatives and figureheads to just the Muslim community. Another interest group leader shown to be deeply self-serving is Debbie Dawson, the self-appointed leader of SAFI. Debbie falsely claims that SAFI is 'feeding and housing' Sean who has had to 'flee his home' after 'standing up to the Islamic threat,' and actively solicits donations for this false cause (2011: 211). Debbie's agenda is mostly about promoting her own burgeoning celebrity and supporting herself financially. Waldman's depiction of unrepresentative representatives gains power because of the diversity of the communities she portrays. This is vivid in the description of the members of the MACC: 'South Asians, African Americans, Arabs; bearded men and clean-shaven, in suits and in djellabas; two women in headscarves and one – striking and black-haired in an aubergine suite – without' (2011: 101).

The novel's depiction of the widespread failure of representations and representatives is powerful in the 'post-truth' era. But while her variously compromised and emotionally-driven characters and organizations speak to the current crisis in the rhetorical power of fact, they are in tension with her own metafictional project. I have examined the ways in which *The Submission* is both about and part of the memorialization of 9/11, elsewhere (Keeble 2014). While it invites reflection on who is excluded from this memorialization and the toxic racism and xenophobia of the period, it remains attached to exceptionalist narratives and rhetoric in its own memorialization of 9/11. In fact, as trenchant as Waldman's critique of Islamophobia is, *The Submission* tacitly endorses the idea of 9/11 as a singular historical moment. This tension is compounded by the fact that the novel's metafiction belongs to a wider postmodernist 'incredulity to metanarratives' and suspicion of overarching 'truth' and reveals an uncomfortable overlap between this mode of cultural criticism (mostly oriented by leftist academics) and new, popular notions of 'post-truth.'

The 9/11 novel debate

Mirroring the internal tensions and anxieties of the 9/11 novels, the critical response to these novels has been polarized. Pankaj Mishra's 2007 *Guardian* article "The End of Innocence," critiqued early 9/11 novels dominated by relationship dramas. Mishra asked, speaking specifically about the novels by McInerney, DeLillo, Messud and Kalfus: 'Are we meant to think of marital discord . . . as a metaphor for post-9/11 America?' (2007: 6). Mishra's broad point about the inwardness of early 9/11 novels was developed in academic articles by Richard Gray and Michael Rothberg. Gray's article "Open Doors, Closed Minds: American Prose Writing at a Time of Crisis," is particularly trenchant. Discussing the same novels, Gray argues that they fail to engage with the wider complexities of the crisis and 'simply assimilate the unfamiliar into familiar structures. The crisis is in every way domesticated' (2009: 134). The problem with this domestication, he argues, is that 9/11 and contemporary America, as subjects for fiction, demand engagement with difference:

> There is the threat of the terrorist but there is also the fact of a world that is liminal, a proliferating chain of borders, where familiar oppositions – civilized and savage, town and wilderness, 'them' and 'us' – are continually being challenged, dissolved, and reconfigured.
>
> (2009: 135)

Rothberg is equally critical and expands on Gray's argument by calling for a more outwardly facing perspective: 'we need a fiction of international relations and extraterritorial citizenship' (2009: 153). For Rothberg, it was vital that 9/11 novels address the 'prosthetic reach' of the American 'empire into other worlds' (2009: 153).

Gray, Rothberg and Mishra are influential and authoritative commentators but their criticisms were roundly challenged. In the introduction to a special issue of *Modern Fiction Studies*, John Duvall and Robert P. Marzec argue that:

> Gray and Rothberg are both unwilling to look very closely at what 9/11 fiction sets out to do because they are both sure that they know what 9/11 fiction ought to be doing. If one retrospectively applied their perspective to fiction after World War I, one might be forced to say that Virginia Woolf's *Mrs. Dalloway* and Ernest Hemingway's *The Sun Also Rises* are failures for their oblique treatment of the root cause of historical trauma, since Woolf's Septimus Smith and Hemingway's Jake Barnes only imagine the private traumas of war veterans.
>
> (2011: 381)

Duvall and Marzec's strongest objections are to the ideas that the domestic is necessarily apolitical and to the prescriptive nature of Gray's and Rothberg's arguments: that 'they know what 9/11 fiction ought to be doing.' However, it is important to note that the counter-arguments they offer are themselves prescriptive as they point to canonical literary representations of the aftermath of World War I as proven models for historical traumas. Catherine Morley also challenges the prescriptive analysis of Gray and Rothberg, noting that they seem to 'transcend the role of the cultural or literary spectator' (2011: 720). Morley's rejoinder is important because it demonstrates the ways in which this debate about the 9/11 novel speaks to wider issues in contemporary literary studies. She rightly questions the idea that 'fiction is no more than a political tool, through which writers can understand (and educate readers about) the United States' place in the world,' and goes on to point out that fraught and sometimes problematic intersections between the domestic and international or private and public have long been prevalent in American fiction (2011: 720). Morley's analysis resonates with current debates about the relationship between art or aesthetics and politics or ideology. In *Politics and Literature at the Turn of the Millennium* (2015), Michael Keren highlights this, pointing to concerns about 'the reduction of literature to ideas,' or the focus on 'ideology, which is not at all the same thing as art' (2015: 16). This debate about the 9/11 novel is evidently central to these larger debates about the role(s) of novels, novelists, literature and culture in the twenty-first century.

Recent critical interventions, however, have returned to the tensions within the novels and have offered compelling ways of reconsidering them. Rachel Sykes' reappraisal of 9/11 fiction – and Sykes includes *Extremely Loud and Incredibly Close*, *Falling Man* and *The Submission* in her analysis – focuses on an 'aesthetic of anxiety and noise' (2016: n.p.). For Sykes any 'focus on a singular event' is a 'noisy' narrative conceit (2016: n.p.) and is potentially ideologically problematic. This is an excellent critical tool for addressing these texts and their roles in the exceptionalisation of 9/11. I see this 'noisiness' as part of the tensions this chapter has worked through: between the private and public; continuity and discontinuity; politics and trauma and within trauma itself: 'the will to deny' and the 'will to proclaim.' Two recent 9/11 novels move away from the singularity that Sykes is rightly suspicious of. Pynchon's *Bleeding Edge* (2013) builds 9/11 into an 'intertwined historical narrative of 9/11 and the internet' which locates the attacks on a broader historical continuum and places great importance on this other before and after (Keeble 2018; n.p.). Similarly, Porochista Khakpour's *The Last Illusion* (2014) uses the framework of the Persian myth of Zal from *The Shanameh*, which imbues the narrative with a wider, international and historical framework that underpins the novel's discussion of otherness. Yet both novels can also be located firmly in the 9/11 canon. They foreground romantic relationships, parents and children, trauma and recovery. Despite its anxieties, tensions, increasingly political and international iterations, the 9/11 novel genre remains relatively cohesive as we approach the twentieth anniversary of the attacks.

Notes

1 Michael Rothberg noted this in an essay entitled "'There is no Poetry in This': Writing, Trauma and Home," from 2003: 'a focus on trauma solely as a structure of reception might . . . actually end up unwittingly reinforcing the repressive liberal-conservative consensus in the United States that attempting to explain the events amounts to explaining them away or excusing them' (2003: 151). More recently, Anna Hartnell has identified the framework of trauma as a 'barrier' to more ethical understandings of 9/11 and Hurricane Katrina (2017: 19).
2 Jonathan Lethem noted that 'most of the novelists in New York were asked . . . to write something, and to me it seems our voices, at that moment, blended into one vast impotent scream' (2012: 227).
3 Directly after 9/11 criticism of US policy was seen by US commentators as unpatriotic. In the introduction to *Dissent from the Homeland* (2003) Frank Lentricchia outlines the ways Sontag's "Talk of the Town" piece which criticized proliferating cries for vengeance, was attacked: 'Vilification swiftly followed. The stalwart New York intellectual was savaged, especially in New York' (4).
4 In 2010 the development of the Park51 Islamic Community Center was challenged by anti-Islam groups who characterized it as the 'Ground Zero Mosque' foregrounding the issues raised in *The Submission*.

Works cited

Beigbeder, F., *Windows on the World* trans. Frank Wynne (London: Miramax Books, 2003).

Boxall, P., *Twenty-First Century Fiction: A Critical Introduction* (Cambridge: Cambridge University Press, 2013).

Cowart, D., '"Down on the Barroom Floor of History": Pynchon's Bleeding Edge,' *Postmodern Culture*, 24.1 (2013), n.p.

Darlington, J., 'Capitalist Mysticism and the Historicizing of 9/11 in Thomas Pynchon's *Bleeding Edge*,' *Critique*, 57.3 (2017), 242–253.

Däwes, B., *Ground Zero Fiction: History, Memory and Representation in the American 9/11 Novel* (Heidelberg: Universitätsverlag Winter GmbH, 2011).

DeLillo, D., *Falling Man* (New York: Scribners, 2007).

—— 'In the Ruins of the Future,' *Harper's*, December, 2001, 33–40.

DeRosa, A., 'The Law of Ruins and homogenous empty time in Don DeLillo's Falling Man' in Morley, Catherine (ed.) *9/11: Topics in Contemporary North American Literature* (London: Bloomsbury, 2016). 41–60.

Duvall, J. and Marzec, R. P., 'Narrating 9/11,' *Modern Fiction Studies*, 57.3 (2011), 382–400.

Eaglestone, R., 'Contemporary Fiction in the Academy: Towards a Manifesto,' *Textual Practice*, 27.7 (2013), 1089–1101.

Gray, R., 'Open Doors, Closed Minds: American Prose Writing at a Time of Crisis,' *American Literary History*, 28.1 (2009), 128–151.

Hamid, M., *The Reluctant Fundamentalist* (London: Hamish Hamilton, 2007).

Hartnell, A., *After Katrina: Race, Neoliberalism and the End of the American Century* (New York: CUNY Press, 2017).

Herman, J., *Trauma and Recovery* (New York: Basic Books, 1992).

Hirsch, M., 'I Took Pictures: September 2001 and Beyond,' in J. Greenberg (ed) Trauma at Home (Lincoln, Nebraska: University of Nebraska Press, 2003). 69–86.

Holloway, D., *9/11 and the War on Terror* (Edinburgh: Edinburgh University Press, 2008).

Houen, A., 'Novel Spaces and Taking Place(s) in the Wake of September 11,' *Studies in the Novel*, 36.3 (2004), 419–437.

—— *Terrorism and Modern Literature* (Oxford: Oxford University Press, 2002).

Keeble, A., *The 9/11 Novel: Trauma, Politics and Identity* (Jefferson: McFarland, 2014).

—— 'Bleeding Edge, Neo-Liberalism and the 9/11 Novel,' *Canadian Review of American Studies*, (2018). Ahead of print edition available here: https://utpjournals.press/doi/10.3138/cras.2017.028

Keniston, A. and Follansbee Quinn, J. (eds.), *Literature after 9/11* (London: Routledge, 2007).

Keren, M., *Politics and Literature at the Turn of the Millennium* (Calgary: University of Calgary Press, 2015).

Lentricchia, F. and Hauerwas, S. (eds.), *Dissent from the Homeland: Essays after September 11* (Durham: Duke University Press, 2003).

Lethem, J., *The Ecstasy of Influence* (London: Jonathan Cape, 2012).

Lorentzen, C., "Review of the Submission," *London Review of Books*, 33.18 (2011), 28–29.

McInerney, J., *The Good Life* (London: Bloomsbury, 2005).

—— 'The Uses of Invention,' *The Observer*, September 05, 2005. Available: www.theguardian.com/books/2005/sep/17/fiction.vsnaipaul

Messud, C., *The Emperor's Children* (London: Picador, 2006).

Millard, K., *Contemporary American Literature* (Oxford: Oxford University Press, 2000).

Mishra, P., 'The End of Innocence,' *The Guardian*, Saturday Review, May 19, 2007, 4–6.

Morley, C. (ed.) *9/11: Topics in Contemporary North American Literature* (London: Bloomsbury, 2016).

—— '"How Do We Write about This?": The Domestic and the Global in the Post-9/11 Novel,' *Journal of American Studies*, 45.4 (2011), 717–731.

Mukherjee, P., 'Review of Dominic Head: The State of the Novel,' *THE*, 15 January, 2009.

Potter, C. L., *Writing the 9/11 Decade: Reportage and the Evolution of the Novel* (London: Bloomsbury, 2016).

Pynchon, T., *Bleeding Edge* (London: Jonathan Cape, 2013).

Randall, M., *9/11 and the Literature of Terror* (Edinburgh: Edinburgh University Press, 2011).

Rothberg, M., '"There is No Poetry in This": Writing, Trauma, and Home,' in Greenberg, Judith (ed.) *Trauma at Home* (Lincoln, Nebraska: University of Nebraska Press, 2003). 147–157.

—— 'A Failure of the Imagination: Diagnosing the Post-9/11 Novel: A Response to Richard Gray,' *American Literary History*, 28.1 (2009), 153–158.

Safran Foer, J., *Extremely Loud and Incredibly Close* (London: Penguin, 2005).

Scott, J., 'Introduction,' in multiple authors, *Portraits: 9/1101: The Collected Portraits of Grief from the New York Times* (New York: Times Books, 2002) ix.

Shamsie, K., 'Review of the Submission,' *The Guardian*, August 24, 2011. Available: www.theguardian.com/books/2011/aug/24/the-submission-amy-waldman-review

Shostak, D., 'Prosthetic Fictions: Reading Jonathan Safran Foer's Extremely Loud and Incredibly Close through Philip Roth's the Plot against America,' in Catherine Morley (ed.). *9/11: Topics in Contemporary North American Literature* (London: Bloomsbury, 2016) 21–40.

Simpson, D., 'Telling It Like It Isn't,' in Kenniston, Ann and Follansbee Quinn, Jeanne (eds.). *Literature after 9/11* (London: Routledge, 2007) 209–222.

Smith, Z., 'Two Paths for the Novel,' *New York Review of Books*, 55.18 (2008), 34–39.

Sykes, R., '"All That Howling Space": "9/11" and the Aesthetic of Noise in Contemporary American Fiction,' *C21 Literature*, 4.1 (2016), DOI: http://doi.org/10.16995/c21.2

Updike, J., in various authors, "Talk of the Town," The New Yorker (September 24, 2001). Available here: https://www.newyorker.com/magazine/2001/09/24/tuesday-and-after-talk-of-the-town

Versluys, K., *Out of the Blue: September 11 and the Novel* (New York: Columbia University Press, 2009).

Waldman, A., *The Submission* (London: Windmill, 2011).

Yaqin, A. and Morey, P., *Framing Muslims: Stereotyping and Representation after 9/11* (London: Stanford University Press, 2011).

25

WAR ON TERROR

Daniel O'Gorman

Since the onset of the 'war on terror' in 2001, the literary fiction market has seen an intensification of interest in authors with a background outside of the West, and particularly from nations
affected by Islamist extremism. On one level, this has been productive, lending a platform to a
wide and diverse range of global authors who might otherwise have struggled to be heard, and
who collectively play an active role in challenging the Islamophobia and racism that sometimes
lends shape to the language of counterterrorism. On another, it has also, at times, been *reductive*,
as this platform is conditional. A publishing industry that shows temporary fascination with
novels about Islam, in the context of debates about terrorism, can have the unintended effect of
reinforcing the media-driven, stereotypical association between the two, even if the content of the
novels themselves attempts to challenge this discourse. Taking the latter perspective, critics such
as Catherine Morely have expressed caution about a trend, in transnationally oriented post-9/11
literary studies, to '[suggest] that fiction is no more than a political tool, through which writers
can understand (and educate readers about) the United States' place in the world' (2011: 720).

Both perspectives have truth to them, but it is also possible – and, indeed, crucial – to see
the tension between them as itself containing a unique political value. Novels that are products
of globalization can simultaneously work to resist its more homogenising tendencies, and, as
this chapter will show, many texts about the global 'war on terror' by authors of 'non-Western'
descent have actively dramatised the complexity and ambivalence underlying racial, cultural and
religious identity negotiations since 9/11. Authors as diverse as Mohsin Hamid, Chimamanda
Ngozi Adichie, Teju Cole and Khaled Hosseini have been widely read, and sometimes highly
praised, for the polyphonic fictional perspectives that they have taken in opposition to what
political scientist Richard Jackson has identified as the dangerous 'us vs. them' binaries that have
'been discursively constructed through the official language of counter-terrorism' (Jackson 59).
Reviewers have favourably drawn attention to the work of these writers as, variously, presenting 'a different voice, a different view of the aftermath of 9/11' (Halaby 2007), 'melding the
personal struggle of ordinary people into the terrible historical sweep of a devastated country'
(Hill 2003), and 'speak[ing] through history to our war-wracked age' (Nixon 2006). Note in
particular the latter's use of the pronoun 'our': the sentence is taken from Rob Nixon's review
of Adichie's *Half of a Yellow Sun* (2006) in the *New York Times*, and identifies resonances between
its depiction of the Biafran war in Nigeria (1967–70) and the aftermath of the 2003 US-led
invasion of Iraq.

Historical echoes, reflections and entanglements are central motifs in the work of all of these authors, in a manner that undercuts the simplistic binaries often championed in politics and the media. The sweeping 'global war on terror' may have been declared 'over' by Barack Obama in May 2013, in favour of 'persistent, targeted efforts to dismantle specific networks,' but this claim has come to seem painfully premature in light of Donald Trump's election to the United States Presidency on a virulently Islamophobic anti-terrorism platform. Works of literature that challenge this divisive rhetoric are as necessary today as they ever have been.

Case study: Pakistan

This chapter will show that one of the most vital things that many authors with roots outside of the West have achieved in their writing on the war on terror is, precisely, a complication of straightforward categories such as 'Western' and 'non-Western,' 'secular' and 'Muslim,' or 'us' and 'them' in the first place. Using as a case in point the recent increase in the Anglophone fiction market for work by authors from Pakistan, I suggest that such texts are best viewed as *global* – rather than 'non-Western' – novels of the war on terror. The novels that I will focus on are *The Reluctant Fundamentalist* by Mohsin Hamid (2007 [2008]), *The Wasted Vigil* by Nadeem Aslam (2008) and *Burnt Shadows* by Kamila Shamsie (2009). All three authors are all prominent in the Anglophone world, and their marketability is underscored by a proclivity for high-profile award nominations: *The Reluctant Fundamentalist* was included on the Man Booker shortlist in 2007, *Burnt Shadows* on the 2009 Orange Prize shortlist, and Nadeem Aslam won the 2005 Kiriyama Prize for his earlier novel, *Maps for Lost Lovers* (2004). Hamid and Shamsie were both shortlisted for the Booker again in 2017 for *Exit West* (2017) and *Home Fire* (2017), respectively, with the latter proceeding to win the Women's Prize for Fiction in 2018.

Written in an accessible register, *The Reluctant Fundamentalist*, *Burnt Shadows* and *The Wasted Vigil* occupy an unstable position in post-9/11 political discourse. On the one hand, they offer a critical reaction against the more Anglo-centric or neo-imperialist aspects of globalization, as well as an alternative to the much-critiqued attempts by established Anglo-American authors such as John Updike and Martin Amis to imagine themselves into the experience of the perceived Muslim 'other' (Kakutani 2008; Shamsie 2012; Chambers 2016). On the other, they are also products of globalization, in line with what Sarah Brouillette has identified as an increasing marketability of global writing, which 'can be explained in part as an aspect of the twinned processes of niche fragmentation and market expansion in the global publishing industry' (Brouillette 2007: 56). However, I suggest that there is a potential for the ambivalence that these texts display towards globalization to be productive. While the relative marketability of the novels emerges from a mildly Orientalist appetite for didactic international writing on Islam and the 'Islamic world' after 9/11, all three texts also demonstrate – sometimes intentionally, sometimes unintentionally – that any such attempt at didacticism is never straightforward. They do this by attempting to enact – whilst simultaneously undercutting – an 'authentic' representation of Pakistan. To borrow a phrase from Gayatri Chakravorty Spivak's "Terror: A Speech After 9/11," the texts raise consciousness whilst simultaneously 'disrupt[ing] confidence in consciousness-raising' (2004: 87).

This chapter will be divided into two main parts. In the first, I analyse this ambivalent, self-reflexive didacticism, suggesting that it is particularly evident in the way that the novels engage with the well-established postcolonial trope of migration. In the second, I go on to show how the novels' ambivalence towards globalization helps them to challenge stereotypes about Muslims that have been prevalent in the global media since 9/11, and encourages new, more interconnected ways of thinking about the many histories of which the war on terror is a part.

Thwarted itineraries: migration and didacticism

The novels that I have selected are all part of an increase in the publication of English-language fiction by Pakistani authors (or authors of Pakistani descent) over the past two decades, including Mohammed Hanif, Daniyaal Mueenuddin, H.M. Naqvi and Uzma Aslam Khan. This development was celebrated in a special issue of *Granta* centred on work by Pakistani writers in 2010. However, what is notable is that none of the three texts that I focus upon in this chapter can be said to be directly 'about' Pakistan, as such: *The Wasted Vigil* is set primarily in Afghanistan, *Burnt Shadows* jumps between multiple countries across three continents, and, although narrated from within Pakistan, most of the action in *The Reluctant Fundamentalist* is constituted by a recollection of its narrator's earlier life in the United States.

The ambivalence that underlies the three novels' representation of Pakistan is particularly evident in the way that the texts play upon the trope of migration. They use it in a way that is, to varying degrees of subtlety, self-reflexive, prompting the reader to think about the hermeneutic or imaginative migration that she is partaking in as she reads. On the one hand, the novels aim to engender an appreciation for what Aslam, in *The Wasted Vigil*, describes as 'the delightful essential idea that tales can travel, or that two sets of people oceans apart can dream up similar sacred myths' (231). On the other, they do so in a style of self-contradiction that draws attention to what Spivak, channelling Derrida, has described as 'the itinerary[, in all texts,] of a constantly thwarted desire to make the text explain' (2006: 143). Through their depictions of characters that migrate both into and out of Pakistan, the novels attempt to educate their readers about the nation by challenging normative perceptions, but in doing so they simultaneously draw attention to the impossibility for any text, on its own, to achieve this in more than a superficial way.

This process of 'thwarting' the readers' desire for explanation is enabled by the way in which, through their ambivalence, all three novels blur the boundary between explanation and *figuration*, foregrounding the element of the latter within the former.[1] *The Reluctant Fundamentalist*, in particular, is narrated in the form of a long, second-person monologue, literally explaining how the protagonist has come to develop a disparaging view on post-9/11 America (a society that, in his opinion, has 'retreated into myths of [its] own difference, assumptions of [its] own superiority' [190]). One might argue that the writing here is clumsy and overly expositional, but I would suggest that there is a degree to which this exposition is necessary if the alterity that any of these novels wish to convey is to be *translated* into a language that mainstream Western audiences can at least get a sense of, if not fully comprehend. In this sense, the texts can be seen to enact what Spivak, in her essay 'Translating into English,' describes as a 'double-bind' in which '[w]e transfer content because we must, knowing it cannot be done' (2005: 100). From one perspective, they are products of an emerging market for an accessible, yet didactic, kind of Anglophone international fiction. From another, they consciously signpost the translational issues that Hamid's narrator is getting at when he says: 'what is natural in one place can seem unnatural in another, and some concepts travel rather poorly, if at all' (143).

The notion of ideas *travelling* – or, rather, failing to travel – is central to the bearing that this double-bind has upon identity and difference. It is upon precisely such ideas that identities are constructed, whether in the form of Pakistani national identity or the more general 'us vs. them' binaries perpetuated in post-9/11 media discourse. Indeed, it constitutes an exception of sorts to the kind of fluid 'traveling theory' that Edward Said describes at the opening of his essay of the same name:

> Like people and schools of criticism, ideas and theories travel – from person to person, from situation to situation, from one period to another. Cultural and intellectual life are

usually nourished and often sustained by this circulation of ideas, and whether it takes the form of acknowledged or unconscious influence, creative borrowing or wholesale appropriation, the movement of ideas and theories from one place to another is both a fact of life and a usefully enabling condition of intellectual activity.

(Said 1983: 226)

The exception is significant not so much because it arguably contradicts Said's argument, but rather because it points to an instance in which such an exception might actually be desirable: an acknowledgement that some ideas cannot travel may in some cases be more ethical than an attempt to understand an idea at all costs. This kind of 'itinerary' of thwarted explanation is frequently highlighted by all three of the novels in question. It is evident, for instance, when Hamid's narrator says 'we have not met before, but you seem to know something about me' (86), or when one of Shamsie's characters declares that she 'is at home in the idea of foreignness' (141).

The Wasted Vigil identifies a kind of 'thwarting' of itineraries at the heart of the conflict that underpins the war on terror. In a short, poetic passage at the exact mid-point of the novel (in the closing section of the first of its two "Books"), the American character David finds his memory drifting back over the events of 9/11:

No one has ever mentioned – anywhere – the dust-and-ash-covered sparrow that a man leaned down and gently stroked on September 11, the bird sitting stunned on a sidewalk an hour or so after the Towers collapsed. It is one of his most vivid memories of that day's television, but no one remembers seeing it. Perhaps he remembers it because he has since read that Muhammad Atta's nickname as a child was Bulbul.

(Aslam 2008: 201–202)

There is an obvious, almost crudely literal thwarting of potential itineraries here in the image of a sparrow physically grounded in state of terror. However, there is also a slightly less obvious thwarting at play: specifically, a thwarting of any straightforward 'explanation' for the attacks. By creating a poetic mirroring between the dust-covered bird and Muhammad Atta (whose childhood nickname, Bulbul, denotes a type of songbird common in Southeast Asia), Aslam imbues the event with a complicated sense of ambiguity. In doing so, he demonstrates that its meaning cannot be explained in a straightforward way. Like the unstable symbolism of the bulbul itself – indicative of both liberty and, in light of Atta's violent 'thwarting' of the itinerary of American Airlines Flight 11, destruction – 9/11 is here shown to be akin to a kind of Rorschach test: that is, an amorphous sign that prompts spectators to project upon it their own personal signification.

By thwarting the itinerary of the reader's desire for a didactic explanation of 9/11, the novel does not play down the importance of the event. Nor does it suggest that all explanation, no matter how thoroughly thwarted, is completely futile. On the contrary, this thwarting of explanation constitutes a kind of educational explanation in itself, as it prompts the reader to think about her *perspective* on the event. In doing so, it reinforces Claire Chambers' argument that

[i]mportant though 9/11 and subsequent events such as the Madrid and London bombings have been for non-Muslim perceptions of Islam, the war on terror has had far greater impact on the lives of Muslims. For writers of Pakistani descent, at least, the war in Afghanistan represents a particular watershed which has had a devastating impact on Pakistan.

(Chambers 2011: 129)

Daniel O'Gorman

The novel's 'stepping back' from 9/11 has the effect of automatically placing the event in a complex geopolitical context, and as such elevating the war in Afghanistan – and Pakistan's involvement in it – to a more prominent position in the Western reader's frame of perception. This, in turn, helps underscore the novel's broader point that, 'everyone [involved] is human and must try to understand each other's mystery. Each other's pain' (Aslam 2008: 230). As the philosopher Judith Butler puts it, in her book on representations of the war on terror, *Frames of War*: 'the boundary is a function of the relation, a brokering of difference, a negotiation in which I am bound to you in my separateness' (2009: 44). Indeed, it is the *attempt* at understanding between identity groups, rather than the act of understanding itself, that *The Wasted Vigil* suggests is potentially most conducive to 'mak[ing] links out of separations' (87).

This attempt to 'make links out of separations' is also evident in *The Reluctant Fundamentalist*. In a recent article on the novel, Anna Hartnell rightly argues that '[Hamid] insists on the potentially radical nature of the American project by suggesting that its meaning eschews fixed understandings of identity based on race or place and thus transcends its old world beginnings' (Hartnell 2010: 346). However, I would add to this that he likewise insists on the potentially radical nature of Pakistan. In drawing attention to the historical connections between America and Pakistan, the novel shows not only that the national identity of neither country is fixed, but also goes further than this by demonstrating that they face a similar challenge. Namely, it indicates that both nations need to formulate a flexible sense of identity that is perpetually open to the kind of radical ethnic and cultural multiplicity upon which each is founded.

The narrative travels between a past in America, where most of the story's action takes place, and a present in Pakistan. The narrator, Changez, recalls his experiences as a young immigrant attempting to be welcomed in America through 'a process of osmosis,' but ultimately feeling so alienated by a post-9/11 suspicion of Muslims that he decides to move back to Pakistan (160). His relationship with the United States is captured microcosmically in the form of a romantic relationship with a young woman called Erica, an admittedly rather unsubtly named cipher for post-9/11 *Am*erica, who is driven to psychosis by a sudden personal trauma. Reflecting on his relationship with Erica – and, by extension, America – after it has fallen apart, he says:

> Such *journeys* have convinced me that it is not always possible to restore one's boundaries after they have been blurred and made permeable by a relationship: try as we might, we cannot reconstitute ourselves as the autonomous beings we previously imagined ourselves to be. Something of us is now outside, and something of the outside is now within us.
>
> (Hamid 2008: 197, emphasis added)

Through his protagonist's affair with Erica, Changez characterises the relationship between Pakistan and the United States as itself a deeply problematic kind of 'journey' or, to use Spivak's phrase, 'thwarted itinerary.' However, despite its frustrations, Hamid shows that this 'thwarting' might also be fruitful. The thwarting of a journey can only take place when some form of attempt to travel has occurred. It is through the collision of cultures and identities that such an attempt at travelling necessarily involves that the novel connects Pakistan with the multitudinous histories of the world, and warns against the perpetuation an overly isolated national history.

In a similarly historicising vein, Shamsie's *Burnt Shadows* opens with a short prologue in which a man sits in a cell in Guantanamo Bay, wondering '*How did it come to this?*' (1). It then shifts back in time to the bombing of Nagasaki by US forces in 1945, and goes on to trace a connection between the two scenes, via such historical moments as the Partition of India, the Soviet invasion of Afghanistan, the 9/11 attacks, and the war on terror. It joins these historical dots not in the manner of a paranoid conspiracy theorist, but rather in such a way that – like in the other two novels – generates a sense of *historicity*; that is, what Hayden White describes as a heightened subjective '*awareness* of the historical process itself' (1973: 97). In doing so, the novel constitutes an answer of sorts to Shamsie's own line of questioning in her essay, 'The Storytellers of Empire': 'Where were the [9/11] novels that could be proffered to people who asked, "Why do they hate us?," which is actually the question "Who are these people and what do they have to do with us?"' (2012).

Instead of dialectically opposing globalization, Shamsie aims to infuse its language with a *sense*, if not an understanding, of the other; a sentiment that is strongly reflected in a melancholy, epiphanic moment that its protagonist, an itinerant Japanese woman called Hiroko Tanaka, experiences when looking at the photo of a missing person in New York shortly after the 9/11 attacks: 'Hiroko thought of the train station at Nagasaki . . . The walls plastered with signs asking for news of missing people. . . . In moments such as these it seemed entirely wrong to feel oneself living in a different history to the people of this city' (274). Passages like this one directly foreground what Shamsie has identified as a need for a post-9/11 'entwining' of histories in a way that fosters new empathic global ties (Shamsie 2012; Butler 2006: 40). As Gohar Karim Khan has argued, the novel can be read 'as an attempt at "psychic healing" – a work that embraces nationalism transnationally, hence propounding an "imagined community" . . . that makes possible the existence of a kind of "horizontal comradeship," transcending national borderlands and cultural boundaries' (Khan 2011: 54). However, the feeling of 'living in a different history' that Shamsie is addressing in the passage above is shown throughout the novel to be 'wrong' not only on an ethical level, but also on a descriptive one. Specifically, by writing in a language that, as I have already argued, adheres to – while simultaneously 'thwarting' – generic conventions determined by the global fiction market, the novel is itself a product of histories becoming 'entwined.'

It is at moments such as these, when the itinerary of explanation is brought to the fore and 'thwarted' that all three novels most overtly challenge their readers' preconceptions about Pakistan. However, they aim to do this in a way that those who speak the language of globalization can understand, even if this simply means understanding the very impossibility of understanding itself. Indeed, it is the novels' attempt to 'uproot' or translate themselves from the localised specificities of regional history – be it Pakistani or otherwise – that enables them to repeatedly draw attention to the inseparability of explanation and figuration. By consciously thwarting their own explanatory trajectories, the novels might be most accurately described not as *anti*-globalist Pakistani texts, but, rather, *ambivalently* globalist ones.

Entwined histories: challenging stereotypes

I have so far argued that the three novels challenge perceptions about Pakistan from both within and outside of the country, and that they do this by manipulating the language of globalisation in a way that might help reshape their readers' perceptions of the nation. I now look in closer detail at the ways in which the novels challenge the stereotypes about the nation – and particularly about Muslims – that have helped construct these perceptions during the war on terror. Each novel presents a vision for Pakistani identity that transcends the nation's frequent reduction to its Islamic and Islamist elements in the global news media, emphasising both its historicity and its place in a complicated post-9/11 geopolitical context. I analyse the ways in which each of the novels productively complicates Pakistani national identity by simultaneously expanding its limits and questioning the usefulness of national identity as a concept in the first place.

In a key passage of *The Wasted Vigil*, one of the novel's American characters, James, watches a DVD of a Hollywood thriller with some Afghan compatriots. '[E]very scene,' we are told,

> was full of sleek cars or shiny women or blasting guns – making him understand why the rest of the world thought Americans were crazy. Only minutes later, however, he wasn't too sure. When you learn that the rest of the world thinks this is what life in America is like, that this isn't just throwaway entertainment, isn't *understood* by sane Americans as fantasy or momentary diversion, you realise how crazy the rest of the world is.
>
> (Aslam 2008: 328)

Despite his orientation towards benevolence, James has internalised the prejudicial urge to lump his comrades together with a vaguely conceived 'rest of the world.' By witnessing the Afghans view the extremely two-dimensional representation of his homeland through the medium of the film, he is shocked into an uncomfortable realisation of just how easy it is to resort to stereotype when contemplating an entire nation. However, he ironically fails to recognise that he is doing exactly the same thing, and is thus, by his own logic, equally 'crazy.' He is maintaining an overly rigid separation between 'us' (the United States, and perhaps by extension the West) and 'them' (everyone else): a division that the novel attempts to complicate by showing how easy it is for *anyone* to fall back upon the 'craziness' of prejudiced or stereotypical thought.

A similar subversion of stereotypes is present in *Burnt Shadows*. For instance, Hiroko's confident, exploratory character goes directly against the grain of common stereotypes about Japanese women being meek or unassuming (a fact to which she consciously draws attention in her dialogue with others). A survivor of Nagasaki, Hiroko has two dark, bird-shaped scars scorched into her back, the symbolic 'burnt shadows' of the title that have resulted from the black design on her kimono absorbing the heat of the atomic bomb in Nagasaki in 1945. Killing her German fiancé, Konrad, the bomb catalyses the start of Hiroko's (and the narrative's) gradual journey across the globe, from India to Pakistan, and eventually to New York. Hiroko is described as 'Fearless and transmutable, able to slip from skin to skin, city to city' (Shamsie 2009: 223). She challenges stereotypes about what it means to be a Pakistani woman when she takes residence in the country and makes it her home for many years. She dresses in Pakistani clothes, learns to speak Urdu, and makes friends with other Pakistani women, but her appearance and attitude mark her as an outsider. As Khan puts it, Hiroko 'presents an alternative to "homeland" in the traditional sense of the term – she is heroic and wise not despite the multiple homelands she inhabits but because of them' (Khan 2011: 67).

This is transposed into her son, Raza, whose mildly Japanese looks lead his peers to make the common mistake of marking him out as ethnically Hazara (the Hazara are an Afghan tribe whose presence is not uncommon in Northern Pakistan, but whose features tend to be noticeably distinct from those of most local people). With his unusual background and appearance, as well as an almost prodigious gift for learning languages, Raza feels like an outcast amongst his peers. When he says, 'I want words in every language, . . . I think I would be happy living in a cold, bare room if I could just spend my days burrowing into new languages,' his mother thinks to herself: '[acquiring language] was a passion that could have no fulfilment, not here. Somewhere in the world perhaps there were institutions where you could dive from vocabulary to vocabulary and make that your life. But not here. "Polyglot" was not any kind of career choice' (Shamsie 2009: 146).

I do not mean to suggest here that the representation of the family's immediate Pakistani surroundings itself resorts to stereotypical views about the country's homogeneity. On the contrary, despite their manifest difference, the family are largely welcomed in the community. Beginning her time in the country as a teacher in the local school, Hiroko establishes herself as a familiar part of the community long before Raza's birth. 'Through the children,' we are told, 'she won over the mothers, whose initial reaction towards the Japanese woman with the dresses cinched at the waist was suspicion. And once the mothers had made up their minds, the neighbourhood had made up its mind' (139). To underline this point, Shamsie writes that the neighbourhood boys all regularly call out 'Sayonara' to Hiroko as they jump on the school bus in the mornings (139). However, Raza remains deeply aware of his inability to truly fit in with his classmates, harbouring a secret shame about his background. He consciously holds back from saying the word himself, choosing 'only [to speak] Japanese within the privacy of his home' (139). 'Why allow the world to know his mind contained words from a country he had never visited?' Shamsie writes, going on to provide an insight into his increasingly depressive thoughts:

> Weren't his eyes and his bone structure and his bare-legged mother distancing factors enough? All those years ago when he'd entered a class of older boys, at an age when a year was a significant age gap, his teacher had remarked on how easily he'd fitted in. He saw no reason to tell her it wasn't ease that made it possible but a studied awareness – one he'd had from a very young age – of how to downplay his manifest difference.
>
> (Shamsie 2009: 139)

Raza's feeling of difference is as much a product of his own psychological processes of self-reinforcement as it is any 'manifest' dissimilarity. What is ironic here, however, is that his experience of difference is itself one that is familiar to many of the nation's citizens. As Cara Cilano notes in *National Identities in Pakistan: The 1971 War in Contemporary Pakistani Fiction*, the textbooks used to teach 'Pakistan Studies' in many schools propagate narratives that 'assert for generations of students a vision of a seamlessly whole Pakistani national identity born of a particular historical, social and cultural construction, that is to say, a discursive construction, at odds with the on-the-ground realities of every decade of Pakistani lived history' (Cilano 2010: 30). The problem is not simply that Raza does not conform to the stereotypical expectations of Pakistani identity that others expect of him, but that he also fails to conform to those that he has been taught to expect of himself. As Hiroko reflects at one point: 'It didn't bother her in the least to know that she would always be a foreigner in Pakistan – she had no interest in belonging to anything as contradictorily insubstantial and damaging as a nation – but this didn't stop her from recognising how Raza flinched every time a Pakistani asked him where he was from' (Shamsie 2009: 204).

This contrast between Hiroko's and Raza'a attitudes towards the notion of home is typified by the scars on the former's back. On the one hand, the birds symbolise Hiroko's freedom and itinerancy, but on the other, they are a reminder of disaster, of her original home being literally ripped up from around her by the bomb. When she hears that Raza's sudden journey into Afghanistan has been prompted by a girl that he has been trying to impress describing him as 'deformed,' we are told that:

> All Hiroko could think of was: the bomb. In the first years after Nagasaki she had dreams in which she awoke to find the tattoos gone from her skin, and knew the birds were inside her now, their beaks dripping with venom into her bloodstream, their charred wings engulfing her organs.
>
> (Shamsie 2009: 222)

The scars, in her mind alternately fixed and fluid depending on how she feels, are shaped by historical trauma in a way not unlike the 'shaping' of Pakistani national identity. The symbolic meaning of the 'tattoos' shifts depending on what one chooses to read into them. For Hiroko, national identity, despite causing her some pain, is what she makes of it; for Raza, it has a rigidly homogenous outline that he cannot reconcile with his own self-perception. The girl's comment only helps to reinforce this, and, thus, through a combination of his own depressive feelings of fundamental difference and a perceived collective notion of national identity (which, while powerful, is actually perhaps less widespread than he believes it to be), a version of Pakistani identity that is heavily reliant upon stereotype ends up being perpetuated and strengthened in Raza's mind.

The Reluctant Fundamentalist also challenges stereotypes about Pakistan, in two key ways. The first constitutes a direct deconstruction of stereotypical views. This is particularly evident in passages such as the following, in which Changez notes the similarities between Lahore and Manhattan:

> Like Manhattan? Yes, precisely! And that was one of the reasons why for me moving to New York felt – so unexpectedly – like coming home. But there were other reasons as well: the fact that Urdu was spoken by taxicab drivers; the presence, only two blocks from my East Village apartment, of a samosa- and channa-serving establishment called the Pak-Punjab Deli; the coincidence of crossing Fifth Avenue during a parade and hearing, from loudspeakers mounted on the South Asian Gay and Lesbian Association float, a song to which I had danced at my cousin's wedding.
>
> (Hamid 2008: 36–37)

As with *Burnt Shadows*, a questioning of the notion of 'home' is taking place here, with Changez' comparison between the two cities epitomising the novel's continuous attempt, throughout its narrative, to create an uncanny parallel between the United States and Pakistan. The notion of a song played on a Manhattan gay and lesbian float being the soundtrack for dancing at a Pakistani wedding might be a little surprising to Western readers. However, Changez notably does not specify what the song is: it could be an American-style pop song or a traditional Punjabi piece, but if the reader makes an assumption either way, then she is once again resorting to a preconceived set of cultural expectations.

The second and more interesting way in which the novel challenges stereotypes about Pakistan is by playing with Pakistani perceptions of the United States. Changez frequently reminds his American listener (and in turn the reader) that 'we have not met before, . . . yet you seem to know at least something about me' (86). Throughout the novel Hamid attempts to make the reader feel a similarly patronising sense of overdetermination, or in other words, a feeling that a restrictive, stereotypical sense of identity is being projected onto her by the narrator. An example of this is evident when Changez recounts a moment soon after 9/11 when he was approached by an abusive stranger in New York who calls him a 'Fucking Arab' (134). He is quick to remind his interlocutor that he '[is] not, of course, an Arab,' and then proceeds to drive the point home by subjecting the abuser to a similar – albeit less abusive – kind of stereotypical thinking:

> What did he look like, you ask? Well, sir, he . . . But how odd! I cannot now recall the man's particulars, his age, say, or his build; to be honest, I cannot now recall many of the details of the events I have been relating to you. But surely it is the *gist* that matters; I am, after all, telling you a history, and in history, as I suspect you – an American – will agree, it is the thrust of one's narrative that counts, not the accuracy of one's details.
>
> (Hamid 2008: 134)

There are two assumptions here. The first is that Americans tend not to be interested in the fine details of a story, and the second is that the man to whom he is speaking necessarily adheres to the same values as other Americans. Whether Changez makes these assumptions consciously or unconsciously is beside the point. What is important is that, once again, the second-person narration puts the reader in the American's position and forces her to vicariously experience the overdetermination to which he is subjected. The idea of America that Changez projects onto his interlocutor reveals its own artificiality when the reader is, in turn, made to feel uncomfortable by the restrictions it forces upon her own sense of identity.

Moreover, it identifies a link between stereotypical thinking and what might broadly be described as 'fundamentalism.' The narrative 'gist' that Changez describes in the quotation above is simply another way of drawing attention to one of the text's key motifs: namely, what it describes as the desire in American culture to '[f]ocus *on the fundamentals*' (112). This is the 'guiding principal' of Changez' New York employer, the valuation firm Underwood Samson: 'drilled into us since our first day at work[,] . . . it mandated a single-minded attention to financial detail, teasing out the true nature of those drivers that determine an asset's value. And that was precisely what I continued to do' (112). On the one hand, this business-driven notion of 'fundamentalism' offers an alternative to a tendency among the post-9/11 news media to use the term almost as a byword for Islamist terrorism. On the other, it draws attention to the narrowness of worldview that any ideology or system which focuses primarily on 'fundamentals' will inevitably produce. The point that the novel makes here is that while Islamist terrorism might be seen to enact more manifest violence than US-style capitalism (at least ostensibly), the drive within each to privilege fundamental detail over the nuanced complexities of world history is necessarily conducive to a reinforcement of arbitrarily delineated – and mutually antagonistic – categories of collective identity. In other words, by complicating the stereotypical representations of fundamentalism so familiar to consumers of the global media, Hamid shows that the only way in which to rationally approach a phenomenon of such complexity is with a measured sense of ambivalence.

This is most clearly evident at the novel's conclusion. The narrative ends with an implied act of fundamentalist violence between Changez and the American, but its ambiguity leaves open to question exactly what happens and to whom. The narrative's final pages follow the two figures as they leave the tearoom and wander through the darkened streets towards the American's hotel, and the closing paragraph is as follows:

> Ah, we are about to arrive at the gates of your hotel. It is here that you and I shall at last part company. Perhaps our waiter wants to say goodbye as well, for he is rapidly closing in. Yes, he is waving at me to detain you. I know you have found some of my views offensive; I hope you will not resist my attempt to shake you by the hand. But why are you reaching into your jacket, sir? I detect a glint of metal. Given that you and I are now bound by a certain shared intimacy, I trust it is from the holder of your business cards.
>
> (Hamid 2008: 209)

The 'waiter rapidly closing in,' waving at Changez to 'detain' the American suggests a degree of threat that would make it easy to initially read the passage as describing the moment when Changez reveals himself as the 'reluctant fundamentalist' of the title, pushed into violent anti-American extremism by a belligerent post-9/11 US foreign policy.

However, this would be too simple a reading, as the language has an ambiguity that resists a single, straightforward interpretation. The passage constitutes the culmination of a series of passing comments that Changez has been making as they walk through the dimly lit city, each working to build the tension a little more ('What? Is somebody following us? I cannot see anyone' [200]; 'I must avoid doing what you are doing at this instant, namely looking over my shoulder' [208]). In addition, while walking, Changez simultaneously recounts the final part of the story of his relationship with America, in which he becomes an outspoken university lecturer highly critical of US foreign policy and, as a result, attracts the attention of international news reporters. He acknowledges that he 'was perhaps more forceful on the this topic than [he] intended,' and even (in one of Hamid's admittedly slightly clumsier metaphorical flourishes) that '[i]f Erica was watching – which rationally, I knew, she almost certainly was not – she might have seen me and been moved to correspond,' but the topic of discussion only adds to the sense of foreboding that builds over the novel's final pages (207).

The quickness with which the reader might jump to the conclusion that Changez is some sort of terrorist – which she may even expect from the start, given the novel's title – becomes part of the point. It is for this reason that I would diverge slightly from James Lasdun's highly astute review of the novel in the *Guardian*, in which he suggests that 'in a neat – arguably too neat – reversal, it transpires that the real fundamentalism at play here is that of US capitalism' (2007). What is more important, I would argue, is the fundamentalist impulse that the novel provokes in the *reader*, experienced vicariously through the figure of the American. With virtually no concrete evidence upon which to suspect that Changez has been transformed into a violent figure (as opposed to one that is simply angry at the United States), the reader is responding, intellectually, in much the same way as the American perhaps does as he reaches into his pocket for what is heavily implied to be a handgun. In the possible circumstance that Changez is innocent and that the American has, in his anti-Islamic paranoia, jumped to conclusions, then it is he, as well as any reader that jumps to the same conclusion, that can most accurately be described as a 'reluctant fundamentalist.'

It is precisely this dangerous instinct to resort to stereotype that all three novels attempt to challenge, and in doing so they simultaneously subvert the kind of simplistic identity binaries – 'Western' and 'non-Western,' 'citizen' and 'immigrant,' 'us' and 'them' – that continue to dominate public discourse as the 'global war on terror' approaches the threshold of its third decade.

Note

1 Spivak gestures towards something similar in *Death of a Discipline*: "The meaning of the figure is undecidable, and yet we must attempt to dis-figure it, read the logic of the metaphor" (2003: 71).

Works cited

Aslam, N., 2008. *The Wasted Vigil*. London: Faber.

Brouillette, S., 2007. *Postcolonial Writers and the Global Literary Marketplace*. Basingstoke and New York: Palgrave Macmillan.

Butler, J., 2006. *Precarious Life: The Powers of Violence and Mourning*. London: Verso.

—— 2009. *Frames of War: When Is Life Grievable?* London: Verso.

Chambers, C., 2011. A Comparative Approach to Pakistani Fiction in English. *Journal of Postcolonial Writing*, 47(2), 122–134.

—— 2016. Book Review: Tabish Khair, Just Another Jihadi Jane and Tariq Mehmood, Song of Gulzarina. *Huffington Post*, 20 Dec. <www.huffingtonpost.co.uk/dr-claire-chambers/book-review-tabish-khair-_b_13674626.html>

Cilano, C., 2010. *National Identities in Pakistan: The 1971 War in Contemporary Pakistani Fiction*. Oxford: Routledge.

Freeman, J. (ed.), 2010. *Granta 112: Pakistan*. New York: Granta.

Halaby, L., 2007. The Return of the Native. *Washington Post*, 22 Apr. Available at: <www.washingtonpost.com/wp-dyn/content/article/2007/04/19/AR2007041903000.html>

Hamid, M., 2008. *The Reluctant Fundamentalist*. London: Penguin.

Hartnell, A., 2010. Moving through America: Race, Place and Resistance in Mohsin Hamid's *The Reluctant Fundamentalist*. *Journal of Postcolonial Writing*, 46(3–4), 336–348.

Hill, A., 2003. An Afghan Hounded by His Past. *Guardian*, 7 Sept. Available at: <www.theguardian.com/books/2003/sep/07/fiction.features1>

Jackson, R., 2005. *Writing the War on Terrorism: Language, Politics and Counter-Terrorism*. Manchester: Manchester University Press.

Kakutani, M., 2008. Novelist's Crash Course on Terror: Review of *The Second Plane* by Martin Amis. *New York Times*, 8 Apr. Available at: <www.nytimes.com/2008/04/08/books/08kaku.html?_r=0>

Khan, G.K., 2011. The Hideous Beauty of Bird-Shaped Burns: Transnational Allegory and Feminist Rhetoric in Kamila Shamsie's *Burnt Shadows*. *Pakistaniaat: A Journal of Pakistan Studies*, 3(2). Available at: <http://pakistaniaat.org/index.php/pak/article/view/122>

Lasdun, J., 2007. The Empire Strikes Back. *Guardian*, 3 Mar. Available at: <www.theguardian.com/books/2007/mar/03/featuresreviews.guardianreview20>

Morley, C., 2011. "How Do We Write about This?" The Domestic and the Global in the Post-9/11 Novel. *Journal of American Studies*, 45(4), 717–731.

Nixon, R., 2006. A Biafran Story. *New York Times*, 1 Oct. Available at: <www.nytimes.com/2006/10/01/books/review/Nixon.t.html>

Said, E., 1983. Traveling Theory. In: *The World, the Text and the Critic*. Boston: Harvard University Press.

Shamsie, K., 2009. *Burnt Shadows*. London: Bloomsbury.

—— 2012. The Storytellers of Empire. *Guernica*, 1 Feb. Available at: <www.guernicamag.com/features/shamsie_02_01_2012/>

Spivak, G.C., 2003. *Death of a Discipline*. New York: Columbia University Press.

—— 2004. Terror: A Speech after 9/11. *Boundary 2*, 31(2), 81–111. Available at: <http://dx.doi.org/10.1215/01903659-31-2-81>

—— 2005. Translating into English. In: S. Bermann and M. Wood, ed. *Nation, Language, and the Ethics of Translation*. Oxford: Princeton University Press.

—— 2006. *In Other Worlds: Essays in Cultural Politics*. Oxford: Routledge.

White, H., 1973. *Metahistory: The Historical Imagination in Nineteenth-Century Europe*. Baltimore: The Johns Hopkins University Press.

26

FROM CIVIL RIGHTS TO #BLM

Anna Hartnell

Around halfway through Jesmyn Ward's most recent novel, *Sing, Unburied, Sing* (2017), the text raises the threat that the self-destructive logic towards which its narrative lurches might take out the character at its heart:

> Jojo raises his arms to a cross. The officer barks at him, the sound raw and carrying in the air, and Jojo shakes his head without pausing and staggers when the officer kicks his legs apart, the gun a little lower now, but still pointing to the middle of his back. I blink and I see the bullet cleaving the soft butter of him. I shake.
>
> (Ward 2017: 164)

By this gut-wrenching moment in the novel it has become apparent that thirteen-year-old Jojo, although just one of three narrators, is the one who matters the most: from the direction of his eyes to the feel of his mouth, the reader's intimacy with the perspective of this young black boy testifies to his role as the text's material and moral centre. His and our exposure to the potentially annihilating effects of police violence also signals Ward's engagement with the politics that animate Black Lives Matter – that rallying cry that has gestured in recent years towards the formation of a new movement that might act as both continuation of and corrective to the African American civil rights struggle of previous generations. Where Ward's twenty-first century literary contributions have come to be emblematic of this new generation of black politics and thought, Toni Morrison's work, straddling the distance between the 1970s and our contemporary moment, celebrates, explores and unravels the legacy of the civil rights movement that culminated in the 1960s. Her most recent novel, *God Help the Child* (2015), like *Sing, Unburied, Sing*, settles on the figure of the child as the vehicle through which America's painful racial dynamics are narrated. This chapter examines Ward's and Morrison's latest novels as contributions to a specifically black literary tradition that has not only constituted a key site of exploration for the black freedom narrative; it has also functioned as one of its most significant voices.

Reflecting recently on racism and US politics, the iconic Black Power activist and intellectual, Angela Davis (2016), claims that 'the overwhelming number of Black people are subject to economic, educational, and carceral racism to a far greater extent than during the pre-civil rights era' (2). In the late 1960s and 1970s Davis was at the heart of black nationalist tendencies that were seeking to push attention away from civil rights struggles and towards economic and social spheres that were barely affected by the signature achievements of the civil rights movement, the Civil Rights Act of 1964 and the Voting Rights Act of 1965. Davis (2016) notes:

> The movement we call 'the civil rights movement', and that was called by most of its participants the 'freedom movement', reveals an interesting slippage between freedom and civil rights, as if civil rights has colonized the whole space of freedom, that the only way to be free is to acquire civil rights within the existing framework of society.
>
> (115)

Davis's call for a more transformative vision of society, first as a member of the Communist Party USA and the Black Panther Party in the 1960s and 70s, and more recently as a prominent voice in the prison abolition movement, gestures towards a global horizon that transcends the parameters marked out by civil rights. While acknowledging the achievements of the civil rights movement, Davis's analysis demonstrates the limitations of a struggle that enabled social mobility for the minority of black Americans while leaving the majority to suffer the backlash against it: increased calls for 'law and order' to police black neighbourhoods; the rollback of federal aid programmes designed to help poor black communities. These were of course entirely unintended consequences of the civil rights movement, but her suggestion is that they occurred because the movement did not go far enough.

In the 2014 protests that took place in Ferguson, Missouri, following the fatal police shooting of Michael Brown – an unarmed black teenager – Davis glimpses the possibility of a more 'capacious' movement that combines a critique of racist state violence and mass incarceration with an economic and intersectional analysis. While Davis herself does not identify the Ferguson protests explicitly with Black Lives Matter, subsequent commentary has done so unequivocally, claiming Ferguson as the most prominent and perhaps the most successful moment for a movement whose slogan appeared the previous year in response to another shooting. Alicia Garza, Patrisse Cullors and Opal Tometi (https://blacklivesmatter.com) created what they describe as a 'Black-centered political will and movement building project called #BlackLivesMatter' in 2013, in response to the acquittal of George Zimmerman, a neighbourhood watch volunteer who shot another unarmed black teenager, Trayvon Martin.

African American Studies scholar Frederick C. Harris (2015) echoes many commentators when he states that 'core activists of the Black Lives Matter movement have been quick to remind us that this current wave of protest "is not your grandmamma's civil rights movement"' (35). Central to this perceived difference is the new movement's emphasis on feminism and LGBTQ issues, as well as a decentralized leadership – in stark contrast to the male leadership model that dominated both the civil rights and black nationalist phases of the black freedom movement in the 1960s and 70s. Perhaps more surprising is Harris's assertion that the civil rights movement 'did not directly confront the racialized degradation of black people'. He cites Tef Poe, a St. Louis hip-hop artist, who claims that 'one of the negligent areas of the civil rights movement is that we did not move the moral compass of racism to the right direction' (2015: 3). It is hard to make such a statement consistent with Martin Luther King's impassioned expression of his dream of racial equality, or indeed the more prosaic but perhaps more important dramatizations of racist state violence that played out on the nation's TV screens as a call to action. While desegregation of the South was the principal aim of the mainstream civil rights movement, the whole strategy of non-violent civil disobedience involved appealing to the conscience of white America.

More convincing is Harris's poignant reflection that 'it is a curious thing for black people in the twenty-first century to once again have to claim their humanity' (40). Davis reflects along similar lines when she points out that

> although racist state violence has been a consistent theme in the history of people of African descent in North America, it has become especially noteworthy during the administration of the first African American president, whose very election was widely interpreted as heralding the advent of a new, postracial era.
>
> (2016: 77)

Citing William Faulkner – 'The past is never dead. It's not even past' – Davis paints a portrait of a United States stalked by 'the ghosts of our past'. The most potent of these ghosts is of course that of slavery. As Davis (2016) commonsensically points out, 'it would not have been necessary to create a mid-century Black freedom movement had slavery been comprehensively abolished in the nineteenth century' (115). Likewise Black Lives Matter inherits the unresolved ghosts of the civil rights past. And yet some of these ghosts that haunt our contemporary moment might be traced back, Davis argues, not so much to slavery as to the new regimes of racialized control over the black body that were introduced in freedom's wake. These various ghosts, of slavery and its afterlife, in turn haunt the pages of Toni Morrison's and Jesmyn Ward's fictions, fictions that not only dramatize Faulkner's dictum but which are deeply marked by his literary legacy.

My analysis of *God Help the Child* and *Sing, Unburied, Sing* suggests that the latter marks a distinct shift in representation in black writing, mapping out new ways to think about race and indeed the future. Before turning to these novels, this chapter will briefly survey the literary tradition of which they are a part – and which has long sustained the ghosts of the nation's unburied victims of white supremacist violence.

Between art and politics: the African American literary tradition

In his landmark 1903 collection of autobiographical essays, *The Souls of Black Folk*, the African American intellectual W.E.B. Du Bois reflects on the American South after Reconstruction, that period immediately following slavery and during which the newly freed slaves were briefly able to make inroads into the political, social and economic worlds previously reserved for white citizens. What quickly followed was a backlash known amongst white southerners as 'Redemption', and it is the results of this backlash that Du Bois's text records. This new order is defined by the establishment of 'Jim Crow' segregation, whereby black people are consigned to 'separate' but supposedly 'equal' social spaces.[1] The world inaugurated by Jim Crow, Du Bois (2003) suggests, is one in which whites reside in a distant 'other world', while black people exist beneath 'a vast veil' (3–4). As many commentators have pointed out, this veil signifies the fact that black southerners continue to labour under the threat of death, even after slavery.

And yet while slavery haunts this post-Reconstruction landscape, Du Bois is most concerned to diagnose the new conditions of black life created by freedom. This diagnosis is most vividly captured in Du Bois's notion of double consciousness, by which he describes the new dilemmas created by citizenship:

> One ever feels his twoness, – an American, a Negro; two souls, two thoughts, two unreconciled strivings, two warring ideals in one dark body, whose dogged strength alone keeps it from being torn asunder.
>
> (2003: 5)

'It is a peculiar sensation, this double-consciousness', Du Bois (2003) explains, claiming that the black American is 'gifted with second sight in this American world – a world which yields him no true self-consciousness, but only lets him see himself through the revelation of the other world' (5). Double consciousness thus emerges as a curse and a gift, as the African American is consigned to viewing himself through the eyes of the white racist.

This 'peculiar sensation', this heightened self-consciousness constantly routed via the eyes of the other, runs through the heart of the post-slavery black literary tradition: writers have variously dramatized, embraced or exorcized it. Literary critical discussion about black American literature has similarly wrestled with the duality of a tradition that has apparently marked itself out for two mutually exclusive roles: exploring what a specifically black identity might be on its own terms, if such a thing is possible or desirable, and dramatizing the horrors of racism in order to educate a white audience. And if, as many scholars have claimed, the African American literary tradition has its origins, at least in part, in the genre of the slave narrative, then a variant of this dilemma was there from the beginning.

The classic slave narratives were penned prior to abolition, usually by runaway slaves who escaped from the slaveholding South to the 'free' North, and who wrote narratives for white liberals in order to persuade them to the cause of abolition. These narratives, the most well-known of which was that of Frederick Douglass, became proving grounds both for the horrors of slavery and for black humanity (See Douglass, 1987). These two aims were tangled and conflicted: in a post-Enlightenment culture where writing was seen as a sign of 'reason', the slave's ability to display not only literacy but literary talent was evidence of their humanity (See Gates, 1988). In turn, the more 'artful' and dramatic these accounts were, the more horrifying and powerful were the depictions of slavery; and yet many white readers then doubted their veracity. Consequently almost all pre-abolition slave narratives included prefaces from prominent white abolitionists, authorizing the texts by verifying their (black) authorship. Here we see a crudely literalized and literary version of double consciousness, whereby the text must be refracted through the eyes of the white other before the black writer can speak.

The ghost of this scenario is very much in evidence in the texts of the Harlem Renaissance, the first great flowering of the black arts in slavery's aftermath that centred on New York City in the 1920s and 30s. The white patrons who sponsored many of these black literary artists – like Langston Hughes and Zora Neale Hurston – in some ways echoed the role of the white abolitionists, in spite of the fact that these works charted a new racial consciousness that could only have emerged after slavery. The Harlem writers were enormously influenced by the work of Du Bois, and their portraits of fractured subjectivity constitute a distinct contribution to modernism.

In spite of this literary experimentation, in 1949 James Baldwin (2012) famously decried what he saw as the tendency of black American writers to adhere to the formula of 'protest fiction'. In Baldwin's view, an overtly anti-racist agenda subjected aesthetics to politics, reducing the complexity of black life: 'the failure of the protest novel is its rejection of life, the human being, the denial of his beauty, dread, power, in its insistence that it is categorization alone which is real and which cannot be transcended' (24). Echoes of Baldwin's searing critique of writers like Richard Wright can be heard today in the insistence of the African American writer Percival Everett that his work not be viewed through the prism of race (see O'Hagan, 2003). Everett's dis-ease with the place he is accorded by publicists and critics within an 'African American literary tradition' is echoed in different ways in the work of Paul Beatty and Colson Whitehead, black writers whose work emerged in the 1990s. These three writers engage variously in postmodern deconstructions of identity that often play with and yet do not quite escape from race as a structuring concept. Much of Everett's work dramatizes his frustration that the racial frame persists, just as Baldwin's work, though ideologically distinct, and despite its similar refusal to be categorized, was unable to turn away from US race relations. Indeed, Baldwin's oeuvre stands as one of the most eloquent and significant bodies of commentaries that we have on the black freedom movement.

Henry Louis Gates's influential 1988 work, *The Signifying Monkey: A Theory of African American Literary Criticism*, provided further insight into these tensions which often shape black writing and writers by diagnosing another condition of duality related to Du Boisian double consciousness. He argued that black writing is marked by the 'double-voiced tongue' appropriated by New World blacks as a means by which to survive. Black texts thus emerge in his work as trickster figures that say one thing and 'signify' another. More recently, and contra the kind of unity that Gates's theory of black American literature and criticism implies, Kenneth W. Warren argued in a controversial 2011 publication, *What Was African American Literature?*, that the tradition had lost its unifying force. Warren suggests that African American literature as it emerged in the twentieth century historically gained its coherence through both upholding and critiquing the racial status quo inaugurated by Jim Crow. Warren argues that with the end of Jim Crow segregation in the South – as a consequence of the success of the civil rights movement – it had lost its *raison d'être*. All subsequent works identified as part of that tradition in fact exhibit nostalgia for the forms of racial solidarity that legal segregation brought into being. Warren's claim is not that racism ended with the demise of the Jim Crow system, but rather that what he characterizes as the fixation on African American *identity* in black literature obscures the more powerful role of class in determining black life. In so doing he echoes voices like Angela Davis, who have long argued that structural racism can only be answered with a critique of capitalism.

The difference between Warren's and Gates's positions reflect very different assessments of the continuation of racism in the aftermath of the 1960s and 70s freedom movements. These movements have also constituted the driving force behind a tradition of black female writers, including Alice Walker, Ntozake Shange and Toni Morrison, whose work explores and dissects the movement from feminist or 'womanist' perspectives[2] – perspectives that critique but simultaneously refuse to relinquish the forms of racial solidarity that Warren claims are no longer helpful in the fight against racial and economic injustice. The next section considers Toni Morrison's work, focusing on her most recent novel and the ghosts that hang over that text.

Toni Morrison's *God Help the Child* (2015)

Morrison's first novel, *The Bluest Eye* (1970), features a young black girl whose internalized racism is reflected in her longing for blue eyes. Morrison's latest novel returns to this theme when she depicts the trauma and arrested development experienced by a neglected young black woman whose mother, herself 'high yellow', is repelled by her daughter's 'midnight black' skin (3). *God Help the Child* is a slim book and has been widely proclaimed as lightweight and insubstantial by critics who have long been suggesting that Morrison's later work does not match the energy and power of her earlier masterpieces.

Morrison's status as one of the most lauded living writers today was sealed by the publication of *Beloved* in 1987. The figure at the centre of this text, Beloved, is the materialized ghost of a girl who was killed by her mother, Sethe, herself a runaway slave, who wants to save her daughter from being taken back into slavery. Morrison's magical realist exploration of the idea that slavery might be a fate worse than death not only dramatized the traumas of slavery for a culture complacent about its history of racial violence in the aftermath of civil rights; it also explored the damage inflicted upon the black family by slavery, proposing, contra racist stereotypes about neglectful parentage, that sometimes black people may love their children too much. 'Your love is too thick' (Morrison, 2005: 193) is a proposition repeated throughout the novel, one which also makes its way into Morrison's 1997 novel, *Paradise*.

While *Beloved* paved the way for Morrison's international recognition in 1993 when she was awarded the Nobel Prize for Literature, *Paradise* was liked much less by critics, who branded this text 'cold' and 'intellectual' (see Kakutani 1998), less befitting a writer whose oeuvre has been credited with performing the work of 'healing' a divided nation, just as Morrison herself has been crowned the 'conscience of America' (see Ghanash 2015). Morrison has been wary of this role, asserting contentiously in interviews that she writes 'for black people'. And yet while she claims to be entirely at ease with the label 'black writer' (Hoby 2015), her work quite deliberately constructs uncomfortable projections of black community that are probed and often unravelled. This is precisely the trajectory of *Paradise*, which opens with the memorable line, 'They shoot the white girl first' (Morrison 1999: 3). This text portrays a separatist all-black town that is based on the black towns founded in Oklahoma following the end of Reconstruction. But it also recalls more recent historical developments in the spatialization of race, namely the formation of racially exclusive all-white suburbs in the postwar period.

The inversion of this scenario that is narrated in *Paradise* is clearly a reaction to white supremacy, and a close reading of the text does not support the idea, suggested by some commentary, that it dramatizes so-called 'reverse racism'. Nonetheless, the opening line and the hostility to white people felt by some of the text's central protagonists clearly plays with this idea. Moreover, these problematic attitudes about race are explored in *Paradise*, set in 1976, the bicentennial of the nation's founding, as unfinished business from the civil rights era. The all-black town portrayed in the novel is divided by an intergenerational divide that can be loosely mapped on to the split that occurred in the movement between an older, southern, rural, Christian demographic committed to non-violence, and the younger, more urban movement in the North which became impatient with what it saw as the passivity of non-violent resistance. And yet the views of this older generation in the novel have congealed and collected around a fatal commitment to ideas of racial superiority linked to their particularly dark complexions – their '8-rock' skin. As the line that opens the novel indicates, this town's non-violent beginnings have given way to aggression as their 'dream' of a free community has twisted into its opposite. Central to the corruption of this dream is the fetishization of money and material possessions that has become disturbingly intertwined with the town's religious commitments. Here Morrison appears to be commenting on the formation of a black middle class in the aftermath of civil rights – a group which, in the novel at least, has embraced a 'prosperity gospel' and become dangerously disconnected from its roots in the experiences of racial and economic oppression.

The horizons of *God Help the Child* are much more modest: Bride, our central protagonist, has similarly suffered abuse for her exceptionally dark skin and has turned it into a principle by which to live. Yet Bride's narrative is deprived of the mythic coordinates explored in *Paradise*, her orientation individualistic rather than collective: her 'Sudanese skin' becomes not an enabling – and deeply problematic – group myth of racial empowerment but rather a commodity for her to sell in the marketplace that the social has become. Bride's style consultant tells her: 'Black sells. It's the hottest commodity in the civilized world. White girls, even brown girls have to strip naked to get that kind of attention' (36). Bride's narcissistic fixation on her newly conceptualized 'beauty' is reflected in her role as the creator of a cosmetics brand and the superficial relationships she entertains both with sexual partners and with her 'friend' Brooklyn, 'the one person I can trust'. Brooklyn's contempt for Bride is in turn demonstrated to the reader in Brooklyn's willingness to betray Bride at every opportunity.

The character of Bride and the plotlines of this novel also echo Morrison's 1981 novel *Tar Baby*, whose central protagonist, Jadine, a fashion model, is similarly consumed by economic models of success. *Tar Baby* is the only other of Morrison's novels to have a contemporary setting and yet, like *Paradise*, it too is graced with mythic coordinates: set on a Caribbean island, it is a text rich with allusion, exploring, among other things, a magical realist, postcolonial reading of Shakespeare's *The Tempest*. As Hermione Hoby (2015) writes of this comparison, in an interview with Morrison shortly after the publication of *God Help the Child*, 'with its island of spirits and talking trees, *Tar Baby*, Morrison points out, is more timeless phantasmagoria than identifiable present reality. So this [*God Help the Child*], really, is her first contemporary novel and she admits that it gave her some trepidation'.

The atmosphere of this contemporary landscape is decidedly bleak. Bride's social isolation is compounded after she has been attacked by Sophia Huxley and the only person she can turn to is Brooklyn. The cynicism of her misanthropic friend is reflected in the hollowed-out arms of state and civil society that do little more than offer a band-aid for Bride's physical and psychological wounds: they find themselves in a 'dump of a clinic' having passed the 'closed-shut police station'. 'Of course it's closed', Brooklyn notes, 'it's Sunday, when only churches and Wal-Mart are open' (22). Brooklyn's gloomy perspective is mirrored in the larger novel, which is populated by paedophiles and murderers. When Booker – Bride's lover – and his family discover that Booker's brother, Adam, has disappeared, the police respond by 'immediately' searching the family home,

> as though the anxious parents might be at fault. They checked to see if the father had a police record. He didn't. 'We'll get back to you', they said. Then they dropped it. Another little black boy gone. So?
>
> (Morrison 2015: 114)

It turns out that Adam has been gruesomely murdered. While the murder is not racially motivated – the other victims indicate, we are told, that this is 'an equal-opportunity killer' (118) – the casually cruel response of the police indicate that this is a world in which black men die, and in which black lives do not matter very much.

This theme is mirrored in the literal 'un-mattering' of Bride. As Bride states to the reader at the start of the novel, 'I feel like I'm melting away' (Morrison 2015: 8). In a direct gesture to *Beloved* and its namesake, whose body and behaviour progress through the early stages of childhood – to ghost what would have been the progression of the murdered infant – Bride's body regresses back into childhood: the holes in her earlobes close up, she loses her pubic hair, and eventually her breasts disappear into her chest. While the immediate cause appears to be her rejection on the part of her boyfriend, Booker, the larger cause of Bride's increasing insubstantiality has something to do with those initially responsible for her care. 'Sweetness', the name by which Bride addresses her mother – having been forbidden to use the terms 'Mother' or 'Mama' – opens the narrative with a cloying attempt to justify her neglect of her child on account of her dark skin. Yet the 'colourism' of Bride's mother is everywhere reflected in the racist structures of state and society that have similarly abandoned Bride. Thus Morrison seems to deploy the classic trope of the absent parent standing in for the withdrawal of the state. Where Morrison's 1997 novel, *Paradise*, similarly tracked the rollback of federal programmes that were the achievements of the civil rights movement, that earlier novel also wrestled with various models of black community that might be embraced in its absence. This is not the case in *God Help the Child*, the title of which speaks to the novel's dystopian tenor and the fact that Morrison seems to no longer be engaging with narratives of national redemption that her richest and most densely plotted texts – *Beloved* and *Paradise* – both problematized and, to an extent, affirmed.

The narrative of US decline towards which *God Help the Child*'s fragmented social landscape seems to gesture is partially explored as an emanation of economics. Poverty stalks this text as with most of Morrison's novels, while one of the central protagonists, Booker, concludes from his university studies of the nation's racist history that 'wealth alone explained humanity's evil' (122).

Certainly his own rejection of materialism contrasts with Bride, just as Bride's uncomfortable refuge with Evelyn and Steve, whose apparent disinterest in material rewards and comforts baffles her, is part of the narrative's learning curve. And yet the glib expression of Booker's revelation undermines its authority in the text. Having learned that materialism and consumption is not the key to happiness, Bride and Booker move on, to discover that if they can love themselves and accept their damage, they can also love each other.

The conclusion to this novel is both moving and formulaic. Its quasi-redemptive ending – a baby is on the way – is a kind of hollow echo of the redemption that is glimpsed at the end of *Beloved*. Where the earlier novel ended with community, this one ends with an atomized nuclear family, unmoored from any bonds apart from those to each other. In a recent collection of published lectures, Morrison (2017) suggests that 'narrative fiction provides a controlled wilderness, an opportunity to be and to become the Other. The stranger. With sympathy, clarity, and the risk of self-examination' (91). Bride and Booker themselves inhabit this wilderness, but stand for a sympathetic (black) other who might mitigate the (white) racist other that Du Bois claims haunts the psychology of black Americans. In this sense, *God Help the Child* reflects Morrison's most enduring preoccupation, the exploration of black racial consciousness and identity. In the contest between race and economics as rationales for injustice, race trumps economics in Morrison's work.

Morrison claims that her work that plays with racial identity and in some cases undermines its authority – in *Paradise* she never reveals to the reader which character in the text the 'white girl' of the first line is – opens her to the charge of 'literary white-washing' and might thus be rejected by other black authors and readers. And yet Morrison has clearly been unequivocally embraced as a kind of spokesperson for black Americans. According to Kenneth Warren's slightly dubious formulation, her work is vulnerable to the critique that it displays nostalgia for the forms of racial solidarity enabled by Jim Crow. I would temper Warren's suggestion by saying that those forms of solidarity were just as much on display in the civil rights movement, which overturned the Jim Crow system, and this is where I would situate the racial solidarity towards which Morrison's texts lean.

This chapter now turns to the very different figure of Jesmyn Ward, whose work represents a new generation of writing about the precarity of black lives. I suggest that while Ward is still very much interested in claiming a black identity for herself and her characters, these identifications are far from nostalgic, and are rooted as much in a politics of class as they are in racial politics.

Jesmyn Ward's *Sing, Unburied, Sing* (2017)

When Trayvon Martin was shot in February 2012, Jesmyn Ward was revising her memoir, *Men we Reaped* (2013), which tells the story of five young black men Ward grew up with – including her brother and her cousin – all of whom died violent deaths in the space of just four years. As Ward describes it, on hearing of the circumstances of Martin's death, 'I took to Twitter. I didn't have anywhere else to go' (3). In this way Ward was part of the Black Lives Matter movement, as it has since come to be known, from the start, as well as the author of a memoir that provides vivid commentary on – and indeed rationale for – the movement.

By this point Ward was already an established writer, having written two previous novels in the wake of what Ward describes as a post-Hurricane Katrina writers block that lasted three years (Hartnell, 2016: 216). Ward's native community on the Mississippi Gulf Coast was devastated by the storm, another moment in recent history that has graphically and brutally highlighted the precariousness of black lives a generation after the civil rights movement and in a new era of state shrinkage and the rollback of social safety nets. Ward's two subsequent novels, *Where the*

Line Bleeds (2008) and *Salvage the Bones* (2011) are both very much marked by a post-Katrina sensibility. *Where the Line Bleeds* charts the divergent paths of twin brothers following high school graduation. The one who manages to find employment performs back-breaking and ultimately unsafe labour at the local shipyard, his periods of rest dominated by the need to sleep. The other, bereft of employment opportunities, slips into the hazy world of drug dealing. Both chart down-ward spirals from a moment that should be a rite of passage, entry into the world of work and progress. *Salvage the Bones*, for which Ward won the National Book Award in 2011 (she won it again in 2017 following the publication of *Sing, Unburied, Sing*), dramatizes Katrina directly, tell-ing the story of a young, pregnant girl, Esch, part of a family already only just hanging on to the edges of survival even before the storm hits. Inhabiting a highly masculine world populated by her father, her brothers and her brothers' friends, Esch's female company is the dog, China, who massacres and eats her own puppies. This episode encapsulates the way in which all of Ward's texts are pregnant with the threat that the characters might be swallowed up in their elemental struggles to survive. Esch's various identifications with China, in the same vein, opens up an exploration of the boundaries between human and animal that has become very much a theme of Ward's writing, as evidenced by her latest work, *Sing, Unburied, Sing*.

Like Ward's two previous fictional works, *Sing, Unburied, Sing* is set in Bois Sauvage, a fictional town in rural Mississippi which might be compared to William Faulkner's similarly constructed Yoknapatawpha County in which most of his novels are set. Ward's 2017 novel characteristi-cally opens with the slaughter of an animal: 'I like to think I know what death is' says Jojo, the text's first narrator, although soon we see him running away and vomiting. Death and erasure shadow the figure of Jojo throughout the text. Despite the love he receives from his maternal grandparents, Jojo is neglected by his mother and father who find it hard to recognize their son as someone who might require their care. Instead, Jojo cares for his three-year-old sister, Kayla, while his mother, Leonie, gets high, and his father, Michael, serves time in prison.

The main narrative of the novel is centred on a road trip to the state penitentiary, also known as Parchman Farm, made by Leonie, Jojo and Kayla, accompanied by Leonie's friend Misty. Michael, Jojo's white and distanced father, is to be released. Despite Jojo's reluctance to accom-pany his mother, and his grandparents' anxiety about the trip, Leonie wants to present Michael and the world with a reunited, nuclear family. The delusion of this vision is punctuated by various obstacles on the way: Kayla is overcome by a high fever and vomiting; Leonie is unable to focus on her daughter's distress because she is distracted by first smuggling and then using drugs with Misty. They are pulled over by a police officer who draws his gun on Jojo, as described in the opening of this chapter. It is at this moment that his mother is able to recognize him as a child:

> He's just a baby. And when he starts reaching in his pocket and the officer draws his gun on him, points it at his face, Jojo ain't nothing but a fat-kneed, bowlegged toddler. I should scream, but I can't.

> (163)

Where in *God Help the Child* the neglectful parent is reflected in a hollowed-out or absent state and indifferent civil society, in *Sing, Unburied, Sing*, the negligent parent is more than matched by a positively malevolent state apparatus. If Leonie's indifference to Kayla's illness is not life-threatening, the intervention of the state at this moment certainly is.

In fact, while it is hard to like Leonie, one of our three narrators, Ward's narrative does provide a rationale for her sometimes shocking indifference to her children. Leonie is haunted by the death of her brother, Given, who was shot by a white man for winning a bet. '*The fucking hothead shot the nigger for beating him*', the killer's uncle says. '*You fucking idiot . . . this ain't the old days*'

(49–50). Retrospectively constructed as a 'hunting accident', Given's murderer is then sentenced to three years. As Ward explains in an interview (Begley, 2017) she felt she had to overcome her own distaste for Leonie and provide an explanation for her behaviour. Reflecting on the fact that her own brother was killed by a white drunk driver who fled the scene – and who was sentenced to just five years in prison and served only three – Ward explains, 'I didn't want people to think that Leonie was some sort of stand-in for me in the book . . . but I felt like at Leonie's center, there's a great loss . . . it's unhealed and it's festering in some ways. I just felt like it motivates so much of what she does that that had to be it, she had to have lost a sibling'.

Leonie's grieving for Given is complicated by the fact that she seeks refuge in a romantic relationship with the cousin of her brother's murderer, Michael. Leonie's infatuation with Michael is so overpowering that she is unable to properly care for the children they have together. When the ghost of Given starts appearing to Leonie when she is high, it is not clear if his presence is a rebuke of her drug-taking or of her veritable betrayal of him. And yet while getting into bed with Given's murderer's family is possibly an unfortunate choice, Ward's narrative is insistent that the poor black rural communities she portrays – not so dissimilar from the one Ward herself was born into – do include interracial relationships in ways that refuse to separate completely black and white life. This in some ways reflects Ward's own mixed background – including African, European and Native American ancestry (see Ward 2016: 89–95) – and the Creole cultures of the Gulf Coast. The characters of different racial backgrounds in her novels are thus to an extent united by shared horizons. In this way the shadow of Parchman Farm that hangs over this text afflicts all of the characters, black and white. While Michael is imprisoned at the start of the text, River, or 'Pop', Leonie's father and Jojo's grandfather, spent a harrowing time there as a young man.

The novel's third narrator, Richie, is himself a ghost from River's time at Parchman. He cannot 'pass on' because he is unable to comprehend the circumstances of his own violent death at the hands of River – who, though himself very young at the time, was like a father to Richie. It turns out that River, in a move comparable to Sethe's infanticide in Morrison's *Beloved*, killed Richie in order to save him from what he believed was his fate – a lynch mob that would subject him to excruciating and prolonged torture. Thus Richie embodies this scene of racial violence, bringing into the narrative present a time when Parchman Farm functioned just like a slave plantation – long after the abolition of slavery. Contemplating the fields of 'endless rows of cotton' with 'men bent and scuttling along like hermit crabs, bending and picking', Richie recalls 'other men walking in circles around them with guns': 'this is where I was worked. This is where I was whipped' (Ward, 2017: 136). In conjuring such images, Ward reminds us of America's contemporary system of mass incarceration, which similarly often exploits the labour of prison inmates and which overwhelmingly and disproportionately affects black men.

Sing, Unburied, Sing thus powerfully dramatizes the racial order described by Michelle Alexander in her influential 2010 study, *The New Jim Crow: Mass Incarceration in the Age of Colorblindness.* Alexander stresses that 'the New Jim Crow' reflects a new set of technologies of racialized control that have arisen in response to late twentieth and early twenty-first century realities. Her focus is on the way in which the 'war on drugs' has decimated black communities, replacing neighbourhood policing with militarized policing and placing grotesque numbers of black people behind bars: 'more African American adults are under correctional control today – in prison or jail, on probation or parole – than were enslaved in 1850' (2010: 180). Alexander's ideas have played a large role in influencing the Black Lives Matter movement and its conceptualization of the criminal justice system, just as Ward's novel animates what Alexander terms the 'cruel hand' of the criminal justice system to play a determining role in her characters' lives. While Michael's prison experience as a white man is, according to Alexander, as a result of the fact that he is 'collateral damage' in a 'war' (on drugs) designed to manage black people, the conflation of Parchman Farm with the slave plantation reveals that *Sing, Unburied, Sing* similarly characterizes the prison system as a form of racialized control.

Alexander's thesis has come under fire for overlooking issues of class in her attempts to diagnose a new condition of racial caste. James Forman's (2012) objection to the Jim Crow analogy is that middle class blacks are largely free from interference by the criminal justice system and so where the original Jim Crow system targeted all black people (in the South), mass incarceration does not. And yet this objection overlooks the fact that Jim Crow itself was designed to subordinate black labour in ways that echoed slavery. It was not until the defeat of Jim Crow and the successes of the civil rights movement in the 1960s that a sizable African American middle class came into being. That this section of the black population – a significant minority – is largely exempt from the criminal justice crackdown does not invalidate the claim that mass incarceration is a new system of racial caste. It shows the ways in which racial caste has always been powerfully articulated through class paradigms that exploit poor whites as well.

While fleshing out many of Alexander's propositions, Ward's constructions of racial identity are at no point disarticulated from those of class. In this sense her work differs significantly from that of Toni Morrison, whose explorations of racial identity often function independently from the economic analysis that her texts nonetheless incorporate. Where Morrison's texts frequently enact uneasy searches for positive constructions of blackness, which are then subjected to rigorous anti-essentialist critique, Ward's work explores the material consequences, the lived experience, of being black and poor.

That said, Ward, much less equivocally than Morrison, is clear about what it means to identify as a black American: in an article about the discovery of, and vague discomfort with, the extent of her mixed ancestry after using an online genetic testing kit, Ward (2016) writes:

> In choosing to identify as black, to write about black characters in my fiction and to assert the humanity of black people in my nonfiction, I've remained true to my personal history, to my family history, to my political and moral choices, and to my essential self: that self understands the world through the prism of being a black American, and stands in solidarity with the people of the African diaspora.
>
> (94)

Ward's is principally a political understanding of black identity that is not particularly interested in chasing, exploring and deconstructing the enigma that is 'race'. This perhaps partly reflects the fact that she has come of age during a time when the poststructuralist deconstruction of essentialist categories is no longer the dominant strand of literary studies. For Ward, race is a political fact. The above quotation is extracted from a collection titled *The Fire This Time: A New Generation Speaks about Race* (2016), edited by Ward herself. This appropriation of James Baldwin's title – The Fire Next Time (1963) – shows the way in which the generation that has felt compelled to insist that black lives matter pays tribute to their forbears while insisting that they face a distinctly new fire. One that demands different conversations from those that defined the civil rights movement and its long aftermath.

This new juncture comes into sharp focus in the concluding pages of *Sing, Unburied, Sing*. Jojo survives his encounter with the gun-wielding police officer and is then shadowed by the ghost of Richie. Rather than exorcize Richie by encouraging Pop to tell his story, the story that Richie says he needs, Jojo goes on to discover an entire tree full of ghosts. 'They speak with their eyes':

> *He raped me and suffocated me until I died I put my hands up and he shot me eight times she locked me in the shed and starved me to death while I listened to my babies playing with her in*

the yard they came in my cell in the middle of the night and they hung me they found I could read and they dragged me out of the barn and gouged my eyes before they beat me still I was sick and he said I was an abomination and Jesus say suffer little children so let her go and he put me under the water and I couldn't breathe.

(282–283)

These ghosts collapse the distance between times and spaces and different phases in the history of black oppression on US soil. In stark contrast to the ghost in Morrison's *Beloved* – who represents the 'sixty million and more' to whom the novel is dedicated, and who perished in the Middle Passage and beyond – that comes to quite literally suck the life out of our central protagonist, the population of ghosts in Ward's novel constitute the knowledge that Jojo needs in order to survive. Their song is his life.

Notes

1 The legal basis for Jim Crow was established in the 1896 US Supreme Court ruling Plessy v. Ferguson, which decided that separate public facilities could be established for black and white people – as long as they were 'equal'.
2 'Womanist' is a term coined by Alice Walker to distinguish black female resistance to patriarchy from a second-wave feminism that Walker and others have argued overly identifies with whiteness and the West.

Works cited

Alexander, M. (2010) *The New Jim Crow: Mass Incarceration in the Age of Colorblindness.* New York: The New Press.

Baldwin, J. (1955; 2012) 'Everybody's Protest Novel.' In *Notes of a Native Son.* Boston: Beacon Press. 13–24.

Begley, S. (2017) 'Jesmyn Ward, Heir to Faulkner, Probes the Specter of Race in the South.' *Time.* 24 August 2017. http://time.com/4913697/jesmyn-ward-heir-to-faulkner-author-profile/ (accessed 25 February 2018).

Black Lives Matter. https://blacklivesmatter.com (accessed 25 February 2018).

Davis, A. Y. (2016) *Freedom Is a Constant Struggle: Ferguson, Palestine, and the Foundations of a Movement.* Chicago: Haymarket Books.

Douglass, F. (1845; 1987) 'Narrative of the Life of Frederick Douglass, an African Slave.' In *The Classic Slave Narratives.* Ed. Henry Louis Gates, Jr. New York: Mentor.

Du Bois, W.E.B. (1903; 2003) *The Souls of Black Folk.* New York: The Modern Library.

Forman, J. Jr. (2012) 'Racial Critiques of Mass Incarceration: Beyond the New Jim Crow.' *New York University Law Review.* 87: 101–146.

Gates, H. L. Jr. (1988) *The Signifying Monkey: A Theory of African-American Literary Criticism.* New York and Oxford: Oxford University Press.

Ghanash, R. K. (2015) 'The Radical Vision of Toni Morrison.' *New York Times Magazine.* 8 April 2015. www.nytimes.com/2015/04/12/magazine/the-radical-vision-of-toni-morrison.html (accessed 25 February 2018).

Harris, F. C. (2015) 'The Next Civil Rights Movement?' *Dissent.* 63.3: 34–40.

Hartnell, A. (2016) 'When Cars Become Churches: Jesmyn Ward's Disenchanted America: An Interview.' *Journal of American Studies.* 50.1: 205–218.

Hoby, H. (2015) '"I'm Writing for Black People . . . I Don't Have to Apologise".' *Guardian.* 25 April 2015. www.theguardian.com/books/2015/apr/25/toni-morrison-books-interview-god-help-the-child (accessed 25 February 2018).

Kakutani, M. (1998) '*Paradise*: Worthy Women, Unredeemable Men.' *New York Times.* 6 January 1998. www.nytimes.com/books/98/01/04/daily/morrison-book-review-art.html (accessed 25 February 2018).

Morrison, T. (2017) *The Origin of Others.* Cambridge, MA: Harvard University Press.

—— (2015) *God Help the Child.* London: Vintage.

—— (1997; 1999) *Paradise.* London: Vintage.

—— (1987; 2005) *Beloved.* London: Vintage.

—— (1981; 1997) *Tar Baby*. London: Vintage.

—— (1970; 1999) *The Bluest Eye*. London: Vintage.

O'Hagan, S. (2003) 'Colour Bind.' *The Observer*. 16 March 2003. www.theguardian.com/books/2003/mar/16/fiction.features (accessed 25 February 2018).

Ward, J. (2017) *Sing, Unburied, Sing*. London: Bloomsbury.

—— ed. (2016) *The Fire This Time: A New Generation Speaks about Race*. New York: Scribner.

—— (2013) *Men We Reaped*. New York: Bloomsbury.

—— (2011) *Salvage the Bones*. New York: Bloomsbury.

—— (2008) *Where the Line Bleeds*. Chicago: Agate.

Warren, K. W. (2011) *What Was African American Literature*. Cambridge, MA: Harvard University Press.

27

THE PAST

Robert Eaglestone

Introduction

William Faulkner's much-quoted dictum that the 'past is never dead. It's not even past' evokes a key characteristic of post-millennial modernity. Instead of dwindling into insignificance, as, in turn, the rhetoric of modernism, then postmodernism and then globalization suggested, the past's grip on the present has become even stronger. Indeed, what I name 'the resurgent past' is a distinctive and dominant theme of much contemporary fiction and the focus of this chapter.

By 'the resurgent past', I don't simple mean that novels deal with 'things that happened earlier' – almost every novel would fall into this category, from the murder mystery that starts with a corpse in the library to the uncovering of George Wickham's previous behaviour in *Pride and Prejudice*. Instead, I mean that for much contemporary fiction there is an intense concern for the impact of the past on the present. This sense of the resurgent past far exceeds the remit of the conventional historical novel, and, indeed, both complements and challenges the concepts that underlie it.

In his analysis of the 'historical novel today' Fredric Jameson identifies the problems and proposes his own answer. He declares that

> we have protagonists in whom we no longer believe, and masses who are at best imaginary, and to this unpromising material we bring our incredulity about the grand narrative of decisive events and genuine historical change or development. What kind of History can the contemporary historical novel then be expected to 'make appear'?
>
> (Jameson 2013: 263)

Jameson argues that to understand 'historicity today' demands 'a temporal span far exceeding the biological limits of the individual human organism' (301) and so turns to the generation-spanning science fiction/alternate histories of David Mitchell's *Cloud Atlas* (2004) and Kim Stanley Robinson's *The Years of Salt and Rice* (2002). These works rely for narrative unity on the idea of the reincarnation of major characters which allows them, Jameson suggests, to fulfil most effectively 'indispensable functions of ideological analysis . . . to show the contradictions in which we are ourselves imprisoned' (308).

However, I suggest that Jameson's view is limited precisely because is he is looking for a kind of (capital H) *History*, and as such a more conventional model of the 'historical novel': instead, if we wonder what *kind* of history, with less of a focus on an 'indispensable function', it's clear that the dazzling range of contemporary fiction about the past offers another form of answer. Indeed, one characteristic of this current preoccupation with the past in fiction is exactly the ever more diverse and contradictory array of modes by which the past is represented, forms which far exceed the historical novel as usually conceived. In this chapter I touch on only some: fable, memory, forms of contrapuntal past (of which Neo-Victorian fiction is the prime example), haunting, possession and trauma.

More, these various different modes, very different *kinds* of history, offer different kinds of *affordances* to the past. In her book *Forms*, Caroline Levine explains that she takes the term 'affordance' from design theory, a term used 'to describe the potential uses or actions latent in materials or designs . . . Cotton affords fluffiness but also breathable cloth when it is spun into yarn': in terms of form, she explores how each 'shape or pattern, social or literary lays claim to a limited range of potentialities . . . Rhyme affords repetition, anticipation and memorisation' (Levine 2015: 6). (The idea of affordances has also been taken up in cognitive criticism too [see Cave 2016: 46ff]). The different modes of fiction I explore below offer different forms of access to a past. These may not be 'History' (with a capital H) as Jameson intends, but instead reflect precisely the multifaceted and heterogeneous engagement with the past which shapes our existence before it is codified into a history or even a 'History'. Each offers a series of different understandings of the past and each brings a different series of ethical and metaphysical questions or commitments.

Past as fable

One example of what I mean is past-as-fable is exemplified in *The Buried Giant* (2015) by the 2017 Nobel Laureate Kazuo Ishiguro. All Ishiguro's fiction, from his earliest novels *A Pale View of Hills* (1982) and *An Artist of the Floating World* (1986), is concerned with the interaction of the past and present, usually involving guilt and complicity, both individual and social. *The Buried Giant* extends these themes. A fable, the novel is set some years after the reign of King Arthur. Narrated by a Charon-like and seemingly immortal ferryman, a type of Death, it weaves together the personal story of an elderly couple of Britons, Axl and Beatrice, and a national and genocidal story: the mass-murder of Saxons and their subsequent subdual by Britons led by Arthur. These stories are linked in two ways. First, neither the couple not the mass population can recall much of the past: Axl and Beatrice can barely remember their son, for example – the novel is, in part, their quest to find him – and the two populations of Saxons and Britons live together mostly in quiescence, rather than peace. It emerges that this forgetfulness is the result of an enchanted mist that emanates from a dragon called Querig, guarded by an aging Sir Gawain. Querig was set by Arthur to keep the gigantic secret of betrayal and mass-murder buried. The second link is that Axl is not really the peasant farmer he takes himself to be: rather, he played a crucial role in Arthur's genocide, as a knight of integrity who led the Saxons to believe they would be safe: a sort of Judas-goat, in fact (and Axl rescues a type of Judas-goat late in the novel, to make the point).

Ishiguro was criticised for his choice of a fable. But the novel's engagement with the past relies less on the fabulous and more on thinking the past as fable: this gives access to a range of complexities and difficulties about the past. The intention of those behind the mist is, as Gawain says, for forgetfulness to 'allow for old wounds to heal for ever and an eternal peace to hold among us' (Ishiguro 2015: 311). But the forgetfulness has terrible insidious effects both personal and social. Individuals lose themselves: as Beatrice says, we 'don't remember our fierce quarrels of the small moments we enjoyed and treasured. We don't remember our son' (49). Communities are stunted, rootless, superstitious (inventing strange and meaningless rituals) and are unable to function fully (they are unable, for example, to use public deliberative reason). Even the landscape becomes a blasted waste land.

But the novel's narrative concerns the end of the dragon and the mist: that is, the return of memory. On their journey, Axl and Beatrice pick up a Saxon orphan, Edwin and also a Saxon warrior, Winstan, able to 'withstand strange spells' (308). He knows the past and makes Edwin promise to 'carry a hatred' of Britons 'in his heart' (264): 'it was Britons under Arthur slaughtered our kind. It was Britons took your mother and mine. We've a duty to hate every man, woman and child of their blood' (264). Indeed, Winstan's secret mission is to kill Querig. And after the dragon is slain 'justice and vengeance await' (322). Even where Briton and Saxon 'mingle village by village' (323), Winstan prophesies that the 'giant, once well buried, now stirs' and the

> friendly bond between us will prove as knots young girls make with the stems of small flowers. Men will burn their neighbours house's by night. Hang children from trees at dawn, The rivers will stink of corpses bloated from their days of voyaging . . . And county by county this will become a new land, a Saxon land, with no more trace of your people's time here than a flock or two of sheep wandering the hills untended.
>
> (324)

One does not need to know all the details of every genocide, ethnic cleansing and atrocity, from (say) Namibia in 1904, though the Holocaust to former Yugoslavia in the 1990s to the Rohingya in Myanmar since 2015, to hear what the novel, as fable, is discussing. Yet what does the novel decide? It stands unresolved between, on the one hand, works like David Rieff's *In Praise of Forgetting* (2016) (the title gives the argument) and, on the other, the general ethical thrust of 'memory studies' that to remember is a good (in, for example, Yerushalmi's influential book *Zakhor: Jewish History and Jewish Memory* (1982) forgetfulness is contrasted not to memory but to justice). The melancholy conclusion, afforded because it is a fable, is that forgetfulness leads to the decay and deformation of personal and social life yet memory leads to more murder, violence and vengeance.

Past as memory

Atrocity is not far from the work of Vietnamese-American writer and academic Viet Thanh Nguyen: his 2015 novel *The Sympathiser* won the Pulitzer Prize (and several others): its themes are echoed in his work of literary theory *Nothing Ever Dies: Vietnam and the Memory of War* (2016). There is much of importance in these twined and profound reflections on memory, ethics and war: here, I focus on one area in order to explore the affordances that the form of the novel offers for his own fiction in relation to the past. Nguyen is interested in the ethics and politics of war remembrance, especially in relation to juridical, popular and cultural memory. He outlines three modes of remembrance in the opposition between 'us' and the 'others'. In the first, the 'the simplest and most explicitly conservative mode', we recall only 'our humanity and the inhumanity of others' (Nguyen 2016, 96). In contrast, the more complex liberal mode recalls the humanity of our side and the humanity of the 'others'; the radical mode recalls only our own inhumanity and the humanity of our enemies. The missing term in these latter two is the 'inhumanity' of our enemies. For Nguyen, the liberal register, like the conservative, is conducive to war ('carried out in humanitarian guise, as rescue operation for the good other' (96)), whereas the radical is the source of most anti-war feeling.

However, he finds in both of these, and especially amplified in the radical form, a crucial deception: recalling our inhumanity and forgetting the inhumanity of the other casts the other in the role of victim, lacking in agency, 'subordinate, simplified, and secondary' (97), a canvas for our full range of existential expression. Nguyen argues that to avoid this, 'the ethics of recognition demands that we remember our humanity and inhumanity, and that we remember the humanity and inhumanity of others as well' (97). Nguyen, here, is thinking of the ways in which discourses of the Vietnam war – conservative, liberal and radical – stripped agency and a full range of humanity from the people of Vietnam through these forms of othering. In parallel, Daniel O'Gorman's work analyses an analogous process for the 'War on Terror': he argues that literature has the potential to disrupt and rethink 'the processes by which the division between the self and the other are conceptualised in the first place' (O'Gorman 2015: 5): and it is this ethical reconceptualization of agency in history and memory that Nguyen's novel, *The Sympathiser*, attempts.

The protagonist is a Vietnamese double agent, 'a man of two faces' (Nguyen 2015: 1), and the book is ostensibly the confession he writes in a Vietnamese prison camp. Sent by his spymasters for an education in the US, 'six idyllic years in the dreamy, sun-besotted world of Southern California' (15), he has become the chief aide of a South Vietnamese general while an intelligence officer for the North Vietnamese army. In this role he not only supplies military information but, to maintain his cover, has to expose and kill other North Vietnamese spies. After the fall of Saigon, he is instructed to accompany the general in to exile in the USA, where, again, he is forced to commit murder for both sides, and works as a consultant for a movie very much in the mould of *Apocalypse Now*. He has much to say about how this misrepresents the war and everyone involved. Later, he accompanies a CIA-funded insurgent force, doomed to failure, and is captured and tortured by his own spymaster. Like Winston Smith, brainwashed at the end, he reneges on his own self-reflexivity 'How dare a man with two minds think he could represent himself, much less anyone else, including his own recalcitrant people' (483).

The novel expresses Nguyen's demand that both sides remember the humanity and inhumanity of the other. The Americans behave in ways which both demonise or victimise the Vietnamese: this is clear in the profoundly orientalist education the narrator receives in the USA, and satirically during an account of the making of a movie – a fictionalised version of Francis Ford Coppola's *Apocalypse now* (1979) – in which stereotypically heroic US marines save a hamlet of suffering peasants from monstrous NVA. The Vietnamese, too, stereotype the Americans. In *The Sympathiser* both sides are presented as both humane and as inhumane and, significantly, as agentic. The protagonist is a sympathiser in two senses: in the euphemistic sense of sympathising with, or being, the enemy – a 'fellow traveller' – and in the more normal sense of sympathising with the people he knows and meets. He helps save one of his closest friends, although he is on the other side; he is deeply upset by the widow of a man he has assassinated and is haunted by the traumatic memories of his actions. His human agency, his oscillation between, to use Nguyen's critical language, humanity and inhumanity are shown precisely through the range of behaviour, from murder to quiet and insistent heroism: he is agent, monster and victim all at the same time. The point of this in terms of engagement with the past in fiction is to question the public construction of memory and to reveal the more complex and damaging commitments behind even apparently radical political forms of memory.

Contrapuntal pasts

This knowingly 'contrapuntal' approach to the past is central to another mode that engages with the past and looks akin to historical fiction: one might think of it as fiction that appropriates the past knowingly and rewrites tropes, narratives, identities from the past. The most significant example of this is neo-Victorian fiction, which has created a small critical industry around it. Tracing a point or origin from Jean Rhys' revolutionary rewriting of *Jane Eyre* in *Wide Sargasso Sea* (1966) and John Fowles' *The French Lieutenant's Woman* (1969), these texts re-inhabit previous stories or genres and, as it were, reconstruct them from other angles. The difference between these novels and others are that – rather than being from the point of view of a famous person from history, or more mainstream romance or adventure-story protagonist – these novels draw out narratives from those marginalised or excluded from accounts of the past and in so doing, almost unavoidably, reflect metafictionally on the conditions of their own making. As a consequence, these kinds of fictions are considered to be progressive and inclusive. They need not be: one of the most celebrated of these neo-Victorian revisionings – but least discussed academically – is George MacDonald Fraser's *Flashman* series, which uses *Tom Brown's School Days* (1857) as a source text, and, with some but not total irony, celebrates sexism, forms of race-thinking and exclusivity. However, the paradigmatic example of this is the neo-Victorian fiction of Sarah Waters. Her novel *Fingersmith* (2002) foregrounds precisely this kind of performative re-inhabitation of past fictions at the start, in a theatre in which *Oliver Twist* is being performed: indeed, the main character lives on Lant Street, where Dickens once lived. The novel is a kind of pastiche of Victorian sensation fiction, all twists and turns, reworking stock clichés and character types. But centrally, rather than passing over issues of sexuality, it places the lesbian sexuality of the two protagonists at the core of the novel and so, as Kaye Mitchell argues, works to queer the text: the pornography collection, central to the plot, is reused as not as a form of objectification but as an archive of the history of female pleasure and desire (see Mitchell 2013).

Sebastian Barry's *Days without End* (2016) also undertakes exactly this kind of knowing revision. Taking the form of the epic western odyssey, of escape and reformation, from films like *The Outlaw Josey Wales* (dir. Clint Eastwood, 1976) and novels like Larry McMurtry's *Lonesome Dove* (1985), Barry's novel is narrated by Thomas McNulty and covers his life from boyhood, beginning in 1851. He is a soldier in the 'Indian wars' but before this, he and his lover John Cole have been actors: boys dressing as women for a saloon owner, until they grew too old. The story, then, with all the western clichés is – like *Fingersmith* – queered: 'We're holding hands then like lovers who have just met or how we imagine lovers might be in the unknown realm where lovers act as lovers without concealment' (Barry 2016: 128). Just as in, for example, *Josey Wales*, they create a family around them of outcasts: an orphaned Native American girl, Winona, for example, and others. And, too, their past, and the atrocities with which they have been involved, catch up with them. However, unlike other fiction and film set in the 'Wild West', the central character is not a gun-toting hero but a former solider in a loving gay relationship who dresses as a woman. The final twist is not one of lawless violence, but of love, and indeed, of law.

The past as haunting

I have discussed novels which, however much they engage with contemporary concerns, are set in the past or recent past. In contrast, another form of representation of the past in contemporary fiction that concerns the haunting of the present by the past: 'hauntology'. This concept stems from Jacques Derrida's book *Spectres of Marx* (1993) which interweaves the relationship of Hamlet and the ghost of his father with the famous beginning of Marx's *Communist Manifesto* ('a spectre is haunting Europe: the spectre of communism'). The ghosts of the past – old Hamlet, Marx's legacy – are both absent (they are dead) and present (as ghosts) and so are ontologically complex (both present and absent): so, naturally, they haunt us demanding something from the future. As Katy Shaw argues in her book on the topic, time is central to the concept of hauntology. Haunting looks back to the past and points forward to the future from the moment of the present. In doing so, it signals towards a legacy as well as to a promise of something to come, drawing attention to the structuring role of absence.

(Shaw 2018: 7)

Aleksander Hemon's *The Lazarus Project* (2008), an allusive, melancholic novel is precisely about the forms of haunting, absence, legacy and the future and so illustrates another form of relationship to the past.

The novel tells two stories which cross over and interweave. The first draws on events from the historical record, the story of a young Jewish immigrant to the USA, Lazarus Averbuch and the controversy over his death. On March 2nd, 1908, Averbuch visited the chief of Police of Chicago, George Shippy, on some undefined errand. Shippy and his driver, taking him for an anarchist intent on murder, shot him dead. This killing is the focus for a panic, with more than a hint of anti-Semitism, stirred up by the yellow press and others, about anarchists and non-Americans threatening the state. Moving seamlessly between historical sources and fiction, the novel explores this panic, its manipulation by the press and impact of this on Averbuch's sister, Olga, who eventually returns to Europe. (Some critics have seen this as a response to hysteria over 9/11 in the USA). The second strand concerns a struggling, underemployed Bosnian-American writer, Vladimir Brik, who is in an unhappy marriage. Brik, by chance, left Bosnia before the war there, and while shaped by the war (the country that was his home has changed utterly) feels keenly his lack of experience of that war. Receiving a grant, Brik uses it to trace Averbuch's story back to Europe and, at the same time, trace his own roots to Bosnia, accompanied by his friend, Rora, a photographer. Rora, who did live through the war in Bosnia, is an endless source of stories which may or may not be true, stories which haunt Brik, just as the Averbuch narrative haunts the text. These hauntings – the war, Averbuch – work to destabilise Brik's identity, his marriage and his writing. Arriving back in Sarajevo, Brik feels like a ghost, uncanny: following Freud, uncanny is *unheimlich*, un–home–ly. The novel is left unresolved. Averbuch and Olga's story is never finally explained or their roots traced (although it seems likely that Olga died in the Holocaust) and the stories in the press remain unanswered. Brik's own life is left in flux, at the mercy of trying and failing to find meaning in his own personal experiences and, through the stories of his friends, his 'collective' experience as a Bosnian. While the novel is about 'living after' some appalling event, like the Lazarus from the Christian Gospels, it is, in its title, a *project*, some thing thrown, pro–jected towards an end or goal, not a finished thing. The lack of closure haunts the novel as the war haunts Brik.

Hauntology is a widely spread cultural phenomena: for example, analysts have found it in music, fashion, contemporary visual art and film, as well as in fiction (for example, see Reynolds 2011: 328–329ff). Shaw argues that its special relation to time (the haunting by the past in relation to the future) means that as a mode it encourages 'readers to revisit important ethical issues as well as historical and cultural heritages that remain unresolved in the present' (Shaw 2018: 106). The ghosts summon us to engage precisely with these challenges.

The past as possession

While haunting is a powerful metaphor for how the past relates to us, it is problematic. We can, to use Derrida's metaphor, engage with the ghost: but equally, we can simply ignore the ghost (in fact, Hamlet considers this option). Statues in city centres – the figures of dead people – might seem to haunt us: but we can simply ignore them. So, despite its critical importance as a term, hauntology might not be quite apt for all form of the past in the present. However, while we can ignore the past, we still inhabit it: literally, in the buildings we use; we tell it, in the stories we narrate and traditions that we accept or reject; and we speak it in our use of the language. To exchange one Halloween vocabulary with another, the past may not haunt us but it does *possess* us. This possession is not a whole, in the way that traditions used to be perhaps, but rather seizes us in fragmented and uncanny ways.

Possession is at the centre of Nicola Barker's huge novel *Darkmans* (2007). Set in the middle of the first decade of the twenty-first century, in Ashford, Kent in the UK, where the forces of the new (the rebuilding for the Channel tunnel, motorways, new roads and roundabouts) run up directly against the old (an ancient medieval town, the landscape and the coast), it links several characters through possession. The characters are possessed by obsessions, by revenge, by grief and, in a literalising metaphor that takes over the book, by the past in the form of a late medieval jester. Daniel Beede, a former merchant seaman, is obsessed with the past, specifically, a mill which has been taken down and reassembled: however, the tiles from this mill were stolen by a developer and Beede is, it seems, possessed by trying to enact a slow vengeance on him. He is, it seems, paying an art forger a huge amount of money to forge perfectly normal things in the developer's home (a mug, for example) with tiny unsettling things wrong with them, to create a sense of unease and un-at-homeliness. Kane is Beede's estranged son. He illegally deals prescription painkillers because he is psychically paralysed by witnessing the abortive assisted suicide and lingering, painful death of his mother. Gaffar, a Kurd and former small time gangster, is employed by Kane to run errands. They also know Elen, a chiropodist, who has a birth mark and may (or may not) be a witch, her husband Dory/Isadore, who is pretending to be German, and their strangely precious and fey child Fleet. Dory has episodes where he loses his memory and behaves in a strange way (abandoning his car and stealing a horse, for example). At first these are thought of as madness, but slowly it becomes clear it may be that the spirit of a jester called John Scogin has possessed him. He behaves in unsettling ways, hurts his wife: the son, Fleet, may, in fact, be Scogin's son. A story that recurs in the novel tells how Scogin imprisoned several beggars in a barn, and then burnt the barn down – his appearance in the novel is often accompanied by the small of wood smoke, and the novel is obsessed by fire, and images of fire. Scogin also seems to inhabit, from time to time, other characters: Kane, for example, and Beede, in one rather horrifying scene that occurs in a disorienting gap in the novel. But the central form of possession in the novel is language itself.

The novel is reminding us that it isn't us who use language but rather, language that uses us. The text is possessed by etymology and our everyday language is possessed by the past. Characters language become unstable in time: Fleet asks a fisherman if he can look 'at your mathek please?' (Barker 2007, 443) and, until it is realised that 'mathek' is an old word for maggots, his meaning is unclear. More, in a recurring trope, characters fumble chronologically through the whole history of a language to get to what they have to say. To say water one stutters 'Weit . . . vaat . . . vaad . . . votur . . . vater . . . water' (428); stunned by blood another goes 'Reudh . . . Ruber . . . Rood . . . Rud . . . Red . . . Red . . . Blut-red' (667); and Dory, while possessed by John, considers his wife's mole 'mal . . . mole . . . moll . . . moll . . . molest . . . moelstus' (467) (he goes on, darkly sinister, 'surely there must be some kind of *joke* in this?' (467). In these whole histories of words, associations swim to the surface and are made clear, as are their continual, if subliminal, impact on us. This is an example of how we are possessed by the past: we may be able to ignore ghosts or statues, but we cannot ignore the very words we use, precisely because they shape us and our relation to the world.

Past as trauma

Another major way in which contemporary fiction engages with the past is through trauma, the eruption into the present of terrible events from the past. Fiction, which frequently deals with subjectivity and experience, has often explored appalling events both personal and communal.

And, of course, there has been no lack of these in recent human experience. However, the increasing understanding of trauma as a psychiatric, psychoanalytic, ethical, cultural and even legal concept over the last century or so has shaped both fiction and criticism (see Luckhurst 2008). Many of the major novels of the last hundred years can be said to be involved with trauma: for example, Toni Morrison's *Beloved* (1987) deals with the memory of slavery and Kurt Vonnegut's *Slaughterhouse-Five* (1969) with the Second World War, specifically the bombing of Dresden. A large critical movement has grown up to address these matters which includes works from psychiatry (for example, Judith Lewis Herman's *Trauma and Recovery* (1992) and from philosophy (say, Judith Butler's *Precarious Life* (2004) and *Frames of War* (2009)). However, a foundational critical text in this area is Cathy Caruth's collection, *Trauma: Explorations in Memory* (1995). In this, she argues that that trauma consists 'in the structure of its experience or reception: the event is not assimilated fully at the time, but only belatedly, in its repeated possession of the one who experiences it'. (Caruth 1995: 4–5). A traumatic event is not 'taken in' at the moment it happens: rather, it presses on the person who experiences it later, in powerful and distressing ways. Reflecting precisely this belatedness of the traumatic experience, much 'trauma fiction', as Anne Whitehead names it (Whitehead 2004), moves backwards and forward in time. More, and revealing the influence of the Holocaust on this form of writing, it is often highly modernist, experimental or postmodern: as Shoshona Felman, and Dori Laub argue in the case of about Paul Celan's poetry, the 'breakage of the verse enacts the breakage of the world' (Felman and Laub 1992: 25). Finally, trauma fiction is involved, in complex ways, with ethics: the act of vicarious witnessing through fiction is tied to forms of contestable and problematic ethical and even political demands.

One paradigmatic contemporary example of a trauma novel is Hanya Yanagihara's novel *A Little Life* (2015). Very long (not at all little), it begins ostensibly as the story of four young men, friends from the same college, Jude, Willem, Malcolm and JB in New York, and, like Virginia Woolf's *The Waves* or Mary McCarthy's *The Group*, it explores the interplay between them. Each forges a successful career. However, as the novel continues, it begins to focus on Jude, an orphan, and it becomes clear that he is the survivor of absolutely catastrophic and profoundly traumatic sexual abuse. As this emerges, the novel jumps backwards and forward in time to uncover the full history of his abuse. Jude is successful, has a wonderful lover, is surrounded by friends, is adopted by a loving couple of older academics and has what he calls 'happy years': yet he never escapes the traumatic events and eventually kills himself. Indeed, the length of the novel, and the wealth and success of the protagonists serve only to act as a counterpoint to the utterly irrevocable damage done by the sexual abuse to Jude. One debate in trauma theory is over whether trauma can be resolved or not: the point of *A Little Life* seems to be that, unlike some other fictions on this topic, that trauma simply cannot be reconciled to life, cannot be resolved.

In partial contrast to this lack of resolution is Ruth Ozeki's *A Tale For the Time Being* (2013), a complex and multi-layered novel which begins with a 'Hello Kitty' lunch box washed up on the shore of Canada containing letters, a diary and a wristwatch, discovered by Ruth, a Japanese American artist. The diary belongs to Nao, a teenager from Tokyo, and is the central part of the book. At first Ruth and her husband think the diary is part of the Tsunami debris – but it is not, although the novel make much of the Pacific Gyre which links Japan and North America. In this novel, no traumatic incident takes precedence. Nao's family are in despair over a failed business endeavour in the US and their return to Japan: her father is suicidal. Nao is bullied (with sexual connotations) at school: she is sent to her great grandmother, and aged nun. From her, she learns the story her great uncle, killed in the war (it's his wristwatch) and about the personal impact of Japan's traumatic history. All these terrible events – personal, national, historical, contemporary – exist in an interconnected way: indeed, the core of the novel is about the connections between people, time and events. These transnational interconnections work as a way to explore these personal and collective traumas reflecting what Michael Rothberg calls 'multidirectional memory' (Rothberg 2009): the way in which different traumatic memories in fact enable each other rather than crowd each out in a competitive way. In Ozeki's novel, these trauma are nor resolved but opened out by each other and – as it were – contextualised within a cyclical understanding of time (presented as Zen, but I lack the expertise to judge how correct the novel is in this): in contrast to the severance of trauma, Ozeki's work is suggesting a multidirectional form of the 'interconnectedness of all things' in a species of time and in terms of the environment.

Trauma fiction is problematic, in terms of the agonizing and demanding content it brings to light, and much critical work in this field addresses exactly these matters: what does it mean to read and respond to such pain? But these extreme contents also beg further challenges. For example, in his *Postcolonial Witnessing* (2013), Stef Craps argues that much criticism in this field marginalizes or ignores the traumatic experiences of non-Western or minority cultures. More, he suggests that western critics adopt a kind on 'psychiatric universalism' of trauma – the idea that trauma works in the same way in different cultures as it does in the West. These two ideas mean that, Craps suggests, Western scholars find it hard to identify trauma outside its accepted model (Craps 2013: 20ff). This is exacerbated by what Rob Nixon calls the damage wrought by 'slow violence'. In contract to understanding trauma as a kind of puncture in normal life-experience, it's the case that many of our world's most damaging events – especially ecological destruction and the effects of extreme poverty – occur slowly, almost imperceptibly, but with no less destructive effects (Nixon 2011: 10ff). Finally, Craps and others argue that critics – influenced by high modernist writers like Beckett – have assumed that only broken, fragmented works can embody trauma (Craps 2013: 40ff): in fact, a whole array of literary forms, including realist and popular, can deal with trauma.

Conclusion

This brief chapter has looked at some of the modes though which the past is represented in contemporary fiction. Some of these modes are new; some are occurring in a new form; each is only the heading for a diverse range of representation. Each mode implies a different philosophy of history, offering conflicting views on such key matters as the reality of the historical past and the ethical responsibilities that we may (or may not) owe to that past. Beyond their particular affordances, the very multiplicity of these modes in the contemporary suggest that how we understand our relation to the past itself is in the process of change.

By this I don't refer to the ways in which the past is rewritten by sinister political powers, either in the classic Orwellian manner or now as 'fake news'; nor do I mean the (quite normal) revaluation of the historical record, which shapes and reconceptualises the history written by historians; nor do I mean that the past has become fractured with no single past but rather a succession of different histories based on divisions or subdivisions of categories of identity – women, Londoners, Bosnians and so on; nor, do I mean, as Jameson argued, that our sense of historicity and that we have lost History (capital H), or that the past is now simply heritage or propaganda: although all these things are symptomatic of our changing sense of the past .

Instead, I want to suggest that the past has grown simultaneously more important – as trauma, as possession, as memory, as shaping force, for example – and at the same time become much harder to control or understand. The forms of narrative – say, written history or historical fiction – which staked a claim to this control now seem unsatisfactory. They no longer function as a form of foundational narrative. It may be that we are casting about for new forms of historical understanding which embody our historicity, less shaped by the established structures of the representation of the past. Contemporary fiction is the crucible in which these new senses of the past and of pastness itself are being made.

Works cited

Barker, N. (2007) *Darkmans* London: Fourth Estate.

Barry, S. (2016) *Days without End* London: Faber.

Caruth, C. ed. (1995) *Trauma: Explorations in Memory* London: Johns Hopkins University Press.

Cave, T. (2016) *Thinking with Literature: Towards a Cognitive Criticism* Oxford: Oxford University Press.

Craps, S. (2013) *Postcolonial Witnessing: Trauma Out of Bounds* Basingstoke: Palgrave Macmillan.

Derrida, J. Spectres of Marx (1993) trans. Peggy Kamuf London: Routledge

Felman, S. and Laub, D. (1992) *Testimony: Crises of Witnessing in Literature, Psychoanalysis, and History* London: Routledge.

Hemon, A. (2008) *The Lazarus Project* London: Riverhead Books.

Ishiguro, K. (2015) *The Buried Giant* London: Faber.

Jameson, F. (2013) *The Antinomies of Realism* London: Verso.

Levine, C. (2015) *Forms: Whole, Rhythm, Hierarchy, Network* Princeton, NJ.

Luckhurst, R. (2008) *The Trauma Question* London: Routledge.

Mitchell, K. (2013) *Sarah Waters: Contemporary Critical Perspectives* London: Bloomsbury Academic.

Nguyen, V. T. (2015) *The Sympathiser* London: Corsair.

—— (2016) *Nothing Ever Dies: Vietnam and the Memory of War* London: Harvard University Press.

Nixon, R. (2011) *Slow Violence and the Environmentalism of the Poor* Cambridge, MA: Harvard University Press.

O'Gorman, D. (2015) *Fictions of the War on Terror* London: Palgrave Macmillan.

Ozeki, R. (2013) *A Tale for the Time Being* London: Canongate.

Reynolds, S. (2011) *Retromania: Pop Culture's Addition to Its Own Past* London: Faber and Faber.

Rothberg, M. (2009) *Multidirectional Memory: Remembering the Holocaust in the Age of Decolonization* Stanford: Stanford University Press.

Shaw, K. (2018) *Hauntology: The Presence of the Past in Twenty-First Century English Literature* Basingstok: Palgrave Macmillan.

Waters, S. (2002) Fingersmith Virago: London.

Whitehead, A. (2004) *Trauma Fiction* Edinburgh: Edinburgh University Press.

Yanagihara, H. (2015) *A Little Life* London: Picador.

28

HOPE

Emily Horton

In this chapter, I explore the importance of affect in relation to two contemporary twenty-first century writers, Ben Lerner and Ali Smith, both of whose work negotiates modernist techniques as a means to reconceiving novelistic sentiment, rejecting irony and cynicism in favour of candour and hope. They do this in distinct but comparable ways. In Lerner's *10:04* (2014), a Benjaminian concern with the artistic reconfiguration of historical time and the projection of alternate futures currently unavailable enables a sense of hope or promise regarding art's potential for social transformation, even in the context of large-scale socio-economic division and environmental catastrophe. Similarly, in Smith's *Autumn* (2016), an Eliotian attention to the possibility alive within the present – to 'timeless moments' which release the individual from temporal constraints – balances a disaffection with the contemporary Brexit experience, suggesting an opportunity for artistically enabled resistance to provincialism and bureaucracy. These writers' experiments with temporality and form thus consciously upset the established social and political order, instead making visible a hope-inspired outlook, which promises to galvanise critical consciousness and to combat present morbidity. In this way, they contribute to what has been called a 'new sincerity' within twenty-first century fiction (see, for example, Kelly 2016), though their understandings of this differ in notable ways.

   The conceptual basis for this argument emerges from an ongoing critical conversation regarding affect's meaning, and its importance in conceiving politics and political community. One central strand of this conversation, much referenced in recent writing, concerns the idea of affect as a mode of reception fundamentally distinct from emotion, the latter being tied to cognition, the former to non-rational and non-narrational 'intensities'. Thus, as Lawrence Grossman writes, 'Unlike emotions, affective states are neither structured narratively nor organized in response to our interpretations of situations'. Rather, '[they point] to a complex set of effects which circulate around notions of investment and anchoring' (Grossman 2013: 81). Likewise, Brian Massumi argues that while 'an emotion is a subjective content' (Massumi 2002: 28), by contrast, affect exists 'outside expectation and adaptation, as disconnected from meaningful sequencing, from narration, as it is from vital function' (Massumi 2002: 25). These explanations make clear a more indefinite or diffuse understanding of affect, as 'indicating what cannot be clearly named, and what tends to be linked to pre-discursive or pre-ontological bodily excitations' (Schippers 2015: 94).

Depending on their agenda, critics have disagreed on how correct or useful this distinction is, sometimes seeing it as problematic in reinforcing the very mind/body division that the theory was intended to challenge (see Ngai 2005: 27; Schippers 2015: 94). With regards to affect's political role, however, at least some sense of affect's difference from rationality is expedient, in so far as it allows critics to challenge a dominant rationalist imperative within Western society and government. Writing on the centrality of hope, for example, as a necessary condition for conceiving democracy, enabling society to 'think that their present condition could be better' (qtd. in Zournazi 2002: 123), Chantal Mouffe explains that hope's significance relates to its ontology as a form of 'passion', seeing it as a 'kind of place holder for all those things that cannot be reduced to interest or rationality', for 'fantasies, desire, all those things that a rationalist approach is unable to understand in the very construction of human subjectivity and identity' (qtd. in Zournazi 2002: 124). For Mouffe, indeed, this affective emphasis allows for a belief in a 'social imaginary', a symbolically invested fantasy, which might reconceive democracy otherwise, in juxtaposition to rational choice or universalistic models (Zournazi 2002: 124). In this way Mouffe underlines affect's primacy as a vehicle for mobilizing political change, in so far as current global institutions are based primarily on calculative rationalism: on self-interest and universal rules of moral conduct (Zournazi 2002: 123, 125–127).

In understanding hope in this way, Mouffe thus provides a key example of affect-centred political philosophy, reasserting the necessity that individuals 'have those affects of their imagination mobilized towards something' (qtd. in Zournazi 2002: 126). Judith Butler, in her writing on grief, also provides a notable instance of this mode of thinking, underlining the priority of affective 'relationality' as a means towards re-envisaging social responsibility. She writes,

> Many people think that grief is privatizing, that it returns us to a solitary situation and is, in that sense, depoliticizing. But I think it furnishes a sense of political community of a complex order, and it does this first of all by bringing to the fore the relational ties that have implications for theorizing fundamental dependency and ethical responsibility.
>
> (Butler 2004: 22)

This reading of grief thus invokes a political understanding of precariousness and vulnerability, a recognition of 'the thrall in which our relations with others hold us [. . .] in ways that challenge the very notion of ourselves as autonomous and in control' (Butler 2004: 23). The importance of this perception lies in the fact that, as with Mouffe's writing on hope, 'it conveys how ethical responsibility is not inherently at odds with the notion of the decentred subject. Rather, ethical responsibility is anchored in the subject's constitution as relational' (Schippers 2015: 91–92).

Indeed, what is crucial to both of these accounts of affect is their awareness of how a non-rational and decentered affective experience might provide a necessary ground for appreciating social interdependency – one which is not provided by more rationalistic or depth-oriented readings of the subject. Birgit Schippers expresses this nicely when she writes that 'affect's equivocal qualities constitute the promise of an affective ethics', one aimed not only at post-traumatic reconciliation but also 'at political transformation' (Schippers 2015: 94). It is, in other words, the non-cognitive and precarious that promise to weld identity and democratic community in the global world; by registering relationality, affect also registers complex ethical ties to an immanent material world, and to an unknown planetary future still unfolding within the present. With respect to the contemporary novel, this emerges as a significant perception both thematically and formally, in so far as it speaks to the centrality of reapproaching selfhood and identity, of mapping out new, affect-centered forms of spatial-temporal consciousness.

In this chapter, as stated above, I aim to explore this understanding by examining two novels in particular: Ali Smith's *Autumn* and Ben Lerner's *10:04*, in each case highlighting the text's attentiveness to questions of affect. This orientation is, notably, a gesture towards a new type of political novel: each text can be read to understand affect as a means towards rereading present political realities, connecting these to alternative notions of possibility or connectivity. Affects are seen, in other words, as intensities that accompany important shifts of creative perception, which in turn facilitate a sense of promise or disappointment regarding future democracy. In accordance with Butler's writing above, there is, unmistakably, an element of equivalence to these depictions: they emerge not as guarantees of positive change or transformation, but instead as, in Lerner's words, 'indeterminacy', a 'possibility of imaginative redescription' (qtd in Smith 2015: n. p.). Nevertheless, in the context of these novels, these affective recognitions are more often than not embraced and enacted, seen as creative openings within which hope and connection might yet be restored.

★★★

In order to appreciate this understanding, I begin by considering the affective dimensions of *10:04*, mapping out its approach to this subject in relation to two corresponding concerns: firstly, time as a source of promise rather than constraint, and secondly, a critique of consumer capitalism as it figures both in various 'practices of everyday life' and in the supposedly more progressive art world. These concerns are interconnected in ways that help explain the structure of the novel, recognizing a fundamental disjunction at the heart of late capitalist temporality.

Thus, while on the one hand the text establishes from the start the author-narrator's plan to 'project [himself] into several futures simultaneously', and in this way to 'work [his] way from irony to sincerity' (Lerner 2014: 4) – a pointedly affective motivation, – on the other hand, the reader confronts the narrator's panorama of professional and existential anxieties, all of which are compounded by the pressures imposed by the global market. Indeed, contemplating the stress of his upcoming submission date, again presented as a condition of his advance for the novel, alongside his best-friend's maternal disquiet, these personal stresses are further augmented by the menace of geological peril, including an upcoming storm which threatens to leave New York City underwater. In this way, from the novel's opening, the fiction situates itself in response to global capitalist crisis, this being seen to impinge not only upon the narrator, but everyone around him.

Indeed, the event of crisis is here underlined not simply via reference to an accumulation of personal and public anxieties, but also to a disjointed bodily condition that encompasses both the narrator and the city itself. Thus, sitting in the pediatric ward of a hospital, where 'a giant octopus was painted on the wall' (Lerner 2014: 4), and having been diagnosed with Marfan syndrome, a disorder specific to 'the long-limbed and flexible' (Lerner 2014: 4), the narrator begins to experience his body in a manner radically different from what he is used to, as a cephalopod, whose poor 'proprioceptive inputs' means that it 'cannot integrate' information regarding its surroundings 'into a larger picture': it/he 'cannot read the realistic fiction the world appears to be' (Lerner 2014: 6–7).

On the one hand, this imagined bodily transformation offers a metaphor for the narrator's sense of displacement within the current world order: his crisis condition threatens his sense of security and reliable self-understanding. At the same time, Lerner's choice of terminology here in referring to the genre of 'realistic fiction' is not incidental: the implication is that this post-millennial crisis demands a new approach to 'realist' representation, one which better registers the tangible estrangement produced by global capitalist order. Indeed, by extending this diagnosis to the city more broadly, as a living 'organism', which confronts the storm also in the form of a giant octopus, 'an aerial sea monster with a single centered eye around which tentacular rain bands swirled' (Lerner 2014: 17), Lerner underlines the geopolitical nature of this literary anxiety;

he seeks to carve out a new form which will speak to the extensive proportions of the current planetary predicament – indeed, to seek out a new constellation for planetary seeing.

As visible within this stated ambition, the text's particular rejoinder to the current world situation can be understood in terms of a pointed injunction towards Benjaminian constellationary thinking: a view towards recognizing connections already existent 'between different objects, registers, and discourses' (Malinowska and Lebek, 2017: 114). In effect, the project involves a Benjaminian dialectical reconfiguration of historical time, shaped by an attention to futurity as well as the past, with a view not simply to contemplating the ruins of history, but also to reconstituting the present and future in new and hopeful ways – ways which allow for the recognition of previously unseen possibilities.

Thus, Benjamin's 'angel of history' is featured here as one significant textual reference, conjured explicitly through a reproduction of Klee's *Angelus Novus*, alongside the passage from the 'Theses on the Philosophy of History' which famously interprets this, and furthermore echoed by the trope of the storm, which likewise functions as metaphor for progress's potential for destruction (see also Vermeulen 2016: 2). Even so, through allusion to two additional cultural reference points – Robert Zemeckis's 1985 *Back to the Future* and Jules Basien Lepage's 1879 *Joan of Arc*, both also reproduced visually within the novel – this historical dialecticism is here notably complicated by an attention to the present, and to the promise of alternative futures currently unimagined. Thus, this unlikely comparison, involving an intermingling of elite and popular culture, also makes explicit a sense of equivocality between two temporal outlooks: the first, like Benjamin's angel, with his 'back to the future', figures the past, when revealed, as capable of erasing any reliable future. By contrast, the second sees the dialectic as capturing the promise of future possibility: 'here it's a presence, not an absence, that eats away at her hand: she's being pulled into the future' (Lerner 2014: 9).

Benjamin's dialectic thus emerges as a crucial artistic means of conjuring the dreamed reality of the past, but also of conceiving a future outside of the apocalyptic. Indeed, what Lerner seems to be drawing on most chiefly here is Benjamin's focus on a dialectical 'awakening': a sense of emergence from a mode of collective daydreaming into historical awareness, wherein 'the past might turn over dialectically to become an inspiration for awakened consciousness' (Benjamin 1982: 490–491).[1] As becomes clear through repeated references to a messianic afterlife, also ascribed to a quotation from Benjamin's writing, wherein '*Everything will be as it is now, just a little different*' (Lerner 2014: 19), Lerner is concerned chiefly with how dialectical awareness might also anticipate a yet unimagined future, a space of 'indeterminacy', as Giorgio Agamben puts it, wherein 'possibility and reality, potentiality and actuality, become indistinguishable' (Agamben 1993: 55). Indeed, as Adorno's writing on Benjamin's constellations argues, the point is to seek out a means to avoid complacency, an outlook via which perspectives can 'be fashioned that displace and estrange the world, reveal it to be, with its rifts and crevices, as indigent and distorted as it will appear one day in the messianic light' (Adorno 2005: 247). In this way, the notions of awakening and constellational thinking carry an expressly political function here, as ways of seeking out a means to change in a context of passive normativity.

The narrator's book project itself can be understood perhaps most clearly in this light, as part of a series of moments of dawning political awareness, which allow for new narrative beginnings and alternative endings. Indeed, the novel works through various individual political awakenings, which function to capture a larger appreciation of time as susceptible to reexamination and reconstruction. One key trope here which makes this project explicit is the novel's focus on auratic moments, or, as Lerner describes them, 'flickering' presences, which 'glow' with 'a certain aura' (Lerner 2014: 15, 19). For Benjamin, these, more than anything, are dialectical images, 'flashing up momentarily' amidst everyday relations, which function as clues to an experience of awakening, allowing for the past to 'be captured' as a function of oppressive consumer realities now revealed (Benjamin 1973: 49). Likewise, the novel's focus throughout on such moments acts as a signal for a new way of seeing, which, while it makes apparent oppressive and hidden relations of production structuring daily practices, also registers alternative, more hopeful and communal, possibilities for a yet unfulfilled future.

The narrator's response to the effect of the storm on the city, and indeed, his register of the city's response more broadly, offers one poignant example of this narrative strategy, reaffirming a Benjaminian emphasis on dialectical awakening. Visiting the supermarket with Alex in the build-up to the storm, and holding a container of instant coffee in his hand, the narrator experiences a moment of sublime demystification: 'estranging the routine of shopping just enough to make me viscerally aware of both the miracle and insanity of the mundane economy' (Lerner 2014: 19). What follows is an explicatory breakdown of the social relations underpinning the coffee trade, which terminates with the impression that the container 'began to glow' (Lerner 2014: 19). Key to this apparently auratic experience is the impression that the threat of the storm itself, with all its Benjaminian philosophical undertones, is what reveals this object's meaning, its capacity to ground planes and close highways refiguring reality in a new and illuminating light. As the narrator puts it again, quoting Benjamin, '*Everything will be as it is now, just a little different*' (Lerner 2014: 19). In consequence:

> what normally felt like the only possible world became one among many, its meaning everywhere up for grabs, however briefly – in the passing commons of a train, in a container of tasteless coffee.
>
> (Lerner 2014: 19)

In other words, the event of the coming storm provokes a rereading of existing social relations, which in turn enables the recognition of alternate futures previously unimagined. In effect, the storm facilitates a reviewing not only of the past, but also of the future, a cognitive reconstruction that registers the existence of multiple possible narratives.

This experience of phenomenal indeterminacy is replayed at various moments throughout the novel, in the build-up to the storm, but also subsequently, as a response to artworks that the narrator experiences, or stories he hears. What is significant about these encounters, however, is how their promise is subject to actual history, the sense of hope or anticipation they provide being potentially shattered by the reassertion of mundane reality. As the narrator puts it with respect to the events he experiences around the storm, it is not as though these moments are 'just over, but retrospectively erased' (Lerner 2014: 24): as they 'had been enabled by a future that had never arrived', he explains, 'they could not be remembered from this future that, at and as the present, had obtained; they'd faded from the photograph' (Lerner 2014: 24). Here, via reference to *Back to the Future*, Lerner underlines the violence of existing historical relations: late capitalism's determinate encroachment on fantasied futures, he implies, shuts down a sense of hope that fiction and art can provide.

Interestingly, this view of mundane reality echoes the writing of Hannah Arendt, whose understanding of politics reiterates Mouffe's affective reading above. For Arendt, also an active defender of Benjamin's dialectical thinking (see Arendt 1968, 1998), a legitimate politics entails a form of collective storytelling, in the sense of an attempt, narratively orchestrated, to confront and potentially modify future experience: 'If the world is to contain a public space, it cannot be erected for one generation and planned for the living only; it must transcend the life-span of mortal men' (Arendt 1998: 55). In this way, a future-looking narrative – or indeed, multiple narratives – regarding the potential revision of social experience, is necessary in order to locate political hope outside the merely intimate, in the realm of public order. As Arendt continues, 'Without the transcendence into a potentially earthly immortality, no politics, strictly speaking, no common realm, is possible. For [. . .] the common world is what we enter when we are born and what we leave behind when we die. It transcends our lifespans into past and future alike' (Arendt 1998: 55). In other words, political practice requires a narrative that extends beyond the daily routine of the present, registering public life's trans-generational character.

Lerner, significantly, reiterates this concern by placing stress on future collectivity, repeatedly discussing conjoint imagining between individuals as a form of 'co-constructing', rather than simply constructing, future worlds (Lerner 2014: 8, 11, 15). This emphasis is underlined through-out the novel through an attention to the movement of the city, such that experience is conceived not as static or molecular, but instead as interwoven, immanent, corporeal, and communal (see, for example, Lerner 2014: 17, 18, 29, 33, 53, 85, 134, 143, 158, 224). As the narrator describes at one point:

> I was aware that water surrounded the city, and that the water moved; I was aware of the delicacy of the bridges and tunnels spanning it, and of the traffic through those arteries, as though some cortical reorganization now allowed me to take the infrastructure per-sonally, a proprioceptive flicker in advance of the communal body.
>
> (Lerner 2014: 28)

In this way, through an understanding of the city as a living organism, an imminent 'communal body' in the making, political unity emerges as a key concern for Lerner, upheld through hope, and complementing a voiced conception of politics as artistic and creational: founded on an affective vision of utopian possibility.

Even so, as Arendt warns, what politics seems to be replaced with in the modern age is a type of fiction that shuts down possibility, substituting creative foresight with a present moment that is bureaucratically managed and standardized, rather than politically understood. As she puts it, 'Statis-tical uniformity is by no means a harmless scientific ideal; it is the no longer secret political ideal of a society which, entirely submerged in the routine of everyday living, is at peace with the scientific outlook inherent in its very existence' (Arendt 1998: 43). Similarly, Lerner laments this reality as he repeatedly bewails the ubiquity of the profit motive, making clear his anxiety that market selfishness co-opts even his most empathetic or artistic of moments, as when he feeds a stranger, imagines having a child, helps at a food co-op, or as he makes plans to write this novel (Lerner 2014: 46–47, 93–94, 95–96, 155–156). This latter concern is underscored at various points throughout the novel, as the narrator repeatedly meditates over art's (often failed) potential to escape a consumer-oriented outlook (see, for example, Lerner 2014: 4, 72–73, 129–134, 153–157, 182).

In the end, however, despite this anxiety, the novel's overall viewpoint is optimistic, appealing, like Mouffe, to hope in art's, and especially experimental art's, democratic potential. This can be seen in particular through two scenes in the novel: firstly, the narrator's reflections on Christian Marclay's *The Clock*, a 'twenty-four-hour montage of thousands of scenes from movies [. . .] each scene indicat[ing] the time with a shot of a timepiece or its mention in dialogue' (Lerner 2014: 52); and secondly, through his engagement with the so-called 'Institute for Totaled Art' (Lerner 2014: 131), a curatorial experiment involving damaged artwork 'declared to have "zero value"' (Lerner 2014: 129). In the first case, *The Clock* is, in effect, what drives the narrator-author's decision to write the novel (Lerner 2014: 54). What is inspiring about the piece is what it says about the distinctive nature of fictional time, how, despite the fact that 'fictional time [is] synchronized with nonfictional duration' (Lerner 2014: 53), the division between fictional time and real time is not 'collapsed': 'while the duration of a real minute and *The Clock*'s minute were mathematically indistinguishable, they were nevertheless minutes from different worlds' (Lerner 2014: 54). In this way, art's temporality retains its political promise, even as it seems (deceptively) to coincide with mundane reality. As the narrator comments, 'I felt acutely how many different days could be built out of a day, felt more possibility than determinism, the utopian glimmer of fiction' (Lerner 2014: 54).

The narrator's encounter with the Institute for Totaled Art also registers this utopian energy, chronicling how art's public value may still be separated from market appraisal. Thus, also based on a real-world project – Elka Krajewska's 'Salvage Art Institute', mentioned in the acknowledgements – the Institute for Totaled Art collects and showcases art damaged in some way or another, which on account of this damage and the relative cost of restoration, has been written off by an insurer as financially worthless, or, as the institute puts it, 'totaled'. What is particularly compelling about this artwork for the narrator are those pieces which, despite having been included here, appear as if they have not suffered 'any perceptible material transformation' (Lerner 2014: 133), thus seemingly retaining their aesthetic value, whilst nevertheless having had their exchange value 'extracted' (Lerner 2014: 134). As the narrator understands it, such instances involve 'a reversal of the kind of recontextualization associated with Marcel Duchamp' and the 'ready-made' (Lerner 2014: 133), achieving 'a kind of magical power' not on the basis of a 'monetizable signature', like any other branded product, but instead on account of this very signature having been extracted. 'What was the word for that liberation?' the narrator pointedly asks, '*Apocalypse? Utopia?*' (Lerner 2014: 133), thus reaffirming a sense of possibility regarding future socio-economic orders.

In drawing attention to this artwork, then, the novel invokes art's capacity to escape 'the fetishism of the market' (Lerner 2014: 134): to regain a value 'before or after capital' (Lerner 2014: 134). Such a conceptualization speaks again to a Benjaminian rereading of space and time, wherein a past or future messianic other-world is envisioned in the dialectical notion of sameness combined with difference: again, '*Everything will be as it is now, just a little different*'. Here, in implicitly invoking this utopian conception, the novel facilitates an affective-political reclamation of art, not simply as an aesthetic object, but as a potentially revolutionary event, capable of envisioning alternative, non-pecuniary future orders. In this way, Lerner echoes Mouffe's appreciation regarding politics' ultimate dependency on hope, adding to this the recognition that it is art that might provide this democratic vision.

★★★

Ali Smith's *Autumn*, like Lerner's *10:04*, also pointedly addresses art's role in responding to a contemporary climate of crisis and in endorsing hope, as opposed to irony, as a pertinent affective outlook. Commenting on this directly, Smith notes, 'Art is one of the prime ways we have of opening ourselves and going beyond ourselves. That's what art is, it's the product of the human being in the world and imagination, all coming together' (qtd. in Laing 2016: n.p.). In *Autumn*, this conjunction of real-world and imaginative forces takes the form of an openly topical reply to the event of Brexit, which nevertheless registers this event's correspondence with an earlier political scandal, the Profumo Affair of 1963. Thus, in investigating Brexit's significance for twenty-first century Britain, *Autumn* also indexes its place within a wider historical panorama of UK governmental mendacity, making it clear that this should not be seen as exceptional in meaning or tenor. Nevertheless, also like *10:04*, the novel explicitly contemplates ways of looking beyond this restrictive moment, and of envisioning alternative perspectives and alternate futures more genuinely committed to democratic values.

One way it achieves this, again as in *10:04*, is through a modernist investigation of time, in this case calling on an Eliotian idea of present possibility, and of seasonal change and organic reconstruction. Thus, while on the one hand *Autumn* chronicles the overwhelming pace of recent current events, making clear contemporary society's entrapment in an onslaught of radical shifts and scandals – including the murder of Jo Cox (Smith 2016: 38); the Brexit referendum (Smith 2016: 53, 59); the Nazi flag displayed in Nice (Smith 2016: 63); environmental crisis (epigraph); and the refugee crisis, accompanied by ongoing debates about (and attacks on) immigration (Smith 2016: 12, 53, 111) – on the other hand, it also underlines a natural order existing outside this fast-paced experience, in which, as in Eliot's *Four Quartets*, there is destruction ('the leaves falling off and rotting into earth' (Smith 2016: 123)), but also restoration and renovation (the naked twigs 'splitting into a million billion brand new buds' (Smith 2016: 123)). This, what–might–be–called 'planetary' understanding of time thus contrasts the astronomical speed of contemporary human centred, or 'anthropocene' life, offering hope in the recognition that time is constant, if constantly changing.

For Eliot, this attention to seasonal change was, of course, a historical response to the Second World War, and to the pervasive destruction and trauma that seemed to erase time's forward movement in favour of endless, unchanging horror. As Charles Bax notes, 'Despite the prominence of violence and destruction during World War II, themes of hope and ideas that humanity can overcome the atrocities of war are interwoven into [. . .] *Four Quartets*' (Bax 2010: 4):

> The themes of humanity's relationship to time, social dissatisfaction, violence, and salvation are present in all four poems through the recurring images of the seasons, destruction, and both physical and purgatorial fire as well as the repetition of beginnings and endings.
>
> (Bax 2010: 41)

In this way, while *Four Quartets* confronts the horror of war, and the sense of inertia and despair that this provokes – an experience that expunges all alternative pasts and makes 'All time [. . .] irredeemable' (Eliot 2009, *Burnt Norton* I, 4), – it nevertheless balances this with an awareness of possibility made available through temporal appreciation, a sense of hope in the consciousness of the present moment's promise, as well as in the cognizance of time's cyclical (and often destructive) nature. As Eliot puts it in *Burnt Norton*, 'Only through time time is conquered' (Eliot 2009, II, 44).

One particularly significant aspect of this temporal awareness, shared by Smith, is Eliot's focus on 'timeless moments', which reflect an appreciation of how time might conquer time through a focus on lived experience. As Kenneth Paul Kramer explains, '*Four Quartets* contemplates [. . .] how timeless moments – of redeeming reciprocity, of graced consciousness – shine through physical landscapes and release the poet from temporal enchainments' (Kramer 2007: xiii). In part this is achieved through meditative contemplation of these landscapes, wherein 'the poet discovers that spiritual substance cannot be found fully in himself', but rather in his relationship to his surroundings, and in particular in 'unforeseen moments of redeeming reciprocity' (Kramer 2007: xiii). These moments, as Kramer reads them, 'are then retrieved and appropriated through an interplay of detached memory and disciplined imagination' (Kramer 2007: xiii), such that through backward and forward movement across time, and through perception of the vital uniqueness of the present moment, the poet learns to engage with his environment more critically. As Pedro Blas González likewise explains, 'Eliot creatively avoids the trap of treating time like an abstraction' (González 2014: n.p.), disfiguring it in terms of 'what might have been', rather than what is. Instead, 'for Eliot, time is best measured in vital moments that metastasize into years, culminating in eternity' (González 2014: n.p.) and in an awareness of 'cyclical time' that ultimately reminds us of how 'memory fails us' (González 2014: n.p.). These are his outlook's defining features.

In *Four Quartets*, this becomes visible in a number of prominent symbols: for example, in the emphasis on the rose garden in *Burnt Norton*, as an emblem of lived experience, as opposed to conjecture ('What might have been and what has been/Point to one end, which is always present' (Eliot 2009, I, 9–10)); in the image of fire in *East Coker* as a figure for life's intensity ('a lifetime burning in every moment' (Eliot 2009, V, 23)); in the preoccupation with travel in *The Dry Salvages*, and what this might suggest regarding passing time's impact upon the self ('You are not those who saw the harbour/Receding, or those who will disembark' (Eliot 2009, III, 27–28)); and in the stress on history in *Little Gidding* as a source of potential redemption based in the remembered moment ('A people without history/Is not redeemed from time, for history is a pattern/Of timeless moments' (Eliot 2009, V, 20–22)). In this way, Eliot underlines his view of temporal knowledge as at once dependent upon awareness of the past, but also attentive to the promise of renewal alive within the present.

Autumn, developing Eliot's thinking, reflects a similar consciousness both of history's weight in the present and of the unmistakable vitality of the lived moment, which is a source of visible hope within the novel. Thus, time appears here, on the one hand, as disturbingly fleeting, the media reflecting 'the usual huge changes there've been in the last half hour' (Smith 2016: 137), and on the other hand, also trapped within a bureaucratic motionlessness and homogeneity that conjures 'a 1950s utilitarian utopia' (Smith 2016: 54): so slow that Elisabeth manages to read 'nearly a whole book' (*Brave New World*) whilst waiting to send her passport application. Nevertheless, countering both of these experiences is an appreciation of lived time or the temporality of the moment, which allows for a sense of hope despite overwhelming constraint. This is visible in *Autumn*'s representation of this season as one of ongoing growth and life – 'the flowers are still coming. The hedgerows are still humming' (Smith 2016: 85) – as well as in its emphasis on particular felt moments, still happening even in the present: for example, when Daniel describes his experience as 'an old story so new that it's in the middle of happening, writing itself right now with no knowledge of where or how it will end' (Smith 2016: 181). What becomes visible in these passages is a discernment of time's immanence and of the ethical and political promise this offers for challenging contemporary cynicism. As Felix Guattari also puts it, 'there is an ethical choice in favour of the richness of the possible, an ethics and politics of the virtual that [. . .] make[s] use of [. . .] procedures that are more collective, more social, more political' (Guattari 1995: 94). In this way, likewise, *Autumn* registers possibility as a source of optimism and strength within the present, defying contemporary society's relentless speed, as well as its petty bureaucracy.

Significantly, then, what the novel is *not* trying to do is to escape politics by insisting upon the present – the narrator, as it were, blinkering herself to the past's importance or to wider present political machinations. As Idelbar Avelar remarks, this is a concern within a contemporary context wherein 'it is proper to the market to live in a perpetual present' and wherein 'the erasure of the past as past is the cornerstone for all commodification': 'the past [. . .] forgotten because the market demands that the new replace the old without leaving a remainder' (Avelar 1999: 2). By contrast, *Autumn*'s focus on lived time repeatedly recalls history's ongoing significance, the structural juxtaposition between Daniel and Elisabeth's voices contrasting contemporary post-Brexit racism and bigotry with memories of WWII atrocities and 1960s scandal. Indeed, Daniel's dream of dead 'washed up' bodies on a beach, their presence without impact on vacationers 'holidaying up the shore', who sit in the shade 'working on a computer' or 'reading a little screen' (Smith 2016: 12), could, ignoring the mention of present technology, as easily be taken as a comment on his own WWII memories, the dream-like status of the scene and the knowledge of his own escape from Nazi persecution leaving the passage open to multiple contextualizations.

Moreover, concentrating on lived time cannot mean here a blocking out of the present political context or a reduction of value to what is private and intimately lived. As Christos Tsiolkas
notes, this is a pressing concern within our current global situation, given that, on account of
'the increasing individualism of the world we live in', we often 'see ourselves as consumers and
individuals' rather than 'members of a community', with 'limited understanding of what kind of
responsibility we have' (Zournazi 2002: 107). By contrast, *Autumn* self-consciously responds to
this anxiety by reading lived time as encompassing both personal and shared experience, registering the need for rebellion against a repressive system (Smith 2016: 250), but also participation
within a polis made of up multiple communities. As Elisabeth notes, what she is fighting for, in
questioning the fence that has been constructed near her house, is 'common land': 'Common land
is by definition not private' (Smith 2016: 140). In other words, she seeks to recognize a wider
community than post-Brexit culture acknowledges.

As with *10:04*, this understanding directly impacts upon the novel's view of art, both in the
style of the novel itself and in its more direct reflections on artistic production. Thus, on the one
hand, the novel addresses precisely 'what it feels like, to feel' (Smith 2016: 7), repeatedly conjuring
a sense of present immediacy concentrated in lived experience and in the hope this proffers for
change. This is visible, for example, in the text's promise to relate Daniel's story despite the failures of Elisabeth's memory, rescuing it 'whole from the place in human brain cell storage which
keeps intact but filed away the dimensionality of everything we experience' (Smith 2016: 123).
In effect, by making this representation possible despite the limitations of Elisabeth's memory, the
novel grants the reader access to Elisabeth's lived past, showing how 'timeless moments' did and
do exist, despite her present cynicism. Similarly, a focus throughout on the act of vision reiterates
a sense that life must be lived (or seen) intensely and relationally, for example when Elisabeth
recalls Daniel's eyes opening and thinks 'how it was like that moment when you just happen
to see the streetlights come on and it feels like your being given a gift, or a chance, or that you
yourself've been singled out and chosen by the moment' (Smith 2016: 74). Here, her sense of
newly gifted potential underlines the importance of seeing (and seeing each other) clearly: her
world is reshaped and given promise simply by being perceived through the eyes of her friend.
As Daniel puts it elsewhere, 'We have to hope [. . .] that the people who love us and who know
us a little bit will in the end have seen us truly. In the end, not much else matters'. (Smith 2016:
160) Thus, relationality is granted pride of place amongst the novel's values.

Interestingly, the text's reflections on artistic production, made explicit through its focus on
the work of Pauline Boty – the British pop artist made famous for painting Christine Keeler in the
context of the Profumo Affair (Smith 2016: 151) – build on this understanding, reiterating the hope
that comes through grasping lived encounters and also registering connectivity between individuals. Thus, for Elisabeth, what is compelling about Boty is not simply her attention to gendered
representation – her focus on 'highly sexualized images' and their relation to patriarchy (Smith
2016: 155) – but, more centrally, her devotion to making society reconceive its received images:
her paintings challenging 'the image everyone thought they knew', precisely by '*not be[ing]* it'
(Smith 2016: 242). Indeed, her focus on 1960s pop culture is intended to wake society from its
stupor, shocking convention in a way that made pictures 'sort of alive' (Smith 2016: 245). Thus,
as Boty herself explains in the novel, her work reflects a desire 'to be vital' (Smith 2016: 245): to
suspend time, 'rather than us be suspended in it' (Smith 2016: 245). In this way, art becomes a way
to 'to catch [life]' and its 'intense happiness' (Smith 2016: 252), to capture 'the moment before
something had actually happened' (Smith 2016: 252) and make it valuable.

In the last few pages of the novel, in which Daniel finally opens his eyes to look at Elisabeth
(Smith 2016: 258), and when Elisabeth's mother takes a stand against the government's immigration policy by throwing objects (notably, antiques) at a detention centre fence (Smith 2016: 255),

the novel reinforces this message by underscoring again both its personal and political value, seeing hope as encapsulated in the moment in which individuals challenge convention in pursuit of justice. As Elisabeth's mother puts it, she is '*bombarding that fence with people's histories and with the artefacts of less cruel and more philanthropic times*' (Smith 2016: 255). The very ending of the novel, in which the text describes a 'wide-open rose' alive with colour, strengthens this picture, echoing Eliot's closing image of a rose bud fighting its way to life despite the cold. Here, unmistakably, is a vision of autumn as full of potential.

★★★

What connects these two fictions conceptually, then, is a concern with contrasting temporal orders, and with how certain temporalities explored within modernism promise more genuine forms of hope for the present day. In Lerner's novel, this is tied to Benjamin's dialectic, and in particular, to his idea of dialectical awakening, this enabling a demystification of everyday experience that in turn makes visible a variety of previously unexplored future possibilities. As Lerner's narrator puts it at one point, 'what normally felt like the only possible world became one among many' (Lerner 2014: 19), and again, '*Everything will be as it is now, just a little different*' (Lerner 2014: 19). Smith's intertextual references to Eliot also reinforce a similar temporal promise, underlining the value of lived experience as a basis for confidence, both registering the past's importance to the present, as well as the moment's potential to envelop meaningful change.

In either case, then, hope is understood both as temporally located and political, oriented towards shared community in such a way as to include and value the presence of difference. As Mouffe writes, the consequence of this project lies in its aim to respond to the supposed stasis of time in the present day, where 'people are told that there is no alternative to the neo-liberal hegemony, and that it is here to stay' (Zournazi 2002: 123). By contrast, for both of these texts, as for Mouffe, hope lies in politics' capacity to offer something 'to look forward to': 'perfect democracy' itself will never be completed, she laments, but at least 'there is something to fight for', despite knowing 'we will never be able to reach it' (Zournazi 2002: 129). Lerner and Smith recognize this and look to provide contingent alternatives; their politics are provisional, yet they resolutely seek out positive change.

Note

1 The translation of Benjamin's work here comes from Goldstein (2006).

Works cited

Adorno, T., (2005). *Minima Moralia: Reflections from a Damaged Life*. Translated by E. F. N. Jephcott. London: Verso.

Agamben, G., (1993). *The Coming Community*. Translated by M. Hardt. Minneapolis: University of Minnesota Press.

Arendt, H., (1998 [1958]). *The Human Condition*. Second Edition. Chicago: University of Chicago Press.

—— (1968). Walter Benjamin. *The New Yorker*, [online] 19 October. Available at: www.newyorker.com/magazine/1968/10/19/walter-benjamin [Accessed: 4 October, 2017].

Avelar, I., (1999). *The Untimely Present: Postdictatorial Latin American Fiction and the Task of Mourning*. London: Duke University Press.

Bax, C., (2010). *The Vortex and World War II: Ezra Pound and T. S. Eliot's Poetic Treatment of Wartime*. [MA theses] Clemson University. *All Theses*. 943. Available at: http://tigerprints.clemson.edu/all_theses/943 [Accessed: 4 October, 2017].

Benjamin, W., (1982). *Gesmmelte Schriften V*. Edited by R. Tiedemann and H. Schweppenhauser with the collaboration of T. W. Adorno and G. Scholem. Frankfurt am Main: Suhrkamp Verlag.

—— (1973). *Charles Baudelaire: A Lyric Poet in the Era of High Capitalism*. Translated by H. Zohn. London: New Left Books.

Butler, J., (2004). *Precarious Life*. London: Verso.

Eliot, T. S., (2009). *Four Quartets*. New Edition. London: Faber and Faber.

Goldstein, W. S., (2006). Dreaming of the Collective Awakening: Walter Benjamin and Ernst Bloch's Theories of Dreams. *Humanity and Society*, 30(1), 50–66.

González, P. B., (2014). Time and Permanence in T. S. Eliot's *Four Quartets. The University Bookman*, [online] 26 October. Available at: www.kirkcenter.org/bookman/article/time-permanence-eliot-four-quartets [Accessed: 4 October, 2017].

Grossman, L., (2013). *We Gotta Get Out of This Place: Popular Conservatism and Popular Culture*. London: Routledge.

Guattari, F., (1995). *Chaosmosis: An Ethicoaesthetic Paradigm*. Translated by J. Pefanis. Bloomington: Indiana University Press.

Kelly, A., (2016). The New Sincerity. In *Postmodern/Postwar: And After*. Iowa City: University of Iowa Press, 197–208.

Kramer, K. P., (2007). *Redeeming Time: T.S. Eliot's Four Quartets*. Lanham, MD: Cowley Publications.

Laing, O., (2016). Ali Smith [Interview]. *The Guardian*, [online] 16 October. Available at: www.theguardian.com/books/2016/oct/16/ali-smith-autumn-interview-how-can-we-live-ina-world-and-not-put-a-hand-across-a-divide-brexit-profu [Accessed: 4 October, 2017].

Lerner, B., (2014). *10:04*. London: Granta.

Malinowska, A. and Lebek, C., (2017). *Materiality and Popular Culture: The Popular Life of Things*. London: Routledge.

Massumi, B., (2002). *Parables for the Virtual: Movement, Affect, Sensation*. London: Duke University Press.

Ngai, S., (2005). *Ugly Feelings*. Cambridge, MA: Harvard University Press.

Schippers, B., (2015). Violence, Affect, and Ethics. In M. Lloyd, ed. *Butler and Ethics*. Edinburgh: Edinburgh University Press.

Smith, A., (2016). *Autumn*. London: Penguin.

Smith, K., (2015). Time Is a Flat Circle: Ben Lerner Interviewed. *The Quietus*, [online] 8 February. Available at: http://thequietus.com/articles/17190-ben-lerner-interview-1004-leaving-atocha-station-poetry-time-knausgaard [Accessed: 4 October, 2017].

Vermeulen, P., (2016). How Should a Person Be (Transpersonal)? Ben Lerner, Roberto Esposito, and the Biopolitics of the Future. *Political Theory*, 45(5), 659–681.

Zournazi, M., (2002). *Hope: New Philosophies for Change*. Melbourne, Australia: Pluto Press.

PART IV

Case studies

29

GRANTA'S 'BEST OF YOUNG BRITISH NOVELISTS'

Katy Shaw

The twenty-first century witnessed the rise of a new literary community, an eclectic collective of tastemakers and trend setters that collectively combine to shape the field of contemporary literature. From authors to agents, publishers to booksellers and critics to book clubs, the digital age has turned everyone into a critic of contemporary writings. Within this dynamic environment, literary prizes, awards and lists fuse the shared interests of the cultural and the economic in their influencing role over the ways in which new fictions are produced, distributed and read. This chapter examines the rise of literary prize culture in the new millennium, its function, potential limitations, and the role of literary prizes, awards and lists in the formation of a canon of contemporary fiction. Through a case study approach to the *Granta* 'Best of Young British Novelists' (BOYBN) list of 2013, the chapter offers a series of reflections on how and why literary prize culture has a significant role in defining 'popular fiction' and shaping which fictions become popular in our twenty-first century world. Critically exploring the significant extension of the scale and impact of literary prize culture on the field of contemporary fiction in the twenty-first century, the chapter considers the role of literary prize culture in both commodifying and canonising contemporary fiction today.

Literary awards enjoy a diverse range of impacts on the reception of future fiction. This impact phenomenon does not begin and end at increased book sales, but extends to adaptation, movie rights, merchandise, translation and ultimately the opening up of fiction to wider audiences. Through award nominations or successes, authors can become brand names, and their fictions recognised cultural products. The financial reward that accompanies such an accolade can transform the fortunes of writers, enabling them to write professionally, or broadening their networks through associated events and mentoring programmes. Significantly, literary awards also create a wider impact on literary culture beyond the immediate author, text and publisher, enabling literary interaction across the industry and between readers and writers through their shared experience of the text.

But contemporary literary award culture is not without its critics. As Claire Squires reflects, 'in terms of the central tension of the publishing industry – between culture on the one hand and commerce on the other – literary prizes are situated on the fault line' (Squires 2004: 41). Literary prize culture overtly combines the commercial and the artistic, offering nominees and winners literary legitimacy as well as money in the bank. This dual demand can lead to tension between the ideal of autonomous literary production and the demands and influences of the market. As Richard Todd argues in his study of the Booker Prize, writers now work 'in increasingly intensified atmosphere, one in which both the promotion and the reception of serious literary fiction have become steadily more consumer-oriented' (Todd 1996: 128). Many authors, readers and critics are also sceptical regarding the increasing influence of literary award culture on the formation of a canon of contemporary fiction. Man Booker winner Julian Barnes likened contemporary literary awards culture to a game of 'posh bingo' (Barnes quoted in Gilmartin 2016), while Man Booker nominated Sunjeev Sahota argued that an over-emphasis on prizes can close down or discourage the development of other opportunities for writer development and arts funding (Sahota in Shaw 2017).

Despite this controversy, literary prize culture expanded exponentially across the globe from the 1970s onwards. As a series of framing devices – each with its own longlist, shortlist, odds and bets, profiles and interviews, podcasts and ceremonies – the increasing number and variety of prizes, awards and lists have continued to expand in the new millennium. Reflecting on this rise, James English claims that somewhere in the world a new literary prize or award is created every six hours (2005: 20). Globally, authors can compete for the Nobel Prize for Literature, and in Europe the EU Prize for Literature has recognised the best emerging authors in Europe since 2009. In Britain, literary awards culture is dominated by a range of established and recognised lists and prizes that carry substantial cultural value as well as economic reward for the nominated and winning authors. Contemporary fiction is dominated by the annual Man Booker Prize, the Women's Prize for Fiction, and the James Tait Black Memorial Prize, but once every ten years literary attentions turn to the *Granta* magazine list of 'Best of Young British Novelists', a list without a single 'winner' but with a strong pedigree of identifying and celebrating the best and brightest rising stars of the British fiction scene.

Granta is the world's leading new writing magazine, profiling some of the most recent fiction and authors from Britain. For more than 40 years, *Granta*'s BOYBN lists have produced lists featuring authors who, in the opinion of the magazine's editors, will go on to define contemporary British fiction. The once-a-decade *Granta* BOYBN list 'purports to predict the shape of British fiction for the next decade' (Merritt 2003) and across the past four decades has 'gained a substantial reputation for an authority beyond literary prizes' and into the shaping of the contemporary fiction canon. As a snapshot of literary leaders of its moment, it also offers 'a way of looking into the future of creativity' (Hensher 2012). As past list-nominee Philip Hensher argues, the *Granta* list 'matters; it genuinely matters; and it matters because, on the whole, this list has got things generally right' (Hensher 2012). Featuring alumni including Martin Amis and Julian Barnes (1983); Jeanette Winterson and Kazuo Ishiguro (1993); and David Mitchell and Sarah Waters (2003), the *Granta* lists have effectively functioned to foreshadow the development and direction of contemporary British fiction.

The 2013 *Granta* list presents a range of fictions that represent the rapidly changing sociopolitical, cultural and economic landscapes of contemporary Britain through the recurring trope of the country and the city. The fictions featured on the 2013 list do not offer a purely pastoral perspective on Britain, but instead use the natural world as a platform to stage wider discussions regarding a range of present-day issues. Across these texts, the country and the city function as critical mirrors to contemporary society, highlighting underlying tensions created by overarching drives for modernity and progress, socialisation and development.

Reframing our relationship with the environment in the new millennium, the 2013 *Granta* BOYBN use the novel form to call for a reshaping of environmental practices, offering historical tensions between the country and the city as a paradigm for contemporary cultures of knowledge. Raising questions that weigh beyond the limits of the natural world – about humanity, modern assumptions about what nature means and nature itself as a form of community – the

2013 *Granta* BOYBN question the relation of humanity to the contemporary natural world. Nature is represented by these fictions as a form of refuge from city life but, significantly, not as an opportunity to shy away from political, social or economic debates. Instead, through a return to nature, or encounters with cityscapes, characters are forced to engage and grapple with contemporary 'state of the nation' questions, as the country and the city become spaces in which to enter intro dialogue about pressing post-millennial concerns.

Fiction plays an important role in shaping our collective image of cities. The city has always enjoyed a pervasive influence on fiction and the development of new writing. As Jonathan Raban argues:

> Cities [. . .] are plastic by nature. We mould them in our images: they, in their turn, shape us by the resistance they offer when we try and impose a personal form on them [. . .] The city as we might imagine it, the soft city of illusion, myth, aspiration, nightmare, is as real, maybe more real, than the hard city one can locate in maps and statistics, in monographs on urban sociology and demography and architecture.
>
> (Raban 1974: 10)

London has historically led the rest of Britain. As Warnes suggests, 'London has dominated the settlement hierarchy of England and Wales for more than a thousand years and now accounts for between 25% and 40% of the population of these two countries' (Warnes 1991: 156). Textual representations of London have become defining elements in the atlas of twenty-first century British literature. Since 'the literature of London [. . .] to a large extent [. . .] also represents the literature of England', literary representations of the city offer a distinct combination of the geography of the real and the imaginative world that they are generated from (Ackroyd 2003: 763). As such, many authors on the 2013 *Granta* BOYBN list use contemporary fiction to stage interactions with the country's capital, positioning London as an apposite site in which to debate issues key to twenty-first century Britain.

Hoggart argues that 'the idea of London is central to the self-image of the British people', and just as the idea of London 'deeply penetrates the rest of the world's view of British life', so literature about London has shaped not only British literature but also world literature written in English (Hoggart 1991: 1). Throughout the fictions featured on the 2013 *Granta* BOYBN list, London is not stable, fixed or static, simple, transparent or readable, but contested, fluid and in conflict, a space as defined by cultural and physical practices and subjective experiences. The selection offers a dynamic consideration of space and place, examining London as both a twenty-first century city and an epicentre for issues pertaining to contemporary society.

Szalay's *Spring* (2011) tells the London love story of James and Katherine, two people living in a busy city but feeling alone and isolated, dislocated from both one other and their environment. Concentrating on the interior life of London and Londoners, his fiction explores the friendships, failures and fortunes, both economic and personal, of James and Katherine, a one-time internet billionaire and a hotel manager currently separated from her husband. The personal failures of the pair highlight an underlying absence that comes to define the landscape of the novel. Reminiscent of a Patrick Marber play in its use of London not as a backdrop to their love story, but a subtle part of it, *Spring* details the lives of individuals fractured by London zones, separated by the divisions of flats and houses, and isolated in empty parks and art galleries.

The protagonist lovers even go on a 'city break' in an attempt to escape their own city, but upon their return they reach an emotional impasse, one which is resolved only by Katherine moving to another city, in an alternative country. Their short-lived romance is framed by contemporary London, with the title *Spring* underlining the fleeting nature of their encounter with each other and the city. The city forces characters to confront their own lack of ambition or sense of direction in their professional and personal lives. As evidence mounts of their inability to communicate with one another, their pervasive isolation and lack of commitment, readers are encouraged to note the transient nature of the city and its inhabitants, as this romantic encounter ultimately ends in pain, against a cityscape in constant and indifferent motion.

For Walter Benjamin, 'reading the urban text' is 'not a matter of intellectually scrutinizing the landscape: rather it is a matter of exploring the fantasy, wish-processes and dreams locked up in our perception of cities' (Benjamin 1968: 236–237). In Zadie Smith's fourth novel *NW* (2012), London is presented through the eyes of four local, but very different inhabitants. Centred on the North West region of its title, her fiction is largely set in Willesden and the Caldwell housing project on which protagonists Natalie, Leah, Felix and Nathan were raised. *NW* is a novel firmly attached to a map of twentieth and twenty-first century London, using the city as a marker of changes in race, class and gender across the new millennium. The first section is narrated by Leah, who expresses a modernist anxiety with time and the passing of time in the city; the next by Felix Cooper, a recovering addict with a tragic past, who is finally happy but is about to meet an awful end; then by Keisha – renamed 'Natalie' in her new, alternative life as a barrister – who offers 185 numbered sections which, like her apparently highly successful (but unhappy) life, are deeply fractured. In a final section, all four plots and narrators meet on the weekend of the annual Notting Hill Carnival.

Drawing upon modernist perspectives on place profiled in texts such as Virginia Woolf's *Mrs Dalloway*, the city is experienced through the eyes of one woman for the first section of Smith's fiction. Leah is a child of the NW zones of London, 'as faithful in her allegiance to this two-mile square of the city as other people are to their families, or their countries' (5). Yet, while her neighbour Ned demonstrates a 'migrant enthusiasm for the city [. . .] Leah, born and bred, never goes anywhere' (44). Instead, she observes the passing of time and its impact on the landscapes of her youth. She notes that the 'church of her childhood [. . .] has been converted into luxury apartments' (49) in this new 'multiverse' (53). Her vision of the city promotes the need for more connected communities and events and considers whether it is better to view the carnival that concludes the text from the street or the privileged balcony of an expensive town house. Presenting London as a space for class and identity transformations, Smith uses the city to stage debates about what it means, and costs, to be 'modern', setting guests against inhabitants to question who can be a native of a city in continual flux.

In a tale of visits and visitations and the haunting of the present by the past, London is presented not as a static spatio-temporal site but as a means of mapping changes in space and people over time. *NW* is assembled freely across the printed page, articulating the context and content of exchanges and the changing forms these can take. Readers follow Leah and Natalie as their narrative moves across visual presentations of emails, texts and electronic communication. With sections entitled 'visitation', 'guest', 'host' and 'visitation', the third section of the novel even breaks down into numbered sections, with each section title reflecting its content and popular culture references from the period. Across *NW*, Smith freely incorporates lyrics from popular music, grave stone inscriptions, menus, internet chat room conversations, satellite navigation directions (and culturally experienced alternatives) in an attempt to capture the forms and sensibilities of late twentieth and early twenty-first century London.

As a form of 'heterotopia', a space in which many different spaces, and many different times within these spaces, meet and interact, the London of *NW* is offered as a threshold, a space for differentiation, a mixing ground where status and identity are destabilised (Foucault 1986: 25–26). In a satirical engagement with the city – a satire that comes from a deep love of and connection to the capital – Smith's fond criticisms centre on the spaces and places forged by individuals in an urban world. Representing both the white host community and the guests who arrive in London, Smith's use of overlapping and competing narratives voices and mix of genders, races and ages encourage her reader to consider the parallel experiences of the characters from differing viewpoints to create a communal, but not concordant, overarching narrative on twenty-first century city life.

Representations of cities in contemporary fiction have an intrinsic role in promoting and making sense of encounters with the urban, reminding readers of their own role in engaging with the reality and future of urban space. Across the 2013 *Granta* BOYBN list, the city environment is presented as deeply influenced by characters' individual experiences of, and interactions, with city space. As a site for transformative social and cultural encounters, London becomes a diasporic urban melting pot of polycultural narratives and interactions between old and new. Featuring alternative mappings of the city environment by the marginalised and alienated, London functions as an enabling space in these fictions, allowing characters to shred the traditions and routines of old and to celebrate and explore individual freedoms. Through a sustained examination of physical places in the city and the individuals who experience them, the 2013 BOYBN authors produce fictions that suggest how and why place effects the development of individuals and communities. Presenting global problems through the microcosm of the city, fictional representations of London combine a celebratory pride and a revelatory frankness about the composition, nature and function of the city in the new millennium and offer the capital as a marker for the development of Britain in the twenty-first century.

The novelists featured on the 2013 *Granta* list interrogate the concept of a contemporary countryside, exploring the corruption of the natural world by humans and the effects of the city on the country. Foregrounding ecological values, these fictions ask readers to question understandings of 'nature' in the twenty-first century. They interrogate the notion of place as a stable category and consider how contemporary interactions with nature are represented in literature, how we interact with the natural world and engage with the concept of wilderness. Focussing of marginalised natural topographies and under-represented regions of Britain, several *Granta*'s 2013 BOYBN take the fate of the natural world, and our engagement with it, as their central narrative concern.

In *Haweswater* (2009), Sarah Hall tells the unwritten human history of the flooding of the Mardale Valley to create a dam in rural Westmorland, UK. The novel is based on real life events in Mardale during the twentieth century when the British government gave permission for their valley to be flooded in order to ensure a safe water supply for the growing conurbation of Manchester in the North West of England. Rather than foregrounding official, historical accounts that stress the necessity of the scheme for the development of the industrialisation of North West England, Hall's fiction re-writes the past from the perspective of the people in this 'drowned village', offering a frontier example of an encroachment of the modern on the natural environment.

Exploring the flooding of a 'Westmoorland valley' (4) to construct a damn for neighbouring conurbation of Manchester, the novel represents the intrusion of the national on the regional, underscoring the unseen human impact of drives for progress and profit. The development is approved without consultation or consideration of the heritage and perceived value of what is being wiped out. Instead, this distant area about which the British government knows and cares little is sanctioned as a dam. The scheme is 'all fact, done and dusted' (50) by a 'parliament [. . .] a long way south, remote from the valleys of the north of England' (53). The dam technology authorised by the government literally drowns the people and traditions of the area in the spread of the city of 'Manchester [. . .] a city leading the way of modernity in the north [. . .] The city would be a defender of this country. Its growth was beneficial to the country entire. It should be nurtured with pride, with sacrifice, hard though that may be' (53). Detailing the transformation of history and human life by technology and placing the good of the many against the suffering of the few, the novel sets a 'village. Not insignificant, but [. . .] a small place', against 'a scheme to benefit the whole nation' (50).

The narrative takes pains to illustrate that apparently simple communities can have valuable histories, heritages and cultures. The country children have 'ruddy complexions, the absence of city reflections in their eyes' (46) and, compared with their city counterparts, 'were template from an entirely different press' (46). Language functions as an important expression of their regional identity. The Mardale accent is 'set and roughened and deepened by the wind and the rain' (5). Although the people appear 'insular, as silent and self-sufficient as monks, closing ranks to off-comers, and uncommunicative and silent' (6) they are linked by silent bonds that are 'strong and necessary and abundantly understood' (6). This local dialect and assumed comprehension is not initially shared by dam representative Jack Liggett, who reflects on the 'old bitten-at language of the area, with its sluggish, ugly vowels, there were words which he did not understand, which sounded brutal, and he could not guess their English equivalent' (91). As a spokesperson of the water company driving the development, Jack Liggett represents modern progress and the intrusion of the city on the countryside. At the beginning of the novel, his car functions a symbol of dislocation from the 'small place' (50) he enters. Locals note 'the mechanical purr of a smooth engine' as the sports car is set against 'the ancient-wheeled tractor struggling up the incline to High Bowderthwaite Farm' (42). They observe 'the automobile was very new and very fine. And utterly incongruous with the environment in which it now found itself' (42).

Haweswater suggests that the people of an area are inherently connected to the land they work and considers why, in the wake of the industrial revolution and the growth of the cities, water becomes a commodity as valuable as land itself. Encouraging a generation of people to question and learn, the narrative follows the lives of those who live off the land and their individual experience of a wider project. In a novel about change, physical and emotional, social and economic, through a distinct blend of the documentary and the imaginary the true tragedy lies at the heart of an onset of modernity, as the city is seen to slowly shadow over the countryside valley of Mardale. The end of the novel makes a wider statement on the role of fiction in re-voicing marginalised perspectives on regional events. Its closing pages remind the reader that:

> In secure, rural places, small villages and insular hamlets where grand events and theatrical schemes rarely take place, enormous human episodes, when they finally do rip apart the fabric of normal life, sometimes come away lacking clarity [. . .] the borders between fact and myth have a tendency to blur in these regions. History fogs, or becomes loose and watery. Bizarre mythologies arise. Half-lives. Half-truths. Events are built up or deconstructed. Leaps of faith are made, often for the strangest of sakes. The past becomes indistinct and subplots continue.
>
> (253)

The flooding of the valley becomes an event of biblical proportions and significance, as modernity encroaches like a plague on the village suggesting the valley as a symbol for the many wider casualties of progress in the natural world. Taking the 'largely unrecorded' event in the history of the reservoir (253), Hall makes a marginalised perspective on a regional historical event very real and immediate, using the flooding of this valley as a microcosm for much wider conflicts and social, political and global changes in inter-war Britain.

Gods Own Country (Raisin 2009) extends this contemporary concern with the perceived impact of the city on the countryside via the gentrification of UK country villages by 'out of towners'. Narrator Sam Marsdyke, a farmer's son on the North Yorkshire Moors, holds a deep seated dislike of city dwellers, torments walkers visiting from the towns and scares away urban intruders on what he perceives to be 'his' moorlands. The novel opens with Sam's analysis of ramblers as 'daft sods [. . .] like a line of drunks, addled with the air' who are 'crapping up Nature's balance' (1). He watches one group 'moving on like a line of chickens, their heads twitching side to side. What a lovely molehill. Look, Bob, a cuckoo, behind the dry-stone wall. Only it wasn't a cuckoo, I knew, it was a bloody pigeon' (1). Satirising a lack of urban awareness about the natural world, Sam presents himself by contrast as the authentic countryside, a 'real, living, farting Nature to their brain of things' (1). Angry at the way urban dwellers use and abuse the countryside, Sam argues that they 'couldn't give a stuff for the Moors, all they wanted was a postcard view out the bedroom window' (9). He reflects that, the 'country was a Sunday garden to them, wellingtons and four-by-fours and glishy magazines of horse arses jumping over a fence' (10). These concerns are actualised when an urban family purchases the farm house opposite his family home. Sam is highly suspicious of 'their sort', their priorities ('the sun hadn't done a lap round their house yet, but the cookbooks were fettled up' – 13) and the impact of an urban drift on the community.

When the local pub is taken over and turned into a base for these new urban drifters, Sam concedes that the 'shadows of the cities were sneaking in both sides of the valley, and there was nothing any of them could do about it' (29). The pub, as 'the heart and soul of the town' (29), becomes a symbol for the wider diluting of the local community and soon even the local butcher is transformed into 'The Green Pepper Deli'. Sam reflects that 'last time I'd been here, there were rabbits strung up and bloody hunks of beef dripping on to the counter, but now it was all shiny jars on shelves and a tray of olives pricked with little sticks' (100). The final straw appears in the form of a new housing development which Sam nick-names 'Off-comed hole [. . .] Twenty or thirty red houses, all bright and glishy like a piece of flesh with the skin torn off. Probably that's what the town used to look like, way back, before it started to snarl up and scab over' (100). This raw, organic image underscores the perceived destruction of the local by new inhabitants from the cities, their immediate impact on the composition of the town, and the shift in dynamics created by twenty-first century population change and land use in Britain.

The first person narrative of protagonist San Marsdyke grants intimate access to his thoughts and feelings on the country and the city, which quickly reveals him to be capable of cruelty, balanced with acts of affection and emotion. Accused of rape against a fellow pupil in his countryside school at the age of sixteen, Sam submits to psychological profiling treatment after the allegations (88). There are undertones of Tennyson's 'Maud' in his relationship with this girl, who comes from the urban family who buy the farm house next door to Sam's country home. As a sustainable exploration of the power of unreliable narration, the narrative makes readers doubt Sam's increasingly instable vision which culminates in nightmares that build towards the conclusion of the text.

The narrator's slow descent into madness and loss of control is initially marked by his fascination with natural objects, both animate and inanimate, and his practice of talking to them. Shunned by the people of the village and enduring a cold and uncomfortable relationship with his family, like Heathcliffe in *Wuthering Heights*, Sam takes refuge in nature and seems to identify more with animals than people. Always on the margins, looking in as a voyeur onto other people's lives, the sublime isolation of the moors encourages imaginative freedom but also enables him to cross the line between imaginary violence and real, as he confesses to killing, beheading and burying a chicken and succumbing to humorous but increasingly paranoid fantasies. When he runs away with Jo from the neighbouring farm house, his subjective first person narrative increasingly makes readers aware that the reality he communicates may not be the actual situation on the ground. Jo seems less and less willing to be part of the plan to escape and his own mental stability clearly weakens as he starts to engage in conversations with animals that encourage him to consider 'breeding her' (191). When he is eventually caught by the police, Jo is revealed to be tied up and in distress. The novel concludes with Sam leaving prison after serving four years for abduction, casting doubt on the claims offered by his narrative in the previous pages and making readers reassess the narrative as a highly subjective account.

The impact of the urban on the rural community is taken to its logical conclusion in Kavenna's *Come To The Edge* (2012). The novel begins at its end, in a scene of rural apocalypse as houses burn and people run. Whether this is a revenge attack or a mutiny is initially unclear, but it is clear that the novel immediately establishes conflict between the city and the country as its key concern. Set in the remote Duddon valley in Cumbria, the novel follows its narrator as she leaves the city to live in the countryside with revolutionary organic warrior Cassandra White. The narrator confesses that 'Suburbia was my chosen idyll, and I was a devout worshipper of my personal pile of bricks, bricks my husband and I were paying off one by one, until the glorious day we would own them all' (7). But in the wake of a failed marriage, she shuns her 'flat-pack totems' (7) and 'twilight suburban half-life' (10) and decides to 'head for the hills' (36), viewing her life with Cassandra as punishment for the many consumer evils of her past.

Cassandra's self-sustaining way of life and opinions on the use of the countryside by the inhabitants of the cities becomes an education for the narrator as she experiences life on the 'edge' of England, sanity and a wider national problem. The text concentrates on the purchase of rural houses as second homes, or holiday homes, by wealthy city inhabitants. Like Sam Marsdyke in *God's Own Country*, Cassandra argues that the 'countryside is just a fantasy for people like this, a place where you roam through the so-called scenery by day, allowing the elements occasionally to ruffle the folds of your expensive outdoor wear, where you can always retreat to your roaring fire, your pristine house' (121). Cassandra calls these second home owners 'perverts' because, in her opinion, they are going against the natural order of local homes for local people. Cassandra believes the fact that city dwellers use a country house once a year while local people suffer in substandard dwellings is simply 'a waste of a house' (91). She argues that these 'people are committing a terrible crime by never using these houses. I have devised a solution, whereby we can save them and others from the terrible consequences of their criminal behaviour' (111). Dubbing these buildings 'pervert dwellings' (114), Cassandra works out that thirty two out of forty such dwellings are never used and sets about organising a system called 'Resettlement' – moving local people, who are in need of new homes, into the deserted or under-employed second houses owned by city dwellers. Her scheme not only highlights the power of the individual but also raises issues of justice, property and ownership rights, morality and ethical behaviour, as well as ecology.

Using 'Resettlement' as system through which to examine the growing gap between rich and poor in twenty-first century Britain, Kavenna's novel encourages an examination of the relationship between humans and the natural world via a proposed utopian scheme. Using humour to flavour a very serious debate about the growing divide between the haves and have nots in twenty-first century Britain, the novel offers a critique of worshipping wealth through the eyes of a reformed capitalist addict who, via a reconnection with the natural world under the guidance of Cassandra, learns the value and liberation of physical labour and the ability to self-sustain through the beauty of free pleasures.

Narrated by a suburban house wife narrator, who starts and ends the novel with a *Thelma and Louise*-style scene of defiant glory, the novel asks whether revolution will always fail and shows the possibility and viability of an alternative to twenty-first century capitalism and city life. Condemning the bourgeois lifestyle formerly occupied by its narrator, the novel offers Cassandra White as a leader and a revolutionary, a liberator, freedom-fighter and law breaker. Cassandra

White's refusal to comply with social norms and commitment to live an alternative life, enables the narrator, 'a nice girl from the suburbs', to turn into a 'gun-toting maniac' (2). Cassandra, 'like a happy ogress' (128), sees conforming to social norms as a form of 'mental illness' (27) and through her innovative 'Resettlement' scheme – which quickly spreads from the valley to Wales, Cornwall and even France – soon 'has disciples at her feet' (225). In the final moments of the novel, one such disciple asks simply: 'What would Cassandra White tell us to do?' (265). By this point, Cassandra as revolutionary leader has led an international movement to its logical, if doomed, conclusion.

Resettlement ends in the burning of the resettlement houses, the denial of the resources to the city dwellers, and Cassandra is finally killed in combat by the police. Although the novel concludes with the narrator returning to her suburban half-life, 'chipboard desk' and 'view of the car park' (292) the exciting message of the novel lies in the glimpse of a possibility of an alternative. In her satire on modern life, Kavenna offers readers an example of a character that rejects the city for the country, capitalist systems for self-sufficiency and individualism for community. Cassandra's note to the narrator whilst giving directions to her country home – 'Carry on along this road. DON'T lose heart! It seems endless, when you don't know where you're going. But you will arrive!' (18) – finally stands as a message for the novel and the personal journey of the individual who chooses a different path through twenty-first century life.

Representing the natural world and engagements between humans and the countryside, 2013 BOYBN use the environment to stage broader debates about social structures and ideologies, culture–nature interactions and ideas about war and peace. In these texts, the natural world is shown to empower the marginalised individual, reconnect communities and enable personal transformation. Challenging prevailing economic and political discourses that put the city before the countryside, the economic before the social, progress before heritage and the collective over the individual, these fictions instead call for a re-engagement between humans and the natural world in the twenty-first century.

In the first decades of the twenty-first century, fiction has continued to dominate as an appropriate form in which to articulate contemporary experiences of, and concerns about, social, political and economic topographies of contemporary society. The 2013 *Granta* BOYBN list contains timely examples of experiments in literary form, voice, language and thematic concerns that are pushing the boundaries of what fiction can offer the contemporary period. As an area of academic and popular cultural study that is still in formation, contemporary literature is resistant to definitive boundaries, categories or labels. Instead, as this literary list suggests, it is characterised by a tendency to develop concerns extended from the old century, and map them onto twenty-first century landscapes to reframe issues central to the new millennium.

Not only representing, but entering into critical dialogue with, some of the more pressing issues and directions of contemporary literature, the 2013 BOYBN selection stands as a testament to the vitality and significance of the novel form in the twenty-first century. As Bentley suggests, the 'novelist at the end of the first decade of the twenty-first century appears to be standing not at a crossroads but at a far more complicated intersection that offers routes in several directions' (Bentley 2008: 196). Carving into old landscapes to offer new representations and historical reverberations that echo across the twenty-first century world, the 2013 *Granta* BOYBN list re-writes a past that continues to assert its role in the present, disrupting narratives and engaging readers in a multiplicity of perspectives on post-millennial society.

Across four decades, the *Granta* BOYBN lists have offered timely insights into the social, cultural and economic function of literary awards in forming the evolving canon of the contemporary, as well as role in the survival of fiction in the twenty-first century. The *Granta* list and its legacies are significant – many of the featured writers have gone on to shape the field of contemporary fiction and in doing so continue to demonstrate the relevance and impact of literary award culture beyond the immediate award itself. *Granta* and its fellow literary awards, lists and prizes continue to enjoy a significant function in moulding our awareness and appreciation of contemporary writings as a direct result of their important role in contributing to the canonisation of texts in the contemporary period. As well as enhancing and extending the production, creation and survival of publishing houses and the literary industry in a new digital age, literary awards and their matrix of admissions criteria and judging frameworks bravely make the otherwise 'unfashionable statement that there is still such a thing as literary writing and that it is alive and well' (Merritt 2003).

In the twenty-first century, literary awards generate new conversations and new subject positions, bringing the literary into the focus of popular attention at a time when it is increasingly competing with a new range of narrative representations. In turn, they exercise a scholarly influence over what is taught and read as the canon of contemporary fiction. The continued success and influence of the *Granta* list is suggestive not only of the wider productive impact of literary award culture for authors, publishers and readers in the twenty-first century, but also of an increasingly popular awareness regarding the frameworks involved in selection and the competing demands of the emerging and diverse field of twenty-first century writings. Offering an evaluation of a year in fiction, literary prizes, awards and lists like the *Granta* BOYBN function to create a recognised canon of contemporary writing that can be communicated effectively to a global marketplace. The role of literary prize culture in the formation of the field of popular fiction is vital, as is their disruptive function is problematizing boundaries between the commercial and the literary, between high and low art, the critical and the popular. While the remit of each prize differs, they all seek to differentiate in an increasingly competitive field and recognise quality, creativity and innovation in new writings. In the twenty-first century literary prize culture has the power to shape a canon of contemporary literary canon, initiate debates about the future of new writing and offer a timely health check on the current condition of contemporary fiction.

2013 *Granta* Best of Young British Novelists list

Naomi Alderman, *The Liar's Gospel* (2012)
Tahmima Anam, *The Good Muslim* (2011)
Ned Bowman, *The Teleportation Accident* (2012)
Jenni Fagan, *The Panopticon* (2012)
Adam Foulds, *The Quickening Maze* (2009)
Xiaolu Guo, *Concise Chinese-English Dictionary for Lovers* (2008)
Sarah Hall, *Haweswater* (2009)
Steven Hall, *The Raw Shark Texts* (2007)
Joanna Kavenna, *Come to the Edge* (2012)
Benjamin Markovits, *Childish Loves* (2012)
Nadifa Mohamed, *Black Mamba Boy* (2009)
Helen Oyeyemi, *Mr Fox* (2009)
Ross Raisin, *God's Own Country* (2009)
Sunjeev Sahota, *Ours Are the Streets* (2011)
Taiye Selasi, *Ghana Must Go* (2013)
Kamila Shamsie, *Burnt Shadows* (2009)
Zadie Smith, *NW* (2012)
David Szalay, *Spring* (2011)
Adam Thirlwell, *Kapow!* (2012)
Evie Wyld, *After the Fire, A Still Small Voice* (2009)

Works cited

Ackroyd, P. (2003) *London: The Biography*. New York: Anchor Books.

Barnes, J. quoted in Gilmartin, S. (2016) 'Literary Awards Pros and Cons', *Irish Times*, 9 March <www.irishtimes.com/culture/books/literary-awards-pros-and-cons-gold-stars-and-black-marks-1.2566177>.

Benjamin, W. (1968) 'The Work of Art in the Mechanical Age of Reproduction', in *Illuminations: Essays and Reflections*, ed. Hannah Arendt, trans. Harry Zorn. New York: Schocken Books.

Bentley, N. (2008) *Contemporary British Fiction*. Edinburgh: Edinburgh University Press.

English, J. (2005) *The Economy of Prestige: Prizes, Awards and the Circulation of Cultural Value*. London: Harvard University Press.

Foucault, M. (1986) 'Of Other Spaces', trans. Jay Miskowiec, *Diacritics*, 16, 22–27.

Hensher, P. (2012) 'Comment: Granta's Once-a-Decade List of Rising Novelists Is More Important Than Ever', *The Independent*, 31 December <www.independent.co.uk/voices/comment/grantas-once-a-decade-list-of-rising-novelists-is-more-important-than-ever-8433998.html>.

Hoggart, K. (1991) 'London as an Object of Study', in *London: A New Metropolitan Geography*, ed. K. Hoggart and D. Green. London: Edward Arnold.

Merritt, S. (2003) 'A Question of Merit', *The Observer*, 12 January <www.theguardian.com/books/2003/jan/12/features.review3>.

Raban, J. (1974) *Soft City*. London: Hamish Hamilton.

Shaw, K. (2017) 'Living by the Pen: Katy Shaw in Conversation with Sunjeev Sahota', *English: Journal of the English Association*, 66:253, 263–271.

Squires, C. (2004) 'A Common Ground? Book Prize Culture in Europe', *Javnost: The Public*, 11:4, 37–47.

Todd, R. (1996) *Consuming Fictions: The Booker Prize and Fiction in Britain Today*. London: Bloomsbury.

Warnes, A. (1991) 'London's Population Trends: Metropolitan Area of Megalopolis', in Hoggart and Green, *London: A New Metropolitan Geography*. London: Edward Arnold.

30

HARI KUNZRU

Lucienne Loh

Introduction

'Rootless but at Home in a Britannia All His Own', the headline from a *New York Times* interview with Hari Kunzru, paradoxically captures Kunzru's sense of 'the mutability of identity' (Lyall 2002: np) refracted through the lens of contemporary British nationhood. This malleability may be in part due to Kunzru's mixed parentage: his father, an orthopaedic surgeon moved to London from India in the 1960's and married a nurse. Brought up in the middle class, predominantly white, suburb of Woodford in Essex, notably Sir Winston Churchill's long term constituency, Kunzru went on to read English at Oxford and his portrait now graces Wadham College's Okinaga Room as one of the college's most celebrated alumni. Like other writers concerned with postimperial Britain such as V.S. Naipaul, Salman Rushdie, Caryl Phillips, Monica Ali and Zadie Smith – all similarly Oxbridge graduates – Kunzru continues to possess a heightened wariness towards the traditions and class privileges epitomised by their alma maters as well as a constant questioning of white Englishness. Yet more so than these writers, Kunzru's challenge to English essentialism flows from a fascination with a highly networked and globalised Britain carved from colonialism's legacies. He most famously proclaimed his solidarity to those who continue to live out these legacies by rejecting the 2003 John Llewellyn Rhys Prize for his novel *The Impressionist*. As 'One of Them', he felt that it was right to turn down 'a literary award sponsored by the xenophobic Mail on Sunday' (Kunzru 2003: np). Kunzru did, however, accept the Betty Trask Award and the Somerset Maugham Award for the same novel and since 2003, has garnered considerable literary accolades. This essay explores Kunzru's major novels to date, focusing particularly on his self-conscious and consistent use of parody to portray a relentless and, at times, frightening but exhilarating globalised postmodern society, one often portrayed as a product of erstwhile European empires. While certainly many critics acknowledge Kunzru's consistent use of parody, this essay also seeks to explore parody's limits and limitations within Kunzru's oeuvre.

The Impressionist (2002): postcolonial personalities

The Impressionist, Kunzru's first novel, established him as a major British novelist. With its success pre-empted by a £1.25 million advance, Kunzru's most widely critiqued novel functions primarily, according to the author, by 'keeping a keen sense of absurdity' (Lyall 2002: np). Indeed, the novel parodies colonial discourse but simultaneously deploys a pastiche of a range of core postcolonial theories, including Edward Said's 'orientalism', Gayatri Spivak's 'epistemological violence' and Homi Bhabha's 'hybridity' and 'mimicry'. Indeed, Murat Aydemir argues for the novel's impressionistic style and supports its self-conscious resistance to realism in the flimsy alignment between setting and character. Certainly the impressionistic performances of the central character's various guises are so wide ranging and farcically incongruous that Kunzru clearly did not intend to depict a traditionally 'rounded' character in his protagonist, Pran Nath. These personas include the degraded 'Rukshana', effectively an imprisoned catamite in a Nawab's palace and 'Pretty Bobby', a domestic servant to a racist Bombay missionary preoccupied with phrenology. The chameleon like protagonist, an orphan of Indian and white English parentage, eventually ends the novel as Jonathan Bridgeman, a research assistant to an august Anthropology Oxford University Professor studying remote West African tribes. Aydemir believes the novel provides 'a theory sampler' (2006: 204) that contests four central terms – 'hybridity', 'travesty', 'mimicry', 'nomadism' – from which postcolonial theoretical staples such as 'migrant metaphors' and malleable identities are forged. While Aydemir does not reflect upon the comic nature of the novel's theoretical engagements, he argues that '[t]he novel resists both a realistic reading and a naively theoretical one', (2006: 205). Homi Bhabha's theory of hybridity, for example, argues for a form of colonial imitation that involved 'a difference that is almost total but not quite' (1994: 91). According to Aydemir, Kunzru's novel troubles the potentially defiant and celebratory politics of Bhabha's theory of 'hybridity' through the racist and purist ideologies purveyed by the Indian characters.

Frederick Luis Aldama traces the novel's unfolding, where Pran 'moves from a blinding belief in civilized order to a sharply focused awareness of the power of chaos and his own racial hybridity' (2009: 89). If the novel demonstrates that hybridity forms a fundamental condition of the postcolonial and postmodern subject in a global context where selfhood is fragmented, unstable and constituted performatively, then *The Impressionist* also serves as Kunzru's most strident critique of the way in which colonialism and its legacies construct the sites of such identities: class, gender, sexuality and, to an overwhelming degree, race. This last category gains such prominence largely because of the central character's ability and keen desire to pass as white English, enabling a performance and 'mimicry' of Englishness which allow him access to spheres of social power and economic privilege. The novel, as Jopi Nyman argues, 'performs Englishness' (2009: 101) and does so 'as elements of postmodern parody not as mere critique of such issues' (2009: 100). Nyman, focussing more specifically on the subversion of the postcolonial *bildungs'* plot believes, too, that the novel is non-realist, and more specifically 'undoes parodically the ideological baggage of the *Bildungsroman* promoting fixed (gendered and racialized) subjects' (2009: 93).

Similarly, Dave Gunning suggests that while the novel promotes a parody of the conventions of the picaresque novel, this implies more disconcerting consequences. Pran Nath's lack of identity as he performs a range of stereotypes constructed by colonialism becomes 'increasingly disturbing' and he succumbs to a despairing 'emptying out of [. . .] selfhood' (2012: 803). Barbara Schaff agrees, arguing '[t]he mimicry of [Kunzru's] protagonist [. . .] produces a non-entity, complete void' (2009: 289). Shane Graham also focuses on the debilitating nature of stereotypes fashioned through the colonial encounter, a realisation that dawns on Pran following his 'confrontation with blackness at the Empire Exhibition' in London in 1924 (2013: 442). At the exhibition, he grasps the shallowness and falsity of his identity, realising his repressed self through his consistent mimicry of the British colonial construction of selfhood.

Many critics thus assume, then, that for most of his life in the novel, Pran subscribes and defers to colonial ideologies and the pageantry of empire enacted all around him. I would like to suggest the novel also undermines colonial stereotypes through parodying colonialists who themselves ironically embody characteristics supposedly requiring the beneficent hand of European civilisation. The novel thus suggests British colonialism as a dissipated mission and corrupt enterprise. Raba Kabbani in *Imperial Fictions: Europe's Myths of the Orient* argues that 'if it could be suggested that Eastern peoples were slothful, preoccupied with sex, violent, and incapable of self-government, the imperialist would feel himself justified in stepping in and ruling' (1986: 18–19). Instead, in most of the instances in the novel, it is the colonialists who are themselves depicted as possessing these wanton elements that colonial discourse ascribed to colonised subjects.

Kunzru acknowledges that the novel's intertextual allusions draw ironically on writers such as Kipling, Waugh and Conrad. They include colonial texts such as E.M. Forster's *Passage to India* and Joseph Conrad's *Heart of Darkness*: 'I play a lot of games with the colonial literary canon' he claims (Aldama 2005: 13), further asserting:

> You can't write a story about colonialism without encountering this whole huge tradition of canonical English literature. There are two ways to approach it. One is to sidestep the whole thing and imagine that you have unimpeded access to the subject, which seemed to me absurd and fake. The other is to write in a kind of playful dialogue with this entire tradition of English literature, which has so much to do with defining Englishness.
>
> (Lyall 2002: np)

It is worth exploring, however, some of the more specific colonial discourses that feed into the novel's self-conscious parodic structure, particularly around the nexus between Orientalism and sexuality. In *Orientalism*, Edward Said stresses that 'the association is clearly made between the Orient and the freedom of licentious sex [. . .] the Orient was a place where one could look for sexual experience unobtainable in Europe' (1979: 190). Eighteenth-century Orientalist and later nineteenth and early twentieth century colonial texts were inundated with Oriental clichés, including, in the earlier periods, the orient as a space where colonials could indulge in sexual forays otherwise censured in restrained bourgeois Europe. As a sexualised space, the Orient proved highly contradictory, at once a site of condemnation and titillation where colonial discipline was both required and relinquished and where repressed colonial sexual fantasies could flourish.

In the chapter 'Rukhsana', Kunzru self-consciously deploys orientalist images in his depiction of the New Fatehpur Palace with its excessive Mughal architecture, coterie of turbaned and bearded courtiers draped in shawls cradling hookahs and a wasted Nawab, all likened to 'the appearance of a Persian miniature painting' (2002: 83). Sexualised Orientalist images are further accentuated as the palace includes an extensive 'zenana', an area where women and girls are secluded and overseen by a powerful eunuch or 'hijra' who also holds sway over Pran. Now named Rukhsana, 'a beautiful boy-girl' (2002: 85), Pran is repeatedly drugged and coerced into sexual service to please the priapic British resident, the Major Augustus Privett Clampe. Yet, through a sustained parodic tone, Kunzru also renders such orientalist sexual fantasies pathetic, reflective of a 'debased age' (2002: 83) of British colonial rule where officers within the Indian Political Service are politically blackmailed by the Nawab's staff through photos of their deviant sexual encounters within the walls of the palace. Kunzru clearly parodies the salacious colonial 'native' stereotype in his reversal of roles here, yet the palace houses grotesque cruelty and sexual abuse towards entrapped children and enables deviant sexual fantasies to be fulfilled. In this sense, the extent of Kunzru's parody is certainly ambivalent and could be seen as representing South Asian Muslim cultures through an orientalist lens. The novel may even be positioned within a more contemporary 'neo-Orientalism', one that 'entails certain discursive repetitions of and conceptual continuities with its precursor'. As Behdad and Williams have argued, '[n]eo-Orientalism should be understood [. . .] as a supplement to enduring modes of Orientalist representation' (2010: 284).

Transmission (2004): confounding cosmopolitanism

Kunzru's novel *Transmission* has received the widest range of scholarly attention within fields such as postcolonial studies, contemporary and postmodern literature, British Asian fiction, and narratology. Most critical work focuses on Kunzru's use of postmodern literary conventions to foreground the vagaries of life under late capitalism and globalised neoliberal culture driven by the signifiers of global wealth and social distinction as well as the concomitant despondency and alienation that accompany life fundamentally imbricated within these systems.

Dave Gunning, comparing *The Impressionist* with *Transmission*, argues that '*Transmission* might ultimately seem to offer the same kind of emptying out of identity as seen in *The Impressionist*' (2012: 805). Similarly, Alan Robinson argues that *Transmission* presents a world irrevocably constructed from simulated images, with 'no regress to an underlying, unmediated reality' (2008: 78). Yet other critics focus on global social and economic inequities as well as the dependency of the rich world on the poor, at times raising the novel's tentative points of resistance through metaphorical explorations of the deterritorialised nature of the Leela virus, a rogue computer virus designed by one of the novel's central character, an Indian computer programmer based in America, Arjun Mehta. The virus wreaks havoc across the world, but through its nebulous yet extensive effects, ties the novel's otherwise disparate characters together, including an English elite global business brand manager, Guy Swift and Leela Zahir, a Bollywood superstar actress who lends the virus its moniker.

For Liam Connell, the virus serves as an attack on those who have privileged from globalization. Various state and international institutions declare the Leela virus an act of 'terror', yet the term, 'terror' can be viewed as a 'misapplication to the actions of all those who act against the structures of organised capitalism' (2010: 283) and as Arjun Appadurai argues, 'as a name for any variety of antistate activity' (2006: 16). Philip Leonard sees hacking computer systems in the same anarchic light. In an age where 'capitalism has now turned to information as its primary commodity' (2014: 280), hacking resists this new mode of information as marketable property. Other critics (Brock 2008; Liao 2013) have explored the virus in terms of various extended metaphors, including seeing it as a reflection of an ironic reversal of the power assumed by developed countries to combat global viruses like HIV/AIDS as the Leela virus causes the most damage amongst the more economically privileged – and consequently more electronically networked – nations of the world.

In other readings of the novel's transnational and global narrative frame, a range of critics draw on theories of cosmopolitanism. Emily Johansen (2013) argues for the reversal of the negative connotations linked to the term 'virus' and its proliferating threat by drawing on theories of cosmopolitanism. For Johansen, the virus' mutability and adaptability offers a new model for global interconnectedness, rather than divisive modes of cosmopolitanism where one is either a privileged consumer or exploited labourer. She thus argues for another framework whereby privileged cosmopolitans are self-reflexive and made consciously aware of the inescapability of everyday global cosmopolitan connections to a range of cosmopolitan others within localised contexts and especially through their reliance on a highly mobile global migrant labour force who are similarly constantly adapting in cosmopolitan ways to local conditions. Similar to Johansen, Dave Gunning's reading of the novel (2012) deploys cosmopolitan theory more conventionally by associating it with the politics of planetary empathy.

Ashley T. Shelden, too, draws on cosmopolitanism, but argues, on the other hand, that *Transmission* critiques the cosmopolitical spirit. He suggests that the purported naturalised link between cosmopolitanism and ethical love for the other is in fact deeply paradoxical for it intimates at once both a collective humanity and the simultaneous impossibility of that collective spirit: 'cosmopolitical love cannot make up for the fundamental discontinuity that structures communal, or global, human relationship' (2012: 355). *Transmission*, on the other hand, 'seems to suggest that love can be universal without attempting to resolve difference into unity' (2012: 356). Global corporate branding's co-option of the superficial image of love as universal is particularly insidious and thoroughly exploited by Guy Swift, the CEO of the brand and marketing consultants, Tomorrow★. For Shelden, Kunzru valorises 'in turn a version of cosmopolitanism that understands the other as *other*, that tolerates difference rather than attempting to assimilate it to sameness' (2012: 366, italics in original). Cosmopolitan love, conceived in this nature, stresses, in particular, the *difference* on which love insists, and consciously incorporates its potential for antagonism, aggression, division, danger and corrosion in any and all 'cosmopolitan' encounters with the other. For Shelden, the Leela virus, figuring both love fulfilment and a corrosive nature, is both sexually alluring and destructive and is a metaphor for this form of cosmopolitanism by accentuating the fundamental disconnect and conflict between individuals.

No criticism, however, has focused on the function of the predominantly parodic narrative point of view in *Transmission* and its intended audience. *Transmission*'s extradiegetic narrator opens the novel with a second person narrative voice which collapses into the voice of any number of forms of internet communication disguised as a personalised exchange.

> It was a simple message.
> *Hi. I saw this and thought of you.*
> Maybe you got a copy in your inbox, [. . .]
>
> (2005: 3)

The novel opens on a point of prolepsis when the Leela virus has already been unleashed upon the world. The novel then proceeds retrospectively to trace the events which led to the release of the virus on the world's electronically networked systems. The parodic fictional world of the novel is assumed also to be the world of the fully networked reader, more than likely male who is functional in English and fully integrated into the world wide web and its libidinal economies. He is the enfranchised consumer of technocratic and corporate capitalism, but also of what David Hill has termed 'the pathology of communicative capitalism' (Hill 2015). The reader clicks on the image of the seductive dancing figure of Leela Zahir that forms the virtual public facing interface of the virus and he enters into the global viral mayhem unleashed. The narrative intimacy is unsettling from the novel's opening because it describes the late capitalist Everyman's computer (also assumed to be the reader) being infected by the Leela virus, lured by the falsity of communicative intimacy underpinning on-line interactions.

Thus this opening conceit draws the reader, perhaps unwittingly, as the virus does, into the fictional world of the novel, which is set in different geographical locations of contemporary life in the late twentieth and early twenty-first centuries. In all of these locations, the narrative is frequently focalised through one of the three central characters – Guy Swift, Arjun Mehta and Leela Zahir – each one seemingly as inauthentic as the other. Yet, the overriding tone is one of parody; Kunzru draws on archetypes, satirising the cultural discourses and identity positions each of the characters represent who, at times, appear like caricatures. Parody also surrounds other minor characters throughout the novel. Arjun's mother smothers her son with the cosseted love of the South Asian variety; heavily tattooed Chris, who provides Arjun with his first sexual encounter, views herself as a cultural and sexual renegade despite working for Microsoft. Guy Swift's girlfriend, Gabriella, is the luscious but vacuous face of the footloose, globally mobile super rich elite. The comforts of bourgeois identity and subcultural quiddities are all revealed to be superficial. Thus, setting, plot and character all conjoin to produce comic and structural irony.

Significantly, the voice of the novel's extradiegetic narrator operates at a degree of detachment from its characters. Later in the novel, less than 24 hours after its release, the reader is once again asked: 'Who clicked? Did you click? Were you curious enough to try?' (2005: 115). At this moment, we are given the option *again* to decide what to do when faced with the Leela virus having been informed of its pernicious effects and the reader is invariably challenged to temporarily reject the simulated world of the internet and everything it offers. The novel thus suggests the promises of security and surety proffered by the knowledge-based global economy and information technology appear misplaced and facile, and those trapped irredeemably within it, including the reader himself, are forever vulnerable to greater rather than fewer contingencies. Indeed, at the end of the novel, in the chapter 'Noise', the extradiegetic narrative voice returns to aver: 'Certainty backslides into probability. Information transmission, it emerges, is about doing the best you can' (2005: 271). When the narrative voice deviates from the overriding parodic tone, offering a very traditional omniscient narrative voice, we are urged to pay attention and often the stark contrast in tenor causes the reader to consider the context of this shift more attentively. For example, the reader is compelled to gaze upon '[a] figure, a walking man, trudging along the margin of a wide California highway' (38), who soon manifests as Arjun recently parted from his home and family in India. At this point Arjun, caught in a visa limbo, stands between the sublime mobility of the frequently air bound cosmopolitan elite (such as Guy), and at the other extreme of this the homeless, the static and destitute who reside at the other end of the spectrum of global privilege. Arjun is simply a forgotten marginal figure – neither raised in public consciousness as the spectre of poverty or the boon of wealth – simply exploited but not to the degree where he might gain either public recognition or sympathy. As Emily Johansen argues, Arjun represents that 'transnational movement to be much more highly delimited than typically presumed' (2013: 426). The image of the figure which we are prompted to scrutinise in such minute detail was in fact the source of Kunzru's initial inspiration for the novel: 'One of the first images I put up was of somebody walking by the side of a major road. This grew into the character Arjun's non-driving experience of California' (Aldama 2005: 13).

As in the example above, the narrative voice which charges us with a moral responsibility is one that is interested in spaces and especially the spaces in which the nameless mass of humanity exists. Committed to the material and built environment, it concentrates on the concrete which grounds identities, rather than the ephemera transmitted through internet waves. Kunzru's world view, his mental model of reality which frames his ideas and attitudes about the world and the human beings that live in it beyond the individual characters depicted in his novel, can be discerned in his very clear images of the built environment. It is a world view which sees economic progress and, in particular, the processes of *state capitalism* in developing economies such as India and the United Arab Emirates as fundamentally corrupt. These states enrich the few, displace the poor and swell millions of people jostling to secure for themselves 'every imaginable variant of discreet low-cost modernism' (Kunzru 2005: 14). The 'new industrial fairyland of the nation', (Kunzru 2005: 14), the North Okhla Industrial Development Area (NOIDA), where Arjun lives before migrating to America, personifies state capitalism and the domination of the world by specialised technocratic elites.

The industrial edifices of NOIDA in developing India contrast with the seat of economic and political power of the developed world: Brussel's EU headquarters, where Guy Swift has been sent to cut a deal to design a 'Pan European Border Agency' (PEBA). Kunzru asserts in

Transmission that in Brussels, and 'like all areas devoted to government and administration, the physical has been ruthlessly subordinated to the immaterial, to the *exigencies of language*. [. . .] [I]n the EU quarter, language is order and with order comes violence, [. . .]. [I]t is a violence that has been coated in language, incrementally surrounded and domesticated by it [. . .]' (2005: 249, emphasis mine). Kunzru is speaking, without parody, in the vein of Paul Ricoeur who argues that 'violence has its meaning in its other: language. [. . .] A violence that speaks is already a violence trying to be right: it is a violence that places itself in the orbit of reason and that already is beginning to negate itself as violence' (1974: 89). Ricoeur also argues that within politics 'the rule of law which gives form to the social body is also power, an enormous violence which elbows its way through our private violences and speaks the language of value and honor' (1974: 94). Bureaucratic and political language, then, as endlessly issued forth from Brussels, isolates the poor and empowers the rich who are invariably further legitimised by their control over this discourse. Despite the novel's parodic tone, *Transmission's* self-conscious narrative strategies are profoundly socially conscious. They seek to raise the privileged reader's awareness that the transnational flows of knowledge and capital, transmitted virtually and which fuel knowledge-based economies from which the reader is likely to benefit, are also everyday reminders of exceptional vulnerability and fallibility.

My Revolutions (2007): circular politics

Kunzru's third novel, *My Revolutions*, is his least critiqued and also the most localised of his novels, being set predominantly in England. The most realist and perhaps most traditional of Kunzru's work, it is also certainly the least parodic of his major novels thus far. While as Andy Beckett argues, '[f]or a few pages this comfortable modern Britain is subjected to slightly obvious satire' (2007: np), Tim Adams rightly asserts that the novel 'is a departure for Kunzru, whose two previous novels, – *The Impressionist* and *Transmission* – were teeming satirical explorations of cultural identity and colonialism' (2007: np). *My Revolutions* centres around the domestic and political life of a protagonist with dual identities, one of which he hides from his friends and family. Michael Frame, an otherwise innocuous middle class British man from suburban west London was once Chris Carver, a fugitive member of an underground revolutionary and at times militant group politically active in the 1970s. In the novel, Chris and his comrades are responsible for the 1971 bombing of the Post Office Tower, an act for which he is never caught. Anticipating his much more audacious fourth novel, *Gods Without Men*, published four years after *My Revolutions*, Kunzru explores the search for meaning and motivation by citizens of the developed world who lead fundamentally materially secure but banal lives in countries regulated by 'the hypnotic dream-show of fuckable bodies and consumer goods' (Kunzru 2005: 202). For his resistance to the presumptions of postmodern prosperity, Michael is imprisoned for protesting against the Vietnam war outside the American Embassy and after his release, lives in a series of London squats. In one sense, an element of parody also exists in the novel. Michael, fleeing from a political imbroglio in Britain flees to the Wat Tham Nok Monastery in Thailand to seek physical and spiritual salvation from a heroin addiction and to steep himself in third world religious asceticism. When finally Michael claims 'It took me a long time to put a name to my disillusionment. I wanted to go home' (2005: 271), this point of view seems all too self-indulgent, privileged and Western.

Beyond these brief moments of parody, Matthew Hart (2009) identifies in Kunzru's work and in *My Revolutions*, in particular, Kunzru's critique of state practices in a post 9/11 world. Hart argues that the novel invokes a radical 'critique of sovereignty', a term, drawing on the work of Georgia Agamben, that describes the inherently coercive nature of state power. The novel, for

Hart, encourages readers to sympathise with the erstwhile political fervour of Chris Carver, despite its tragic repercussions as the novel progresses. The time period in which the novel is set is important. It begins in 1998, a few years prior to 9/11, when Britain's sovereign power was less ubiquitous and the state could convince its citizenship that a retreat from social obligation was for the best through the promotion of a neoliberal hegemony under the New Labour government (Hart 2009: 1067).

Yet I would further argue that Chris/Michael himself remains convinced that the state's social function is crucial to social citizenship and he fails to relinquish this fundamental belief in the state's ability to construct a better future, despite his profound resistance to state sovereignty at an earlier, more radical, point in his life. The novel is thus an exploration of sovereignty, the nature of the contemporary British state and the extent of its biopolitical hold over its citizens. The state's paring back of its social democratic functions under Blair's Britain while claiming to be protective underpins a contradiction absorbed by everyone (including Chris) who passively complies but who cannot extricate himself from this quandary. The novel suggests that his own revolution is thus doomed and circumscribed by the state itself. Even though Chris chooses to reject 'the states' claim to mediate collective life through the juridical structure of citizenship' (Hart 2009: 1065), he nonetheless eventually subscribes to these citizenships in deference to his role within the sureties of the bourgeois family.

Gods Without Men (2011): endless faith

As a departure from his other novels, Kunzru's fourth novel is set entirely in the United States, a terrain made both more familiar and confounding to him after a move to New York City in 2008 to research the book at the New York Public Library. 'I'd underestimated what it would mean to be in America, surrounded by Americans, having to deal with and understand America in a way that I hadn't before. It seemed the only sensible thing I could write about was America'. (Gilbert 2012: np). Discussing *Gods Without Men*, published in 2012, Douglas Coupland situates Kunzru's work amongst other contemporary authors such as Michael Cunningham and David Mitchell. Coupland locates parallels in these writers' works in 'a new literary genre' he labels 'translit'. For him, these narratives 'span geography without changing psychic place', inserting 'the contemporary reader into other locations and times, while leaving no doubt that its view-point is relentlessly modern and speaks entirely of our extreme present' (2012: np). Frequently set against the 'blank' canvass of a vast Mojave desert landscape in Southern California, the novel coalesces Native American myth, the diary of an eighteenth century Spanish Franciscan friar, contemporary celebratory pop culture as well as records of a hippy alien worshipping cult during the 1960s. These narratives intertwine against the backdrop of a media whirlwind generated over the mysterious disappearance of a young mixed race boy in the desert.

In terms of the novel's 'translit' elements, critics often focus more specifically on the 'cross-time' effect of the novel, spanning the eighteenth century to present contemporary times in the first decade of the twenty-first century. From a cosmopolitan viewpoint, Carmen Zamorano Llena argues that the novel's 'signifiers such as place, borders, locality and nation do not dilute in the mesh of globalising influences; the signifiers are maintained, though repeatedly throughout the times, they have new layers of interpretation added, which are shaped by their socio–historical context' (2016: 10). Similarly drawing on theories of cosmopolitanism, Berthold Schoene (2012) sees Kunzru's *Gods Without Men* as an example of what he calls 'cosmopoetics', a term defined against 'cosmo-kitsch'. He argues that David Mitchell pioneered 'cosmopoetic devices' in *Cloud Atlas* (2004) and in Mitchell's and Kunzru's novels, the characters typify 'cosmopoetic paradigms, anticipating and seemingly replicating one another, each individual existence reverberating with the life-stories of a multitude of contemporaries, ancestors and descendants' (Schoene 2012: 110). In *Gods Without Men*, these paradigms wend through disruptive yet congruent narrative threads, enabling both a celebration and a critique of the myth of America's founding principles of diverse democracy. Individuality emplaced within highly disparate communities is relentlessly pursued by the novel's characters but found endlessly lacking. Kunzru parodically represents this particular conception of the American self within a collective national identity to be delusional and often self destructive.

Daniel O'Gorman also draws parallels between Mitchell's *Cloud Atlas* and Kunzru's *Gods Without Men* (2015b: 95). Reflecting on the novel's engagement with more contemporary political times, O'Gorman has recently placed the novel within 'Fictions of the War on Terror' and deems it a 'transnational 9/11 novel' (2015b). Borrowing from a term in Roger Luckhurst's article 'In War Times: Fictionalizing Iraq' (2012), O'Gorman argues that the 'novel demands to be read "polytemporally"' (2015b: 95), where there is constant interplay of the old and the new. O'Gorman focuses his idea of polytemporality, in particular, on the different raids depicted in the novel that forces references to more recent historical conflicts. Scenes of a police raid on the drug addled alien worshipping cult camped in the desert as well as simulated raids on volunteer Iraqi refugees organised by a military training camp preparing soldiers for deployment to Iraq are transferable onto images of both the Vietnam War and the protracted Iraq War. But the desert wilderness that is transformed into a fictitious Iraqi village by a postimperial America is also reminiscent of 'the memory of [America's] annihilated Native communities at the same time as [Kunzru] satirizes the "counter-insurgency" tactics of the U.S military [. . .]' (2015b: 548). Critics such as Schoene and O'Gorman have focused on the novel's 'cross-time' effects but have yet to stress that one of the novel's most consistent motifs across its multiple time zones reflects the history of exploitative capitalism and responses to its alienating effects.

Indeed, the novel appears to form part of Kunzru's self-admitted interest in 'the more general (and ultimately quixotic) project of trying to understand capitalism' (Kumar 2012: np). *Gods Without Men* parodies the strange ephemeral, alienating effects of individual and family life attenuated under late capitalism and dominated by global financial mechanisms and social machines which persistently demand cycles of personal and public projects of 'prediction and control' to engage with, in Kunzru's words, 'the extraordinary transnational web that has been created by globalization' (Kumar 2012: np). Kunzru suggests, however, that religion, which works as a counterforce to these uncertainties, remains just as elusive. Many of these themes are repeatedly explored with the same ironic self-consciousness in the 2005 collection, *Noise*, in stories such as 'Bodywork' (Kunzru 2005) and 'Godmachine™ V.I.0.4' (Kunzru 2005). This sentiment is perhaps aptly encapsulated in the claim by the narrator of the short story 'Deux Ex Machina' (Kunzru 2005) that 'as is well known, God moves in mysterious ways' (Kunzru 2005: 16).

Yet the irony within *Gods Without Men* lies in the family plot which unfolds around Jaz' family. Despite possessing access to vast reams of detailed financial information as a financial analyst which he deploys to predict and simulate market trends, it is him and his family who are subjected to the most inexplicable events in the novel: his autistic son suddenly goes missing during a family outing to the desert and then just as mysteriously reappears. The novel endeavours to explore a range of sites of meaning people seek to combat uncertainty, sites which are themselves ever proliferating products of consumer capitalism under globalization. Some of these are more innocuous than others. On the one hand there are Eastern religions, the worship of music celebrities, a belief in the extra terrestrial, and on the other there are predatory cults and a military-masculinity industrial complex led by the United States. The novel's parodic touch implies that despite these individual and collective searches for respite from seemingly irrational and inarticulable pain – what Kunzru calls 'people yearning for the on-high to come and infuse their lives with meaning' (Romig 2012: np) – these are efforts that are always already flawed. Certainly the novel's panoply of characters, drawn together to the desert through their confrontations with the endless possibilities for meaning, reflects the success of the novel's extended metaphor, the blank and sublime desert itself.

Memory Palace (2013): can't you see how we are diminished?

In 2013, Kunzru publishes *Memory Palace*, a 10,000 word novella specially commissioned by the Victoria and Albert Museum in London which in turn inspired 20 international multimedia artists who created works for the museum's exhibition 'Sky Arts Ignition: Memory Palace'. Set against a post-apocalyptic London ravaged by a magnetic storm which has destroyed the world's information infrastructure, Kunzru's dystopian novella is unremittingly bleak. Amidst the ruination wreaked by 'the Withering', where all memory, art, writing and recording – indeed, all knowledge and technology – has been lost and banned, the novel is set against a landscape that is recognisably London of the early twenty-first century. Addressed to 'fellow Londoners' (2013: 15), the narrative traces one man's endeavours to rehouse his memory palace (an imaginary location in the mind organised around mnemonic images) in his cell as he mnemonically relives fragments of a bygone past up to the point known as 'the Booming', in other words, a period of late capitalism or postmodernity.

'The Thing' consists of a group of men who seek a return to 'The Wilding', a wholly natural state of existence. They hold the unnamed narrator prisoner for being a fellow of the Memorialists, a banned sect of members who seek to remember facts. While suffering intermittent scenes of torment by 'The Thing', the narrator also recollects frequently erroneous facts and descriptions of a waste strewn and decaying London remembered collectively by the Memorialists which serve as a palimpsest of scientific technological and cultural advancements across the centuries. These memories include the use of 'pewters' to perform the complex financial transactions that structure late capitalism.

If our heroic narrator stands for some of the foundational cornerstones of civilisations across time – intellectual life, culture, society and crucially, language, notably referenced as 'sign' throughout the narrative – then his enemies represent a regressive, violent and primal state. Indeed, if Kunzru so frequently parodies the excesses of contemporary life, this novella appears as an unambiguous celebration of human society's monumental achievements and potential, timed perhaps as an oblique condemnation of present day fundamentalist movements which seek to destroy everyday freedoms. Nonetheless, a *Guardian* review of the exhibition inspired by Kunzru's moral tale suggests that *Memory Palace* is 'part satire of contemporary life' and perhaps these satirical elements are most critical of the presumed privileges of life in the developed world. Even in a world in which terrorism often looms large, Kunzru asserts that 'Britain is a wealthy country, and a safe country' (2003: np). But this should not be taken for granted. Zoe Pilger also rightly argues, in a review of the book, that '[p]ublic services, literacy, museums, free expression – are rooted in dazzling leaps of the imagination and must be defended' (2013: np).

The futuristic dystopia of *Memory Palace* and the nexus between advanced technology and a capitalist world system are clearly themes which Kunzru would like to develop. In March 2015, *Granta* published Hari Kunzru's short story 'Drone', extracted from a forthcoming novel. Unlike the London of *Memory Palace*, the short story is set in a post-apocalyptic, but identifiably, Indian landscape where the earth's resources have been stripped bare. The story portrays a hideous society completely overlaid with both huge industrial technology as well as nanotechnology, some biologically embedded into every human being; human exploitation and rampant capitalism are heightened to the point where every part of everything and everybody is for sale. Jai, the name of the autistic child in *Gods Without Men*, is also the name of an impoverished Indian miner in the short story who tragically dies from hybrid complications of both digital and biological sources following a botched transplant of a mechanical arm which he had hoped would help him mine raw metals more efficiently. Placed on the other end of the social spectrum is the Seth, an all powerful and encompassing business overlord with a penchant for Italian Renaissance art. The Seth's particular cultural affiliation with European civilisation places him as a futuristic neocolonial figure, suggesting Kunzru's rather dire prognosis for the ongoing process of neocolonial exploitation.

White Tears (2017): black lives

Hari Kunzru's latest and fifth novel *White Tears* (2017), is set against the wider backdrop of the United States as a late twentieth century/early twenty-first century Empire whose wealth was established on the back of the transatlantic slave trade. The legacies of the trade in black bodies resonate throughout the novel which was written in the wake of the growing international momentum behind the Black Lives Matter movement, born in 2013 following the murder of Trayvon Martin, and glibly dismissed by one of the novel's most privileged characters, Leonie Wallace, as pointless for white people to support: '[e]ven if you did something, I don't know, really selfless. Black lives matter or whatever. They [black people] still wouldn't like you'. (153). As with Kunzru's previous novels, parody operates through capturing the colloquially quotidian to critique the narcissistic excesses of economic wealth within a system of global capitalism. In this novel, parody is also directed against the farcical sense of 'a post-racial America' (263). Kunzru parodies the white characters who dominate the novel through what he calls 'a plot that is mostly a sort of carnival of white pathology' (Barron 2017). In contrast, the black characters – often ghostly and surreal – receive serious historical attention, refracted through the assiduous research Kunzru conducted into the history of black American music: 'It occurred to me that if America is still haunted by racism, then this novel should take the form of a ghost story'. (Barron 2017). In this postmodern cross-time, non-linear narrative, black history literally and figuratively fills the margins of the novel and denudes the 'disabling caucasity' (17) of white men in pursuit of black authenticity.

White Tears 'starts as a satire about the search for authenticity' (Tait 2017) as Kunzru introduces two white college graduate music geeks, Carter Wallace and Seth, who obsess with recapturing the 'authentic' sound of blues music. They artificially produce a seemingly unique old blues track – replete with elemental distortion and crackle – ironically via the gadgetry of highly sophisticated and exorbitant state of the art music technology and equipment. Their ability to do so speaks of Carter's immense class entitlement hailing from a family empire who are leading federal providers of detention and correctional services boasting the use of 'advanced networked monitoring technologies' (260). The parallel, albeit different, technologies that endow the Wallaces across different generations with social, economic, cultural and racial power are linked to the systemic oppression of African-Americans through the ages: from the post-emancipation era during which the Wallaces reaped a fortune, to the contemporary era of black urban music which the Wallaces also exploit through the music industry. The novel thus explores the motivations behind those who maintain America's racial hierarchies and the telos of black disempowerment.

The spectre of black trauma and disenfranchisement that comes to haunt the Wallaces and possess Seth in phantasmagorical scenes takes the form of the elusive figure of Charlie Shaw, a talented and long lost blues musician whose voice the young music producers unknowingly sample on their track. Originally from the Jim Crow South, Shaw's career in the 1920s is tragically cut short when a white policeman arrests him under the pernicious vagrancy laws while on his way to his first recording. Unable to pay his fines, he ends up on the chain gang labouring for Wallace Construction. His broken spirit appears throughout the novel in malevolent forms as he seeks reparations and ekes revenge on the Wallace family by destroying both Carter and Leonie. But these appearances/apparitions also manifest themselves – in various surreal settings – as contemporary racist African-American stereotypes upon which white fear and hatred of the black other depend. Thus Charlie Shaw partially materialises in the novel as Leonie's rapist murderer and as a thuggish gangster adorned with gold rings in a low slung car with a thumping bassline. In this sense, the novel uses Shaw to critique black archetypes which are reinvented and resurrected through different periods, both past and present.

Kunzru initially parodies Seth and Carter's supercilious preoccupation with being true to, and honouring, black music by their quintessentially postmodern fetishisation of a retrograde musical sound underpinned by a fundamental disregard for its material history. However, as the novel's plot unfolds, this parodic tone serves as a strident and unequivocal condemnation of white appropriation of black cultural self-expression wrought from suffering, poverty and deep seated racial injustice. Sukhdev Sandhu argues that '[a]t the heart of the book is an exploration, or perhaps dark satire, about cultural appropriation' (2017). The novel further suggests that this co-option may at times be a violent hijacking of a communal form of black identity and a plundering of black heritage, all in the name of white cultural custodianship or curatorship. The blues, as Ron Eyerman argues, 'is the memory of slavery [. . . it] gave expression to black subjectivity, [. . .] being intimately connected to a collectivity, to being black in America'. (119). One of the novel's triumphs, then, must thus be Kunzru's efforts to entwine the gravity of slavery's contemporary legacies with self-conscious parody of the purportedly highly self-conscious, but in truth, profoundly ignorant, performance of white hipster culture.

Kunzru's oeuvre to date, then, captures with nuance, precision and a prevailing tone of parody and satire the zeitgeist of twenty-first century globalised societies networked through both capital and technology. Yet, despite his highly contemporary tone and style, he remains equally attentive to the historical foundations underwriting those individuals and nations who have benefited from these networks. On the other hand, Kunzru's parodic tone frequently departs in his portrayals, often with profound sympathy, of individuals and communities marginalised, victimised and killed by the advancement of such networks. Following his move from London to New York in 2008, we also see Kunzru's works more consistently depicting the United States as Britain's heir to the multifarious excesses and egos of global imperial power.

Works cited

Adams, T. (2007) September 2, Rev. of *My Revolutions*. *The Guardian* [online] Available at <www.theguardian.com/books/2007/sep/02/fiction.features3> [Accessed 12 September 2016].

Aldama, F.L. (2005) Hari Kunzru in Conversation. *Wasafiri* 20(45), 11–14.

—— (2009) Fictional World Making in Zadie Smith and Hari Kunzru. *A User's Guide to Postcolonial and Latino Borderland Fiction*, 86–106.

Appadurai, A. (2006) *Fear of Small Numbers*. Durham and London: Duke University Press.

Aydemir, M. (2006) Impressions of Character: Hari Kunzru's *The Impressionist*. In Boer, I.E., Bal, M., and Eekele, B van. eds. *Uncertain Territories: Boundaries in Cultural Analysis*. Amsterdam and New York: Rodopi, 199–217.

Barron, M. (2017) May, Interview with Hari Kunzru. *White Review* [online] Available at <https://www.thewhitereview.org/feature/interview-hari-kunzru/> [Accessed 6 March 2018].

Beckett, A. (2007) August 25, Rev. of *My Revolutions* [online] Available at <www.theguardian.com/books/2007/aug/25/featuresreviews.guardianreview15> [Accessed 12 September 2016].

Behdad, A. and Williams, J. (2010) Neo-Orientalism. In Edwards, B.T. and Parameshwar, G.D. eds. *Globalizing American Studies*. Chicago: University of Chicago Press, 283–299.

Bhabha, H. (1994) *The Location of Culture*. London and New York: Routledge.

Brock, R. (2008) An 'Onerous Citizenship': Globalization, Cultural Flows and the HIV/AIDS Pandemic in Hari Kunzru's *Transmission*. *Journal of Postcolonial Writing* 44(4), 379–390.

Connell, L. (2010) E-Terror: Computer Viruses, Class and Transnationalism in *Transmission* and *One Night @ the Call Center*. *Journal of Postcolonial Writing* 46(3–4), 279–290.

Coupland, D. (2012) March 8, Rev. of *Gods without Men*. *The New York Times* [online] Available at <www.nytimes.com/2012/03/11/books/review/gods-without-men-by-hari-kunzru.html?_r=0> [Accessed 12 September 2016].

Deleuze, G. and Guattari, F. (1972) [1983] *Anti-Oedipus: Capitalism and Schizophrenia*. Minneapolis: University of Minnesota Press.

Gilbert, E. (2012) 13 January. That's Where Coyote Comes In: *PW* Talks with Hari Kunzru. *Publishers Weekly* [online] Available at <www.publishersweekly.com/pw/by-topic/authors/interviews/article/50172-that-s-where-coyote-comes-in-pw-talks-with-hari-kunzru.html> [Accessed 23 September 2016].

Graham, S. (2013) Memories of Empire: The Empire Exhibition in Andrea Levy's *Small Island* and Hari Kunzru's *The Impressionist*. *The Journal of Commonwealth Literature* 48(3), 441–452.

Gunning, D. (2012) Ethnicity, Authenticity and Empathy in the Realist Novel and Its Alternatives. *Contemporary Literature* 53(4), 779–813.

Hart, M. (2009) The Politics of the State in Contemporary Literary Studies. *Literature Compass* 6(5), 1060–1070.

Hill, D. (2015) *The Pathology of Communicative Capitalism*. Basingstoke: Palgrave Macmillan.

Johansen, E. (2013) Becoming the Virus: Responsibility and Cosmopolitan Labor in Hari Kunzru's *Transmission*. *Journal of Postcolonial Writing* 49(4), 419–431.

Kabani, R. (1986) *Imperial Fictions: Europe's Myths of the Orient*. London: Macmillan.

Kumar, A. (2012) March 6. Hari Kunzru on *Gods without Men*. *Paris Review* [online] Available at <www.theparisreview.org/blog/2012/03/06/hari-kunzru-on-%E2%80%98gods-without-men%E2%80%99/> [Accessed 13 September 2016].

Kunzru, H. (2002) [2003] *The Impressionist*. New York and London: Plume.

—— (2003) November 22, I Am One of Them. *The Guardian* [online] Available at www.theguardian.com/books/2003/nov/22/immigration.pressandpublishing [Accessed 12 September 2016]

—— (2004) [2005] *Transmission* London: Penguin Books.

—— (2005) *Noise* London: Penguin Books.

—— (2007) [2008] *My Revolutions* London: Penguin Books.

—— (2011) *Gods without Men* London: Penguin Books.

—— (2013) *Memory Palace* London: V & A Publishing.

—— (2015) Drone. *Granta* [online] Available at <https://granta.com/drone/> [Accessed 16 September 2016].

—— (2017) *White Tears* London: Hamish Hamilton.

Leonard, P. (2014) 'A Revolution in Code?' Hari Kunzru's *Transmission and the Cultural Politics of Hacking*. *Textual Practice* 28(2), 267–287.

Liao, P.-C. (2013) Crossing the Borders of the Body Politic after 9/11: The Virus Metaphor and Auto-immunity in Hari Kunzru's *Transmission*. In *'Post' -9/11 South Asian Diasporic Fiction: Uncanny Terror*. Basingstoke: Palgrave Macmillan, 53–84.

Luckhurst, R. (2012) In War Times: Fictionalizing Iraq. *Contemporary Literature* 53(4), 713–737.

Lyall, S. (2002) July 2, Rootless But at Home in a Britannia All His Own. [online] Available at <www.nytimes.com/2002/07/02/arts/02ARTS.html?pagewanted=2> [Accessed 12 September 2016].

Mitchell, D. (2004) *Cloud Atlas*. London: Sceptre.

Nyman, J. (2009) The Politics of Self-Making in Post-Colonial Fiction: The *Bildung* of Pretty Bobby in Hari Kunzru's *The Impressionist*. In *Home, Identity, and Mobility in Contemporary Diasporic Fiction*. Amsterdam and New York: Rodopi, 93–107.

O'Gorman, D. (2015a) Refiguring Difference: Imaginative Geographies and 'Connective Dissonance' in Three Novels of the Iraq War. *Critique: Studies in Contemporary Fiction* 56(5), 545–559.

—— (2015b) *Fictions of the War on Terror: Difference and the Transnational 9/11 Novel*. Basingstoke: Palgrave Macmillan.

Pilger, Z. (2013) Art Review: Memory Palace, V&A Museum, London. *The Independent* [online] Available at <www.independent.co.uk/arts-entertainment/art/reviews/art-review-memory-palace-va-museum-london-8663549.html>[Accessed 16 September 2016].

Ricoeur, P. (1974) Violence and Language. In Bien, J. trans. *Political and Social Essays by Paul Ricoeur*. Athens, OH: Ohio University Press, 88–101.

Robinson, A. (2008) Faking It: Simulation and Self-Fashioning in Hari Kunzru's *Transmission*. In Murphy, N. and Sim, W.-C. eds. *British Asian Fiction: Framing the Contemporary*. Amherst, New York: Cambria Press, 77–96.

Romig, R. (2012) March 13, Staring into the Void with Hari Kunzru. *The New Yorker* [online] Available at <www.newyorker.com/books/page-turner/staring-into-the-void-with-hari-kunzru> [Accessed 16 September 2016].

Said, E. (1979) *Orientalism*. New York: Vintage.

Sandhu, S. (2017) Rev. of *White Tears*. *The Guardian* [online] Available at <www.theguardian.com/books/2017/apr/28/white-tears-hari-kunzru-review> [Accessed 6 March 2018].

Schaff, B. (2009) Roots, Genes and Performativity in Zadie Smith's *White Teeth* and Hari Kunzru's *The Impressionist*. In Schulze-Engler, F. and Helff, S. eds. *Transcultural English Studies: Theories, Fictions, Realities*. Amsterdam and New York: Rodopi, 281–292.

Schoene, B. J. (2012) Cosmo-Kitsch vs. Cosmopoetics. *The Review of Contemporary Fiction* 32(3), 105–113.

Shelden, A.T. (2012) Cosmopolitan Love: The One and the World in Hari Kunzru's *Transmission*. *Contemporary Literature* 53(2), 349–373.

Tait, T. (2017) 27 July, Three Minutes of Darkness, Rev. of *White Tears*. *London Review of Books* 39(15), 37–38.

Zamorano Llena, C. (2016) A Cosmopolitan Conceptualisation of Place and New Topographies of Identity in Hari Kunzru's Gods without Men. *Transnational Literature* 8(2), 1–11.

31

JENNIFER EGAN

Dorothy Butchard

Jennifer Egan's work traces shifting perceptions of time, memory and technological change in the contemporary era, offering keenly observed and often prescient insights into American culture in the twentieth and twenty-first centuries. 'Freakishly,' Egan observed of her 2001 novel *Look at Me*, a decade after it was first published, 'almost every aspect I invented has come to pass in some way, including the terrorist who fantasises about blowing up the World Trade Centre' (Fox 2011: n.pag.). The 'freakish' predictions which occasionally emerge in Egan's writing are the result of careful social observation, demonstrated in her depictions of New York-based celebrity and media scenes, the inexorable intertwining of commercial interests with new technologies, and the frustrations of social conformity and suburban life. *Look At Me* explores a feverish schism between reality, virtual reality and marketing prompted by the advance of new media and blogging platforms, and this interest in the effects of changing technologies is central to much of Egan's published work. In *The Keep* (2007), *A Visit from the Goon Squad* (2010) and the short story 'Black Box' (2012a), Egan pursues her interest in technologised intersections of culture and commerce, while retaining the skilful depiction of memory and loss central to earlier short stories and her first published novel, *The Invisible Circus* (2012c). Egan's most recent novel, *Manhattan Beach* (2017), reconfigures these concerns in a historical context, setting the possibilities offered by technological progress in 1930s New York against the perilous backdrop of the second world war. This chapter examines the evolution of these themes across Egan's oeuvre, reflected in her subtle experimentation with style, genre and narrative structure.

Egan insists that her fictional works are written in what she calls a spirit of discovery. 'I discover the plot as I go,' she explained in a 2009 interview, "writing in an exploratory way . . . In fact, if I know too much at the beginning, it's a bad sign' (Reilly 2009: 442). This 'exploratory' impulse is evident in the omnivorous referencing of narrative styles and genres found across Egan's writing, as well as her expansive approach to plot and characterisation. In *Look at Me*, Egan cycles between the viewpoints of four different protagonists – ex-model Charlotte, who agrees to publish every detail of her life online, the fundamentalist Z, still trying to come to terms with his encounter with America, troubled college professor Moose, and a younger character, also named Charlotte, struggling through awkward teenage years. This structural experimentation and use of multiple protagonists has become a frequent feature of Egan's work. Reviewing *The Keep* in 2006, Bell described Egan as an 'unclassifiable novelist'

(Bell 2006: n.pag.), and this novel finds Egan experimenting with increasingly complex narrative layers. With three separate author-figures each writing in a distinctive narrative voice, *The Keep* delights in a mixture of gothic pastiche and 1960s metafictional devices, as it darts between different modes of expression deployed by the novel's insouciantly wayward narrators. The exploratory qualities of this 'unclassifiable' approach are also apparent in Egan's treatment of a near-future scenario in 'Black Box,' whose cybernetically modified protagonist narrates her experiences as direct 'instructions,' originally published online as a series of tweets. Egan's most recent publication, *Manhattan Beach*, is more easily classifiable as a historical novel – but as Anna Diebel observes, it is also 'a crime story, and, to its credit, a self-reflexive one' (Diebel 2017: n.pag.). Just as *Look at Me*, *The Keep* and 'Black Box' dabble with noir, detective fiction, gothic stylings, and speculative fiction, *Manhattan Beach* incorporates stylistic traits and plot devices drawn from the thrillers and pot-boilers enjoyed by its protagonists, while the move into the realm of historical fiction marks another direction in Egan's continuing journey through literary categories.[1]

The genre-bending qualities and structural complexities of Egan's writing are most immediately apparent in the Pulitzer Prize-winning *A Visit from the Goon Squad* (henceforth *Goon Squad*), her most critically acclaimed work to date. Like David Mitchell's *Cloud Atlas* (2004) and Colum McCann's *Let the Great World Spin* (2009), *Goon Squad* encompasses a wide variety of narrative perspectives, with thirteen loosely 'entangled' (Ciabattari 2010: n.pag.) stories each focusing on a different character, location and chronological moment. The lives of *Goon Squad*'s characters play out across a number of destinations from San Francisco to southern Africa, with a broad chronological sweep stretching from the punk scene of the 1970s to a near-future version of New York. The book is structured as discrete sections which overlap and intertwine, a 'mash-up of forms' (Blythe 2010: n.pag.) whose characters are constantly engaged in forging and breaking links, endeavouring to discover truths about one other, only to discover further layers of meaning which remain obscured. While she was writing *Goon Squad*, Egan described it as 'a constellation of intersecting lives' (Reilly 2009: 440), and has since suggested that she altered its structure to emphasise these intersections. In a 2010 interview, Egan explains that she had originally intended the stories to cycle backwards through time, but changed her mind, instead choosing to scramble the stories' chronology. The eventual structure in the print version was the product of Egan's 'own curiosity' (Julavits and Egan 2010: n.pag.), arranged according to the author's sense of which story would be most 'satisfying' to encounter next, 'based on these little tingling awarenesses of other people and other possible stories that might interest the reader' (Ibid).[2] The result is a text whose shifting chapters play with the possibility of readerly 'discovery'; for each of the 'possible stories' that flicker into life amidst this pattern of recurring characters and imagery, many others will inevitably remain untold.

Egan's reference to 'tingling awarenesses' sparked by possible stories indicates a crucial aspect of her literary approach: the tendency to unlayer characters' lives by offering a series of brief, intense glimpses of significant moments. In an essay on memory, A.S. Byatt recalls the '"glittering" quality' of certain childhood experiences, 'excessively bright, strongly outlined, *recognised* so to speak as important, even when they were met for the first time' (Byatt 1998: 47). Egan's fictional representations rely on a similar impression of the glittering quality of moments marked out for future recollection. This is one of the more striking aspects of her fiction, and its most recognisable stylistic trait, as narratives zoom in on characters in moments when they pause to imagine the significance of particular events and sensations for their own future recollection. Examples of this technique abound throughout Egan's oeuvre, beginning with the earliest short stories. Bernadette, a character in 'The Stylist,' 'longs for this moment as if it had already passed' (Egan 2012b: 68), while the teenage narrator in 'Sisters of the Moon' imagines looking back from her own future:

> When I'm thirty-four, tonight will be a million years ago, I think – the St Francis Hotel and the rainy palm tree sounds, Silas with the bandage on his head – and this makes me see how everything now is precious, how someday I'll know I was lucky to be here.
>
> (Egan 2012b: 170)

The flashfoward in 'Sisters of the Moon' exemplifies Egan's use of this technique to emphasise the emotional import of certain moments, rendered 'precious' by anticipated nostalgia. In Egan's first novel, *The Invisible Circus* (2012c), protagonist Phoebe has a sensation of 'hurtling forward in time until she was looking back from an imaginary future' (Egan 2012c: 297), and finds herself reassured by the idea that 'she would stand somewhere and look back, she would live a life' (Ibid.). In *Look at Me*, Charlotte experiences 'an anticipatory nostalgia for the sweet, small life I would soon cast off; its every detail felt precious' (Egan 2011b: 172). Each of these instances serves to emphasise characters' sense of the present moment's precious ephemerality.

Mark Currie defines such moments as 'the anticipation of retrospection' (Currie 2007: 31), describing this particular kind of flashfoward as 'structural prolepsis,' where '[t]he present is experienced as the object of a future memory' (40). In Egan's writing, the emotional impact varies according to the reader's knowledge of an eventual outcome. Whereas Phoebe and Charlotte are soothed by 'anticipatory nostalgia' in *Invisible Circus*, moments of structural prolepsis can also reveal the bitterness of false comfort. At the conclusion to *Invisible Circus*, Faith's boyfriend Wolf recalls watching her stand on a cliff face, reassuring himself that '[s]omeday we'll look back on all this and die laughing' (327). Faith falls to her death while Wolf is left still 'reaching for that time, that calm, sweet place out ahead' (Ibid). In *Goon Squad*, the removal of the 'calm, sweet place' of an anticipated future is further exacerbated by the novel's use of a scrambled chronology.[3] Analysing the non-chronological form of *Goon Squad* as an exemplar of her definition of a 'networked novel,' Caroline Edwards finds that amidst its 'narrative loops, thematic eddies and. . . . expanding network of people' the 'theme of loss coalesces into a central novelistic concern' (Edwards 2018: insert pag at proof stage). This is not only the loss of bereavement – as with Phoebe's mourning for her sister in *Invisible Circus* – but also the loss of future experiences snatched away from the individuals who hope to live them. Shortly before his own death, Rob in *Goon Squad* anticipates a future which will never transpire. '[F]or a second,' he announces, 'the future tunnels out and away, some version of "you" at the end of it, looking back' (Egan 2011a: 209). A few pages later, he is drowning, in a death already foretold by *Goon Squad*'s opening chapter.

By combining nostalgic sentimentality with pitilessly direct declarations of character's fates, Egan's writing demonstrates how the 'anticipation of retrospection' (Currie 2007: 31) can be rendered bittersweet by a reader's foreknowledge of impending disaster. In *Goon Squad*, Egan tends to disrupt descriptions of a character's narrative 'present' by offering stark presentiments of their future from the viewpoint of an omniscient narrator. Thus the chapter titled 'Safari,' first published as a short story in the *New Yorker*, undercuts a child's moment of unselfconscious delight by revealing the bleak future which awaits him. A description of twelve-year-old Rolph, thrilled to be dancing with his older sister, is brutally spliced with a flashforward to his traumatised adulthood:

> As they move together, Rolph feels his self-consciousness miraculously fade, as if he is growing up right there on the dance floor, becoming a boy who dances with girls like his sister. Charlie feels it too. In fact, this particular memory is one she'll return to again

and again, for the rest of her life, long after Rolph has shot himself in the head in their father's house at twenty-eight: her brother as a boy, hair slicked flat, eyes sparkling, shyly learning to dance.

(Egan 2011a: 87)

Folding the news of Rolph's eventual suicide into his delight at the sensation of 'growing up,' and using Charlie's future recollection as a route into this information, Egan destabilises a scene of childish contentment, foreshadowing the instability and uncertainty of future events. Rolph in 'Safari' is a vulnerable boy, already beginning to wrestle with difficult aspects of his relationship with his father, and the significance of this paternal strife is implied by the revelation that his suicide will take place 'in their father's house.' Against this impending tragedy, the beauty of the moment between Rolph and his sister consists in its 'glittering quality,' its simplicity outlined against the mess that will overtake the adult lives of both children.

In moments of narrative anticipation and recollection, Egan uses descriptions of shared objects recurring across time to draw connections between events and characters. Objects can function as significant markers to connect disparate characters and moments, as when 'Safari' reveals that a Kikuyu warrior's iron hunting dagger – 'now hanging at his side' (Egan 2011a: 64) – will be bequeathed to his future grandson, Joe and eventually 'displayed inside a cube of Plexiglas' in Joe's New York apartment. The dagger's appearance concludes a significant flashforward – Bruce Robbins calls it 'epic' in his article on 'Deep Time' – which draws together hitherto disparate sets of characters. Robbins notes that these instances of 'extended prolepsis' produce 'an aesthetically successful and morally valuable uncertainty as to whose story this really is' (Robbins 2012: 201). This is an important function of Egan's flashforwards, as each story is briefly expanded by a reminder of the other, absent lives folded within it. The artefact of the dagger works to compress narrative time by aligning individuals across a dispersed chronology; we learn that it will be displayed in the apartment Joe shares with his future wife Lulu, who features in other chapters of *Goon Squad* as an uncannily composed young child and later as a self-possessed young woman. Here, narrative prolepsis serves a practical structural purpose, used to emphasise points of convergence between the novel's constellation of loosely interlinked characters. The object's significance also transcends the boundaries of its book; years after *Goon Squad*'s publication, the same dagger will make a brief reappearance in the short story 'Black Box,' which features Lulu as a cybernetically enhanced spy who has volunteered for an undercover mission overseas. When Lulu soothes herself by picturing her home in New York, where her husband's 'grandfather's hunting knife is displayed inside a Plexiglas box' (Egan 2012a: Section 42), the object of the dagger reappears as a signifier of safety and familiarity.

The significance of objects in Egan's novels extends beyond their role as convenient markers of plot. Bill Brown refers to 'the slippage between *having* (possessing a particular object) and *being* (the identification of one's self with that object)' (Brown 2003: 13), and Egan explores this slippage in her portrayal of protagonists who define aspects of their identity in relation to certain objects. In *Look at Me*, struggling model Charlotte has carefully assembled the furnishings in her living room, where the 'fluffy white carpeting' (Egan 2011b: 5) and 'soft white upholstery' (38) of her sectional couch provide a consoling space for her gradual recovery from physical injury. Yet when Charlotte snoops through the journal of her ghostwriter, Irene, she is disturbed to find a note observing that Charlotte is 'v. proud' of her apartment, 'esp. sect. couch' (340). Finding that 'reading it in someone else's hand made that pride seem ludicrous' (Ibid.), Charlotte is shocked to discover that her wounded vulnerability emerges through acknowledgment of these objects' value, particularly the couch on which she slumps, sleeps, seduces and collapses. Like Charlotte, Sasha in *Goon Squad* finds herself rendered vulnerable through attachment to her own apartment, which has ended up 'solidifying around [her], gathering mass and weight' until she feels 'both mired in it and lucky to have it' (Egan 2011a: 14). In Sasha's case, the significant objects collected within her apartment comprise a small table filled with items she has stolen from others over the years, and she feels a mix of pride, tenderness and shame at the idea that others might observe the significance of this 'raw, warped core of her life' (15). For Sasha, these objects signify 'glittering moments' from her own past, containing 'years of her life compressed' (15).

Just as Sasha fetishises items she has stolen as a way of pinioning certain moments in her personal history, characters elsewhere in Egan's fictions use objects in a deliberate effort to resurrect memories of others' lives. Egan's works are filled with instances which reclaim the value of solid objects, as in *Invisible Circus*, where sisters Phoebe and Faith recall their deceased father by 'touching the very things their father had touched' (51). 'He was gone forever,' Phoebe acknowledges, 'but he was everywhere. It felt miraculous' (Ibid.). After her sister's death, Phoebe is convinced that 'the key to a mystery was buried among the forgotten moments of her sister's life' (29), and she devotes her efforts to 'finding that trace, placing her hand upon some relic from the scene of Faith's death' (317). These secular relics acquire a totemic power, anticipating Sasha's compulsion to collect objects as a way of compressing 'years of her life.' For Phoebe, the power of objects also extends to significant landscapes, and after reaching the location of Faith's death, she clings to her belief that 'so gigantic an event did not just disappear' (317). Certain that evidence of her sister's suicide must be somehow etched on the landscape, Phoebe compares it with the endurance of fossils amongst 'the earth's shifting plates,' where 'everything left a print, no matter how stark or faint or deeply buried' (317). This conviction that a residue must be etched or perceptible in some way reappears in various modes of expression in Egan's writing, often in the form of haunted and haunting objects and environments. Ray's cellmate in *The Keep* is convinced he can hear ghostly voices through a carefully wired contraption. 'All that love, all that pain, all the stuff people feel,' he explains, 'how can all that disappear when somebody dies? It can't disappear, it's too big. Too strong, too . . . permanent' (Egan 2007: 98). The longing for permanence is palpable in *The Keep*, as characters repeatedly endeavour to overcome seemingly irrevocable absences and ruptures.

In *Manhattan Beach*, even a move from 'the earth's shifting plates' to the changeable surface of the sea cannot overcome a conviction that some signifier of a past presence must remain. When Eddie Kerrigan's ship sinks mid-ocean, it initially seems that he has been forced to accept its disappearance, as he contemplates a blank surface on which 'nothing marked the spot where seven thousand tons of welded steel loaded with nine thousand tons of cargo had floated thirty minutes before' (Egan 2017: 368). The repetition of figures and elements in this phrase works to emphasise the heft of the ship, and the scale conjured by its thousands of tonnes of weight and solidly constructed steel recalls the certainty that some things are 'too strong, too . . . permanent' to disappear (Egan 2007: 98). At first it seems that this solid mass has indeed vanished, since the sunken ship has left 'not a depression, not even a patch of effervescence' on the sea's surface (368). Yet the kind of 'trace' Phoebe yearns for in *Invisible Circus* is subsequently offered up to Eddie, when a glow of plankton appears like 'an emanation from the ocean floor: the *Elizabeth Seaman* and other lost ships, hundreds over centuries, signaling up from the deep' (369). The scene echoes a significant moment in the novel's opening pages, where Eddie's daughter Anna speculates that the ocean's surface must conceal 'a landscape of lost objects: sunken ships, hidden treasure, gold and gems and the charm bracelet that had fallen from her wrist into a storm drain' (6). The sea's concealment of lost objects opens up to the false promise of rediscovery. After Anna achieves her goal of becoming a Navy diver, she ends up scouring the ocean floor for the 'lost object' of her father's absent body; she believes she has achieved this when, with 'an icy shock,' an object becomes 'legible' in the water. The discovery of her father's watch on the seabed prompts Anna to believe she has found his body; the convergence of object, time and memory is complete when she states simply, 'I found him' (338). In these moments, a reality of loss or disappearance is counterbalanced by a longing for – and belief in – the enduring trace of what cannot be restored.

The insistence on the past's permanence in *Invisible Circus*, *The Keep* and *Manhattan Beach* chimes with a recurring metaphor of the present as a permeable layer. Observing others going about their daily routines, Phoebe is convinced that '[b]eneath all this lay a frame of past events, a structure upon which the present was stretched like a skin' (Egan 2012c: 22). In *Goon Squad*, a similar sense of time as layered rather than linear is encapsulated by the representation of shifting and interspersed chronologies. Egan has suggested that this approach is an expression of her own personal 'experience' of time:

> I don't experience time as linear. I experience it in layers that seem to coexist. I feel like 20 years ago was really recent even though I was much younger and had a different kind of life. Yet at the same time I feel like I'm still kind of there.
>
> (Julavits and Egan 2010: n.pag.)

The impression of a possible slippage between layers of time is captured in the hopes and sensations of many of Egan's protagonists; in *Look at Me*, troubled college teacher Moose feels 'the past unroll suddenly from behind the present panorama . . . as if a phony backdrop had toppled, exposing a labyrinth' (Egan 2011b: 71), while ex-model Charlotte becomes enthralled by the ghostly remnants of old advertisements still visible on the walls of New York buildings. In the gothic pastiche of *The Keep*, the past's persistent presence is rendered via a character's ghostly journey through 'a tunnel of memories, stuff, information,' building to the conclusion that '[i]t was all still there. *Nothing disappears*' (Egan 2007: 210, original emphasis). This interweaving of objects and landscapes with individuals' sense of the present as a permeable layer complements Egan's use of flashforwards, where physical traces are deployed as a way of drawing connections between people and moments.

The quotation from Marcel Proust which serves as an inscription to *A Visit from the Goon Squad* refers to 'the unknown element of the lives of other people,' a citation which perfectly captures Egan's fascination with unlayering lost or hitherto unrevealed existences. Discussing portrayals of anxiety and mental illness in *Look at Me* and *The Keep*, Egan suggests that she finds herself particularly drawn to describing individuals who have been 'left out of the general flow of everyday life':

> I find myself writing about human beings whose misfortune it is to have minds that are slightly askew, people who are left out of the general flow of everyday life and normal social interaction. In a sense, they have an almost subterranean existence. They are the ones who aren't quite 'there,' who have somehow fallen through the cracks.
>
> (Reilly 2009: 453)

Egan's ambition to unveil aspects of society and individuals' existence that might otherwise be overlooked has prompted her to conjure an array of characters who feel themselves to be distanced or distinct from the societies in which they function. In *Look at Me*, ex-model Charlotte is cast out of her already-waning career and dissociated from former acquaintances, while each of the narrator-figures in *The Keep* feel detached from those around them, whether due to physical imprisonment, geographical and emotional displacement, or the challenges of single parenthood. In *Manhattan Beach*, Anna is struck by an intense solitude that abruptly jerks her away from 'the general flow of everyday life.' Egan personifies this solitude as a grasping thing with 'a pulse and a heartbeat,' whose 'clutch removed Anna from the realm of mothers pulling children by the hand, and men hurrying home with evening papers under their arms' (Egan 2017: 209). The depiction is complex; Anna finds a 'macabre comfort' in the clutch of isolation, while Egan's choice of imagery – the pulse, heartbeat, mothers and fathers – prefigures the terrified thrill Anna will experience when concealing her pregnancy later in the novel. *Manhattan Beach* eventually casts the ability to fall 'through the cracks' as a source of opportunity. Despite her friend's warning that her illegitimate pregnancy will render her an 'outcast' (Egan 2017: 414), the social vicissitudes of wartime enable Anna to restart a new life on the West coast. 'Amid those shifts and realignments,' we are told, 'Anna had slipped through a crack and escaped' (Egan 2017: 431).

In Egan's reference to individuals with 'an almost subterranean existence,' the 'almost' is significant. Though she frequently describes individuals in moments when they find themselves acutely separated from the 'flow' of others' experiences and expectations, Egan's fiction seldom lingers on characters at moments when they find themselves entirely detached from functional society. Instead, the novels and short stories tend to focus on those who endeavour to maintain outwardly conformist existences despite feeling a sense of profound disconnection. Though Charlotte in *Look at Me* is convinced that she has 'fallen through the cracks,' stepping outside the familar flow of her former life when she is briefly forced to exchange her dreams of becoming a supermodel for a job in a supermarket, her involvement with PersonalSpace and the 'Extraordinary People' project corresponds with a growing awareness of her own longing for a perceived version of normalcy. The novel ends with Charlotte asserting her right to occupy 'everyday life' and 'normal social interaction' (Reilly 2009: 453), selling her celebrity identity and the associated trappings of wealth for a sum that will 'keep myself and two or three others comfortable' (Egan 2011b: 513). Charlotte's wish to be 'comfortable' is echoed in the penultimate chapter of *Goon Squad*, where former kleptomaniac Sasha has settled in Arizona with a new husband and two young children. As a young woman in the opening chapter, Sasha disrupts the tedium of a dispassionate date by stealing a woman's purse, opposing the 'dull,' 'life-as-usual' prospect of leaving the purse with a longing to 'throw caution to the wind, to live dangerously' (Egan 2011a: 3). In the later chapter, her 'askew' nonconformity has been transformed into creativity, as she constructs sculptures from the discarded objects of her family's life.

Among the characters who appear to have genuinely 'fallen through the cracks' of American society in Egan's fiction, perhaps the most viscerally outspoken is Scotty in *Goon Squad*, who is homeless for most of his life before eventually being persuaded by his former friend, Bennie Salazar, to perform a gigantic, virally promoted open-air concert. *Goon Squad* is preoccupied by the technological alterations affecting the music industry, and Bennie Salazar offers a voice of dissent, hating the increasingly commercial aspects of an industry which is about 'reach' rather than 'sound' (Egan 2011a: 319). Against an onslaught of cynical marketeering and smoothly digitised blandness, Bennie is convinced that Scotty is special because he is 'absolutely pure,' 'untouched' (321). Having emerged from his 'subterranean existence' (Reilly 2009: 453) with rage intact, Scotty's detachment from the perceived ills of a slick, corruptible society lead to his reception as a totemic figure, ushered into the 'realm of myth' (Egan 2011a: 344) as a huge crowd responds to his music with rapturous euphoria. His perceived detachment from the gradual commodification of social communications lends him an aura of unimpeachable realness: he is 'no one's data':

> Anyone who was there that day will tell you the concert really started when Scotty stood up. That's when he began singing the songs he'd been writing for years underground, songs no one had ever heard, or anything like them – 'Eyes in My Head,' 'X's and O's,' 'Who's Watching Hardest?' – ballads of paranoia and disconnection ripped

from the chest of a man you knew just by looking had never had a page or a profile or a handle or a handset, who was part of no one's data, a guy who had lived in the cracks all these years, forgotten and full of rage, in a way that now registered as pure. Untouched.

(Egan 2011a: 343–344)

Even in the midst of describing the performance, however, the omniscient narration wearily anticipates its consequences: Scotty's performance will become the stuff of trend legend, as 'more people claim it than could possibly have fit into the space' (344). Although his appeal is rooted in the idea that he is 'no one's data,' Scotty's 'ballads of paranoia and disconnection' are enjoyed by a mass of people who continue to check their handsets mid-gig. *Goon Squad*'s preoccupation with the intertwining of celebrity and technology prompts the revelation that Scotty's newly mythic status means that 'everyone wants to own him' (344), and his perceived 'purity' only serves to augment his status as a commodified cultural object.

Throughout Egan's oeuvre, commentaries on the anodyne nature of slick, market-based cultural phenomena are woven into characters' observations of the environment surrounding them. An earlier scene in *Goon Squad* considers the acquisition of celebrity at the expense of privacy, as ageing ex-rocker Bosco proposes to turn his ill health into a PR novelty by staging a 'Suicide Tour' (Egan 2011a: 136). Determined that his death should be 'an attraction, a spectacle, a mystery,' Bosco is encouraged by the example of reality TV, and his key weapon is the proliferation of opportunities to narrate his demise in various media: 'I want interviews, features, you name it [. . .] Let's document every fucking humiliation' (134). 'Hell,' he persuades his friend and PR, 'it doesn't get any realer than this' (137). Thematically, Bosco is a direct successor to Charlotte in *Look at Me*, whose encounter with American culture anticipates the popularisation of the internet, the legacy of reality TV, and an increasing commercial demand for performed versions of individuals' 'authentic' lives. Charlotte is hired to offer herself as a superannuated version of 'real' American celebrity, agreeing to release every detail of her life for publication on a brand-new platform named PersonalSpace. Her increasing anxiety about the interface between her existence as a private individual and her public presence online exposes the faultlines of public celebrity to which Bosco is so acutely attuned.[4] In both cases, Egan's sardonic depiction neatly skewers the false suppositions and cultural assumptions encountered by each character.

Both Charlotte and Bosco enter into their contracts with performed realness because they crave the fame of a celebrity spotlight. Bosco is determined that he will '*flame* away,' not 'fade away' (136, emphasis in original), while Charlotte pictures total celebrity as a 'transcendent existence' (Egan 2011b: 14), a 'mirrored room' (Egan 2011b: 163) which she longs to enter. For these characters, the marketing of supposedly 'real' lives receives scathing treatment from Egan. As with the media frenzy in response to Scotty's seemingly authentic purity and Bosco's pledge to provide absolute realness, *Look at Me* offers a sardonic depiction of a 'mania for real people' (44), where models are recruited from news coverage of warzones, and a fashion shoot requires that the models' faces are cut to draw blood. When Charlotte refuses to have her face sliced, the photographer explains his reasoning: he is 'trying to get at some kind of truth . . . something pure,' and the sacrifice of blood, like Bosco's Suicide Tour, is 'the most real thing there is' (179). Charlotte's sardonic response neatly cuts through the faulty logic in this fetishistic aestheticisation of the 'real': 'It's too bad Oscar didn't call you when my face was mashed to a pulp last August,' she retorts, 'Every bone was crushed, you would've loved it' (180). Anticipating the references to reality TV and manipulated media in *Goon Squad*, *Look at Me* summarily dismisses the use of impressions of 'realness' and 'purity' for commercial profit.

Look at Me and *Goon Squad* offer an acerbic vision of a cultural milieu obsessed with the authentic – 'real' – representation of individuals' lives, mired in an inexorable process of commercial performativity. Egan's apparent scepticism about a counterintuitive obsession with performed 'realness' is often voiced by specific characters. Among these, two of the most forceful are Z and Moose in *Look at Me*, who both offer apocalyptic visions of America's inevitable demise; Moose rails against those who enjoy a seemingly frictionless existence, bemoaning the ascension of 'quicksilver creatures' in a 'world remade by circuitry' (Egan 2001: 483). The potential terrorist, known variously as Aziz, Z and Michael West, is used to offer an outsider's view as he endeavours to study and assimilate a range of experiences he deems to be quintessentially 'American.' Z seeks out, but is disgusted by, 'real' American experiences, providing a counterpoint to the enthusiasms of the imagined audience for whom characters such as Charlotte, Bosco and Scotty are invited to perform. *Look at Me* was released a mere fortnight after the 9/11 attacks on the Twin Towers, and the author's carefully phrased afterword suggests that the novel's portrayal of a character with terrorist intentions should be treated as an 'imaginative artefact of a more innocent time' (Egan 2011b: 516). Z is a crucial aspect of this effort to produce an 'imaginative artefact' of millennial America, since his chameleon shapeshifting in a variety of scenarios and environments across the novel provides a counterpoint to the introspection and obsession with celebrity depicted elsewhere in the text.

Although individual characters critique the effects of luxurious commercialisation and the dehistorising consequences of technological progress, Egan's representation of these themes actively avoids didacticism. As Zappen notes, Goon Squad is 'neither the dystopian world of hyperconsumerism and hypermediation . . . nor an unabashed apology for either its flawed characters or its new and imagined future media' (Zappen 2016: 306–7). Though they are often based in exaggerated versions of American culture, Egan's extrapolations regarding the excesses and possibilities of an imagined future tend to be explorative rather than scathing. This is particularly evident in the account of a near-future version of New York in the concluding chapter of *Goon Squad*, which portrays a society dominated by the rise of social media and populated by permanently wired individuals. Titled 'Pure Language,' *Goon Squad*'s final chapter treats new media as simultaneously fascinating, oppressive and all-pervasive in a city filled with the kind of 'quicksilver creatures' loathed by Moose. These are the thematic descendants of Danny in *The Keep*, who cannot bear to be parted from his mobile phone, and they have reached a level of power and influence that Danny can only yearn for. Bloggers are paid to provide 'authentic' recommendations for new products, individuals find it simpler to communicate by text than in spoken conversations, and the development of 'kiddie handsets' (Egan 2011a: 320) has spawned a new generation of trend-dominating toddlers and babies, meaning that commercial success in popular culture is now dependent on the fleeting approval of preverbal children.

As with *Look at Me*, the depiction of children's use of digital devices and social media in the final chapter of *Goon Squad* can be seen as 'prescient' for its extrapolation of existing cultural trends. Mere months after the novel's release, an article for the *New York Times* hailed the iPhone as 'the most effective tool in human history to mollify a fussy toddler' (Stout 2010: n.pag.), and the market has subsequently seen a 'flood of baby and toddler apps' (Kang 2011: n.pag.) targeted at young children.[5] In *Goon Squad*, the younger generation's preference for communication by 'T-ing' – texting – is explored carefully, even lyrically. Youthful marketing guru Lulu explains her preference for this mode of communication: 'It's pure – no philosophy, no metaphors, no judgments' (Egan 2011a: 329), and 'Pure Language' does not dismiss this view; in the final scenes, protagonist Alex's sentimental message of love for his wife is enhanced, rather than diminished, by being communicated by 'T.' The simplicity of the message he sends – 'pls wAt 4 me, my bUtiful wyf' (Egan 2011a: 345) – is touching partly because of the restrictions of its medium, whose economy of space reduces Alex's longing for his wife and child to a childlike plea. This attention to changing trends within language and new media extends to Egan's literary experimentation with new technological forms, most notably in *Goon Squad*'s much-praised 'PowerPoint chapter' and the serialisation on Twitter of the short story 'Black Box.'

Egan's use of PowerPoint and Twitter explores the creative possibilities of new technological media, in her most formally experimental pieces of writing to date. Her engagement with the software platform itself is limited; in both cases, she wrote the content out by hand first, before painstakingly transferring it to the technological medium. Nevertheless, the Power-Point chapter of *Goon Squad*, titled 'Great Rock and Roll Pauses,' has been rightly acclaimed as one of the most striking sections of the novel. Framed as the journal of a young girl – Sasha's daughter, Alison – the constraints of the technological medium provide an incongruous setting for the contents' emotional impact. Alison describes her autistic brother's project to document pauses in rock music, a simple conceit which builds to a touching depiction of her father's struggle to understand his son's attempts to express affection. Points of disconnection and miscommunication are starkly outlined in Alison's diagrams, as when she describes the gulf between her brother's words and his intended meaning. Just as Egan's use of prolepsis undercuts sentimental moments elsewhere in *Goon Squad*, the businesslike aesthetics and concise tone of the PowerPoint chapter ensure that it avoids cloying sentimentality, with its seeming mismatch of form and content working to emphasise, rather than undermine, the work's emotional impact.

As in 'Great Rock and Roll Pauses,' 'Black Box' uses the character restrictions of the Twitter format to ensure that its portrayal of a heroine in the midst of dangerous, unpleasant and life-threatening situations does not sink into sentimentality or melodrama. Cast as a series of 'field notes,' the aphoristic messages of *Black Box* betray personal hardship thinly concealed in the clipped form of an official dispatch. When the narrator must endure a sexual encounter with one of her targets, the brutality of the experience is interspersed with tweet-by-tweet reminders of personal duty – 'Your voluntary service is the highest form of patriotism' – and detailed instructions for survival, in this case the 'Dissociation Technique,' which must begin 'only when physical violation is imminent,' and whose countdown proceeds inexorably. 'By three,' the instructions intone, 'you should feel fully detached from your physical self' (Egan 2012a: Section 8). Performing a similar feat to Egan's use of PowerPoint in *Goon Squad*, 'Black Box' explores the productive restrictions of a new technological medium, balancing sentiment and suffering against the formal discourse of new technologies.

Throughout her fictional works, Egan's distinctive approach interweaves ideas about the perception of time and memory in contemporary culture with a range of technological possibilities – and problems – associated with new media. In *Goon Squad* and other novels, characters' longings for purity, transcendence and mutual understanding are thwarted or complicated by a background of commercial interests and a pace of technological transition which often leaves them reeling. When Charlotte in *Look at Me* finally casts off her celebrity skin, it is with the recognition that '[l]ife can't be sustained under the pressure of so many eyes' (514), and this impression of an endeavour to sustain 'life' amidst a variety of pressures and threats pervades Egan's later novels. Holding up a mirror to contemporary American society, however, Egan ultimately offers hopeful conclusions based in the restoration of person-to-person communications, offering a sharp contrast with an alternative scenario of cynical, bloodless lives dominated by misunderstandings and sensations of profound disconnection. In *The Keep*, Danny's cousin informs him that 'Old-fashioned "reality" is a thing of the past. It's gone, finito – all that technology you're so in love with has wiped it out' (Egan 2007: 130). Egan's fiction explores this possibility, but consistently returns to an idea of personal 'reality' rooted in human encounters and communications.

Notes

1 Egan joins a number of contemporary authors in using tropes and structures commonly associated with genre fiction; Tim Lanzendörfer lists her among a list of 'literary luminaries' described as '"frantically borrowing" from the often-disparaged "popular" genres' (Lanzendörfer 2016: 3).
2 An app version of *A Visit from the Goon Squad* was released in 2012, which scrambles the order of chapters on readers' second encounter.
3 Time and chronology have proved to be a preoccupation in critical discussions of Egan's 2010 novel; see for example Cowart (2015), Moling (2016), and Strong (2018).
4 For analysis of how Egan's novels tackle the intersection of public and private selves in the context of data and surveillance, see Johnston (2017) and Lederer (forthcoming 2019).
5 The increasing ease of child purchases facilitated by tablets and smartphones became evident in early 2014, when technology behemoth Apple reluctantly agreed to refund over $32.5m (£19.9m) spent by children downloading in-app purchases (Holpuch 2014: n.pag.).

Works cited

Bell, M. S. (2006) Into the Labyrinth. *The New York Times*. 30 July. [online]. Available from: www.nytimes.com/2006/07/30/books/review/30bell.html (Accessed 12 May 2014).

Blythe, W. (2010) To Their Own Beat. *The New York Times*. 8 July. [online]. Available from: www.nytimes.com/2010/07/11/books/review/Blythe-t.html (Accessed 12 May 2014).

Brown, B. (2003) *A Sense of Things: The Object Matter of American Literature*. Chicago: University of Chicago Press.

Byatt, A. S. (1998) 'Memory and the Making of Fiction', in Patricia Fara and Karalyn Patterson (eds.) *Memory*. Cambridge: Cambridge University Press. 47–72.

Ciabattari, J. (2010) *The Book on Aging Rockers* [online]. Available from: www.thedailybeast.com/articles/2010/06/29/jennifer-egan-interview-a-visit-from-the-goon-squad.html (Accessed 12 May 2014).

Currie, M. (2007) *About Time: Narrative, Fiction and the Philosophy of Time*. Edinburgh: Edinburgh University Press.

Cowart, D. (2015) Thirteen Ways of Looking: Jennifer Egan's A Visit from the Goon Squad. Critique: *Studies in Contemporary Fiction* [online] 56(3), 241–254. Available from: https://doi.org/10.1080/00111619.2014.905448 (Accessed 2 February 2018).

Diebel, A. (2017) Anna Papa Mama Liddy. *London Review of Books* [online] 39 (23), 41–42. Available from: www.lrb.co.uk/v39/n23/anne-diebel/anna-papa-mama-liddy (Accessed 30 November 2017).

Egan, J. (2011a) *A Visit from the Goon Squad*. London: Corsair. (Original work published 2010)
—— (2011b) *Look at Me*. London: Corsair. (Original work published 2001)
—— (2012a) *Black Box*. London: Corsair. (Original work published 2012)
—— (2012b) *Emerald City and Other Stories*. London: Corsair. (Original work published 1993)
—— (2012c) *The Invisible Circus*. London: Corsair. (Original work published 1994)
—— (2007) *The Keep*. London: Abacus. (Original work published 2006)
—— (2017) *Manhattan Beach*. London: Corsair.

Fox, K. (2011) Jennifer Egan: 'I Would Have Accepted a Marriage Proposal from Roger Daltrey on the Spot'. *The Guardian*. 21 August. [online]. Available from: www.theguardian.com/books/2011/aug/21/jennifer-egan-interview-observer (Accessed 12 May 2014).

Holpuch, A. (2014) Apple to Pay $32.5m over Practice That Let Children Make in-App Purchases. *The Guardian*. 15 January. [online]. Available from: www.theguardian.com/technology/2014/jan/15/apple-practice-children-make-in-app-purchases (Accessed 12 May 2014).

Johnston, K. D. (2017) Metadata, Metafiction, and the Stakes of Surveillance in Jennifer Egan's A Visit from the Goon Squad. *American Literature* [online] 89(1), 155–184. Available from: https://doi.org/10.1215/00029831-3788753 (Accessed 2 February 2018).

Julavits, H. and Egan, J. (2010) Jennifer Egan. *BOMB Magazine* [online]. Available from: http://bombmagazine.org/article/3524/jennifer-egan (Accessed 12 May 2014).

Kang, C. (2011) Kid Apps Explode on Smartphones and Tablets: But Are They Good for Your Children? *The Washington Post*. 17 November. [online]. Available from: www.washingtonpost.com/business/economy/kid-apps-explode-on-smartphones-and-tablets-but-are-they-good-for-your-children/2011/11/07/gIQAq2enVN_story.html (Accessed 12 May 2014).

Lanzendörfer, T. (2016). 'Introduction: The Generic Turn? Toward a Poetics of Genre in the Contemporary Novel', in T. Lanzendörfer (ed.) *The Poetics of Genre in the Contemporary Novel*. Lanham: Lexington Books. 1–17.

Lederer, R. (2019). 'Jennifer Egan and the Database', in R. Ferguson, M. M. Littlefield, and J. Purdon (eds.) *The Art of Identification: Forensics, Surveillance, Identity*. University Park, Pennsylvania: The Pennsylvania State University Press.

Maslin, J. (2010) Jennifer Egan's 'Visit From the Goon Squad'. *The New York Times*. 20 June. [online]. Available from: www.nytimes.com/2010/06/21/books/21book.html (Accessed 12 May 2014).

Moling, M. (2016). "No Future": Time, Punk Rock and Jennifer Egan's A Visit from the Goon Squad. *Arizona Quarterly: A Journal of American Literature, Culture, and Theory*. [online]. Available from: https://doi.org/10.1353/arq.2016.0000 (Accessed 2 February 2018).

Reilly, C. (2009) An Interview with Jennifer Egan. *Contemporary Literature* [online] 50 (3), 439–460.

Robbins, B. (2012) Many Years Later: Prolepsis in Deep Time. *The Henry James Review* [online] 33 (3), 191–204.

Strong, M. J. (2018). Found time: Kairos in A Visit from the Goon Squad. *Critique: Studies in Contemporary Fiction* [online] 59(4), 471–480. Available from: https://doi.org/10.1080/00111619.2018.1427544 (Accessed 2 February 2018).

Stout, H. (2010) iPhones for Toddlers. *The New York Times*. 15 October. [online]. Available from: www.nytimes.com/2010/10/17/fashion/17TODDLERS.html (Accessed 12 May 2014).

Zappen, J. P. (2016). Affective Identification in Jennifer Egan's A Visit from the Goon Squad. *Lit: Literature Interpretation Theory* [online] 27(4), 294–309. https://doi.org/10.1080/10436928.2016.1236519 (Accessed 2 February 2018).

32

DAVID MITCHELL

Sarah Dillon

Beginning

In 2014, a British short film called *The Voorman Problem*, directed by Mark Gill and staring Martin Freeman and Tom Hollander, appeared on the list of nominees for the Academy Award for Best Live Action Short Film. This Oscar category has been known under its current name only since 1974, but there have been various categories of award for short film since the fifth Academy Awards in 1932. Despite this longstanding Academy recognition of the short form, winners and nominees of this category receive little attention in press coverage of the Oscars which focuses almost exclusively on the feature film awards. Critical and popular attention to the writing of David Mitchell commits a similar oversight, focusing again almost exclusively on his long, rather than his short, fiction. This might not be surprising, given the richness of Mitchell's novelistic canon to date: seven published novels, as well as one unpublished novel (his first, *The Old Moon*) and one time-locked novella (*From Me Flows What You Call Time*, on which more later). These range across time, space and genre with an insouciant disregard for limits or boundaries of any kind. But Mitchell now also has an established body of published short stories including 'The January Man' (2003), 'What You Do Not Know You Want' (2004b), 'Acknowledgements' (2005a), 'Hangman' (2005b), 'Preface' (2006), 'Dénoument' (2007a), 'Judith Castle' (2007b), 'The Massive Rat' (2009b), 'Character Development' (2009a), 'Muggins Here' (2010b), 'Earth Calling Taylor' (2010c), 'The Siphoners' (2011a), 'The Gardener' (2011b), 'An Inside Job' (2012a), 'In the Bike Sheds' (2012b), 'Lots of Bits of Star' (2013), 'Variations on a Theme by Mister Donut' (2014b), 'The Right Sort' (2014c), 'My Eye on You' (2016a) and 'A Forgettable Story' (2017).

It is necessary to pay attention to these stories both for reasons beyond and specific to Mitchell. Paying attention to Mitchell's short fiction is part of a wider push back against the hegemony of the novel in big business publishing and UK literary prize culture, a push being headed most prominently by the BBC National Short Story Award launched in 2008. But the short story also has a unique and crucial place in Mitchell's writing, since the short form – whether short story or novella – always serves as the building blocks for his longer works, which in turn serve as building blocks for what I will call Mitchell's *storyverse*: a sophisticated fictional universe of which his short stories, novellas and even 595 page novels, are all just a small part. Mitchell's storyverse is built out of his short stories, as well as his novels which are themselves 'compounded short stories' (Mitchell in Birnbaum 2006: n. pag). Whereas other authors might work hard to conceal the borders,

Mitchell does not plaster over the cement between the short story bricks to provide an illusion or delusion of unity. Rather, he delights in exposing and playing with the consequences of the persistent visibility of the separate story blocks. The result is an ever-present thematic concern with connectivity, which is mirrored in the formal structures of his work. This chapter explores these formal and thematic connectivities as a way to enter into Mitchell's storyverse. At the end, it will become clear how *The Voorman Problem* is also a part of it . . .

Form

Mitchell's first novel *Ghostwritten* (1999) is constructed out of nine stories set in Okinawa, Tokyo, Hong Kong, Holy Mountain in China, Mongolia, Petersburg, London, New York and Clear Island in Ireland respectively. Each story has a different main character, and a different generic feel: Quasar is a doomsday cult terrorist on the run after carrying out a gas attack in Tokyo; Saturo is an endearing young musician and record shop boy who falls in love with a beautiful Hong Kong schoolgirl; Neal Brose is a Nick Leeson–type lawyer whose life disintegrates due to untreated diabetes and his dodgy business dealings. From Holy Mountain, the Tea Shack Lady watches the history of modern China unfold around her, whilst in Mongolia we meet a disembodied spirit, or 'noncorpum', who transmigrates from host to host searching for the mystery of its origin. In contrast, the distinctly corporeal Margarita Latunsky is a pitifully self-deluded former courtesan embroiled in a Petersburg art theft ring, and the equally corporeal Marco is a lovable rogue, professional ghost writer and musician, who maps London by 'trigonometrical shag points' (Mitchell 1999: 290). Dr. Mo Muntervary, a scientist with a conscience, goes on the run after her quantum cognition technology is put to military uses, and the loquacious Bat Segundo presents a late-night radio show during which he unwittingly helps out the advanced artificial intelligence Mo invents – the Zookeeper – who is having moral trouble with the Isaac Asimov–inspired laws which govern his behaviour. Mitchell's second novel, *number9dream* (2001), might offer up a *Bildungsroman* coming-of-age story arc but the whole work is in fact built out of interruptive fantasies, video games, a fabulist's children's stories, memories, flashbacks, excerpts from a wartime journal and dreams.

Cloud Atlas (2004a) is perhaps Mitchell's most well-known novel, thanks to the 2012 film adaptation by the Wachowskis. It is fabricated out of six short stories, with the added structural twist that the first five stories begin but are then interrupted by the next, only to be completed each in turn after the central uninterrupted tale is told. Like *Ghostwritten*, *Cloud Atlas*'s story blocks range across time and space and are drawn from distinct generic traditions: historical fiction in 'The Pacific Journal of Adam Ewing' set in the nineteenth century; epistolary novel in Robert Frobisher's 'Letters from Zedelghem', written in the 1930s; crime thriller in the 1970s 'Half-Lives: The First Luisa Rey Mystery'; picaresque memoir in the present day 'The Ghastly Ordeal of Timothy Cavendish'; and two SF future dystopias, 'An Orison of Sonmi~451' and 'Sloosha's Crossin' an 'Ev'rythin After'. Mitchell's fourth novel, *Black Swan Green* (2006) is carefully structured with one story for each of the thirteen months of the narration's duration. In this relative simplicity, it might at first appear to be the least indebted structurally to the short story form. But many of Mitchell's short stories – 'The January Man', 'Acknowledgments', 'All Souls Day', 'Preface', 'Dénouement', 'The Massive Rat', 'Character Development', 'Muggins Here', 'Earth Calling Taylor' – feature characters from the Black Swan Green world. Seen in this context, *Black Swan Green* becomes part of a much larger picture of which it is in fact just one small part.

The boundaries between the short story bricks are perhaps most porous in *The Thousand Autumns of Jacob de Zoet* (2010a), a historical fiction set in the late eighteenth century on the man-made island of Dejima in Nagasaki bay. But the separate stories are present, and Mitchell did write them as such: Jacob's experiences on Dejima; his love, Orito's, incarceration at the mountain shrine; Uzaemon's mission to rescue her; and Captain Penhaligon's attack on Dejima. *The Bone Clocks* (2014a) moves across time and place in a similar fashion to his earlier work. It is put together out of six novellas, beginning in 1984 and ending in 2043, told from the perspective of five different people and with action taking place across the world in places as diverse as Cambridge, Gravesend, Switzerland, Manhattan, the Hudson Valley, Toronto, Vancouver, Russia, Australia, Colombia, Shanghai, Iraq and Iceland. But piercing this world in the novel is a fantasy plot in which two powerful groups battle against each other over human souls. The Anchorites are a group of Carnivores who, whilst mortal, feed off human children's souls in order to prevent ageing and thus attempt to avoid death. In opposition to them, the Atemporals of Horology are immortal souls who are reincarnated in new bodies 49 days after whichever body they have been then inhabiting dies. The reader has in fact already encountered one such Horologist in *The Thousand Autumns of Jacob de Zoet* – Dr Marinus, who was on his/her 28th life in 1799, now resurfaces as the narrator of the fifth novella, 'An Horologist's Labyrinth' in 2025. Marinus reappears again in 'Astronauts 2015', the final story in Mitchell's most recently published novel *Slade House* (2015). *Slade House* is built out of five short stories – 'The Right Sort 1979', 'Shining Armour 1988', 'Oink Oink 1997', 'You Dark Horse You 2006', 'Astronauts 2015' – which together tell the story of two Anchorites, twins Norah and Jonah Grayer, and their struggle to sustain their defiance of death. In *Slade House*, Marinus is embodied in the early twenty-first century as Dr Iris Marinus-Fenby, a black female psychiatrist who is in fact one of the narrators in *The Bone Clocks* and had, before that, appeared in Mitchell's libretto for Michel van der Aa's opera *Sunken Garden*.

Marinus is just one of a myriad of recurring characters in and across Mitchell's long and short fiction. In my introduction to *David Mitchell: Critical Essays* (2011), I elucidated some of these character repetitions. Since then, many more have been delightedly discovered by Mitchell critics and fans across the world. Whilst this is often a playful exercise, character repetitions across the short stories that comprise the novels, and between the novels and the published short fiction, in fact serve to weave those stories together in intricate and complex ways. Along with repeated phrases, places, plot moments and themes, these character repetitions weave Mitchell's story blocks together to create what he calls his überbook, what I am calling his *storyverse*. For instance, as well as appearing in *Slade House* and *Sunken Garden*, Marinus recurs across *The Bone Clocks'* stories, protecting Holly as a child from the Anchorites not once but twice (Mitchell 2014a: 21 and 63) in 'Hot Spell', before the narrative shifts to his/her perspective in 'An Horologist's Labyrinth'. S/he then returns in 2043 in 'Sheep's Head' – reincarnated as Icelandic presidential adviser Harry Veracruz – to offer escape and asylum to the children in elderly Holly's care. Likewise, Hugo Lamb, narrator of the second bone clock novella, 'Myrrh Is Mine, Its Bitter Perfume', appeared as Jason Taylor's visiting cousin in *Black Swan Green*, and his multiple appearances across *The Bone Clocks'* novellas weave its separate story blocks together. He reappears outside of his own novella in 'Crispin Hershey's Lonely Planet', a satire of the contemporary publishing industry, after he has been turned into an Anchorite. But his brief affair with Holly before he is converted, narrated in his novella, provides the background plot necessary for the unfolding of the climactic escape at the end of 'An Horologist's Labyrinth'. His lasting love for Holly prevents him from using the only means of escape from the labyrinth behind the Anchorites' Way of Stone – she is saved, and he and Marinus are left to work together to summon an alternative means of escape. We know they succeeded, since Marinus reappears in the final novella, but we do not know what Hugo's fate was thereafter. We are left to wait and see if we will discover it in a future Mitchell novel; it is not impossible, in fact, that Hugo lies buried in Oslo's Nordmarka forest in the pages of Mitchell's novella *From Me Flows What You Call Time* (2016b), to be resurrected when that work is finally published in 2114 as part of artist Katie Paterson's Future Library project.

Hugo Lamb is by no means the only character from *Black Swan Green* to have a life beyond the pages of that novel. Clive Pike, one of Jason's classmates, appears first in 'Acknowledgements' (2005a), published a year prior to the novel, as the author of a nine hundred page work which details the field of Psychomigration, a theory he conceives on the 15th March 1999 whilst working in the Customs and Excise House in Potters Bar:

> I was sitting in my cubicle on the ninth floor, gazing out at traffic on the M25, when a binary metaphor coalesced in my brain. Bodies are vehicles: minds are drivers. These six words and their colon were the ova of what became the Book. Bodies are vehicles: minds are drivers. As I dunked a KitKat into my coffee on that momentous morning, I tested the metaphor to breaking point. A car doesn't only carry one person, obviously. A driver can get out of one car and climb into another, obviously. However, as Mr Nixon points out in chapter 7, 'obviously' hides the unobvious as cleverly as a walnut hides a walnut tree.
>
> (Mitchell 2005a: n. pag)

Clive is narrating the 'Acknowledgements' to his magnus opus whilst hiding in a hay loft after having killed his former head teacher – Mr Nixon, also a character in *Black Swan Green* – under the impression that it was necessary to free Nixon from his terminally ill body before it was too late. He believes that he is now hosting Mr Nixon's soul. Timothy Cavendish, from *Cloud Atlas*, is Pike's publisher, and Clive himself appears again as the psychiatric patient in 'Muggins Here' (2010b) who leads the narrator Pearl to leave her job of twenty years. Clive returns as the narrator of the story 'All Souls Day' – an unpublished draft of which Mitchell shared with me in 2010 – now 'Re-integrated into the Community', in which he stumbles across an island on which he seems to have been marooned after a day trip. Peering in through a bungalow window, he watches a family watching television, 'a hospital drama on a big old 1970s TV' (Mitchell 2016c: 84). What he recounts is not, however, what he sees on the family's television, but an episode of the same series that he remembers his mother and father watching – spying on a family, and then watching their TV, takes him back into his memories of his mother and father watching TV, and into the episode they were watching where, to our surprise, we find Marinus:

> Mother never missed an episode, so neither did Father.
> Mother is hard of hearing: subtitles flash up on the screen.
> *Will he make it, Doctor Marinus?*, asks doe-eyed Nurse Gilchrist.
> Cut to Marinus, a rugged Indian, removing his surgical mask.
> *His stomach's pumped, Nurse. From now on, it's up to him . . .*
> Lipsticked Nurse Gilchrist: *I don't understand, Doctor.*
> Marinus: *Was it death he sought, or something else?*
> *You mean*, cut to Nurse Gilchrist, *um . . . what do you mean?*
> Nurse Gilchrist – never the brightest bulb on the Christmas tree.
> Marinus: *Who can tell what psychodramas unfold . . .*
> Cut to the patient's skinny torso, his drip. Pan upwards.
> *. . . unfold in the hidden theatre of the mind.* Pan upwards.
>
> (Mitchell 2016c: 84)

Marinus was indeed, in one reincarnation, an Indian – he refers to that life in *The Bone Clocks*, 'as my Indian self, Choudary, I taught Unalaq' (Mitchell 2014a: 497) – but here the 'real' world of *Black Swan Green* and its cast, leads into the fictional (the television they watch), only for that fictional television to be inhabited by a character that is 'real' in the rest of Mitchell's storyverse. Such structural slippage between reality and fiction occurs throughout Mitchell's work, not least for instance in *Cloud Atlas*, in which the reader begins each story believing in its reality, only for each subsequent story to then call that reality into question. But such slippage also occurs generically in the way in which Mitchell's writing transgresses the supposedly rigid boundary between realism and fantasy in contemporary fiction publishing.

In *The Bone Clocks*, formerly best-selling author Crispin Hershey pitches his new book project to his despairing agent:

> 'But this one's got legs, Hal. A jetlagged businessman has the mother of all breakdowns in a labyrinthine hotel in Shanghai, encounters a minister, a CEO, a cleaner, a psychic woman who hears voices' – gabbling garbling '– think *Solaris* meets Noam Chomsky via *The Girl With the Dragon Tattoo*. Add a dash of *Twin Peaks* . . .'
>
> Hal is pouring himself a whiskey and soda: hear it fizz? His voice is flat and accusative: 'Crispin. Are you trying to tell me that you're writing a fantasy novel?'
>
> 'Me? Never! Or it's only one-third fantasy. Half, at most.'
>
> 'A book can't be a half-fantasy any more than a woman can be half pregnant.'
>
> (Mitchell 2014a: 348–349)

The story in this pitch recalls in parts Crispin's earlier experiences in the hotel in which he plants cocaine on the critic who savaged his most recent novel. Crispin's novella recalls Timothy Cavendish's tale in *Cloud Atlas* – realist in style, picaresque and satirical in tone, despite some deeply serious threats. But the pitch also recalls Mitchell's deeply disturbing short story 'What You Do Not Know You Want' (2004b), very different in style and tone to Crispin's novella, much more closely resembling the disturbing supernaturalism of *Twin Peaks* or, to give a literary example, Edgar Allen Poe. In this tale, the businessman in question is attempting to retrieve a valuable ornamental knife found by his business partner but now lost since that partner jumped to his death from the very same hotel in which he is now staying. The narrator strikes up something of a relationship with Wei, the hotel owner's imported bride who, positioned between two mirrors, informs him that 'If you look at your face from different places [. . .] you are reminded that we are not a Me, but an It who lives in a Me' (Mitchell 2004b: 14). The idea that our bodies are, or might be, possessed by souls which may or may not be our own is a constant theme in Mitchell's work from the noncorpum that moves though his first novel *Ghostwritten*, to the souls crossing time and space in *Cloud Atlas*, to Clive Pike's theory of psychomigration in 'Acknowledgements'. This theme becomes fully fledged as the transtemporal battle in Mitchell's storyverse between the Anchorites and the Atemporals is fully revealed to us *The Bone Clocks*, 'The Right Sort' and *Slade House*. Despite their clear generic differences, 'What You Do Not Know You Want' also reverberates with Crispin's story, however, at the level of pronouns. Crispin is not – or at least we are not told that he is – possessed by any other soul, but his narrative constantly and unnervingly shifts from the first to the third person, throughout his tale, changing point of view within even the same paragraph. On March 11 2016, for instance, we are told that 'Up on his balcony, Crispin Hershey taps ash into his champagne glass . . . ' (Mitchell 2014a: 294), only to find a few lines later that the first person has returned, 'as far as I can see' (Mitchell 2014a: 294). Crispin's narrative divides himself from himself linguistically, if not actually, echoing the way in which the Horologists in this novel divide themselves from themselves literally, a soul moving from different body to different body at will, or the way in which, her body providing asylum for Esther Little, Holly Sykes is for so many years both herself and not herself.

Clive's realisation that bodies are cars that minds can drive is directly recalled, also linguistically, in *The Bone Clocks* when Marinus is benignly co-occupying Holly's body in order to help them escape from the Anchorites and the encroaching, all consuming, Dusk:

> Panic surges through Holly. I psychosedate it back down.
>   We hear the hum of the Dusk. *Shall I drive?*
>   'Yeah', Holly croaks. 'Please'.
>
>   (Mitchell 2014a: 516–517)

Just as Clive says of his metaphor, the obvious realism of Mitchell's fiction germinates its unobvious fantastical elements – the realism is the walnut out of which the tree of fantasy grows; Clive develops the idea of psychomigration whilst dunking a kitkat in tea. Just as Holly experiences in *The Bone Clocks*, when reading Mitchell 'the gears of what's real slip' (Mitchell 2014a: 58). The protagonist of 'What You Do Not Know You Want' may well simply be hunting down a lost artefact crucial to his business and economic prosperity, but he ends up being sliced open by that artefact at the hands of what appears to be the first soul-eating Anchorite to appear in Mitchell's published work. Here, the Carnivore's realist name 'Wei' morphs homophonically into the much more sinister 'We':

> My right arm spasmed and the razor-sharp metal bored through my stomach wall. Left to right, *rip*. Severing cartilage, intestines, notching my spinal cord. Pain firecrackered, but the It in Wei kept my backbone erect and stopped the blackness swallowing the lights. It was feeding.
>
>   (Mitchell 2004b: 31)

Now that *The Bone Clocks* and *Slade House* have been published, and the transhistorical existence of soul carnivores who feed on human souls to prolong life has been explicitly explained, Mitchell's readers can look back across his work and see their presence throughout. In this light, Enomoto's sinister spiritual order in *The Thousand Autumns of Jacob de Zoet*, whose members believe in achieving immortality through drinking the blood of newborn babies, becomes not an isolated sect but just one instance of this transhistorical phenomenon.

Content

The explicit focus on the confrontation between mortality and immortality in *The Bone Clocks* and *Slade House* serves to bring Mitchell's longstanding interest in this theme throughout his writing into sharper focus. It now takes its place at the forefront of an array of recurrent themes that can similarly be organised into tense pairings: colonialism and resistance; slavery and freedom; apocalypse and hope; fate and causality; mis(communication). And here we find a parallelism between Mitchell's formal structuring of his writing and his thematic explorations. Structurally, Mitchell creates and retains discrete story blocks whilst at the same time weaving connections between them that challenge, without destroying, their distinctness. The same pattern can be seen in his thematic explorations, paradigmatically in his concern with mortality and immortality. Human beings are mortal – we live finite lives in finite bodies. This is the trouble with being bone clocks. Throughout history, the grand narratives of myth and religion have promised alternatives to this reality, variations on the promise of everlasting life. Mitchell imports and develops some of these alternatives into his storyverse, extrapolating from the idea of reincarnation to the possibility of more temporary pyschomigrations – what in *The Bone Clocks* is called 'ingressing' – as well as telepathy and other 'psychosoteric' powers. In doing so, Mitchell's writing both accepts the limit that we are mortal, and weaves fantastic connections across mortal bodies that defy our very limitation. In *The Thousand Autumns of Jacob de Zoet*, Jacob's fear that 'this *engine of bones* [. . .] *is a man's entirety*' (Mitchell 2010a: 141) is countered by Marinus' assertion that 'The soul is a verb . . . not a noun' (Mitchell 2010a: 141).

It is important to note, though, that such connections are not entirely, or exclusively, fantastical. And again we have a parallel here between form and content. Just as we have seen how Mitchell's writing generically moves across the boundaries between realism and fantasy, likewise his concern with the possibility of immortality challenges any stark division between what is real and what is fantastical. Souls may not literally cross ages like clouds cross the skies, possessing different bodies as they go, but one human being can, indeed is, a multitude of beings in one lifetime – Holly Sykes the teenager in 'Hot Spell' is a very different person to Holly Sykes the grandmother in 'Sheep's Head'. They are the same person, and elderly Holly's memories link her with her childhood self, but they are also very different people, her soul changed by age and time and experiences. Whilst these changes might not be wholly positive, they do demonstrate a very real division between body and soul, between the mortal body we inhabit and the 'I' we understand ourselves to be: 'Once upon a time "my body" meant "me", pretty much, but now "me" is my mind and my body is a selection box of ailments and aches' (Mitchell 2014a: 558). Ageing and memory are therefore two key realistic ways in which we bone clocks transgress the limitations of our bodies, transcending space and time, changing into a myriad of different people as we make our way through life: '"A film is all its stills", says Mr Nixon. "We are all our ages"' (Mitchell 2016c: 56).

More than this, we do in fact achieve immortality in some very real senses: in the continuation of our DNA in our children, and in the memories others retain of us after we die. Again, Holly in *The Bone Clocks* provides examples of both. In 'Sheep's Head', her daughter Aoife has now died in a plane crash, but she lives on in her own daughter Lorelei, and the likeness to Aoife Holly sees in her: '"It's almost ten", says Lorelei, "and school tomorrow", and if I close my eyes I can almost imagine it's Aoife at fifteen years old' (Mitchell 2014a: 524). As she watches Aoife and Rafiq leave for safety with Marinus, Holly treasures that moment, creating an explicit parallel between the fantastical immortality of Esther Little and the real immortality of two generations of her lost loved ones:

> if I could choose one moment of my life to sit inside for the rest of eternity, like Esther Little did for all those decades, it'd be now, no question. Aoife's in here too, inside Lorelei, as is Ed.
>
> (Mitchell 2014a: 594)

Hugo Lamb might regret that 'sex may be the antidote to death but it offers life everlasting only to the species, not the individual' (Mitchell 2014a: 120), but the narrator of 'What You Do Not Know You Want' celebrates the fact that 'sex is not, as cliché claims, a little death – sex is man's *fuck you!* to death' (Mitchell 2004b: 20). The fact that some of us have children, the fact that people who remember us outlive us; these facts give one person a very real sort of immortality, beyond the short confines of their corporeal presence on earth.

Since Shakespeare's Sonnet 18 proclaimed 'So long as men can breathe, or eyes can see,/So long lives this, and this gives life to thee' (Shakespeare 1993: 11), it seems something of a truism to assert the immortalising power of the written word, but this form of immortality also has its place in Mitchell's work. Every conceivable form of 'writing' in the sense of 'technologies of communication', can be found in Mitchell's texts, from the most real and ancient to the most futuristic and imagined; from word of mouth, diaries, letters, scrolls, novels, poems, music, to film, voice messages, text messages, ethered tabs, Net patching and orisons. All of these technologies create connections across divides of time and space whether it be each of the characters in turn in *Cloud Atlas* finding the communication that is the previous story, or, more simply, the communicative lifeline Marinus hands to Holly so that she can keep in touch with Lorelei and Rafiq:

> He took out a pack of four sheathed tabs and handed me one, explaining they were ethered to one another, so wouldn't need the Net to thread a connection. 'One for you, me, Lorelei and Rafiq. Not the same as having them in your kitchen, of course, but this way they're not gone from your life once we round the headland'.
>
> (Mitchell 2014a: 593)

The tabs are 'powered bioelectrically just by holding them, too, so they'll function without solar panels' (Mitchell 2014a: 593), Marinus informs Holly. In a future dystopia where power is scarce, this independence from an external power source is crucial to the communicative effectiveness of the tabs. Mitchell has productively engaged with modern communication technologies and recognises their proliferative power – the Twitter story 'The Right Sort' germinated *Slade House* with surprising and uncharacteristic speed; media savvy writer Crispin Hershey in *The Bone Clocks* stages public forgiveness of his harshest critic, knowing that 'Crispin Hershey's magnanimity will be reported and retweeted and so it will become the truth' (Mitchell 2014a: 299). But one also gets a sense that Mitchell would not be unsympathetic to Ray Bradbury's now infamous comment to The Associated Press at BookExpo America in 2008, that 'e-books smell like burned fuel' (Italie 2008: no pag). Current communicative technologies depend on power in order to survive. As such, they are incredibly fragile. Lose power and we lose the internet, computers and all the knowledge and communication that comes with them. As Bradbury's *Farenheit 451* makes clear, it would take a lot more effort to destroy all the books in the world. '"Books'll be back"', says precognitive Esther Little in *The Bone Clocks*, 'Wait til the power grids start failing in the late 2030s and the datavats get erased. It's not far away. The future looks a lot like the past' (Mitchell 2014a: 478–479). One letter, one poem, one book can, like a body, carry a soul. Similar to the Anchorites in *The Bone Clocks*, one letter, one poem or one book is not immortal – it can be killed, burnt, lost, otherwise destroyed – but that end can be perpetually delayed, well beyond the lifespan of a human body. Such writing technologies, then, can carry the souls invested in them across space and time. Writing in general, and Mitchell's writing in particular, has an uncanny vitality that connects us with our past, present and our future. Writing itself is a form of escape from our mortal boundedness. In a chain of continuances that performs the point, in 'Dénouement' Mitchell recalls Mr Nixon, the headmaster from *Black Swan Green*, who himself rediscovers Montaigne in his essay 'That to Philosophize is To Learn How To Die', in which Montaigne resurrects Cicero via his reflection that 'philosophizing is nothing more than preparing for death', which Nixon interprets as such: 'that is as much to say that study and contemplation in some sort withdraw our soul outside of us, and keep it occupied apart from the body' (Mitchell 2007a: no pag). This may indeed be 'a kind of resemblance to death' (Mitchell 2007a: no pag), but it is also the beginning of the possibility of immortality. In this sense, Marinus is right to reflect that 'at certain rare moments, a library is a kind of mind' (Mitchell 2014a: 481).

Not the end

Mitchell's writing creates – is in fact still creating – a storyverse. It is world building of the most ambitious and impressive kind, across and through texts, with a recurrent cast populating that world and repeated themes haunting it. As such, despite its local genre-bending in specific works,

Mitchell's project as a whole is generically much more closely aligned to the world building of science fiction and fantasy literature than it is to the real-world inhabitation of realist fiction. It is no surprise, then, that in interview Mitchell enthuses about the British comic 2000AD which, he says, 'taught me a lot of things about storytelling' (Poole 2001: no pag). His storyverse contains all the same qualities which he so admires, for instance, in Mega-City, the fictional city-state of the Judge Dredd comic book series and its spin-offs: 'so huge, so dense, so consistent' (Poole 2001: no pag). And similar to comic books like 2000AD, the Marvel universe, or, to give another literary example, Iain M. Banks' Culture novels, Mitchell's work creates not just readers, but fans – fanatical readers, devoted to his works and nerdily knowledgeable about all their details and all the interconnections that connect them and shore up his storyverse. Mitchell's readers might in fact be described as Mitchell's followers, which brings us back at last to the short film, *The Voorman Problem* mentioned in the opening of this chapter. Mitchell himself would no doubt appreciate this critical mirroring of one of his favourite fictional techniques: the slow reveal. In interview he reflects on the strangeness that in a culture supposedly 'addicted to instant gratification' our most popular fictions are long novels, such as those by himself or George R.R. Martin, or TV dramas such as *True Detective*, *Mad Men* or *Sherlock* in which 'despite all the hurly burly – the fast cutting and so on – it also trusts the audience enough to do slow reveal' (Poole 2001: no pag). To get to my reveal, then, I did not select *The Voorman Problem* at random from the Academy Award list of nominees for Best Live Action Short Film 2014; I selected it because the film is based on a short section from near the beginning of Mitchell's novel *number9dream*.

Waiting in a café opposite the offices of his father's lawyer, Eiji Miyake indulges in a range of fantasies about how he might confront her and discover the name of his father. In one such fantasy, just as he decides to launch his attack on the PanOpticon building, the lawyer, Akiko Katō strides past the window of the café. Eiji follows her to a backstreet cinema and into the showing of a movie called '*PanOpticon*' (n9d 26). And within Eiji's fantasy we then get a description of the plot of the film, in which a psychiatrist is called to assess a prisoner, Voorman, who maintains he is God. 'The Voorman problem' (Mitchell 2001: 30) is not the individual's delusion itself, but the fact that he has persuaded all the other prisoners to believe and worship him. The Warden fears riots. If the psychiatrist assesses him as mad, he can be moved to an asylum and the Warden's troubles are over. In the next scene, we witness the psychiatrist's first interview with Voorman, in which we learn that his main professional responsibility as God is 'on-going maintenance. Of my universe' (Mitchell 2001: 31), a universe he created only nine days ago, together with all the evidence and memories that would imply it is much older: 'everything in this universe is a figment of my imagination' (Mitchell 2001: 32). To prove that he is telling the truth, he suggests an experiment – 'Belgium'. In the next scene, we see the doctor and his wife talking over supper, and we learn the nature of the experiment, and its outcome:

'Is he the slave, or the master, of his imagination? He swore to make Belgium disappear by teatime.'

'Is Belgium another prisoner?'

Polonski chews. 'Belgium.'

'A new cheese?'

'Belgium. The country. Between France and Holland. Belgium.'

Mrs Polonski shakes her head doubtfully. [. . .]

The doctor turns to the general map of Europe and his face stiffens. Between France and Holland is a feature called the Walloon Lagoon. Polonski gazes, thunderstruck. 'This cannot be. This cannot be. This cannot be.'

(Mitchell 2001: 33–34)

In a macabre twist, when Polonski visits Voorman the following day, the bored, weary, immortal God decides that they will change places: '*You* can juggle time, gravity, waves and particles [. . .] I'm going to make your wife smile in a most involuntary way and partake of the chief warden's brandy' (Mitchell 2001: 36).

Here we have a textual description of a scene in a film, a description that takes place within a character's fantasy which is itself part of a *bildungsroman* written by Mitchell, that then becomes a real film *The Voorman Problem*, only for us to learn, in *The Bone Clocks*, that 'The Voorman Problem' was written by Crispin Hershey (Mitchell 2014a: 381 and 423). There could not be a more excellent example of the bewildering and exultant, in equal parts, hyper-interconnectedness of Mitchell's storyverse, drawing inexhaustibly into itself not just its own fictions but the world outside it as well. And 'The Voorman Problem' is a story about an omniscient immortal God who maintains an entire universe only by his constant acts of imagining . . .

Can you hear it here and now? (As Polonski does when he enters the prison.)
The distant singing, the far off chanting, of the God's devoted followers?

Herein I give to you only one part of the great CriticFanBook:

The Psalms of Mitchell

Blessed be the Lord.

Long may He live.

Works cited

Birnbaum, R. (2006), 'David Mitchell', *The Morning News*, 11 May, URL (consulted December 2017): www.themorningnews.org/archives/birnbaum_v/david_mitchell.php
Dillon, S. (2011), *David Mitchell: Critical Essays*, Canterbury: Gylphi.
Italie, H. (2008), 'Bookseller Talk Big, Act Quietly at Convention', *USA Today*, 1 June, URL (consulted December 2017): http://usatoday30.usatoday.com/money/economy/2008-06-01-1819108364_x.htm
Mitchell, D. (1999), *Ghostwritten*, London: Sceptre.
—— (2001), *number9dream*, London: Sceptre.
—— (2003), 'The January Man', *Granta 81: Best of Young British Novelists 2003*, URL (consulted December 2017): https://granta.com/the-january-man/
—— (2004a), *Cloud Atlas*, London: Sceptre.
—— (2004b), 'What You Do Not Know You Want', in *McSweeney's Enchanted Chamber of Astonishing Stories*, edited by Michael Chabon, London: Vintage, 11–31.
—— (2005a), 'Acknowledgements', *Prospect Magazine*, 22 October, URL (consulted December 2017): www.prospectmagazine.co.uk/magazine/acknowledgements
—— (2005b), 'Hangman', in *New Writing 13*, edited by Ali Smith and Toby Litt, London: Picador, 90–105.
—— (2006), *Black Swan Green*, London: Sceptre.
—— (2007a), 'Dénouement', *The Guardian*, 26 May, URL (consulted December 2017): www.theguardian.com/books/2007/may/26/originalwriting.fiction
—— (2007b), 'Judith Castle', in *The Book of Other People*, edited by Zadie Smith, London: Hamish Hamilton, 1–18.
—— (2009a), 'Character Development', *The Guardian*, 2 September, URL (consulted December 2017): www.theguardian.com/books/2009/sep/02/david-mitchell-character-development

—— (2009b), 'The Massive Rat', *The Guardian*, 1 August, URL (consulted December 2017): www.theguard ian.com/books/2009/aug/01/david-mitchell-short-story-rat

—— (2010a), *The Thousand Autumns of Jacob de Zoet*, London: Sceptre.

—— (2010b), 'Muggins Here', *The Guardian*, 14 August, URL (consulted December 2017): www.theguard ian.com/books/2010/aug/14/david-mitchell-summer-short-story

—— (2010c), 'Earth Calling Taylor', *The Financial Times*, 30 December, URL (consulted December 2017): www.ft.com/content/3e898e58-121c-11e0-92d0-00144feabdc0

—— (2011a), 'The Siphoners', in *I'm with the Bears: Short Stories from a Damaged Planet*, edited by Mark Martin, London: Verso, 129–142.

—— (2011b), 'The Gardener', in Kai and Sunny, *The Flower Show*, Limited Edition Box Set, available in audio-visual at *The Guardian*, URL (consulted March 2018): www.theguardian.com/books/audioslideshow/2011/jun/06/davidmitchell

—— (2012a), 'An Inside Job', in *Fighting Words*, edited by Roddy Doyle, Dublin: Stoney Road Press.

—— (2012b), 'In the Bike Sheds', *The Bookseller*, 20 June, URL (consulted March 2018): www.thebookseller. com/feature/bike-sheds-short-story-david-mitchell-338886

—— (2013), 'Lots of Bits of Star', in Kai and Sunny, *Caught by the Nest*, Limited Edition Box Set.

—— (2014a), *The Bone Clocks*, London: Sceptre.

—— (2014b), 'Variations on a Theme by Mister Donut', *Granta* 127: Japan, 24 April, URL (consulted March 2018): https://granta.com/variations-on-a-theme-by-mister-donut/

—— (2014c), 'The Right Sort', *Twitter* @david_mitchell, collated by *The Guardian*, 14 July, URL (consulted December 2017): www.theguardian.com/books/2014/jul/14/the-right-sort-david-mitchells-twitter-short-story

—— (2015), *Slade House*, London: Sceptre.

—— (2016a), 'My Eye on You', in Kai and Sunny, *Whirlwind of Time*, Limited Edition Box Set.

—— (2016b/2114), *From Me Flows What You Call Time*, Future Library Project, URL (consulted March 2018): www.futurelibrary.no/

—— (2016c), 'All Souls Day', in *Francis Upritchard: Jealous Saboteurs*, Exhibition Monograph, Curated by Charlotte Day and Robert Leonard, Melbourne: Monash University Museum of Art, and City Gallery Wellington, 78–86.

—— (2017), 'A Forgettable Story', *Silkroad Magazine*, 30 June, URL (consulted December 2017): http://discovery.cathaypacific.com/a-forgettable-story-david-mitchell/

—— (no date), 'Preface', *Penguin Random House*, URL (consulted December 2017): www.penguinrandomhouse. com/authors/20870/david-mitchell

Poole, S. (2001), 'I Think I'm Turning Japanese', *The Guardian*, 10 March, URL (consulted December 2017): www.guardian.co.uk/books/2001/mar/10/fiction.davidmitchell

Schulz, K. (2014), 'Boundaries Are Conventions. And *The Bone Clocks* Author David Mitchell Transcends Them All', *Vulture*, 25 August, URL (consulted December 2017): www.vulture.com/2014/08/david-mitchell-interview-bone-clocks-cloud-atlas.html

Shakespeare, W. (1993), *The Sonnets*, London: Everyman.

Filmography

The Voorman Problem, directed by Mark Gill, URL (consulted December 2017): www.thevoormanproblem.com

33

JONATHAN LETHEM

Joseph Brooker

The American novelist Jonathan Lethem (b. 1964) has expressed scepticism about literary canons. He argues that the American novel resembles a Mount Rushmore on which only three or four heads are carved, and those belong to white males. Lethem admits that he himself has occasionally been carved on the latest version of the figurative Rushmore, alongside a selection of contemporaries. But he thinks that we should beware declarations about 'America's three or four greatest living novelists', and instead be open to the unmasterable and still growing abundance of books (Lethem 2011: 367–372).

If we follow Lethem's own view, we should be careful about applying to him the sort of terms he rejects here. Nonetheless the case for his significance, among contemporary writers in the English language, can be made a few ways. First, in the most Rushmore-like mode, he has received a measure of official recognition, with the MacArthur Fellowship ('Genius Grant'), National Book Critics Circle Award and World Fantasy Award. In 2010 he was appointed to a prestigious chair of Creative Writing at Pomona College in California. A volume of collected interviews, *Conversations with Jonathan Lethem*, was published in 2011.

Second, Lethem is extraordinarily prolific. From 1994 to 2017 he produced ten novels, one novella, three full short story collections and two more slim volumes containing short stories; three substantial collections of essays and memoirs and two critical books on film and music. To this one can add his role as writer for a revived superhero comic; extensive labour as co-editor of the writings of Philip K. Dick; editing of multiple anthologies of others' essays; and many other uncollected short stories. With many contemporary writers, one is necessarily dealing with a nascent oeuvre of uncertain weight and longevity. With Lethem, the mass of work has reached a point where it is difficult for any one reader to be sure that they have read everything.

Third, Lethem's work connects strongly to certain tendencies in recent literary history. First is the use he has made of genre. In his writing, 'literary fiction' and the genres of science fiction and crime, in particular, are united, or the difference between them becomes more doubtful. Lethem's use of genre's tropes connects with a subsequent development in his non-fictional writing, towards ideas of intertextuality, appropriation and collage as the basis of creativity. At the same time, Lethem has also come to partake in another trend in American letters: autobiographical writing and the foregrounding of personal experience. He has at times blurred further lines here: between creative and critical writing, personal and cultural history. Lethem's writing on his home town of New York City relates closely to contemporary interests in the experience of space and the qualities of place, and how they may be refracted through memory. His work also aspires to a political dimension, addressing such issues as the US prison system, the goals of the Occupy movement and the history of the American Left. Even the recent critical surge of interest in animals and their representation can find a recurring echo in the curiously insistent kangaroos, dogs, tigers and eagles that vividly occupy Lethem's fictional worlds. In all these areas, his work has been an invitation to juxtaposition and exploration. A writer never given to hermeticism, he is keen to serve as the occasion for new thought and creativity in others.

The essay that follows proceeds primarily as a chronological account of Lethem's career. Along the way, that eventful story will generate issues for critical consideration, and signal points of connection between Lethem and others in the evolving world of contemporary literature.

Origin stories

Lethem's background bears recounting, both because it is plainly formative and because it would eventually become an unmistakable model for his fiction. He was born and raised in Brooklyn, New York City, the child of bohemian radicals. His father Richard Brown Lethem is a painter. Jonathan Lethem's own aspirations to visual art were displaced by the parallel course that he developed on the typewriter that his mother Judith gave him at fourteen. A social worker and activist, she was of German Jewish background; Lethem can thus define himself as a Jewish writer, though this aspect has not thus far been prominent in discussion of his work. Far more crucial is her death from cancer in 1978, a loss that would leave its trace on his fiction.

From his upbringing Lethem drew an easy openness to art and creativity: 'a lot of my parents' friends were [my father's] students or colleagues, and so this activity – specifically, going into the studio every day and trying to make paintings – seemed normal to me' (Clarke 2011: xiv). This sense of the openness of art to life, and vice versa, can be viewed as an enabling condition of Lethem's later output: continuous, garrulously expansive, and often making light of boundaries between fact and fiction, between pictures and writing, or between intellectual property and common inheritance. Lethem also inherited his parents' politics. Even when not ostensibly political, his fiction has consistently tended to a sceptical view of the world and those in power.

This sceptical view derived also from his reading. When still a teen, Lethem read much literature that would be formative for his work; but most distinctively and significantly he discovered science fiction, consuming the genre 'like a machine' (Clarke 2011: 35). The California-based novelist Philip K. Dick (1928–1982) quickly became the master author of Lethem's life. Lethem read his voluminous body of work multiple times, becoming not only an expert but an early member of the Philip K. Dick Society. He would eventually introduce editions of Dick's work for the Library of America (making Dick the first science fiction author to be granted entry to this notably official canon), and co-produce a vast edition of Dick's late journals known as his *Exegesis*. Meanwhile, Lethem also consumed the rest of the science fiction canon, and that of hard-boiled crime fiction (Dashiel Hammett, Raymond Chandler, Stanley Ellin). The overall effect – of many of these writers, but especially Dick – was to instal paranoia and dystopia as default settings for Lethem's imagination. Much later, Lethem's 2010 short book on John Carpenter's 1988 film *They Live* would confirm his fascination with how a 'pulp' narrative could productively articulate political paranoia.

Lethem spent a year at Bennington College in Vermont, a setting that he would later fictionalize. So would his contemporaries Bret Easton Ellis and Donna Tartt, in *The Rules of Attraction* (1987) and *The Secret History* (1992) respectively. In hindsight, Lethem's college year (also featuring the novelist Jill Eisenstadt) seems quite a distinguished literary generation. But Lethem himself soon dropped out and relocated to San Francisco, drawn in part by the spell of

Philip K. Dick – who had inconveniently died shortly before. Settling a few streets from Dick's old home, Lethem worked for years in bookshops, honing his knowledge of literary obscurities and the backroads of the canon. He also wrote short stories, publishing (from 1989) mainly in genre-based magazines such as *Isaac Asimov's Science Fiction Magazine* and *Interzone*. His career as a novelist began with the debut novel *Gun, With Occasional Music* (1994). The novel is a hard-boiled detective story after Chandler, but set in a near-future dystopian California akin to Dick's, in which animals have been genetically modified to act like humans. Lethem describes the work as 'a piece of carpentry' located at 'the exact midpoint between Dick and Chandler' (Clarke 2011: 51).

This functional, craftsmanlike account indicates Lethem's readiness to think of art in terms of ideas and techniques, consciously applied and admitted. In an essay he suggests that, by polite convention, novelists are not supposed to be overt about their estimation of their contemporaries, their influences or their own career's arc: in this mode, 'We [writers] don't know why we do what we do, but we're not *too* amazed with ourselves for being the lucky keepers of this universal flame' (Lethem 2011: xviii). His own approach to literature can profitably be understood as a counter to these polite conventions. Lethem's work, from the start, has resulted from strategies, choices, open adaptations of other artistic models. His extensive comments on his own work freely demonstrate how continuously aware he has been of what he has been doing all this time, and his readiness to share these ideas with others who might take them up in turn.

Lethem's second novel *Amnesia Moon* (1995) drew on numerous attempts at fiction that he had written since his teens (Lethem 2011: xix). They added up to another near-future dystopia, this time particularly preoccupied with a multiplicity of worlds or distinct zones of reality. As the protagonist Chaos travels across an America apparently blighted by a nuclear war, he learns that no war has in fact taken place, and that he himself has an earlier identity as Everett Moon. In picaresque mode, the novel stages a series of distinct, peculiar communities: a city on a mountain shrouded in green fog, a post-apocalyptic McDonald's restaurant, a town whose inhabitants are frequently compelled to move house and whose politicians are television stars. *Amnesia Moon* also features such non-naturalistic items as a girl covered in fur, or a clock in which Everett becomes trapped as a disembodied spirit. Here Lethem produces what the critic of science fiction Darko Suvin (1979) has influentially called 'nova': items of radical novelty and strangeness that take us distinctly out of the naturalistic realm and into a fantastic one.

As a slim campus novel, *As She Climbed across the Table* (1997) seems closer to life as we know it. But it centres on a particle physics laboratory which has discovered a portal in reality that becomes called Lack. Lack mysteriously captures the affection of Alice, partner of the protagonist Philip. The novel thus recounts his doomed romantic quest to regain her love, and it can be read as a reflection on love and loss alongside, say, Roland Barthes' *A Lover's Discourse* (1977). But it also stages still larger questions about reality, perception and the production of worlds. Philip eventually finds a multiplicity of alternative worlds beyond Lack, only partially reminiscent of the universe he usually inhabits. The novel is not quite science fiction in a familiar sense, but it does make estranging fiction out of ideas of science.

Lethem had moved back to Brooklyn in 1996, and his next three novels would treat of the borough in some way. *Girl in Landscape* (1998a) is Lethem's last indisputable science fiction novel to date. It commences in a thinly sketched future Brooklyn from which the Marsh family departs to begin a new life on a distant planet. The mother dies of a mysterious illness early in the novel, in Lethem's plainest refraction thus far of his own mother's death. Most of the novel relates the Marsh family's experience as interplanetary colonizers, along with a handful of other human beings and the strange, seemingly harmless alien race the Archbuilders. The book's protagonist is Pella Marsh, a teenage girl entering puberty: a life experience which is mixed with the sometimes dreamlike strangeness of the new planet. The novel is comparable to various precursors in science fiction. But its signal distinction is in fact to derive from the Western: specifically John Ford's film *The Searchers* (1956). The film dramatizes an ambivalence about the Native American, which Lethem transposes to space in the unease around the Archbuilders. This unease and potential for violence centres on the film's protagonist Ethan Edwards, played by John Wayne, and the figure of Efram Nugent who partially echoes him in Lethem's novel. Once again Lethem has been open about the derivation of his work from an earlier source, writing an entire essay about his own ambivalence toward *The Searchers* and adding other reference points (including Forster's *A Passage to India*) to enrich the picture (Lethem 2005: 1–14).

Through the 1990s Lethem had continued to publish short stories located between science fiction, contemporary realism and conceptual allegory. A significant selection of these appeared in the volume *The Wall of the Sky, The Wall of the Eye* (1996; in 2002 the UK edition offered a slightly different selection). But at the decade's end he issued a novel that withdrew from science fiction, while enriching his engagement with genre. *Motherless Brooklyn* (1999) was Lethem's most commercially successful novel thus far, and might be counted his crossover work into high visibility in the American literary field. The novel's narrator Lionel Essrog has Tourette's syndrome – a neurological condition which Lethem creatively adapts for literary effect. Lionel narrates the action to us without complication, but his speech to others is punctuated by outbursts of 'word salad' and extraneous verbal content. This adds significantly to the novel's semantic texture, and Lionel's compulsion to tic or repeatedly touch things also plays its part in his passage through the story. Lionel is an orphan, raised in St Vincent's Home for Boys: hence the title, with its evident autobiographical pertinence for the author. Lionel and three fellow orphans have been taken under the wing of Frank Minna, a shady, wisecracking local businessman who has effectively become their father figure. The book commences with Minna's murder. Its remainder comprises Lionel's attempt to solve the crime. He thus becomes, by default but with growing enthusiasm, a kind of detective. The novel has all the intricacy and intrigue of a successful crime novel; it won the Gold Dagger award for achievement in that genre. Yet it also comes at the genre from a deliberately skewed angle: in centring on a would-be detective rather than an established professional; in letting Lionel's Tourette's distort its verbal texture and become a major theme in its own right; and in its self-consciousness about genre, as in Lionel's quotations from Raymond Chandler and comparisons of his own experience to generic fictional ones (Lethem 1999: 307, 119, 205). Working in multiple ways at once while remaining compactly formed, *Motherless Brooklyn* remains among Lethem's finest achievements.

The claims of genre

We may pause here to consider the position in the literary field that Lethem had developed through the 1990s. It depended in part on the distinctiveness of particular genres. At its broadest, genre is a multivalent term for a type or mode (such as, for the ancient Greeks, tragedy and comedy in drama). But in the present context it refers to the modern development of popular genres in mass-market formats, from the paperback and comic book to the radio serial and Hollywood film. Within these media, genres were types of story: the Gothic and its descendant horror; romance; the Western; science fiction; crime. Each of these might hold numerous sub-genres (cavalry Western, space opera, the hard-boiled detective story). The particular genres essayed by Lethem derived from these traditions.

Genre fiction is defined in part by that which is contrasted to it. This is a body of work comparatively bereft of the iconography of the popular genres (cowboys, robots, vampires), and often considered, at least on average, to be better written and more fully achieved as art. Terms for such work include 'literary', 'realist' and 'mainstream' fiction. All these labels have their particular connotations, and problems. It is even feasible to argue that 'literary fiction' itself is a genre, as comfortably convention-bound as the Western, and that to distinguish it from genre is thus misleading. Yet for practical purposes, it is difficult to relinquish reference to 'literary', 'mainstream' and related terms in discussing popular genres and what lies beyond their borders.

By the time Lethem's literary career commenced, the boundary between fictions considered as 'genre' and as 'art' had already been ostentatiously crossed a number of times. In the late 1960s the maverick American critic Leslie Fiedler had urged that writers should 'turn frankly to Pop forms' to revitalize US fiction. He included the Western and science fiction as good sources of inspiration, but ironically already, thirty years before *Motherless Brooklyn*, considered detective fiction 'hopelessly compromised by middlebrow condescension' (Fiedler 1972: 69). In the decades from Fiedler to Lethem, numerous ventures were indeed made into genre territory by writers who had started outside it. William S. Burroughs' *Red Night* trilogy (1981–7) brought elements of different generic types (gunfighters, pirates, detectives) into its fractured montage; Robert Coover's *A Night at the Movies* (1987) offered a collection of gross parodies of Hollywood film; Paul Auster's *New York Trilogy* (1985) staged a cool encounter with the mystery genre.

Lethem's early work belongs in the same historical continuum as these creative and critical tendencies. It might be distinguished in two ways. One, which seemed his signature in the 1990s, is his tendency to collide genres (crime, science fiction, the Western) and make them work together: not in a montage of irreconcilable icons, but as an internally coherent narrative world. A second point, phrased figuratively, is that Lethem occupied his genres from the inside. His science fiction novels were written with the emergent artistic awareness of a devotee of Calvino and Borges. But they were also written by a devotee of science fiction itself. Lethem had learned the genre on its own terms, rather than merely toying with its images from a distance; and this strongly affects his novels. The detective plots in *Gun, with Occasional Music* and *Motherless Brooklyn* are as compelling as Chandler's; the dystopia of *Gun* is as fully realized and dismaying as those of Dick or Ray Bradbury (which were indeed sometimes sketchy themselves). In this regard, *Motherless Brooklyn*'s achievement is telling in winning prizes not only for literary fiction, but among other detective novels. Whatever his awareness of the literary and artistic history beyond specific popular modes, Lethem also occupied his chosen forms so that the works succeeded on the internal terms of their genres, rather than as amusements lightly mocking genre from the outside.

Lethem himself has reflected on the place of genre in literary history. He recalls spending his apprentice years attending science fiction conventions and perpetually appearing on panels discussing 'Science Fiction and the Mainstream'. Lethem himself could claim the privilege of a liminal role, one who knew science fiction better than mainstream critics but also 'knew more about contemporary writing than anyone else' in the seemingly hermetic zone of science fiction (Lethem 2011: 68). The 'quarantine' of science fiction from the mainstream seemed antiquated to Lethem, whose tendency in such discussion is to run the two lineages together: he lists Pynchon, DeLillo and Angela Carter alongside Samuel R. Delany and the inherently ambiguous J.G. Ballard. In Lethem's presentation of the issue, the emphasis is often on a single space of imaginative writing, which has been unnecessarily complicated and fenced about by genre distinctions. In such a space Kafka and Dick, Borges and Ballard could belong together, perhaps under the capacious roof of 'the fantastic'. Such an ecumenical approach fuelled Lethem's 1998 polemic 'The Squandered Promise of Science Fiction', which argued that the genre had gone wrong the day in 1973 that Pynchon's *Gravity's Rainbow* was not awarded the Nebula award. Pynchon's nomination, Lethem declared, 'now stands as a hidden tombstone marking the death of the hope that science fiction was about to merge with the mainstream'. Ideally,

Lethem (1998b) proposed, 'the notion of science fiction ought to have been gently and lovingly dismantled, and the writers dispersed'.

By these lights, work like *Gun* and *Girl in Landscape* was ideally intended to belong to a realm in which the reifying labels of genre would not apply. Lethem's fiction would simply be judged alongside all other imaginative literature. Yet the aspiration occludes the way that Lethem's own fiction was fired and given definition by its roots in science fiction, rather than in a vaguer literary space. Boundaries can be productive, as the Oulipo would insist. (Indeed in 2013 Lethem would corroborate this view, in a science-fictional context, by contributing a cyberpunk parody to a neo-Oulipan anthology (Lethem 2013b).) Roger Luckhurst has noted that declarations of the dissolution of genre are rarely convincing: games played at generic margins take their force from the power of genres, rather than from their weakness (2005: 243). Lethem's ecumenical aspiration seems laudable, especially in bidding for greater respect for science fiction writers; but some of the most dynamic gestures of his own fiction were predicated on the barriers whose dismantling he urged.

In any case, since Lethem's first forays the claims of genre have increased both on contemporary fiction and in discussion of it. As Rob Latham notes, generic hybridity 'has only served to spawn a host of efforts to coin fresh terms to describe new kinds of cross-border fictions: "new wave fabulism", "interstitial fiction", "transrealism"', and what Bruce Sterling called 'slipstream' writing (2015: 107). In a rich account, Gary K. Wolfe (2011) ponders an 'evaporation' of genre, but we should also continue to notice the potency of genre – in aesthetic terms and also for commercial and institutional purposes. As Latham points out (2015: 104–105), Lethem and his contemporary Michael Chabon have both been glad to accept nominations for genre awards as well as mainstream prizes. And a genre may be enlivened, rather than diminished, by writing that cuts athwart its borders. In 1997 the interviewer Fiona Kelleghan suggested to Lethem that science fiction should thank him 'for being a crossover writer. It makes the whole field look good' (Clarke 2011: 5).

Whether genre has been dissolved or re-emphasized, it is true that the landscape has altered, allowing new thinking and writing. In a British context, so much is well attested by a dialogue which in 2015 the fantasy author Neil Gaiman conducted with Kazuo Ishiguro: a 'literary' author and past Booker Prize winner who yet recounted his increasing ventures into territories that seemingly belonged to popular genre. Earlier in his career, Ishiguro reflected, he would not have cast *Never Let Me Go* (2001) in the science fiction mould it assumes. But: 'Some time in the Nineties I felt a change of climate in the mainstream literary world. [. . .] I sensed that there was a whole generation of people emerging who had a very different attitude to sci-fi, and that there was a new force of energy and inspiration because of that. I may have had the crusty prejudices of somebody of my generation but I felt liberated by these younger writers' (Gaiman and Ishiguro 2015). Lethem's endeavours made a significant contribution to this still developing state of affairs.

Lethem in the twenty-first century

Lethem's first book of the new century was *This Shape We're In* (2001), a fantastic novella which portrays an eccentric alternative society living inside a giant (effectively Trojan) horse. Some of the world-conjuring tools of science fiction are on display here, though – characteristically enough for Lethem – deployed not in a hi-tech far-future setting but a sketchily fabulistic, uncertainly allegorical one. But it was his next novel that would do most to define Lethem's career.

The Fortress of Solitude (2003) confirmed the return to Brooklyn while further shifting Lethem's relation to genre. The novel comprises three parts. The first details, in the third person, the childhood and youth of Dylan Ebdus in the Brooklyn of the 1970s and 1980s. The second brief section offers the liner notes that Dylan has written for a CD reissue. In the third, Dylan himself narrates from the late 1990s as he returns from California to settle accounts on the East Coast. Throughout, what is especially at stake is 'race' in America, the relations between black and white people and cultural traditions. Plainly Dylan Ebdus is the closest character yet to a Lethem alter ego, literally growing up on the same street as his creator.

In one typical writerly trajectory, a novelist starts with thinly veiled autobiography then gradually gains the confidence and knowledge to move outwards to other experiences and scenarios. Lethem's first decade of novels inverts this trajectory: the fiction starts with fantastic and imaginative settings, then eventually turns to an extended treatment of the autobiographical material that had been excluded or sublimated by earlier works. (One comparable case is the British novelist David Mitchell, arguably another 'slipstream' artist, who saved his fictional autobiography for his fourth novel.) What made this unusual trajectory possible in Lethem's case was genre. The genres in which he had installed himself, especially science fiction, allowed him to evade the familiar path of personal growth and to start somewhere stranger and more conceptually adventurous. From this perspective, *Fortress* marks a return to literary normality. This *Bildungsroman* can largely be called a realist novel, layered with historically authentic detail. Considerably longer than Lethem's earlier novels, it is an American epic, writing on a 'Rushmore' scale.

Yet one element drastically complicates this picture: Dylan's discovery of a magic ring that enables him and his friend Mingus to fly. (Later, almost inexplicably, the ring changes and confers invisibility instead.) The ring is recovered from a washed-up, homeless black superhero, and its power chimes with the comic books that Dylan and Mingus already cherish. Popular genre, therefore, has not entirely been cleared from the stage of Lethem's writing. What initially seems a realist monument bears the streak of the superhero genre: a distinct mode which, heavily associated with comic books (and later, blockbuster films), actually has still lower cultural status than the science fiction or crime genres from which it partly derives. (Remarkably, the prominent critic James Wood reviewed the novel without even mentioning the magic ring; Lethem (2011: 384–389) would make public his infuriation with this treatment, which he believed reflected Wood's myopically fastidious distaste for popular culture.) Reclaiming the superhero mode known fondly from his childhood, Lethem grants it a kind of literary seriousness: simultaneously the superhero genre injects energy and strangeness into the book's otherwise naturalistic world. In this venture Lethem's novel found a strong parallel with Michael Chabon's *The Amazing Adventures of Kavalier and Clay* (2000), a re-imagining of the early history of comic books. In both writers' work, superhero comics at once attained new weight and offered a rejuvenating force in American literature.

Lethem's major works sometimes bring additional writing in their prolific wake. In the story collection *Men and Cartoons* (2004) Lethem again worked with figures ('The Vision', 'Super Goat Man') who were ambiguous versions of superheroes. He had already essayed that terrain in a fragmentary treatment of Batman in *Kafka Americana* (1999), a brief but sophisticated collaboration with Carter Scholz. Some of the same concerns were evident in Lethem's first collection of essays, *The Disappointment Artist* (2005), whose defining strategy is to make memoir from cultural analysis and vice versa. Throughout Lethem's essays, life and the art one has experienced are understood as profoundly entwined: there is little distinction, for him, between writing about his childhood and writing about the Fantastic Four.

That deeply personal approach to cultural history would be enduring in Lethem's work, through to his book-length analysis of Talking Heads' *Fear of Music* (2012). But the most formally remarkable offshoot of Lethem's preoccupation with superheroes appeared in 2007–8 when he wrote a new series of an actual Marvel comic, *Omega the Unknown*. The 10-issue run revived a character who had been dormant since his brief run in 1976–7, but mentioned in *The*

Fortress of Solitude. The character completed a circle of remediation, from 1970s comics through a twenty-first-century novel and back into graphic form again. This process also continued a curiously close parallel with Michael Chabon, who had brought his fictional historical super-hero The Escapist from novel into graphic form in 2004. Lethem's revival of *Omega* might also be framed in a broader trend of the fan as artist, in which writers and directors who had grown up with iconic narrative brands were hired to produce new versions of them. The American director J.J. Abrams' refashioning of *Star Trek* and *Star Wars* and the British actor Mark Gatiss's corresponding influence over the renovation of *Dr Who* and Sherlock Holmes are relevant cases; both are just two years younger than Lethem.

You Don't Love Me Yet (2007) is in part a rejection of the scale achieved in *Fortress*. Lethem defied expectations of a weighty follow-up by issuing his lightest novel, a romantic comedy set in 1990s Los Angeles. The novel does, though, circle a significant cluster of themes that Lethem was now exploring: authorship, borrowing, the ownership of ideas and culture. He expanded on these in the essay 'The Ecstasy of Influence', a 2007 essay for *Harper's* and his most cited piece of non-fiction. The essay is a polemic against the jealous protection of cultural rights (as in copyright) and for a more open world of intertextuality in which characters and motifs can be borrowed and reused in new contexts without legal reprisal. Lethem sides with the emergent category of 'The Commons' as one name for such cultural sharing in the digital age. But 'The Ecstasy of Influence' is distinctive in another way. Subtitled 'A Plagiarism Mosaic', it is in fact composed of numerous sections from other texts, subtly adapted for their new context and forged into what appears a seamless whole by Lethem. In a performative coup, it enacts as well as states its theme. The essay would find a distended likeness in another patchwork text, David Shields' book-length manifesto for contemporary writing *Reality Hunger* (2010), which was acclaimed by Lethem among numerous others.

The Ecstasy of Influence also became the title of a large volume of Lethem's 'Nonfictions, etc' in 2011. The reused title confirmed the importance of the essay in his thinking, but in a subsidiary piece (Lethem 2011: 121–124) he also expressed regret at having been taken for an extremist in the matter of copyright and intellectual property. The collection, in any case, was the fullest gathering yet of Lethem's voluminous work as essayist and journalist, collecting long pieces on pop music and framing some of his earliest stories and essays in a retrospective narrative. Beyond the specific issues of intellectual property that Lethem had ventured into, the book's title suggested a general joy in being 'influenced' by other artists and narratives, and Lethem's defiant determination to wear them on his sleeve rather than sublimate them out of view. By now he had issued another hefty novel which also corresponded to that approach, with its extended meditations on Norman Mailer, Marlon Brando and the Rolling Stones.

Chronic City (2009) shifts Lethem's narrative focus from Brooklyn to Manhattan; such had been his identification with his native borough that this move across the East River could be drolly presented as a migration of continental scale. The novel's world also differs from earlier ones in taking in wealth, high society and municipal political influence, as the bland, passive protagonist Chase Insteadman moves through the margins of charity balls and gala opening nights. This Manhattan partly corresponds to that of the mid-2000s, but is also 'reality-shifted' (Clarke 2011: 170) into a more mysterious world. A grey fog seeps over Lower Manhattan, the *New York Times* is available in a 'war-free edition', and a tiger is rumoured to be loose around the city. In forging this estranged, mildly dystopian Manhattan, *Chronic City* is the closest thing Lethem has produced to a specifically post-9/11 novel. It is also (as of 2017) the closest he has come to producing a science fiction novel since *Girl in Landscape*. Rereading Dick's work for the Library of America edition, Lethem had returned to Dick's mode of creating 'real characters in an unreal world', 'the ground [. . .] falling away under the characters' feet' (Clarke 2011: 175–176). Thus

Chase Insteadman lives out a media-fuelled relationship with a lost astronaut, his fiancée Janice Trumbull, whose fate turns out to be a simulation, part of the bread and circuses that divert public attention from real issues. Perhaps the book's most vital figure, though, is Perkus Tooth, a battered and embittered rock journalist and cultural activist. Tooth is the novel's voice both for dissections of musical and film history and for furious conspiracy theories about contemporary America. A cultural obsessive and paranoiac dissident, he might be seen to voice Lethem's own preoccupations, but distanced from the author and given fanatical intensity.

With *Dissident Gardens* (2014) Lethem issued his third large-scale novel of New York City. The geographical focus again shifted fractionally, to the Borough of Queens and specifically the housing development Sunnyside Gardens where the Jewish Communist Rose Zimmer is a dominant figure – though the book also spends much time in Greenwich Village and outside the city. More distinctive within Lethem's corpus is *Dissident Gardens*' historical range. Scenes are laid in the 1950s, the early 2010s and each decade in between. No linear movement through time is offered, as the book swings back and forth between periods: confronting each new chapter, a reader must navigate its unpredictable moment in history without particular guidance from the narrative.

The Fortress of Solitude was in various ways a social and political inquiry, above all in its climactic exploration of America's prison-industrial complex and the extensive incarceration of young black males. Nonetheless, *Dissident Gardens* is Lethem's most politically explicit novel. It seeks to compare different versions and generations of the political Left. Rose Zimmer's generation avers that 'Communism is twentieth-century Americanism', seeking to make their movement mainstream in the mid-century USA. Yet Rose's husband ultimately moves to East Germany and the re-education camp that gives the book its title. His daughter Miriam Zimmer, by contrast, belongs to the New Left of coffeehouse and Dylanesque folk scene. Versed in the American Communist past, she nonetheless stands against the Old Left and her father's Stalinism and for a hippy and dissident generation corresponding roughly to that of Lethem's own parents. Rose Zimmer's affair with a black police captain introduces another strand. The captain's son Cicero Lookins is schooled by Rose, but as an overweight gay black boy he also comes to explore identity politics, and becomes an academic iconoclastically teaching critical theory in Maine. Cicero in turn is interviewed by Miriam's son Sergius, who is inspired by an encounter with a member of the Occupy movement. This signals the arrival of a third or fourth generation of post-war American leftism.

All this radical history might seem inspiring material for a novelist of the left. Yet the mood of *Dissident Gardens* is not inspirational. The novel spends more time detailing the failures, dubious motivations and grubby compromises of its characters than expounding the values they espouse. It might be said that given the travails of the American Left in the relevant period, Lethem is being realistic. Realism is also at stake here in formal terms. *Dissident Gardens* is unprecedented among Lethem's major works in not engaging at all with popular genre (like science fiction or crime), standing instead as a work of 'literary' fiction that does not contain elements of the fantastic. The novel's actions can be outlandishly dramatic or symbolic (as in the scene, frequently recalled in the novel, where the Jewish mother Rose bids to commit suicide in her own gas oven) or its characters larger than life (as when Miriam's cousin Lenny Angrush hurtles through New York dressed as Abraham Lincoln for Halloween), yet these arguably do not take the novel outside the precincts of literary fiction and into those of fantasy. Accordingly, *Dissident Gardens* could be said to complete a gradual journey on Lethem's part – underway at least since *The Fortress of Solitude* – to the realist 'mainstream'. Its political pessimism might be of a piece with this. Fantastic or utopian possibilities are not readily available in this mode; rather, a detailed naturalism drags Lethem's characters down from political dreams into their sordid, limiting circumstances.

In its eschewal of the fantastic, its complex movement through history, and its multi-generational cast of characters, *Dissident Gardens* is a very different brand of fiction from the novels Lethem first issued two decades before. The 'influence' in question seems more Philip Roth than Philip K. Dick, though the novel's winding long sentences also pay stylistic homage to Pynchon. It is perhaps ironic that Lethem should move in this direction while much contemporary fiction moves the other way, into the slipstream zones that he had already explored. Yet we cannot assume that this trajectory represents the definitive rejection of one mode (science fiction) for another (the realist novel). Lethem's career is ongoing; there is no guarantee that his next novel will not be set in outer space rather than the Outer Boroughs. It is worth recalling the cautious, nuanced pledge he gave in 1997 to a question about his future in science fiction: 'What I can promise is that I won't ever betray my own sense of the complexity of that question and suddenly pretend to have nothing to do with science fiction' (Clarke 2011: 5).

Accordingly, in his short fiction – most recently collected in *Lucky Alan* (2015) – Lethem has continued to move between more naturalistic and more experimental or stylized modes. Five of *Lucky Alan*'s stories first appeared in the *New Yorker*, the canonical home for short fiction in America, and these are mainly the closest to literary realism. The book's title story, not far from a bleak Woody Allen scenario, even has an Upper East Side setting that seems primed for its place of publication. 'Realism' here is relative: scarcely a matter of the rugged workaday life of much American short fiction from Raymond Carver to David Means and Wells Tower, Lethem's brand includes such eccentric material (in 'The King of Sentences') as an obsessive literary couple pursuing a reclusive writer and being stripped naked by him in a hotel room. But Lethem's recent stories are apt to be most intriguing when most experimental. 'Their Back Pages' revives the fascination with comics in positing an island on which a set of comic book characters are stranded. Boldly varying modes of narration, Lethem shifts in and out of the characters' florid journals and poems, while narrating via instructions to a comic book illustrator: 'Page forty-two, panel two, a campfire in a clearing' (2015: 83). Another story imagines an online blog as a real place, and narrates its fate backwards, beginning with the blog's demise and concluding with its euphoric origin. In 'Traveler Home' Lethem finds a striking new narrative voice, telegraphically condensed ('Quandary of toothbrush solved, laid on briefcase for ease of notforgetting' (2015: 41)), and narrates the fantastical gift of a baby from a pack of wild wolves: rather as though he were now seeking the midpoint between Beckett and Angela Carter, in the landscape of Richard Ford.

The story 'Procedure in Plain Air' invites us to consider again the political impulse of Lethem's writing. A *New Yorker* publication from 2009, it starts amid the daily detail of the twenty-first-century city, with the protagonist Stevick scanning the regulars in his local coffee shop. The story swiftly modulates into something more sinister, as a hole is dug in the street and a dark-skinned man in an orange jumpsuit is lowered silently into it. Seeking to protest at the situation, Stevick finds himself drawn into it, somehow taking on the job of holding an umbrella over the prisoner. The reader may well consider the story a refraction of the treatment of terrorist suspects since 9/11, most notoriously seen in Guantanamo Bay. Notably, the story does not simply cultivate outrage but traces complicity. Stevick becomes part of the system of incarceration precisely because of his attempt to ameliorate it. A grey area seems to blend good intentions and participation in the security state. Most significantly, what begins as bizarre is swiftly accepted. The initially protesting Stevick ends the tale 'certain he was going to do a good job' (Lethem 2015: 70). The 'realist' setting amid which the story begins thus has its dramatic function: all this takes place in an essentially plausible environment, not a sparsely allegorical one in which the sinister events would be less incongruous. The major model here is surely Kafka, one of Lethem's touchstones. What Lethem reenacts in this story is what Michael Wood has identified as Kafka's theme of 'the taming of surprise', a process in which the protagonist 'fails to hang on to the sense of strangeness the situation seems to call for. He treats it as if it were almost normal, or as if it could soon be made normal. [. . .] And gets himself, in most instances, further and further into trouble as a result' (2003: 25).

In Wood's terms, Kafka's project was partly to shadow our capacity to tame surprise, and partly, by extension, to make us once again as surprised as we ought to be. That is also one of the vocations of science fiction, sometimes under the guise of Suvin's (1979) 'cognitive estrangement'. This offers one way to appreciate Lethem's avowal that he will 'never betray my powerful sense of origin in and indebtedness to and involvement with science fiction' (Clarke 2011: 6). His unceasing literary output has been peculiarly varied, and its future trajectory is harder to predict than that of many contemporary novelists: in large part because he has from the start awarded himself the space to move in and out of the real and the fantastic, the naturalistic and the allegorical. We may hope that his work remains true to his own description (2011: 83) of the value of contemporary literature: 'the most advanced radiation suit yet devised for wandering into the toxic future'.

Coda: tumbling dice

Lethem's next novel would start with a deliberate nod to his first novelistic treatment of that future. 'It was there when I woke up, I swear. The feeling' (1994: 3): with that reflection from private eye Conrad Metcalf, Lethem's career as a novelist began. In 2016 his tenth novel commenced: 'It was there when he woke up. Presumably also when he slept. The blot' (2016: 3). The echo is unmistakable, suggesting the author's awareness of his own trajectory and a readiness to string intertextual connections across the decades. Yet the larger relation between Lethem's tenth novel and his earlier work is less plain. Even the novel's own identity is ambiguous: issued as *A Gambler's Anatomy* in the US, it was then published as *The Blot* in the UK a few months later. The two titles might appear to represent the divergent options of elegant literary respectability and pulp directness. Lethem compounded the ambiguity by collaborating with the academic Laurence A. Rickels on *The Blot: a Supplement* (2016), a textual dialogue circling the novel and other shared themes.

A Gambler's Anatomy itself follows the international backgammon player Alexander Bruno. We see Bruno roll the dice at backgammon tables in Singapore and Berlin, where he falls victim to a disabling tumour inside his head – the source of the 'blot' across his field of vision. (The novel points out that 'blot' is also jargon for a vulnerable piece in backgammon; it draws much of its structure and imagery from the game.) Bruno is flown to California for specialist surgery at the expense of his old acquaintance Keith Stolarsky, who turns out effectively to own a whole urban community. His face reshaped by surgery, Bruno dons a surgical mask as he keeps a low profile in Berkeley, before eventually taking part in a climactic riot against Stolarsky's domination of the neighbourhood. The novel closes with the masked Bruno once again playing backgammon in Singapore, content to be anonymous. He has also apparently gained psychic powers, and can plant suggestions in his opponents' minds. Bruno in fact believes himself to have had such powers since childhood: the blot, he reasons, developed as a 'barricade' against it (2016: 160).

Beyond the first sentence, echoes of Lethem's past work are discernible, yet distorted. Bruno meets a 'couples therapist from Kansas City' called Cynthia Jalter, who seems to have resurfaced from a previous appearance in *As She Climbed Across the Table*. But the new novel's Cynthia is 'peroxided' (2016: 74–76) while the earlier incarnation was 'the least blond woman I had ever met' (1997: 103), and the novels' contrasting narrative styles and worlds make them seem entirely separate characters. The later novel's Berlin dimension recalls the German family saga running through *Dissident Gardens*, which was in part a fictional response to Lethem's own family history. The Californian setting of its second half reprises the San Francisco Bay settings of the first two novels, but as a zone of contemporary corporate power rather than a futuristic dystopia. The insertion of Bruno's psychic powers into a relatively realistic narrative world might recall the presence of the magic ring in *The Fortress of Solitude*, but is accompanied by a gruesome physicality unprecedented in Lethem's writing: the novel's central set piece is an extended close description of the neurosurgeon's operation on Bruno's tumour, which Lethem himself suggests is his first venture into horror fiction (Laity 2017). If Bruno's mysterious powers offer a trace of the fantastic, the international casino settings also hint at another genre: the spy thriller. This would be another new generic turn for Lethem (as Singapore is a new setting, in a novel that never ventures near New York), and the characters' references to James Bond indicate his awareness of it (2016: 76).

Yet a clearer continuity with Lethem's literary heritage is the flavour of Thomas Pynchon, who seems the closest precursor to what becomes a loose, roaming narrative of bohemian, sometimes profane and promiscuous interactions in Berkeley. Keith Stolarsky's control of local land and business recall Pierce Inverarity, the deceased mogul who in Pynchon's *The Crying of Lot 49* (1965) has founded an entire California town, San Narciso, that threatens to entrap the paranoid protagonist. The symbiotic relation between Stolarsky and his supposed political antagonist Garris Plybon echoes that between Inverarity and a Mexican anarchist, and even the conflagration that destroys Stolarsky's property and enables him to claim insurance recalls a similarly convenient fire in San Narciso (Lethem 2016: 200, 281; Pynchon 1996: 82–83, 102–103). In sum, *A Gambler's Anatomy* contains various traces of the Lethem we have known thus far – occasionally as though subjecting his own work to the playful remix of 'The Ecstasy of Influence' – yet scrambles them into a story not quite like anything he has previously offered.

Perhaps the simplest connecting thread through Lethem's career is productivity. Since *A Gambler's Anatomy* he has already seen into print a co-edited anthology of rock writing, *Shake It Up*, and a substantial new collection of essays on literature, *More Alive and Less Lonely*. 2017 also brought a feature-length film about his life and work. For those seeking to make sense of Lethem's universe, the most elementary challenge is the rapidity with which that universe continues to expand, generating multiple worlds as it goes.

Works cited

Clarke, J. (ed.) (2011) *Conversations with Jonathan Lethem*, Jackson: University Press of Mississippi.

Fiedler, L. A. (1972) *Cross the Border: Close the Gap*, New York: Stein & Day.

Gaiman, N. with K. Ishiguro (2015) 'Let's Talk about Genre', *New Statesman*, 4 June.

Laity, P. (2017) "'I've Always Thought of Myself as a Dark Writer, But This Is Utterly Different": "The books interview" with Jonathan Lethem', *Guardian*, Saturday, 11 February 2017, Review, 13.

Latham, R. (2015) 'American Slipstream: Science Fiction and Literary Respectability', in E.C. Link and G. Canavan (eds.) *The Cambridge Companion to American Science Fiction*, Cambridge: Cambridge University Press, 99–110.

Lethem, J. (1994) *Gun, with Occasional Music*, San Diego, CA: Harcourt Brace.

—— (1995) *Amnesia Moon*, San Diego, CA: Harcourt Brace.

—— (1996) *The Wall of the Sky, the Wall of the Eye*, San Diego, CA: Harcourt Brace.

—— (1997) *As She Climbed across the Table*, New York: Doubleday.

—— (1998a) *Girl in Landscape*, New York: Doubleday.

—— (1998b) 'The Squandered Promise of Science Fiction', *Village Voice*, June, available at http://hipsterbook club.livejournal.com/1147850.html.

—— (1999) *Motherless Brooklyn*, New York: Doubleday.

—— (2001) *This Shape We're In*, San Francisco: McSweeney's.

—— (2003) *The Fortress of Solitude*, London: Faber.

—— (2004) *Men and Cartoons*, New York: Doubleday.

—— (2005) *The Disappointment Artist*, London: Faber.

—— (2007) *You Don't Love Me Yet*, London: Faber.

—— (2008) *Omega: The Unknown*, New York: Marvel Comics.

—— (2010a) *Chronic City*, London: Faber.

—— (2010b) *They Live*, Berkeley: Soft Skull.

—— (2011) *The Ecstasy of Influence*, New York: Doubleday.

—— (2012) *Fear of Music*, New York: Bloomsbury.

—— (2013a) *Dissident Gardens*, New York: Doubleday.

—— (2013b) 'Cyberpunk', in Raymond Queneau and Barbara Wright (eds.) *Exercises in Style*, New York: New Directions, 247–248.

—— (2015) *'Lucky Alan' and Other Stories*, New York: Doubleday.

—— (2016) *A Gambler's Anatomy*, New York: Doubleday.

—— (2017) *More Alive and Less Lonely: On Books and Writers*, ed. by Christopher Boucher, New York: Melville House.

Lethem, J. and K. Dettmar (eds.) (2017) *Shake It Up: Great American Writing on Rock and Pop from Elvis to Jay Z*, New York: Library of America.

Lethem, J. and L. A. Rickels (2016) *The Blot: A Supplement*, Fort Wayne, IN: Anti-Oedipus Press.

Lethem, J. and C. Scholz (1999) *Kafka Americana*, New York: Norton.

Luckhurst, R. (2005) *Science Fiction: A Cultural History*, Cambridge: Polity.

Pynchon, T. (1996 [1965]) *The Crying of Lot 49*, London: Vintage.

Suvin, D. (1979) *Metamorphoses of Science Fiction: On the Poetics and History of a Literary Genre*, New Haven and London: Yale University Press.

Wolfe, G. K. (2011) *Evaporating Genres: Essays on Fantastic Literature*, Middletown, CT: Wesleyan University Press.

Wood, M. (2003) *Franz Kafka*, Tavistock: Northcote House.

34

ALI SMITH

Daniel Lea

Ali Smith's fiction demands of its reader some basic requirements. Firstly, one must be the bearer of a sense of humour, and, if possible, a sense of the ludicrous, for we are everywhere treated to a stream of in-jokes and puns that reflect their author's fondness for both whimsy and surreality. Secondly, one must give up any reliance on the conventions of narrative realism for though her works are often explicitly set in recognisably contemporary worlds, they rarely limit themselves to the visible parameters of social reality, preferring audacious imaginative flight over intricate description or plot trajectory. Finally, one needs to tune emotionally to the pitch of writing that while fearsomely clever is also hauntingly affecting. Smith does not manipulatively wring from her reader an emotional reaction to the heart-breaking concerns with loss, vulnerability, grief, and loneliness about which she often writes, rather through echoes and associations one comes obliquely to appreciate and empathise with the difficult work of being human that Smith captures. Armed with these prerequisites the reader can feel prepared to tackle one of the most innovative, thoughtful, and witty writers of her generation.

Alison Smith was born in Inverness, Scotland on 24th August 1962 to an English father, who was an electrician, and a mother from the very north of Ireland, who worked as a bus conductress. The last of five children, Smith recalls a happy childhood but one in which she, as the youngest by seven years, spent much time amusing herself. She learned to read at the age of three and had devoured her siblings' book collections before her teenage years. A profound sense of her differ-ence to many in her Highland community preceded her recognition of her lesbianism; she fell deeply in love with another girl in her teens and though she experienced straight relationships during her student years – which she describes as 'terrible and [. . .] fine' (Bowditch 2001) – her sexuality never seems to have been in serious doubt. Smith studied as an undergraduate at the University of Aberdeen, taking her Bachelors in English Literature, and had planned to enrol for a PhD at the University of Edinburgh before receiving an offer to continue her study at Newnham College, University of Cambridge. There, she wrote her doctoral thesis on William Carlos Williams, Wallace Stevens, and James Joyce, though she was not awarded her degree on her examiners' judgement that the topic was too broad. By this point, Smith seems to have been losing faith in the fustiness and pomposity of academia, but she did take up a lecturing post in English and American Studies at the University of Strathclyde, an experience which appears to have been disheartening: 'I'd be talking about *To the Lighthouse* and people would be waiting for an answer! [In giving it] I knew I was lying' (Akba 2012). In her late twenties, whilst working at

Stratchlyde, Smith developed the chronically debilitating condition ME (Myalgic Encephalopathy), and though her illness was relatively short-lived, it did prove a turning point in her artistic development: 'It was a visionary experience. You're faced with a different world and, if you are going to live, you have to renegotiate this world. The illness was the catalyst for my next stage. It allowed me to write' (Bowditch 2001). It also provided her with the personal experience to create the chronically fatigued character of Lise in her break-through novel *Hotel World* (2001). After six months sick leave, Smith gave up her job in Strathclyde and returned to Cambridge with her partner – the artist and film-maker Sarah Wood, who had been an undergraduate at Robinson College, Cambridge – determined to commit herself to writing, which, at this stage largely took the form of short stories and poetry.

Her first collection of stories, *Free Love* was published in 1995, and over the course of four further collections (*Other Stories and Other Stories* (1999); *The Whole Story and Other Stories* (2003); *The First Person and Other Stories* (2008) and *Public Library and Other Stories* (2015)), and eight novels (*Like* (1997); *Hotel World* (2001); *The Accidental* (2005); *Girl Meets Boy* (2007); *There But For The* (2011); *How To Be Both* (2014); *Autumn* (2016) and *Winter* (2017)), she has established a reputation for narratives of great virtuosity and depth. She is undoubtedly prolific – to the above should be added *Shire* (2013), a collaboration of stories and images with her partner Wood, *Artful* (2012), a series of lectures that Smith gave whilst Weidenfeld Visiting Professor at St Anne's College, University of Oxford, and a number of plays. The regularity of this output has led to some criticisms of diminishing return. Sophie Gee for instance, when reviewing *The First Person and Other Stories* felt that her characteristic caprice and subversion of literary culture 'are no longer jolts from the margins; they are comfy and relaxed, too much at home' (Gee 2008), and as I have argued elsewhere (Lea 2016), the stylistic quirks of some of her stories in particular have become repetitive. Indeed it is for her novels, which continue to be consistently ground-breaking, that she has received the critical acclaim that she deserves. She has been shortlisted for the Booker Prize three times, for the Orange Prize for Fiction twice, winning its most recent incarnation as the Baileys Women's Prize for Fiction in 2015 for *How to be Both*, has won the Whitbread Novel of the Year (for *The Accidental*), and has been awarded the Scottish Arts Council Book of the Year Award twice (for *Hotel World* and *Girl Meets Boy*). *How to be Both* also claimed the 2014 Goldsmith's Prize for fiction and the Costa Novel of the Year award.

She has repeatedly turned to a number of issues across her career and rather than try to give an exhaustive account of her contribution to contemporary writing, what follows here will address only the most salient and recurrent concerns of human connectedness, technology, and the transformative capacities of language. Though many of her novels and stories critique the nature of individualism in a hyper-technologised contemporary world where intimacy has given way to solipsism, many also address more universal concerns with love and its failure, death, the search for meaning through art, the human compulsion to tell stories, and, encompassing all of these, the existential problem of connecting with other people. The difficulty of understanding how the self connects with an other is one of the most consistent themes of Smith's work, but in fact it might be more accurate to say that it is the failure of connection between people that is a more persistent trope. In many of the short stories especially, the absence of empathy or simple understanding provides context for Smith's analysis of human interaction as perennially caught between conflict and resolution. Her narratives are filled with contrasting points-of-view, which often forcefully express their right to primacy. These voices explain the world as it appears to them, but none are allowed the ultimate satisfaction of determining the meaning of another's experience. Instead Smith relishes the argumentative grist of opposed perspectives, replacing singular with plural truths. Her novels, and many of her stories tend to be constructed as duologues or multilogues, with characters' differing versions of the world built around shared events or experiences. These 'you–me' stories (Murray 2006: 220) pitch voices against each other but never with the intention of establishing an authorised account. The real point of interest is not the victory of one voice over another but the profusion of different registers, *paroles*, tones, vocabularies, accents, and pitches that feed into the dialogic ambiguity inherent in communication.

Smith is one of the great contemporary writers of domesticity, and much of her questioning of the nature of human connectedness is set in and around the home. Her stories display an acute awareness of the pain of individual loneliness and the cost that is involved in combatting that emptiness by placing other people and other things in our lives. Repeatedly she portrays the emotional and moral difficulties of being with others, and emphasises the fragility of understanding and potential for disruption that overshadow even the strongest and most intimate of human bonds. The voices that emerge are often conflicted, fearful, melancholic, and in thrall to the hurtful memories that have defined, and limited them. Yet, at the same time, these voices are also often hopeful, daring, altruistic, and open to the possibilities of transformation that being touched by the other can bring.

Three interconnected tales in *The First Person and Other Stories* illustrate well her even-handed treatment of different perspectives. 'The First Person', 'The Second Person', and 'The Third Person' tackle, from different thematic and grammatical positions, not only the problem of knowing the other, but also the temptations of speaking for, over, and about the other. 'The First Person' plays on the double sense of first person as a point-of-view (the 'I' of the story) and an agent (the first person to do something). As with many of Smith's stories, it involves a couple in bed imagining how they will tell the story of their relationship to others, and there is a sweet tenderness to the banter as they tease each other with the accusation 'you're not the first person to . . . '. Yet the slight underlying defensiveness that this intimates, the warning to the other not to get above themselves, is touchingly resolved by the novelty that fresh love brings. Actually the narrator experiences a stripping away not just of her cynicism about intimacy, but also of her identity to reveal her first-personage in an originary sense: 'You have peeled the roof off me and turned the whole library into a wood. Every book is a tree. Above the tops of the trees there's nothing but birds' (Smith 2008, 196). The connection with a lover is transformative here, turning a spirit calcified through experience back into youthfulness and hopefulness. And this reversion to first-ness brings with it a new, but welcome, awareness of the self as strange and malleable.

In 'The Second Person', Smith opposes two squabbling lovers, each recounting what the other is 'like', and each upsetting the other with their analogy. One is the 'kind of person' who would make nonsensical impulse purchases out of unrealistic ambition, the other is the kind of pedant who points out to a pianist all the historical nuances of the songs s/he is playing. Of course each protagonist is like and unlike these character sketches, but each sees in the other's story their own self-doubt about how the world sees them. Neither sees the romantic sub-text that the other implies, the open-hearted acceptance of another's enlivening and maddening totality; in the heat of an argument, they hear only the accusatory 'you'. The story ends with reconciliation and the uplifting, wry, 'You're something else, you' (Smith 2008: 134), a phrase that combines the acknowledgement of the other's strangeness with the recognition that we are equally mysterious to ourselves. 'The Third Person' opens with a characteristically vivid metaphor for that strangeness: a relationship, Smith claims, is like being trapped in a small room with another person and a piano which is just too big to make moving around comfortable. This comic image captures well the clumsy intimacy of many of the relationships she describes, and the story then unfolds to explore the interpretive trouble involved in being in the outsider position of the third person. Presented as a series of unconnected vignettes, the story involves moments of anxiety and self-doubt: a petty theft on holiday, a theatre visit for a couple nearing the end of their relationship, a man's fear of being observed as he is cruel to a cat. In each case the perspective is singular, the thought-processes of the other an unreadable blank, and the reader is left with a clear sense of the piano in the room that underpins all intimacies – closeness and awkwardness as inseparable bedfellows.

These stories encapsulate the contrary impulses of selfishness and selflessness that Smith positions at the core of many of her protagonists' relationships. Intimacy is the simultaneous desire for what is to be denied to the other, the recognition that the needs of the other are legitimate but demand a troubling degree of self-sacrifice. These contradictory motivations can lead to cruelty such as in the intemperate locking of one partner out of the home ('The Start of Things' in *The Whole Story and Other Stories*) or the denial of another's feelings (as in the exclusion of Ash from Amy's diaries in *Like*), but they can also lead to moments of tenderness and wordless identification such as the unquestioning acceptance by one protagonist of their partner's romantic love for a tree ('May' in *The Whole Story and Other Stories*) or the humanitarianism that Lise shows in *Hotel World* in allowing the homeless Else to sleep in one of the unoccupied rooms at the Global Hotel. Finding momentary common ground with a would-be combatant, or sharing the sadness of another's life through wordless physical contact, infuse Smith's stories with a humane acceptance of life's trials and triumphs. The intimacy that Smith describes is quarrelsome and destabilising precisely because it involves the surrender of oneself to another whom one does not understand, and it demands a commitment to connect with that other. That commitment is not a predicate of love, but an ethical choice that human beings have to choose to make, or not make. Smith's fiction – both short and long – presents connection with the other therefore as a challenge to the boundedness and self-interest of the individual. It is an offer to explore beyond the known, to open oneself to the caprice of the other and the mutability of connection. As she says in conversation with Boddy:

> There's something which is really exciting and something which is the same about the places of connection and disconnection. They're about either acceptance or decision to connect or to be part [. . .] They are like a kind of interstice, they're like the stitches. Even the disconnections are the things that hold things together.
>
> (Boddy and Smith 2010: 69)

Understanding the whole of the other is as impossible as understanding the whole of the self, but to live in the way that Smith seems to advocate requires a deliberate decision to reach out to the possibility of a life-enhancing connection that is guaranteed to bring with it the painful knowledge of difference.

Contemporary society's infatuation with technology as a means of augmenting human connectedness is a facet of this issue to which Smith has returned increasingly regularly in recent fiction, and without a great deal of optimism. Far from decreasing loneliness and social exclusion she suggests, the Internet, 24-hour television, celebrity culture, and mobile technology have simply generated new kinds of soul desolation where profound connection with others has been replaced by superficial coincidence. The 'Intimate' as one of the older characters in *There But For The* (2011) tellingly misnames the Internet, typifies the retreat from meaningful relationships in a culture of obsessive observation and instantaneous gratification. Information technology supposedly offers unprecedented and uninhibited access to data from every spectrum of human experience, yet Smith wonders at the extent to which this allows us to know things, and particularly others with any depth. It might seem curious that a writer as celebratory of the carnivalesque and anti-hierarchical as Smith would reject the open architecture of the Web – in many ways it would seem an ideal metaphor for her narrative anti-authoritarianism. However, the kind of passing attention that the Web tends to facilitate is diametrically opposed to the considered, ethically committed focus that she believes underpins true empathy. For Smith, the 'great sea of hidden shallows' (Smith 2011, 159) opened up by the Internet is the consequence of allowing machine technology to replace genuine connection. Or rather, of allowing it to become the excuse we use to absolve ourselves of the responsibility of connecting with another, for real intimacy demands a morally engaged and humane recognition of the other, not the superficial kind of knowledge that an Internet search engine can provide. As one of the characters in *There But For The* muses: 'Google is so strange. It promises everything, but everything isn't there. You type in the words for what you need, and what you need becomes superfluous in an instant, shadowed instantaneously by the things you really need, and none of them answerable by Google' (Smith 2011: 159).

Part of the problem with the information revolution lies in its excessive surplus, a surplus that inevitably turns to unfulfillable promise, in Smith's eyes, because it cannot come close to conveying the depth of human experience, nor the diversity of desire. The structural advantage of the Internet is its proliferative tendency that promises the answer to all desire through sheer informational bulk, but in embracing its democratic diversity we are at risk of mistaking breadth of reference for depth of understanding. This leads, as one character in the novel remarks, to a hollow and ultimately soul-destroying individualism: 'the charm is a kind of deception about a whole new way of feeling lonely, a semblance of plenitude but really a new level of Dante's inferno, a zombie-filled cemetery of spurious clues, beauty, pathos, pain, the faces of puppies, women, and men from all over the world tied up and wanked over in site after site [. . .]' (Smith 2011: 159).

The same dilemma of 'how to walk a clean path between obscenities' (Smith 2011: 159) in an age of over-exposure assails George in *How to be Both* (2014) who, following her mother's death, tries to commemorate her feminist politics by ritually watching a demeaning pornographic film on the Internet in the hope that repetition will engender empathy with the young woman portrayed:

> *This* really happened, George said. To *this* girl. And anyone can just watch it just, like, happening, any time he or she likes. And it happens for the first time, over and over again, every time someone who hasn't seen it before clicks on it and watches it. So I want to watch it for a completely different reason. Because my completely different watching of it goes some way to acknowledging all of that to this girl.
> (Smith 2014: 224; italics in original)

Watching the film, she believes, generates a connection with the woman, offering at least a token acknowledgement of the humiliating disempowerment endured. It thus grows from a creditable ethical impulse, but like the digital format in which it is distributed, George's viewing is automatic, repetitive, and identical. Sympathising with the pain of others is a reaching towards something that matters, an attempt to feel like/for the girl in the film, but her repeated viewings are superficial. In watching over and over without getting any closer to understanding the suffering that the girl endures she is merely seeing rather than connecting.

Though Smith clearly does not believe that the Internet is the 'cesspit of naivety and vitriol' (194) that Sophia describes in *Winter* (2017), she does warn against mistaking its ubiquity for reality. For all its allure to the curious – and Smith's writing clearly reflects the increasing Wikipediation of contemporary fiction – the Internet-age is characterised by systems of ideological simplification and covert control that run counter to genuine expressive freedom. Though the prospect of multiple, crowd-sourced answers to any conceivable question appears to democratise and extend access to knowledge, Smith's conviction is that technology is a false god, in that it offers a system for ordering the world but misinterprets human desire as satiable by pornography and consumerism. The bland reduction of needs to shopping and fucking drastically undersells the human capacity for inquisitiveness, iconoclasm, transformation, and transcendence, qualities that attest to the richness and wonder of lived experience. Moreover these qualities need not be traduced by online extremity nor mediated by technology for they already exist in the domestic and the ordinary settings in which self and other collide, a collision that generates more mystery than the Web can capture.

If our submissive dependence on contemporary technology highlights our discomfort with life's unanswerable questions, Smith celebrates the compensatory solace offered by an older *techne* – storytelling. She writes about the value of words as microcosmic universes for grander stories; she is a crafter of narratives in which wordplay is central not only to the diegetic energy, but also to the thematic investigation. Puns, neologisms, jokes, and metatextual references dominate her stories, but above and beyond this technical attention to the vitality of words, Smith's writing also emphasises the intimacy of our relationships with books, joyously celebrating them as some of the most significant and fulfilling of our lives. 'Text for a Day' from *Free Love* for instance follows a character in crisis who literally disassembles her library – tearing out page after page after they have been read – in a bid to reattach herself with the unrepeatable experience of discovery. 'The Universal Story' in *The Whole Story* constructs biographies for the contents of a second-hand bookshop, detailing their experiences with consecutive owners and lovingly drawing out the ways in which the intersection of life and literature affects both. Each book's history is enshrined in another story, a form of endless recession that indicates the continual resonances of stories through each other and through their tellers/readers. Smith's book/story is like her relationship: always open to fresh interpretation and analysis, but also subject to surprising transformation and redirection.

In 'Believe Me' in *The Whole Story* we see how this transubstantiation of word and person can occur:

> [. . .] because I can read you like a book and because the thing about a beloved book, if it's a good one, is that it shifts like music; you think you know it, you've read it so many times, of course you know it, of course the pleasure of it is in how well you know it, but then you hear, in the background, the thing you never heard in it before, and with the turn of a page you see a combination of words you know you've never seen before, you thought you knew this book but it dazzles you with the different book it is, yet again, and not just that but the different person you have become, the different person you are now, reading it again, and you, my love, are an excellent book for me, and then us both together, which takes some talent with rhythm, but luckily we are quite talented at reading each other.
>
> (Smith 2003: 146)

Reading and loving are thus closely related for Smith – her characters love to read, but they also read to love. Both practices come with costs and benefits and they both offer ways of understanding the world. Throughout her collections books act as forms of distraction, forms of consolation, forms of shaping the past in new ways, and forms of ordering the difficult lives we live. This can be seen in 'Erosive' (2003) where the narrative structure of a story about loss is reordered in order to better comprehend the shifting nature of grief, and in 'The Book Club' (2003) where the ordering of the story and the algorithmic protocols of a sat-nav device overlap as metaphors for control of the disorienting realities of the physical world. Narrative is alive for Smith, it is organic, and as a consequence, it has the ability to be disruptive and disorderly, challenging with a voice as loud and ornery as any of her protagonists.

Stories as constitutive means of self-knowing and self-deception play central roles in the novels too. From the overlaying voices of the four narrators in *Hotel World*, through the self-deluding stories of the parents in *The Accidental*, the messianic hagiographies of Miles/Milo in *There But For The*, and Art's hopelessly pretentious blogging in *Winter*, Smith's protagonists narrate themselves, and are narrated in ways that are frequently elliptical and ambiguous and always point towards the mystery of being that eludes them. Self is elusive in Smith because of the limited means it has to express itself, as for all the productive mutability of language it frequently fails to live up to the task of capturing the meaningful connection between things. In *Like* – a novel that Smith describes as 'a nasty warring book' (Murray 2006: 222) because of the way that it sets one view of knowing and telling the world against another – Amy contemplates the disjunction that language produces: 'The word and the thing it means, the barbed dark between the word and the world; nothing but a rope bridge hanging by knots across a ravine, dropping loose slats as soon as you put your weight on it. A path around a chasm, that's all there is' (Smith 1997: 96). Language is the primary but precarious mechanism we have to combat the barbed darkness of our uncomfortable relationship with the world and with the other. As with the path around the chasm it always represents a detour into metaphor, which while suggestive is often painfully vague as a form of self-expression. Smith's treatment of language in *Like* reveals an interesting contradiction that is evident elsewhere in her longer fiction: on the one hand, she is committed to the idea of language as forever open to playfulness and transformation, and regards this as a foundational aspect of language's anti-authoritarian ability to avoid cliché and hierarchy. Stories are told and retold, language is formed and reformed, and words are shifted from their accepted moorings to take up temporary residence in other semantic regimes. But on the other hand, there is a palpable regret that language does not perform the task of describing the individual's experience of the world with any degree of accuracy. Words, for all their potential, are endlessly frustrating and imprecise and cannot encapsulate authentic human experience in a way that is ultimately true to it.

'True Short Story', an autofiction from *The First Person and Other Stories* illustrates this paradox well. The story begins with the narrator over-hearing the conversation of an older and a younger man sitting in a café who are discussing the relative sexual merits of the novel and short story, with the former described as a 'flabby old whore', the latter 'a slim nymph [. . .] in very good shape' (Smith 2008, 4). The incident allows the narrator to make a diegetic leap to Smith's hospitalised friend Kasia Boddy, an academic and expert in the short story, and to introduce the idea of contrast as a form of play. As a patient, Boddy is subject to the pathological determination of a mirthless disease, and to a hospital system that is characterised by well-meaning indifference. Systematised logic underpins the decisions made by health professionals about their patients' care, most pointedly in Boddy's case over whether to administer the effective, but costly, breast cancer drug Herceptin. The unenviable choices about who should and shouldn't receive the treatment are shrouded in defensive acronyms such as PCT (Primary Care Trust) and NICE (National Institute for Health and Care Excellence), and Smith's resistance to authority butts against these euphemisms with undisguised ironic emphasis: '"Primary". "Care". "Trust". "Nice"' (Smith 2008, 11). Each term is punctuated not just to highlight the distance from reality of these terms in the context, but also to open those terms out to the many, and varied meanings that each one contains, many of which fly from the limited and dishonest co-option by institutional speech.

For Smith, language is captured and perverted by authority, used to mask the small truths such as the two-centimetre tumour in Boddy's breast, whose undeniable and irreducible reality defies description. Yet the story suggests that the only answer to these truths and the hard twists of language made to cover them, are the lies of stories. Smith is not romantic about the healing power of imagination but rather she suggests that the invented is all that can be offered in the face of the coldness of things as they are. Words transform reality through their refusal to be monologic, so, in telling Boddy of her experience in the café, the nymph transmutes between a dirty joke; a fishing fly; and ultimately the mythological story of Echo, which is retold by Smith as a tale of answering back against the immovable power of disease. 'True Short Story' becomes a celebration of the litheness of language, and of the possibility of responding to the seeming immutabilities of the physical world with a defiance born of humour and multiplicity. However, the story never claims that such strategies are anything more than compensation. Narrative, imagination, and a creative unwillingness to accept the way things are, will not prevent them being thus, but they at least provide a temporary respite and the sense of a small victory.

The importance of language and storytelling as a tool of resistance to monoliths of authoritarianism is everywhere apparent in Smith. She gleefully mocks the territorial pretensions of 'official' culture whether that is manifest in the philistinism of the Pure Corporation seeking to marketise Scottish water in *Girl Meets Boy*, the pomposity of the power-crazed Borse D'Este in *How to be Both*, or the esoteric sterility of academia. As her irreverent treatment of institutional literary study in *Like* and *The Accidental* suggests, Smith loves undermining the claims to ownership of language by any privileged clique and is intent instead on reminding her readers that Literature (in its most emphatically capitalised form) is not the preserve of those of us whose job it is to objectify and decode it. Rather she glories in the ways that readers live in and through the stories that they encounter and create, continuously repurposing them for the different challenges that life offers. She had the opportunity to convey this creative approach when she gave a series of lectures on her own engagement with literary criticism whilst Weidenfeld Visiting Professor at St Anne's College, Oxford. Published as *Artful*, they are distinctly unlecture-like in format, blending literary criticism with the first person narrative of a bereaved woman whose partner has died whilst writing a series of invited lectures. The device displays Smith's formidable literary erudition without ever falling into the dry impersonalism of the academic. Rather the lectures playfully slip between fiction and criticism emphasising how the two feed, and feed off, each other, and reminding the reader again, that reading without a personal, moral engagement leads to the kinds of intellectual and emotional paralysis that she has resisted throughout her career.

Smith is creatively restless, and believes that stories become sterile once they are structured into a narrative in a specific way and for a specific purpose. Instead, narrative is most vital, intriguing and perceptive she argues when it is allowed to form itself outside the imperative of order. This led to her most metafictional experiment with *How to be Both*, which consists of two distinct accounts, both identified as book/part/chapter 'One', but ordered differently depending on the copy of the text that a reader held. Half the print-run of the volume was published with the narrative of a transgendered Renaissance painter, Francescho del Cossa first, and half with the narrative of George Martineau, a precocious teenager in present day Cambridge. There is nothing in the book's front or back matter to advertise this narrative device, so the reader falls into an interpretational pattern which is at once likely to be both predetermined by the ordering of the text they hold, and provisional depending on the happenstance of selecting one copy from a bookshelf rather than the one next to it. This is an intriguing attempt to circumvent the problem of plot progression by offering an illusion of simultaneity – two interchangeable narratives each dealing with past, present, and future – even though readers are ultimately likely to consume whichever text they choose sequentially. Nevertheless, within the narratives, there is a concerted effort to problematise linear diegesis, especially in the use of time. Smith blends temporal positions, slipping between each frame within the space of several lines and creating, if not simultaneity, then at least a blurring of temporalities. The effect is to generate a sense of disorderliness, but one that is open to limitless reshaping and reinterpretation. The novel is thus never closed but remains aesthetically and morally mobile just as the relationship between George and Franchesco remains chronologically fluid.

Trying to capture the texture of a writer's range of work for a volume such as this is tricky, but if I were to sum up the fiction of Ali Smith in a word, it would probably be 'but'. Though it might seem an inelegant and uncritical way of describing the achievements of Smith, the contingency of 'but' encapsulates a stand-out quality of her fiction that might be termed conjunctional. Smith's novels and short stories are always concerned with the pivots that balance alternative perspectives and world views, and gain their richness from the divergence from singularity that is implied by 'but-ness'. If what precedes the 'but' is a forceful statement of subjective point of view, that which succeeds it brings depth, polyvocality and, crucially for Smith, opens up the creative possibilities of ambiguity. As one of the main characters in *There But For The* comments: 'the thing I particularly like about the word "but" [. . .] is that it always takes you off to the side, and where it takes you is always interesting' (Smith 2011: 175). Being taken off to the side, detoured, disoriented, or derailed are adventures to which the reader of Smith must get accustomed, for her style, though often directly personal in its address, is characterised by a quirky roundaboutness that demands a continuous openness to others' ways of seeing the world. That those ways often embrace the voices of children, outsiders, the dead, or inanimate objects, points us back to the liminality of the 'but', which sits between, conjoining disparate stories and forging difference into a grammatical coherence. As the title of one of her collections of stories suggests, our stories, like the voices which tell them are always, and never, whole.

Works cited

Akba, A., (2012) 'Conversations with the Undead'. *Independent* 27 October, 27.

Boddy, K. and A. Smith, (2010) 'All There Is: An Interview about the Short Story'. *Critical Quarterly* 52(2), 66–82.

Bowditch, G., (2001) 'From the Bucket to the Booker'. *Sunday Times* 14 October, 14.

Gee, S., (2008) 'Mad for It'. *Financial Times* 11 October, 19.

Lea, D., (2016) *Twenty-First Century Fiction: Contemporary British Voices*. Manchester, Manchester University Press.

Murray, I. (ed.), (2006) *Scottish Writers Talking 3*. Edinburgh, John Donald.

Smith, A., (1995) *Free Love and Other Stories*. London, Virago.

—— (1997) *Like*. London, Virago.

—— (1999) *Other Stories and Other Stories*. London, Granta.

—— (2001) *Hotel World*. London, Hamish Hamilton.

—— (2003) *The Whole Story and Other Stories*. London, Hamish Hamilton.

—— (2005) *The Accidental*. London, Hamish Hamilton.

—— (2007) *Girl Meets Boy*. Edinburgh, Canongate.

—— (2008) *The First Person and Other Stories*. London, Hamish Hamilton.

—— (2011) *There But for The*. London, Hamish Hamilton.

—— (2012) *Artful*. London, Hamish Hamilton.

—— (2013) *Shire*. Woodbridge, Full Circle Editions.

—— (2014) *How to Be Both*. London, Hamish Hamilton.

—— (2015) *Public Library and Other Stories*. London, Hamish Hamilton.

—— (2016) *Autumn*. London, Hamish Hamilton.

—— (2017) *Winter*. London, Hamish Hamilton.

35

A. L. KENNEDY

Carole Jones

A. L. Kennedy is a prolific contemporary writer who is difficult to categorise. Often praised for her ease with postmodern literary strategies, including her metafictional preoccupations with the purpose of writing, such interpretation is often quickly qualified by reference to the ethical seriousness of her method and intent; her stylistic expertise is not 'an empty technical exercise or a display of postmodern knowingness, but rather works in the service of some more traditional, humanistic purpose' (Mitchell 2008: 146). 'Humanistic' here may refer to the specifically *humanist* conceptions of truth, reality and a coherent selfhood, and also to the more broadly understood *humanizing* ideas of freedom and equality and their ethical connotations. The implication of the lesser moral consciousness of postmodern writing, that an ethical discourse can only be adequately realised in more humanist modes, is one encouraged by Kennedy herself when in interviews she rejects all labels but can assert 'I'm a humanist' (March 1999: 107). However, her work is aptly summarised in Patricia Waugh's description of Muriel Spark:

> [She] embraces neither a complacent liberalism nor an anarchic postmodernism. Her stories [. . .] are neither 'true' nor simply 'lies'; they are neither mimetic representation nor simply the play of signification; they neither assume a fixed human moral order nor abjure morality altogether. For these reasons, her novels, too, cannot easily be assimilated to the dominant aesthetic categories of realism, modernism, or postmodernism.
>
> (Waugh 1989: 217)

Kennedy's work slips through the gaps between literary theory's complacent groupings, and from these interstices her writing challenges dominant interpretive frameworks, particularly those which privilege a postmodern point of view. Philip Tew (2003: 53) believes that 'in many ways [. . .] Kennedy's fiction offers an example of the limits of a postmodern or "historiographic metafictional" reading of texts'. Kennedy's writing, then, offers an example of going beyond postmodernism, of a developing mode of fictional engagement, 'resistant to the broadly anti-realist and relativistic conceptions underpinning the postmodernism(s) that have dominated the literary–critical scene' (Tew 2003: 51). This essay investigates the accuracy and usefulness of this claim by taking Kennedy's short story collection *What Becomes* (2009) as an extended case study. Both individual stories and the text as a whole demonstrate what I will refer to as an ambivalent return of the referent in her work which pays cogent attention to the relation between text and reality. The crux of this argument, then, is that Kennedy employs the techniques of postmodernism to counter the most radical effects of postmodernist discourse, particularly its moral relativism and textualizing of reality.

Setting Kennedy's writing in the context of contemporary challenges to postmodern frameworks of interpretation, I explore the humanist impulses of the text and their implications for the radicalism of a 'new realism'. Questioning the authority of the discourse of postmodernism in contemporary literary studies and beyond is now a commonplace, particularly since the turn of the millennium, challenging what was seen by some critics as the routine interpretive framework based on uncertainty, fragmentation, and a radical scepticism towards the real. In books titled *After Postmodernism* (2001) and *Beyond Postmodernism* (2003), for example, the concept is written of insistently in the past tense. Philip Tew for one has repeatedly voiced this challenge:

> Whatever the ongoing and seemingly interminable debates concerning the exact parameters of the terms 'postmodern' and 'postmodernity', it appears to have occurred to many academics and philosophers that the intellectual activities that these two terms have come to represent are either at a radical turning point or they are facing an insurmountable crisis in terms of conceptual credibility.
>
> (Tew 2003: 29)

Though such critiques can emerge from a reductive notion of postmodernism, prioritising its radical relativism and anti-realism, this critical atmosphere is also associated with a new 'postsecular' worldview becoming apparent in the wake of the 9/11 attacks which articulates a need for certainty and meaning.[1] A perception, or desire even, that we are *beyond postmodernism* calls attention to what can be termed a *return of the referent*, a 'tendency towards a new anchoring of what is characterised as the free-floating signifiers or the irresponsible playfulness of the more "radical" versions of postmodernism to a system of referents and values, however tentative or contingent' (Stierstorfer 2003: 4). In the search for a new critical framework, Tew (2007: 13) keenly maintains 'as a central tenet the need in criticism and fiction for referentiality and a "reality principle" to locate the imaginary'. Certainly the need for new models and frameworks of interpretation is emphasised by the commodification of postmodernist techniques in contemporary writing, challenging its radical nature, and the normalisation and institutionalisation of the discourse in academic departments and a plethora of readers, manuals and introductions since the turn of the millennium.[2]

The issue of form raises questions as to whether circumstances necessitate a return to realism. This might reiterate the post-World War Two context in Britain when modernist experiment was rejected by one constituency of a new generation of writers such as Kingsley Amis who instituted a new wave of postwar realism, often concerned with class and related to the 'gritty realism' of kitchen sink drama. However, radical experiment in literature is often made with aspirations to a greater realism, to more effectively represent the contemporary experience. As Pam Morris (2003: 75) points out in line with Brecht, 'Experimental art is necessary to keep pace with social transformations of everyday reality'. Similarly the strategies of the modernist novel can be seen 'to serve a higher realism' (Bradbury and MacFarlane 1991: 408). Tew characterises his own call for greater referentiality not as a return to the notion of a 'simple correspondence' between reality and text, but as a move towards a range of 'meta-realist thinking [which] offers a recuperation of an appeal to a reality principle that involves an extension of an ongoing complexity of understanding of being and objectivity, incorporating an acknowledgement of provisionality' (Tew 2003: 37). By this I understand him to be affirming a greater complexity in the engagement of literary writing with the real, one grounded in intersubjectivity, the experiential, and a pre-existing, shared reality; 'One must insist that all literary texts [. . .] whatever their imaginative excursions and deviations presuppose a reality both as constituent of themselves and existentially independent of themselves' (Tew 2003: 46). Tew is certainly calling for more complexity in our approach to thinking about our rumble with real life and the manner in which we represent it, a meta-realism which involves 'thinking about our thinking about reality' (Tew 2001: 202).

The pervasive deploying of postmodern writing strategies in contemporary fiction has not gone without criticism, in some instances for its conservatism. For example, in a thoughtful essay on Ian McEwan's celebrated novel *Atonement* (2001), Alistair Cormack argues against the characterisation of McEwan's self-conscious metafictional strategies (in a final denouement the narrative turns out to be a fictional and inaccurate version of the narrator, Briony's, experiences) as part of a radical postmodern textualizing and ontological destabilisation. Instead Cormack demonstrates that McEwan enacts an attack on imagination and presents fiction as a lie which obscures the truth and unarguable certainty of reality and produces 'unethical action' (Cormack 2009: 81). McEwan's method constructs 'a novel that passes through modernism and postmodernism to arrive back at a more traditionally realist form' (Cormack 2009: 70). Considering McEwan's 'profound interest in the ethical dimension of the processes of reading and writing fiction' (Cormack 2009: 82) such a reading suggests that his novel promotes realism as an ethical mode over the dangerous moral relativism of postmodernism, and thus reinstates the real as a recountable, reliable and stable point of reference.

The frequent allusions to the ethical dimensions of Kennedy's writing may produce the expectation of similar implications. For Eleanor Bell (1999: 112) 'throughout Kennedy's work there is blatant concern with the ethical, the political and the truthful which cannot easily be dismissed'. While remarking on the frequency of religious models and references, Sarah M. Dunnigan (2000: 154) observes that 'The underlying structure of Kennedy's novels is loss and their "quest" a restoration, whether moral, sexual or spiritual'. Kennedy herself often refers to her work process in terms of a revelation: 'Writing is a complex sensual and spiritual experience of enormous power' (Kennedy 1995b: 100), she has said, invoking issues of faith. Her narratives have been characterised as expressing a search for faith and a yearning for transcendence, even if this is inevitably undermined and thwarted by physical materiality (Jones 2009). The ethical concerns and the allusions to spirituality in themselves could characterise Kennedy as reacting against postmodernism. But it is also the materiality in her writing, the work's 'poetics of particularity' (Mitchell 2008: 58), which draws us back to the claiming of Kennedy as an anti-postmodernist and to issues of realism.

At the same time Kennedy's metafictional narrative strategies are also widely recognised and her texts often comment on their own construction, directly involving the reader in questioning the nature of the relation between fiction and reality. In an increasingly typical instance, 'Story of My Life' in *What Becomes* opens, 'In this story, I'm like you. Roughly and on average, I am the same: the same as you' (Kennedy 2009: 139). In its intense intimacy, Kennedy's work engages the reader, but all the while she disrupts and disturbs the act of reading, employing various narrative techniques to destabilise the text and ultimately our sense of the reality portrayed within it. Often the narration shifts, particularly in these short stories, between direct and indirect discourse, moving fluidly between first person and free indirect discourse. Kennedy also plays with time, winding and rewinding a narrative forwards and backwards with a similar disturbing virtuosity as that of Muriel Spark and that writer's infamously disorientating deployment of prolepsis in her fiction. Such strategies contribute to Kennedy's defamiliarisation of the ordinary and everyday; allusion to the supernatural is a disruptive tactic in earlier novels and short stories, such as the mysterious incidental appearances of the devilish Mr Webster in *Looking for the Possible Dance* (1993), the reincarnation of Sauvinian Cyrano de Bergerac in a grittily real contemporary

Glasgow in *So I Am Glad* (1995a), and the strange haunting in 'Christine' in *Now that You're Back* (1994). The repetition of incidents from different viewpoints is a pervasive device which puts chronology and causality out of joint, such as the increasingly significant smashing of a café window in *Looking for the Possible Dance*. The ordinary and everyday – stereotypically constituted in fiction through a unified perspective and a causal and consecutive conception of time – become strange and unfamiliar, so that our sense of what is safe and homely is troubled. This writing disrupts our expectations and perceptions and so effectively disturbs our sense of ourselves, of our own knowingness and ability to be known. In these techniques we have, of course, a familiar postmodern destabilisation of universals and coherence.

In the light of these perspectives on Kennedy's work we can ask whether, similar to the example of McEwan's *Atonement*, this writing deploys postmodern techniques to return us to a more traditional realism and the implied certainties of self and reality this entails. Indeed, whereas a postmodern perspective is always questioning whether there is a real world, real people, real bodies, Kennedy takes great care to remind us of the materiality of the world, of ourselves and our bodies; this could be construed as a return of the referent. Does she therefore re-discover humanist categories in the postmodern context of her fiction? Or, alternatively, does she re-create them in 'a *new* anchoring of free-floating signifiers' within a framework of contingency and provisionality?

The title story 'What Becomes' presents us with a cogent exploration of these issues. In this affecting portrait of a traumatised individual Kennedy fragments the trajectory of the narrative and fractures the time frame so that the reader has to work hard to piece the story together. The narrative opens with the male protagonist, Frank, in a cinema waiting for a film to begin; a few pages later it is revealed that he is travelling, staying in a hotel, that he has 'run away' (Kennedy 2009: 6). What follows is a detailed memory of a particular event in the kitchen of his home; while cooking, he badly cuts his finger, and this eventually leads to a confrontation with his wife. His behaviour is odd as the 'gash that almost woke the bone' (Kennedy 2009: 7) prompts him to scatter his blood over the kitchen:

> Then he'd paused for a few millilitres before he needed to swipe his whole arm back and forth in mid-air, blood hitting the dark glass of the doors in punctuated curves [. . .] he'd thrown overarm, underarm, tried to get a kick out of his wrist until the hurt in his hand felt anxious, abused.
>
> (Kennedy 2009: 7–8)

At this point Frank's behaviour is unexplained, and so is his wife's anger when she returns home to find him in the blood-splattered kitchen. It is not until several pages later, after returning to the scene of the cinema, that we find out that Frank is responsible for the accidental death of their daughter, that his wife blames him 'for one terrible thing which had been an accident, an oversight, a carelessness that lasted the space of a breath and meant he lost as much as her' (Kennedy 2009: 17).

In the manner of Kennedy's telling the story circles around this traumatic event and attempts to approach it but turns away several times, never describing it. This is a way of broaching the unthinkable and the unbearable, a technique which, Mitchell (2008: 52) observes, 'mimics the workings of a traumatised consciousness, where memories are initially repressed'; Kennedy explores here how memory works and how consciousness is structured to resist the consequences of the event. She narrates the deferring of the traumatic moment, an expression of Freudian belatedness common in many late twentieth-century novels, from Toni Morrison's *Beloved* to Pat Barker's *Regeneration* trilogy.[3] Here Frank's lack of acknowledgement of his odd behaviour is a sign of his disconnection and inability to feel or express his grief, a situation which in this story effectively puts him outside human relations. However, the language of childcare envelops him in the narrative discourse, chillingly signifying the unconscious presence of his inexpressible loss: his cooking makes 'the whole house smell domestic and comforting' as he 'rocked the knife, setting a comfy rhythm' and 'tucks his ingredients into the pan' (Kennedy 2009: 6); in the cinema the darkness 'cuddled at his back' (18). Yet for the reader, struggling to piece together the narrative, the elliptical structure coupled with the violently detailed immediacy of the text promotes a critical engagement with this complex portrait in order to achieve an understanding. Through this process Kennedy resists a reductive, sentimental understanding involving the securing of blame and cathartic expression of pity.

The narrative technique, this slow and interrupted revelation, fulfils our expectations of a familiar postmodern fiction: fragmentation, more digression than progression, and a lack of closure creating uncertainty, incoherence and disorientation. This strategy structures an absence as the text skims the unrepresentable death. Yet in its disturbing intimacy the narrative brings us closer to the experience of trauma than the experience of the event which caused it, a facet of the story which promotes the breakdown of rational thought and action as personal to the individual rather than general to the received worldview. This is underlined by the foregrounding of the material reality, drawing particular attention to Frank's actions and self-harmed body. Kennedy effectively employs postmodern strategies to bring us closer to an individual human experience structured by trauma, one that is perceived as irrational and difficult to understand. Such a presentation is not easily broached in our dominant genres as Kennedy points out when she writes, in reference to the blood-spattered kitchen, 'Read the blood here and you'd see perhaps a blade that rose and fell, or the clash of victim and attacker: blows and fear and outrage, shock' (Kennedy 2009: 8). And of course we would be wrong in our reading; our genre-driven expectations of sensational, entertaining violence potentially limit our interpretation and dissuade us from forming an alternative narrative of a quieter domestic personal trauma. Kennedy aims to challenge these expectations by normalising and desensationalising the context of the tragic events and shocking the reader with their disturbing proximity to familiar everyday experience.

The incorrect reading of signs is a great concern in these stories and often Kennedy will suggest or even demonstrate the presence of a deep or inner reality masked by surface disguise or distraction. For example, the teacher in 'As God Made Us' tells the six amputees, survivors of recent and ongoing military campaigns, that she has told her school-children 'you were as God made you' (Kennedy 2009: 122), deliberately distorting and suppressing the violent reality embodied in the men. Also in 'Marriage' a man uses the image created by his bespoke coat to hide his violence under its cover of civility, propriety and chivalry:

> And he brushes the warm of her hair, cradles her head and then winds both arms around her, stills her: the shape of his coat, he imagines, bringing more than a dash of romance to the scene. They will be admired, a little focus of attention for the street. And everyone who sees them will be sure – this is what it looks like. This is exactly what it looks like. Marriage.
>
> (Kennedy 2009: 135)

The use of prolepsis here – 'they will be admired' – completes the character's control, not only in this moment but for the future. But in the galling irony of the story we have been shown the truth – the man's habitual violence towards his wife – indicating that there is a single and incontrovertible reality here. Similar to McEwan, Kennedy appears to encourage us to question appearances but insists on an immanent truth. However, Cormack argues that McEwan refers to

and portrays the willful use of art to distort the truth whereas Kennedy employs fictional strategies to suggest the fictional nature of dominant appearances and ideologies. In effect, she uses
her art to expose this fiction; it works to relate and reveal a truth rendered invisible by a more
straightforward realist narrative form. In this story in particular Kennedy exposes the unequal
power relations between the couple, illustrating the direct relation between the man's dominance
and his control of his own and the couple's projected public image, and the coinciding of this
image with expectations generated by dominant discourses.

The point is, however, that there are no inviolable, single truths to be extracted from Kennedy's
narratives. In 'Marriage' and 'As God Made Us' she explores which possible version of the truth
(for instance, whether 'God' or 'war' is responsible for the men's disabled bodies in the latter story)
is the most ethically sustainable. Kennedy effectively poses the question of which interpretation
promotes an ethical sense of the human (if made by God, the veterans' condition can be judged
as fate, and perhaps punishment, whereas as victims of war that fate is a result of human power
relations and politics, and therefore avoidable) and which is most useful in critiquing the prevalence of violence, whether domestically or internationally. The reader takes part in this moral
odyssey focusing on issues of justice not on the implications of literary tricks. To promote this
reaction Kennedy employs a variety of modernist and postmodernist tactics, strategies which
amount to a challenge to realism though they do not create a unified methodology in her work.
There is an aspiration here towards a greater realism, signalled by the engagement with the ethical
dimensions of humanism such as equality and justice; an attempt to find a mode of representation
more suited to critically engaging the contemporary social context and existential circumstance.

This impulse describes Kennedy's work even at its most radically metafictional in narratives
which announce very loudly their own fictionality. The aforementioned 'Story of My Life' is a
trenchant example, which may be characterised as a satire of the 'misery memoir' and some of
the assumptions of that genre. Though offering the reader an insight into the real world – the
narrator begins 'I'm like you' – the text draws attention to its own pretence by highlighting the
falseness of stories:

> Roughly and on average, I am the same: the same as you.
> The same is good. The same is that for which we're meant. It's comforting and
> gently ties us, makes us unified and neat and it tells us the most pleasant kinds of story,
> the ones that say how beautifully we fit, the ones that summon up their own attention,
> make us look.
> I understand this.
> I understand a lot – very often – almost all the time – especially the stories. They
> are an exercise of will: within them whatever I think, I can wish it to be. They are the
> worlds that obey me, kinder and finer worlds: in many of them, for example, I'd have
> no teeth.
>
> (Kennedy 2009: 139)

The narrator then goes on to recount a series of dreadful experiences at the dentist, and a life
of failed romance. She closes, in contrast with the opening, by imagining a story which begins
with the line 'In this story, you are not like me. All my life I'll take care we are never the same'
(Kennedy 2009: 150). She begins the story asserting similarity because it is comforting, but ends
with an acceptance of difference and individuation. Considering the horror of the recounted
events the reader may feel relieved. However, the narrator has tricked the reader, initially offering stories that will flatter us with their kinder and finer worlds but then relating a bizarre and
uncomfortable narrative of tooth extraction, bleeding, social alienation and existential anxiety.

In its accumulation of painful events the story disrupts the initial expectations leaving the reader dismayed and disorientated. Moreover, the vividly detailed and insistently repellent materiality of the narrative attempts to invoke an equally nauseated reading experience, capitalising on the corporeal and existential discomfort of the protagonist in graphic, sensual descriptions of blood, pain and loneliness. On a failing romantic date, the narrator describes her frustrated attempts at conversation with her uncommunicative companion:

> My roots are 23 millimetres long, which is not unimpressive, is almost an inch. I tell him about my root canals. I summarise the activities involved in an apesectomy – the gum slicing, tissue peeling, the jaw drilling, the noise.
>
> This is not romantic, because I no longer wish to be, not any more. I am watching a space just above his head and to the right where another part of my future is closing, folding into nowhere, tasting coppery and hot.

(Kennedy 2009: 146)

The disturbing sensuality of this story, combined with its occasional scientific specificity, as above, makes an appeal to the real which suggests Kennedy is attempting to bridge the gap between representation and experience, even though the narrative revels in the absurd: 'the dentist gives me more anaesthetic and I notice his hands smell a little like cornflakes [. . .] "Perhaps a touch more there". *Whad? No, no thass a bid mush* [. . .] *I can'd feed by arms*' (Kennedy 2009: 148).

The return of the referent amidst a restless, self-interrupting and self-interrogating narrative illustrates Kennedy's use of postmodern literary techniques, not simply to point out the fictionality of her story, but to highlight both a reality principle and its provisionality. In the above quotation, for example, the future has a 'taste' as much as the 'oddly tasty' (Kennedy 2009: 141) blood of the dental surgery, giving physical sensation to both corporeal and conceptual-temporal realms of experience, the present and the absent. Such sensual paralleling of blood and impossible future evokes the contingency and uncertainty of both, where the loss of either puts the life so depleted in danger. The extraction of a tooth and the extraction of a future is vividly conjured through blood, provoking a visceral reaction in the reader from a story that 'in its essentials, was never anything other than true' (Kennedy 2009: 149).

Kennedy's foregrounding of truth and the physical individual brings me to the crux of her fiction: as stated above, she engages the techniques of postmodernism to counter the most radical effects of postmodernist discourse, specifically its moral relativism and textualizing of reality. The profound postmodern scepticism which undermines unified conceptions of a stable selfhood and reality, and threatens notions of community and communal understanding, is challenged by a return of the referent, which should be a point of unambiguous shared reality. However, this approach is aptly summarised in Kennedy's early comment on her writing, that 'I will be telling whatever lies are necessary to give some appreciation of what my truth is' (1995b: 101). Her aim, then, is not to confer a universal truth on this referent but to explore the ethical implications of its stabilisation through interpretation; here the 'truth' is not fixed but produced. This is, of course, a postmodern issue and Kennedy's re-emphasis of the referent and its materiality does not signify a return to the traditional liberal humanist model of the world and the subject; this is not a singular and irreducible referent. In the instance of 'Story of My Life' singularity and sameness, the foundation of the humanist model of the subject, are rejected for a self based in difference and relationality; she writes 'I have only these words and *no others* [my italics] and this makes my stories weak, impossible – impossible as the Christmas cards – *with love from all of us*' (Kennedy 2009: 149). Stories, their 'kinder and finer worlds', are impossible without significant others, and for Kennedy of course this includes the reader.

However, rather than embrace a postmodern characterisation of the contingent nature of her work, Kennedy often construes the relationship of the writer with writing, reality and the reader as in some way mystical and spiritual. 'I believe', she has said, 'that writing can have a spiritually nourishing dimension' (Kennedy 1995b: 100). If this does not necessarily refer to a religious schema, Kennedy's conception retains a certain enigmatic vagueness; writing involves 'an absence of self [. . .] It's a meditative occupation' (March 1999: 107–8). The terms and tone of these statements construct art as a revelatory process which, in its sidelining of the author's conscious control, can be likened to postmodern intertextuality arising from the 'death of the author'. Yet the terms she chooses deliberately reject the alienation of the postmodern approach; and if they invoke a notion of faith she refuses to impose a moral code associated with any organised religious discourse, but presents art and creativity as redemptive and humanising practices in themselves. Notwithstanding the obfuscation of some of Kennedy's reflections, she sees in the work of art its potential as a point of communal unity, an occasion for communication, togetherness and contact between individuals. It thus provides an opportunity, perhaps the only one, to overcome the postmodern relativism and disconnection which Kennedy clearly perceives as structuring the world. Yet this is not because of its presentation of enduring truthful depictions of that world, but because art is an occasion of contestation – of meaning and interpretation. The magic, Kennedy would aver, is not in the message but in its prompting of human communication and convergence.

The final story in the *What Becomes* collection, 'Vanished', goes some way to illustrating this point. Here Paul the protagonist has tickets to see a famous magician perform live. His girlfriend having left him, he ends up giving her ticket to a random stranger in the queue. Simon is an obsessive fan of the magician and at the end of the night Paul finds himself joining him and a few others to wait for the performer to emerge from the stage door. At the end of the story, then, we are left with a diverse group of people waiting in the cold outside a theatre for a magician who never turns up; 'Waiting for Godot' as 'Waiting for Derren Brown'. As in Beckett's *Godot* the central absence keeps the group together: 'Paul understands the magician isn't coming. He also understands it doesn't matter any more. They won't leave: Simon, Barry, Gareth, Lucy – they'll stand here and he'll stand with them – they're all going nowhere. Together' (Kennedy 2009: 217). The magic resides in that togetherness. Kennedy commits a cultural blasphemy here because it is not high art but popular culture which creates this epiphany; and this experience of communion is produced by a performance based on illusion. Though not grounded in a stable rationally understood reality, the instance of convergence this illusion produces suggests that Kennedy undermines her own postmodern sensibility with intimations of coherent selfhood, unified communities and perfectly realised communication, even if these are only momentary. This is the light which brightens the commonly observed bleakness of these stories.

From this point of view the trajectory of *What Becomes* is perhaps not so bleak. It begins with an individual and ends with a group; it opens with the isolation of the cinema and closes with the collective participation of a live theatre show. In effect it travels from the distant and virtual conjured by the cinema to the tangible reality of the theatre, even if the performance is a magic show that foregrounds illusion and trickery. The story suggests that only faith or the suspension of disbelief engendered by such an event can bring individuals together in this uncertain, unstable, relative and hyperreal world.

> When it lifted, when the chain lifted . . . It's a trick, I know it's a trick – but it was right . . . It was the way that you need it to be.
> She squeezes his fingers now. 'Like something coming true. [. . .] That's why I come. To see that. Because it isn't real anywhere else.'
>
> (Kennedy 2009: 215)

This communal creation of a stable reality or truth defies immanence and, even if transient, provides a model for existential connection in the face of postmodern pressures of fragmentation. In moving from inexpressible grief to comfy community over the course of its journey, *What Becomes* offers new faith in human relationships.

For Kennedy fiction writing is fraught with ethical responsibilities. In her 2011 novel *The Blue Book* she continues with the theme of magic by depicting a fake medium, a symbol of the writer with the power to create convincing illusions and the ethical choices this enforces. Reality is a process for Kennedy and her attempts to capture this preclude her returning uncritically to established humanist categories. She re-creates those categories to set that process in motion, emphasising provisionality and contingence to present sensitively considered and poised constructions of the self and the world. This is postmodernism channelled to a humanist cause to portray a world founded on relationships and interrelationality. Kennedy's 'deep realism' begins with postmodern uncertainty but aims towards humanist stability; it counters unbearable anxiety with the achievable security of love. In its faith in magic Kennedy's work confirms the modernist assertion that art is the secular replacement of religion; fiction is not a lie but a revelatory key to a greater understanding of the inescapable fragility and uncertainty of the world and the individuals and their relations in it. This may appear to be a backwards glance to previous literary moments, but Kennedy takes us beyond postmodernism while accepting its premises. This is new writing in need of new critical frameworks to begin to elucidate its radical referentiality.

Notes

1 On the 'postsecular' see, for example, During, S. (2005) 'Toward the Postsecular', *PMLA* 120.3: 876–877; Huggan, G. (2010) 'Is the Post in Post-Secular the Same as the Post in Postcolonial?', *MFS* 56.4: 751–768; Braidotti, R. (2008) 'In Spite of the Times: The Postsecular Turn in Feminism', *Theory, Culture & Society* 25: 1–24.

2 In emerging critiques of postmodernism the notion of a *post-postmodernism* is becoming more widespread. For example, see Nealon, J. T. (2015) *Post-Postmodernism or the Cultural Logic of Just-in-Time Capitalism*. Stanford: Stanford UP, where he describes post-postmodernism as 'an intensification and mutation within postmodernism' (ix); also McLaughlin, R. L. (2012) 'Post-Postmodernism', In Bray, J., Gibbons, A. and McHale, B. (eds.) *Routledge Companion to Experimental Literature*, Abingdon: Routledge: 212–223. Other challenges include Felski, R. (2015) *The Limits of Critique*. Chicago and London: University of Chicago Press, where she calls for an alternative model of 'postcritical reading' in line with Eve Kosofsky Sedgwick's (2003) conception of 'reparative reading' in her *Touching Feeling: Affect, Pedagogy, Performativity*. Durham and London: Duke University Press.

3 For an excellent account of this in *Beloved* see Nicolls, P. (1996) 'The Belated Postmodern: History, Phantoms and Toni Morrison', In Vice, S. (ed.) *Psychoanalytic Criticism: A Reader*, Oxford: Polity: 50–74.

Works cited

Bell, E. (1999) 'Scotland and Ethics in the Work of A. L. Kennedy.' *Scotlands* 5.1: 105–113.

Bradbury, M. and MacFarlane, J. (1991) *Modernism 1890–1930: A Guide to European Literature*, London: Penguin [1976].

Cormack, A. (2009) 'Postmodernism and the Ethics of Fiction in *Atonement*.' In Groes, S. (ed.) *Ian McEwan: Contemporary Critical Perspectives*, London and New York: Continuum: 70–82.

Dunnigan, S. M. (2000) 'A. L. Kennedy's Longer Fiction: Articulate Grace.' In Christianson, A. and Lumsden, A. (eds.) *Contemporary Scottish Women Writers*, Edinburgh: Edinburgh University Press: 144–155.

Jones, C. (2009) *Disappearing Men: Gender Disorientation in Scottish Fiction 1979–1999*, Amsterdam: Rodopi.

Kennedy, A. L. (1993) *Looking for the Possible Dance*, London: Secker and Warburg.

—— (1994) *Not That You're Back*, London: Jonathan Cape.

—— (1995a) *So I Am Glad*, London: Jonathan Cape.

—— (1995b) 'Not Changing the World.' In Bell, I. (ed.) *Peripheral Visions*, Cardiff: University of Wales Press: 100–102.

—— (2009) *What Becomes*, London: Jonathan Cape.

—— (2011) *The Blue Book*, London: Jonathan Cape.

López, J. and Potter, G. (eds.) (2001) *After Postmodernism: An Introduction to Critical Realism*, London and New York: Athlone.

March, C. L. (1999) 'Interview with A. L. Kennedy.' *Edinburgh Review* 101: 99–119.

Mitchell, K. (2008) *A. L. Kennedy* (New British Fiction), Basingstoke: Palgrave Macmillan.

Morris, P. (2003) *Realism*, Abingdon: Routledge.

Stierstorfer, K. (ed.) (2003) *Beyond Postmodernism: Reassessment in Literature, Theory and Culture*, Berlin and New York: Walter de Gruyer.

Tew, P. (2001) 'Reconsidering Literary Interpretation.' In López, J. and Potter, G. (eds.). *After Postmodernism: An Introduction to Critical Realism*, London and New York: Athlone: 196–205.

—— (2003) 'A New Sense of Reality? A New Sense of Text? Exploring Meta-Realism and the Literary-Critical Field.' In Stierstorfer, K. (ed.) *Beyond Postmodernism: Reassessment in Literature, Theory and Culture*, Berlin and New York: Walter de Gruyer: 29–49.

—— (2007) *The Contemporary British Novel*, London and New York: Continuum.

Waugh, P. (1989) *Feminine Fictions: Revisiting the Postmodern*, London: Routledge.

36

HILARY MANTEL

Jenny Bavidge

Introduction

In the summer of 2017, Hilary Mantel delivered the BBC's prestigious Reith Lectures. Over five lectures, Mantel provided her audiences with wide-ranging discussions around her own preoccupations and concerns: the presence of the past within the present, the value of historical fiction, especially in the excavation of women's lives, and discussed the potential dangers of the artist's immersion in her subject. Sketch shows may have subsequently mocked her light, high-pitched speaking voice but the lectures were full of her characteristic mix of lightness and gravity, with comic twists buried in discussions of dark subjects. Such contrasts are part of her writerly persona: Hilary Mantel is a Dame of the British Empire who writes short stories imagining the assassination of the Prime Minister, and a historical novelist fond of pointing out the limitations of our historical knowledge.

Mantel may be primarily thought of as a writer of 'historical novels' but she has often poked suspiciously at this term in her critical and journalistic writing. When she writes about real figures from history she presents them with the same ambiguity and slant as she does her fictional characters. Mantel's phantasmagoria is drawn from a complex sense of interaction between the living and the dead and the particular style of her work has recast the critical descriptors of historiographic fiction mobilised to describe the work of authors such as Peter Ackroyd or A. S. Byatt. Mantel's writing career began three decades before 2000, but the twenty-first century has seen her established as one of Britain's foremost writers of literary fiction. In the era of 'tl:dr', Mantel's wordy novels have been widely read, much-judged and frequently rewarded. She has won the Man Booker Prize on two occasions, for the first and second novels of her *Wolf Hall* trilogy, which charts the rise and prefigures the fall of Thomas Cromwell. *Wolf Hall*, published in 2009, met with enormous commercial and critical success and although it was not initially intended to have a sequel, the second volume, *Bring Up the Bodies*, arrived in 2012 to a similar response. A third instalment is promised to bear us towards the spike waiting for Cromwell on London Bridge.

Wolf Hall, and its stage and screen adaptations, produced by national cultural institutions the RSC and BBC respectively, have made Mantel famous and so her interventions into debates on the historical novel or royal personalities often receive attention beyond the pages of the literary magazines or broadsheet review pages in which they're first published. The mainstream success of the Cromwell novels can draw critical attention away from the experimental nature of much of

Mantel's oeuvre, particularly her use of the gothic mode, her sustained focus on the strangeness of bodies and her treatment of the precariousness of identity. The controlled style and scholarly historical research which characterises *Wolf Hall* may conceal or filter the weird imagination and comically bleak outlook present in her earlier works, but its pulse and presence complicates the works in ways which resist a definition of the Trilogy as 'merely' historical fiction.

Context

Mantel has written domestic gothic, historical fiction, fiction featuring historical characters and alternative histories. She has lectured on literature and has also written autobiographically. Her novels up to the publication of *Wolf Hall* are interestingly eclectic although certain themes reappear from book to book and each, in its own way, discusses the pressures and the pleasures of narrative. Mantel's work frequently enacts the problems of narrative as truth-telling or bearing witness, whether to personal, familial or historical events. Each of the pre-2000 works is quite different in tone, style and genre. *Every Day is Mother's Day* (1985) and its sequel *Vacant Possession* (1986) tell of spiritualist Evelyn Axon and her daughter Muriel, and Muriel's dark revenge against those who wrong her and her baby; *Eight Months on Ghazzah Street* (1988) draws on Mantel's experience of living in Saudi Arabia and charts tensions between Western expats and their Saudi neighbours, with a Gothic-claustrophobic sense of incipient threat throughout; *Fludd* (1989) is set around a convent and church in a northern village and narrates the arrival of a strange Mephistophelean character, who is presumed to be a curate by the community but who works an uncanny alchemy on them all. In 1992, Mantel published a long novel, *A Place of Greater Safety*, which prefigures *Wolf Hall's* conjuring of historical figures into fiction, in its epic recounting of the events of French Revolution. The next novel, *A Change of Climate* (1994) is set once again in present day, among a seemingly happy family in Norfolk, but deals with the breakdown of the parents' marriage under the pressure of a long-repressed and traumatic incident which occurred in Botswana many years before. *An Experiment in Love* (1996) recalls some of the mental territory and atmosphere of the Muriel novels, but takes its protagonists Carmel and Karina from their Lancashire convent school to their claustrophobic halls of residence at the University of London. Like the other novels of the 1980s and 90s, this is a story of hauntings, and also one of one hunger, physical and emotional.

Mantel's final novel of the twentieth century was *The Giant O'Brien* (1998). In a Postscript to the 2010 edition of the novel, Mantel tells how her initial plan for telling the true story of the eighteenth century figures John Hunter and Irish 'giant' Charles Byrne was to write a 'big realistic, historical novel' (2010: 8). In the writing of the story though, she found herself overwhelmed by a more pressing sense of her own 'Irishness', and particularly of an Irish voice forced into English, 'as if something came into the room, opened its mouth and sang. I just wrote the song out [. . .]' (9). This tension or synergy between an impulse to record and know the past, and an equally strong awareness of the more chaotic energies of the body or repressed memory or identity is perhaps the strongest characteristic of Mantel's writing across the years.

My discussion here will focus on the novels and other writing which continued to expand this extraordinary range of works and stories into the first decades of the twenty-first century. Despite their differences in tone, setting and genre, *Beyond Black* (2005), her two collections of short stories (*Learning to Talk* (2003) and *The Assassination of Margaret Thatcher: Stories* (2014)) and the *Wolf Hall* novels, share many of the same concerns as the earlier work. They tell stories of generational conflict and the working through of trauma and revenge. Often, they present characters experiencing altered states of mind or a sense of freakishness; they depict the humiliations and mysteries of childhood transformed by time into adult anger and uncomfortable relationships.

Life-writing

Mantel's own scepticism about how difficult it is to understand our own motives and intentions and those of even our closest friends and family should make us very wary of trying to understand her characters as manifestations of her own biography. However, she has tempted readers to make those connections by frequent use of the places in which she has lived and through her autobiographical writings. Mantel was born in 1952, and spent her early years in the Derbyshire mill-town of Hadfield. Her own account of her childhood in her memoir *Giving Up the Ghost* (2003) describes complex family dynamics, and a recurrent theme of secrecy and shame so powerful it left her, for a period, unable to speak. This experience is articulated in literary terms as a struggle to find a voice or a representational form through which to express things which seem unsayable, whether because of trauma or the lack of a language adequate to frame them. Mantel describes the strength of her internalisation of being 'wrong and bad' resulting from her Catholic education (she says she lost her faith at 12) and her parents' separation: her surname came from the man who suddenly appeared in the family home, replacing the father who became a 'ghost'. After convent school, she read Law at LSE, a trajectory explored in *An Experiment in Love*'s story of London students. She married in 1972 and her husband's career as a geologist took her to Botswana and then to Jeddah. The delight she felt when her work was first accepted for publication is tempered in her accounts of this period by the physical suffering she endured as a result of long-term debilitating illness and misdiagnosis. Much of Mantel's life-writing happens in the present tense, with the sense of on-going immersion in the most intensely felt memories. Apart from the immediacy of the prose, the use of the present tense is a reminder of the persistence of physical suffering, linking incidents of often overwhelming sensory and physical experience of Hilary as a child with the physical suffering Mantel endures as an adult. In her 2010 account of an agonising period of treatment and recovery she writes: 'pain is a present-tense business. [. . .] Remembering to breathe. Studying how to do it. Plotting to get your feet on the floor, inching a pillow to a bearable position' (2010: 10).

In *Giving up the Ghost*, Mantel writes of the effects of long-undiagnosed endometriosis on her body, and the terrible experience of akathisia, triggered by antipsychotic drugs which were prescribed to treat the depression which doctors thought was causing her physical collapse:

> You force yourself down into a chair, only to jump out of it. You choke; pressure rises inside your skull. Your hands pull at your clothing and tear at your arms. Your breathing becomes ragged. Your voice is like a bird's cry and your hands flutter like wings [. . .] Every fiber of your being is possessed by panic.
>
> (2003: 175)

Here the writing is in the second person, a mode Mantel slips into when the self becomes so split and uncertain that there's a sense of observing oneself, holding the fracturing persona at bay in a desperate attempt at control. The memoir as a whole holds out the promise of recovery and a successful rediscovery or reinvention of the self, crucially through the power and the process of writing.

Giving Up the Ghost describes Mantel's struggle to 'seize the copyright in myself', from the bullies, doubters and the drag of her own ill health. In different hands, such a story might seem likely to follow a familiar and conventional trajectory from misery to recovery, but as Prodromou (2012) has suggested, Mantel's depiction of her illness and sense of alienation from her body refuse easy compensation or resolution. What Mantel does win from her experience is a sense of ownership of *knowledge* of her body, which had been denied her by the insistence of doctors that her illness was psychogenic.

Away from her own experiences, all bodies remain terribly vulnerable in Mantel's writing, but especially the bodies of women: they are beheaded, infected, penetrated, haunted, cut open, trussed up and broken down. The description in *Bring Up the Bodies* of the execution of Anne Boleyn does not cut away (as the BBC television adaption must, at this moment) but keeps its focus on the precise effects of cutting Anne in two:

> There is a groan, one single sound from the whole crowd. Then a silence, and into that silence, a sharp sigh or a sound like a whistle through a keyhole: the body exsanguinates, and its flat little presence becomes a puddle of gore.
>
> (397)

The bodies of women in power, or tenuously attached to power, are always doubly significant in Mantel's work. She reads them as she has Thomas Crowell size up every person who crosses his path: like him, she shows us how to quantify an individual's relative wealth in the cut and quality of their clothes. But underneath the show of power suits or crowns, or the gauzy peach costume adopted by the tortured Alison of *Beyond Black*, are bodies which wear different kinds of meaning.

Mantel's interest in royal bodies got her into tabloid-led trouble when she wrote a knife-sharp article tracking a continuity between the decapitated, drained body of Anne Boleyn and the 'irreproachable [. . .] painfully thin [. . .] precision-made, machine-made' body of contemporary royal, Kate Middleton (Mantel 2013: 5). What annoys Mantel most in this piece is Middleton's silence and the cultural expectation of that silence because what is most hard won in Mantel's life-writing is voice and self-expression, whether threatened by family trauma, societal censorship or self-limitation. Along with physical pain, illness threatens to steal identity: 'there is no me, really, any more'. Against this loss is set the insistent presence of writing and communication, and of ownership of that writing. The phrase 'her book' is an essential one in Mantel, appearing in her autobiographical work, but also in *Wolf Hall* and *Bring Up the Bodies*. Bodies are no guarantor of safety or identity, but a body which can master writing, which can hold a book and write in it has a promise of communication, at least, if not longevity. The last paragraph of *Giving up the Ghost* is a promise to the dead:

> I will always look after you, I want to say, however long you have been gone. I will always feed you and try to keep you entertained; and you must do the same for me. This is your daughter 'Ilary speaking and this is her book.
>
> (252)

Thomas Cromwell's love for his daughters, dead from sweating sickness one third of the way into *Wolf Hall*, is one of the best gifts Mantel can bestow on her character. Their presence in his life is felt throughout the tumult of the political events and the many other deaths he witnesses and instigates. The littlest girl Grace has 'left no trace' of herself but he has his other daughter's copy book: 'sometimes he takes it out and looks at it, her name inked in her bold hand, Anne Cromwell, Anne Cromwell her book' (2012b: 405).

Gothic and ghosts

While ghosts, benign or malign, are everywhere in Mantel's writing, it would be a false step to label her work 'gothic'. Where she does employ the gothic mode it is often ironic or dealing in a horror of such grim mundanity that it hardly warrants the spurious glamour 'gothic' might suggest. Both Sarah Knox and Catherine Spooner (2010) have detailed the grubby landscapes of *Beyond Black*, a world far removed from the highly coloured state violence of *Wolf Hall*. This mundane domestic gothic takes place in a world of sinister garden sheds, scrubby wastelands, and the sullen sodium circle of the M25, around which medium Alison travels to ply her trade. On the other hand, Knox suggests, 'the Gothic seems too small a handle for Mantel's work' (Knox 2010: 313), so we should think of her work as being 'super-realist – as *fantastically* real'. Her use of hauntological paraphernalia is never only about the supernatural but always about the unmythologised, unromanticised real.

Alison's professional success is enabled by the malign spirits of the men who terrorised her in childhood. *Beyond Black* believes in the spirit world and also in the hope of retribution for wrong-doers and rewards for the good at heart. Alison is surrounded by monsters; weighted by the memory of her vindictive mother, haunted (literally) by her abusers, 'the fiends' and attended by her assistant Colette, who begins the novel as a terribly banal person and ends it as a banally terrible one. In order to rid herself of her vile 'spirit guide', Morris, Alison must face her violent and traumatic childhood, whilst handing out cheerfully trivial messages from the Beyond to her audiences. In the midst of this fantastical storyline, Mantel slyly inserts the real-life death of Princess Diana in 1997, allowing her to diagnose the nation's tendency to summon ghosts for its own emotional purposes: 'Diana is the Queen of Hearts; every time the card turns up in a spread, this week and next, she will signify the princess, and the clients' grief will draw the card time and time again from the depth of the pack. [. . .] If you look hard you will see her face in fountains, in raindrops, in the puddles on service station forecourts' (x).

What does Mantel see when she sees ghosts? What are they in her work? In her life-writing, the confused world of the child Hilary is charged with a sense of the supernatural particularly when she writes of the most terrifying moment of her childhood: in the chapter entitled 'The Secret Garden' (deep in the present tense) she sees *something* which changes her forever. The chapter is entitled 'The Secret Garden', an ironic reference to Frances Hodgson Burnett's children's novel wherein the secret garden is a place of grace and recuperation. In this garden, Mantel encounters something which marks her out for evermore as 'a graceless creature, abandoned' (109).

> There is nothing to see. There is nothing to smell. There is nothing to hear. But its motion, its insolent shift, makes my stomach heave. I can sense – at the periphery, the limit of all my senses – the dimensions of the creature. It is as high as a child of two. Its depth is a foot, fifteen inches. [. . .] Grace runs away from me, runs out of my body like liquid from a corpse.
>
> (109)

The hovering between the present and the absent, here queasy and terrible, elsewhere in her work the source of a powerful ambiguity, may stem from childhood terrors but becomes throughout the novels an intense study of how a person, a house, a court, a nation, may be, in a phrase Mantel has used in interview, 'penetrated by ghosts'. Her interviewer asks if she 'believes' in ghosts, and Mantel's answer is 'For practical purposes, yes' (Pollard 2015: 1042). 'All houses are haunted', she says, by the lives you 'might have led' or the children you might have had, '[t]he wraiths and phantoms creep under your carpets and between the warp and weft of fabric, they lurk in wardrobes and lie flat under drawer-liners' (2003: 12). The ghosts of *Beyond Black* live in the domestic world in just this way, Alison can hear them talking behind sofas and under carpets but most of the haunting in Mantel's novels is figurative; characters are haunted by their own pasts, their rotten childhoods, their present failings, or terrorised by the 'the half-animated corpses of forbidden childhood thoughts crawling out of the psychic trenches we have dug for them' (2016: 68).

Suggestions of the uncanny find their way into the historical fiction too: *Wolf Hall*, with its suggestively Gothic title deals with the realist terrors of state tyranny and bereavement, but there is an awareness too of the construction or the performance of the gothic mode. Mark Smeaton, the young musician whom Cromwell sets up as a witness to Anne Boleyn's supposed crimes, is terrorised at Crowell's home by being threatened with torture and then shut up in the dark of a lumber room, surrounded by the household's Christmas decorations and paraphernalia. Mark believes he has been shut in with a ghost and, in a scene both comic and chilling, Cromwell wakes to the sound of Mark screaming. As he stumbles in the dark, he has brushed against peacock feathers 'out of their shroud' and his panic results in a complete breakdown and capitulation to Cromwell's demand for a 'confession', one which will also implicate a number of innocent men, and Anne Boleyn herself. The story of Mark's supernatural encounter is reported to Cromwell in the early morning and we remember with him that the peacock feathers which have tormented Mark were once a symbol of grace in this household: they were Anne Cromwell's treasured Christmas fancy dress. Cromwell has often remembered her in them, how she loved them, along with 'her book'. The smallest of details placed here by Mantel show us how, like Cromwell, she may use a ghost 'for practical purposes' but the most persistent haunting might come from the loss and longing embedded in family homes.

History

So far, we have discussed Mantel's twenty-first century work in terms of the themes of the body and the disembodied. These motifs, as well as her interest in the daylight world of politics, return us to her greatest preoccupation: the past and how we might encounter it, imagine it and represent it. History, she suggests in one of her Reith lectures, is what is left in the sieve. It can only ever be the sketchiest of outlines of the whole, rich, chaos of lived experience. Mantel's innovative mode of representation of that complex past has been the most-commented upon aspect of her writing, most specifically her use of the historic present and of the extremely close third person. We are cheek-by-jowl with Cromwell throughout the Wolf Hall novels.

Stylistically, Mantel could be contrasted with a writer against whom she has been judged for the literary prizes, and has mostly beaten to those prizes: Will Self. Self's *Umbrella* was also on the shortlist for the 2013 Booker Prize and is a much more aggressively modernist, experimental work. Some of its sections are historical, although set in a twentieth rather than a sixteenth century context. Self's work continues the modernist project of taking the novel form apart, breaking the narrative into multiple perspectives, jostling stream of consciousness with sentences which break mid-flow and throwing out intertextual references and allusions as fast as the reader can move to catch them. Both authors keep faith with the form and the idea of the novel, but Mantel is reworking realism using different tools from those of Self. There is in her work a presumption of a shared understanding of how the world is perceived, even while she questions the reliability of a shared sense of reality. Just as with the use of first person and second person in the memoir, Mantel uses her close third person to create 'the "reality effect" of the familiar mind' (Wilson 2015: 157). This is a strategy she uses across her range of writing. For example, she manages to create the same sleight of hand in the article which reflects on royal bodies, when she moves into a consideration of the status of royal *minds*; here, Mantel describes the experience of meeting Prince Charles and falls into an empathetic understanding of what his experience of being continually *looked at* might be like; she provides the documentary detail that away from the grand reception room, just out of sight, is the 'depressing, institutional, impersonal sight' of a room full of stacking chairs.

> I thought, Charles must see this all the time. Glance sideways, into the wings, and you see the tacky preparations for the triumphant public event. You see your beautiful suit deconstructed, the tailor's chalk lines, the unsecured seams. You see that your life is a charade, that the scenery is cardboard, that the paint is peeling, the red carpet fraying, and if you linger you will notice the oily devotion fade from the faces of your subjects, and you will see their retreating backs as they turn up their collars and button their coats and walk away into real life.
>
> (2013: 7)

This passage slides so cleverly into Charles' imagined viewpoint, invents sights he might see, speculates on his feelings about these sights, persuades us that this is what he *does* feel. Just as Mantel includes aspects of the Gothic in realist works, her treatment of real figures and real minds is constructed through knowing fantasy and invention. The job of the historical novelist she suggests, is to be as rigorous as possible about checkable, knowable detail (what sort of wallpaper would have hung on Robespierre's walls or how a person might have travelled from the City to Greenwich Palace in 1535), measured in the use of reported historical detail (how Jane Seymour reacted to receiving a letter from Henry while Anne Boleyn still lived, as recorded by a French diplomat) and from this respectable historian's basecamp, the novelist is free to roam and invent.

Mantel's treatment of the past involves assuming the voices of historical figures and translating them for a modern ear, but in a manner very different to a writer such as Peter Ackroyd. Ackroyd's description of his own writing and work like it as forming a new genre of 'transitional writing', writing which moves between past and present, 'with one foot in each' also suggests that this wavering is not only the property of fiction but, post-2000, increasingly of biography and non-fiction (Vianu 2006). Ackroyd's novels and biographies summon Wilde, Dickens or Hawksmoor and write their voices as a kind of ventriloquist performance, often attempting to recreate the speech of the day. Cromwell's voice is familiarly modern to us, no recalibration is necessary on the part of the reader. Neither is Mantel's fiction purely 'historiographic metafiction' to use Linda Hutcheon's term for the postmodern version of the historical novel, popular in the 1980s. Such novels summoned the past while simultaneously questioning our ability to know or grasp it, allowing fictional reconstruction and historical 'evidence' to wrestle with the problem of representing and witnessing the past. Ackroyd's suggestion in 2006 that 'transitional' historical narrative was now a genre in itself is borne out by Mantel's continuation of this mode without some of the more self-conscious 'postmodern tricksiness' of earlier writers. In her 2017 Reith lectures, Mantel gives a detailed account of her own understanding of the status and purpose of the historical novel:

> it is impossible now to write an intelligent historical novel that is not also a historiographical novel, one which considers its own workings. But I have tried to find a way to talk about the past without, day by day, using terms like 'historiography'. I became a novelist to test the virtue in words that my great-grandmother would recognize, from that journey she made, Ireland to England, from one damp green place to another: words like thread and loom and warp and weft, words like dockside, and ship, and sea, and stone, and road, and home.
>
> (2017, transcript)

This description suggests that Mantel keeps faith with the stubborn existence of things. In fact, her writing might have less in common with postmodern literary historiography than with the turn towards material history, the 'history of things', exemplified by the British Museum series 'The History of the World in 50 Objects' or academic work in material history which examines the history of a single objects, such as potatoes or the colour red. Human experience may be a wavering, ghostly presence to bring to the page but *things*, a style of shoe or a method of accounting, are good markers of change.

This is not to say though, that Mantel has abandoned the investigation of how the fractured and ghostly self might find a way to set down interior experience in 'her book' in favour of the material or the superficial. Mantel's writing style is invested not just in the setting down of the experience of existing in a historical moment and of expressing consciousness of that moment but the movement of thinking itself, the action and recall of thinking. While her work takes place within the bloody grandeur and theatre of Tudor history, her sentences might find kin with the wry everyday expression of the inner voice by contemporary writers such as Gwendoline Riley or George Saunders. Mantel has herself said of her writing of history that: '*Wolf Hall* attempts to duplicate not the historian's chronology but the way memory works: in leaps, loops, flashes'. (2012a) Rather than give us a narrative of the past which underlines its fictive state with switches back and forth between present and past, Mantel focuses on the construction of encompassing narrative voice which convinces us of its reality. The urgency and immediacy of the narrative form of *Wolf Hall* however, should recall to us the use of the present tense in Mantel's life-writing, as described above. Cromwell may not be describing the present tense 'business' of coping with physical pain but perhaps a more general existential sense of the precariousness of identity, and a hyper-awareness of the vulnerability of the self engendered by threat and uncertainty.

In the *Wolf Hall* novels Mantel uses the tricks of the realist trade: Dickensian detail and in depth knowledge of the cost of things and a Balzacian range of characters (she lists them as the 'Cast of Characters'), but then overlays the busy canvas with modernist acknowledgement of the slippery stuff of subjective thought, dipping into a (controlled) stream of consciousness or building a series of experiences and echoes towards epiphany. An occasionally jokey postmodernism skitters over these layers as well, making itself felt in authorial commentary and intervention: there are self-reflexive moments in Mantel's work, moments of blurring in the narrative voice or invoking of mock authorial intent. *Wolf Hall* begins with the animating aggression of Cromwell's father's command: 'So now get up' (2009: 3). Likewise, *Bring up the Bodies* ends with an acknowledgement of its narrative status. In its final paragraph, the narrative voice seems to move away from Cromwell as he is installed as Baron Cromwell of Wimbledon, at the height of his power and political success. It begins to know something he doesn't yet know – how the story will eventually end:

> The word 'however' is like an imp coiled beneath your chair. [. . .] There are no endings. If you think so you are deceived as to their nature. They are all beginnings. Here is one.

> (2012b: 407)

Leigh Wilson is right to say that Mantel reasserts a realism founded in a faith in a recognition of 'like minds' and does not develop her study of consciousness into a modernist questioning of the limits of perception, but I would also argue that indeterminacy both as a theme and as a style has a stronger presence in her work than might be expected in an author so closely connected with satisfyingly convincing historical novels, of the sort that can be adapted into full-scale costume dramas. Placing the Tudor novels alongside the experimental aspects of Mantel's other 21st writing reveals a series of common themes, though the texts are distributed so widely across space and time. Hauntings, ghostliness, the insistent pressure of memory and childish interpretations slipping away into equally baffling adult experience, suggest that identity is always under threat, by the living in the form of oppressive relationships or an uncaring society, or from the dead and the weight of history.

Works cited

Knox, S. L. (2010) 'Giving Flesh to the "Wraiths of Violence": Super-Fiction in the Writings of Hilary Mantel.' *Australian Feminist Studies*, 25(6), 313–323.

Mantel, H. (2003) *Giving Up the Ghost*. London, Fourth Estate.

—— (2005) *Beyond Black*. London, Fourth Estate.

—— (2009) *Wolf Hall*. London, Fourth Estate.

—— (2010) 'Diary.' *London Review of Books*, 32(21), 41–42.

—— (2012a) 'How I Came to Write *Wolf Hall*.' *The Guardian*. Retrieved from www.theguardian.com/books/2012/dec/07/bookclub-hilary-mantel-wolf-hall

—— (2012b) *Bring Up the Bodies*. London, Fourth Estate.

—— (2013) 'Royal Bodies.' *London Review of Books*, 35(4), 3–7.

—— (2016) '"Blot, Erase, Delete": How the Author Found Her Voice and Why All Writers Should Resist the Urge to Change Their Past Words.' *Index on Censorship*, 45(3), 64–68.

Pollard, E. J. (2015) '"Mind what gap?": An Interview with Hilary Mantel.' *Textual Practice*, 29(6), 1035–1044.

Prodromou, A. (2012) 'That Weeping Constellation': Navigating Loss in 'Memoirs of Textured Recovery.' *Life Writing*, 9 (1), 57–75.

Spooner, C. (2010) '"[T]hat Eventless realm": Hilary Mantel's *Beyond Black* and the Ghosts of the M25.' In Phillips L. (ed.) *London Gothic: Place, Space and the Gothic Imagination*. London, Continuum, 80–90.

Vianu, L. (2006) 'Interview with Peter Ackroyd.' Retrieved from http://lidiavianu.scriptmania.com/peter_ackroyd.htm

Wilson, L. (2015) 'The Historical Novel and the Crisis of Fictionality.' In Hubble, N., Bentley, N. and Wilson, L. (eds.) *The 2000s: A Decade of Contemporary British Fiction*. London, Bloomsbury, 145–172.

37

MARILYNNE ROBINSON

Rachel Sykes

Marilynne Robinson has long been considered America's most un-contemporary living novelist. Known for her fiction's complex combination of rhetoric, religiosity, and American history, the author has fans as diverse as former US president Barack Obama, former Archbishop of Canterbury Rowan Williams, and controversial American novelist Bret Easton Ellis.[1] Despite mainstream success, however, critical appreciation of Robinson largely centres on her reputation as a historical novelist, the Christianity of her central characters further marking her as an outlier in the landscape of twenty-first-century literary fiction. When her debut novel *Housekeeping* was published in 1980, the author's slow and richly metaphorical prose, which is deeply indebted to nineteenth-century American authors like Herman Melville, Emily Dickinson, and Henry David Thoreau (Robinson 2012: xiv), was described as a 'transfiguration' of 'the ordinary human condition' (Broyard 1981) in a rave review for *The New York Times*. As Joan Acocella (2005) later wrote: '[R]eviewers loved it and, seemingly, were also grateful to it, for while *Housekeeping* had all of modernism's painful knowledge, it showed none of the renunciations of clarity and unity that the modernists – not to speak of the postmodern types, who were already around – felt that such knowledge required.'

This chapter outlines Robinson's opposition to the 'postmodern types' of her literary generation while also critiquing the willingness of critics and reviewers to assign the style and concerns of her writing to the past. Robinson's second novel, *Gilead* (2004), was published twenty-four years after *Housekeeping* when the author was sixty-one-years-old. Although the novel won the Pulitzer Prize for fiction in 2005, it too was celebrated for its 'old fashioned' (Wood 2004; Hadley 2005: 19) qualities. According to novelist Ali Smith (2005), *Gilead* 'reads like something written in a gone time' and in everything from the novel's setting in 1956, its secluded location in the small fictional town of Gilead, Iowa, and the Christian (specifically Congregationalist) beliefs of its seventy-six-year-old narrator, the Reverend John Ames, *Gilead* was widely perceived as a book that felt 'out of time' (Wood 2004) for the twenty-first-century moment in which it was written and published. When two partner novels, *Home* (2008) and *Lila* (2014), followed in quick succession, revisiting the same characters, the same location, and set in the same year as *Gilead*, Robinson's 'old fashioned' reputation seemed assured.

This chapter argues for the importance of reading Robinson as a twenty-first-century author who is no less engaged in the politics of the contemporary United States for her tendency to evoke historical and fictional worlds that are 'remote enough' to avoid 'the intractability of the language of contemporary experience' (Robinson 1985). Understanding Robinson solely as a historical novelist, and as a religious outlier in contemporary fiction, not only radically diminishes the interpretive possibilities of her work but also neglects her record as a public intellectual, her authorship of six volumes of political and theological non-fiction, and, before her retirement, nearly thirty-years teaching writing as a professor at the Iowa Writers' Workshop. Through consideration, first, of Robinson's representation of rural communities in the Midwest and Pacific Northwest regions of the United States and, second, her commitment to Christian theology, I argue, third, that what I describe elsewhere as Robinson's 'quiet' (Sykes 2017: 108), uneventful, or even 'antievental' (Sayeau 2013: 5) aesthetic presents a way of understanding the twenty-first century through its philosophical and political continuities with the past and diminishes claims of our present moment's exceptionalism. In this way, Robinson's understanding of history is neither nostalgic nor 'old fashioned' but rather privileges historical and theological inquiry as a way of understanding longer histories of inequality that might speak, as Robinson (2018) herself argues, to '[w]hat is at stake now in this rather inchoate cluster of anxieties that animates so many of us' (23).

Region: *Housekeeping* (1980) and *Mother Country* (1989)

Two ideas dominate critical readings of Robinson and arguably account for the author's 'old fashioned' reputation. The first is her fierce love and intellectual appreciation of the mid- and north-western United States. All of Robinson's novels are set in small and pointedly isolated towns during the mid-1950s: *Housekeeping* takes place in the fictional town of Fingerbone, Idaho on the edge of a vast and mysterious lake while *Gilead*, *Home*, and *Lila* are all set in the small fictional town of Gilead, Iowa where life 'on the prairie' provides its characters with 'nothing to distract attention from the evening and the morning, nothing on the horizon to abbreviate or to delay' (Robinson 2004: 246). Robinson's interest in mid- and north-western experiences of rurality is in the first instance biographical. Born Marilynne Summers on 26 November 1943, she entered a family of fourth-generation Idahoans and self-describes as 'an American of the kind whose family sought out wilderness generation after generation' (Robinson 1998: 246).[2] During her early childhood, the Summers family moved with her father's work in the timber industry, living in a succession of small towns in northern Idaho and western Washington, one of which, Sandpoint, became the model for Fingerbone in *Housekeeping*.

Robinson insists on her intensely intellectual relationship with what might commonly be perceived as the 'flyover' states of America. In a 2012 essay, 'When I Was a Child,' she writes that 'the hardest work in the world is to persuade easterners that growing up in the West is not intellectually crippling' (68). *Housekeeping*, she continues, demonstrates 'the intellectual culture of my childhood': Robinson's narrator, Ruthie, reads from the same Latin textbook that she and her brother used in high school and draws from Robinson's favourite works of literature as a child, the collected poems of Emily Dickinson and the Bible (Mason 2014: 24). Robinson (2012) refers similarly to Iowa, the setting of all three Gilead novels, as her second 'adopted state' (35); the only region after Idaho that she 'learned' to love since moving to join the Iowa Writers' Workshop in 1991. Robinson's phrasing here ('learned') is not a slight to Iowa but rather confirms that she sees the production of fiction as deeply connected, if not reliant, on a cerebral relationship with her surroundings. Her connection with both Idaho and Iowa is not, therefore, part of a conservative drive to commemorate a forgotten American heartland but symbolic of Robinson's broader attempt to add nuance to the portrayal of rural areas in contemporary American culture, which regularly empties rural life of both historical event and intellectual presence.

A surprising and often neglected example of Robinson's engagement with the environment is her first and highly controversial work of non-fiction, *Mother Country: Britain, the Welfare State, and Nuclear Pollution* (1989), which she began researching as a visiting professor at the University of Kent, UK in the late 1980s. With uncharacteristic directness, Robinson accuses the British government of contaminating the Irish Sea with waste from the Sellafield nuclear power plant, controversially naming the environmental activist group Greenpeace as complicit. Arguing that Britain is 'the most abused landscape in the industrial world' (Robinson 1989: 19), Robinson claims to write *Mother Country* 'in a state of mind and spirit I could not have imagined before Sellafield presented itself to me' (3) and which she has not replicated since. Greenpeace successfully sued Robinson for libel, banning the book from publication in Great Britain but its importance to Robinson's later work is clear. In *Mother Country*, the author's uncharacteristically 'political' stance at once distances the writer from contemporary environmental movements and reframes their shared interest in conservation as an extension of both her Congregationalist beliefs and the wider intellectual project of her writing:

> I'm profoundly critical of the environmental movement. Not because I have any prob-
> lem with the idea that the environment needs to be rescued, but in the sense that I think
> that they have been stunningly ineffective and in many cases a major part of the prob-
> lem. [. . .] I am who I am, and I write about landscape and the human investment in
> landscape and vice versa, I mean the investment of soul, because I want to make people
> love where they are. I think that the best defense, the best sort of on-the-ground defense
> for any landscape is to have people love it, and any landscape deserves that.
>
> (Robinson 1989: 114–117)

Rejecting current trends in environmental activism, Robinson writes about conservation as a philosophical and moral imperative that falls outside and certainly predates any current political movement. Importantly, *Mother Country*'s wider evisceration of the British political system, par- ticularly the Welfare State, also reaffirms her belief in American democracy, highlighting a need, she writes, 'to rediscover the complexity of our own political history' (Robinson 1989: 104) so as to avoid the mistakes of the British.

Mother Country therefore contextualises the representations of American rurality found in Robinson's fiction. *Housekeeping*, for example, tells the story of two sisters, Ruthie and Lucille Stone, who are orphaned and raised by a succession of female relatives in Fingerbone, a remote, misty, and mountainous settlement bordering a vast lake. It is an environment that exists, as the narrator Ruthie suggests, at several 'puzzling margins' (Robinson 1980: 4); a town that is so intertwined with the lake and mountains beyond it that residents speak about Fingerbone as if it 'belonged' to the water. The sisters' eventual caretaker, their eccentric Aunt Sylvie, gives up a life riding freight trains across the country for a settled and pseudo-domestic existence where she gradually and literally dismantles the family home. The novel reaches its climax with Sylvie and Ruthie putting 'an end to housekeeping' (Robinson 1980: 209), setting fire to a broom and leaving the house in flames as they readopt Sylvie's transient lifestyle and enter the ghostly world of the wanderer.

The novel's evocation of liminal spaces, patriarchal erasure, and domestic destruction has led to several feminist readings. Aviva Weintraub (1986) describes *Housekeeping* as an 'essentially female novel' and Lake Fingerbone as an 'essentially female image' (69). Similarly, Joan Kirkby (1986) reads the novel as a clear rejection of 'the patriarchal values that have dominated American culture and a return to values and modes of being that have been associated in myth and imagery with the province of the female' (92). These interpretations have been complicated by subsequent critics

(Burke 1991; McDermott 2004; Engebretson 2017) and ultimately challenged by Robinson herself, who insists not only on the text's essential ambiguity but also on her dislike of critical theory and what she sees as the conceptual dead-end of 'identity politics' (Robinson 2017).

For the purpose of this chapter, debate about whether *Housekeeping* can be read as a feminist text reaffirms Robinson's wider resistance to the language of contemporary politics. Although deeply indebted to the women's movement of the 1960s and 70s, who provided Robinson's generation, as she writes in 'Imagination and Community' (2012), with '[a]lmost suddenly an expanding field of possibility' (29), the author doesn't discuss 'feminism' and doesn't refer to herself as a 'feminist' in interview or in print. As Alex Engebretson (2017) suggests, '[p]erhaps it is Robinson's humanism, its skepticism toward gender-based descriptions of identity, that causes her to avoid using the word "feminism"' but either way critics have largely abandoned early attempts to read Robinson's work through the lens of feminism or, indeed, through many other strands of contemporary theory. The Gilead novels, for example, which I discuss below, focus just as prevalently on the prescription and constriction of gender roles within the rural American home yet the only reference to feminism in Shannon Mariotti and Joseph Lane Jnr.'s ambitious volume, *A Political Companion to Marilynne Robinson* (2016), comes in a digressive footnote. Overall, the editors suggest, '[i]t might seem somewhat vulgar [. . .] to call what Robinson offers a "political theory,"' because her writings rarely advocate for conventional politics in a direct fashion and her unique constellation of beliefs, values, and advocacies don't fit into our usual categories of Republican or Democrat, red or blue, conservative or liberal.' In this way, Robinson has been framed not only as a novelist who doesn't 'fit' with expectations of contemporary authorship but also as a writer who can only be read through the lens of her older influences.

Religion: the Gilead novels (2004)

A second strand of Robinson criticism has therefore overtaken early eco-feminist readings of her work, further marking the author as 'unique' (Mariotti and Lane Jr 2016) and 'out of time' (Wood 2004) within the landscape of contemporary American fiction. This strand attends to the author's representation of religion: Robinson is not only a Christian but also a serving Congregationalist minister who, since the millennium, has used her fiction and non-fiction to examine the complexities of religious belief, particularly notions of grace, repentance, and predestination (Liese 2009; Hungerford 2010; Thurston 2010; Douglas 2011).

Although best known for what is currently a trilogy of Gilead novels, Robinson's six volumes of essays, including *The Death of Adam* (1998), *The Givenness of Things* (2015), and *What Are We Doing Here?* (2018), demonstrate a clear and sometimes confrontational style that recalls the manifesto-like tone of *Mother Country* but remains largely absent from her fiction. Her essays on John Calvin, for example, the sixteenth-century French theologian popularly associated with a rule-bound, puritanical, and largely unforgiving mode of Christianity, redraw the thinker as a misunderstood humanist who is 'more or less entirely unread' by contemporary Americans but who has proven 'of the great historical consequence, especially for our culture' (Robinson 1998: 12). Again, Robinson's desire to reinterpret lesser known works of literature, philosophy, and theology provides the author with a way of understanding the present that roots current issues in centuries of debate and allows Robinson to reject exceptionalism by suggesting that no intellectual or moral problem is ever truly new.

This philosophy extends to her fiction. The trilogy of novels for which Robinson is best known, *Gilead*, *Home*, and *Lila*, focus on two Christian families, the Ames and the Boughtons. Narrative episodes overlap around 1956 but through family anecdote and inherited memory, the trilogy details events dating back to the 1850s. *Gilead* is an epistolary novel written from the perspective of Congregationalist minister John Ames and addressed to his seven-year-old son, Robby, in the months after he is diagnosed with heart failure (in the novel: *angina pectoris*). *Home* retells the events of *Gilead* from the household of Ames' oldest friend and confidante, the Presbyterian minister Robert Boughton, whose daughter Glory returns 'home' at the age of thirty-eight to care for her elderly father. *Home*'s third-person narrative is often focalised through Glory's perspective but her younger brother, John 'Jack' Ames Boughton, is the black sheep and would-be 'prodigal son' (Robinson 2004: 84) whose search for redemption structures both *Gilead* and *Home*. A third novel, *Lila*, provides the history of Ames' much younger second wife who is a marginal and peaceful figure in the preceding novels and the only central character to have been born outside of Gilead. Through a closely focalised third-person perspective, Robinson revisits themes of drifting, transience, and gender identity last fully explored in *Housekeeping*. Yet, while the end of Robinson's debut sees the Stones destroy their family home, Lila depicts the opposite transition as the second Mrs. Ames comes to terms with her vagrant and sometimes criminal past, converts to Christianity, and struggles to make Gilead her physical and spiritual home.

What Mariotti and Lane Jr (2016) refer to as the 'unfashionable' and 'alien' qualities of Robinson's style result, at least in part, from the philosophies her characters reference. Reverend Ames and Reverend Boughton, for example, discuss many of the Christian thinkers considered in Robinson's non-fiction. From the works of John Calvin to those of Karl Barth, the Swiss Reformed theologian, and Ludwig Feuerbach, the German philosopher, Ames discusses the theology that Robinson (1998) claims is 'more or less entirely unread' (12) in her essays. Notably, however, and although their work is unpopular, the theology that Ames and Boughton quote is more radical than conservative. On the surface, Ames seems to follow a traditional conception of God as a transcendent Creator who judges sinners and offers eternal salvation to a worthy few. However, as Andrew Ploeg (2016) argues, in the concepts he introduces throughout *Gilead*, Ames 'embraces progressive and even atheistic ideas regarding the divine' (2) and, in claiming to keep many 'old boxes of sermons' (Robinson 2004: 43) in his attic, the Reverend further conceives of writing as a kind of communion with God: 'as that which facilitates and renders perceptible man's proximity to divinity' (Ploeg 2016: 2). Although on first reading, that is, Ames seems so old fashioned that, to return to Ali Smith's (2005) review, 'when [his] child draws Messerschmitts and Spitfires, it is actually shocking,' on closer inspection the reverend entertains a wide range of philosophies that are markedly open-minded for a seventy-six-year-old who has served a small rural congregation in Iowa since the 1890s. As Amy Hungerford (2010) also notes, 'John Ames is a character fully imagined to be living in Charles Taylor's secular age: he emerges in *Gilead* as a believer profoundly aware of the possibility – even the plausibility – of unbelief' (114). Ames is, in other words, mindful of the potential secularity of his son, to whom *Gilead* is addressed, and his wife, Lila, who is completely 'unschooled in Scripture' (Robinson 2004: 67), just as Robinson anticipates the likely secularity of her twenty-first-century reader.

The reverend's concept of writing as a form of communion further reflects the larger project of Robinson's fiction. Both, for example, evoke a 'capacious' (Hungerford 2010: 121) form of Christianity based in Congregationalist and therefore Calvinistic principles of individual autonomy for congregation and congregant. Although the Gilead novels may read as 'old fashioned' or even 'out of time' to some readers, Robinson's commitment to largely forgotten or marginalised theologies, philosophies, and, as I discuss below, regional histories may be 'unfashionable' (Domestico 2014: 12) but they are also clearly relevant to America's present. In the final words of *Gilead*, Ames tells his son: 'I'll pray that you grow up a brave man in a brave country. I will pray you find a way to be useful. I'll pray and then I'll sleep' (Robinson 2004: 247). Turning attention away, finally, from his 'weary' hometown and considering the idea that his family might leave Iowa, Ames ends *Gilead* with a plea that his son might have the bravery to reckon with the forgotten and often brutal threads of American history that he spent his life ignoring. What better words for an American reader facing feelings of futility in the wake of the Iraq War; what better words to leave for a child in the age of Trump?

History in the present

In the final part of this chapter, I want to consider the relationship between the rural setting of Robinson's fiction and her characters' engagement with history. Robinson's novels take place in what some might consider historically insignificant locations. In *Housekeeping*, residents of Finger-bone describe the town and the state of Idaho as 'chastened [. . .] by an awareness that the whole of human history had occurred elsewhere' (Robinson 1980: 62). Similarly, the Reverend Ames, a fierce defender of the small town that he has devoted his life to, contemplates with increasing frequency what the loss of local history might mean for his community. 'The President, General Grant,' he writes towards the end of *Gilead*, 'once called Iowa the shining star of radicalism. But what is left here in Iowa?' (Robinson 2004: 175). The historical 'insignificance' of Idaho and Iowa serves two purposes. First, as detailed above, from *Housekeeping* and the Gilead novels to *Mother Country* and *What Are We Doing Here?*, Robinson reclaims rural states and historic events that are both local to her and that have in some way been forgotten, misread, or undervalued. Second, and although she is rarely read this way, the author considers what is historically forgotten or neglected as deeply indicative of ongoing inequalities in the contemporary United States.

A key way in which the past of the Gilead novels relates to the twenty-first-century moment in which they are written is their ambiguous and almost atemporal setting. At the beginning of *Gilead*, Ames states that he was born in 1880 and has lived seventy-six years in the town from which the reader can work out, if they want to, that he is writing in 1956. By writing a letter for his son to read when he becomes an adult, Ames' narrative is further divorced from its present moment because, as Ali Smith (2005) argues, the epistle is 'a conscious narration to the future from someone whose time was different and is over.' Ames lovingly imagines Robby as an old man: 'Why do I love the thought of you old? That first twinge of arthritis in your knee is a thing I imagine with all the tenderness I felt when you showed me your loose tooth' (Robinson 2004: 210). And if Robby turns seven in 1956–7, he would be fifty-six and old enough to be in pos-session of his letter in 2004, the year *Gilead* was published. It is in this way that Robinson writes an abstract notion of temporality that gestures towards contemporaneity but remains rooted in the past. The Gilead novels pointedly occupy 'an ambiguous present in which the political and cultural "now" is vague scenery to the emotional landscape of the characters' (Sykes 2017: 115). Put simply, very few dates or historic events are stated or referenced in *Gilead* and its partner texts and although we might deduce that the novels take place in the 1950s, Robinson writes three historical novels that are curiously and pointedly non-topical, or abstract enough to take place any time between the 1880s when Ames was born and 2004 when the novel was published.[3]

What Lee Spinks (2017) calls Ames' radical ambivalence towards the political climate of the 1950s is also important to any argument about the text's contemporaneity (141). In *Gilead*, we learn that Ames' grandfather, John Ames I, was a radical preacher who fought to end slavery both prior to and during the American Civil War of 1861–65. Robinson modelled Ames I on the Reverend John Todd, a leading abolitionist and 'conductor' on the Underground Railroad who co-founded the town of Tabor, Iowa in the 1830s to serve as a fall-back for abolitionists fighting pro-slavery factions in Kansas (Robinson 2012: 180). According to Robinson, the town of Gilead is the fictional 'offspring' of Tabor and through the memories and stories of three generations of the Ames family, the Gilead novels contrast Iowa's radical past with the generalised political disengagement now associated, however simplistically, with the 1950s.[4] Both Ames' father and grandfather served in the Union Army during the Civil War but disagreed about the necessity of continued activism during the period of Reconstruction that followed. Ames then represents the ethical outcome of their conflict; he is reluctant to narrate or engage with the political climate of either his progenitors or his present moment. 'All best forgotten,' he writes, as 'my father used to say' (Robinson 2004: 76).

A major theme of both *Gilead* and *Home* is the difficulty of inheritance as the act of passing on knowledge, bequeathing memories, and achieving ethical consensus proves difficult even between three generations of Iowan, Congregationalist preachers. *Gilead*, of course, is also an epistle: a letter and record of Ames' 'begats' (Robinson 2004: 9); a familial and local history that the reverend will leave for his son to read as an adult. Yet the potential failure of patrilineal relationships to achieve moral and political consensus haunts all three novels. The confession of 'Jack' Boughton, for example, the wayward son of Ames' oldest friend, is the closest to a narrative climax in either *Gilead* or *Home*. In both novels, Jack returns to Iowa after twenty years of self-imposed exile, causing Ames, Jack's father the Reverend Boughton, and his sister Glory, ceaseless anxiety and worry. A major turning point then occurs when Jack 'confesses' to Ames that he wants to return to Iowa with his African American partner, Della, and their young son, Robert. In Missouri, where the family have been living, Jack's lack of income, Della's distrustful father, and the state's anti-miscegenation laws, which enforce racial segregation, and which Iowa, the 'shining star of radicalism' (Robinson 2004: 175), rejected in 1851, conspire to keep the couple apart. Jack therefore returns to Iowa to find work and a home for his young family.

The religious arguments against slavery debated by Ames' father and grandfather foreground and, in some way, anticipate the crisis of purpose that afflicts Ames from this point in *Gilead* through the rest of the novels. Presenting long since marginalised debates about the use of violence in social action and the necessity of activism in religious life, the memories of Ames' father and grandfather serve to condemn the reverend's political apathy and ignorance of the Civil Rights Movement (1954–68) in the narrative present. Jack's revelation provokes a strong reaction in Ames who finally despairs at Iowa's forgotten radicalism. He notes that the black communities his grandfather welcomed to Gilead in the 1850s all left in the 1880s when a mysterious fire destroyed their church. Gilead, Ames writes, was set up as 'part of an old urgency that is now forgotten' (Robinson 2004: 254) and, in realising this, the reverend cannot tell Jack that his interracial relationship would be welcome.

This confrontation is a crucial moment in the Gilead novels; one that is revisited in *Home* and informs the events of *Lila*. Still, because of academic fascination with Robinson's religiosity, it has only recently gained critical attention. As Lee Spinks (2017) writes:

> Variously entranced by Ames's unwavering commitment to self-knowledge and right perception in the face of his own impending death and his rapturous celebration of the transcendent beauty of a natural world which incarnates the miracle of divine creation, much of Robinson's audience has elected to read his letter either as a type of sublime secular ethics or a materialized spiritual vision rather than a fraught meditation upon the burden of a historical inheritance.

> (147)

Any doubt of *Gilead*'s commitment to debating the individual's moral and political responsibilities in the present would be further dismissed by a reading of *Home*. The second Gilead novel both contextualises its predecessor and provides evidence of Ames' political beliefs beyond the brief allusions made in *Gilead*. In *Home*, for instance, Glory describes what Ames calls 'conversations' (Robinson 2004: 212) between Ames and Boughton as 'incomprehensible . . . shouting matches' (Robinson 2008: 222). Boughton's own account of their fights further complicates the persona that Ames writes for himself. '[Ames] pretends to be mulling it over,' he says, 'but I know he will vote Republican again. Because his grandfather was a Republican! [. . .] Whose grandfather was not a Republican?' (Robinson 2008: 43). In *Home,* Boughton presents himself as a moderate outsider, suggesting that his family, who arrived in Iowa in 1870, could not understand the 'fanaticism' (Robinson 2008: 213) of abolitionists like Ames' grandfather. Whether or not Boughton is right about the vehemence of Ames' convictions, and his surprisingly thoughtless support of the Republican party, *Home* connects both novels with a radical politics that critical categorisation of the trilogy as either 'sublime secular ethics or a materialized spiritual vision' (Spinks 2017: 147) would exclude.

Moreover, *Home* amplifies the political events of the 1950s excluded from Ames' letter. Although the dates are, again, never stated, it is clear that Jack follows news of the 1956 civil rights demonstrations over segregation in Montgomery when he argues with his father about the 'provocation' (Robinson 2008: 214) of non-violent protest. The events of *Home* therefore seem bleaker after *Gilead.* Whatever else it might achieve, the primary function of Ames's epistle is to communicate; to memorialise the reverend's affection for his young wife and son so that '[w]e as readers become, in effect, Ames's son, encountering his words a half century after he writes them' (Chodat 2016: 356). *Home,* by comparison, returns to the point where *Gilead* began and, from Jack's return onward, details the Boughtons' repeated failure to connect with each other. If the reader knows *Gilead,* they read *Home* with the knowledge of Jack's secret and anticipate the repetition of his 'confession' scene in *Home.* When, in that second novel, Jack's confession doesn't materialise, Robinson's elision seems significant, evading a sense of resolution and catharsis for the reader but also confirming that repetitions of the same historical moment can only ever be partial, unrecoverable, and highly subjective in the present.

This, I argue, is how Robinson's fiction best engages with the unexceptionalism of her contemporary moment: through an unmoored and almost atemporal rendering of history that gestures forward as much as it looks back. However, Robinson's commitment to taking the long-view of American politics and pointedly distancing herself from contemporary movements may be changing. In an essay to mark the one-year anniversary of President Donald Trump's election in November 2016, Robinson (2017) pivots from a discussion of the 'older, deeper problems' of American society, characteristic of much of her writing to date, and launches a direct attack on the 'so-called "theory"' taught in universities, blaming this 'twaddle' for the decline of public rhetoric and ultimately for the election of Trump. Her latest essay collection, *What Are We Doing Here?,* similarly opens with a dismissal of the 'contemporary Left and Right' (Robinson 2018: xiii) for the 'maelstrom of utter fatuousness' that they introduce to public rhetoric. Robinson, who turns seventy-five in 2018, concludes the preface with the following: 'I say this all because I am too old to mince words' (Robinson 2018: xiv).

Notes

1 Obama names Robinson as one of his favourite novelists and famously flew to Iowa in the final year of his presidency to interview the author for the *New York Review of Books* (2015). Williams frequently reviews Robinson's work and Ellis (2006) suggests in an interview that, although he found *Gilead* 'boring,' it's a text that he has 'to pick it up again because it's so beautifully written, the prose gives me the chills when I read it.'

2 Following William Cronon's famous critique of how wilderness protections have promoted conceptions of exotic locales for massive environmental destruction, Robinson's concept of 'wilderness' is not stable; the essay, 'Wilderness' (1998), from which this quote is taken, criticises a colonial structuring of 'civilisation' that constructs wilderness as an absent space over which humanity can exert their 'onerous dominion' (245) in the belief that it is a location 'where actions would not have consequences' (247).

3 This temporal ambiguity is also true of *Housekeeping*, which the reader might suppose is set in the mid-1950s due to several references to issues of *Good Housekeeping* and a 1954 bestseller, *Not a Stranger* by Morton Thompson. The date however is never stated.

4 As Simon Hall (2016) notes, contrary to popular opinion, 1956 was a year 'on the cusp of dramatic change' which 'saw ordinary people, all across the globe, speak out, fill the streets and city squares, risk arrest, take up arms and lose their lives in an attempt to win greater freedoms and build a more just world' (xiv). Not only was Dwight D. Eisenhower re-elected in a landslide but, as Hall argues, a series of 'rapid' changes and events including the Suez crisis, US involvement in the Middle East, and clashes over race in the South, undercut the 'small-town conservative values' (iv) that historians associate with the period.

Works cited

Acocella, J., 2005. 'A Note of the Miraculous.' *The New York Review of Books* [online]. 9 June. www.nybooks.com/articles/2005/06/09/a-note-of-the-miraculous/.

Broyard, A., 1981. 'Books of the Times.' *The New York Times* [online]. 7 January. www.nytimes.com/1981/01/07/books/books-of-the-times-books-of-the-times.html.

Burke, W. M., 1991. 'Border Crossings in Marilynne Robinson's Housekeeping.' *MFS: Modern Fiction Studies* 37.4. Winter. 716–724.

Chodat, R., 2016. 'That Horeb, That Kansas: Evolution and the Modernity of Marilynne Robinson.' *American Literary History* 28.2. 328–361.

Domestico, A., 2014. 'Blessings in Disguise: The Unfashionable Genius of Marilynne Robinson.' *Commonweal*. 12–17.

Douglas, C., 2011. 'Christian Multiculturalism and Unlearned History in Marilynne Robinson's Gilead.' *Novel* 44.3. 333–353.

Ellis, B. E. 2006. Interviewed by Robert Birnbaum. 'Bret Easton Ellis.' The Morning News. 19 January. http://www.themorningnews.org/article/bret-easton-ellis.

Engebretson, A., 2017. *Understanding Marilynne Robinson*. Columbia: The University of South Carolina Press. Ebook.

Hadley, T., 2005. 'An Attic Full of Sermons.' *London Review of Books* 27.8. 21 April. 19.

Hall, S. 2016. 1956. *The World in Revolt*. London: Faber & Faber.

Hungerford, A., 2010. *Postmodern Belief: American Literature and Religion since 1960*. Princeton: Princeton University Press.

Kirkby, J., 1986. 'Is There Life after Art? The Metaphysics of Marilynne Robinson's Housekeeping.' *Tulsa Studies in Women's Literature*. Spring. 91–109.

Liese, C., 2009. '"That Little Incandescence": Reading the Fragmentary and John Calvin in Marilynne Robinson's Gilead.' *Studies in the Novel* 41. Fall. 348–367.

Mariotti, S., and Lane, J., Jr, 2016. *A Political Companion to Marilynne Robinson*. Lexington: The University Press of Kentucky. Ebook.

Mason, W., 2014. 'The Revelations of Marilynne Robinson.' *The New York Times*. Sunday Magazine. 5 October. 24.

McDermott, S., 2004. 'Future-Perfect: Gender, Nostalgia, and the Not Yet Presented in Marilynne Robinson's *Housekeeping*.' *Journal of Gender Studies* 13.3. 259–270.

Obama, B., and Robinson, M., 2015. 'President Obama & Marilynne Robinson: A Conversation in Iowa: Part One.' *The New York Review of Books* [online]. 5 November. www.nybooks.com/articles/2015/11/05/president-obama-marilynne-robinson-conversation/.

Ploeg, A., 2016. '"Trying to Say What Was True": Language, Divinity, Difference in Marilynne Robinson's Gilead.' *Journal of Language, Literature and Culture* 63.1. 2–15.

Robinson, M., 1980. *Housekeeping*. London: Faber & Faber. 2005.

—— 1985. 'Writers and the Nostalgic Fallacy.' *The New York Times* [online]. 13 October. www.nytimes.com/1985/10/13/books/writers-and-the-nostalgic-fallacy.html?pagewanted=all.

—— 1989. *Mother Country: Britain, the Welfare State, and Nuclear Pollution*. New York: Farrar, Strauss & Giroux.

—— 1998. *The Death of Adam: Essays on Modern Thought*. Boston: Houghton Mifflin.

—— 2004. *Gilead*. London: Virago.

—— 2008. *Home*. London: Virago.

—— 2012. *When I Was a Child I Read Books*. London: Virago.

—— 2014. *Lila.* London: Virago.

—— 2017. 'Year One: Rhetoric and Responsibility.' *The New York Review of Books* [online]. 14 November. www.nybooks.com/daily/2017/11/14/year-one-rhetoric-responsibility/.

—— 2018. *What Are We Doing Here? Essays.* London: Virago.

Sayeau, M., 2013. *Against the Event: The Everyday and the Evolution of the Modernist Narrative.* Oxford: Oxford University Press.

Smith, A., 2005. 'The Damaged Heart of America.' *The Guardian* [online]. 16 April. www.theguardian.com/books/2005/apr/16/fiction.alismith.

Spinks, L., 2017. '"The House of Your Church Is Burning": Race and Responsibility in Marilynne Robinson's *Gilead.' Journal of American Studies* 51.1. February. 141–162.

Sykes, R., 2017. 'Reading for Quiet in Marilynne Robinson's Gilead Novels.' *Critique: Studies in Contemporary Fiction* 58.2. 108–120.

Thurston, A., 2010. 'Marilynne Robinson and the Fate of Faith.' *Studies: An Irish Quarterly Review* 99. 396. 1 December. 449–454.

Weintraub, A., 1986. 'Freudian Imagery in Marilynne Robinson's Novel Housekeeping.' *Journal of Evolutionary Psychology.* March. 69–74.

Wood, J., 2004. '*Gilead*: Acts of Devotion.' *The New York Times* [online]. 28 November. www.nytimes.com/2004/11/28/books/review/28COVERWOOD.html.

38

COLSON WHITEHEAD

Christopher Lloyd

An elevator inspector. A junketeer and steel driver. A nomenclature consultant. Black kids in Long Island. Apocalypse survivors. Escaped slaves. These are the diverse protagonists of Colson Whitehead's often uncategorisable novels. Alongside this fiction, Whitehead has also published essays on New York City, and a memoir about poker. Whitehead's extremely varied writing transcends genre and time, but it is always firmly rooted in the complexities and vicissitudes of race and national identity in the United States. While his work can be connected to other African American writers of his generation – say Toni Morrison or Percival Everett – Whitehead's oeuvre is distinct. Born in New York City in 1969, Whitehead is a Harvard graduate, a recipient of the Guggenheim ('Genius Grant') Fellowship, and winner of numerous prizes (The Pulitzer Prize, The National Book Award for Fiction, Carnegie Medal for Excellence in Fiction). Yet, until the publication of *The Underground Railroad* in 2016, he was not as well-known as some of his fellow American writers; he has not been, until now that is, included in the same list as Jonathan Franzen, Michael Chabon, Annie Proulx, and others. This chapter will survey Whitehead's fiction and show how the imagination that created *The Underground Railroad* has been burrowing into American soil for a number of years. This chapter will suggest that the complex meanings of race and nation are at the heart of Whitehead's literary imagination; yet, it will also argue for the idiosyncrasy and particularity of each book. In short, the chapter will show how, across his oeuvre, Whitehead is consistently revealing how African American history and memory suffuse every corner of US identity.

In broad literary terms, we might easily contextualise Whitehead's work with Peter Boxall's summary of twenty-first-century fiction. As with the examples in Boxall's book (2013: 11), Whitehead is also concerned with 'the shifted temporality that characterises the new century', a 'new attention to the nature of our reality', and the preoccupation with 'embodiment' and the 'way we experience our own bodies'. The six novels that this chapter surveys continually strive (in very different ways) for a 'poetic language with which to describe the shifted, estranged experience of being in the new century' (Boxall, 2013: 12). Even *The Intuitionist* from 1999, which seemingly looks back at the early twentieth century, also attempts to reconfigure how we see the contemporary world. But in more particular ways, Whitehead spins these broader preoccupations through the lens of race. That is, the author's six novels are not simply further examples of a broad trend in contemporary writing but offer specific interventions into the genre of African American literature. While that term has been queried and discussed in recent years (see Warren,

2011; and responses to it, by Ross, 2012; or Edwards and Michaels, 2011, for example), the persistence of a literary output by African American writers about African American experiences and identities, among much else, is significant. Whitehead clearly fits into this category.

In the introduction to a recent special issue of *American Literary History*, Stephanie Li (2017: 631) suggests that there is a struggle to find a prefix capacious enough to articulate the place of African American literature today: 'post-black, post-soul, the newblack, even the new new black' do 'little to illuminate the contours of our contemporary moment'. Her special issue is thus an attempt to 'historicize and contextualize the flourishing of black literature in [. . .] an era defined by horror and anxiety if also by the hope of new possibilities' (Li, 2017: 632). Li's introduction charts the impact on black literature of historical events such as the September 11, 2001 attacks, the Crash of 2008, Hurricane Katrina, as well as the numerous police shootings of black people. She also notes the significance of black intellectuals (Ta-Nehisi Coates, Roxanne Gay), pan-African diasporic writers (Teju Cole, Chimamanda Ngozi Adichie), in addition to new and established black writers fostering dynamic modes of writing (Toni Morrison, Jesmyn Ward) in these contexts.

If, as Kenneth W. Warren would argue, African American literature flourished – emerged – in relation to the conditions of Jim Crow segregation, Li rightly points out that contemporary black writing is now responding to the 'most significant uprising since the Civil Rights era: the Black Lives Matter movement' (2017: 633). Black art and history have always gone hand in hand, and the twenty-first century is no different; African American literature today 'seconds the urgency, vision and hope that we associate with [BLM]' (Li, 2017: 633). The essays that Li gathers in this special issue testify to the breadth of black writing today: its reflection of the past, present and future; its engagement with diaspora; its illumination of intersectional identity and assemblages; as well as a 'deep commitment to resistance and multiplicity', a reminder that there is not a 'unitary black subject' (Li, 2017: 634).

This definition of African American literature is important because it seems to so precisely summarise Colson Whitehead's place in this canon. Through his novels, Whitehead has remade and recast the meanings of race, identity and history innumerable times. Like James Baldwin and Zora Neale Hurston before him, Whitehead continues to explore the transformative potentials of blackness in his writing. He embodies the complex lineage of African American literature – as a multifaceted, shifting and fluid genre – taking its legacies into both established and uncharted territories. The following outline of his novels will show, one-by-one, how Whitehead's fiction is vital to understanding twenty-first-century literature and culture, and the United States more broadly. To do this, the chapter will illustrate how Whitehead returns to a few preoccupations such as memory and place. Through novels about elevators and town-names and zombies, we will see how Whitehead exemplifies the expansiveness of twenty-first-century African American fiction.

'Verticality is such a risky enterprise': *The Intuitionist* (1999)

Colson Whitehead's first novel, *The Intuitionist*, establishes some of the major themes, concerns and literary strategies that will come to define his writing up to the present day. Set in a New York-like city, somewhere in the early to mid-twentieth century, the novel follows Lila Mae, an African American elevator inspector, as she is drawn into a noirish plot-line. Its genre is ever-shifting, but we might follow Ramón Saldívar, who calls it '*Afrofuturism*, or simply *black speculative fiction*, offering an *alternate Americana* of a past that was not quite this one' (2013: 7). In re-envisioning the US past and present, then, Whitehead plays out race-relations and ideologies through physical structures and spaces.

The novel opens with the sudden fall of an elevator at the Fanny Briggs Memorial Building: 'It's a new elevator, freshly pressed to the rails, and it's not built to fall this fast' (1). At stake here is the fact that Lila was the last person to assess the elevator, and now it has failed; even so, she says throughout, 'That's impossible. Total freefall is a physical impossibility' (35). On top of the fact that Lila is black and a woman (both of which, in this city, are unprecedented), she is also is an Intuition-ist, as opposed to an Empiricist. Where Empiricists turn to physical and material 'evidence' to do their inspecting, Intuitionists depend on 'meditation and instinct' (Saldívar, 2013: 9). The racialisa-tion of Lila's method – Intuitionism is called 'voodoo', and she a 'witch docto[r]' (7) – ties into the novel's broader investigation into knowing, seeing and understanding race. For, the elevator falls in a building dedicated to an escaped slave; as Lauren Berlant (2008: 852) glosses, 'now the building, symbolically embodying a US that supports racial uplift, is the scene of a catastrophe that reveals the machinery of white supremacy' at the heart of society. Indeed, the notion of verticality – what the elevator literally and metaphorically enables – fosters uplift and progression. As Lila and other black characters in the novel try to make a life in this northern city, the racial politics of the South still haunts them. Lila, like the countless African Americans who moved to northern cities in the Great Migration, 'moved up here because here is where the elevators are' (168). Yet, as Lila is scapegoated for the elevator's failing, and is drawn into the life of James Fulton – author of the Intuitionist bible, *Theoretical Elevators* – verticality becomes 'a risky enterprise' (44).

Such questions of verticality (of spatiality more broadly) engage a longer history of modern-isation in the American city. As Christoph Linder agues (2015), cities like New York grew – in actuality, and in their representations – through two axes: vertical and horizontal. Where bridges, roads and subway lines opened the city up to horizontal movement, skyscrapers and other build-ings evidenced upward and vertical movement. This dual dynamic was 'particularly conspicuous during the boom years of architectural and infrastructural modernization in the late nineteenth and early twentieth centuries' (Linder, 2015: 9). In both physical senses – up and out – the city (and the modernity it so embodied) also enabled and produced social movement and habitation. What Colson Whitehead's novel shows us is the sense in which this history of modernisation and a renewed spatiality is also one of white supremacy. Lila's place in this urban world is tense: the elevator's crash is a catalysing moment for the war between Intuitionists and Empiricists. The Elevator Guild is holding an election, and in blaming a black woman Intuitionist for its failure, attention can be directed 'away from the reproduction of structural inequality' (Berlant, 2008: 852). Yet, in the end, neither the Intuitionists or the Empiricists are to blame for the elevator's fall, and neither can explain why it happened.

Mitchum Huehls argues that, rather than thinking about the novel as a clear allegory for race (as many reviewers have pointed out), it rather forces us to rethink the way we talk about race altogether. While Intuitionism and Empiricism are clearly racialised throughout the novel, Hue-hls (2016: 116) suggests that it is the 'crashed elevator [. . .] that embodies blackness' because 'race remains illegible, an object in its own right. Race cannot be intuitively detected, rooted out, or uncovered; and it cannot be empirically observed, measured or calibrated'. As such, the elevator's ontological status – like race – is one that cannot be easily captured or understood. And, as 'black speculative fiction', *The Intuitionist* explores the 'subsistence and persistence of race' (Huehls, 2016: 116) in ways that are far from easy to pin down. The United States Whitehead depicts in this book – tangibly real, yet estranged, deeply rooted in its racial history, but complexly so – is further explored in his follow-up, *John Henry Days*.

'Just a tale someone started': *John Henry Days* (2001)

After the imaginative and metaphoric reach of Whitehead's first novel, he published *John Henry Days*, a broad and 'polyphonic novel that strives to capture the spirit of a nation' (Jaggi, 2001). The novel follows J., a freelance junketeer/journalist, who travels from New York to West

Virginia to follow the launch of a postage stamp and small festival to celebrate the renowned John Henry, a black folk hero who was a steel driver in the nineteenth-century. Henry, according to legend, raced against a steam drill but ultimately lost, dying on the job. While J. is the protagonist of *John Henry Days*, the book follows other junketeers, motel owners, a stamp collector, and other figures. The novel is told in short chapters, jumping from one perspective to another. Peter Collins (2013: 289) suggests that unlike other postmodern novels (including *The Intuitionist*), this book 'makes an effort to stay within the bounds of historical plausibility'. However, through its 'multiple characters, multiple times, multiple viewpoints, [. . .] multiple literary forms', the text depicts history as plural and far from objective; indeed, the novel asks 'what power history (real or fictitious) exercises over us' (Collins, 2013: 289). Thus, much *like* Whitehead's first novel, *John Henry Days* revitalises and interrogates US history and memory, for the ways in which it shapes narratives in the present.

The novel begins with a variety of voices that claim to know and understand the *real* John Henry. 'I would say he was a real live and powerful man' (3), one says; 'John Henry was a white man they say' (4), claims another; 'My Uncle Gus [. . .] said he was Jamaican' (4) says someone else. This conflictual portrait of Henry is summarised by the line: 'I think this John Henry stuff is just a tale someone started' (5). The history of the man is complex, and his name is known largely through song: according to Scott Reynolds Nelson (2006: 2), 'There are almost two hundred recorded versions of the ballad of John Henry' and is perhaps the 'most researched folk song in the United States'. Indeed, the iconicity of Henry – especially among working-class African Americans – meant that for a long time, historians 'assumed that John Henry was just a legend, a story designed to inspire pride, an invention' (Nelson, 2006: 2). Yet, Whitehead's novel explores Henry as *both* mythic figure and real person; the novel allows us access to his perspective in some chapters. His ghost, too, haunts the motel room where J. is staying. The presence of Henry, then, suffuses the book's pages, and as such it invokes African American history more broadly.

J.'s junketeering leads him around the country to many events; as the book starts, he is attempting to break a professional record of one press event each day. These journalists are, J. thinks, 'quintessential Americans': 'They want and want now and someone else is picking up the check' (137). However, his trip to West Virginia is not like his other jobs. Travelling to the South to explore Henry's legacy evokes many racial fears and histories. Where *The Intuitionist* explored the perils of 'verticality', here, J. thinks, 'There is the problem of horizontal space' (18). Stretching for miles, the rolling hills of this landscape evoke the railroads that cut through it (and that killed Henry, among many other black workers). Such a spatial imaginary continues into Whitehead's *The Underground Railroad*, examined below. J.'s anxiety about this landscape stems from his idea that 'The South will kill you. He possesses the standard amount of black Yankee scorn' for the region. 'He has arrived', he thinks, 'at a different America he does not live in' (14). J.'s response to the South taps into a long history, from emancipation and the Great Migration, of black people moving North to escape the region. Yet, in coming to the John Henry Days festival, J. confronts both the commodification of this man and his very real heritage. In becoming attracted to Pamela Street, a woman who comes to the town to bury her father's ashes (a man who collected black memorabilia), J. is forced literally and figuratively into southern soil.

At the end of the book, J. and Pamela make their way to a woodland clearing where the men who built the railroads were apparently buried, including Henry: 'He had expected tombstones but there were none' (375). They 'sit there in the dirt', digging a hole, finding a way to connect the past and present. They inter Pamela's father's ashes, offering a form of mourning that is at once personal and cultural. So, while the novel overall slowly charts 'the commodification of John Henry' though the gradual 'erasure of his race and class' (Collins, 2013: 294) – his legacy is turned from a specific one to something broadly 'American' – Whitehead also shows how the past is always reconstructed and remade. J.'s trip to West Virginia is just one more in his junket-eering life, but its effects are profound.

'He came up with the names': *Apex Hides the Hurt* (2006)

In *John Henry Days*, Whitehead explored the ways in which the United States constructs its past(s). In *Apex Hides the Hurt*, Whitehead traces this idea even further back than the nineteenth-century, to a dominant narrative of America's founding. The novel concerns an unnamed black nomen-clature consultant who is hired by council-members in a small town named Winthrop. The town is debating whether it should have a new name: one person wants it unchanged to reflect his family's business that 'established' the town's economy; another wants to change it to New Prospera, to reflect the technology company taking over; and a third, the mayor, wants to change it to Freedom, which was the name given to the settlement started by her ancestor, an escaped slave. As such, the protagonist descends on Winthrop because, we are told at the book's opening, 'He came up with the names' (3), usually for 'new detergents and medicines and stuff like that' (22). In this case, the consultant actually engages in a process of rebranding, or rewriting, the idea of American origin-stories.

As far as names go, Winthrop calls up one key figure from US history: Puritan lawyer John Winthrop. Winthrop is well-known for his sermon, 'A Model of Christian Charity', possibly delivered aboard the Arbella ship, around 1630, as the settlers made their way to American shores. In this sermon, Winthrop utilises the Biblical phrase 'a city upon a hill' to describe the new American project: 'The eyes of all people are upon us' (2017: 188). Whitehead capitalises on this figure and his legacy. When the consultant reaches the town, he stays in the 'Winthrop Suite of the Winthrop Hotel on Winthrop Street', and so on (13). Whitehead's point here – that Winthrop so suffuses this town's (and nation's) idea of itself – echoes throughout the novel, and broader culture. As I have discussed elsewhere (Lloyd, 2014: 160), the 'city upon a hill' idea has become a bedrock for notions of 'American exceptionalism' from the Puritan era to contem-porary political life. While, indeed, Winthrop's speech was as much a warning to the colonists as it was a celebration of their Providential mission, that gleaming city lingers. Exceptionalism, Donald Pease writes (2009: 8), is not a unified ideology, but a 'fantasy through which U.S. citizens bring [. . .] contradictory political and cultural descriptions into correlation with one another through the desires that make them meaningful'. In this way, the town of Winthrop draws on one version of its history in the same way that the United States clings to its founding myths of exceptionalism.

Whitehead's novel thus reconfigures this past (or at least, the past's significance in the present). In other words, *Apex* joins *John Henry Days* and later Whitehead novels in the project of cultural memory. As Leise writes (2014: 287), 'To modify the cultural memory of [. . . any] perceived originary period is thus to change the idea of America itself'. As Winthrop, in the novel, was 'a colored town once' (24), or 'only a settlement really' where some escaped slaves 'dropped their bags' (76), its history lies in slavery and its aftermath. Salamishah Tillet (2012: 2) notes that many contemporary writers return to 'the site of slavery as a means of overcoming racial conflicts that continue to flourish'. Where *Apex* and Whitehead's previous two books visit 'sites of slavery' only tangentially, he will later explore its vast mechanisms of power in *The Underground Railroad*. But, in revealing the palimpsestic nature of US identity and place ('Winthrop' is built upon 'Freedom'), Whitehead skewers and questions notions of heritage, history and memory altogether. Indeed, as the protagonist finds out, the co-founder of the original settlement wanted to name Freedom something else: Struggle. Both men saw the act of naming this place as a way of substantiating (and describing) their place in the world. *Apex* thus confronts the power of naming, of language, especially as it relates to the myths and realities of American national fantasy. The novel's title comes from a Band-Aid that the protagonist names 'Apex'; the tagline being 'Apex hides the hurt'. When the consultant hurts his foot, and puts an 'Apex' over it, Whitehead's love of metaphor takes over: taking off the Band-Aid, after 'hourly stubbings had taken their cruel toll', 'fresh blood seeped out'. If it were a shoddier product, he reflects, it might have fallen off and 'he would have been aware of the horrible transformation going on under there' (150). This grisly corporeal turn illustrates the power of a name: its ability to cover over, and obscure, the very real and messy truth beneath. Winthrop – the town, the person, the idea – covers as much as it reveals about American history.

Where good branding, the protagonist thinks, needs a 'name that got to the heart of the thing', this possibility is merely 'miraculous', as all he can do is put 'a bandage on it to keep the puss in'. He thinks, 'What is the name for that which is always beyond our grasp?' (183). What is so elusive and painful, *Apex* reveals, is the complex and multifaceted past of the United States. Haunted by the scars of slavery, Native American removal, and so much else, American exceptionalism can only ever be a flimsy fantasy hiding *struggle*. So, by returning to 'Struggle' as a name for the town, our nomenclature consultant settles on a word with a 'broad semantic range' (Leise, 2014: 297). Though he likes the name Apex, he 'had to admit that Struggle got to the point with more finesse and wit. Was Struggle the highest point of human achievement? No. But it was the point past which we could not progress [. . .]. Exactly the anti-apex' (211). The city upon a hill has always been built on struggle, and only by pulling off the bandage of myth will that be revealed.

'When did you get out?': *Sag Harbor* (2009)

'When did you get out?' is the question that opens *Sag Habor*. 'First you had to settle the question of out' (1). This out-ness is a mark of escape from the city (New York) and a claim on the summer landscape of Sag Harbor in Long Island. Whitehead's novel is a remarkable shift in tone and style from his other books; indeed, Touré (2009) calls it a 'memoiristic [. . .] coming of age story'. The story follows Benji, a fifteen-year old black boy from the city, who, with his friends, spend their summer in the small beach town of Sag Harbor. The narrative is slow and leisurely, rarely offering the dramatic tension or imaginative reach of Whitehead's other texts. As Touré (2009) suggests, 'It's easy to come away thinking not much happens [. . .] but *Sag Harbor* mirrors life, which is also plotless'. As such, the novel begins as Benji – now wanting to be called Ben – and his brother Reggie get 'out' to the coast and wait for their other friends. From there, Benji works a job at an ice-cream parlour, he and his friends hang out and talk about life, they enjoy the sunshine. Beyond that, the height of narrative tension occurs when Benji is hit in the face with a BB. In short, this novel seems quite different from Whitehead's last book, *Apex Hides the Hurt*. Yet, as that novel unravelled the narrative myths of American identity, and placed slavery and blackness at the story's core, so too does *Sag Harbor* represent the complexities of African American identity.

We learn of Benji's relationship to blackness through an early scene in which he describes his time in the city. He attends numerous events – 'It was Bar Mitzvah season' (6) – but was 'used to being the only black kid in the room – I was only there because I had met these assorted Abes and Sarahs and Dannys in a Manhattan private school, after all' (7). Benji's simultaneous insider and outsider status drives the novel in various ways; he's both part of this wealthy Manhattan culture, but also outside of its overwhelming whiteness. Every Bar Mitzvah, Benji says, 'should have at least one black kid with a yarmulke hovering on his Afro', which is both a 'nice visual joke' and (though this isn't the character's lexis) a complex cultural signifier (7). Later, Benji notes, when the Jewish relatives spy him at the party, they comment 'Who's that?' and 'So regal and composed – he looks like a young Sidney Poitier' (7). The layers of awkwardness and racism Benji experiences here are treated with a wry touch by Whitehead. Indeed, the narrative thrust of the protagonist's relationship to his blackness – as well, of course, to his more general teenage identity crises – ranges from an understanding of W. E. B. DuBois to the kind of shoes to wear. In the case of the former, Benji's parents often talk about how DuBois once stayed at Sag Harbor; though Benji 'had no idea who DuBois was', he nonetheless 'fell into the category of Famous Black People' (13). Later, describing his father's drive out to the town, Benji notes: 'it was potholes of double consciousness all the way. There were only two things he would listen to on the radio: Easy Listening and Afrocentric Talk Radio' (14). Comically referencing DuBois' famous conception of 'double consciousness' – of black people seeing themselves doubly, as 'looking at one's self through the eyes of others' (DuBois, 1994: 2) – Whitehead points to Benji's own internal split. For instance, talking to a friend, NP, was 'to start catching up on nine months of black slang and other sundry soulful artifacts' he'd 'missed out on' in his white school; the rest of the time he feels like he'd 'been blindfolded and thrown down a well' (29). This disorientation, Benji's attempt to inhabit his idea of blackness, subtly underscores his time at Sag Habor. Moreover, it exemplifies the complex representation of race in the novel.

Touré (2009), and other critics like Leader-Picone (2015) see this book as another example of Whitehead's 'post-racial' writing. Among many other qualities of *Sag Harbor*, the depiction of Benji as a 'Smiths-loving, Brooks Brothers-wearing son of moneyed blacks who summer in Long Island and recognise the characters on "The Cosby Show" as kindred spirits' (Touré, 2009), reveals the expansiveness of black identity. Elsewhere, Touré (2012: xvii) has argued that post-blackness is not 'the end of Blackness; it points, instead, to the end of the reign of a narrow, single notion of Blackness'. As such, the term illuminates the range of black identities today that aren't locked into static and often historical conceptions of race. Many critics cited in this chapter see Whitehead's work in this light (see Saldívar, 2013, for the fullest treatment), but here I merely want to argue that *Sag Harbor* extends Whitehead's larger investigation into the shifting and capacious meanings of blackness in the twenty-first century United States. In his following novel, this exploration takes a darker, and more apocalyptic turn.

'Normal meant "the past"': *Zone One* (2011)

Zone One, Kate Marshall notes (2015: 532), 'isn't much of a zombie novel', due to its lack of suspense. Instead, the book spends much of its time in flashback, in memories of the protagonist, known as Mark Spitz. Set across three days, in which Mark and a team of 'soldiers' – a sweeper team made up of 'unemployable man-children, erstwhile cheerleaders, salesmen of luxury boats' and so on (31) – clear a section of Manhattan called 'Zone One'. In this United States, zombies (skels) have overtaken, but a few camps have been set up around the country, especially Buffalo, where the human population is surviving. The next area to clear is Manhattan, so Mark and the others in his team are scouring the city for the remaining undead. Many of these were wiped out by an earlier army attack, but there are skels here that are locked into the past, mindlessly repeating the tasks they were doing in their previous life. Whitehead plays with the zombie genre, and with looping temporalities throughout, not least with the novel's 'primal scene' in which, at age six, Mark 'walked in on his mother giving his father a blow job. [. . .] there she was, gobbling up his father' (70). That memory is twinned with a more gruesome moment later in life: on returning home, he opens the door to his parents' bedroom, and 'witnessed his mother's grisly ministrations to his father. She was hunched over him, gnawing away with ecstatic fervor on a flap of his intestine, which, in the crepuscular flicker of the television, adopted a phallic aspect' (70). Quoting this at length illustrates not only Whitehead's wry and lush writing style, but also the nightmarish return of the past that suffuses this book.

At the heart of this wasted world is a reconfiguration of what went before: 'Normal meant "the past". Normal was the unbroken idyll' (65) of life before the outbreak. In this catastrophic future, nearly everyone is struck by 'PASD, or Post-Apocalyptic Stress Disorder' (55). Whitehead explicitly plays with the pun on 'past', as this condition is a contemporary malaise of the new world. Symptoms include 'sadness or unhappiness; irritability [. . .]; reduced sex drive; insomnia or excessive sleeping' and so on. Mark thinks, it's 'Not so much a criteria for diagnosis but an abstract of existence itself' (55). In short, the novel concerns itself with a new cultural pathology. Critics like Mitchum Huehls see *Zone One* as exemplifying neoliberalism – 'our very own zombie plague' (2016: ix) – and the structures of contemporary capital. At the end of the novel, Mark 'walk[s] into the sea of the dead' (259) attempting to escape an embattled Zone One; Huehls sees this as a 'concerted willingness to begin mapping [a] new dispensation' out of the ruins of apocalypse and 'annihilation' (2016: ix). Whether we see in the novel such optimism (in Mark, in neoliberalism), the link between zombies and capital are well-trodden. As Roger Luckhurst notes (2015: 150), George A. Romero's *Dawn of the Dead* (1978), set in a shopping mall, is clear in its 'critique of consumption' and late-twentieth century consumerism. But Luckhurst and many other critics also remind us the zombies are rooted in the transatlantic world of slavery, often emblematising the workings of life and death, self and other, free and unfree. As such, in Ramón Saldívar's words (2013: 13), *Zone One* is a 'memoir of a future America in ruins', and for Andrew Strombeck (2017: 260), 'Whitehead depicts past and present as porous': the focus on memory and history is ever present.

As we've seen so far in Whitehead's work, an American history that refuses to vanish is slavery itself. Though un-noted by many of the critics who have written on the novel so far, *Zone One* makes a number of references to the institution: skels 'trudged like slaves higher and higher into midtown' (8); 'untold Americans still walked [outside the camps . . .] beyond order's embrace, like slaves who didn't know they'd been emancipated' (39); 'In reconstruction, you knew where you stood' (89). These slight, but repeated, references to slave bodies and post-slavery Reconstruction in the United States encode an antebellum and postbellum history into the novel's fabric. Such historical texture is focalised through the protagonist Mark Spitz. The joke of his name, in fact, relates to the character's race: 'the black-people-can't-swim thing' (231). It is notable that only two hundred pages in does Whitehead reveal the protagonist's blackness. This delay in revelation is just one of the novel's interesting elements. Why Whitehead chooses to keep this information from the reader is debatable; perhaps, as Saldívar (2013) argues, this is a 'post-racial' novel that reconfigures and rethinks blackness. Or perhaps this is just another one of Whitehead's games, a way of wrong-footing the reader, so that we cast back over the preceding book in a new light. As with his other novels, African American identity is central to *Zone One*, but here we just don't know it until the very end. As Saldívar suggests (2013: 13), 'Whitehead proposes that it may well be necessary first to imagine the end of the world before we may imagine the historical end of racialization and racism'. Not even the apocalypse can wipe away such an American plague.

'America, too, is a delusion': *The Underground Railroad* (2016)

Where *Zone One* subtly surfaced histories of race, *The Underground Railroad* is an explicit work of cultural memory, recalling and remediating slavery in the United States. As such, it joins an ever-growing list of films and literary texts interested in the system and effects of slavery, from Octavia Butler's *Kindred* (1979) to Steve McQueen's *12 Years a Slave* (2014). Whitehead's novel has a fairly simple plot: two slaves, Cora and Caesar, escape from a southern plantation and head north on the underground railroad. Where, historically, the railroad was metaphorical (it relates to the networks of people helping African Americans escape slavery), in Whitehead's novel it becomes literal.

The novel, for the first fifty-or-so pages, is strictly realist and depicts the brutalities of the antebellum South in exacting detail. At the book's opening, we meet Ajarry, who is transported across the Middle Passage as a slave: 'The noxious air of the hold, the gloom of confinement, and the screams of those shackled to her [. . .]. She twice tried to kill herself on the voyage to America, once by denying herself food and then again by drowning' (4). To begin the novel in memories of the slave ship, *The Underground Railroad* enacts what Christina Sharpe has called thinking in 'the wake'. For Sharpe (2016: 17–18), wakes are at once 'keeping watch with the dead, the path of a slave ship, the consequence of something, in the line of flight and/or sight, awakening, and consciousness'. To acknowledge these wakes of Blackness is 'to occupy and be occupied by the continuous and changing present of slavery's as yet unresolved unfolding' (Sharpe, 2016: 12–13). Such unfolding begins in Whitehead's novel with the trauma of the slave ship, and slavery's broader reconfiguration of personhood. The narrator notes: 'In America the quirk was that people were things. [. . .] If you were a thing – a cart or a horse or a slave – your value determined your possibilities' (6–7). The horrors of slavery – what Sharpe elsewhere (2010) calls the 'monstrous intimacies of slavery' – are further depicted in scenes on the Georgia plantation. The master's brother, for instance, 'violated the bonds of affection, sometimes visiting slaves on their wedding night to show the husband the proper way to discharge his marital duty' (3). The brutalities of slavery on the black body are laid out in visceral and shocking detail.

Yet, the novel takes a different turn when Cora and Caesar escape from the Georgia plantation. They run away through dense forest and swampland, ending at the first stop on the underground railroad. Literalised as an underground network of rail lines and stations, Cora and Caesar escape north in a boxcar. The train driver tells them, 'If you want to see what this nation is all about [. . .] you have to ride the rails. Look outside as you speed through, and you'll find the true face of America' (69). The true face, we then learn, is nothing like we or the characters imagine: each state is radically different from the last. Eric Foner, in *Gateway to Freedom* (2015: 4), argues that we cannot know how many slaves escaped through the nineteenth-century network, but it is possibly between '1,000 and 5,000 per year' from 1830–60, which was a 'cause of alarm in the slave states'. When the term is invented in 1839 (in a newspaper article quoting a slave), it becomes widespread and numerous writers 'went overboard with the railroad metaphor' (Foner, 2015: 11). In a sense, that is exactly what Whitehead does here, tipping from realism to fabulism, not just metaphorizing but literalizing the railroad's complexity and breadth. By offering recollection that transcends and remediates the literal past into an imaginative one, Whitehead's novel allows readers to rethink the escape from slavery in ways that the historical record cannot reveal.

Travelling to South Carolina, Cora obtains a job in a museum, acting out scenes from the history of slavery, often in reverse: it is 'like going back in time, an unwinding of America', from 'Plantation to Slave Ship to Darkest Africa' (125). In North Carolina, a white-only state, Cora must hide in the attic of a somewhat sympathetic white family, recalling Harriet Jacobs' famous slave narrative *Incidents in the Life of a Slave Girl* (1861). Beyond the Carolinas is the apocalyptic Tennessee, a charred and ashy wasteland. From there, Indiana and beyond. The novel ends, after numerous attempts at capture by slave catchers – very real figures from the time of the Fugitive Slave Act of 1850 – with another escape by Cora. This time without a conductor, Cora has to pump the handcar alone, 'throwing all of herself into movement. Into northness. Was she travelling through the tunnel or digging it?' (303). Cora thinks, 'Was she going deeper in or back from where she came?' (304). At once creating and travelling on the railroad, Cora's final journey is far from her last: the concluding pages offer more movement, a future of escape. As cultural memory, *The Underground Railroad* is wake-work that is not locked into the past but is spurred by it.

In short, Colson Whitehead's work fits both seamlessly and uneasily into the broader map of twenty-first-century fiction. While his novels might be called postmodern, because of their generic, formal and linguistic play, they are also explicitly concerned with depicting the complex realities of the contemporary United States. Like his contemporaries – Percival Everett, Paul Beatty, Jennifer Egan, Danzy Senna, and Toni Morrison (among many others) – Whitehead is concerned neither with conforming to existing literary movements nor honing a singular aesthetic. Rather, across these six novels, we see experimentation and tradition, narrative tension and linguistic excess; but above all, we can identify a writer who is reimagining the meanings and textures of racial life in the contemporary United States.

Works cited

Berlant, L. 2008. 'Intuitionists: History and the Affective Event', *American Literary History*, 20.4: 845–860.

Boxall, P. 2013. *Twenty-First-Century Fiction: A Critical Introduction*, Cambridge: Cambridge University Press.

Collins, P. 2013. 'The Ghosts of Economics Past: *John Henry Days* and the Production of History', *African American Review*, 46.2–3: 285–300.

DuBois, W. E. B. 1994. *The Souls of Black Folk*, New York: Dover Publications.

Edwards, E. and Michaels, W. B. 2011. '*What Was African American Literature?* A Symposium', *Los Angeles Review of Books*, June 13, https://lareviewofbooks.org/article/what-was-african-american-literature-a-symposium/#

Foner, E. 2015. *Gateway to Freedom: The Hidden History of the Underground Railroad*, New York: W. W. Norton and Co.

Huehls, M. 2016. *After Critique: Twenty-First-Century Fiction in a Neoliberal Age*, Oxford: Oxford University Press.

Jaggi, M. 2001. 'Railroad Blues', *The Guardian*, June 23, www.theguardian.com/books/2001/jun/23/fiction.artsandhumanities

Leader-Picone, C. 2015. 'Post-Black Stories: Colson Whitehead's *Sag Harbor* and Racial Individualism', *Contemporary Literature* 56.3: 421–449.

Leise, C. 2014. 'With Names, No Coincidence: Colson Whitehead's Postracial Puritan Allegory', *African American Review*, 47.2–3: 285–300.

Li, S. 2017. 'Introduction: What Is Twenty-First-Century African American Literature?', *American Literary History*, 29.4: 631–639.

Linder, C. 2015. *Imagining New York City: Literature, Urbanism, and the Visual Arts, 1890–1940*, Oxford: Oxford University Press.

Lloyd, C. 2014. 'Introduction: American Exceptionalism, a Reconsideration', *European Journal of American Culture*, 33.3: 159–164.

Luckhurst, R. 2015. *Zombies: A Cultural History*, London: Reaktion Books.

Marshall, K. 2015. 'What Are the Novels of the Anthropocene? American Fiction in Geological Time', *American Literary History*, 27.3: 523–538.

Nelson, S. R. 2006. *Steel Drivin' Man: John Henry, The Untold Story of an American Legend*, Oxford: Oxford University Press.

Pease, D. E. 2009. *The New American Exceptionalism*, Minneapolis and London: University of Minnesota Press.

Ross, M. B. 2012. 'Kenneth W. Warren's *What Was African American Literature?* A Review Essay', *Callaloo*, 35.3: 604–612.

Saldívar, R. 2013. 'The Second Elevation of the Novel: Race, Form, and the Postrace Aesthetic in Contemporary Narrative', *Narrative*, 21.1: 1–18.

Sharpe, C. 2010. *Monstrous Intimacies: Making Post-Slavery Subjects*, Durham, NC and London: Duke University Press.

Sharpe, C. 2016. *In the Wake: On Blackness and Being*, Durham, NC and London: Duke University Press.

Strombeck, A. 2017. '*Zone One*'s Reanimation of 1970s New York', *Studies in American Fiction*, 44.2: 259–280.

Tillet, S. 2012. *Sites of Slavery: Citizenship and Racial Democracy in the Post-Civil Rights Imagination*, Durham, NC and London: Duke University Press.

Touré. 2009. 'Visible Young Man', *New York Times*, May 1, www.nytimes.com/2009/05/03/books/review/Toure-t.html

—— 2012. *Who's Afraid of Post-Blackness? What It Means to Be Black Now*, New York: Free Press.

Warren, K. W. 2011. *What Was African American Literature?* Cambridge, MA: Harvard University Press.

Whitehead, C. 2002. *John Henry Days*, London: Fourth Estate.

—— 2007. *Apex Hides the Hurt*, New York: First Anchor.

—— 2011. *Sag Harbor*, London: Vintage.

—— 2012. *Zone One*, London: Vintage.

—— 2016. *The Underground Railroad*, London: Fleet.

—— 2017. *The Intuitionist*, London: Fleet.

Wintrhop, J. 2017. 'A Model of Christian Charity', in Sandra M. Gustafson and Robert S. Levine (eds.), *The Norton Anthology of American Literature*, Vol. A, 9th edn, New York: W. W. Norton and Co.

INDEX

445